Progress in IS

Progress in IS encompasses the various areas of Information Systems in theory and practice, presenting cutting-edge advances in the field. It is aimed especially at researchers, doctoral students, and advanced practitioners. The series features both research monographs, edited volumes, and conference proceedings that make substantial contributions to our state of knowledge and handbooks and other edited volumes, in which a team of experts is organized by one or more leading authorities to write individual chapters on various aspects of the topic. Individual volumes in this series are supported by a minimum of two external reviews.

The Series is SCOPUS-indexed.

Constantinos K. Coursaris • Joerg Beringer •
Pierre-Majorique Léger • Burak Öz
Editors

The Design of Human-Centered Artificial Intelligence for the Workplace

Springer

Editors
Constantinos K. Coursaris
HEC Montreal
Montreal, QC, Canada

Joerg Beringer
ProContext
Redwood City, CA, USA

Pierre-Majorique Léger
HEC Montreal
Montreal, QC, Canada

Burak Öz
HEC Montreal
Montreal, QC, Canada

ISSN 2196-8705 ISSN 2196-8713 (electronic)
Progress in IS
ISBN 978-3-031-83511-7 ISBN 978-3-031-83512-4 (eBook)
https://doi.org/10.1007/978-3-031-83512-4

This Springer imprint is published by the registered company Springer Nature Switzerland AG
The registered company address is: Gewerbestrasse 11, 6330 Cham, Switzerland

Foreword

Ben Shneiderman

This book's editors wisely advocate Human-Centered AI (HCAI) to ensure that when the AI technologies are embedded into enterprise and workplace solutions they amplify, augment, empower, and enhance human performance. They recognize that devotion to user experience design is necessary to bring the benefits of machine learning, deep learning, and generative AI to our professional and personal lives, while reducing the dangers of malicious actors, biased data, and flawed software.

The editors have chosen contributors who offer diverse examples and emerging principles, which are meant to guide designers, implementers, researchers, business leaders, and government agency staffers. The contributors propose HCAI processes and principles, which they hope will lead to AI-infused tools that are not only functional but also empowering and inclusive.

Readers who design systems that cater to the diverse needs of users will ensure accessibility and usability for everyone. Aspiring to universal usability requires that designers consider the diverse abilities of users and the infinitely varied contexts of use. This means going beyond compliance with laws and more than acceptable designs, to a world in which users feel valued and empowered. By doing so, the designers achieve commercial success and contribute to a more equitable digital world.

By striving for consistency, offering informative feedback, and preventing errors, designers can create environments where users feel more than just confident and in control. The truly satisfied user has an enhanced sense of self-efficacy and the capacity to carry out their tasks.

The editors and contributors demonstrate a commitment to excellence in design. This book is a call to action for designers, developers, and all stakeholders to collaborate and innovate, always keeping the users at the heart of their efforts. When they succeed, their technology products enhance human potential and foster a more connected and compassionate world.

As designers delve deeper into the intricacies of human-computer interaction that underlie HCAI, it becomes clear that their mission extends beyond mere functionality. They create experiences that resonate on a human level, fostering a sense of trust and satisfaction. By prioritizing user-centered design, they can anticipate the needs of users and deliver solutions that are both intuitive and delightful.

Generative AI Amplifies Human Performance

Let us move forward with a shared vision of creating interfaces that not only meet but exceed the expectations of our users, making their interactions with technology seamless, intuitive, and delightful. Together, we can build a future where technology serves as a bridge to greater understanding and connection, enhancing the human experience in meaningful ways. The launch of ChatGPT triggered global excitement and adoption of Artificial Intelligence (AI) in the domain of enterprise and workplace support. Applications based on Large Language Models (LLMs) include decision-making, prediction, and generative tasks that users invoke by a natural language dialogue interface to produce written text, images, sound, and computer programming code. This unprecedented flexibility in generating artifacts, which until today have been considered as being exclusive to knowledge-based workers with special technical skills, has become the poster child of AI in the press.

While these generative AI applications are startlingly impressive, they are disturbingly flawed.

The Great Debate

This book brings timely contributions to a great debate about whether AI-infused systems should be designed as tools that amplify, augment, empower, and enhance human performance or as teammates, partners, companions, and collaborators. Machine autonomy is the opposite of human-centeredness. I believe in tool-like designs that build users' self-efficacy, support creativity, clarify their responsibility, and facilitate social connectedness with other humans.

Strong examples of HCAI are digital cameras, which embed AI for focus, aperture, color balance, lighting, and reduced hand jitter, but give users control over the composition, zooming, and decisive moment when the photo is taken. Photographers get continuous feedback of what their photo will be and a wide range of controls to prepare and revise the photo. Then they can easily delete their photos or share them with friends and family.

However, the devotees of the AI-teammate notion dominate the discussion, even though this breaks with historical precedent and has yet to produce commercial success. The development of Generative AI applications, such as ChatGPT, Gemini, Claude, Copilot, Midjourney, and many of the new systems based on Large Language Models, has enlivened the discussion. These applications typically have a text-based natural language user interface, enhancing the suggestion that these applications are like friends, colleagues, or assistants.

Selected Chapters

In this Great Debate, I especially liked Sean Koon's chapter with six guidelines for "Reasoning with AI" (in Part 2). It contains this memorable quote, which is in harmony with my beliefs: "However, such tools will not arise from a preoccupation with AI capabilities but by emphasizing human expertise and its application in a domain. This focus on expertise is a specialization of human-centered design emphasizing human needs, capabilities, and behavior."

Among the other valuable chapters, we find Rong and Konstan's analysis of how to improve email at the University of Minnesota. They use the term "socially embedded agents" but advise designers to "consider the limitations of applying agents in workplaces. For example, an agent that is not well-trained might miss relevant audiences when targeting bulk messages. Therefore the targeting process cannot be fully automated by agents."

Djartov and Wurfel's case study of an Intelligent Pilot Advisory System has insights for both sides of The Great Debate. Dov Te'eni also sees a world in which human-AI collaboration is the norm, but chooses to focus on the situation in which "humans always have ultimate control over collaboration and are responsible for the result and conduct of the collaboration."

Tanabiki and Yamamura describe an image-sensing technology called Image AI to help railroad train operators monitor crowds on station platforms. They are clear about the limitations of autonomous systems and recognize that "Human operators play a crucial role in the functional effectiveness of Image AI. They make important decisions in high-risk situations and are responsible for keeping stations safe. When Image AI alerts them to possible issues, they decide what actions to take."

Maxim's case study of a banking chatbot gives hope for those who believe that customer service chatbots will become success stories, even in light of the long string of failures that left unhappy customers. Those who believe in chatbots might reflect on why Amazon has not implemented this technology on its astonishingly successful website. Chatbot enthusiasts are confident that Amazon will do it, while I believe that its well-designed visual interfaces provide good service in finding products, placing orders, and resolving problems.

A devastating report from the US Consumer Financial Protection Bureau found that ten leading bank chatbots "may be useful for resolving basic inquiries, but their effectiveness wanes as problems become more complex." The report warns of chatbots providing inaccurate and misleading information, then points to even deeper problems: "Financial institutions risk violating legal obligations, eroding customer trust, and causing consumer harm when deploying chatbot technology... Deficient chatbots that prevent access to live, human support can lead to law violations, diminished service, and other harms." It closes with a warning that "The shift away from relationship banking and toward algorithmic banking will have a number of long-term implications that the CFPB will continue to monitor closely."

The analysis of the two deadly crashes of the Boeing 737 MAX by Lescieux, Singh, and Doyon-Poulin was very effective in pointing out the potentially tragic outcomes of systems with excessive autonomy. They conclude "The findings of this research underscore the importance of a human-centered approach in improving the safety and efficiency of highly complex automated systems." However, the complexity and confusion of The Great Debate is revealed by their closing comment, which encourages development of "a teammate that pilots can count on, and not just as a tool that needs to be supervised. As the civilian aviation industry investigates uncrewed air vehicles, developing more resilient automation will also support the transition from system automation to system autonomy." As you may guess, I do not share the view that full autonomy is a virtue and instead advocate for the design of systems where humans are ultimately in control.

Many chapters maintain a sympathy for "intelligent systems," "AI teammates," and similar terms, which are troubling to me as they are antithetical to my views of the design space of AI solutions. However, these terms are widely accepted, so readers will have to decide for their own context whether to use or replace such terms with more user-centered phrases. Overall, the book is a balanced set of papers that offers a holistic perspective, and inspires future research to clarify design guidelines and further validate the importance of human-centeredness in AI systems.

Summary

In summary, this book is a valuable contribution to the current lively discussions of how advanced computing, especially AI-based systems, can be fruitfully applied in business. The diverse perspectives and case studies will enable managers and designers to understand the evolving principles, guidelines, and strategies that lead to successful products and services.

While some perspectives elevate AI capabilities, there is a strong devotion to the human-centered approach which celebrates the remarkable abilities of people and the dramatic benefits of supporting human-human collaboration.

Bravos to the editors for bringing this collection together.

University of Maryland
January 2025

Ben Shneiderman

Preface

This book synthesizes diverse perspectives on designing and implementing AI in organizational contexts by offering a comprehensive overview of scholarly conceptual perspectives and applied case studies presented in four parts with each comprising several chapters. The first part introduces foundational theories such as the Situation Awareness theory and the Decision Ladder framework that have been used as lenses through which to view and explain AI related phenomena. The second part then explores extant research and emergent design recommendations for AI-enabled systems within organizational processes. Chapters within the third part focus on AI users, ranging from their cognitive and emotional responses during use to factors contributing to perceptions, adoption, and effective use of AI-driven systems. Chapters within the fourth part present real-world AI implementation and use cases in fields such as aviation, manufacturing, logistics, and security, among others, highlighting key challenges and solutions across these diverse contexts. By presenting these various viewpoints, the book provides researchers with a holistic conceptual understanding that can be leveraged in future AI research thereby advancing the field further. The book also offers practitioners insights and approaches for implementing AI systems in a human-centered, effective, and responsible manner. Altogether, this comprehensive overview of design considerations for AI solutions in an organizational context is about not losing sight of the most important piece in this complex sociotechnical puzzle: the people—the designers, managers, and users of AI solutions in the workplace.

Montreal, QC, Canada — Constantinos K. Coursaris
Redwood City, CA, USA — Joerg Beringer
Montreal, QC, Canada — Pierre-Majorique Léger
Montreal, QC, Canada — Burak Öz

Acknowledgments

We would like to thank the authors of individual contributions for having chosen to disseminate their ideas, findings, and recommendations through our edited book.

This book would not have been possible were it not for the tremendous effort invested by the scholars who served as double-blind peer reviewers of manuscripts received for publication consideration. We thank them for their service to the scientific community.

We are grateful for the financial support provided by Blue Yonder Group Inc. [Grant number ALLRP 57332-22], which was instrumental in our ability to produce this edited book. The support of Blue Yonder Group Inc. reflects its commitment to advancing human-centered design and enhancing the user experience in innovative supply chain management systems and, more broadly, Artificial Intelligence solutions for organizations, i.e., the focus of this book.

We are also grateful for the financial support provided by the Natural Sciences and Engineering Research Council of Canada (NSERC) [Grant number ALLRP 57332-22], and Prompt Innov. The support of NSERC and Prompt was instrumental in enabling the research and ideas being described in several chapters of this book.

We extend our heartfelt appreciation to Dr. Ben Shneiderman for his relevant and insightful Foreword. We are also grateful for the intellectual exchanges we had throughout our journey of producing this comprehensive collection of perspectives on the design of AI solutions for the workplace anchored on the principle of human-centeredness.

Lastly, we would like to extend a special thanks to the Tech3Lab team at HEC Montréal and our HEC Montréal colleagues for their unwavering support and dedication throughout this extensive project.

Contents

Part IV Case Studies

Introduction

The Design Space of Human-Centered AI Solutions

Constantinos K. Coursaris, Joerg Beringer, Pierre-Majorique Léger, and Burak Öz

Abstract The rapid advancement and adoption of AI technologies, including large language models (LLMs) and chatbots, marks a new era in workplace and enterprise support by enabling the generation of human-like artifacts. Through a broad range of machine learning (ML) algorithms and deep neural networks, AI enables mission-critical functions such as pattern recognition, decision-making, and automation. To navigate this exciting albeit complex technological landscape, we introduce a human-centered AI (HCAI) solution map, which classifies AI solutions according to two dimensions: human-centered AI purpose, i.e., whether the AI solution is primarily intended to assist, augment, automate, or replace the human expert, and human-centered AI cognition, i.e., the type of cognitive function support such as sensing, decision-making, and action execution. Moreover, the HCAI solution map organizes AI solutions into roles ranging from assistants and tools to orchestration agents and automation agents. These roles vary in the way they support users and reflect different levels of human involvement during the process (i.e., in-the-loop, on-the-loop, or out-of-the-loop). Designing AI systems with human-centered qualities such as empathy, transparency, and explainability fosters positive user experience and trust. Characteristics such as context awareness, human-centeredness, and human-control, in turn, determine the effectiveness of AI solutions in adapting to situational needs and corresponding user interactions. Ultimately, by considering these human-centered dimensions, characteristics, and qualities when designing AI solutions, organizations can align the AI solution with the intended users' needs and empower users and maintain human control while creating value for all stakeholders.

C. K. Coursaris · P.-M. Léger · B. Öz (✉)
HEC Montreal, Montreal, QC, Canada
e-mail: constantinos.coursaris@hec.ca; pierre-majorique.leger@hec.ca; burak.oz@hec.ca

J. Beringer
ProContext, Redwood City, CA, USA
e-mail: joerg.beringer@procontext.ai

C. K. Coursaris et al. (eds.), *The Design of Human-Centered Artificial Intelligence for the Workplace*, Progress in IS, https://doi.org/10.1007/978-3-031-83512-4_1

1 Human-Centered AI Solutions

With the public launches of chat applications based on large language models (LLMs), we are experiencing global excitement and adoption of artificial intelligence (AI) in enterprise and workplace support—mainly in the form of natural language dialogue interfaces in combination with generative capabilities to produce human-like artifacts such as written text, images, sound, and computer programming code. This unprecedented capacity to generate artifacts, which until today have been considered exclusive to knowledge-based workers with special technical skills, has become the poster child of AI in the press.

However, such LLM-based solutions are only one flavor of AI systems, i.e., advanced technologies that leverage large and diverse data inputs to perceive and respond rationally to the world around them. Machine learning (ML) and AI technology have been in production for several decades in different forms in the consumer and business world. ML algorithms are powerful in classifying and clustering information even predicting critical events. Deep neural networks successfully recognize patterns in visual information or human preferences to extract meaning or make personalized recommendations based on historical data.

As can be seen by these seemingly heterogeneous examples, there is a diverse set of enabling technologies such as ML, deep neural networks, LLM, and problem solvers and a broad spectrum of purposed solutions that are either built to support users, perform functions intended to augment human performance, or aim to establish automated decision-making and execution. This broad spectrum is also reflected by the variety of topics presented in this book's 25 chapters.

To help readers navigate this book, we introduce a solution map for human-centered AI (HCAI) applications (see Fig. 1), which is arranging the different flavors of AI solutions not by the underlying technology rather by the following two human-centered dimensions:

- *Human-Centered AI Purpose:* What role does the AI solution play in relationship to the user? Should the solution assist, augment, orchestrate, or automate?
- *Human-Centered AI Cognition:* What type of cognitive function support is provided by the AI solution to help the user sense information, make decisions, and enact decisions?

This two-dimensional canvas is used to map out popular solution paradigms of human-centered AI systems according to their locality of the provided intelligence and their primary purpose.

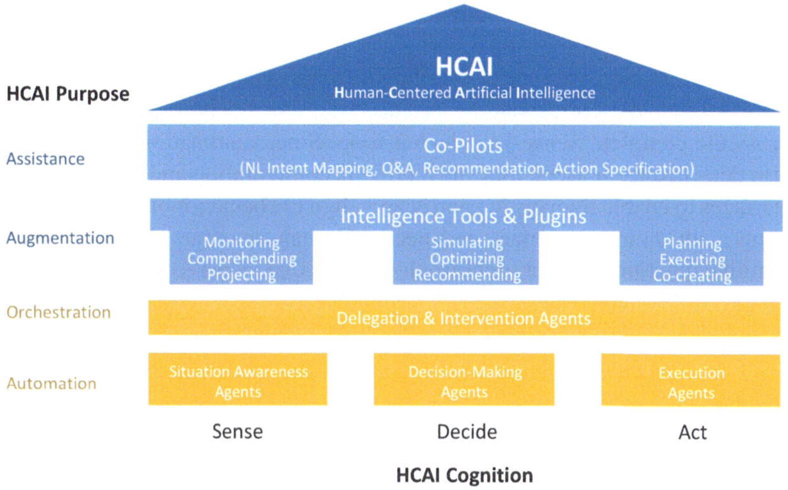

Fig. 1 Human-Centered AI solution map

2 Human-Centered AI Purpose

Each AI solution is explicitly or implicitly designed with a certain purpose in mind. A human-centered purpose defines the relationship between the human and the AI system:

- *AI assistants* directly support users by typically providing natural language interfaces, answering questions, giving recommendations, and/or triggering/executing actions specified by the user. For example, a copilot assists in writing code, choosing between decision options, making the user aware of a risk, and more.
- *AI augmentation tools* provide packaged AI-enabled functionality that augments a user's abilities and/or capacity. Such technology solutions are used exclusively in a direct, interactive manner to accomplish a specific user task. For example, an AI-powered graphics tool may help the user edit images with just a few clicks. The more generative the tool is, the more it serves the role of an assistant that performs task-related actions on behalf of the user upon request.
- *AI orchestration agents* function in support of human-centered purpose or human-centered cognition. In the former, orchestration agents manage delegation and human control. They are the human interface layer for coordinating and supervising AI systems and setting interventions points. In the latter, orchestration agents coordinate across multiple agents in different cognitive realms. For example, in autonomous driving, a situation awareness agent in a moving vehicle senses (i.e., detects) a pedestrian who is anticipated to step on the street; a decision-making agent decides that there is a need to slow the vehicle down; and an execution agent acts by controlling the brakes as needed to stop the vehicle in a safe way.

- *AI automation agents* are AI systems that run decoupled from user interaction to provide specific cognitive function support, including sensing the environment to establish a situation awareness, deciding on what task(s) needs to be carried out, and executing the corresponding task(s). In doing so, they enable automation across the complete Sense-Decide-Act loop. Since automation agents can perform detached from users, they must provide configuration and intervention user interfaces to enable humans to control and align the behavior of these automation agents with their preferences and needs. Human operators delegate a task or cognitive function to either orchestration agents that map a recognized user intent to an available agent (e.g., LLM plug-in sourced by ChatGPT in response to a user input) or automation agents (e.g., a surveillance system that automatically recognizes strangers on a property).

3 Human-Centered AI Cognition

By "cognition," we refer to the set of human abilities as described and modeled in cognitive psychology. Every human has foundational mental skills such as perception, working memory, memory recall, and more sophisticated executive cognitive skills such as problem-solving, decision-making, planning, reasoning, and creativity. While LLM systems are impressive in their reasoning and generative capabilities, they lack the concept of fact-based retrieval, decision-making, and foremost perception. This is why they are primarily used as an assistant or generative tool, and not as a decision or automation tool.

Human-centered cognition describes the foundational type of cognitive skill that is provided by AI systems. We focus on three cognitive realms that are required to create end-to-end automation loops:

- *Sense:* The capabilities of an AI system are perceptual or help the user to monitor some task-relevant state of the external environment. This can be an AI-powered fraud detection agent at a bank that discovers an unusual combination of financial transactions, or a call center service that recognizes the risk of customer churn based on interactions with the call center agent. What all these AI solutions have in common is that they run independently of the user to observe, comprehend, and detect a critical event that requires a decision or action.
- *Decide:* AI systems that are specialized in making decisions are traditionally rule-engines that can take an input and make a rule-based decision. For complex problems, domain-specific problem solvers can generate decision options or plans that represent a short list of the best solutions. Those systems depend on input from humans or sensing agents. Complex decisions involve the creation and simulation of decision options and related action plans that are complex mental activities. Users must know typical approaches of how to respond and must be able to anticipate the outcome.

- *Act:* To enact a decision, an automation agent must have the ability to trigger actions or execute actions. Those automation agents are typically integrated with other generative plug-ins or Enterprise Resource Planning (ERP) systems to trigger a specific action (e.g., block financial transactions; generate personalized email; and send it to customers). While generative actions are intrinsically cognitive skills, not all actions are of cognitive nature. However, the planning of multiple actions and the specification of an action requires context knowledge and domain knowledge even after the decision has been made.

4 Elasticity and Interoperability of HCAI Agents

The two-dimensional canvas illustrated in Fig. 1 helps to classify AI solution paradigms according to their locality on the dimensions of human-centered purpose and cognition, but also illustrates the interoperability and necessary elasticity on both dimensions. While an assistant may be optimized to understand user preferences and map intents to action, it may still require other automation agents that are specialized on a specific cognitive function and operate in support of any cognitive realm.

A copilot experience may also allow the user to delegate certain functionality to automation agents to reduce mental workload and to define policies for intervention points. In this role, the copilot becomes the tool to meta-manage and oversee delegated and automated cognitive functions provided by AI-based automation agents.

When users directly engage with automation agents, the interaction paradigm extends from using a tool to one of coordinating, collaborating, and sharing information between humans and AI-powered automation agents. The structure of such multi-agent automation networks may either be designed and bounded a priori by business stakeholders, or adapted ad hoc by human agents based on situational needs.

Having an explicit understanding of the to be supported solution paradigms is important as it sets the stage for the design and technical implementation. Each paradigm maps to typical requirements and design patterns and sharpens the identity of each automation agent contributing to a larger solution. Since usage patterns of AI systems vary over time depending on trust and situational needs, the role of an AI solution may shift from assistance to delegation, to automation, and then back to assistant if there is a need for human intervention.

5 Characteristics of HCAI Solutions

The human-centered AI solution map presented in Fig. 1 focuses on the primary purpose and cognitive functions supported by the AI systems. Depending on those two aspects of the AI solution, certain design principles and user experience qualities are likely to be dominant and of paramount importance. Figure 2 puts forth a set of characteristics corresponding to each AI solution type according to its human-centered purpose:

- *Context Awareness:* Each AI system is linked to the external reality relevant in the context in which it operates. The AI system represents this context in the form of user history, time series, behavioral graphs, or dedicated digital twins among other data-driven representations of the external state within the system. Such context representations enable the AI system to establish a specific kind of awareness among user awareness, task awareness, agent awareness, situational awareness, and mission awareness. Each kind of awareness is characterized by attributes, which are included as a non-exhaustive list in Fig. 2.
- *Human-Centeredness:* Human-centered design objectives describe which quality dimensions of an AI solution should be optimized for a given use case to evoke a favorable user experience. When developing design requirements for AI-based solutions, additional qualities such as empathy, trust, explainability, transparency, intervenability, and goal alignment, among others, are important. While these and other AI solution qualities apply to all layers of Fig. 1, a few of them become more prominent depending on the level of human control characterizing the AI solution, as proposed in Fig. 2.
- *Human Control:* Distinguishing AI solutions according to the primary human-centered purpose they support also reflects the level of human control maintained in the process. To what extent do direct or indirect users have control over the use, behavior, and outcome of the AI solution? Is the human at the center of all actions, using AI for consultation? Or are AI systems decoupled from direct user interaction and instruction, becoming increasingly self-sufficient in executing tasks? Depending on how deeply the user remains involved, those usage patterns with AI-based systems are referred to as keeping humans in-the-loop, on-the-loop, or out-of-the-loop. Each level presents its own ergonomic, ethical, and safety challenges.

For an AI solution to be successfully adopted by users, it is important not only to identify the business case but also to clearly define the human-centered role the AI solution should play. The posture of an AI solution should align with its human-centered role. For example, common postures are evolving for copilots, as well as for supervision and user intervention in automation agents. Once mapped to one of these roles, the AI solution's design can focus on supporting the corresponding stakeholder requirements, technical requirements, and data requirements for generating reliable context awareness and human-centered qualities.

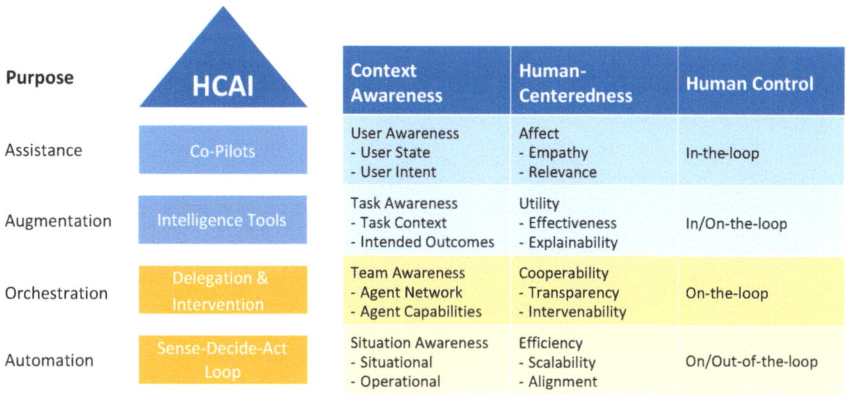

Fig. 2 Characteristics of HCAI solutions

6 What to Expect from the Book?

Each chapter in this book is authored by different experts who are specialized on one of the aspects outlined in this introductory chapter. Authors either deep-dive into a specific topic or discuss more holistically broader topics such as automated AI decision loops, interaction (including author-referenced teaming and collaboration) scenarios between human and system agents, or the impact of AI systems on the entire work system.

Several chapters approach an AI topic from a theoretical perspective and provide concepts and frameworks to help you, the reader, better understand design patterns and principles of designing AI solutions for the workplace. Other chapters share specific use cases of designing and implementing an AI solution to help you learn from their examples and be better prepared for your own AI projects.

Our book also features chapters that explore best practices related to DevOps and requirements engineering, specifically for AI solutions that must be trained and allowed to evolve over time while in production.

We hope this collection of chapters on the design, user experience, and applications of human-centered AI solutions in the workplace provides you with a comprehensive perspective that is both enlightening and empowering.

Part I
Human-Centered AI in Business

The Situation Awareness, Decision, and Execution (SADE) Ladder: A Framework for Human-AI Collaborative Decision-Making

Joerg Beringer, Alexander J. Karran, Constantinos K. Coursaris, and Pierre-Majorique Léger

Abstract In order to implement intelligent systems that exhibit autonomous behavior, the system must develop its own situation awareness and ability to execute the decisions being made. To model these end-to-end decision loops, we propose a framework that combines situation awareness, decision-making, and action-planning theories into one decision ladder that helps to understand the requisite anatomy and ergonomics of intelligent systems.

This Situation Awareness and Decision Execution (SADE) Ladder acts as a catalyst bringing together different research disciplines specialized in each of the three referenced domains. This synergistic view across multiple research agendas manifests in a conceptual framework to understand better the interaction dynamics in human-AI interactions and the importance of transparency and explainability in multi-agent networks to help the human experts understand the locality of artificial system intelligence and the underlying rationale of system-generated decisions and action plans.

Identifying the different cognitive demands and sub-functions within the SADE Ladder enables practitioners to derive the appropriate requirements from cognitive work analysis and design intelligent systems for workplaces that are trusted and accepted by their users.

J. Beringer (✉)
ProContext, Redwood City, CA, USA
e-mail: joerg.beringer@procontext.ai

A. J. Karran · C. K. Coursaris · P.-M. Léger
HEC Montreal, Montreal, QC, Canada
e-mail: alexander-john.karran@hec.ca; constantinos.coursaris@hec.ca; pierre-majorique.leger@hec.ca

C. K. Coursaris et al. (eds.), *The Design of Human-Centered Artificial Intelligence for the Workplace*, Progress in IS, https://doi.org/10.1007/978-3-031-83512-4_2

1 Introduction

Artificial intelligence (AI) systems are used increasingly in workplaces not only to augment capabilities of the human operators and domain experts but also to automate human work and business processes. Unlike traditional automation systems, which support well-defined repetitive work, AI-based automation agents can deal with significant uncertainties in the environment and have sufficient reasoning and problem-solving capabilities to make autonomous decisions about responding to contemporary conditions and initiating actions. Given those higher-level cognitive functions, AI systems are often referred to as intelligent systems.

The level of autonomy of an automation agent depends on its capability to perform an end-to-end decision loop comprised of being aware of the current situation, making decisions, and turning decisions into action without the need for human intervention. While the goal is to deploy such systems to offload work from the human experts and improve scalability and quality of results, it is also important to keep the human in the loop to oversee system performance and avoid deskilling and detachment from operational awareness. Moreover, if direct human input is not needed in the specific context of system use, maintaining the human on the loop assures their ultimate control, oversight, and action override if and when they deem it appropriate.

To better understand the potential of integrating human expertise and AI-based automation systems, we propose a holistic conceptual framework of human/system-agent decision-making, referred to as Situation Awareness, Decision, and Execution (SADE) Ladder. The SADE Ladder benefits designers, developers, implementers, and users of automation intelligent systems by disentangling the prerequisites to unfolding the full potential of distributed cognitive skills and human-AI interactions.

The ultimate goal of process automation is to create end-to-end understand/decide/act control loops that use situation awareness as a basis from which to initiate and inform decisions that trigger actions to reach a desired outcome or state. However, full autonomy, i.e., the human agent *out-of-the-loop*, is achieved only when one or multiple automation agents support the entirety of these functions. In most cases, human will be on- or in-the-loop and perform a task or process in a more collaborative way—often referred to as human-AI teaming.

Teaming as a verb refers to the fact that all agents that contribute to a task or process must form an ad hoc team and collaborate and coordinate in some form to achieve an intended outcome (Edmondson 2012). An AI system agent supporting some or all of the aspects described in the SADE Ladder will not only be capable of performing tasks in a self-directed autonomous way, but must possess team awareness and collaboration skills to successfully coordinate and communicate across all members of a human agent and autonomous agent team (HAT) (O'Neill et al. 2022).

In this chapter, we introduce the different phases and levels of the SADE Ladder in more detail and refer to research related to each phase. The SADE Ladder not only is helpful to understand the core component of autonomous decisions loops but also affords an understanding of the collaboration dynamics between human and AI systems along the end-to-end decision-making cycle of any automation system that can make decisions and respond to situational needs. Through an understanding of the underlying theoretical concepts, we identify requirements and patterns that must be met to ensure the successful implementation and adoption of autonomous AI systems in the workplace.

2 End-to-End Decision-Making Loops

One of the key motivations for automating human tasks is to free the human agent from performing the task and to allow the reallocation of their cognitive and other resources (e.g., time) elsewhere. However, such task reallocation comes with the inherent risk of the human operator over time unlearning the requisite task skills and becoming detached from the task context in general, which can pose a challenge when the human agent is asked or needed to take over control having low situation awareness.

For this reason, much of the research related to cockpit automation (Jones and Endsley 1996; Munir et al. 2022; Politowicz et al. 2021; Salotti and Suhir 2019) and driver assistance (Golestan et al. 2016; McCall and Trivedi 2007; Rockl et al. 2007; Wulf et al. 2014) focuses on the concept of situation awareness and how to ensure that a basic level of situation awareness is shared between human and system agents to sustain the human agent's readiness to intervene if and when necessary.

Situation Awareness (SA) as a concept was initially presented by Endsley (1995). The need for SA in many task domains is self-evident, from aerospace to military planning, where obtaining and maintaining SA is critical to assuring safety or mission success. However, the concept of SA has been applied to many other contexts. Its relevance for the workplace context has been shown when studying the usage patterns of AI systems of real business users (Beringer et al. 2022; Jiang et al. 2022). SA differences were a typical cause for tensions within human-AI teams.

Regarding our interest in autonomous end-to-end decision loops, SA is one important step of the ladder, comprising three levels: perception, comprehension, and projection. In the original conceptualization of SA (Endsley 1995), the decision-making process itself was not considered. Specifically, the actual mechanics of decision-making and the role of human expertise in the decision-making process were neither considered nor included in the original conceptualization of SA. Furthermore, when considering the addition of AI systems, which are becoming more capable and granted greater autonomy, it would be fair to conclude that an appraisal of more formal decision-making models and how they fit within an SA framework is warranted.

In this regard, early work from Rasmussen (1983) and Parasuraman and Riley (1997) introduced models outlining different decision-making stages to explain the different behaviors and cognitive demands for humans when making decisions at different levels of complexity.

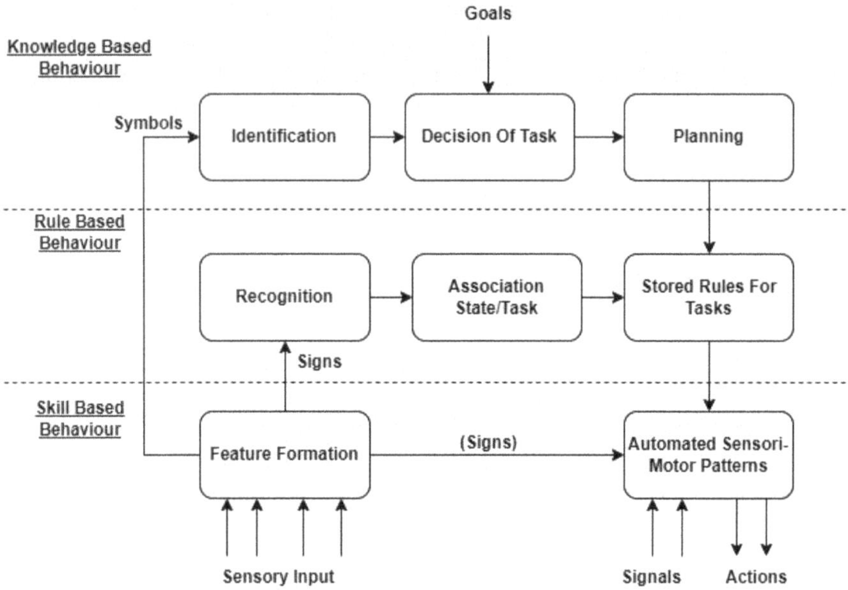

Fig. 1 Rasmussen skills-rules-knowledge decision template (adapted from Rasmussen 1983)

Rasmussen (1983) investigated human-machine control systems and formalized (Fig. 1) how decisions transform inputs (information) into outputs (action). These transformations can be perceived as end-to-end decision loops. Similar to Endsley's work on SA, Rasmussen introduced a formal model of human performance comprising three levels on the basis of conscious planning involved when processing information as inputs for decision-making.

At the lowest level, sensory input is directly transformed into simple actions or skill-based behavior control loops without conscious control. These control loops do not require higher-level mental processes and hence can often be assimilated into autonomic (automated) behaviors. For example, drivers maintaining a specific distance from the car in front of them is a skill-based behavior requiring no conscious planning and is instead a smooth and automated decision-making process. A similarly automated process can be embedded in AI-enabled systems such as self-driving cars, which are often referred to as autonomous vehicles (a misnomer as no vehicles exist to date that are fully autonomous).

At the next higher level of conscious planning, decision-making concerns the application of rules to map an input (condition) to an output (action). This decision-making mode requires rules to be in place and known by the AI agent, allowing a transformation of an input into a known set of actions by applying a rule set. For example, if the temperature reaches a specific level that is deemed a priori to be "too high" by the human, the AI agent would turn on the cooling function of an air conditioner; and conversely, if the temperature reaches a level that is defined a priori as being "too low," it would turn on the heating function of the same air conditioner. At a higher level of system autonomy, an AI agent may be designed to "learn" over time, for example, by considering the human overrides performed over time in association with turning on the cooling and the heating functions, respectively, and subsequently adjusting the temperature levels associated with the activation of the corresponding function in an ongoing continuous, dynamic process.

The highest level of conscious planning reflects situations of greater uncertainty (e.g., due to incomplete situation information) and increased mental workload during decision-making, as it is either unclear what rules apply or the rule set may not be exhaustive to support decision-making. If these elements are missing and cannot be easily provisioned, then decision-making shifts from rule-based to the highest level—knowledge-based. The agent gathers additional information to perform causal analysis and generates decision options based on experience and technical understanding of the domain. This process can result in a lengthy investigation to understand the problem (situation) and planning exercises to generate action plans with the desired impact.

3 The Situation Awareness and Decision Execution Ladder

Inspired by the work on situation awareness (Endsley 1995) and Rasmussen's levels of human-machine control (Rasmussen 1983), and the visual metaphor of a decision ladder, (Rasmussen 1976), to connect upstream sensing with downstream action, we propose the Situation Awareness and Decision Execution (SADE) Ladder framework (see Fig. 2), which integrates the concepts of situation awareness and action planning with an iterative decision-making process to form a model of an end-to-end decision-making loop. The left side of the ladder considers the three levels of Endsley's situation awareness model (i.e., detect, comprehend, project). It introduces a hierarchy of cognitive functions, from the simple observation of facts to comprehension and transformation into meaningful information and further diagnosis to project the future state. These levels also relate to Rasmussen's conscious planning levels, given that direct feedback loops are typically based on simple data inputs that are automatically (or subconsciously by the human) translated into action. In comparison, rule-based decisions are grounded on understanding conditions requiring comprehension and synthesis and interpretation of input data as meaningful information that, in turn, drives action.

Elaborating on the SADE Ladder shown in Fig. 2, Endsley's situation awareness model and Rasmussen's decision ladder metaphor are not perfectly aligned. However, by harnessing the respective strengths of each perspective, an integrative framework can help guide the design of a successful human-AI agent interaction that preserves cognitive heterogeneity across both human and AI agents. The proposed SADE Ladder is composed of a left side concerned with the building of situation awareness, a central pillar concerned with the decision-making process, and a right side concerned with the execution of actions pertinent to a decision.

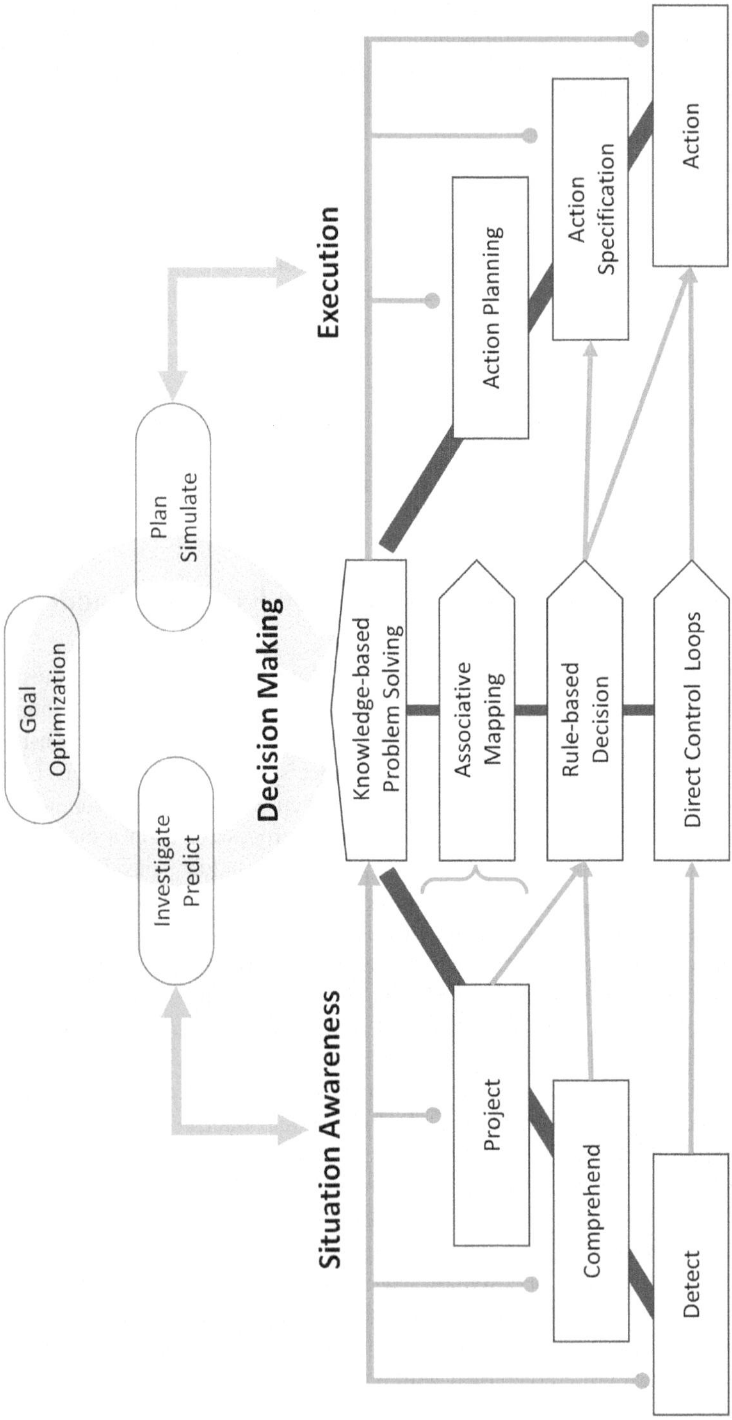

Fig. 2 SADE ladder: Situation Awareness, Decision, and Execution ladder

Phase 1: Situation Awareness

The left side follows Endsley's model of situation awareness: *detect* is the initial stage involved with identifying or detecting a new fact or event; this is followed by *comprehend*, where once detected, the next step is to understand, interpret, and synthesize this information to recognize patterns or anomalies; and finally, *project* involving predictions or forecasting events. These elements align with building situation awareness.

Phase 2: Decision-making

The central pillar consists of discrete, dynamic decision-making processes informed by a decision-maker's situation awareness. The pillar does not comprised levels that are interconnected in a linear manner; instead, each level represents a decision-making "mode," whereby the developing situation awareness of the decision-maker maps to a decision-making mode that, when coupled with prior knowledge or action plans for a given event, can lead to the execution of an action.

The *direct control loops* relationship represents decisions where incoming information directly leads to an action based on a closed, algorithmic feedback loop. For example, keeping the temperature within a certain range or maintaining the speed of a vehicle requires only low-level detection of temperature or speed and making immediate, necessary adjustments. In this, the results of actions are monitored, and direct feedback is used to proceed with further action executions or to achieve or maintain the intended outcome.

Rule-based decisions are based on recognizing known conditions in the environment that can be mapped to predefined actions. Identifying conditions typically requires comprehension of incoming raw or discreet information after converting it into higher-level, meaningful information; for example, in the case of a self-driving car, the AI system is synthesizing low-level image data into the recognition of an object as a person who is walking and about to cross or crossing the street.

Associative mapping is a heuristic applied by experts who instinctively map fuzzy situations to established action plans based on similarity with past symptom patterns. Similar to neural networks, the exact rationale of such decisions cannot be clearly articulated and is based on experience.

More complex issues may require *knowledge-based* reasoning utilizing decision-making strategies that require an iterative, focused, problem-centric analysis of the situation in reference to an intended outcome or goal. This knowledge-based decision is modeled as a higher-level strategic loop involving investigation, prediction, and simulation to establish a better understanding of the situation and causal relationships, develop action plans that consider constraints, and compare anticipated outcomes against agreed goals.

Phase 3: Execution

The right side of the SADE Ladder encompasses execution. It includes *action planning*, where plans are detailed after solutions have been found and decisions have been made, specifying what actions are required, by whom, when, and in what sequence. Informed by the decision-making process and cumulative situation awareness, the action *specification* details actions, potentially down to the operational level, including concrete resources and precise parameters for implementation. *Action* is the actual implementation of a decision or solution; any stage in the decision ladder can lead to action and implementation given sufficient cumulative situation awareness and existing solution frameworks. Examples of actions are sending control commands to a system, initiating a business transaction, or creating an artifact.

4 Design Implications of the SADE Ladder

The SADE Ladder is a framework that improves our understanding of the anatomy and characteristics of AI systems that have the potential to perform tasks or entire business processes in an automated manner. Grounded in this framework, we next discuss selected topics related to human-AI interactions and deep-dive into the two areas of decision-making and execution that complement Endsley's situation awareness model.

4.1 Designing with Humans In, Over, or Out of the Loop

The SADE Ladder helps to understand the different levels of automation and enabled degree of system autonomy. Typically, human experts still own the decision-making step, particularly when complex knowledge-based decisions have to be made. In these cases, the human is "in the loop" and directly involved in a hybrid loop, which consists of human experts and AI systems supporting the three phases of the loop. In a hybrid loop, AI is only used selectively to improve situation awareness, generate decision options, simulate scenarios, or plan and perform actions. The human expert may exclusively own one entire phase or may team up with automation agents that augment or scale human cognitive skills to achieve better outcomes. Only if automation agents cover all aspects of a decision-making loop, we will have a fully autonomous system where the human will be "over the loop" (or "on the loop") or "out of the loop." "Over the loop" refers to workflows where the human still provides supervision of the system and tightly monitors the quality of results on an ongoing basis. In contrast, "out of the loop" means the human is detached from concrete work and only manages the AI systems on a meta-level, for example, setting goals and boundaries or facilitating the AI system's learning.

The level of autonomy may be designed upfront at the organizational level, but in reality, the level of autonomy evolves from the trust and acceptance of the human experts in the AI system, which may vary based on the complexity of the task at hand. If rule-based decisions can be made based on information AI-based agents can reliably derive from the external environment, an autonomous rule engine can make the decision that triggers a predefined action.

For example, an AI-powered marketing solution detects an anomaly in a customer's behavior and automatically triggers an email to make a discounted offer to this customer. If a marketing analyst trusts the detection algorithm and is aligned with the decision-making of the rule engine to send the offer, the analysts will be happy to let the system run and make autonomous decisions and actions.

However, there are also situations where human expertise is needed to analyze a complex situation or define high-impact actions. For example, the same AI system may notify the marketing expert that a key account is at risk of moving to another vendor. In this case, the marketing expert would install a task force to analyze the situation further and propose mitigation actions. In this example, the autonomous systems escalated to the human expert and switched from autonomous agent mode into an "interactive tool" mode to support human-driven problem-solving activities and action planning.

Given these changing requirements, depending on the situation's complexity and the human expert's trust in the AI system to produce intended outcomes, an AI-based system must be flexible enough to support different levels of autonomy and the transition between these modes. The question is then not so much if or if not the human should be in the loop, but when. At the highest level, the human is always in control to engage or disengage an autonomous system, which makes the autonomy of a system always a bounded autonomy (Schraagen 2024).

4.2 Designing for Human Expertise

In the SADE Ladder, we model knowledge-based decision-making as its own iterative process aiming to deeper analyze a situation in the context of a specific problem and to create and compare decision options on the execution side as potential responses to a specific problem. The role of AI systems, in this case, is to augment this human-driven decision-making with AI systems that can process massive amounts of data and recognize relationships to inform human decisions, as well as optimizations and simulators to evaluate or recommend solutions.

AI agents employ vast data resources to create customized knowledge bases, enabling comprehensive decision-making for designated use cases. Their capability to swiftly retrain and optimist within specific contexts outpaces human cognition, not only in speed but also in comparative optimization. Nonetheless, the value of human expertise within this cooperative decision-making framework appears undervalued and under-researched, and the loss of expertise is of growing concern (Fügener et al. 2021).

Expertise refers to the knowledge, skills, and experiences an individual has acquired throughout a lifetime or career. There is also a perception, specifically in industry, that the expert is someone who knows the rules, range of procedures, and routines required to perform a given task or decision with high performance (Farrington-Darby and Wilson 2006), but who also knows when to step outside of the bounds of the task to apply novel strategies to novel problems. Expertise is often posited as both static and cumulative, whereby any decisions the expert makes are based upon explicit deliberation (i.e., logical reasoning). However, research has shown that in many cases, experts bypass logical reasoning in favor of a more intuitive process (Naikar 2010), formalized as expertise-based intuition (Salas et al. 2010) and more recently referred to as naturalistic decision-making (Klein 2015).

Naturalistic decision-making (NDM) is rooted in the dual systems thinking theory of human cognition posited by (Kahneman 2011). Dual-process theory differentiates between two cognitive modalities: System 1, representing heuristic-driven, automatic thought, and System 2, denoting methodical, effortful reasoning. Moreover, NDM accentuates the significance of experience, intuition, and situation awareness in complex environments while acknowledging the necessity of analytical deliberation in certain circumstances.

Various approaches have been applied in cognitive work analysis to analyze decision-making processes and inform decision support systems design (Banks et al. 2020). These frameworks, including the SADE Ladder, describe the different demands and sub-functions associated with System 2 decision-making in a normative fashion. To acknowledge the existence of intuitive experience-based decision-making, we added an associative mapping mode in addition to the rule-based mapping mode to indicate that mapping a situation to a response can also be based on a fuzzy association of a situational pattern in the left pillar to an established action pattern in the right pillar. This type of intuitive decision-making is the focus of the Recognition-Primed Decision Model (RPDM). The RPDM describes how experts develop heuristics that resemble a pattern-matching paradigm where situations are mapped to known situations and then to the corresponding procedures associated with the known situation. Instead of rule mapping, RPDM describes how the entire situations are mapped (Naikar 2010).

The RDPM touches on an interesting aspect of the decision ladder, which relates to how the knowledge-based decision process works in ecologically valid contexts. These contexts vary across decision-making domains but may include conditions where situation awareness has a high level of uncertainty because it includes a probabilistic assumption about the future (using projection, prediction, and/or simulation), which transforms the decision-making step into a discussion of influencing and causal factors rather than the application of simple rules. Other conditions that may arise from ecologically valid decision-making include if the set of facts or insights that built the current situation awareness model is incomplete and requires more focused investigation or diagnostic analysis, if no rule set or model exists that translates a condition into an action, or if the optimization criteria and decision strategy itself become the topic of the discussion or if the impact of an action has an uncertainty of outcome. The SADE Ladder integrates knowledge-based decision-making by including *investigation*, *prediction*, and *simulation* iterative cycles for application in problem contexts where situation awareness is fluid or incomplete between decision agents. Solutions subsequently emerge from a gestalt of agent situation awareness, prior learning, and simulated action-execution-feedback cycles.

AI is currently developing rapidly, with new foundation models being adapted for specific and general purposes appearing almost weekly (Wang et al. 2023). System agents developed using machine learning approaches can be deployed to transform complex situations into actionable information that can help reduce decision-making from knowledge-based problem-solving to a rule-based/associative mapping decision in part or in full. As the technology develops further, it will have the potential to help deal with uncertainty, perform large-scale simulations of outcomes, and replace deterministic rule sets with self-learning pattern recognition to increase adaptability to new situations. However, as previously discussed, caution must be taken to preserve cognitive heterogeneity between decision-making agents through task, agent, and interface design. Such design should consider that the human counterpart in an AI-powered automated decision environment possesses by virtue of expertise a superlative ability to utilize intuitive cognitive processes to perceive, comprehend, and project (within a shared SA framework) either at the global maxima (goal) or local minima (action) of a decision to intervene in the decision process to force an adaptation of an action or goal.

Pertaining to the decline in expertise, contemporary findings in neuroscience reveal that expertise is not necessarily lost, but rather, the velocity of decision-related action potentials is reduced (Yewbrey et al. 2023). Indeed, the evidence suggests that a mechanism exists to "package" expertise (tacit knowledge and sequencing) into neural substructures. That is, moving structured motor and cognitive, logical sequences from the low-level specification of individual actions to high-level sequence features (or heuristics), thus moving from system two explicit planning and action to system one intuitive action.

4.3 Designing Autonomous Execution

To realize autonomous end-to-end business processes, one or multiple AI-based automation agents must possess the capacity to contribute to the situation awareness and decision elements of the SADE Ladder (see Fig. 2) in order to respond to a new situation and make situated decisions without human intervention. In addition, these agents must have the functional agency to implement the decision in the form of concrete actions to complete the end-to-end decision loop. The execution of a decision can develop into more or less complex processes depending on the need, which can include the creation of an execution plan, the selection of the resources needed to enact the plan, and the performance of individual actions. This aspect of execution is the right pillar of the SADE Ladder. Like situation awareness and decision-making, the execution pillar relates to a very different body of research and touches on the question, "what is the difference between automation and autonomy?"

Traditionally, workflows have been used to standardize and automate business processes (Riss et al. 2005; Schulz and Orlowska 2004). An AI-based workflow would be a workflow that is either triggered by an AI-based awareness agent or launches AI-based automation agents to perform steps within the larger workflow. However, this concept falls short, given that a network of cooperating multiple agents differs from a simple workflow model in that each participating agent generates an action plan based on its situation awareness and decision-making capabilities.

An example of complex action planning is AI-based logistics systems (Chien et al. 2020; Afanasenko and Borisova 2021; Winkelhaus and Grosse 2020), which plan and execute a series of business functions in response to a customer order, such as allocating inventory, scheduling picks in the warehouse, and booking carriers to get the items delivered from the fulfillment center to the customer. In this example, multiple systems must make many micro-decisions about the best fulfillment strategy and which resources to select to enact the fulfillment. Multiple independent agents will typically cooperate in executing such a complex fulfillment plan. A sourcing agent might find the nearest inventory, a dynamic tasking agent may assign the picking tasks to human shop floor workers or robots, and a transport scheduling agent may dispatch trucks to deliver the items as part of an optimized multi-stop route. Each step is optimized and enacted by domain-specific automation agents.

Such action-execution is typically the domain of workflow engines (Stohr and Zhao 2001), which perform a series of predefined business operations or system operations to achieve a particular outcome according to some predefined set of rules. In the above example, within the SADE Ladder, a network of cooperative automation agents transforms this deterministic workflow paradigm into an adaptive workflow, wherein agents make intelligent micro-decisions to optimize each step within the larger fulfillment flow to respond to needs stochastically. Each agent acts on domain-specific situation awareness (SA) and makes decisions (D) to define the best action plan (E).

In many cases, decisions depend on the simulation of actions. If, as a driver, one sets the destination of a subsequent trip, the navigation system of a self-driving car will recommend different routes based on the estimated driving time, traffic forecast, and other factors of relevance per its configuration. Based on the system-generated recommendations, the driver will decide which route to take and then delegate the navigation back to the navigation system. In this scenario, the navigation system is primarily the execution system but facilitates decision-making regarding choosing the optimal route by generating and simulating decision options, presenting this information to the human operator, who ultimately decides to either accept the recommended route or choose one of the alternative routes available (or rejecting all system-recommended routes, thus taking full control of the car and driving it).

Another example of an execution agent is the parking assistant: the driver decides where to park and then explicitly initiates the parking assistant to execute the parking maneuver. Again, the execution agent may facilitate the decision-making by notifying the driver if the parking slot is big enough to park, but its primary purpose is to execute the maneuver. The driver maintains the ability to cancel the parking maneuver if desired.

Therefore, to implement fully autonomous business processes, multiple agents must be orchestrated to cover the situation awareness, the decision-making, and the execution of the decision. Imagine a scenario where the parking assistant would be a fully autonomous agent that uses the destination of a car navigation system as the input. Based on this input, the parking assistant would decide what type of parking to use and automatically route the car to the parking garage or a reserved parking slot on the street, stop the car, and maneuver into the parking slot.

Following best practices of workflow modeling and human action planning, a human or a system agent must be capable of covering the following three aspects:

- Orchestration: Defining what type of resources are needed and in what order, steps, or services should be executed. This step is typically associated with the selection of the basic overarching strategy. For example, if one decides to take public transportation to the airport, one will plan the trip by considering public transportation infrastructure.
- Resource allocation: Once the overall plan has been defined, all resources must be secured and allocated in advance of executing the orchestrated plan. For example, if one decides to take a taxi to the airport, one must select an existing taxi service that, according to available data and experience, has a reasonable price, quality, and availability.
- Action: This is the actual enactment of a plan. It could, for example, be placing the order for a taxi service.

As with the other two phases of the conceptual framework, the levels of action planning are optional and depend on the situation's complexity. If procedures are well-known, there is no need for ad hoc action orchestration. If a simple action is needed (e.g., changing the price of a product), then no resources are needed either. The more strategic a decision is, the more likely the upper levels of each phase are involved.

Executing a decision is often not considered "intelligent," given the assumption that the action plan is fully specified. However, this is only true if the decision maps a situation to a known procedure, and the steps of this procedure are fully specified so that it can be executed canonically without further situational adjustments. However, the reality is that even simple workflows often include micro-decisions to follow policies and business rules. It is for this reason that Business Process Modeling and Notation (BPMN) representations are often complemented by Decision Model and Notation (DMN) representations that, when combined, model complex rule sets to determine the exact steps to take depending on available context variables (Aguilar-Savén 2004).

If we consider other domains like cockpit automation (Wiener 1988) or driver assistance systems (Piao and McDonald 2008), there are many cases where the purpose of the AI system is primarily execution and not decision-making. For example, in a fly-by-wire mode, the pilot makes decisions about maneuvering the airplane, but the system electronically executes the pilot commands by performing a sequence of flight parameters and mechanical parts adjustments. In the case of a car, the driver might decide to park and delegate the execution to the parking assistant system, which then parks the car on behalf of the driver. In both examples, the user is making the decision or expressing the intent, and the AI system's task is to execute the decision.

Execution is offloaded to systems for enhanced productivity and management of complex dependencies and constraints during plan generation. These systems decipher extensive dependency trees and optimize resource utilization, such as logistics and shop floor task scheduling. Additionally, their performance often surpasses human abilities, exemplified in driver assistance and robotic surgery. These systems necessitate dynamic adjustments, environmental comprehension, and precise motion, transcending basic automation.

One could argue that during execution, numerous micro-decisions must be made, with their nature contingent upon perspective. Decision-making may involve generating action plans as simulated scenarios for comparison against a baseline (current reality). This type of situation does not negate the SADE Ladder; rather, it implies that fully autonomous business processes necessitate orchestrating multiple automation agents, each with its loops within the SADE Ladder for autonomous action generation.

4.4 Designing for Artificial Intelligence Transparency and Explainability

The relevance of transparency and explainability in the context of designing AI systems is well-known (Ehsan et al. 2021). With AI systems interpreting information, recommending decision options, making decisions, and planning actions, there is an increased demand for transparency of the cognitive capabilities of the underlying AI system and for the explainability of specific insights, recommendations, and actions.

The SADE decision ladder, with its phases and cognitive sub-functions, can serve as a conceptual model that illustrates how a multi-agent network contributes to an understand/decide/act task cycle or a more complex analyze/simulate/plan/act journey. Intelligence is distributed not only between human experts and AI agents but also between AI agents across those phases and different sub-functions. This underpins the importance of helping users understand the behavior of AI systems and the locality of artificial intelligence contributing to the outcome. We could argue that this concept model describes an AI-based tool's "under-the-hood" system reality. However, since the interaction dynamics between human experts and AI agents resemble a teaming approach, it is of utmost importance to help users establish a proper understanding of the system's capabilities, boundaries, and limitations to gain trust and maximize its utility.

One aspect of transparency is understanding the contributing network of agents. In her reappraisal of the situation awareness (SA) model (Endsley 2023), Endsley expands on the notion of awareness by merging the initial conceptualization of SA with human-AI collaborations to arrive at three levels of collaborative SA: taskwork

SA, agent SA, and teamwork SA. Furthermore, Endsley states that human-AI SA is best supported by AI transparency that is both current and prospective.

Similar to human collaboration, one member must understand other members' capabilities and motivation and how work is orchestrated among the members. The SADE framework provides some guidance on how to communicate such a concept model by grouping cognitive functions into phases and incremental levels of cognitive complexity. This creates a lineage of AI-based capabilities and outcomes, which is important to understand when interacting as a user with an AI system that is composed of multiple AI agents.

For example, suppose a workforce planner disagrees with the number of hourly workers scheduled by the system for a given time of the day. In that case, the source of the disagreement may be the planner's perception that there is an inaccurate demand prediction, a situation awareness function; an erroneous conversion of labor demand to resources, a decision strategy function; or the wrong assignment of resources, a decision implementation function. Each function may be provided by independent complex AI systems, including personal assistants for each hourly worker who act as a broker between the shift planning engine and the preferences of one worker. In the absence of an underlying mental model, the workforce planner simply perceives inappropriate staffing and will not accept the system-generated plan. If she knew about the locality of the problem (e.g., demand, labor index, profiles of hourly users) or would be aware of the applied optimization strategy (e.g., costs vs. customer experience vs. hourly worker satisfaction), she would not only have more trust but also may be able to intervene at the right step of the chain of incremental decision-making and provide qualified feedback. This example illustrates how a black-box approach, which does not provide any insight into the locality and orchestration of AI systems, may lead to the rejection of the entire AI solution since the human expert cannot rationalize system decisions and effectively intervene.

The SADE Ladder also depicts incremental or alternative cognitive functions inside one phase, with higher-level functions increasing the desire to understand why and how an AI system came to a specific conclusion, decision, or action plan. It makes a difference if a decision is based on a simple fact (the "signal" in Rasmussen's model) or is based on a cognitive comprehension, projection, and classification process that leads to an insight that triggers a rule-based decision. In this case, the human expert may want the system to explain why an AI agent came to a specific conclusion or decision. The SADE Ladder suggests that explainability must be aligned with the available cognitive resources and support backward navigation along the chain of thought within the ladder.

Both transparency and explainability are important design principles to empower the human expert to understand and contribute to a decision-making process and to maintain a level of situation awareness (passive in the loop) so that intuitive processes such as pattern recognition are engaged to allow a sudden takeover of control without reconstructing situation awareness from scratch (Cummings and Guerlain 2005).

5 Summary

While Rasmussen's decision ladder and Endsley's situation awareness model are not perfectly aligned, by harnessing the respective strengths of each perspective, the integrative view afforded by the SADE Ladder can help guide the design of successful human-system-agent interactions that preserve cognitive heterogeneity across both human and AI agents.

Regarding cognitive functions and skills, both models introduce different cognitive sub-functions or mental processes for a single phase in the automation loop. Wherein, the cognitive resources (mental workload) required in both models increase similarly in each phase, i.e., levels 1–3 of situation awareness and skill-based, rule-based, and knowledge-based in decision-making. Besides combining those two pillars, the SADE Ladder extends this concept of increasing cognitive demands to the execution phase by performing actions, specifying actions, and orchestrating action plans.

Using a conceptual framework such as the SADE Ladder allows us to better understand the ergonomic aspects of embedding AI systems into the workplace and the interaction dynamics between human and AI teaming to get work done.

The SADE Ladder allows us to discuss human-centered aspects of AI-based task and process automation holistically across historically disconnected research domains. Combining research on situation awareness, decision-making, Computer-Supported Collaborative Work (CSCW), and business workflow gives us a new wide-angle lens to look at the challenges and opportunities of AI systems in the workplace. The scope of the design of AI systems goes far beyond the user interface; it expands to human-AI teaming and how to achieve transparency and controllability of hybrid socio-technical systems where multiple human experts and AI agents deliver meaningful business outcomes.

The anatomy of the SADE Ladder also suggests that an end-to-end decision loop covering a meaningful task or responsibility will depend on the orchestration of multiple cognitive sub-functions distributed within and across the three pillars assigned to one or multiple human- or AI-based agents. Such AI agents can be specialized in one cognitive function (e.g., detection of a moving object), on a pillar (an AI-based surveillance system monitoring a house and notifying the homeowner in case an unknown person is entering the property), or across pillars (a surveillance system interrogating the intruder and calling the police if not identified as entitled to enter the premise).

The SADE Ladder also makes it evident that different decision modes suggest structurally different networks of AI-based automation agents. At the same time, the situational adaptability of the decision loop to different levels of decision complexity is essential. We posit that taking an integrative approach to human-AI teaming that balances these aspects and trains human experts to utilize the strengths of intuitive decision-making while simultaneously providing an AI agent to automate and enhance system two-style decision-making would benefit a human-AI collaborative context. This strategy maintains cognitive diversity in the human-AI partnership, potentially mitigating concerns like overreliance, habituation, and distrust. Nevertheless, this method necessitates a decision-making framework that enables human experts and AI to effectively utilize critical decision processes for task completion, for which we posit the SADE Ladder.

References

Afanasenko ID, Borisova VV (2021) Artificial intelligence in digital type logistics systems. In: Meta-scientific study of artificial intelligence book series: advances in research on Russian Business and Management, pp 233–240

Aguilar-Savén RS (2004) Business process modelling: review and framework. Int J Prod Econ 90(2):129–149

Banks VA, Plant KL, Stanton NA (2020) Leaps and shunts: designing pilot decision aids on the flight deck using Rasmussen's ladder. In: Contemporary ergonomics and human factors

Beringer J, Coursaris CK, Léger PM, Karran AJ, Oz B (2022) Teaming models with intelligent systems at the workplace. In: Wirtschaftsinformatik 2022 proceedings, p 2

Chien CF, Dauzère-Pérès S, Huh WT, Jang YJ, Morrison JR (2020) Artificial intelligence in manufacturing and logistics systems: algorithms, applications, and case studies

Cummings M, Guerlain S (2005) The decision ladder as an automation planning tool. Cognition, technology, and work

Edmondson AC (2012) Teaming: how organizations learn, innovate, and compete in the knowledge economy. John Wiley & Sons, New York

Ehsan U, Liao QV, Muller M, Riedl MO, Weisz JD (2021) Expanding explainability: towards social transparency in ai systems. In: Proceedings of the 2021 CHI conference on human factors in computing systems, pp 1–19

Endsley MR (1995) Toward a theory of situation awareness in dynamic systems. Hum Fact 37(1):32–64

Endsley MR (2023) Supporting human-ai teams: transparency, explainability, and situation awareness. Comput Hum Behav 140:107574

Farrington-Darby T, Wilson JR (2006) The nature of expertise: a review. Appl Ergon 37(1):17–32

Fügener A, Grahl J, Gupta A, Ketter W (2021) Will humans-in-the-loop become borgs? Merits and pitfalls of working with ai. In: Management information systems quarterly, vol 45

Golestan K, Soua R, Karray F, Kamel MS (2016) Situation awareness within the context of connected cars: a comprehensive review and recent trends. Inform Fusion 29:68–83

Jiang J, Karran AJ, Coursaris CK, Léger PM, Beringer J (2023) A situation awareness perspective on human-ai interaction: Tensions and opportunities. Int J Hum–Comput Interact 39(9):1789–1806

Jones DG, Endsley MR (1996) Sources of situation awareness errors in aviation. In: Aviation, space, and environmental medicine

Kahneman D (2011) Thinking, fast and slow. Macmillan, New York

Klein G (2015) A naturalistic decision making perspective on studying intuitive decision making. J Appl Res Memory Cogn 4(3):164–168

McCall JC, Trivedi MM (2007) Driver behavior and situation aware brake assistance for intelligent vehicles. Proc IEEE 95(2):374–387

Munir A, Aved A, Blasch E (2022) Situational awareness: techniques, challenges, and prospects. AI 3(1):55–77

Naikar N (2010) A comparison of the decision ladder template and the recognition-primed decision model. Defence Science and Technology Organisation Fishermans Bend, Australia

O'Neill T, McNeese N, Barron A, Schelble B (2022) Human–autonomy teaming: a review and analysis of the empirical literature. Hum Fact 64(5):904–938

Parasuraman R, Riley V (1997) Humans and automation: use, misuse, disuse, abuse. Hum Fact 39(2):230–253

Piao J, McDonald M (2008) Advanced driver assistance systems from autonomous to cooperative approach. Transp Rev 28(5):659–684

Politowicz MS, Chancey ET, Glaab LJ (2021) Effects of autonomous sUAS separation methods on subjective workload, situation awareness, and trust. In: AIAA SciTech 2021 Forum, p 1176

Rasmussen J (1976) Outlines of a hybrid model of the process plant operator. In: Monitoring behavior and supervisory control. Springer, Berlin, pp 371–383

Rasmussen J (1983) Skills, rules, and knowledge; signals, signs, and symbols, and other distinctions in human performance models. IEEE Trans Syst Man Cybern (3):257–266

Riss UV, Rickayzen A, Maus H, van der Aalst WM (2005) Challenges for business process and task management. J Universal Knowl Manag 2:77–100

Rockl M, Robertson P, Frank K, Strang T (2007) An architecture for situation-aware driver assistance systems. In: 2007 IEEE 65th vehicular technology conference-VTC2007-Spring. IEEE, Piscataway, pp 2555–2559

Salas E, Rosen MA, DiazGranados D (2010) Expertise-based intuition and decision making in organizations. J Manag 36(4):941–973

Salotti JM, Suhir E (2019) Degraded situation awareness risk assessment in the aerospace domain. In: 2019 IEEE 5th international workshop on metrology for aerospace (MetroAeroSpace). IEEE, Piscataway, pp 39–43

Schraagen JM (2024) Responsible use of ai in military systems. Taylor & Francis, London

Schulz KA, Orlowska ME (2004) Facilitating cross-organisational workflows with a workflow view approach. Data Knowl Eng 51(1):109–147

Stohr EA, Zhao JL (2001) Workflow automation: overview and research issues. Inform Syst Front 3:281–296

Wang H, Fu T, Du Y, Gao W, Huang K, Liu Z, Chandak P, Liu S, Van Katwyk P, Deac A (2023) Scientific discovery in the age of artificial intelligence. Nature 620(7972):47–60

Wiener EL (1988) Cockpit automation. Elsevier, Amsterdam, pp 433–461

Winkelhaus S, Grosse EH (2020) Logistics 4.0: a systematic review towards a new logistics system. Int J Prod Res 58(1):18–43

Wulf F, Rimini-Döring M, Arnon M, Gauterin F (2014) Recommendations supporting situation awareness in partially automated driver assistance systems. IEEE Trans Intell Transp Syst 16(4):2290–2296

Yewbrey R, Mantziara M, Kornysheva K (2023) Cortical patterns shift from sequence feature separation during planning to integration during motor execution. J Neurosci 43(10):1742–1756

The Dynamics of Human-AI Interactions in Organizational Decision-Making

Burak Öz, Alexander J. Karran, Joerg Beringer, Constantinos K. Coursaris, and Pierre-Majorique Léger

Abstract Information systems (IS) are increasingly being used to support more complex and knowledge-intensive decision-making tasks. Contemporary systems often rely on machine learning, artificial intelligence (AI), and deep learning methods. While these technologies are promising in processing complex problems and large datasets, their black-box nature poses challenges for these systems' adoption in organizational settings, where understanding the rationale used by AI-driven decision-support tools is important. This study examines supply chain experts' interactions with AI systems through the lens of the situation awareness (SA) model. We identify factors leading to a user's decision to either delegate decision-making tasks to AI or intervene in the AI-driven processes. Our findings suggest that mismatches between the AI's SA and the expert user's SA create tensions that impact the delegation of tasks to the AI system. We discuss additional sources of tension and propose human-centered design practices to mitigate these issues.

1 Introduction

Information systems (IS) play a critical role in enabling employees to make better decisions in today's organizational environments. With continuous technological improvements in data processing capabilities, decision support has evolved from simple computations to providing recommendations in complex problem-solving scenarios. Consequently, this shift has transformed IS from simple tools to artificially intelligent agents that support, and in some cases, work together with, domain

B. Öz · A. J. Karran · C. K. Coursaris · P.-M. Léger
HEC Montreal, Montreal, Quebec, Canada
e-mail: burak.oz@hec.ca; alexander-john.karran@hec.ca; constantinos.coursaris@hec.ca; pierre-majorique.leger@hec.ca

J. Beringer (✉)
ProContext, Redwood City, CA, USA
e-mail: joerg.beringer@procontext.ai

C. K. Coursaris et al. (eds.), *The Design of Human-Centered Artificial Intelligence for the Workplace*, Progress in IS, https://doi.org/10.1007/978-3-031-83512-4_3

experts. This shift highlights the importance of collaborative decision-making models between humans and Artificial Intelligence (AI), which are becoming more common in organizational processes (National Academies of Sciences, Engineering, and Medicine 2021).

As the extent of decision support from IS extends beyond simple calculations to autonomous decision-making, the relationship between the user and IS becomes more complex. Users may either rely excessively on the IS, potentially losing their ability to understand how future events impact their decision-making environment, or distrust the IS, thereby not fully benefiting from its capabilities in processing large volumes of data and deriving relevant insights (Chiang and Yin 2022). Balancing these two tendencies is critical for optimal operational outcomes.

Previous research has extensively studied the impact of IS investments on organizational outcomes (Brynjolfsson 1993; Sabherwal and Jeyaraj 2015). Extant theories and models, particularly the technology acceptance model (TAM) and its extensions, highlight factors such as perceived usefulness and ease of use as drivers of IS adoption (Davis 1989; Venkatesh and Bala 2008). While TAM has been used extensively to explain user interactions with traditional IS, the complexities of AI-powered systems necessitate further research on the topic. Unlike traditional IS that function within defined parameters, AI systems are dynamic and adaptive. In other words, AI systems possess the capability to continuously learn and modify their operational patterns based on new data inputs (Schuetz and Venkatesh 2020). While the benefits of using AI in complex decision-making tasks are clear, this continuously evolving and often opaque nature of AI presents unique challenges (Endsley 2022). One such challenge is understanding how users perceive and adapt to a dynamic AI-driven decision support system and how they make ongoing decisions regarding task delegation to AI. Therefore, in this chapter, we aim to answer the following research question:

RQ: What factors influence professionals' decisions on whether to rely on AI in organizational decision-making processes?

To understand users' decisions about delegating tasks to AI, situation awareness theory emerges as a promising lens (Endsley 1995). Situation awareness (SA) is defined as "the perception of the elements in the environment within a volume of time and space, the comprehension of their meaning, and the projection of their status in the near future" (Endsley 1995, p. 1). While the SA concept was initially defined to understand and explain human decision-making with automation tools in aviation, it can be extended to the context of human-AI interactions (Endsley 2022).

This chapter presents a study conducted to answer our research question by considering the perspectives of professionals shared through expert interviews. The rest of the chapter is organized as follows: first, we provide an overview of the SA concept and its relevance to human-AI interactions. We then describe our methods for collecting and analyzing stakeholder interview data within a supply chain management (SCM) context. Results are discussed in two parts: first, we introduce six contextual factors influencing users' meta-decisions whether to delegate decision-making to AI; then, we incorporate these factors into the

SA model and propose a conceptual extension. The chapter concludes with key considerations for successful AI implementation projects.

2 Background

2.1 *The Adoption and Use of IS and AI*

Information systems have been integral to organizational decision-making environments for several decades. As the success of an IS depends on its use, the factors leading to acceptance have been extensively studied in the literature. The technology acceptance model (TAM) (Davis 1989) is one of the well-known perspectives, which presents perceived usefulness and perceived ease of use as predictors of user acceptance. Over the years, the set of constructs predicting user acceptance has expanded, leading to models such as TAM2, the unified theory of acceptance and use of technology, and TAM3 (Venkatesh and Davis 2000; Venkatesh et al. 2003; Venkatesh and Bala 2008).

While these attitude-based theories and other richer theoretical lenses provide valuable insights regarding the use of traditional IS, they assume that an IS is deterministic and behaves predictably according to the rules it was designed to follow (Schuetz and Venkatesh 2020). AI, however, does not rely on a predetermined set of rules. Instead, AI-driven systems continuously learn from new observations and adapt their behavior accordingly (Czako et al. 2021). Therefore, to address the need to better understand human-AI interaction dynamics in organizational decision-making, we borrow the concept of situation awareness from the scientific discipline of human factors.

2.2 *The Situation Awareness Model*

Situation awareness (SA) is defined as "the perception of the elements in the environment within a volume of time and space, the comprehension of their meaning, and the projection of their status in the near future" (Endsley 1995, p. 1). This definition of SA is human-centric, focusing only on the human operators. According to this model, situation awareness is characterized by three levels:

1. Perception of elements in the current situation: This consists of the observations of data points relevant to decision-making.
2. Comprehension of the current situation: This level is about the use of the SA elements from the first level to create a meaningful synthesis that represents the current reality.

3. Projection of future status: This is achieved by integrating SA elements from the first two levels to provide a foundation for anticipating future changes in the environment.

The SA theory initially aimed to explore the relationship between pilots and automation systems in aircraft (Endsley 1995). The high volume of sensory data to be processed and the time-sensitive nature of this context make it important for pilots to maintain their SA. Similarly, modern organizational decision-making environments exhibit similar characteristics. With digital technologies increasingly involved in data generation and processing, the speed and accuracy expected from organizational decision-making processes have also risen (Danilova 2019). Therefore, the conditions in modern decision-making environments are parallel to those targeted by the initial SA theory.

To address the complexities of multi-agent decision-making environments, the original SA model was extended into the distributed situation awareness (DSA) model (Salmon 2008). The DSA model considers both human decision-makers and technical systems as agents capable of building and communicating their own SA. This socio-technical approach is suitable for contexts where different agents need to share their SA.

The DSA model examines the notion of team SA and the communication between actors that builds this collective SA. Moreover, the DSA model also examines how various members of a decision-making team form their interrelationships concerning system, team, task, and individual factors (Salmon 2008). The team SA includes not only the team members' SA but also their awareness of other members' activities, beliefs, and intentions. This aligns well with the IS acceptance literature, which indicates that users' actions regarding an IS are dominantly shaped by their beliefs and intentions (Venkatesh et al. 2003). In summary, the DSA model emphasizes the suitability of SA as a promising theory to investigate human-AI interactions in complex decision-making scenarios.

In summary, existing research and literature involving SA suggest that it is a promising theoretical lens through which to investigate human-AI interactions in complex decision-making scenarios. In this study, we explore the decision-making process of experts who have access to AI-driven decision support systems in their daily work. Through this exploration, we aim to extend our understanding of underlying factors that influence experts in either relying or ignoring AI systems during decision-making.

3 Methods

Our primary method for data collection employed a qualitative interview methodology consisting of a combination of free-form and structured interview questions. The structured questions draw from the SA and DSA models. Following the conceptualization of task factors, individual factors, and system factors in the DSA model, we initially started the interviews with the structured part of the interview, specifically with questions regarding tasks and their influence and interaction with the system within the participants functioned. In this context, individual factors included elements such as experience, training, and workload. Task factors focused more on the characteristics of the task such as complexity. System factors were concerned more with the decision-making environment created by the decision support systems that were in effect and their design. Our interview structure allowed follow-up questions to be asked to explore unforeseen themes and ideas. Such an approach offered a balance between a focus on the relevant concepts and new insights unaddressed in the existing set of questions. Each interview lasted for about 90 minutes.

Our participant sample comprised a variety of stakeholders working in the supply chain management field: individuals from AI development teams, consultants advising on these systems' installation and use, and end users. Each interviewee had experience using an AI-driven decision support engine or configuring it for use in SCM decisions such as truckload management, demand forecasting, and employee shift allocation. A purposive sampling method was employed to select participants based on their roles, and their association with, and their experience with AI decision support tools. We interviewed a total of 20 participants. Data collection was terminated according to the informational redundancy criteria, meaning that the sampling procedure can be concluded when additional interviews do not add new information to the dataset (Lincoln and Guba 1985; Miles and Huberman 1994) or, in other words, when the dataset reaches saturation (Glaser and Strauss 1967).

3.1 Analysis of Collected Data

In the early stages of this study's design, situation awareness (SA) theory was identified as a suitable framework for investigating the dynamics between human decision-makers and AI agents in organizations. However, as SA theory has primarily been applied in other fields, unique insights may emerge from applying it in our study's specific context. We adopted the multi-grounded theory (MGT) approach, which provides a balanced approach between inductive and deductive reasoning in an iterative process, making it possible for additional findings to emerge (Goldkuhl and Cronholm 2010).

In line with MGT, our analysis included three grounding phases: empirical, theoretical, and internal. Beginning with the empirical phase, interview data were meticulously coded without any preconceived biases. NVivo software was used in this coding process, and two researchers from the team collaboratively analyzed one fifth of the data to ensure consistency. After this initial coding, data were categorized using the SA framework. The final phase involved theory condensation, wherein observations were systematically evaluated for their coherence with established theories, and potential expansions to these theories were pinpointed. During data collection, the three grounding phases were followed iteratively within and across participants.

4 Results

As this study's research focus was on understanding the dynamics between human and AI systems during decision-making, we structure the findings across decision-making process stages. A typical decision-making process involves three key stages: sensing, deciding, and acting (Endsley 1995). As we consider human decision-making processes assisted by AI, we focus on the first two stages, sensing and deciding, where the sensing step also consists of three levels, akin to the three levels of SA (Endsley 1995): detect, comprehend, and predict.

4.1 Decision-Making with AI Support and Meta-decision-making

Our findings confirm that decision-makers often follow the three-step decision-making process when faced with decision-making problems, but with a slight difference caused by the presence of AI support. SCM decision-makers tend to view AI more than mere tools. Instead, they consider AI as their counterparts working in the same decision-making process. They continuously evaluate the AI's performance and reliability at various stages of the decision-making process. We refer to this ongoing evaluation and reflection of the decision-making process and strategy as meta-decision-making.

Meta-decision-making can be defined as "deciding how to decide" (Kottemann 1986). It involves choosing the techniques and information that will guide the primary decision-making process. In the context of human-AI interactions, our results indicate that the decision to delegate certain aspects of the decision-making process to AI is not a one-time choice but a continuous consideration.

Our results suggest that depending on which stage of the decision-making process is evaluated, different factors influence the meta-decision of delegating a decision to an AI-system or not.

The sensing phase of the decision-making aligns with the three levels of situation awareness: detecting, comprehending, and predicting. Given the central focus on situation awareness, we have organized the results section according to the stages of decision-making process and the different levels of SA as described by Endsley. We discuss these influencing factors summarized in Table 1 in the following sections.

Table 1 The factors influencing meta-decisions at each stage of the decision-making

Sense			
Detect	Comprehend	Predict	Decide
– Input data – User control – Data volume	– Data volume – AI transparency – AI configurability	– AI explainability	– AI interactivity
– Task complexity – User workload – User perceptions of AI – Task importance – Presence of an exception in the environment			

4.2 *Factors Influencing the Meta-decisions at the "Sense, Detect" Phase*

Our results indicate that decision-makers are comfortable with delegating the perception of elements in the current situation when they are confident that it is safe to do so. In the context of AI-supported decision-making in supply chain management, this confidence depends on factors such as input data, data volume, complexity, and workload.

4.2.1 Input Data

An AI system's SA depends on the quality and relevance of the data it receives as input. Our interviews revealed that discrepancies often exist between the data AI systems use and the data human experts consider relevant, especially in exceptional circumstances—for example, when plans deviate from the baseline values. Participants noted that the AI system lacked awareness of the root cause of such deviations due to missing variables or data points in their dataset. If the AI system does not allow users to add these additional facts as input, users may hesitate to delegate the subtask of monitoring the environment to the AI. Since detecting the environment is the first step in the decision-making process, choosing not to delegate this task means that users will likely complete the entire decision-making process manually.

> (Decision-makers) want to see every price because they are used to doing that. They know they spend a lot of time, but they still want to continue. They say—I want to look at each and every price, and if I am okay (with that), I will go to the next step. — Participant 4

Participants frequently reported evaluating the AI's perception of reality, especially when they are trying to learn more about a newly installed system's abilities. Establishing and communicating that the AI correctly perceives reality is essential before users feel comfortable delegating subsequent stages of SA and decision-making to AI. Without this assurance, users may prefer not to delegate any steps of the decision-making process.

4.2.2 User Control on Input Data

In addition to the input data the system considers, users' ability—or lack thereof—to configure or adjust input variables influences their meta-decision to delegate the first level of SA to an AI. For instance, one participant explained that they had no way of knowing whether the AI planning tool accounts for an employee's experience level, which can impact the expected time required to complete tasks. Without a way of understanding or adding such contextual variables, users often take over the task at the sensing stage instead of delegating any decision-making responsibilities to AI.

> I just heard ten new associates (just started), and they are not experienced. So, I know that I can not look at the freight planning tool and put that exact amount of people (based on what the planning tool says). I am going to need a little bit more (associates) because they are going to be slower. — Participant 8

When exceptions in the environment that the AI cannot perceive occur frequently, users may begin to disregard AI outputs in subsequent stages of the decision-making process. In other words, they dismiss the AI's model of reality and its predictions for the future, based on their perceptions that AI lacks an accurate perception of reality to begin with.

> There are some circumstances that we make a business decision (to apply) aggressive promotions due to market conditions, and we switch this (AI forecasting) system off for this period. — Participant 3

These findings highlight that an AI's ability to incorporate user input related to decision-making environment is critical at the first stage of decision-making, sensing the environment. Moreover, the results indicate that a user's choice not to delegate the perception of the environment to AI can lead to the dismissal of AI throughout all subsequent stages of decision-making.

4.2.3 Data Volume

Another factor that influences the meta-decision of whether or not to delegate a task to AI is the volume of data that must be processed to develop the SA required for a business decision. Our interview data indicates that users rely on AI not only to improve decision accuracy but also to handle vast quantities of data points that would be challenging or impossible to process manually. Participants stated an increased possibility of delegating the task to AI as the data volume increases.

> Having millions of items, ... it becomes very difficult to do it manually. That is where it (AI-driven decision support system) comes in. It automates the manual task, and it is highly scalable. — Participant 4

Participants reported that when working with large datasets, they often choose to delegate the analysis of individual data points to AI, effectively delegating the initial phase of SA development to the system. According to our interview data, this delegation allows them to focus on higher-priority tasks, as they are freed from the time-intensive task of developing the first level of SA from large datasets.

4.3 *Factors Influencing the Meta-decisions at the "Sense, Comprehend" Phase*

4.3.1 Data Volume

As reliance on data increases in SCM, users report having limited time to evaluate every detail, often finding it necessary to delegate subsequent stages of decision-making to AI.

> There are thousands of (AI-generated decision) proposals each week and (we have) only six parallel meetings of one hour each (to evaluate these proposals). — Participant 3

Our interview data suggests that the greater the volume of data, the more likely users are to rely on AI not only to build the initial level of SA but also to handle later decision-making stages.

4.3.2 System Transparency

System transparency refers to "the understandability and predictability of the system" (Endsley et al. 2003, p. 146). A highly transparent system allows users to understand the data sources and inner logic behind its predictions (Chen et al. 2014). Our findings indicate that users' expectation regarding the level of transparency may change according to task type, complexity, and user preferences.

> (some users) want to challenge everything and they are never happy with the solution, and they look at it as a suggestion and then they're constantly trying to modify it. — Participant 12

Participants also stated that their trust in AI is influenced by system transparency, which in turn affects the degree of control they allow AI to exert in the decision-making process.

> All it said was these (are) your demand hours based on your trends, and these are the hours. . . . I like to understand how things work. — Participant 8

Since system transparency is essential for understanding how an AI system constructs a model of the environment, it influences users' decision to delegate the development of level 2 SA to AI.

4.3.3 System Configurability

Before deciding to delegate the comprehension of a decision-making to AI, participants reported that they sometimes need to seek ways of controlling and influencing the AI system's understanding of the environment. They shared that adjusting model parameters not only improves their understanding of the decision-making context but also offers insights into how the AI system works to generate its suggestions.

> The biggest value that the (AI-driven decision support system) brings is quickly modeling it (a scenario) and then playing around with it, such as changing parameters quickly and running it once again. — Participant 2

The interviews suggest that participants view model configurability as a natural next step of system transparency. While transparency helps users understand the input values and AI logic, configurability enables them to actively experiment with different scenarios.

4.4 Factors Influencing the Meta-decisions at the "Sense, Predict" Phase

4.4.1 System Explainability

Explainability of an AI system is "the degree to which a human observer can understand the reason behind a decision (or a prediction) made by the model" (Vilone and Longo 2021, p. 91). Unlike transparency, which relates primarily to the broader understanding of the system and its underlying model, explainability focuses specifically on a given prediction and the factors influencing that outcome. Our findings indicate that users expect a certain level of system explainability when receiving AI recommendations.

> We still need to understand, in what scenarios, what is triggering this forecast, which feels off (compared to our expectations). — Participant 9

> It would be helpful to have some explanation on why a given product has a specific price (recommendation). — Participant 3

When the level of explainability does not meet the users' needs, particularly regarding AI's prediction for the future, users reported that they tend to disregard the system's recommendations. In other words, they refrain from delegating the task of predicting future states to the system, as they find its reasoning unclear or insufficient.

> ...all these parameters say (to me), do not look at (the profit) margin, just get rid of this item. And we see that the system still does not recommend any price decrease. ... We do not understand why the system does not want to decrease the price. ... (this pricing task) is very manual right now. — Participant 3

Overall, the interviews highlight that users' willingness to delegate decision-making tasks to AI depends on the system's ability to justify its recommendations through clear explanations.

4.5 Factors Influencing the Meta-decisions at the "Decide" Phase

The decision-making process concludes at this phase, where a commitment is made to implement the selected course of action. This phase is typically considered irreversible, making it a critical point in the decision-making process. As a result, decision-makers typically conduct a final assessment that draws on the meta-decisions formed during prior stages.

In this final stage, meta-decisions about whether to delegate or intervene in AI are made using a combination of all inputs from previous stages. When decision-makers perceive gaps in their under standing of the system's reasoning, they are more inclined to intervene rather than fully delegate the final decision to the system.

4.5.1 Task Importance

Another factor influencing whether decision-makers intervene in automation is the importance of the task and the potential risks associated with an incorrect decision. When a decision is perceived as critical for the organization, decision-makers would be more thorough in evaluating AI recommendations.

> Planners do not want to take the risk, especially with important products, especially if the order (suggested by AI) is way lower (than our anticipations). — Participant 5

Users also reported that they may be more inclined to delegate to AI in case of lower perceived task importance and higher perceived workload.

> It is not that time consuming to filter those less important items and decide whether we accept (AI recommendations) or not. — Participant 3

Insights extracted from the interviews indicate that perceived task importance plays a role in whether decision-makers choose to delegate to AI.

4.5.2 Task Complexity

Complex decision-making in a supply chain management scenario requires building a comprehensive mental model of reality, which can be challenging given the multifaceted context.

> Modeling (the) complex reality is not always easy, and there is typically a lot of discovery that has to happen. — Participant 2.

Participants reported difficulties in maintaining level 1 SA when the decision complexity and the number of variables were perceived as high. Without this foundational level, users may struggle to develop level 2 SA and fully comprehend the situation.

> It is to a quite low extent (the end-user gets the knowledge of the system), because there are so many factors affecting the final price proposal. And sometimes even [...] when we collaborate with the developers, it is really difficult to understand and explain why the system recommended a particular (solution). — Participant 3

Our findings indicate that contextual complexity impacts users' task delegation to AI both directly and through the system design. Participants noted that as complexity in the context increases, interacting with the AI system's interface becomes more challenging, which limits user's control over the system's configuration.

> It is complex to run. If you open one of those files and you change one parameter without knowing what the impact is, you are likely to break it. — Participant 1

In summary, findings highlight the role of increased task complexity in shaping users' decision to delegate various stages of the decision-making process to AI. As the number of observations grows, decision-makers become more inclined to rely on AI in identifying trends in large datasets.

4.5.3 User Workload

While task complexity challenges users' understanding of the environment and their ability to build SA, high workloads increase their likelihood of accepting AI recommendations without hesitation.

> If (we) start doing this (task) manually, that is a couple of planners doing that and creating multiple stops to make sure about the distribution of loads across drivers. ... It can take (us) hours, or days. — Participant 2

Users reported being more willing to delegate tasks to AI when their workloads were perceived as unmanageable within the available time constraints.

> For the short-term forecast, the responsiveness to what is actually happening in the stores is really strong in that (AI recommender). That is something that we would never have achieved manually. — Participant 5

4.5.4 Exceptional Cases

In predominantly automated processes, participants report switching to manual mode in exceptional cases to handle specific needs more efficiently.

> We work mostly in automatic (mode), but sometimes the supply team sends us some emergencies that are standby manual internal order forms. We work in manual (in these cases). — Participant 13

As mentioned in previous sections, the results indicate that users' tendency to take over mainly stems from a combination of case specificity, lack of transparency, and limited user control and system configurability.

4.5.5 System Interactivity

The level of interactivity provided by an AI system's user interface impacts users' meta-decision to involve AI in their decision-making process. Participants emphasized their satisfaction with being able to adjust AI recommendations and observe the outcomes in real time, as this interactivity allows for a more dynamic and supportive partnership with the system.

> If I accidentally schedule someone seven days in a row, it is going to flag. . . . I do love those warnings and those reminders that it gives us. — Participant 8

By enabling experimentation, interactive features help users understand the AI's reasoning better and apply adjustments to match real-world conditions.

4.5.6 User Perceptions of AI Decision Performance

User perceptions regarding AI and its potential play a role in decisions to delegate specific tasks to AI. Our findings indicate that users are continuously evaluating the system's outcomes in order to update their understanding of its performance over time.

> We need to have more cases where we also build trust to actually think the other way around (having the task fully automated). — Participant 9

> (I) need to have a good, clever way of judging afterwards, who was right. I think that would really help building the trust in the system. — Participant 5

User perceptions of AI performance are often shaped by the alignment, or fit, between user expectations and the system's recommendations. When there is a mismatch, it becomes essential for the system to facilitate a comparison of both options. In line with previous factors discussed, enhanced system configurability enables such comparisons of user expectations and system recommendations. This experimentation not only improves users' comprehension of the AI's decision logic but also enables them to refine the AI's understanding of real-world conditions.

5 An Extended Process Model of Decision-Making with AI

The situation awareness (SA) model highlights the importance of achieving an adequate level of SA to make informed decisions in complex environments (Endsley 1995). At its core, SA involves gathering relevant information to construct mental models that enable decision-makers to understand the current situation and predict possible outcomes.

While the SA lens provides a foundational viewpoint in examining the decision-making process with AI-driven decision support systems, certain aspects of human-AI interactions fall beyond its traditional scope. Specifically, as AI systems learn and adapt within their environments, users must continually recalibrate their mental models, assessing the conditions under which AI can operate effectively.

A unique aspect of human AI interactions is the continuous evaluation of an AI's performance, which leads to an ongoing process of secondary decision-making to determine when, and to what extent, they should delegate tasks to AI. Given this dynamic, we propose modeling the SA of both the user and the AI in a decision-making process model to understand and explain meta-decisions within the primary decision-making process. The proposed process model is illustrated in Fig. 1.

5.1 Meta-decision-making

Meta-decision making, or the act of "deciding how to decide" (Kottemann 1986), represents an important layer in the decision-making process with AI support. Traditionally, meta-decision-making involves selecting the techniques, information, and strategies guiding a primary decision. However, in AI-supported decision-making scenarios, meta-decision-making expands to include the human's ongoing assessments of both the primary decision and the AI's ability to do it, resulting in a more complex, iterative process due to AI's evolving nature.

Figure 1 presents an extended decision-making process highlighting users' meta-decisions about task delegation to AI. This model includes the AI-driven decision support system's SA in parallel to the user's SA, with two-sided arrows representing the interactions between the two. These arrows signify that each decision-making task involves a series of meta-decisions regarding which steps to delegate to AI, influenced by the level of alignment, or fit, between users' SA and their perception of AI's SA regarding the primary task.

In this partnership, the type of primary task to be performed dictates the cognitive skills and information (in terms of mutual SA elements) required from both human and AI. The meta-decision-making aspect, however, becomes a continuous cycle in which users assess the role, reliability, and relevance of AI. Through this ongoing and iterative process, elements from AI become extensions of or augments to human cognition, making the decision-making process more nuanced and therefore moving it into the "meta" realm.

In summary, the concept of meta-decision in human-AI interactions makes it possible to view AI-supported decision-making processes in layers where delegation is an ongoing negotiation rather than a one-time choice. This negotiation requires both parties to be able to effectively communicate their SA to the other. Our results indicate that such human-AI SA alignment can be maintained through increased AI transparency, AI explainability, and human control over AI inputs and parameters.

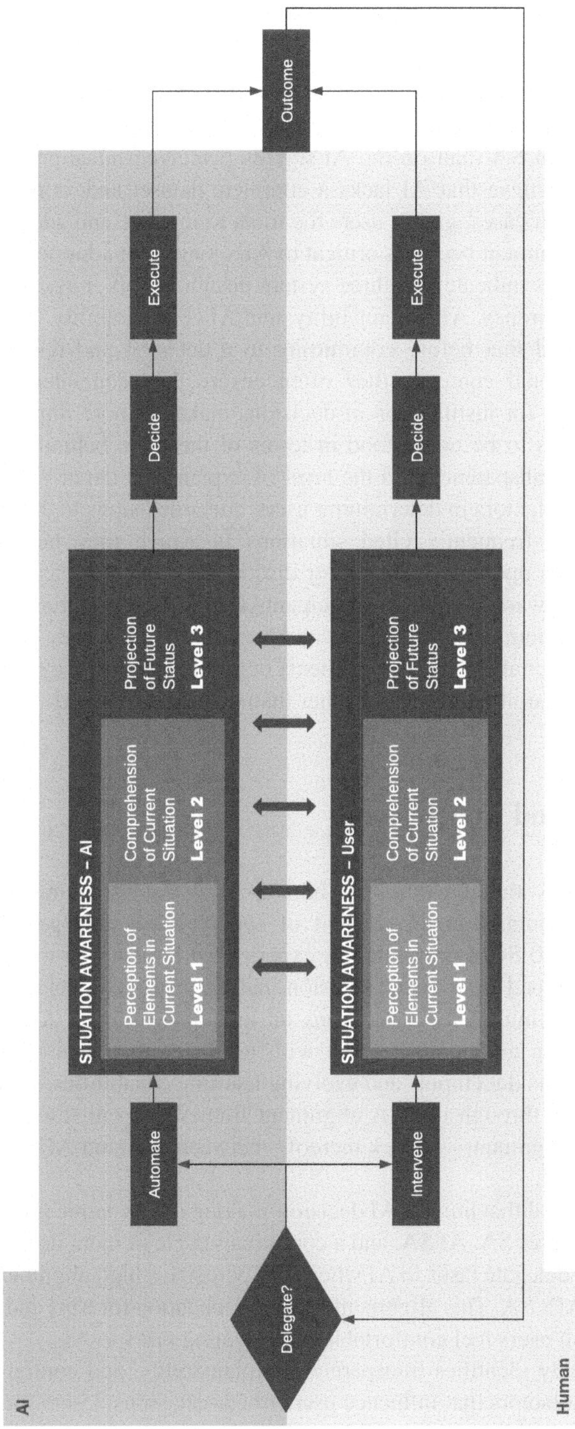

Fig. 1 The process model of a user's decision to automate a complex decision-making task

5.2 *System Design as a Factor in Meta-decisions*

When users perceive a misalignment, a tension manifests (Jiang et al. 2023). In such cases, experts who are highly confident in their domain knowledge may rely more heavily on their own SA than on the AI's. This perceived misalignment is often amplified if users believe that AI lacks a complete dataset and, consequently, an adequate SA. In such cases, giving users the tools to manage and address this lack of perceived misalignment becomes critical to AI's long-term adoption in decision-making. Our findings indicate that three system design factors impact users' meta-decisions: AI transparency, AI explainability, and AI configurability.

Participants noted that before committing to a decision and taking action in complex organizational contexts, they often ensure they can later justify their decisions. This need for justification of decisions makes it more important for the AI recommendations to be understood in terms of the logic behind the decision. Therefore, system transparency and the level of explanation detail within the user interface are crucial factors in determining users' meta-decisions to delegate to AI.

Participants also frequently cited situations in which they held contextual knowledge—such as upcoming competitor discounts or unique seasonal events—that the AI was unaware of. While participants stated their preference toward AI systems that allow them to adjust for such additional variables, they also indicated that when AI does not allow such adjustments or configurations, they tend to retain control over the decision-making task rather than delegating it to AI.

6 Discussion and Conclusions

This study explores the dynamics of human-AI decision-making in complex environments, particularly in the context of supply chain management (SCM). After interviewing 20 SCM professionals experienced in using AI to support their decisions, we developed an extended decision-making process model that highlights how they make continuous meta-decisions on task delegation to AI. This model emphasizes AI as an autonomous agent with its own situation awareness (SA), which is shaped by its data inputs and evolving learning capabilities. By examining user-AI interactions through this SA alignment framework, our research provides insights into how alignment—or lack thereof—between user and AI SA influences task delegation to AI.

Our findings reveal that human-AI decision-making is a dynamic process shaped by the interplay of user SA, AI SA, and a continuous cycle of meta-decisions. Users are more likely to delegate tasks to AI when they perceive a high alignment between their SA and the AI's SA. This alignment sets the foundation for trust and influences the extent to which users feel comfortable in delegating tasks to AI.

Finally, our study identifies transparency, explainability, and configurability as key system design factors that influence users' meta-decisions. Users stated relying on these features to facilitate an alignment between their SA and AI SA through an increased understanding of AI's logic and the ability to make adjustments to input variables.

From a research perspective, this study contributes to the literature on decision-making, AI, and SA by extending the SA theory to model AI as an independent agent with its own SA. By representing AI and human as entities with their own SA, this study reframes human-AI interaction as a two-agent decision-making process. The proposed model also introduces meta-decision making as a key layer of human-AI interaction, in which users continuously evaluate the delegation of tasks. Our findings also contribute to SA and decision-making literature by identifying how alignment between user and AI SA drives trust, adaptation, and delegation. This perspective suggests that future research should examine SA alignment as a core element of human-AI interaction, exploring its role in various aspects of AI use, including trust development, system acceptance, and task performance.

Our research offers actionable guidance for IT project managers and practitioners aiming to implement AI in decision-making environments. First, the decision-making model highlights the need for transparent AI systems that allow user control in both input data and system parameters. When combined with AI transparency, configuration interfaces can help users understand AI processes by letting them adjust parameters and observe how these adjustments affect outcomes. Second, the cyclical nature of the proposed decision-making model suggests that integrating real-time user feedback loops can also improve user and AI SA alignment by enabling AI to learn and adapt its SA based on users' final decisions. In conclusion, emphasizing transparency, explainability, configurability, and user feedback mechanisms in AI implementations can increase the chances of AI-driven decision support system adoption in complex operational settings.

References

Brynjolfsson E (1993) The productivity paradox of information technology. Commun ACM 36(12):66–77. https://doi.org/10/ct4fx4. ISBN: 0001-0782

Chen JY, Procci K, Boyce M, Wright J, Garcia A, Barnes M (2014) Situation awareness-based agent transparency: Tech. rep., Defense Technical Information Center, Fort Belvoir, https://doi.org/10.21236/ADA600351

Chiang CW, Yin M (2022) Exploring the effects of machine learning literacy interventions on Laypeople's reliance on machine learning models. In: 27th international conference on intelligent user interfaces. Association for Computing Machinery, Helsinki, pp 148–161. https://doi.org/10.1145/3490099.3511121

Czako Z, Sebestyen G, Hangan A (2021) Automaticai–a hybrid approach for automatic artificial intelligence algorithm selection and hyperparameter tuning. Expert Syst Appl 182:115225

Danilova OV (2019) The place and role of decision making in the process of modern enterprise management. In: Popkova EG, Chesnokova AV, Morozova IA (eds) Specifics of decision making in modern business systems. Emerald Publishing Limited, pp 57–67. https://doi.org/10.1108/978-1-78756-691-020191008

Davis FD (1989) Perceived usefulness, perceived ease of use, and user acceptance of information technology. MIS Q 13(3):319–340. https://doi.org/10.2307/249008

Endsley MR (1995) Toward a theory of situation awareness in dynamic systems. Hum Fact J Hum Fact Ergon Society 37(1):32–64. https://doi.org/10/ftd9tz

Endsley MR (2022) Supporting human-AI teams: transparency, explainability, and situation awareness. Comput Hum Behav. https://doi.org/10.1016/j.chb.2022.107574

Endsley MR, Bolté B, Jones DG (2003) Designing for situation awareness: an approach to user-centered design. CRC Press, Boca Raton

Glaser B, Strauss A (1967) Discovery of grounded theory: strategies for qualitative research. Routledge, London

Goldkuhl G, Cronholm S (2010) Adding theoretical grounding to grounded theory: toward multi-grounded theory. Int J Qualit Methods 9(2):187–205. https://doi.org/10/gcdtsr

Jiang J, Karran AJ, Coursaris CK, Léger PM, Beringer J (2023) A situation awareness perspective on human-ai interaction: tensions and opportunities. Int J Hum-Comput Interact 39(9):1789–1806

Kottemann JE (1986) Some requirements and design aspects for the next generation of decision support systems. In: Proceedings of the 19th annual Hawaii international conference on systems sciences, pp 339–343

Lincoln YS, Guba EG (1985) Naturalistic inquiry. Sage, New York

Miles MB, Huberman AM (1994) Qualitative data analysis: an expanded sourcebook. Sage, New York

National Academies of Sciences, Engineering, and Medicine (2021) Human-AI teaming: state of the art and research needs. National Academies Press, Washington. https://www.nap.edu/catalog/26355. https://doi.org/10.17226/26355

Sabherwal R, Jeyaraj A (2015) Information technology impacts on firm performance: an extension of Kohli and Devaraj (2003). MIS Q 39(4):809–836. https://doi.org/10/gfxztb

Salmon PM (2008) Distributed situation awareness: advances in theory, measurement and application to team work

Schuetz S, Venkatesh V (2020) The rise of human machines: how cognitive computing systems challenge assumptions of user-system interaction. J Assoc Inform Syst 21(2):460–482

Venkatesh V, Bala H (2008) Technology acceptance model 3 and a research agenda on interventions. Decis Sci 39(2):273–315. https://doi.org/10.1111/j.1540-5915.2008.00192.x

Venkatesh V, Davis FD (2000) A theoretical extension of the technology acceptance model: four longitudinal field studies. Manag Sci 46(2):186–204

Venkatesh V, Morris MG, Davis GB, Davis FD (2003) User acceptance of information technology: toward a unified view. MIS Q 27(3):425. https://doi.org/10/gc8zn2

Vilone G, Longo L (2021) Notions of explainability and evaluation approaches for explainable artificial intelligence. Inform Fusion 76:89–106. https://doi.org/10.1016/j.inffus.2021.05.009

Part II
Design of Socially-Embedded AI Solutions at Workplaces

The Design Challenge of Using Intelligent Agents to Make Work Systems Smarter

Steven Alter

Abstract This paper presents a new approach to the design challenge of using intelligent agents to make work systems smarter. It starts by summarizing the main ideas in a work system perspective that outlines the context. After adding concepts and assumptions concerning intelligent machines, it discusses the smartness of systems or devices in terms of capabilities grouped under the categories of processing information, self-regulation, action in the world, and knowledge acquisition. It presents a spectrum of roles that intelligent agents might perform for a work system. It also presents facets of work (such as making decisions, communicating, and coordinating) to which any of those roles might be applied. It presents an example to illustrate how those ideas might be used and concludes by summarizing its integrated approach to designing intelligent agents to make work systems smarter.

1 Introduction

The design challenge of using intelligent agents to make work systems smarter requires integrating ideas about work systems and ideas about intelligent agents despite inconsistent terminology in each area. For example, the words intelligent and smart have been applied to many things that are largely unrelated, e.g., smart watches, smartphones, smart cities, smart contracts, and smart refrigerators. Explaining how intelligent agents might make work systems smarter requires defining those terms and explaining how they can be used in an integrated way.

This paper aims to provide an organized way to think about opportunities for obtaining better results by making systems more intelligent even when different observers disagree about their intelligence. It applies ideas developed at different times to contribute to the real-world design of socio-technical systems that use entities that might be described as smart or intelligent in some way. Those ideas assume that metaphors and yes/no definitions of smart or intelligent are not directly

S. Alter (✉)
University of San Francisco, San Francisco, CA, USA
e-mail: alter@usfca.edu

C. K. Coursaris et al. (eds.), *The Design of Human-Centered Artificial Intelligence for the Workplace*, Progress in IS, https://doi.org/10.1007/978-3-031-83512-4_4

useful for design or analysis, even though they may be useful for analyzing survey research results, for punditry, or for philosophical discussions about visions of the future. Instead, ideas presented here highlight a spectrum of possibilities that design efforts might try to achieve to varying extents depending on available resources and needs.

Organization This paper combines older ideas about work systems with ideas from recent articles related to the smartness of systems and devices, facets of work, AI usage as the usage of digital agents, and an agent-role framework called the agent-responsibility framework in earlier publications. Section 2 summarizes the main ideas in a work system perspective based on work system theory. Those ideas are fundamental for understanding the context for designing intelligent agents to make work systems smarter. Section 3 adds concepts and assumptions concerning intelligent machines that are inherent in this paper's interpretation of using intelligent agents. Section 4 unpacks the idea of smartness of devices and systems based on degrees of smartness and groups of capabilities that might be smart to varying degrees. Section 5 combines the ideas from previous sections by identifying a spectrum of roles that intelligent agents might perform for a work system and facets of work (such as making decisions, communicating, and coordinating) to which any of those roles might be applied. Section 6 summarizes this paper's integrated approach to designing intelligent agents to make work systems smarter.

2 The Work System Perspective

The work system perspective has evolved over three decades. It covers all operational systems in organizations, including totally automated WSs and sociotechnical WSs that use intelligent agents. It covers systems built to aid humans in specific human tasks, systems that use automation to replace people who previously performed specific tasks, and systems that perform totally automated tasks that were never performed by people. Thus, it covers both work systems with various forms of interactions between humans and computers and work systems where responsibilities of humans and computers are structured to be completely separate.

The development of the work system perspective started with an attempt to create a systems analysis method for business professionals, which was articulated as the work system method (WSM)—(Alter 2006, 2008). The ideas underlying WSM were formalized as work system theory (WST). Subsequent developments related to service systems, workarounds, design principles, and other topics are extensions of WST (Alter 2013). WST applies equally to WSs in general and to ISs, projects, totally automated work systems, and other special cases of WS. As will be discussed briefly, the WST's three components are the definition of WS, the work system framework, and the work system life cycle model. Since these ideas have been presented many times, this section will focus on key points to minimize misunderstandings of the entire approach.

Work For current purposes, *work* is defined as the use of resources to produce products or services for human or non-human customers or for oneself. Resources include human, informational, physical, financial, and other types of resources. Work involves activities that try to be productive and may occur in any business, societal, or home setting. This definition of work is not directly related to careers, jobs, or business organizations.

Work System This term appeared in the first edition of *MIS Quarterly* (Bostrom and Heinen 1977) and is a natural unit of analysis for thinking about systems in organizations. *A work system* is a system in which human participants and machines perform work (processes and activities) using information, technology, and other resources to produce specific products or services for internal or external customers. Nontrivial work systems typically involve multiple participants and machines serving multiple customers. The work in work systems may be structured to varying degrees, e.g., unstructured (designing a unique advertisement), semi-structured (performing typical medical diagnosis), workflows (processing invoice payments), or highly structured (manufacturing semiconductors or pharmaceuticals).

Workplace A physical or virtual place where work is performed. Except for situations where most work is highly improvised, most workplaces contain multiple work systems that perform different aspects of the required work. Also, most nontrivial work systems can be subdivided into interacting subsystems that are work systems in their own right.

Special Cases of Work System The most important distinction in describing special cases of WS is the difference between a socio-technical WS, in which human participants perform some of the activities, and a totally automated WS, where all activities are performed by machines and the slot for participants is blank.

An information system (IS) is a WS with activities devoted to capturing, transmitting, storing, retrieving, deleting, manipulating, and/or displaying information. This definition differs from 20 previous definitions in Alter (2008) and was one of 34 definitions of IS noted in Boell and Cecez-Kecmanovic (2015). An example is a socio-technical accounting IS in which accountants decide how specific transactions and assets will be handled for tax purposes and then produce monthly or yearly financial statements. This example is an IS because its activities are devoted to processing information. It is supported by a totally automated IS that performs calculations and generates reports. In both cases, an IS that is an integral part of another WS cannot be analyzed, designed, or improved thoughtfully without considering how changes in the IS affect that WS.

Projects, service systems, self-service systems, and some supply chains (interorganizational WSs) are other important special cases. For example, software development projects and others are WSs designed to produce specific products or services and then go out of existence. Thus, a project that creates or customizes an intelligent agent is a WS in its own right.

Work system framework: a basic understanding of a WS. The nine elements of the WS framework (Fig. 1) are the elements of a basic understanding of a

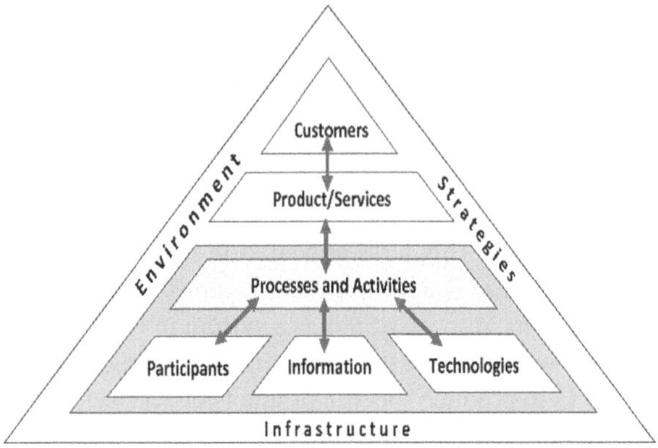

Fig. 1 The work system framework

WS's form, function, and environment during a period when it is stable enough to retain its identity even though incremental changes may occur, such as minor personnel substitutions or technology upgrades. *Processes and activities, participants, information*, and *technologies* are completely within the WS. *Customers* and *products/services* may be partially inside and partially outside because customers often participate in activities within a WS and because products/services take shape within a WS. *Environment, infrastructure*, and *strategies* are outside of the WS even though they have direct effects within a WS and may be affected by major changes in significant WSs.

The following clarifications are often useful: *Customers* refer to people or organizations that receive and use products/services produced by a WS. It includes internal and external customers. The term *product/services* is used to bypass controversies about special characteristics of products versus services. The term *processes and activities* is used because the activities in some WSs are not structured as explicitly defined processes. *Environment* includes organizational and national culture, competition, regulation, demographics, and organizational politics, policies, and procedures. *Infrastructure* refers to human, informational, and technical resources that are viewed as shared by multiple WSs instead of being associated primarily with one WS. An example of human infrastructure is an IT group that serves as a resource for multiple WSs.

Work System Life Cycle Model (WSLC): How WSs Change over Time ISs and other WSs evolve through a combination of planned change through projects and unplanned change through adaptations and workarounds (Fig. 2). WSLC phases (initiation, development, implementation, operation, and maintenance) may be performed differently. Typical activities and responsibilities, e.g., designing, debugging, and training, associated with specific phases apply for waterfall, agile, prototyping, use of off-the-shelf applications, and shadow IT, even when several phases overlap or iterate.

Both planned and unplanned changes often affect multiple WS elements, not just technologies. The *development* phase creates or acquires and then tests software and

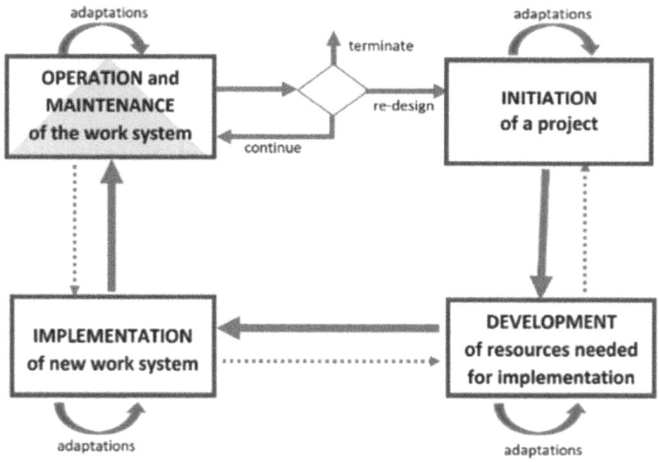

Fig. 2 The work system life cycle model (WSLC)

other resources needed for implementation in the organization. The *implementation* phase involves much more than installation of software on computers. The WSLC's four idealized phases (and related sub-phases) express a waterfall-like approach to identifying things that should happen as a WS evolves iteratively. Many WSLC topics remain valid when agile approaches are used for developing software, such as the importance of WS changes rather than just software development, evolution over time rather than one-time projects, the simultaneous importance of planned and unplanned change, and the relevance of key activities and responsibilities within each phase. The key activities and responsibilities remain even if the phases are partially merged, regardless of whether the WS uses homegrown software, commercial application software, or external platforms. For example, regardless of whether aspects of development and implementation overlap, it remains necessary to determine requirements (at an appropriate level of detail), acquire, produce, or fix software that is needed, test and debug software, decide how to implement WS changes, identify implementation problems, train WS participants, and so on.

Efforts to make WSs smarter can extend throughout any or all of the WSLC phases. Discussions in the initiation phase might consider the extent to which the current WS is smart (based on the capabilities and dimensions mentioned and explained later) and, in general, how to improve it in terms of any of those capabilities. Some of those approaches could involve creating or enhancing intelligent agents, while others could focus mostly on other aspects of the WS. The development phase would specify details of the proposed changes and would produce or update related technical capabilities. The implementation phase would make the new capabilities operational and would make sure that WS participants understood ways in which the new or improved capabilities require action or attention on their part. The operation and maintenance phase would use the new or improved capabilities and be supported by actions or corrections needed to achieve operational goals.

3 Intelligent Agents in the Context of Work Systems

Visualizing how intelligent agents might make work systems smarter requires concepts for describing intelligent agents. This section provides a brief introduction to terms related to machine intelligence and intelligent agents. In subsequent sections, those concepts form a basis for describing roles that intelligent agents might perform for work systems, describing what smarter means in the context of work systems, and describing specific areas in which work systems might become smarter.

Machine Intelligence Discussions of the general notion of machine intelligence go back at least to the 1830s (e.g., Daston 2018; Ashford 2017; Hollerith 1894; Kurzweil 1985; Von Neumann 2012; Hodges 2019; Wiener 2019). The notion of intelligent systems and devices has been defined differently (or not at all) by many researchers and pundits in the years since the seminal Dartmouth AI workshop (McCarthy et al. 1955), which is often viewed as an important impetus for AI research and applications that extend to today (Berente et al. 2021). Definitions published since 2000 in numerous application areas include various combinations of topics such as perceiving the environment, exhibiting humanlike intelligence, recognizing patterns, processing large amounts of data, taking actions, improving performance through learning, reasoning, and making decisions without human intervention.

In combination, those definitions do not resolve ambiguities about whether existing applications in medical diagnosis, facial recognition, language translation, or large language models such as ChatGPT involve "intelligent systems" or "intelligent machines." Instead of trying to improve on those definitions, this paper focuses on a more important goal in practice. The goal is to explain how intelligent agents might make work systems smarter regardless of whether different observers attribute different levels of intelligence to those devices or systems.

Discussing the uses of intelligent agents in the context of work systems requires several ideas about algorithms and agents that were not mentioned in the previous section's discussion of work systems. An additional comment about the concept of situation awareness leads to a subsequent discussion of the smartness of intelligent agents.

Algorithm An algorithm is a detailed method for achieving specified goals within stated or unstated constraints by applying specific resources such as data inputs.

Agent In the context of work systems, an agent is a human or non-human entity that performs tasks delegated by another entity (which may be human or non-human) and can sense, decide, and act autonomously. Agents may be reactive (taking immediate action based on environmental stimuli) or proactive (taking initiative and planning actions in advance).

Digital Agent Digital agents operate by executing algorithms encoded in software. A digital agent can be viewed as a work system because it performs work using information, technologies, and other resources to produce products/services for its direct customers, which may be human or non-human entities.

Intelligent Agent An intelligent agent operates by executing algorithms and exhibits a nontrivial level of "smartness" with processing information, self-regulation, action in the world, and knowledge acquisition (categories explained in the next section). The operation of an intelligent agent can be viewed as a work system. This definition's use of the term *nontrivial* follows this paper's purpose of focusing on design choices that are significant enough to require deliberation.

Situation Awareness This idea (SA) helps in seeing the value of this chapter's approach of considering different degrees of smartness related to different types of capabilities instead of seeing smartness in terms of metaphors or yes/no distinctions. A widely cited article about SA (Endsley 1995), starts with important examples related to aircraft crews, air traffic control, and complex manufacturing and power systems. It defines SA as "the perception of the elements in the environment within a volume of time and space, the comprehension of their meaning, and the projection of their status in the near future" (p. 36). By that definition, SA applies well to human operators in those situations. It applies in a more limited way to devices such as thermostats that operate through a simple algorithmic feedback loop between target and actual temperature with no complex rules, projections into the future, or knowledge-based decision-making. Recognizing the increasing power of automation, some researchers have proposed the idea of distributed situational awareness (DSA) to describe socio-technical systems in which "SA is held by human and non-human agents. Technological artifacts (as well as human operators) have some level of SA (at least in the sense that they are holders of contextually relevant information). This is particularly true as technologies are able to sense their environment and become more animate" (Stanton 2016, p. 2). This paper's discussion of using intelligent agents to make work systems smarter assumes that intelligent agents might exhibit SA in a variety of ways. It contributes to the discussion of SA and DSA by identifying many different types of capabilities that might perform roles in socio-technical or totally automated systems. Its focus on continuous variables related to different aspects of smartness provides ideas that are directly useful for analysis and design.

4 Smartness of Intelligent Agents

A conceptualization of smartness of devices and systems is explained in Alter (2020a), which provides a general way to look at smartness using four categories to organize numerous capabilities that might be built into devices or systems and operate with different degrees of smartness.

The smartness of an intelligent agent or work system in relation to almost any type of capability that involves information can be characterized along the following dimensions (Alter 2020a):

- **Not smart at all.** Does not perform activities that exhibit the capability
- **Scripted execution.** Performs capability-related activities according to prespecified instructions
- **Formulaic adaptation.** Adaptation of capability-related activities based on prespecified inputs or conditions
- **Creative adaptation.** Adaptation of capability-related activities based on unscripted or partially scripted analysis of relevant information or conditions
- **Unscripted or partially scripted invention.** Invention of capability-related activities using unscripted or partially scripted execution of a workaround or new method

Most work systems with human participants have many capabilities under each of four groups of capabilities and may execute related activities with occasional adaptations or inventions. Each group of capabilities includes between five and seven separate capabilities that may exist independently or be intertwined with other capabilities:

- **Information processing.** Capture information, transmit information, store information, retrieve information, delete information, manipulate information, and display information.
- **Action in the world.** Sensing, actuation, coordination, communication, control, and physical action.
- **Internal regulation.** Self-detection, self-monitoring, self-diagnosis, self- correction, and self-organization.
- **Knowledge acquisition.** Sensing or discovering, classifying, compiling, inferring or extrapolating from examples, inferring or extrapolating from abstractions, testing, and evaluating.

With the possible exception of work systems that focus on totally routine and repetitive activities, most work systems with human participants operate with a nontrivial level of smartness for most of those capabilities. In contrast, very few intelligent agents exhibit a high level of smartness related to most of those capabilities. The design challenge of using intelligent agents to make work systems smarter involves designing intelligent agents whose limited smartness nonetheless enhances the smartness of a work system that uses intelligent agents.

5 Making Work Systems Smarter

Incorporating an intelligent agent into an existing WS creates what might be called an augmented WS, i.e., the original WS augmented by the capabilities of the intelligent agent. The elements of the work system framework can be used to describe the structure and characteristics of both the original WS and the augmented WS. The topics for describing the augmentation by the intelligent agent are not obvious, however, because augmentation by an intelligent agent may change many aspects of the WS.

5.1 Analyzing a Work System from a Business Viewpoint

The work system method (WSM) mentioned earlier provides an analysis approach for thinking about making work systems smarter. The WSM is a flexible systems analysis and design method developed to help business professionals analyze work systems for themselves, to support both their own work and their interactions with IT professionals in system-related projects. During 2003–2017 (mostly), MBA and EMBA students demonstrated the usability of that general approach by applying various work system analysis templates in assignments that produced over 700 management briefings about possible improvements in real-world work systems, mostly in their organizations, e.g., Truex et al. (2010). In every case, producing any required software would have called for additional analysis and specifications concerning the details of the software itself. Different versions of WSM have been tailored to different uses. However, the following WSM steps outline an analysis approach that can be taken much further when thinking about using intelligent agents to make work systems smarter:

1. Identify the smallest work system that has the problem or opportunity at hand.
2. Summarize the "as-is" work system using a work system snapshot, a stylized one-page summary that identifies the main constituents of the six central elements of that work system.
3. Evaluate the work system's operation using perceived strengths and weaknesses, metrics, key incidents, social relations, and other factors.
4. Drill down further as necessary using any relevant ideas, including both published WSM tools, e.g., Alter (2006), Alter (2020b), Alter and Bork (2020), and other tools and approaches such as design thinking and Six Sigma methods.
5. Propose changes by producing a work system snapshot of a proposed "to be" work system that should perform well.
6. Describe likely performance improvements and explain why the effort of creating the new work system or making the proposed changes seems justified.

5.2 *Roles that an Intelligent Agent Might Perform for a Work System*

An attempt to use an intelligent agent to make a work system smarter might consider any of a spectrum of roles that an intelligent agent might perform in a WS. The spectrum of roles shown below goes from the lowest to the highest direct involvement of an intelligent agent in executing a WS's activities. That set of roles emerged from many iterations of trying to expand the horizontal dimension of Shneiderman's human-centered AI (HCAI) framework (Shneiderman 2020a,b), which applies to many situations where both automation and human control are design variables. The HCAI framework's two dimensions are low versus high computer automation and low versus high human control. Those dimensions directly lead to useful questions for evaluating and designing WSs by emphasizing that deficiency or excess along either dimension may lead to worse results for organizations, WS participants, and customers. For design, however, the low versus high distinctions in the HCAI framework's two dimensions provide too little detail to inspire vivid visualization and discussion of how or why an intelligent agent might be applied in a WS's operation or might affect its stakeholders.

One of the early iterations in trying to make the HCAI framework more specific involved three roles, i.e., support, control, and perform. Specific instances of those roles might support HCAI values and aspirations or might oppose those values and aspirations (e.g., micromanagement or surveillance capitalism). The following comments about the six types of roles emphasize promoting human-centric values and addressing human-centric issues:

Monitor a Work System An intelligent agent might monitor and measure aspects of work to ensure that a WS's processes and activities are appropriate for WS participants. In some cases, intelligent agents might generate alarms when aspects of work start going out of accepted boundaries regarding health, safety, or cognitive load.

Provide Information An intelligent agent might provide information that helps people achieve their work goals safely and comfortably without infringing on the privacy or other rights of people whose information is used.

Provide Capabilities An intelligent agent might provide analytical, visualization, and computational capabilities that help WS participants achieve their assigned goals safely and appropriately.

Control Activities An intelligent agent might control work activities directly to prevent specific activities from going out of bounds related to worker safety, time on the job, stress, or other variables that can be measured and used to control a work system.

Coproduce Activities An intelligent agent might be deployed in a division of responsibility where the intelligent agent and people have complementary responsibilities for performing separate parts of the work. Either humans or intelligent agents might take the lead in human-computer interactions within coproduction activities. In some situations, initiative might shift back and forth between people and intelligent agents depending on the status of the work.

Execute Activities An intelligent agent might execute activities that should not or cannot be delegated to people. For example, an intelligent agent might perform difficult, dangerous, or impossible activities for people to perform as the WS produces products/services.

5.3 Facets of Work

Looking more deeply at how an intelligent agent might make a work system smarter calls for considering the possibility that any of the above roles might be applied to any of a set of facets of work, i.e., aspects of work that can be observed or analyzed, such as making decisions, communicating, processing information, and coordinating. The idea of facets of work grew out of research for bringing richer and more evocative concepts to systems analysis and design to facilitate interactions between analysts and stakeholders, as is explained in (Alter 2021, p. 342–344). The notion of "facet" is an analogy to how a cut diamond consists of a single thing with many facets that can be observed or analyzed. Psychology, library science, information science, and computer science have used the idea of facets but with quite different meanings and connotations.

All 18 of the facets of work in Table 1 apply to both socio-technical and totally automated WSs, are associated with many useful concepts, bring evaluation criteria and design trade-offs, have sub-facets, and bring open-ended questions for starting conversations (Alter 2021). Some facets overlap in many situations (e.g., making decisions and communication). The selection of the 18 facets resulted from an iterative design process that might have led to some other set of facets, perhaps 14 or 27. Determination of whether or not to include a type of activity as one of the 18 facets of work in Table 1 was based on the extent to which that type of activity was associated with concepts, evaluation criteria, design trade-offs, sub-facets, and open-ended questions that could be useful in analysis and design. The central contribution of facets of work for thinking about intelligent agents is that

Table 1 Eighteen facets of work (Alter 2021)

Making decisions	Communicating	Providing information
Representing reality	Learning	Coordinating
Performing physical work	Providing service	Applying knowledge
Planning	Improvising	Performing support work
Creating value	Thinking	Controlling execution
Processing information	Interacting socially	Maintaining security

the facets of work provide a path toward paying attention to requirements for many types of capabilities that might have been overlooked.

There is no assumption that the facets of work should be independent. On the contrary, the facet of making decisions often involves other facets, such as communicating, learning, and processing information. The main point is that each facet can be viewed as a lens for thinking about where and how WSs might use intelligent agents.

5.4 *Applying Agent Roles to Specific Facets of Work*

The ideas of agent roles and facets of work can be combined as an organized approach for thinking about designing intelligent agents that might make a work system smarter. This approach is organized around an agent-role framework (AR framework) that was called the agent-responsibility framework in previous publications (Alter 2022a,b).

As shown in Fig. 3, the horizontal dimension of the AR framework is the spectrum of roles described in Sect. 5.2, and the vertical dimension is the different facets of work described in Sect. 5.3. The abbreviated version of the AR framework in Fig. 3 shows only 6 of the 18 facets to make it easier to visualize the structure of the AR framework as a pointer toward considering how different roles of intelligent agents might affect different facets of work. The choice of which facets to include in the abbreviated version was based on showing several that are the most obvious (making decisions and communicating) and several that otherwise might not be considered explicitly (creating value and maintaining security). Tools that support the use of this framework in practice could display any convenient view of the 18 facets in Table 1 (or any other set of facets that might be tailored to specific types

<<< **Facet of work** >>>							
	Making decisions						
	Communi-cating						
	Processing information						
	Coordinating						
	Creating value						
	Maintaining security						
		Monitoring work system	Providing information	Providing capabilities	Controlling activities	Coproducing activities	Executing activities
		<<<<<<< **Spectrum of roles and responsibilities** >>>>>>>					

Fig. 3 Agent responsibility framework with six roles and six facets of work

Table 2 Six types of intelligent agent roles applied to different facets of work

Facet	Illustration of how a specific intelligent agent (IA) role *(in parenthesis and italicized)* might be applied to a specific facet of work in a medical case study
Making decisions	*(monitor)* The IA might *monitor* clinical *decisions* to ensure that hospital standards are followed and that people from different socioeconomic classes are treated equitably
Communicating	*(provide information)* The IA might *provide information* that would expedite *communication* between overscheduled medical staff members
Processing information	*(provide capabilities)* The IA might *provide data reduction and visualization capabilities* to help physicians process information they need without expending much effort
Coordinating	*(control activities)* The IA might *control* aspects of *coordination* between staff members by ensuring physician entries in problem lists for patients with complex medical conditions adhere to standards that typically help when other physicians treat the same patients
Creating value	*(coproduce activities)* The IA might help create *value* for physicians and patients by helping them coproduce active monitoring of medical conditions and treatments requiring follow-up and attention
Maintaining security	*(execute activities)* The IA might help maintain *security* and patient privacy by *executing activities* that monitor the content of incoming and outgoing electronic messages that involve security- or privacy-related issues

of situations) and could prompt users to select the specific facets of work that seem worthwhile to analyze or explore concerning the situation at hand.

Combining the AR framework's two dimensions leads to pinpointing design issues, e.g., the extent to which an intelligent agent should perform roles such as monitoring work, providing capabilities, or performing activities automatically. Table 2 shows how different intelligent agent roles in the abbreviated version of the AR framework might be applied to the six facets of work in Fig. 3 that were mentioned in a medical case study (Gawande 2018). Alter (2022a) presents similarly formatted tables related to e-commerce, digital auctions, and self-driving car examples.

The use of the AR framework does not rely on considering all combinations of roles and facets. Also, other roles and facets might be especially relevant to specific situations. Focusing on different facets of work could encourage designers or managers to wonder about the benefits of enhancing specific facets of work in a specific WS. Similarly, the spectrum of roles in the horizontal dimension encourages considering possible roles that intelligent agents might perform. It is unnecessary to consider all or even many of the 36 combinations of six facets of work and six types of roles in the abbreviated AR framework (or 108 combinations of 18 facets of work presented in Alter (2021) and six types of roles in the complete AR framework). Only combinations that are important for a specific WS should be considered.

6 An Integrated Approach for Designing Intelligent Agents to Make Work Systems Smarter

This paper's main premise is that broad generalizations about intelligent machines and AI in the workplace are interesting in many ways but often are not specific enough to be useful for describing, analyzing, or designing WSs. The ideas presented here bypass ambiguities related to the terms *intelligent agent* or *intelligent machine* by providing an integrated approach to understanding intelligent agents and their roles in specific WSs in workplace settings. The basic assumption is that intelligent agents are used by WSs and that incorporating a new intelligent agent into a WS should augment the WS's capabilities in predictable ways that can be described based on roles that the intelligent agent plays concerning specific facets of work.

There are many possible paths for designing intelligent agents to make work systems smarter. The integrated approach proposed here starts by using the general outline of the work system method to understand the context and the related opportunities and problems. Additional ideas that can be used in the design effort include a spectrum of possible roles of intelligent agents, facets of work that can be affected by those roles, and different degrees of smartness that might be pursued concerning capabilities in four categories. This approach is not meant to be mechanical or formulaic. Instead, it is meant to illuminate possibilities for designing intelligent agents with maximum benefit.

The ideas presented here can be applied in describing, analyzing, and designing WSs in many workplaces by asking questions such as the following:

- How smart is the current WS concerning the various capabilities that were grouped previously under processing information, self-regulation, action in the world, and knowledge acquisition?
- What are practical directions for making the WS smarter by enhancing those capabilities in directions that might be beneficial?
- How do those possible directions link with the roles and facets of work identified using the AR framework?

An important caveat is that most intelligent agents have limited smartness in their own right due to the current limitations in how automated devices can understand their own purposes, behaviors, or environments. The key issue is to try to make the work system smarter through an integrated combination of changes, some of which might involve new or improved intelligent agents.

Many earlier papers have applied this paper's ideas about WSs in a variety of situations. However, the new ideas about the smartness of devices and systems and the roles of intelligent agents regarding facets of work within WSs have not been used in practice. Future applications in practice are needed to determine how useful they are for analyzing and designing intelligent agents and WSs that use them.

References

Alter S (2006) The work system method: connecting people, processes, and IT for business results. Work System Press, Larkspur

Alter S (2008) Defining information systems as work systems: implications for the is field. Eur J Inform Syst 17(5):448–469

Alter S (2013) Work system theory: Overview of core concepts, extensions, and challenges for the future. J Assoc Inform Syst 14(2):72–121

Alter S (2020a) Making sense of smartness in the context of smart devices and smart systems. Inform Syst Front 22(2):381–393

Alter S (2020b) Ten lightweight sa&d tools based on work system theory and its extensions. In: Proceedings of AMCIS 2020

Alter S (2021) Facets of work: Enriching the description, analysis, design, and evaluation of systems in organizations. Commun Assoc Inform Syst 49(13):321–354

Alter S (2022a) Agent responsibility framework for digital agents: roles and responsibilities related to facets of work. In: 27th international working conference on exploring modeling methods for systems analysis and development (EMMSAD)

Alter S (2022b) Responsibility modeling for operational contributions of algorithmic agents. In: Proceedings AMCIS

Alter S, Bork D (2020) Systems analysis and design toolkit based on work system theory and its extensions. J Database Manag 31(3):1–13

Ashford D (2017) The mechanical Turk: enduring misapprehensions concerning artificial intelligence. Camb Q 46(2):119–139

Berente N, Gu B, Recker J, Santhanam R (2021) Managing artificial intelligence. MIS Q 45(3):1433–1450

Boell SK, Cecez-Kecmanovic D (2015) What is an information system? In: 48th Hawaii international conference on system sciences

Bostrom RP, Heinen JS (1977) Mis problems and failures: a socio-technical perspective. Part I: the causes. MIS Q 1(3):17–32

Daston L (2018) Calculation and the division of labor, 1750–1950. Bull German Hist Inst 62:9–30

Endsley MR (1995) Toward a theory of situation awareness in dynamic systems. Hum Fact J 37(1):32–64

Gawande A (2018) "the update: why doctors hate their computers". New Yorker pp 62–73

Hodges A (2019) Alan turing. The Stanford Encyclopedia of Philosophy. https://plato.stanford.edu/entries/turing/. Accessed 25 April 2023

Hollerith H (1894) The electrical tabulating machine. J Roy Stat Soc 57(4):678–689

Kurzweil R (1985) What is artificial intelligence anyway? As the techniques of computing grow more sophisticated, machines are beginning to appear intelligent—but can they actually think? Am Sci 73(3):258–264

McCarthy J, Minsky ML, Rochester N, Shannon CE (1955) Dartmouth artificial intelligence project proposal. http://jmc.stanford.edu/articles/dartmouth/dartmouth.pdf. Accessed 25 April 2023

Shneiderman B (2020a) Human-centered artificial intelligence: reliable, safe & trustworthy. Int J Hum-Comput Interact 36(6):495–504

Shneiderman B (2020b) Human-centered artificial intelligence: three fresh ideas. AIS Trans Hum-Comput Interact 12(3):109–124

Stanton NA (2016) Distributed situation awareness. Theor Issues Ergon Sci 17(1):1–7

Truex D, Alter S, Long C (2010) Systems analysis for everyone else: empowering business professionals through a systems analysis method that fits their needs. In: Proceedings of the European conference on information systems

Von Neumann J (2012) The computer and the brain. Yale University Press

Wiener N (2019) Cybernetics or control and communication in the animal and the machine. MIT Press, Cambridge

Human-Centered Requirements Engineering for Intelligent Systems

Thomas Geis and Joerg Beringer

Abstract In this book chapter, we discuss the human-centered perspective on the design of intelligent systems and argue that intelligent systems can be designed and evaluated in the same manner as any other interactive system. We must identify the right stakeholders and their core tasks and clearly identify the user needs to derive the correct requirements for such intelligent systems.

We introduce the concept of human-centered quality and continue with two essential concepts:

Context of Use: This is the context in which an intelligent system is used. A context of use description identifies user profiles and core tasks to define requirements for specific user groups and their tasks. As we will see, intelligent systems can take over some of these tasks, but they also may introduce new (meta) tasks that must be supported by the user interface of the intelligent system.

Stakeholder Requirements: In modern requirements engineering, human-centered requirements are derived from stakeholder needs. The portion of the stakeholders who use the intelligent system (i.e., the users) are success-critical in terms of acceptance and productivity for the organization. However, there are also indirect users and other organizational roles such as business owners, people managers, and team supervisors. This stakeholder view is important when discussing ethical issues such as intelligent systems' purpose, fairness, authority, and controllability.

T. Geis
ProContext, Koeln, Germany
e-mail: thomas.geis@procontext.com

J. Beringer (✉)
ProContext, Redwood City, CA, USA
e-mail: joerg.beringer@procontext.ai

C. K. Coursaris et al. (eds.), *The Design of Human-Centered Artificial Intelligence for the Workplace*, Progress in IS, https://doi.org/10.1007/978-3-031-83512-4_5

1 What Is Artificial Intelligence from the User's Perspective?

We recently have been hired to help a medical equipment manufacturer come up with new innovative products. This project triggered a round of interviews with eye doctors ("ophthalmologists") to learn about their daily work and find out which unsatisfied needs they have that point to missing system support. Such work is commonly referred to as "user research, or to use a more technical term, "context of use analysis." The goal is to identify unsatisfied user needs in the context of a product's use and derive user requirements for new systems or new versions of updated systems (software, hardware, and combinations of both).

During the interviews, one part of the work that eye doctors described was how they analyze a variety of data about the eyes of patients produced by different measurement systems and how to "combine" these datasets to diagnose a patient's underlying disease. Based on this diagnosis, they decide on a therapy that solves the patient's problem. Although all measurement systems are in place in the eye doctor's practice, synthesizing their outputs into an appropriate diagnosis was experienced as time-consuming, expensive, and dissatisfactory work that cries for relief.

Interestingly, all of the interviewed eye doctors pointed out that "AI will help us with this in the future," irrespective of whether the recognition of a pattern (e.g., a likely diagnosis of an eye disease based on given data) would be done by an intelligent system or by the user of the system. From the user's perspective, any solution that helps to surface hidden information and insights is perceived as extremely helpful and associated with intelligence because it outperforms the user's cognitive capabilities. The opposite is also true. The manufacturer may claim that a new solution for measurement instruments is intelligent because it uses some machine learning algorithm to discover patterns within the diagnostic data. However, doctors (users) will only care if those insights are insightful and actionable.

From a human-centered perspective, the "coolness" of the underlying technology does not matter; rather, it depends on how that technology can be adopted by the user to be more effective and productive. The foundational process principles and concepts of a human-centered system development process are described in ISO 9241-210 (International Organization for Standardization 2019a), and the product-related interaction principles that lead to usable and useful interactive systems are described in ISO 9241-110 (International Organization for Standardization 2020a).

A comprehensive set of processes and process outcomes for institutionalizing human-centered design on project, infrastructure, and management levels has been published in ISO 9241-220 (International Organization for Standardization 2019b). A formal assessment model for identifying the process capability of an organization is available in ISO 9241-221 (International Organization for Standardization 2023). From a user's perspective, adherence to these principles can be measured by subjective questionnaires such as the "System Usability Scale" (SUS) (Brooke 1996) or the more recent "User Experience Questionnaire" (UEQ) (Laugwitz et al. 2008).

In 2020, the International Organization for Standardization (ISO) published ISO/TR 9241-810, "Ergonomics of human-system interaction – Robotic, intelligent and autonomous systems" (International Organization for Standardization 2020b), which addresses ergonomic issues specific to the design of intelligent systems. The document classifies diverse types of intelligent systems, including intelligent agents, autonomous agents, and autonomous robots. Whether you develop a traditional interactive system or an intelligent system, a human-centered perspective is always essential to ensure that a system design satisfies the needs of the intended user group related to their daily work. Successful products are those that fulfill underserved needs better than the competition (Ulwick 2016).

In this chapter, we will substantiate the concept of human-centeredness by explaining the concept of human-centered product quality and how it extends from a user-centered approach to a more holistic requirements management approach where all stakeholder needs are considered when deriving requirements based on a context of use analysis. Using the concrete example of a window cleaning robot, we will illustrate how to contrast an as-is task flow and a to-be task flow, assuming the presence of an intelligent robot. With the introduction of system intelligence, there will always be a transformation of work processes and task ownership, which has to be envisioned and prepared to introduce an intelligent system to the workplace successfully.

Finally, we will discuss how to repurpose user requirements to identify system requirements for intelligent systems. When identifying user needs for cognitive skills related to accomplishing a task, we can derive user requirements that can be directly translated into system requirements for intelligent systems. The reasoning is that if an intelligent system covers cognitive functions performed today by humans, the related user requirements will also apply directly to the intelligent system.

2 Human-Centered Quality of Intelligent Systems

Every software development project aims to build a high-quality new system (or a new release of an existing system). Quality is one of the central undisputed concepts in product design and development. However, what exactly is quality? Furthermore, what is the quality of intelligent systems?

- *Quality* is the extent to which requirements on a system have been met. It is important to understand that the quality of interactive systems has two dimensions:
- *Technology-centered quality* is the extent to which technical system requirements are met.
- *Human-centered quality* is the extent to which requirements for using the system are met. These requirements focus on using the system (user requirements) rather than the technical part of the system.

While both human-centered quality and technology-centered quality must be achieved to ensure that the overall quality of the system is appropriate, in this chapter, we focus on the human-centered quality, which is especially relevant to the design of intelligent systems. Human-centered quality is more than just the usability of interacting with a system. ISO 9241-220 (International Organization for Standardization 2019b), which was published in 2019, defines "human-centered quality" as the "extent to which requirements for usability, accessibility, user experience and avoidance of harm from use are met."

Human-centered quality is also not limited to the direct use of an interactive system. Human-centered quality is what direct users (e.g., medical doctors) and those affected by the system (e.g., patients or relatives of patients) experience when the system is in use. The concept of affected users or stakeholders is especially important when designing intelligent systems that can run autonomously without the user in the loop.

One of the important design considerations is identifying who is a direct user, an indirect user (who only interacts with the system's output), or an affected stakeholder. In traditional interactive systems, which are used as a tool in the context of a task, the primary user is typically the task owner. With intelligent systems, this task ownership might shift to the intelligent system, downgrading the original user to a stakeholder interested in the outcome or occasionally interacting directly with the system but not as the sole task owner. To understand those subtle differences, we must take a closer look at how to analyze the context of use of intelligent systems.

3 Context of Use of Intelligent Systems

"Context of use" is defined as a "combination of users, goals and tasks, resources, and environment" (International Organization for Standardization 2018). In practice, this means that the context of use for a system is a group of people who share the same needs (Ulwick 2016). These people are also called a user group. The clearer the attributes of each user group are described, which tasks they perform with which intended outcomes (goals), in which environment they are when performing their tasks, and which resources they use besides the system to be built, the more the designers that design the system are enabled to identify the true user needs.

In traditional system design, the objective was to design a system that snaps into the existing work practice as a tool and helps the user group to streamline work. With the introduction of intelligent systems, the goal is rather to change work practice in a more disruptive way. If an intelligent system performs tasks autonomously, the work practice itself will be radically affected because task ownership is intrinsically shifting between humans and systems, and processes are changing due to the unprecedented new cognitive capabilities of intelligent systems.

3.1 Core Tasks

A core component in the context of use is the tasks that people perform. The term "task" is defined in ISO 9241-11 (International Organization for Standardization

Contextual pre-condition: The tenant perceives their windows that dirty that visitors might feel uncomfortable with the situation

Plan:
- Decide when to clean the windows
- Decide who to clean the windows

Prepare:
- Provide cleaning agent, cleaning cloth, stepladder if necessary
- Clear the windowsill

Perform:
- Soap each window
- Wipe each soaped up window

Assess result:
- Inspect each window for absence of dirt
- Inspect each windows for absence of stripes

Deliver result:
- Present the cleaned windows to the next person coming in

Intended outcome: The tenant perceives the windows as clean.

Fig. 1 Life cycle of the core task "cleaning the windows at home" without the support of an intelligent system (adapted from Geis and Polkehn 2018)

2018) as a "set of activities undertaken in order to achieve a specific goal." The majority of user needs are implied within those tasks people perform. In general, humans perceive tasks as a set of activities that lead to a meaningful outcome. Tasks in terms of a meaningful set of activities can also be referred to as core tasks. The activities that people perform as part of a core task are also referred to as subtasks. Work science has found that how people perform tasks follows a generic task life cycle (Hacker and Sachse 2014). The more a project team understands each core task that a system must support and (their) subtasks—also referred to as "task model"—the better the project team is suited to identify a comprehensive set of user needs and derive a comprehensive set of user requirements.

Figure 1 describes the life cycle of the core task of "cleaning the windows at home" (Geis and Polkehn 2018). Every core task starts with a contextual precondition that triggers the core task and an intended outcome that describes what will have been achieved once the task has been completed.

3.2 Automating Subtasks

When designing an "intelligent" solution that makes it easier for the user to clean the window, we must decide how this solution will fit into the current task model and affect task ownership. Using a window cleaning robot can eliminate the subtasks "provide cleaning agent, cleaning cloth, stepladder if necessary "clear the windows

Contextual pre-condition: The tenant perceives their windows that dirty that visitors might feel uncomfortable with the situation

Plan:
- Decide when to clean the windows
- Decide who to clean the windows

Prepare:
- Provide cleaning agent, cleaning cloth, stepladder if necessary
- Clear the windowsill
- Provide the robot with cleaning agent
- Place the robot on the window
- Turn on robot

Supervise task to be performed by robot:
- Observe the robot cleaning the window

Assess result produced by robot:
- Inspect each window for absence of dirt
- Inspect each windows for absence of stripes

Train robot:
- Point the robot to locations that are still dirty

Deliver result:
- Present the cleaned windows to the next person coming in

Intended outcome: The tenant perceives the windows as clean.

Fig. 2 Life cycle of the core task "cleaning the windows at home" with the support of a robot (adapted from Geis and Polkehn 2018)

sill." The subtasks "soap each window" and "wipe each soaped up window" will be carried out by the robot, and the new (optional) subtask "observe the robot cleaning the window" is now present at the user's side. In case the robot has not fully achieved the intended outcome (clean windows), the user can point the robot to locations that are still dirty/contain stripes, e.g., using an integrated camera, so that the robot can redo those locations (now or next time).

Reconsidering the life cycle of the core task "cleaning the windows at home" in the light of a window cleaning robot that is certainly supposed to take over the cleaning efforts, the life cycle of the task changes, as shown in Fig. 2 (Geis and Polkehn 2018).

What is important to note is that by automating subtasks with the help of an autonomously moving robot, we implicitly introduce new subtasks that did not exist in the original task model. The user must provision the robot, observe the robot's task performance, assess the outcomes achieved by the robot, and potentially "educate" the robot regarding suboptimal outcomes. These additional tasks are not unique to cleaning a window but are representative of managing or supervising an independently acting agent. Therefore, we can decouple them from the specific core task of cleaning a window and describe them as reusable coordination tasks related to supervising other intelligent (human or non-human) agents and collaborating with them.

3.3 Cooperating with an Intelligent System

We learned from the simple example of the cleaning robot that the original worker becomes the supervisor of the newly introduced intelligent system. This is a "redesigned" core task that comes with typical subtasks augmenting the original task flow, as shown in Table 1. A successful introduction of intelligent solutions must systematically analyze how this solution augments the existing task flow and treat this additional interaction according to the user needs originating from the core task of supervising an autonomous intelligent agent.

The (human) user decides which subtasks to assign. Once the (human) user has assigned the work to each intelligent system, the (human) user must monitor the progress achieved by the intelligent system and control the situation up to the point where taking over again what had been assigned to an intelligent system. Once each intelligent system has delivered results, "feedback" must be provided to each agent to improve future outcomes.

In light of forthcoming intelligent systems at business workplaces, we can assume that traditional human subtasks (within core tasks) will be delegated to and shared with intelligent systems. The (human) user and their intelligent systems become increasingly a team. Nowadays (2024), "Alexa" and "Google Home" are assistants that respond to instructions from their (human) users, but in the near future, intelligent systems will also actively instruct (human) users. This results in a mixed-initiative cooperation and requires explicit management of the teaming between the user (human) and the intelligent system in the larger organizational context.

What we learned from above is that the introduction of system intelligence creates a set of additional meta-tasks to manage and orchestrate the relationship between one or multiple intelligent agents (human to human, human to non-human,

Table 1 The changed life cycle of completing a task in the light of intelligent systems

User as task owner Without intelligent system	User as supervisor With intelligent system
Plan	Request
	Assign
	Take over
Prepare	Provision
	Activate
Perform	Observe
	Assist
Assess	Review
	Audit
Deliver	Accept/reject
	Modify
Optimize	Feedback
	Configure

and non-human to non-human) and to train the intelligent system to improve over time. These tasks suggest new job roles, such as task supervisor, team manager, and agent trainer, which must be considered relevant user profiles when designing intelligent systems. Supporting these (new) tasks will lead to a trustful relationship between the user and the intelligent solution where established usability principles such as self-descriptiveness, conformity with user expectations, and controllability are applied.

3.4 Stakeholder-Centric View

Setting the design focus for an intelligent system on the larger organizational context of use, the user is just one of many stakeholders within a larger socio-technical context (see Fig. 3). As depicted in Fig. 3, stakeholder groups represent technical, business, or regulatory interests. This is true for any system being used in an organizational context. However, it is especially interesting for intelligent systems to explicitly call out the influence of those stakeholders on the design and adoption of intelligent systems:

- *Business owners:* Typically have control over training, decision rules, optimization criteria, and teaming models
- *Technical experts:* Decide about an intelligent system's situational awareness, decision capability, and enactment capabilities

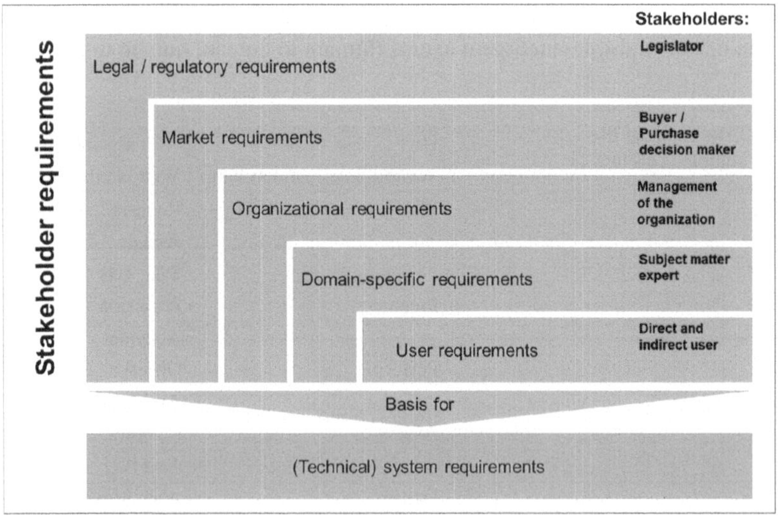

Fig. 3 Types of stakeholders and stakeholder requirements (adapted from Geis and Polkehn 2018)

- *Consultants:* Have the technical know-how to train and configure an intelligent system
- *Regulatory auditor:* Sets policies and boundaries and approves teaming models on how to use an intelligent system
- *Indirect users:* Affected by decisions of an intelligent system

Looking at this larger group of stakeholders expands the design focus from designing user interaction to a more systemic view where cooperative networks of intelligent agents collaborate to achieve desired outcomes.

A human-centered design approach attempts to consider all stakeholder needs and strengthen, specifically, the needs of the direct users who typically fall behind in a classic ERP software implementation project. Each stakeholder comes with a set of typical requirements that reoccur in every systems development project:

- *Legal requirements* are set by authorities, and they represent constraints that must be followed by the organization that is building, introducing, and operating a system.

  Example: "Personal data must only be stored if the individual agrees."
- *Market requirements* are set by those who intend to buy the system (buyers/purchase decision-makers).

  Example: "The system must reduce the turnaround time for the task at hand by at least 50%."
- *Organizational requirements* are set by those who manage an organization and prescribe how people perform their core tasks/interact with other roles when completing them.

  Example: "The sales representative has to get quotations signed off by the sales director if they exceed a price of USD 100.000."
- *Domain-specific requirements* are set by those who ensure the correct output of the system as specified in the business.

  Example: "The invoice must contain the order number of the purchase order before it can be accepted for payment."
- *User requirements* are determined by the needs of the direct users (i.e., those who perform the core tasks with the help of the system) and indirect users (i.e., those who use the system or are affected by its outputs)

  Example: "With the system, the flight manager shall be able to recognize which flight passengers are eligible for a business upgrade."

Regarding intelligent systems, an important question is who has the authority to decide about the cooperation model between users and intelligent systems, and who is empowered to control the intelligent system agent when it comes to autonomous decision-making and actions.

3.5 Aligning Intelligent Systems with Stakeholder Needs

Business software is typically designed and configured according to technical and business perspectives (so-called functional requirements). It tends to neglect the needs of end users performing the tasks. This can quickly become a fundamental showstopper for adopting intelligent systems because the tacit knowledge of experts and the unwritten business rules of how to get the job done are typically not considered in the design. If an intelligent system only embodies official business goals (e.g., minimizing costs or maximizing resource utilization), the resulting decision strategy of an autonomous system may not be accepted by the expert users or affected stakeholders.

During implementation, business owners, technical experts, and consultants collect requirements and configure standard ERP software according to agreed requirements. Those requirements typically represent the official view of the business and the domain experts on how the business works or should work. What typically falls behind is the tribal (tacit) knowledge of the expert users and the unwritten business rules that define the actual work practice. In the old days, user requirements were treated as nonfunctional requirements and were more of an afterthought than a primary focus.

Neglecting user needs not only leads to sub-optimal usability, but, in the case of intelligent systems, ignoring user needs will also result in system intelligence that only reflects the formal business rules and interests and not the tacit knowledge and practices applied by the users. Consequently, systems will be trained on features exclusively associated with business goals and will likely ignore relevant situational contexts experts use to make decisions.

It is, therefore, important to rely on organizational stakeholders and consider user needs related to situational awareness and decision-making. The main question to ask is what users have to know in order to make the right decisions and what the desired outcomes are when making decisions. This context analysis will lead to user requirements complementing formal business and technical requirements.

In the case of intelligent systems, these requirements will not only influence the user interface design but also feature engineering, training, and design of each decision-making step. If an intelligent system is supposed to augment users' situational awareness, it is important to understand what kind of information these users need to make decisions. If an intelligent system is also making autonomous decisions, it is important to align the rationale of the decision with the expert users.

Intelligent systems require a continuous improvement and learning approach that is balanced between user-driven feedback loops and optimization of outcomes represented by other organizational stakeholders. Intelligent systems need guard rails and boundaries to mature during use, and they also need smart oversight to avoid learning the undesired bias of human users while not ignoring the tribal knowledge of experts. If intelligent systems have only limited situational awareness and use static business-oriented decision rules that are not aligned with actual work practice, the practitioners will not accept the outcomes of those systems and will try to work around the system. Such an ignorance of the system may easily result in shadow work, duplicating the intelligent system, or simply ignoring it.

Organizations must continuously monitor the alignment of intelligent systems with their context of use and be prepared to optimize features and decision rules continuously. If this alignment requires technical consultants or is exclusive to data scientists, then end users or domain experts will have no power to configure and adjust the running system for optimal outcomes. As a result, an intelligent system may drift away from being aligned with the most recent business needs and decision strategies.

Introducing intelligent systems to organizations always requires redesigning business processes and human work practices. However, organizations typically make top-down decisions about which subtasks to automate to optimize business results and increase productivity. This top-down approach usually imposes a specific teaming model on their employees, which forces them to use the system either as an expert system or to fully delegate specific steps to the intelligent system.

Research shows that teaming models are not static and highly depend on the situational complexity of the task. For example, pilots can turn off the autopilot if their situational awareness suggests overruling it. In the same way, an intelligent system may escalate and hand over control to the user if it believes it cannot handle the current situation. If business owners and technical experts make fixed assumptions about the teaming model and do not allow users to choose different teaming models depending on the situation, then the risk is that systems are not accepted at all because users disagree with the outcomes they produce.

Users who are empowered to choose the teaming model will develop usage patterns when engaging with intelligent systems to achieve the best results under given circumstances. They will incorporate the output of the intelligent system into their workflow based on their experience with the system and the anticipated outcomes. To achieve this level of elasticity in engaging with intelligent systems, requirements should be explicitly defined for different teaming models to ensure that the resulting system design supports flexible ways of integrating and consuming the intelligent system into the work practice of the human experts.

Finally, the concept of indirect users is important for designing socially responsible intelligent systems that make autonomous decisions. An indirect user is not directly interacting with a system but is affected by the output of a system. In the case of intelligent systems, the output consists of predictions and decision proposals with reasoning, decisions, or actions. Those can have a high impact on indirect users. For example, a supplier classified as high risk by an autonomous tendering system will lose all business if they cannot counteract and improve their reputation in the system.

If an intelligent workforce scheduling application is implemented with invalid estimates about labor standards, then the lean workforce will impose continuous stress on the shopfloor workers. If these systems are not controllable and configurable by users, these issues cannot be resolved and cause frustration on the side of the indirect users, but also on the side of the user who recognizes these issues but cannot intervene to correct the undesired decision behavior of an intelligent system.

4 Requirements for Intelligent Solution Spaces

When deriving user requirements, common pitfalls should be avoided. One common pitfall is to phrase requirements as proposed solutions, which does not help solve users' problems in their use context. It is essential to first derive user requirements from user needs and state them in terms of what the user must be able to do with a to-be-designed system rather than describing the properties of the to-be-designed solution (International Organization for Standardization 2019c; UXQB 2022). Before deriving user requirements, it is essential to have identified the user needs. Generally, users find it difficult to state user needs in a style suitable for project teams. Users also tend to develop proposed solutions rather than stating their implied needs.

Figure 4 illustrates the general approach to ground a discussion about requirements and solutions in a solid understanding of the problem space. After user needs are identified in the context of use for the targeted user group, innovative solutions can be brainstormed that fulfill the user's task-related requirements (Geis and Polkehn 2018).

Ideally, the problem space is first identified and described to give a clear picture of what problems must be solved and which user needs to be satisfied. The problem space consists of the context of use for the system, and the user needs embedded in the context of use. The solution space, in turn, describes the system's design ("solution") that will support the derived user requirements of a specified user group. Requirements are defined as part of the solution space because they are derived and

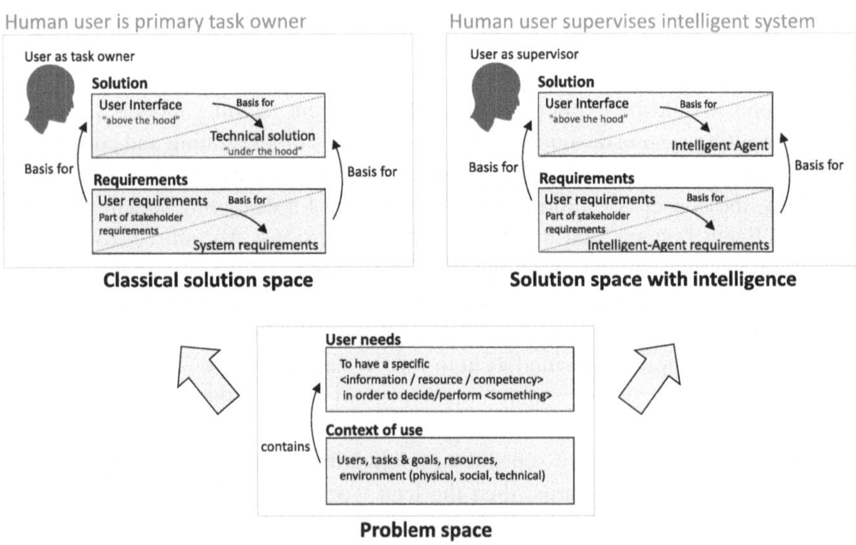

Fig. 4 Problem space and solution space for intelligent systems (adapted from Geis and Polkehn 2018)

formulated by the project team in the context of an envisioned solution instead of being a solution-agnostic users' need.

User requirements describe what information the user shall be enabled to recognize, which choices the user shall be enabled to make, and which information the user shall be enabled to input into the system. In contrast, system requirements prescribe what the system has to provide "under the hood" to enable users to do what is specified in the user requirements.

In the light of intelligent systems, this difference between user and system requirements is not so strict anymore because task ownership shifts from the (human) user to an intelligent system. If the intelligent system takes ownership of subtasks that have so far been performed by the (human) user of the system, the identified user requirements become system requirements for an intelligent agent. Such system requirements will specify what cognitive skills and activities should be accomplished by the intelligent agent. For users interacting with the intelligent system, the user requirements for the user interface will focus on supporting intervention and coordination, which the user shall be able to do in the role of a supervisor or team member.

Table 2 illustrates the shift in focus. (Human) user requirements lead to (intelligent) system requirements that support sensing and recognizing information on behalf of the (human) user, as well as performing subtasks for the (human) user in an autonomous way.

Repurposing user requirements as system requirements in the context of intelligent systems does not invalidate the classic human-centered requirements management approach. Instead, it is the consequence of extending the solution space

Table 2 Transforming user requirements into intelligent-system requirements

Classical view	Intelligent system view
The system supports the user in performing a task	The system takes over parts of or the entire task
User requirements – To recognize information – To make choices – To make inputs	User requirements – To recognize information – To make choices – To make inputs
Lead to	Lead to
System requirements – To provide system function and user interface behavior so that the (human) user can • Recognize information • Make choices • Make inputs	Intelligent-system requirements – To recognize information for the (human) user and inform the (human) user – To make decisions for the (human) user and explain the rationale to the (human) user
Needed as part of their core tasks and subtasks	To initiate actions on behalf of the (human) user based on recognized information

to incorporate autonomous cognitive skills provided by intelligent systems, which would otherwise have been a prerequisite for users to perform the same task. Let us use an example of a surgeon who is removing a cancerous tumor to illustrate this thinking. The text below describes an as-is scenario of the current practice of how a surgeon is removing a cancerous tumor that is situated on the lung of a patient:

> One challenge with cancerous tissue is that, in many cases, it looks the same as healthy tissue. It differs in its reduced elasticity. When I remove a tumor with an appropriate instrument, it is quite straightforward to resect (cut out) large parts of the tumor as long as I have not reached those parts that border with the lung. Once I reach this border, it is important to make sure you exactly and only cut cancerous tissue at the border to not unnecessarily harm the lung. On the other hand, you have to make sure you eliminate the tumor completely. We always cut out pieces of the healthy tissue to ensure the tumor has been taken out completely. So, we do the undesirable, harming healthy tissue. This seems to be a contradiction, but this is our practical challenge when we remove tumors.

The above as-is scenario can be analyzed for implied user needs, e.g.:

(a) The surgeon or the intelligent system *must know which tissue is cancerous and which is healthy* to resect (cut) cancerous tissue only.
(b) The surgeon or the intelligent system *must have the skill to cut cancerous tissue only at the margin of healthy tissue* to maintain its function.
(c) The surgeon or the intelligent system *needs to have a suitable means* to cut to resect (cut) cancerous tissue.

In particular, the information need in (a) and the competency need in (b) are unsatisfied needs from the perspective of the (human) user. The surgeon does not always know which tissue is cancerous and which is not. Furthermore, the skill to resect ("cut out") a tumor at the border to an organ without (unnecessarily) cutting healthy tissue seems almost impossible. These are the opportunities to let robotic systems "do the job" with high precision and reliability. Such a "robotic surgery" is already in place and is valuable for improving surgery outcomes.

Part of the design process is now to identify those user requirements that are better served by an intelligent system. Some of the user needs can be transformed into user requirements for designing the interaction between the user (human) and the intelligent agent; other user needs lead to cognitive requirements specifying the capabilities of the robotic system itself:

- The intelligent system must recognize (sense) which tissue is cancerous and which is healthy.
- With the system, the user must be able to select that the intelligent system resects the cancerous tissue at the margin to the healthy tissue.
- The intelligent system must be able to select (decide) which tissue shall be cut and which tissue shall remain.

We have successfully identified user needs in the existing context of use and mapped the derived user requirements that an interactive system and the intelligent agent must fulfill.

5 Conclusion

Human-centered requirements engineering is an essential part of designing intelligent systems. Intelligent systems are typically "something new" to their users and, therefore, must prove their usefulness and trustability in the context of the use of their users. It is important to understand the capabilities and limitations of users and where the capabilities of intelligent systems can truly help them. Identifying unsatisfied user needs and deriving user requirements for the intelligent system as early as possible in the development process helps to steer predictable success for the intelligent system. Users must be confident that they will achieve better outcomes with the help of system intelligence.

To successfully adopt intelligent systems, all stakeholder requirements should be explicitly derived and managed to understand the human-centered design objectives of introducing system intelligence. Since intelligent systems are typically designed based on organizational objectives, they will embody the interests of organizational stakeholders and optimize business outcomes, e.g., minimizing costs or maximizing revenue. It is, therefore, important to understand and consider the point of view of those stakeholders who are closer to the actual operation, including subject matter experts and the actual direct users of a system.

Complete transparency about the underlying design rationale of an intelligent system, its purpose, and its boundaries is the foundation of responsible AI. End users should be empowered to influence and adjust the teaming model based on situational needs to optimize outcomes within the guard rails of stakeholder interests. Furthermore, the impact on indirect users should be considered to ensure social fairness and adherence to ethical standards.

Human-centeredness does not end with understanding user needs but must consider the needs of all stakeholders. It is also not limited to defining user requirements for user interfaces of interactive systems. However, it is of utmost importance to define system requirements for intelligent systems and understand the new interaction dynamics between users and intelligent systems.

References

Brooke J (1996) Sus: a "quick and dirty" usability scale. In: Jordan PW, Thomas B, Weerdmeester BA, McClelland AL (eds) Usability evaluation in industry. Taylor & Francis, London, pp 189–194

Geis T, Polkehn K (2018) Praxiswissen user requirements. dpunkt.verlag

Hacker W, Sachse P (2014) Allgemeine Arbeitspsychologie: psychische regulation von Tätigkeiten, 3rd edn. Hogrefe, Göttingen

International Organization for Standardization (2018) ISO 9241-11:2018 ergonomics of human-system interaction—usability: definitions and concepts

International Organization for Standardization (2019a) ISO 9241-210:2019 ergonomics of human-system interaction—part 210: human-centred design for interactive systems

International Organization for Standardization (2019b) ISO 9241-220:2019 ergonomics of human-system interaction—part 220: processes for enabling, executing and assessing human-centred design within organizations

International Organization for Standardization (2019c) ISO/IEC 25065:2019 systems and software engineering—systems and software quality requirements and evaluation (SQuaRE)—common industry format (CIF) for usability: user requirements specification

International Organization for Standardization (2020a) ISO 9241-110:2020 ergonomics of human-system interaction—part 110: interaction principles

International Organization for Standardization (2020b) ISO/TR 9241-810:2020 ergonomics of human-system interaction—part 810: robotic, intelligent and autonomous systems

International Organization for Standardization (2023) ISO 9241-221:2023 ergonomics of human-system interaction—part 221: human-centred design process assessment model

Laugwitz B, Schrepp M, Held T (2008) Construction and evaluation of a user experience questionnaire. In: Holzinger A (ed) HCI and usability for education and work. Springer, Berlin, Heidelberg, pp 63–76

Ulwick AW (2016) Jobs to be done: theory to practice. Idea Bite Press

UXQB (2022) Curriculum: certified professional for usability and user experience—foundation level

Reasoning with AI: Six Essential Factors for Augmenting Human Expertise in the Workplace

Sean Koon

Abstract This chapter examines the possibilities and challenges of augmenting expert reasoning in complex, high-risk work settings like healthcare, the judicial system, engineering, military defense, public safety, and more. While AI-augmented reasoning has immense potential in such domains, there is no clear developmental pathway for how such tools should be designed. AI is problematic because it does not follow a human reasoning process nor collaborate as humans do. It can lack transparency and consistency, and its inconsistent outputs can cause unreasonable errors. These characteristics of AI make it potentially incompatible with human experts and the accountabilities of their domain. Creating reliable methods to integrate AI and human participation in reasoning tasks remains an open question. Toward this aim, this chapter presents six factors as foundational considerations for studying and designing tools for AI-augmented human reasoning. The factors include contextual adaptation; situated accountability; roles, boundaries, and interdependencies; domain-specific reasoning strategies; new interaction modes; and shared knowledge and values.

1 Introduction

A particularly interesting but challenging notion is the idea of AI as a "cognitive teammate" (Beringer et al. 2022; Lyons et al. 2021; Seeber et al. 2018). With its ability to leverage large amounts of information, we might imagine it supporting expert workers in reasoning, decision-making, and problem-solving tasks in complex, high-risk settings such as healthcare, the judicial system, engineering, military defense, research, and public safety.

S. Koon (✉)
Kaiser Permanente, Fontana, CA, USA
e-mail: sean.e.koon@kp.org

C. K. Coursaris et al. (eds.), *The Design of Human-Centered Artificial Intelligence for the Workplace*, Progress in IS, https://doi.org/10.1007/978-3-031-83512-4_6

However, the challenging reality is that AI has neither the innate nor the enculturated characteristics that human teammates possess. Human teammates have common conceptual models and expressive language for collaboration and debate. They possess education and experience that gives them essential background knowledge for their tasks. Human teammates develop a nuanced understanding of their socio-technical system and its processes, accountabilities, and barriers. Humans can exert their common sense, creativity, values, and ethics, which technology does not possess (Brenner et al. 2021).

Despite their remarkable capabilities, AI tools are not a reliable substitute for human collaborators, and there may be substantial risks if we relate them as if they were (Shneiderman 2022). It may be especially true in settings where the risk of human impact is high, where humanistic concerns abound, and where experts apply a combination of intuitive and analytical processes (Kahneman 2011; Patel et al. 2002). Nevertheless, it is precisely for such settings, e.g., healthcare, public safety, and the judicial system, that AI development is targeted (Deloitte United States 2022).

The ideal paradigm is AI-augmented reasoning, where the full spectrum of human capabilities and values is employed, along with the technical capabilities of the AI (Dellermann et al. 2019; Xu et al. 2021). This idea, while conceptually satisfying, lacks a clear developmental pathway. In the spectrum between "mostly AI" and "mostly human," there is a "missing middle," as Dave et al. (2023) describe, and the path to creating tools that have a high degree of human and AI integration remains an open question (Beringer et al. 2022; Lyons et al. 2021; Daugherty and Wilson 2018; Oswald et al. 2022).

This chapter explores the unique potential of cognitive tools that are highly compatible with expert workers. It takes the specific vantage point of the expert worker-in-task who needs tools that align with their reasoning capabilities and needs, situated within a socio-technical system of processes and accountabilities. Six factors are proposed that represent the practical considerations that will support the creation and adoption of such highly advanced reasoning tools.

2 The Six Factors

- Factor 1: Design for contextual adaptation
- Factor 2: Support situated accountability
- Factor 3: Define roles, boundaries, and interdependencies
- Factor 4: Consider domain-specific reasoning strategies
- Factor 5: Employ new interaction modes
- Factor 6: Pursue shared knowledge and values

2.1 Factor 1: Design for Contextual Adaptation

Understanding where tools are desired, feasible, and viable is essential in making AI tools available in the workplace (Brenner et al. 2021; Yildirim et al. 2021). Discerning where to place a cognitive tool can be more crucial than the design itself since only adopted tools can be effective. Tool placement depends upon understanding the reasoning task and the larger context in which it is performed. Work "as imagined" can be quite different from "work as done" (Hollnagel 2014), resulting in tools that do not align with the work process or team strategy (Lintern and Motavalli 2018). For example, decision-making support tools in healthcare can suffer from low adoption rates for various reasons, including interference with workflows, time burden, redundancy, unhelpful content, and poor fit for individual cases (Kawamoto and McDonald 2020; Khairat et al. 2018).

Beyond the reasoning task is its socio-technical context. The term "socio-technical" refers to the idea that the function and outcomes of technology are highly dependent on the informal and formal human-human and human-technology interactions within the setting in which it is deployed. As stated by Gerlings et al., "A sociotechnical approach takes a holistic view where relations among people, technology, tasks, and organization are sustainable" (Gerlings et al. 2021, p. 1285). Socio-technical systems have workflows, communication practices, rules, constraints, responsibilities, and institutional culture, all essential to understand when designing and placing tools (Beringer et al. 2022; Ehsan and Riedl 2020; Miller et al. 2017). Analysis of these socio-technical factors may assist in determining the potential settings for human-AI interactions (Sittig and Singh 2010).

By exploring a cognitive task within its socio-technical context (Jiancaro et al. 2014; Read et al. 2015), it is possible to create a realistic model of the work-as-done, understanding the people, processes, and cognitive tasks involved. With this understanding, designs can be insightful and precise about "if" an AI tool should be used, "where" the tool should be deployed, e.g., in a particular aspect of a task, with a specific user type, in a stage in the process, and "how" it should exist, e.g., specific design decisions regarding the degree of AI participation, user control strategies, management of complexity, and user attention (Jiang et al. 2022).

Also, between a well-placed and well-used tool lies the work of implementation and iterative improvement. These efforts may benefit from the emerging learnings of implementation science (Camacho et al. 2020; Lewis et al. 2015; Peters et al. 2014; Bauer et al. 2015), which is "the scientific inquiry into questions concerning implementation—the act of carrying an intention into effect..." (Peters et al. 2014, p. 1). As the tool's life cycle progresses, gaining feedback on user acceptance can streamline the placement of tools and guide ongoing improvements. There are several proposed methods to predict technology acceptance (Taherdoost 2018); for example, the technology acceptance model (TAM) and its revisions have extensive application within the healthcare setting (Hollnagel 2014). The TAM models have also been extended with different variables to suit particular purposes (Ducey and Coovert 2016), and such an extension explicitly designed for AI-enhanced tools may be essential.

2.2 Factor 2: Support Situated Accountability

The Burden of Accountability

Experts bear a burden of accountability for their decisions and the reasoning behind them (Ferreira and Monteiro 2021). Here, being accountable refers to being "responsible for one's actions and expected to explain them" (Oxford University Press 2011). Bearing these accountabilities with a degree of excellence is how, in part, experts experience satisfaction, provide value, and confirm their trustworthiness in their role. For experts to delegate some part of their reasoning to an AI tool, it must demonstrate clear benefits and align with the domain-specific ways that experts justify their reasoning to others. While creating "better-than-human" AI tools may be technically feasible, such tools may remain unadoptable if they fail to support the expert in explaining their decisions. Viewing AI implementations through this lens of accountability should inspire the design of more adoptable tools. The following are examples of the considerations that emerge when we focus on accountability.

Good Decision-Making Versus Good Outcomes

Experts are embedded within systems and processes that involve an accepted knowledge base, methods of explanation or justification, work standards, and documentation practices. In these settings, making good decisions is not synonymous with having good outcomes, a vital distinction when considering AI-enhanced decision support. While uncontrollable factors may create poor outcomes, experts can still justify their decision-making based on adherence to accepted decision-making practices, such as following due process or case law in the legal field (Deeks 2019; Lim 2021), evidence-based medicine recommendations in healthcare (Sackett 1997), quality standards, or other standards and conventions pertinent to a domain.

In contrast, AI tends to be optimized for an algorithmic outcome rather than a defensible decision-making process. With this approach, in addition to being unreliable in some cases, AI tools also rely on complex pattern extraction that is foreign to human reasoners, such that the user may be unable to understand how the AI reached a result (Kelly et al. 2019). Consequently, conflicts may occur between conventional reasoning and the AI algorithm. Does the expert make a justifiable decision by accepted standards, or do they choose the AI recommendation arising from a powerful but mysterious tool? Rejection of the tool is likely in this scenario, but so is the possibility of trusting the tool when it is incorrect. Without a strategy to resolve such conflicts, the expert's ability to justify their decision-making with AI is imperiled. In contrast, an adoptable AI tool would integrate with the existing ways that experts explain, justify, defend, or document their reasoning in the domain.

Explaining Reasoning Versus Explainable AI

Developing "explainable AI" (XAI) is the next logical step in making AI more accessible to human reasoning. XAI may allow users to calibrate their trust, compare AI factors with their thinking, and potentially avoid errors (Adadi and Berrada 2018; Arrieta et al. 2020). Various forms of XAI will be essential to creating AI-augmented reasoning tools. Unfortunately, the "explanations" themselves can be complex and problematic (Antoniadi et al. 2021; Rudin and Radin 2019), potentially making them impractical for real-time use and perhaps better suited to engineers (Miller et al. 2017).

In some cases, workers may see XAI as a new and unreasonable accountability to bear. It is unlikely that users will be proficient with AI, statistics, or even computers, nor will the people to whom they must justify their decisions. Analyzing complex AI outputs may become an inappropriate burden (Jacobs et al. 2021) or cause delays in time-critical decision-making (Narayanan et al. 2018). Also, AI explanations may be seen as a form of risk-shifting that makes the user accountable for design flaws (Naikar 2017; Elish 2019).

From an accountability perspective, however, the chief problem may be that XAI is simply not explaining the right things. XAI often quite literally attempts to explain what the AI is doing, while an expert needs to be able to explain how and why they chose to factor the AI result into their reasoning (Gunning et al. 2021). An expert should be able to make justifications regarding the tool, such as "It is validated by a certifying body," "It gave me a useful insight that I could explore and validate," "It is known to perform well in the scenario I used it," "The model emphasized the same factors that I observed," "I was able to improve the model by removing irrelevant factors," "The AI tool reported a high degree of confidence in this result," or "I have extensive experience with this model in this scenario."

The choice of AI model and explainability must directly support the act of justification. Importantly, this may or may not require an explanation of algorithm behavior. Trustworthiness could also be confirmed through validation (Wing 2021), regulatory oversight (Shneiderman 2022), experimental interactions with the tool (Cai et al. 2019a), "trustworthiness heuristics" (Liao and Sundar 2022), or situational awareness of the AI's reliability in a task (Jiang et al. 2022).

Case-by-Case Accountability Versus Overall Performance

Ultimately, humans bear the practical and emotional impacts of actions taken by or influenced by AI. While AI models may be optimized for overall performance, workers tend to be held accountable on a case-by-case basis. Decision-makers such as police officers, healthcare workers, judges, and military leaders are individually accountable for each scenario or case they encounter. Addressing the personally experienced, case-by-case accountability of experts in a domain is a vital step in designing adoptable AI.

A concern with AI in this regard is that it may be able to outperform humans generally but will also make unreasonable errors that a human would not. For example, if a self-driving car makes an error that a human would not (Eykholt et al. 2018), the driver still bears the responsibility or consequences (Elish 2019). An AI that interprets X-rays may make errors that a human never would, leaving the radiologist responsible for an indefensible error by all human standards (Park and Han 2018). Thus, tools that statistically outperform humans overall may still be unacceptable if they make critical errors in individual outlier cases, such as when applied to a member of an underrepresented population in the dataset (Nushi et al. 2018).

From a case-to-case perspective, clarifying when to use a tool may be more important than understanding its overall performance. In healthcare, for example, many medications, devices, and tests are essentially "black boxes." However, they can be deemed trustworthy based on testing, validation, and a knowledge of the circumstances in which they work well (London 2019). Experts may find a rather poorly performing tool to be acceptable if there is an understanding of the "situations where the model may fall short" and "why the model underperforms" (Tonekaboni et al. 2019). Myers confirms the importance of understanding the scenarios or "subgroups" for which a tool could be safely applied (Myers et al. 2020). Similarly, in military settings, it is necessary to understand when a model can be trusted, when it may fail, and how to correct it (Gunning and Aha 2019). From this perspective of case-to-case accountability, one goal might be to optimize the tool such that users can quickly identify the cases or scenarios for which it will perform poorly and those for which it will perform well. Such an approach represents a strategy different from optimizing an algorithm for overall performance and could have significant upstream implications for algorithm choice, optimization, tuning, explainability, and user interface design.

An understanding of accountability becomes foundational to creating adoptable tools. The expert's concerns are a sort of proxy for the concerns of multiple stakeholders, whether they be regulators, administrators, peers, clients, or others whom the expert's decisions and actions might impact. By understanding what the expert thinks about, worries about, and the kinds of critiques they may have to defend against, we can better design informational tools, display layouts, alerts, or other necessary situational awareness features. Increasingly, however, the question will involve AI participation in general: What should AI be "allowed" to do? It is not only the capabilities of AI but also the situated accountabilities of the user that should shape the manner and degree to which AI can participate in an expert reasoning task.

2.3 Factor 3: Define Roles, Boundaries, and Interdependencies

Combining human and computer capabilities aims to achieve a better, or at least similar, result than either one could achieve individually (Ezer et al. 2019; Friedman 2009). In concept, this is not altogether different from our aim with human teams, where we purposefully include people with differing and complementary capabilities. Similarly, we could aspire to have AI that summarizes evidence, offers supportive information or predictions, offers critique or arguments, proposes solutions, provides situational awareness, and much more.

However, it is easy to overlook how intuitive these types of collaborations are for humans, who have an implicit understanding of how to cooperate. People generally know when and how to contribute to a discussion. They know their area of expertise and its boundaries, i.e., they "know what they do not know." They seek input to fill in knowledge gaps or to address their uncertainties. They experience personal accountability, which adds a degree of caution to what they express and the confidence with which they express it. In contrast, AI (and computers in general) will readily and indifferently present erroneous information if no safeguards exist.

There needs to be a strategy to coordinate human and AI interactions such that the capabilities of each are fully applied and their shortcomings do not lead to errors. Furthermore, there must be an understanding of the specific types of input each might need from the other, thus approximating a sort of "cooperation." These considerations are referred to here as the roles, boundaries, and interdependencies, and they represent high-level precursors to what will ultimately become an interaction design.

Roles

The roles refer to the various functions within a reasoning task that might be allocated to an agent. An agent's role is generally aligned with its capabilities. However, there are situations where a human may need to perform a task that a computer could have done, such as an ethically sensitive decision-making task. Roth et al. (2019) reviews historical paradigms for "function allocation" and discusses methods to determine the cognitive work that might be performed jointly by humans and AI. Roles may need to be flexible (i.e., transferring tasks to another agent) in cases where the scenario is dynamic or when an outlier circumstance may "exceed the boundaries of the automated agents…" (Roth et al. 2019). Importantly, as Johnson et al. (2017) reinforced, the primary challenge for design is not allocating the individual roles or tasks but creating the interdependencies between humans and AI that will support joint activity.

Boundaries

Boundaries refer to the circumstances or conditions where an agent's contribution could be faulty. Moreso than measures of overall model performance, experts are particularly concerned about the specific boundaries of an AI agent's capabilities (Myers et al. 2020; Gunning and Aha 2019; Bansal et al. 2019; Cai et al. 2019b). Given their case-by-case accountability, experts need to know if the tool is suitable and "working right" for the immediate case or scenario in front of them (Antoniadi et al. 2021; Tonekaboni et al. 2019; Anderson 2004). Irregular or "off-nominal cases" (Roth et al. 2019) may represent situations where the expert is likely to perform better and where AI influence should be minimized (Amann et al. 2020). Experts have long used tools that are essentially "black boxes" in that they do not understand their inner workings but do understand their use and limitations (London 2019; Ghassemi et al. 2021).

The boundaries require special attention when planning the interaction design. They may represent opportunities for AI to provide situational awareness of its own uncertainty (Jiang et al. 2022), perhaps giving "trustworthiness cues" (Liao and Sundar 2022). There may also be points where the expert may act upon the AI model to improve its performance (Gunning and Aha 2019). Importantly, humans have boundaries, too, with the potential for errors or cognitive biases that may benefit from computer-aided debiasing and error checking (Blumenthal-Barby and Krieger 2015; Croskerry et al. 2013; O'Sullivan and Schofield 2018). An augmentation model's reliability does not come from overall enhancements in AI performance but rather through an ability never to give AI (or a human) a high-risk task for which it is unmanageably unreliable.

Interdependencies
Interdependencies refer to the points of opportunity where agents might act upon each other in various ways to prevent errors, add supportive information, or otherwise enhance the performance of the other agent in their role. Johnson et al. (2017, p. 3) explore the issue of roles and describe a spectrum of human involvement versus computer involvement for shared tasks. They conclude, "All 'intermediate levels' of automation are joint activity, not cleanly separable functions...." The automation design should focus on the potential interdependencies between humans and computers rather than simply focusing on adding the tool's capabilities to the task. They offer "interdependence analysis" methods to support this (Johnson et al. 2017).

The goal of attending to these roles, boundaries, and interdependencies is to ensure that experts can fully apply their capabilities and AI capabilities to support their accountabilities. Experts are expected to treat each scenario individually, applying background knowledge and values, using perhaps a variety of decision-making strategies (Djulbegovic and Elqayam 2017), applying tacit knowledge (Klein 1998) and intuition (Lee 2020), considering the larger problem-solving context (Patel et al. 2002; Ferreira and Monteiro 2021), and employing human traits such as common sense, fairness, and empathy. They must be able to justify their decisions (Ferreira and Monteiro 2021), follow accepted decision-making practices, and avoid "unreasonable errors," as discussed previously.

AI capabilities are enticing, but if the boundaries of these capabilities cannot be well defined or the expert cannot act on the tool to improve its performance, then the tool is unlikely to support the user's accountabilities and perhaps fails to fit the task. Thus, a thoughtful analysis of the potential roles, boundaries, and interdependencies is a crucial precursor to designing the features of the user interface.

2.4 Factor 4: Consider Domain-Specific Reasoning Strategies

The expertise of professionals is a result of having learned domain concepts and practiced with them extensively in reasoning tasks. As Patel et al. (2001, p. 335), "expertise in medicine and in other domains involves the construction of clusters of concepts that have great explanatory power (facets) and serve to partition a problem space." These concepts or clusters of concepts ("cognitive chunks") refer to useful cognitive intermediates between low-level data and high-level concepts or decisions. For example, "hypovolemia" is a common concept in healthcare and refers to a low fluid volume in the circulatory system. This term consolidates the meaning behind a set of findings but not so far as to make a specific diagnosis. Experts may also have a "cognitive scaffold," essentially a network of the informational gaps they attempt to fill when approaching a particular problem (Patel et al. 2002; Fiore et al. 2010). Concepts and a cognitive scaffold can provide a substrate for decision-making and problem-solving. While reasoning strategies may be complex and varied (Kahneman 2011; Patel et al. 2002; Djulbegovic and Elqayam 2017), an expert trained in the domain can typically participate in another's reasoning process because of the shared mental model built upon these shared concepts and strategies.

The main challenge in "reasoning with" AI is that it does not share a human conceptual model or a reasoning strategy. Instead, many AI tools are innately opaque, leaving users unaware of how the output was achieved (Adadi and Berrada 2018; Rudin and Radin 2019). Without conceptual alignment, it is difficult for experts to leverage their skills with AI, and they may also have difficulty knowing when to trust it (Wing 2021). It becomes problematic if an AI tool competes with, rather than augments, the user's mental model, which could result in decision-making conflicts between AI and human recommendations without a satisfying method to resolve them.

Explainable AI (XAI) aims to improve this "conceptual gap." In some cases, AI explanations are well aligned with concepts of the reasoning task (Alkan et al. 2018; Caruana et al. 2015). In other cases, and perhaps more often, XAI can be "too complex and high-dimensional to be easily understood" (Ghassemi et al. 2021, p. 745) and diverge from how an expert would explain their reasoning.

XAI designs may also attempt to serve too many aims. Explainability can be used to "justify, control, improve, and discover" (Adadi and Berrada 2018), and any jack-of-all-trades explanations that try to suit all purposes simultaneously might suit them poorly. For example, XAI used by engineers to validate or improve the algorithm should be significantly different than the XAI used by an end user to decide whether to trust a particular AI output. If the AI and its explanations are intended to support a reasoning process, then the choice of algorithm (Rudin and Radin 2019) and the design of explanations should explicitly align with the concepts and analytical process of the domain reasoning task (Wang et al. 2019; Lai et al. 2021). The alignment of AI explanations and reasoning requirements in the domain may be informed by analysis of the cognitive task to understand the reasoning and key concepts involved (Read et al. 2015; Naikar 2017). Also, if AI is to support interactive reasoning, it should be both "explainable and tellable" (Premack and Woodruff 1978) so that workers can not only review AI's explanations but also provide feedback to improve the AI's performance (Cai et al. 2019b; Tomsett et al. 2020).

This aim of aligning AI tools with an expert's conceptual model serves multiple purposes. Accountability is supported through conceptual alignment since it is these domain concepts that workers use to document or justify their reasoning. Usability at the interface is also improved if the visualizations and available actions align with the domain reasoning strategies. Collaboration is supported if a team is reasoning about a task with AI. Realistically, AI-augmented reasoning is unreachable without AI tools that accommodate the concepts and reasoning strategies of the domain.

New possibilities may lie in hybrid AI models that combine both opaque "connectionist" or "sub-symbolic" models (such as deep neural networks) with knowledge and logic-based approaches that are conceptually more aligned with human reasoning, for example, by enhancing tools with ontologies (Asunción et al. 2005; MacAvaney et al. 2019; Mishra 2022), knowledge graphs (Dhani et al. 2021; Thakker et al. 2020), and neuro-symbolic reasoning (Hitzler 2022).

2.5 Factor 5: Employ New Interaction Modes

The advent of AI-augmented reasoning will lead to new kinds of interactions and considerations of "usability." Advanced reasoning interactions might leverage the use of critics (Ali et al. 2010; Fischer et al. 1991; Irandoust 2006) and argumentation-based interactions or dialogue (Azhar 2015; Sklar and Azhar 2018). As Irandoust (2006, p. i) suggests, critic systems can take a "problem description and the user's partial or final result as inputs and provide a critique of the user-proposed solution as output." Because they can operate with limited knowledge, they may work well, especially in complex or vague decision-making tasks where "the potential background knowledge relevant to the task cannot be wholly articulated" (Irandoust 2006, p. 14). Argumentation-based interactions can provide a "means for organizing evidence for (or against) particular claims (or decisions)" using an "extended form of negotiation where agents can not only exchange claims, but also their reasons for believing (or disbelieving) those claims" Sklar and Azhar (2018, p. 277). Ideally, the language of these critic or argumentation interactions would align with the terminology and cognitive concepts of the domain (Factor 4). Also, giving the tool access to domain values and priorities might enhance the performance of these tools (Factor 6).

Other interactional possibilities exist as well. Experts often use mental simulation to explore options in their decision-making process (Klein 1998). Users could explore "what if..." scenarios with counterfactual explanations (Verma et al. 2020), potentially using visual sliders to include "more" or "less" of a contributing factor (Cai et al. 2019a; Shneiderman 2020a). AI might be used for simulations and strategy generation in warfighting (Schubert et al. 2015; Mercado et al. 2016), disaster management (Sun et al. 2020), firefighting (Asunción et al. 2005), and other decision-making applications. Users could respond to AI recommendations with "plan repairing" (Asunción et al. 2005) in an iterative problem-solving process. Simulations might employ a "digital twin," a rich virtual model of a physical entity that can be used for simulations (IBM 2023; Rasheed et al. 2020). New transformer models, popularized by tools such as DALL-E[1] and ChatGPT[2], might also support problem-solving tasks. Such tools might catalyze problem-solving if access to a large and relevant data source is available. Also, any simulation or

---

[1] https://openai.com/index/dall-e/

[2] https://openai.com/index/chatgpt/

strategy modeling tools could include critique or argumentation-based techniques to refine the reasoning outcome further.

The Need for New Usability Models and Principles for Augmented Intelligence New interactions with AI will require us to extend our study and evaluation of "usability." For example, AI and its explanations may add a new and different cognitive load. Predictive tools may create new ambiguities or uncertainties in decision-making, compounded by AI's potentially erratic outputs. Some AI tools will be dynamic, with machine learning producing different results for the same type of problem as new data and training are employed. Aiding the user in "calibrating trust" will be essential for usability in some designs. Choices in the timing of when AI outputs are presented can influence whether an anchoring bias will occur, i.e., where the "decision-maker forms a skewed perception due to an anchor (AI decision) available to them, which limits the exploration of alternative hypotheses" (Rastogi et al. 2022). With new transformer models, usability may involve how well a tool helps the user refine their prompts or verify the accuracy of information. Attention management will be a concern, especially in a "mixed-initiative interface" (Horvitz 1999) where AI might spontaneously initiate an interaction. These can potentially increase the cognitive burden and uncertainty (and thus stress) in decision-making. Whether these considerations are called "cognitive usability" or some other apt term, there remains a need for distinct efforts to understand the usability issues of tools that intend to "help people reason." Of note, multiple significant efforts around AI interface design standards are emerging, including Google PAIR[3] and several other academic publications (e.g., Wang et al. 2019; Amershi et al. 2019; Wright et al. 2000) that would benefit from in situ research, consolidation, and standardization.

The computer tools experts use can also impact their job satisfaction or overall well-being (Gardner et al. 2019). As we incorporate AI into the workplace, our interest in usability must extend beyond the user's experience of an interface, per se, to now consider the reasoner's internal experience of decision-making with AI. Frustration with navigating a user interface differs from the stress of using a poorly designed AI tool in a decision with high human risks. Ambiguity, uncertainty (Attema et al. 2018; Bussone et al. 2015; Eastwood et al. 2017; Iannello et al. 2017), need for cognitive closure (Raglan et al. 2014), regret (Becerra Pérez et al. 2016; Connolly and Zeelenberg 2002; Djulbegovic et al. 2015), and decisional conflict (Lipstein et al. 2016; Vickers 2017) are all potential human factors deserving fresh study in the context of augmented intelligence. As the Industrial Revolution had many new physical impacts on workers, we might imagine a cognitive revolution to have cognitive and emotional impacts, thus deserving early and ongoing investigation.

[3] https://pair.withgoogle.com/

2.6 Factor 6: Pursue Shared Knowledge and Values

Regardless of whatever decision we may model, there is generally a broader context of important background information, circumstantial factors, and human values that are outside the model (Pomerol and Adam 2006). For example, a marketing tool that optimizes a price point may not consider the benefit of establishing a long-term customer with a low initial price. An AI recommender could promote one medical treatment over another, potentially without regard to side effects, cost, or some other valued consideration. In sum, the decision may be only one part of a larger goal, important factors may not be included in the model, and the valued outcomes may be broader than what the algorithm is programmed to optimize.

Human collaborators can readily consider this larger context. We can expect that teammates in the workplace will share a similar knowledge of the world, the domain, things that people generally value, and things that are specifically valued in a task. Through common background knowledge and communication, a shared mental model can be developed to support cooperation (Lyons et al. 2021).

With AI, the need for shared goals remains, but with the caution that AI will not have the broader perspective, shared knowledge, and common sense that a human teammate possesses. Unfortunately, attributing human characteristics to technology is both problematic (Shneiderman 2020b) and likely (Nass and Moon 2000), such that users may assume that AI is "thinking about" contextual factors that are not in the model (Cabitza et al. 2017). Users may also base their decisions (or need to) on a "theory of mind" (Premack and Woodruff 1978) of the agent, e.g., what its goals or intentions are, whether it is risk-averse or not, and what it is considering (Cai et al. 2019a). While XAI may give some insight into AI's reasoning, users must also have onboarding (Cai et al. 2019a) and in-task clarification of what the AI does not consider or analyze. In short, the paradox of AI is that we must aim for better-than-human performance while somehow ensuring that users do not attribute full human capabilities to it.

Adding Knowledge and Values

A basic augmentation strategy is to rely on human input wherever background knowledge or values are important. However, creating AI "teammates" that are increasingly useful will require them to access key human concepts and background knowledge. AI that is augmented with background knowledge may more efficiently summarize and supply relevant information for tasks, alert the user to important events, and support situational awareness. In addition, ontologies, knowledge sets that "organize domain knowledge into structures that computers can read, and humans can understand" (Dissanayake et al. 2020, p. 160), can also be used to support cooperative reasoning tasks. Augmenting AI with ontologies can enhance machine learning capabilities with the benefits of formal information structures (Asunción et al. 2005; MacAvaney et al. 2019; Mishra 2022). Related approaches, such as knowledge graphs (Asunción et al. 2005; Dhani et al. 2021; Thakker et al. 2020) and neuro-symbolic AI (Hitzler 2022) (as mentioned in Factor 4), represent important efforts to integrate the nonintuitive "sub-symbolic" approaches of many

AI tools with the deductive, knowledge-based reasoning that experts are familiar. Certainly, generative AI will be an important method of incorporating general and specialized knowledge into decision support and problem-solving tools. However, reliability must be ensured in high-risk tasks (Dave et al. 2023).

A specialized form of human knowledge is that of "values." If humans and machines are to co-process tasks in any advanced way, then AI must have access to human values and priorities. Embedding human values into AI is far from straightforward, as many human values are implicit and may require explicit translation into priorities for the computer. However, to the degree that AI is supplied with formalized information about values, it may assist in reasoning tasks in a more useful and trustworthy fashion. Furthermore, AI could eventually evolve to access a more elaborate collection of priorities that approximate a limited set of "human values." Table 1 elaborates on the six factors and their various considerations.

3 Augmenting Versus Delegating Expertise: User-Directed and Pre-conclusive AI Support

The six factors described here all point to the same underlying philosophy that AI-augmented reasoning is primarily about the capabilities of humans, not AI. Experts may face decisions that are high risk, high accountability, and high uncertainty, with important factors that cannot be incorporated into an AI model (Xiong et al. 2022). They must always be able to apply their full capabilities to support their accountabilities. AI must be given a role that does not obscure or prevent the inclusion of essential background knowledge, practical experience, creative potential, or human values in decision-making. Furthermore, reasoning tools must align with how experts apply their expertise, i.e., considering the work process and the concepts and strategies involved in reasoning, justification, and collaboration in the domain context. Finally, there must be a pathway for workers to rapidly increase their proficiency with the tools; we must presume that domain experts are not experts in machine learning or statistics. In short, AI reasoning tools must become increasingly powerful, simple, and accessible.

It is important to contrast this vision with an often more prevalent vision of AI that focuses on technical capabilities. For many years, the goal has been to create "expert systems" that provide directive decision support to users. Similarly, modern explainable AI often takes a "recommend and defend" approach where AI presents its recommendations and explains why AI came up with that result. This approach, where AI takes a directive role, may sometimes result in anchoring bias (Rastogi et al. 2022) or overtrust (Bussone et al. 2015), cognitive burden, and generally a shift in the agency from the expert to the tool.

An alternative strategy would be to give AI a role that is both pre-conclusive and user-directed. Rather than presenting final answers, advanced reasoning tools

Table 1 The six factors with potential goals and considerations

Factor	Goals	Considerations
1. Contextual adaptation	Deploy desirable, feasible, and well-positioned tools in the work domain. Understand the "work as done" and employ only tools that align with it.	What reasoning support is most desired or needed in this context? Is an AI a good fit for this? Who are the stakeholders, and what are their interests regarding an AI tool? What are the barriers to acceptance? Who takes part in the reasoning task, and how do they communicate and cooperate? Which specific aspect of the reasoning or decision-making process should involve AI?
2. Situated accountability	Ensure that poor decisions do not arise from inappropriate AI influence or errors. Ensure that experts can justify their reasoning and decision-making when using the AI tool.	How are AI explanations made to align with human justifications? If AI and traditional methods present different results, how are these conflicts resolved or harmonized through the interface? How do experts justify their reasoning in this context, and how will they justify it when using AI?
3. Roles, boundaries, and interdependencies	Plan human and AI participation to accentuate strengths and limit shortcomings. Determine the necessary interdependencies between humans and computers as a prelude to interface design.	How does the user know when the AI model can be trusted or when it may fail? How might the user act upon the tool to correct errors or improve the model? How might AI input enhance human reasoning or reduce error and bias? What errors must never happen? How can human or AI input be orchestrated to prevent them?
4. Domain-specific reasoning strategies	Ensure that the user can interact with the tool using the concepts with which they have expertise. Ensure that the reasoning strategies of the domain are understood and can be supported.	What are the important terms and concepts used in the domain to discuss, reason about, or justify a decision? What are the important factors, hypotheses, decisional trade-offs, or other key aspects of the reasoning task? How will explainable AI (XAI) and its interface support the user's reasoning behavior regarding these? With large language models, how do we ensure that the concepts referred to by AI are equivalent to the concepts with which the user is reasoning?
5. New interaction modes	Give users control of the reasoning process and the agency to apply their expertise. Assess and improve cognitive usability issues relating to trust, bias, cognitive load, or decisional stresses.	How does understanding accountabilities, boundaries, interdependencies, and domain concepts translate to what is visualized or actionable in the interface? How might the AI provide pre-conclusive support, i.e., supporting analysis of factors, hypothesis testing, simulation, weighing trade-offs, critique, and argumentation? What interface features can reduce AI overreliance, for example, from anchoring bias or anthropomorphism? How will decisional stressors such as complexity and cognitive load, ambiguity, and decisional conflict be evaluated and improved in the tool over time?
6. Shared knowledge and values	Ensure that the larger context, background information, and human values are relevant to the reasoning process.	What information or values are important in this decision but inaccessible to the AI model? How is it made clear what the tool is "not thinking about"? What does the tool "lean toward," e.g., are its recommendations "conservative" or "moderate risk"? How might the tool better incorporate human priorities?

(AI or otherwise) might help experts analyze all the factors that must be considered before making a conclusion. For example, AI's role could support the user in various ways, such as weighing factors, exploring options, providing critique, predicting specific events that affect a decision, providing error checking, creating situational awareness, and generating simulations while ultimately leaving the conclusions to the human expert.

Miller (2023) elaborates on a helpful approach that gives the user control over the reasoning process and avoids the issues around AI recommendations. This model emphasizes that expert reasoning is "hypothesis-driven" and that the appropriate AI tool should be "evaluative." This type of AI would evaluate evidence for or against a hypothesis, assist in weighing decisional trade-offs, and generally be compatible with human experts' intuitive and analytical reasoning processes.

The term "mastery" might fairly encapsulate the aim of AI-enhanced reasoning. It does not refer to AI's mastery of a task, nor any burdensome human effort to master the AI tool fully, but rather the ability of an expert to master their task while using the tool. This type of mastery involves knowing how and when to use a tool and how to avoid harm caused by its deficiencies. AI participation would be under the control of the expert, such that the user determines the direction and depth of analysis for any aspect of the problem. Prioritizing human mastery over technical performance is essential when developing tools that experts will adopt and use effectively in their reasoning tasks.

4 Case Study in Healthcare: Using "SMILY" for Diagnosing Cancer

Overview

This case study refers to an AI-enhanced image-based decision support tool to assist pathologists in cancer diagnosis (Cai et al. 2019a,b). Pathologists review highly enlarged images of a patient's tissue (biopsies) for any cell changes that might indicate cancer. This task requires a deep understanding of anatomical concepts and extensive visual experience in recognizing patterns in normal and abnormal tissues. What is notable with SMILY is the efforts made to understand and align with the reasoning of expert decision-makers, ultimately resulting in valuable refinements to the tool (Cai et al. 2019a).

Design for Contextual Adaptation

Pathologists may refer to a reference text or online resource when uncertain of a diagnosis to compare their patient's slide with other examples of slides with the suspected diagnosis. Similarly, SMILY accesses a large database of slides, uses a reverse-image search to collect similar images, and sorts them by feature, mimicking the existing diagnostic approach but extending it in particularly desirable ways.

Support Situated Accountability

To correctly diagnose images and explain their decision-making, pathologists must consider the similarity between their image and previously diagnosed cases. They compare them by considering specific anatomic structures, visual features, and frequencies of a feature. This tool aligns well with both the clinical concepts and the reasoning process that pathologists use to make, confirm, and explain their diagnoses to others, thus improving the defensibility of their decisions. Importantly, the tool is pre-conclusive; it does not make a diagnosis nor require the user to interpret its reasons for doing so, i.e., "recommend-and-defend," avoiding to some degree the safety and trust issues with decision support tools.

Define Roles, Boundaries, and Interdependencies

This tool is framed as an "assistant," supporting the physician in exploring alternate hypotheses by presenting relevant images. In terms of roles, the user supplies the reasoning process and background knowledge, and the system gives them the "cognitive reach" of a massive image database, which can be filtered by clinical concept. Users understood that by "playing" with the sliders, they could test the tool's behavior to determine the boundaries of its capabilities.

Consider Domain-Specific Reasoning Strategies

Before creating the prototype, designers "asked pathologists to enumerate diagnostically important concepts such as 'fused glands'." This feedback inspired a "refine-by-concept" enhancement, allowing doctors to use their knowledge of clinical concepts to act upon the tool, such as exploring the counterfactual, "If this image had more fused glands, how would it affect diagnosis?" The exploratory tools allow the expert to satisfy their hypotheses and diagnostic "scaffold" through exploration and experimentation.

Employ New Interaction Modes

The previous factors informed the creation of a straightforward yet powerful interface. As described, the tool uses reverse-image search and concept-based "more or less sliders" that allow doctors to explore features essential to their diagnostic process. Cognitive burden and trust were explicitly considered using standardized measures, and considerations were made to avoid cognitive overload from excessive images. The interface is "tellable" in that the users can intervene to improve the diagnostic support that the AI provides iteratively.

In sum, this AI tool is expert-driven in terms of control and pre-conclusive in terms of decision-making. It supports the exploration of the problem space and hypothesis testing. It aligns with the domain's existing reasoning process and enables the user to leverage their conceptual knowledge, thus supporting their ability to reason and justify their reasoning.

Pursue Shared Knowledge and Values

Users sought a "theory of mind" about the tool, wanting to know "the extent to which it tends to be more liberal or conservative when considering cancer severity" or what it was "tuned to optimize for" in decisional trade-offs (Cai et al. 2019b). Users also wanted to understand the "categorical limitations and potential pitfalls, especially on well-known edge cases that are difficult for humans" (Cai et al. 2019b). An essential aspect was the creation of onboarding materials to help users understand "the general design objectives" and its "global behavior and tendencies."

5 Discussion

These modern tools that we loosely term "AI" will create unprecedented opportunities to augment human reasoning across many domains. There is also a genuine concern that these tools might introduce unreasonable errors or prevent essential human input or control. While we may be awed by AI's sometimes superhuman performance, we can be equally surprised by the odd ways it can fail. This capricious magic can be useful for many purposes but could be problematic in decision-making tasks where risks are high or crucial human factors are present.

This chapter proposes that highly advanced reasoning tools are within reach and can be reliable and trustworthy. However, such tools will not arise from a preoccupation with AI capabilities but by emphasizing human expertise and its application in a domain. This focus on expertise is a specialization of human-centered design emphasizing human needs, capabilities, and behavior (Norman 2013). However, expert reasoning involves highly specialized capabilities and primarily internal behaviors, so the users' needs may not be self-evident to those who would study or design these tools.

In the case study, we discussed an AI tool that is exemplary in the way that it reflects an understanding of the cognitive task, supports expert accountability, and aligns with the concepts and reasoning strategies of the domain. Notably, the tool encourages an exploratory approach, allowing experts to test their hypotheses, try counterfactual possibilities, and test the boundaries of the tool's capabilities. As new AI tools are rapidly developed for the workplace, they must align similarly with the needs and behaviors of the experts for whom they are intended.

Thus, one goal of the six factors is to create a basic set of lenses that are empathetic to the expert in their context. Of note, these factors are not necessarily comprehensive. They are also not wholly distinct from each other but have significant overlap in their aims. Finally, they are presented in an introductory and cursory fashion and require more exploration. Human-AI interaction, a facet of human-computer interaction, will require what any new scientific field would require: new terminology, specific research techniques, broader application of those techniques, and the consolidation and standardization of knowledge (Shneider 2009). At the very least, the six factors may highlight this "augmented expert reasoning" topic as a distinctive part of that work and point to the considerations that may be useful in future research and design.

The other main goal of the six factors is to serve as "boundary objects" (John et al. 2004; Fong et al. 2007) or shared concepts that could facilitate goal setting and collaboration between scientists, engineers, designers, domain experts, and other stakeholders. For example, an awareness of the expert's accountabilities and an understanding of their reasoning could affect decisions about model choice and tuning, explainability, interface design, implementation, and onboarding. A whole spectrum of existing research, from cognitive psychology to computer science, might be reconsidered through this new lens of augmented intelligence. Nevertheless, the greater challenge may involve integrating these areas of study.

Any "human-AI" collaboration would have to arise from a parallel collaboration between experts from very diverse disciplines. The six factors may help to ground such collaborations in a shared perspective.

As Kranzberg's second law states, "Invention is the mother of necessity" (Kranzberg 1986, p. 548). Technology evolves exponentially, while human reasoning remains much the same. The importance of creating AI tools that prioritize human mastery cannot be overstated. The importance of human mastery in human-AI interactions is true not only for experts in professional settings but also for consumers, leaders, patients, parents, and any members of society who will incorporate AI into their reasoning. In the challenges of our future, it is a combination of humanistic priorities and the ability to reason that will serve us in many next steps.

References

Adadi A, Berrada M (2018) Peeking inside the black-box: a survey on explainable artificial intelligence (xai). IEEE Access 6:52138–52160

Ali NM, Hosking J, Grundy J (2010) A taxonomy of computer-supported critics. In: 2010 international symposium on information technology, vol 3. IEEE, Piscataway, pp 1152–1157. https://doi.org/10.1109/ITSIM.2010.5561592

Alkan O, Daly E, Vejsbjerg I (2018) Opportunity team builder for sales teams. In: Proceedings of the 23rd international conference on intelligent user interfaces, pp 251–261

Amann J, Blasimme A, Vayena E, Frey D, Madai V, consortium P (2020) Explainability for artificial intelligence in healthcare: a multidisciplinary perspective. BMC Med Inform Decis Making 20(1):310

Amershi S, Weld D, Vorvoreanu M, Fourney A, Nushi B, Collisson P, Suh J, Iqbal S, Bennett PN, Inkpen K et al (2019) Guidelines for human-ai interaction. In: Proceedings of the 2019 CHI conference on human factors in computing systems. ACM, New York, pp 1–13. https://doi.org/10.1145/3290605.3300233

Anderson J (2004) The role of ethics in information technology decisions: a case-based approach to biomedical informatics education. Int J Med Inform 73(2):145–150

Antoniadi A, Du Y, Guendouz Y, Wei L, Mazo C, Becker B et al (2021) Current challenges and future opportunities for XAI in machine learning-based clinical decision support systems: a systematic review. Appl Sci 11(11):5088

Arrieta A, Díaz-Rodríguez N, Del Ser J, Bennetot A, Tabik S, Barbado A et al (2020) Explainable artificial intelligence (XAI): concepts, taxonomies, opportunities and challenges toward responsible ai. Inform Fusion 58:82–115

Asunción M, Castillo L, Fdez-Olivares J, García-Pérez Ó, González-Muñoz A, Palao F (2005) SIADEX: an interactive knowledge-based planner for decision support in forest fire fighting. AI Commun 18(4):257–268

Attema AE, Bleichrodt H, L'Haridon O (2018) Ambiguity preferences for health. Health Econ 27(11):1699–1716. https://doi.org/10.1002/hec.3800

Azhar M (2015) Toward an argumentation-based dialogue framework for human-robot collaboration. PhD thesis, City University of New York. https://academicworks.cuny.edu/gc_etds/846

Bansal G, Nushi B, Kamar E, Lasecki W, Weld D, Horvitz E (2019) Beyond accuracy: the role of mental models in human-ai team performance. In: Proceedings of the AAAI conference on human computation and crowdsourcing, vol 7, pp 2–11

Bauer M, Damschroder L, Hagedorn H, Smith J, Kilbourne A (2015) An introduction to implementation science for the non-specialist. BMC Psychol 3(1):32

Becerra Pérez MM, Menear M, Brehaut JC, Légaré F (2016) Extent and predictors of decision regret about health care decisions: a systematic review. Med Decis Making 36(6):777–790. https://doi.org/10.1177/0272989X16636113

Beringer J, Coursaris C, Léger P, Karran A, Oz B (2022) Teaming models with intelligent systems at the workplace. In: Wirtschaftsinformatik 2022 Proceedings. https://aisel.aisnet.org/wi2022/workshops/workshops/2

Blumenthal-Barby J, Krieger H (2015) Cognitive biases and heuristics in medical decision making: a critical review using a systematic search strategy. Med Decis Making 35(4):539–557

Brenner W, van Giffen B, Koehler J (2021) Management of artificial intelligence: feasibility, desirability and viability. In: Aier S, Rohner P, Schelp J (eds) Engineering the transformation of the enterprise: a design science research perspective. Springer Cham, pp 15–36. https://doi.org/10.1007/978-3-030-84655-8_2

Bussone A, Stumpf S, O'Sullivan D (2015) The role of explanations on trust and reliance in clinical decision support systems. In: 2015 international conference on healthcare informatics. IEEE, Piscataway, pp 160–169. https://doi.org/10.1109/ICHI.2015.26

Cabitza F, Rasoini R, Gensini GF (2017) Unintended consequences of machine learning in medicine. JAMA 318(6):517–518. https://doi.org/10.1001/jama.2017.7797

Cai C, Reif E, Hegde N, Hipp J, Kim B, Smilkov D et al (2019a) Human-centered tools for coping with imperfect algorithms during medical decision-making. In: Proceedings of the 2019 CHI conference on human factors in computing systems. ACM, New York, pp 1–14

Cai C, Winter S, Steiner D, Wilcox L, Terry M (2019b) "hello ai": uncovering the onboarding needs of medical practitioners for human-ai collaborative decision-making. In: Proceedings of the 2019 CHI conference on human factors in computing systems. ACM, New York, pp 1–14

Camacho J, Zanoletti-Mannello M, Landis-Lewis Z, Kane-Gill S, Boyce R (2020) A conceptual framework to study the implementation of clinical decision support systems (bear): literature review and concept mapping. J Med Internet Res 22(8):e18388

Caruana R, Lou Y, Gehrke J, Koch P, Sturm M, Elhadad N (2015) Intelligible models for healthcare: predicting pneumonia risk and hospital 30-day readmission. In: Proceedings of the 21th ACM SIGKDD international conference on knowledge discovery and data mining. ACM, New York, pp 1721–1730

Connolly T, Zeelenberg M (2002) Regret in decision making. Curr Direct Psychol Sci 11(6):212–216. https://doi.org/10.1111/1467-8721.00203

Croskerry P, Singhal G, Mamede S (2013) Cognitive debiasing 1: origins of bias and theory of debiasing. BMJ Q Safety 22(Suppl 2):ii58–ii64

Daugherty P, Wilson H (2018) Human + machine: reimagining work in the age of AI. Harvard Business Review Press, Boston

Dave T, Athaluri SA, Singh S (2023) Chatgpt in medicine: an overview of its applications, advantages, limitations, future prospects, and ethical considerations. Front Artif Intell 6:1169595. https://doi.org/10.3389/frai.2023.1169595

Deeks A (2019) The judicial demand for explainable artificial intelligence. Columbia Law Rev 119(7):1829–1850

Dellermann D, Calma A, Lipusch N, Weber T, Weigel S, Ebel P (2019) The future of human-ai collaboration: a taxonomy of design knowledge for hybrid intelligence systems. Electron Markets 29(1):49–68

Deloitte United States (2022) The ai dossier. https://www2.deloitte.com/us/en/pages/consulting/articles/ai-dossier.html Accessed 10 Oct 2022

Dhani JS, Bhatt R, Ganesan B, Sirohi P, Bhatnagar V (2021) Similar cases recommendation using legal knowledge graphs. arXiv preprint arXiv:210704771. http://arxiv.org/abs/2107.04771

Dissanayake PI, Colicchio TK, Cimino JJ (2020) Using clinical reasoning ontologies to make smarter clinical decision support systems: a systematic review and data synthesis. J Am Med Inform Assoc 27(1):159–174. https://doi.org/10.1093/jamia/ocz193

Djulbegovic B, Elqayam S (2017) Many faces of rationality: implications of the great rationality debate for clinical decision-making. J Eval Clin Practice 23(5):915–922

Djulbegovic M, Beckstead JW, Elqayam S, Reljic T, Kumar A, Paidas C, Djulbegovic B (2015) Thinking styles and regret in physicians. PLOS ONE 10(8):e0134038. https://doi.org/10.1371/journal.pone.0134038

Ducey A, Coovert M (2016) Predicting tablet computer use: an extended technology acceptance model for physicians. Health Policy Technol 5(3):268–284

Eastwood JL, Koppelman-White E, Mi M, Wasserman JA, Krug III EF, Joyce B (2017) Epistemic cognition in medical education: a literature review. Int J Med Educ 8:1–12. https://doi.org/10.5116/ijme.587a.0f2a

Ehsan U, Riedl M (2020) Human-centered explainable ai: towards a reflective sociotechnical approach. arXiv preprint arXiv:200201092. http://arxiv.org/abs/2002.01092

Elish M (2019) Moral crumple zones: cautionary tales in human-robot interaction. Engaging Sci Technol Soc 5:40–60

Eykholt K, Evtimov I, Fernandes E, Li B, Rahmati A, Xiao C et al (2018) Robust physical-world attacks on deep learning models. arXiv preprint arXiv:170708945. http://arxiv.org/abs/1707.08945

Ezer N, Bruni S, Cai Y, Hepenstal S, Miller C, Schmorrow D (2019) Trust engineering for human-ai teams. In: Proceedings of the human factors and ergonomics society annual meeting, vol 63. SAGE Publications, Los Angeles, pp 322–326

Ferreira J, Monteiro M (2021) The human-ai relationship in decision-making: Ai explanation to support people on justifying their decisions. arXiv preprint arXiv:210205460. http://arxiv.org/abs/2102.05460

Fiore S, Rosen M, Smith-Jentsch K, Salas E, Letsky M, Warner N (2010) Toward an understanding of macrocognition in teams: predicting processes in complex collaborative contexts. Hum Fact 52(2):203–224

Fischer G, Lemke AC, Mastaglio T, Mørch AI (1991) Critics: an emerging approach to knowledge-based human-computer interaction. Int J Man-Mach Stud 35(5):695–721. https://doi.org/10.1016/S0020-7373(05)80143-9

Fong A, Valerdi R, Srinivasan J (2007) Boundary objects as a framework to understand the role of systems integrators. Syst Res Forum 2(1):11–22. https://doi.org/10.1142/S1793965907000122

Friedman C (2009) A "fundamental theorem" of biomedical informatics. J Am Med Inform Assoc 16(2):169–170

Gardner RL, Cooper E, Haskell J, Harris DA, Poplau S, Kroth PJ, Linzer M (2019) Physician stress and burnout: the impact of health information technology. J Am Med Inform Assoc 26(2):106–114. https://doi.org/10.1093/jamia/ocy145

Gerlings J, Shollo A, Constantiou I (2021) Reviewing the need for explainable artificial intelligence (xai). In: Proceedings of the 54th Hawaii international conference on system sciences, pp 1276–1285. http://hdl.handle.net/10125/70768

Ghassemi M, Oakden-Rayner L, Beam A (2021) The false hope of current approaches to explainable artificial intelligence in health care. Lancet Digit Health 3(11):e745–e750

Gunning D, Aha D (2019) Darpa's explainable artificial intelligence (XAI) program. AI Mag 40(2):44–58

Gunning D, Vorm E, Wang J, Turek M (2021) Darpa's explainable ai (XAI) program: a retrospective. Appl AI Lett 2(4):e61

Hitzler P (2022) Neuro-symbolic artificial intelligence: the state of the art. IOS Press

Hollnagel E (2014) Human factors/ergonomics as a systems discipline? "the human use of human beings" revisited. Appl Ergon 45(1):40–44

Horvitz E (1999) Principles of mixed-initiative user interfaces. In: Proceedings of the SIGCHI conference on human factors in computing systems, ACM, New York, pp 159–166. https://doi.org/10.1145/302979.303030

Iannello P, Mottini A, Tirelli S, Riva S, Antonietti A (2017) Ambiguity and uncertainty tolerance, need for cognition, and their association with stress: a study among Italian practicing physicians. Med Educ Online 22(1):1270009. https://doi.org/10.1080/10872981.2016.1270009

IBM (2023) What is a digital twin? https://www.ibm.com/topics/what-is-a-digital-twin. Accessed 20 Feb 2023

Irandoust H (2006) Critiquing systems for decision support. Tech. Rep. DRDC Valcartier TR 2006-070, Defence R&D Canada–Valcartier. https://apps.dtic.mil/sti/pdfs/ADA462355.pdf
Jacobs M, He J, Pradier M, Lam B, Ahn A, McCoy T et al (2021) Designing ai for trust and collaboration in time-constrained medical decisions: a sociotechnical lens. In: Proceedings of the 2021 CHI conference on human factors in computing systems. ACM, New York, pp 1–14
Jiancaro T, Jamieson G, Mihailidis A (2014) Twenty years of cognitive work analysis in health care: a scoping review. J Cogn Eng Decis Making 8(1):3–22
Jiang J, Karran A, Coursaris C, Léger P, Beringer J (2022) A situation awareness perspective on human-ai interaction: tensions and opportunities. Int J Hum-Comput Interact 38(13):1225–1241
John BE, Bass L, Kazman R, Chen E (2004) Identifying gaps between HCI, software engineering, and design, and boundary objects to bridge them. In: Extended abstracts of the 2004 conference on human factors in computing systems. ACM, New York, p 1723. https://doi.org/10.1145/985921.986201
Johnson M, Bradshaw J, Feltovich P (2017) Tomorrow's human–machine design tools: from levels of automation to interdependencies. J Cogn Eng Decis Making 12(1):77–82
Kahneman D (2011) Thinking, fast and slow. Macmillan, New York
Kawamoto K, McDonald C (2020) Designing, conducting, and reporting clinical decision support studies: recommendations and call to action. Ann Internal Med 172(11_Supplement):S101–S109
Kelly C, Karthikesalingam A, Suleyman M, Corrado G, King D (2019) Key challenges for delivering clinical impact with artificial intelligence. BMC Med 17(1):195
Khairat S, Marc D, Crosby W, Al Sanousi A (2018) Reasons for physicians not adopting clinical decision support systems: critical analysis. JMIR Med Inform 6(2):e24
Klein G (1998) Sources of power: how people make decisions. MIT Press
Kranzberg M (1986) Technology and history: "kranzberg's laws". Technol Culture 27(3):544–560. https://doi.org/10.2307/3105385
Lai V, Chen C, Liao Q, Smith-Renner A, Tan C (2021) Towards a science of human-ai decision making: a survey of empirical studies. arXiv preprint arXiv:211211471. http://arxiv.org/abs/2112.11471
Lee J (2020) Is artificial intelligence better than human clinicians in predicting patient outcomes? J Med Internet Res 22(8):e19918
Lewis C, Fischer S, Weiner B, Stanick C, Kim M, Martinez R (2015) Outcomes for implementation science: an enhanced systematic review of instruments using evidence-based rating criteria. Implement Sci 10(1):155
Liao Q, Sundar S (2022) Designing for responsible trust in ai systems: a communication perspective. arXiv preprint arXiv:220413828. http://arxiv.org/abs/2204.13828
Lim S (2021) Judicial decision-making and explainable artificial intelligence: a reckoning from first principles. Revista Forumul Judecatorilor 2021:52
Lintern G, Motavalli A (2018) Healthcare information systems: the cognitive challenge. BMC Med Inform Decis Making 18(1):3
Lipstein EA, Lovell DJ, Denson LA, Kim SH, Spencer C, Ittenbach RF, Anthony KL (2016) High levels of decisional conflict and decision regret when making decisions about biologics. J Pediatric Gastroenterol Nutrition 63(6):e176–e181. https://doi.org/10.1097/MPG.0000000000001308
London A (2019) Artificial intelligence and black-box medical decisions: accuracy versus explainability. Hastings Center Rep 49(1):15–21
Lyons J, Sycara K, Lewis M, Capiola A (2021) Human–autonomy teaming: definitions, debates, and directions. Front Psychol 12:589585. https://doi.org/10.3389/fpsyg.2021.589585
MacAvaney S, Sotudeh S, Cohan A, Goharian N, Talati I, Filice RW (2019) Ontology-aware clinical abstractive summarization. arXiv preprint arXiv:190505818. http://arxiv.org/abs/1905.05818

Mercado JE, Rupp MA, Chen JY, Barnes MJ, Barber D, Procci K (2016) Intelligent agent transparency in human–agent teaming for multi-UXV management. Hum Fact 58(3):401–415. https://doi.org/10.1177/0018720815621206
Miller T (2023) Explainable ai is dead, long live explainable ai! hypothesis-driven decision support using evaluative ai. In: Proceedings of the 2023 ACM conference on fairness, accountability, and transparency. ACM, New York, pp 333–342. https://doi.org/10.1145/3593013.3594001
Miller T, Howe P, Sonenberg L (2017) Explainable ai: beware of inmates running the asylum or: how i learnt to stop worrying and love the social and behavioural sciences. arXiv preprint arXiv:171200547. http://arxiv.org/abs/1712.00547
Mishra K (2022) Role of ontology engineering in artificial intelligence. Int J Swarm Intell Evol Comput 11(2):1–2. https://doi.org/10.4172/2090-4908.1000175
Myers P, Ng K, Severson K, Kartoun U, Dai W, Huang W et al (2020) Identifying unreliable predictions in clinical risk models. NPJ Digit Med 3(1):1–8
Naikar N (2017) Cognitive work analysis: an influential legacy extending beyond human factors and engineering. Appl Ergon 59:528–540
Narayanan M, Chen E, He J, Kim B, Gershman S, Doshi-Velez F (2018) How do humans understand explanations from machine learning systems? An evaluation of the human-interpretability of explanation. arXiv preprint arXiv:180200682. http://arxiv.org/abs/1802.00682
Nass C, Moon Y (2000) Machines and mindlessness: social responses to computers. J Soc Issues 56(1):81–103. https://doi.org/10.1111/0022-4537.00153
Norman DA (2013) The design of everyday things, revised and expanded edition. Basic Books, New York
Nushi B, Kamar E, Horvitz E (2018) Towards accountable ai: hybrid human-machine analyses for characterizing system failure. arXiv preprint arXiv:180907424. http://arxiv.org/abs/1809.07424
Oswald F, Endsley M, Chen J, Chiou E, Draper M, McNeese N, et al. (2022) The national academies board on human-systems integration (bohsi) panel: human-ai teaming: research frontiers. In: Proceedings of the human factors and ergonomics society annual meeting, vol 66. SAGE Publications, Los Angeles, pp 130–134
Oxford University Press (2011) Oxford English dictionary online: accountable. https://www.oed.com/dictionary/accountable_adj. Accessed 24 Sept 2024
O'Sullivan E, Schofield S (2018) Cognitive bias in clinical medicine. J Roy College Phys Edinb 48(3):225–232
Park S, Han K (2018) Methodologic guide for evaluating clinical performance and effect of artificial intelligence technology for medical diagnosis and prediction. Radiology 286(3):800–809
Patel V, Arocha J, Kaufman D (2001) A primer on aspects of cognition for medical informatics. J Am Med Inform Assoc 8(4):324–343
Patel V, Kaufman D, Arocha J (2002) Emerging paradigms of cognition in medical decision-making. J Biomed Inform 35(1):52–75
Peters D, Adam T, Alonge O, Agyepong I, Tran N (2014) Republished research: implementation research: what it is and how to do it. Br J Sports Med 48(8):731–736
Pomerol JC, Adam F (2006) On the legacy of Herbert Simon and his contribution to decision-making support systems and artificial intelligence. In: Intelligent decision-making support systems. Springer, Berlin, pp 25–43. https://doi.org/10.1007/0-387-33419-7_2
Premack D, Woodruff G (1978) Does the chimpanzee have a theory of mind? Behav Brain Sci 1(4):515–526. https://doi.org/10.1017/S0140525X00076512
Raglan GB, Babush M, Farrow VA, Kruglanski AW, Schulkin J (2014) Need to know: the need for cognitive closure impacts the clinical practice of obstetrician/gynecologists. BMC Med Inform Decis Making 14(1):133. https://doi.org/10.1186/s12911-014-0133-7
Rasheed A, San O, Kvamsdal T (2020) Digital twin: values, challenges and enablers from a modeling perspective. IEEE Access 8:21980–22012. https://doi.org/10.1109/ACCESS.2020.2970143

Rastogi C, Zhang Y, Wei D, Varshney KR, Dhurandhar A, Tomsett R (2022) Deciding fast and slow: the role of cognitive biases in ai-assisted decision-making. Proc ACM Hum-Comput Interact 6(CSCW1):1–22. https://doi.org/10.1145/3512921
Read G, Salmon P, Lenné M, Stanton N (2015) Designing sociotechnical systems with cognitive work analysis: putting theory back into practice. Ergonomics 58(5):822–851
Roth E, Sushereba C, Militello L, Diiulio J, Ernst K (2019) Function allocation considerations in the era of human autonomy teaming. J Cogn Eng Decis Making 13(4):199–220
Rudin C, Radin J (2019) Why are we using black box models in ai when we don't need to? A lesson from an explainable ai competition. Harvard Data Sci Rev 1(2):1–9
Sackett D (1997) Evidence-based medicine. Seminars Perinatol 21(1):3–5
Schubert J, Moradi F, Asadi H, Luotsinen L, Sjöberg E, Hörling P, Persson M, Fiedler M (2015) Simulation-based decision support for evaluating operational plans. Oper Res Perspect 2:36–56. https://doi.org/10.1016/j.orp.2015.05.002
Seeber I, Bittner E, Briggs R, de Vreede G, de Vreede T, Druckenmiller D et al (2018) Machines as teammates: a collaboration research agenda. In: Proceedings of the 51st Hawaii international conference on system sciences, pp 115–122
Shneider AM (2009) Four stages of a scientific discipline; four types of scientist. Trends Biochem Sci 34(5):217–223. https://doi.org/10.1016/j.tibs.2009.02.002
Shneiderman B (2020a) Bridging the gap between ethics and practice: guidelines for reliable, safe, and trustworthy human-centered ai systems. ACM Trans Interact Intell Syst 10(4):26:1–26:31. https://doi.org/10.1145/3419764
Shneiderman B (2020b) Design lessons from ai's two grand goals: human emulation and useful applications. IEEE Trans Technol Soc 1(2):73–82. https://doi.org/10.1109/TTS.2020.2992669
Shneiderman B (2022) Human-centered AI. Oxford University Press, Oxford
Sittig D, Singh H (2010) A new sociotechnical model for studying health information technology in complex adaptive healthcare systems. Quality Safety Health Care 19(Suppl 3):i68–i74
Sklar EI, Azhar MQ (2018) Explanation through argumentation. In: Proceedings of the 6th international conference on human-agent interaction. ACM, New York, pp 277–285. https://doi.org/10.1145/3284432.3284470
Sun W, Bocchini P, Davison BD (2020) Applications of artificial intelligence for disaster management. Natural Hazards 103(3):2631–2689. https://doi.org/10.1007/s11069-020-04019-w
Taherdoost H (2018) A review of technology acceptance and adoption models and theories. Proc Manuf 22:960–967
Thakker D, Mishra BK, Abdullatif A, Mazumdar S, Simpson S (2020) Explainable artificial intelligence for developing smart cities solutions. Smart Cities 3(4):1353–1382. https://doi.org/10.3390/smartcities3040067
Tomsett R, Preece A, Braines D, Cerutti F, Chakraborty S, Srivastava M, Harborne D (2020) Rapid trust calibration through interpretable and uncertainty-aware ai. Patterns 1(4):100049. https://doi.org/10.1016/j.patter.2020.100049
Tonekaboni S, Joshi S, McCradden M, Goldenberg A (2019) What clinicians want: contextualizing explainable machine learning for clinical end use. arXiv preprint arXiv:190505134. http://arxiv.org/abs/1905.05134
Verma S, Dickerson J, Hines K (2020) Counterfactual explanations for machine learning: a review. arXiv preprint arXiv:201010596. http://arxiv.org/abs/2010.10596
Vickers AJ (2017) Decisional conflict, regret, and the burden of rational decision making. Med Decis Making 37(1):3–5. https://doi.org/10.1177/0272989X16687010
Wang D, Yang Q, Abdul A, Lim B (2019) Designing theory-driven user-centric explainable ai. In: Proceedings of the 2019 CHI conference on human factors in computing systems. ACM, New York, pp 1–15
Wing J (2021) Trustworthy ai. Commun ACM 64(10):64–71
Wright PC, Fields B, Harrison MD (2000) Analyzing human-computer interaction as distributed cognition: the resources model. Hum-Comput Interact 15(1):1–41. https://doi.org/10.1207/S15327051HCI1501_1

Xiong W, Fan H, Ma L, Wang C (2022) Challenges of human–machine collaboration in risky decision-making. Front Eng Manag 9(1):89–103. https://doi.org/10.1007/s42524-022-0195-y

Xu W, Dainoff M, Ge L, Gao Z (2021) Transitioning to human interaction with ai systems: new challenges and opportunities for HCI professionals to enable human-centered ai. In: Proceedings of the human factors and ergonomics society annual meeting, vol 65. SAGE Publications, Los Angeles, pp 501–505

Yildirim N, Zimmerman J, Preum S (2021) Technical feasibility, financial viability, and clinician acceptance: on the many challenges to ai in clinical practice. arXiv preprint arXiv:210504128. https://arxiv.org/abs/2105.04128

The Contextual Framing of the Interplay Between Human and AI: A Socio-technical Perspective

Joerg Beringer and Thomas Herrmann

Abstract If users consider intelligent systems not as tools but as intelligent agents that take on some tasks in a more autonomous way, the design of such systems must consider the interplay between human and non-human agents from a socio-technical perspective. How can we use established requirements methods and conceptual frameworks to model such an extended context of use? Instead of extending the traditional task-oriented context of use itself, we are proposing to embed the task context into an additional team context and the larger organizational context. With such a three-layer context framework, we provide a conceptual framework that supports designers to identify stakeholder requirements for the application of intelligent system agents. These requirements should be related to these context layers or originate from the dynamics and tensions between those layers. This framework will help formalize and model the interaction dynamics between intelligent system agents and human stakeholders along the different levels of task, team, and organizational context. This holistic design focus is necessary to support the dynamic evolution of task sharing between human and non-human agents within a work environment.

1 Introduction

Traditionally, the design of interactive systems focuses on the user needs implied by tasks to be performed with the help of this to-be-designed system. This task-centric view falls short when designing AI-/ML-based intelligent systems because the challenge is not only to optimize the design of the human-machine interaction for one task, since using AI is much more about the relationship between multiple

J. Beringer (✉)
ProContext, Redwood City, CA, USA
e-mail: joerg.beringer@procontext.ai

T. Herrmann
Ruhr-University Bochum, Institut für Arbeitswissenschaft, Bochum, Germany
e-mail: Thomas.Herrmann@ruhr-uni-bochum.de

C. K. Coursaris et al. (eds.), *The Design of Human-Centered Artificial Intelligence for the Workplace*, Progress in IS, https://doi.org/10.1007/978-3-031-83512-4_7

agents that interact as actors in a mixed-initiative mode (Allen et al. 1999). Therefore, designers have to envision how a solution will be integrated and adopted within a larger socio-technical work system, where various ways of task sharing between humans and AI become possible, as demonstrated by Muller and Weisz (2022), who extend the one-dimensional human information processing model of Parasuraman et al. (2000). Parasuraman et al. (2000) describe a continuum where a task is completely taken over by a human on the one side, and on the other side, the same task is carried out by a technical agent. The six levels of development toward autonomous vehicles are typically described by such a continuum that includes driver assistance and conditional automation (Kukkala et al. 2018). Muller and Weisz (2022) point out that such a continuum is inappropriately one-dimensional since it assumes that every subtask taken over by AI is taken away from the human side. They propose to consider a further dimension where the usage of AI extends the possibilities of the human agent and increases the subtasks being carried out on both sides. For example, using generative AI to support programming might enhance the possibilities of people to take over more software-engineering subtasks than they were able to take over without AI.

To describe an extended variety of interaction and dynamics of task sharing between human agents (H-agents) and intelligent system agents, we propose a nested context model that conceptually frames the interplay between human agents and IS agents as a task-oriented multi-agent team acting within a larger business context:

- **Inner Layer—Task Context:** On the inner level, the core task needs to be done. Core tasks consist of multiple subtasks that must be performed to accomplish the main result. There are proposals for differentiations on the task level (Jiang et al. 2022; Pacaux-Lemoine and Flemisch 2019) to be considered. We are using a sense/decide/act model, which resembles the decision ladder proposed by Rasmussen (1976). These models describe the high-level sub-steps within a core task that an intelligent system agent must support to act autonomously. Each phase requires specific cognitive functions, e.g., detecting and comprehending information, making decisions, and planning and executing actions. The task context is nested into the team context.
- **Middle Layer—Team Context:** The introduction of IS agents implies the interaction of multiple human- and AI-based agents that share various tasks. This interplay between multiple agents can be described as a team context (Dubey et al. 2020) where task sharing and collaboration are coordinated between agents with specific competencies or capabilities that contribute to accomplishing the core tasks. The team context is nested into the organizational context.
- **Outer Layer—Organizational Context:** In real life, tasks are performed within a larger corporate context, including stakeholders with some business interest in the work results or the AI agent as a product. They have the resources and power to choose and design the AI agents and the teaming model. The different roles and interests between the end user interacting with the AI agent in the team context and the business stakeholders configuring the AI agent to align with business interests cause tensions and affect the acceptance of intelligent systems.

These three layers together represent the perspective of socio-technical systems (Fischer and Herrmann 2015; Herrmann et al. 2022), which must be considered to optimize the acceptance and effective use of intelligent systems (Beringer and Latzina 2015). This socio-technical perspective is critical if task execution and responsibility are partially or entirely shifted to intelligent system agents (IS agents) and thus redefines the responsibilities between human and non-human intelligent agents. Understanding the interplay between humans, technology, and organization is important for analyzing task handling (Kirsch et al. 1995). With this framework, we can describe the interaction and task sharing of distributed intelligence and decision-making within an organizational context or when operating machines such as driving a car or flying an aircraft. Concerning the literature that can be employed to describe the three layers mentioned above, it becomes apparent that most of it is limited to the task or team levels. As pointed out by Herrmann and Pfeiffer (2023), the organizational layer is widely neglected in the literature on human-AI task sharing. What is significantly missing is an integration of the different layers into one framework that allows discussing the interdependencies between these layers from a holistic viewpoint of contextual analysis and design.

In the following section, we will introduce each of these context layers in more detail by modeling the task assignments and work relationships of human users and intelligent systems at each of these layers. Building on this foundation, we will discuss the interplay between human and non-human agents originating from task- and team-centric needs to coordinate work distributed among multiple agents.

2 Context Framework of Human-AI Collaboration

This nested contextual framework describes the collaboration between human and intelligent system agents (IS agents) as a multi-agent team that aims to optimize results within a larger organizational context. This framework will help us formalize and model the interaction dynamics between agents and stakeholders at different levels of task, team, and organizational context.

For illustrating the working relationship between a human user and an intelligent agent, we are using a conceptual diagram notation (see Fig. 1), which connects an agent (the user or the system agent) with a task context or task object and annotating this connection with the activity the agent is performing in relationship to this task context.

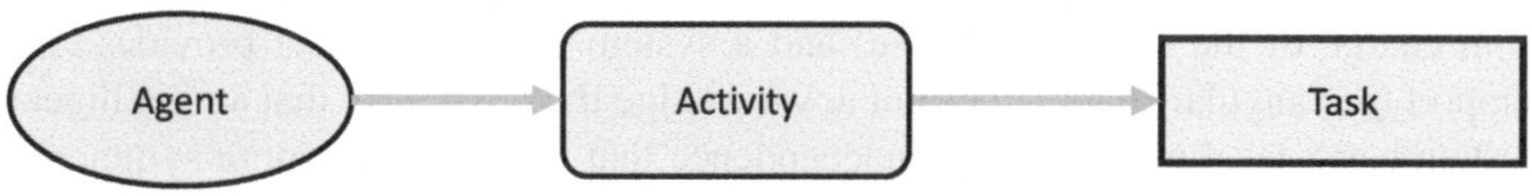

Fig. 1 Notation to illustrate task assignments and work relationships (adapted from SeeMe Herrmann et al. 2004)

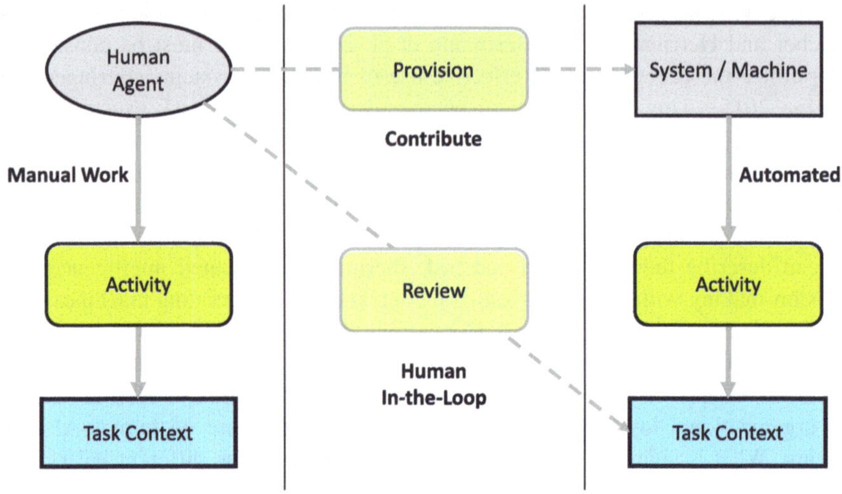

Fig. 2 Manual, semiautomated, and automated task execution (dotted lines are optional meta-activities to facilitate semiautomated delegation of work)

2.1 Task Context

In the task context, we describe how one agent (a human or system) performs an activity to execute a task or subtask related to a task context or task object. Traditionally, we have a human agent performing a task and technical systems that support the human agent or automate specific subtasks.

As depicted in Fig. 2, a simple conceptual diagram allows us to describe who (the actor) is doing what (the activity) concerning a task to be performed (task context) with the help of a system. The human agent (oval shape) may perform a task on his or her own, or the system (rectangular shape) may perform a task in an automated way. Besides this strict separation of task ownership, we have situations where the system assists the human agent by providing input. However, this human agent is still performing the task, or where the human agent is still in the loop to assist and review the output of the automated task performed by the intelligent system agent and declare it as done.

While Fig. 2 describes manual and automated work and some variants of interaction between the human agent and the automation system, it falls short of showing the potential of intelligent systems to learn and make autonomous decisions like a human agent. The asymmetric view between a human agent who is in charge of the task (oval shape) and a system or machine that provides task support (rectangular shape) does not acknowledge the possibility that an intelligent system has a level of ability and independence that will lead to a more symmetric agency between human and system.

We, therefore, suggest modeling the intelligent system just as another non-human intelligent agent (oval shape) to reflect the fact that not only is task execution divided

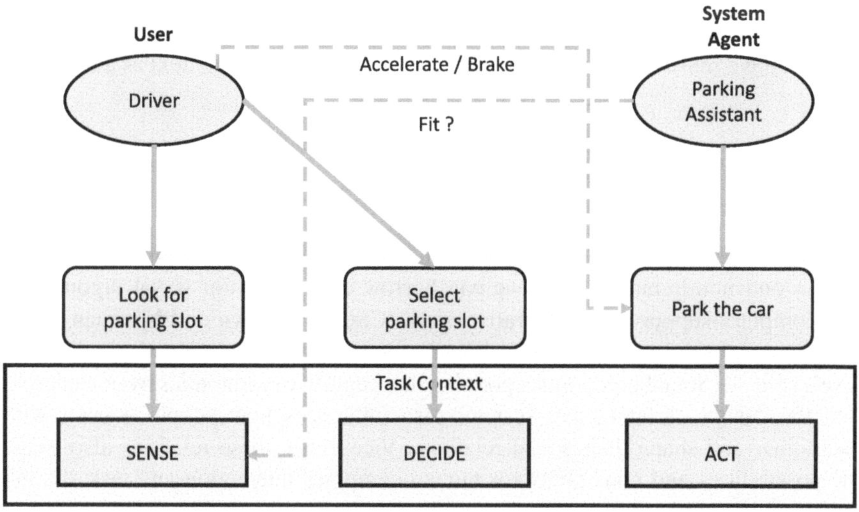

Fig. 3 Functional allocation between driver and parking assistant (solid lines, task ownership; dotted lines, contributions)

into sub-steps, but intelligence is distributed between multiple agents. One IS agent may support a core task or subtask entirely or contribute only specific cognitive skills to one of these phases.

For example, Fig. 3 models the driver (human agent) and a parking assistant (system agent) as oval shapes. With this change in notation, we can describe the relationship between both agents in a much more symmetric way and illustrate how two agents are involved in mastering the three basic phases of parking a car:

- **Sense:** The parking assistant's sensors may help identify an empty parking slot and notify the driver that a parking lot is big enough to fit the car. However, the driver's situational awareness established in the SENSE phase goes far beyond this basic information. For example, the driver knows the current traffic, which might make parking difficult, the proximity to the destination, the ease of opening the doors, and the type of adjacent car models. In this illustrative scenario, the parking assistant only contributes information by detecting the parking slot and comprehending the information into fit/not fit. However, the driver is still the primary owner of the sensing phase.
- **Decide:** Based on the overall situational awareness of the parking assistant and driver, the driver decides whether to go for this parking slot. This decision is made without any contribution from the parking assistant.
- **Act:** Once the driver has decided to park, the driver delegates the parking maneuver to the parking assistant. The parking assistant is now autonomously steering the car, but the driver stays in the loop by controlling speed and monitoring the maneuver in real time.

By representing intelligent systems as agents, we are flexible in describing more symmetric relationships between human and non-human agents and implicitly introducing a multi-agent network, working on the same task context as a team.

2.2 Team Context

When introducing the concept of teaming to describe the relationship between human and non-human agents, we can borrow concepts from social ergonomics and computer-supported collaborative work (CSCW) (Brown and Newman 1985) to describe the interplay between humans and system agents on three different levels (Fig. 4). Social ergonomics goes beyond cognitive ergonomics by considering that the design of interactive systems also influences how people interact with each other and shape their social relations. Vice versa, these relations also shape the possibilities and constraints for human-computer interaction and task sharing between humans and machines. This reciprocal influence was intensively studied by CSCW research that analyzes—for example—how software can support work in groups; how communication, collaboration, and coordination can be facilitated by information systems; or how social relationships can be maintained via social networks. An important CSCW concept is "awareness," which refers to the perception of aspects of a situation that are important for coordinated task execution:

- **Agent Awareness:** This particular type of awareness concerns the social relations that form a team. Team members should know each other's existence, involvement in tasks, purposes, skills, interests, values, availability, reliability, trust,

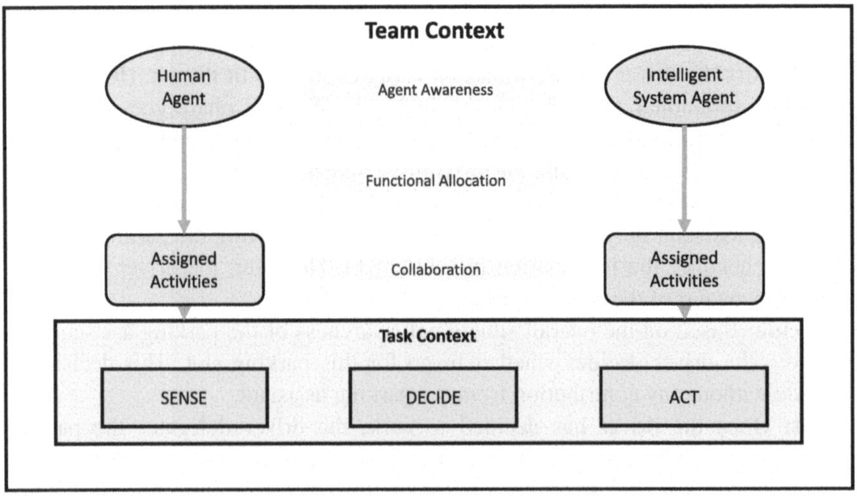

Fig. 4 Team context with embedded task context

and ability. In a human-to-system relationship, this awareness is developed as a mental model of the system agent. The human agent can decide what subtasks to delegate to the system agent only if there is transparency about an IS agent's purpose, cognitive skills, and boundaries. As in real life, a lack of transparency and conflict of interests reduce the trust in the IS agent (Okamura and Yamada 2020).

- **Task and Functional Allocation:** This layer is about managing the available intelligent agents as team resources and developing a team setup that leverages each agent's skill profile and bandwidth to optimize the overall work result. This team setup may assign entire tasks or just selected cognitive functions to IS agents. Depending on the larger business context, this functional allocation may be defined as a priori or (re)defined during task execution, depending on situational needs.
- **Collaboration:** The collaboration layer enables team members to communicate, coordinate, and share work artifacts while performing tasks. Such functions are essential prerequisites for distributed task handling within a team. This collaboration highly depends on the interdependency of tasks and the confidence that each agent delivers the expected quality. Thus, the coordination must consider whether subtasks are highly interdependent or independent.

When forming teams, tasks and functions must be allocated to available agents, and the workflows between agents must be defined based on the anticipated type of cooperation mode and trust. These team characteristics are often shaped by stakeholders in the organizational context; for example, management, as part of the organizational context, may already decide which subtasks are allocated to intelligent system agents and which to the human team members. However, functional allocation and cooperation modes often evolve by aligning teamwork to task requirements and mutual trust levels between agents. For example, a task as a whole may be delegated to a team, and—subsequently—the agents decide which subtasks to allocate to whom, including the intelligent system agents. On the other side of the spectrum of possibilities, it might be that the management, as part of the organizational context, already decides which subtasks are allocated to AI and which to the human side. Based on the literature on job design—for example, Grote et al. (2000)—we assume that flexible task sharing allows for more efficiency. Teams with the flexibility to change functional allocation and coordination between the team members can react more efficiently to the varying requirements of their environment.

2.3 Organizational Context

Finally, any multi-agent team executing tasks acts within the larger context of an organization or business. This larger socio-technical context must be considered when embedding new intelligent agents into the workplace because the organizational context introduces a set of additional stakeholders who are not team members but may also be indirect or secondary users of the AI system. These stakeholders typically have control over the design of the team context and IS agents (Fig. 5).

Although a detailed discussion of the organizational context is not within the scope of this chapter, some common design tensions between business goals and user/team goals are worth mentioning:

- **Power of Design:** As with other enterprise software solutions, there is typically a disconnect between the design and the in-use phase. Business interests, technology, and data availability dominate the design and implementation phase. After going live, users have limited control over the system's configuration. This waterfall model does not work for intelligent systems, which, by definition, are learning, and system behavior and usage patterns evolve during use time. It is therefore important to enable end users to participate in the design over time (Fischer and Herrmann 2011) and have a multidisciplinary project team of domain experts and data scientists continuously monitor and improve the intelligent system to ensure user acceptance, alignment with business strategy, and optimal business outcomes.

  In many cases, the multi-agent team is not empowered to define its setup with an intelligent system. However, technical or business stakeholders define the teaming model a priori during implementation. This top-down configuration of team structure may work for tactical teams, where the task allocation can be predefined a priori how to perform well-defined tasks in a repeated way. However, creative and problem-solving teams need more flexibility and must be empowered to define the teaming model on the fly based on situational needs. Therefore, empowering team members to control functional allocation is an important design aspect that influences user acceptance and the flexibility to deal with new situations.

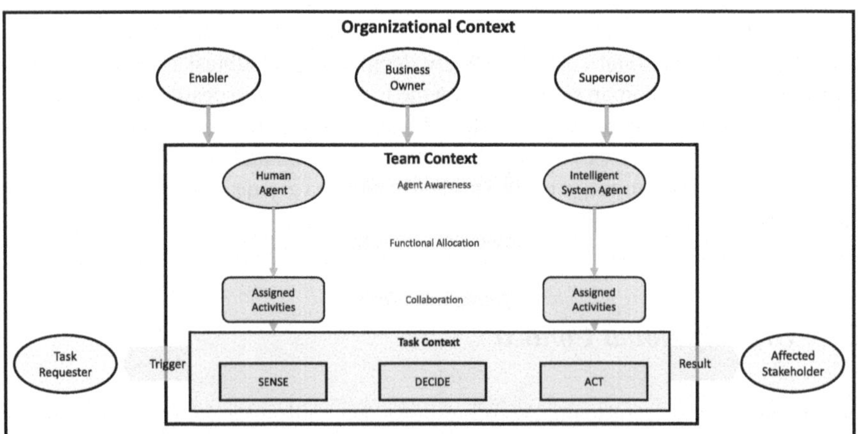

Fig. 5 Organizational context with embedded team and task context

- **Situated Decision-Making:** IS agents that autonomously make decisions and plan actions are set up to optimize specific business outcomes, such as minimizing costs and optimizing utilization of resources. Such decision and optimization strategies may conflict with the human agent's unwritten business rules and actual work practice. This potential misalignment typically causes the rejection of the intelligent systems. Moreover, such a case possibly leads to ongoing frustration on the user side, especially if the system agent continuously produces results that are not in line with the user's preferences or situational needs.
- **Affected Stakeholder:** IS agents that make decisions and plan actions make decisions that affect stakeholders or businesses. For example, a system agent might develop assumptions about the quality of resources and begin to prefer certain people or service providers over others. Alternatively, a system agent trained to optimize costs may not understand human qualities such as social fairness principles of continuity. This lack of understanding will lead to dissatisfaction not only with the primary user but also with all stakeholders affected by these decisions or ratings.

3 Interaction Dynamics Between Human and Non-human Agents

The three context layers introduced above help us identify stakeholder requirements and their perspectives. We also recognize that the dependencies between the task and team context, and between team and organizational context, can easily cause tension if not supported by the design.

The contextual framework suggests specific requirements and design challenges related to the design of intelligent agents, which in many cases can be grounded in conceptual frameworks specific to each context.

3.1 Task-Related Coordination

When considering the team context on top of the task context, it becomes evident that the interaction with intelligent systems is not only driven by the task itself but also by coordination between multiple participating agents.

There is a long history of modeling coordination among two or more agents as a conversational flow of speech between team members (Twitchell et al. 2004; Winograd and Flores 1987). The assumption is that agent interactions follow certain patterns imposed by specific teaming models, authorization models, and preferred collaboration modes.

Agents may work in a horizontal relationship by using the output of one agent as the input of the other agent. Alternatively, they can work in a vertical relationship, where the output from multiple agents is synthesized into the result for one subtask (Millot and Mandiau 1995). In these vertical collaboration models, the merging of multiple inputs may be augmentative (complementary outputs are combined), integrative (different expertise is leveraged to achieve the best result), or debative (multiple agents debate what the best solution is) (Schmidt et al. 1991).

These different modes of collaboration and coordination between agents are relevant for the design of IS agents because each mode comes with a set of use cases and functional requirements. If we want to enable specific collaboration patterns, the user interface of the IS agent must enable the corresponding speech acts or user intents and different modes of embedding the output of an agent into the overall flow of teamwork. The user interface design highly depends on the collaboration mode and how interdependent the agents work.

As an example of interdependent task handling, we take the interaction with a set of ML-based refinement tools (Cai et al. 2019b) with which humans can improve the searching of medical images related to the case at hand. These tools are considered an example of interactive ML. Independent tasks can typically be complementary, where one agent employs the results of another agent to go on with a subtask. Alternatively, independent tasks can be redundant in supporting quality assurance. In this case, the AI or human agent can come first to propose a decision (Fogliato et al. 2022). Concerning quality assurance, agents within team workflows must be able to accept, reject, or modify (Barros et al. 2007) what others deliver, including the intermediate results of AI agents (Rasmussen 1976).

Depending on the user's confidence in the quality of the output of the system agent, the user may decide to delegate, merge, debate, or override the output of an IS agent (Beringer et al. 2022). For example, a work schedule may consider the generated plan of an intelligent workforce scheduling system not as the final result, and, therefore, it may modify the schedule to optimize criteria other than the system that was used. In this case, the output of the IS agent is used as input for a further refinement phase of the workforce schedule. Since the planner understands the advantages and limitations of the workforce scheduling system, they adopted a collaboration model in which the human agent completes the same work artifact that the IS agent (the scheduling system) has generated. The collaboration model is more integrative because the user respects the skill of the IS agent to generate an optimized work schedule for hundreds of workers but is also confident that they can add more value by further refining the schedule.

This example illustrates how collaboration modes between human and non-human agents evolve based on their experience and satisfaction with the quality of the result. If the design of the IS agent is not flexible enough to support different patterns of collaboration models, then the likelihood of rejecting intelligent systems is high.

In many cases, this results in hybrid teaming models and optimizing the sense/decide/act task journey for each phase in different ways. Users make individual meta-decisions for each phase on incorporating and collaborating intelligent systems. These meta-decisions suggest modeling each phase as an independent situational frame, with agents and activities specific to the phase (Beringer et al.

2017). For example, in the *sense* phase, users may use system-generated demand forecasts as input but adjust this forecast based on external knowledge. In the *decide* phase, the user may debate the most likely planning scenarios with the system and then completely delegate the implementation of the supply logistics (*act*) to the system.

3.2 Team-Related Meta-interactions

It becomes evident that the experience design of intelligent systems must not only consider the primary task-related functions but also support meta-tasks originating from the organizational or team context. To understand the interaction dynamics induced by team and organizational context, we can borrow many concepts from classic research and literature on social ergonomics, computer-supported collaborative work (CSCW), and teaming models (Larson and LaFasto 1989).

In a traditional automation scenario, systems perform human tasks. However, these tasks are typically repetitive, feel more like a chore than core, and require a level of scale and quality that exceeds human capacity. These automation systems are designed to perform specific tasks in a specific way with high speed and accuracy.

If, however, higher-level cognitive functions and underspecified tasks are delegated to IS agents, agents must develop distributed situational awareness and cognitive skills and work in a mixed-initiative mode to get the job done. There is a much higher relevance of the social context than in automation, and delegation is not limited to simple repetitive tasks but to more knowledge-based activities and higher-level cognitive functions.

Consequently, the design of intelligent systems must not only focus on the core task itself but also consider the coordination among multiple agents collaborating as a team and the evolution of new teaming models over time.

Functional Allocation To form effective teams, it is crucial to understand the team's intended working mode and the required skills to fulfill the respective roles in the team. Based on the mental model of an IS agent, these skills will be mapped to IS agents based on their perceived capabilities (Fig. 6).

Therefore, mutual awareness of agents' existence and availability and competency profile is essential to form and coordinate effective teams. For this reason, the user interface design of non-human intelligent agents should allow the human agent to develop a correct mental model of each agent and understand its purpose and capabilities for establishing situational awareness, making decisions, and initiating actions. Mutual awareness of others' competencies requires considering that competencies can dynamically develop, which can be supported by the AI itself (Herrmann 2022).

For example, if users do not understand what (sensor) data is available for an agent, they will not be able to understand what situational awareness this agent

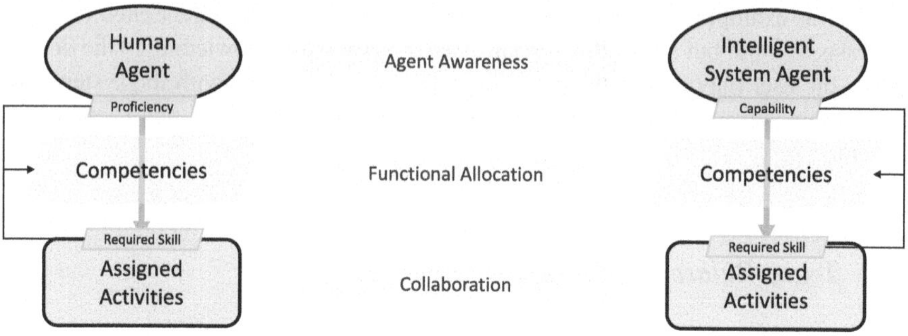

Fig. 6 Agent-competency mapping

has. If the user does not understand the rationale of decisions on the IS agent side, they will not trust these agents. To help users establish the correct mental model, non-human agents should communicate their purpose and be transparent about their boundaries or dependencies to other non-human agents.

This competency mapping also includes transparency about the information flow between IS agents. Often, an orchestration of multiple intelligent systems implements an autonomous business process. For example, an IS agent may monitor edge reality or forecast future demand; another IS agent will take this as input to make decisions. If a user disagrees with the recommended actions, the root cause may be situational awareness and not decision-making. Depending on the locality of these disagreements, user intervention options may be very different.

Trusting Non-human Agents Another aspect of agent awareness is trust. The primary question is to what extent agents can trust each other that they have the competencies and capabilities imputed to them. It must also be transparent about the boundaries of the intelligent system.

Furthermore, in a human-to-human relationship, it is not sufficient to understand the task-related proficiency of an agent. However, it is also important to trust that the agent will be motivated and engaged to apply the skills. While this motivational aspect can be ignored when delegating work to system agents, it is still important to trust that the agent works in the user's interest and is strategically aligned when making decisions.

For example, when activating a speed control system that automatically keeps distance to the car in front, the driver must trust this assistant that it properly discovers the car in front (situational awareness) and maintains a safe but not too large distance to the next car (strategy). The driver must also trust that this system works in more complex conditions, such as windy weather and multilane roads (boundary conditions).

If trust is lacking, the intelligent system's benefit might be dramatically reduced since increased reviewing and intervention might be needed. Instead of performing a relatively simple task, the user will start speculating about the system agent's capabilities and not fully detach from the delegated task. As a result, the user will

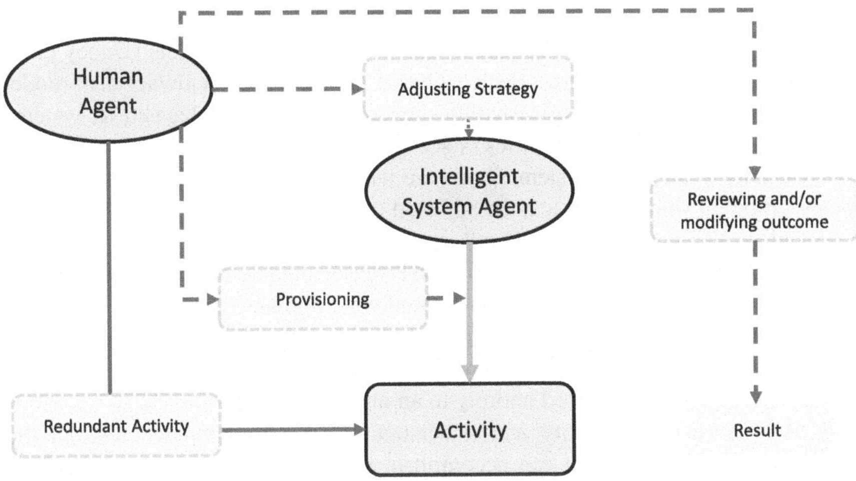

Fig. 7 User interventions and redundant activity of an untrusted agent

start supervising and reviewing the AI agent and, in the worst case, continuously intervening or deactivating the IS agent because this mental workload of supervising the IS agent is higher than the effort to perform the original task (Fig. 7). Thus, interaction design and managerial decisions have to provide possibilities for trust calibration.

In particular, an additional mental workload will initially be necessary after an AI agent is introduced, and trust-building must be supported (Cai et al. 2019a). In addition, over-trusting has to be avoided by appropriate measures that maintain people's awareness of possible faults of AI agents (Croskerry 2003). As a result, trust calibration has to take place (Okamura and Yamada 2020). The trust calibration process concerns the meta-interactions within the team context since trust is also based on social networks (Lee and See 2004) where someone—e. g., named A—trusts in B if A trusts in C and C trusts in B.

If it becomes apparent during supervision or reviewing that something is going wrong and the expectations of the human agents are not being met, intervention might become necessary that has not been planned. Following Schmidt and Herrmann (2017), we consider intervention a temporally limited phase where human agents adjust parameters that influence AI agents' task handling or take over control by fine-grained interaction (Herrmann 2025). A prerequisite of intervention is the possibility of supervision and inspection of AI results, including the possibility of providing explanations by AI (Chromik and Butz 2021). Concerning the nested context framework, intervention could also affect the teaming model: The whole subtask allocated to the AI agent could then be allocated to another agent for a while.

Defining the Teaming Model When delegating work to human agents, each task should be a meaningful activity to motivate the human worker. In contrast, individual cognitive functions may be allocated to intelligent systems if this specific function outperforms human workers. This results in hybrid models (Dubey et al. 2020; Herrmann 2020) where selected phases of the sense/decide/act task model or individual cognitive functions within the same phase are delegated to systems because of their superior capabilities or scalability.

If capacity is an issue, system agents are usually better at scaling than humans because modern web services can be adjusted to the workload.

For example, as depicted in Fig. 8, an intelligent system may be specifically used to detect and comprehend massive IoT sensor data or mine imaging data to establish a basic situational awareness beyond what humans can achieve. However, the classification of how critical an event is and the decision of what approach to take may still be under the user's control. After the user has chosen the approach, the execution may be delegated entirely to an intelligent agent.

If users have the authority and understanding of the competencies and the boundaries of what an agent can accomplish, they will shape the teaming model to optimize the overall outcome.

Managing the Team Context from an Organizational Perspective The introduction of system intelligence directly impacts roles and work processes. In extreme cases, it may change the role of a planner to the role of a supervisor who supervises and manages an intelligent planning system, or it may convert the role of a troubleshooter to a trainer of an autonomous monitoring system. Such high-impact design decisions are primarily made by business stakeholders in the organizational context in the roles of consultants and technical experts. While the lack of consideration of the point of view of an end user typically reduces the usability of any ERP solution, it is a fundamental mistake to believe that intelligent

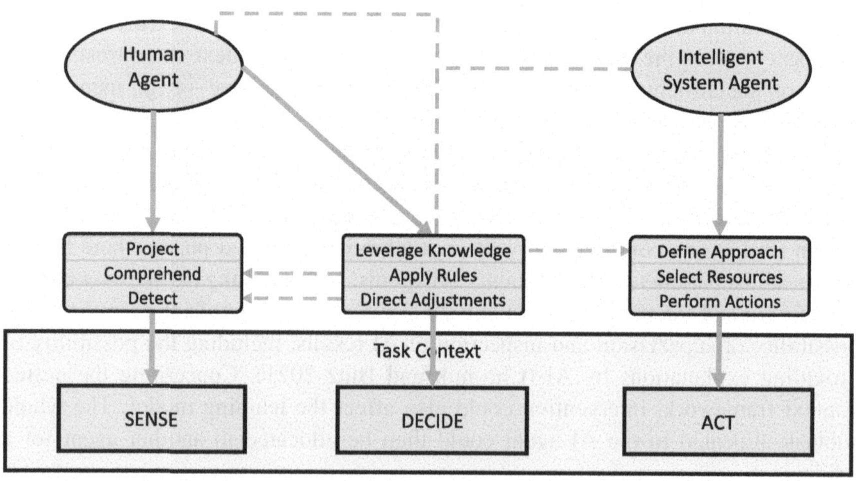

Fig. 8 Teaming model with delegation of subtasks or cognitive functions

systems can be implemented and run as is after being implemented by business stakeholders.

Organizations must identify opportunities to implement fully autonomous business processes that require no or minimal human assistance or intervention. These roadmaps must consider the existing point of view of the human expert and anticipate the changes induced by system intelligence. In a multi-agent team, the team must be empowered to choose the agents' degree of involvement in a task actively.

If the intelligent system supports situational awareness, decision-making, and implementing actions, the expert who has performed the action may be entirely out of the loop. This detachment is dangerous because the user loses their situational awareness and expertise over time to take over. While these radical changes might be the long-term vision of migrating to ML-/AI-supported business processes, the reality is that organizations must have defined a roadmap of how to incrementally shift from human work to intelligent automation and assistants, where humans are still in the loop.

Symmetric Empowerment Considering the speed of innovation and improvements in AI, we project that partial symmetry between human and non-human agents is not unrealistic and must be considered a design objective for multi-agent teams. Symmetry relates to various interactions between agents.

For example, the mutual assistance between the agents should be flexibly and symmetrically distributed concerning the possibilities described in the subsection on task-related coordination. The assistance comprises several activities, such as providing information, explaining intermediate results, and taking over a subtask upon request. AI can provide assistance to humans, for example, through chatbots in the healthcare domain (Ayanouz et al. 2020). Kamar (2016) proposes the other way around, where machine learning-based systems have a model of their own and the humans' competencies and ask humans for help if necessary.

Similarly, interventions are not necessarily only issued by the human agent in the direction of AI (Schmidt and Herrmann 2017), but AI can also intervene in human task handling, such as process monitoring (Teinemaa et al. 2018). For example, regarding explainable AI, it appears reasonable to design AI that can intervene, ask a human for explanations, and seek to learn from them.

Rejection can also be symmetrically distributed. The reasons behind a rejection might be different on both sides. AI might reject requests for help or tasks allocated to it because of its inability to carry out the task or because of implemented rules. For example, when asked about the moral orientation of a political leader, ChatGPT answers: "It is not within my capabilities to make judgments about the moral orientation of individuals ...." Also, humans can refuse to take on specific tasks because they cannot or are unwilling to do so because of psychological or ethical reasons (Mumford 1995).

Figure 9 summarizes central activities on the human side:

- Maintaining an appropriate degree of awareness of the activities and results provided by the other side

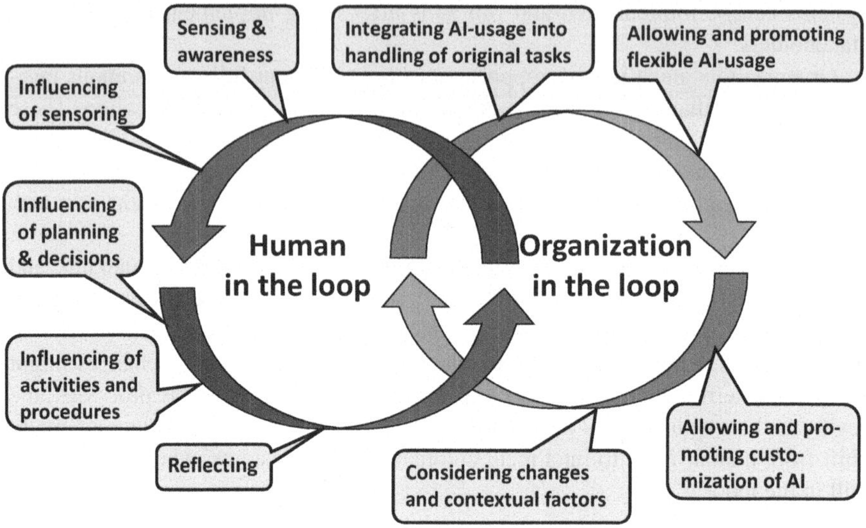

Fig. 9 Keeping the organization in the loop (Herrmann and Pfeiffer 2023)

- Influencing the activities and outcomes of the other side on different levels, such as:
  - Sensing a situation
  - Interpreting the characteristics of the situation to plan further activities or make decisions about them
  - Carrying out processes
- Reflecting on the activities and outcomes of the other side

From the viewpoint of symmetry, these five types of possible reactions can not only occur on the human side but are also possible for the AI agent. Reflection might also indicate an asymmetric relationship since it has to be considered a typical meta-activity and will be quite different on the human side compared to what is possible on the side of the IS agent. To our knowledge, there is no literature about AI that can reflect its own activities and outcomes. However, it would be reasonable if AI performed a critical evaluation of its decisions or forecasts as soon as their effects become apparent.

Social Feedback Loops: How far humans or AI can maintain these types of activities depends on decisions in the organizational environment. Thus, Herrmann (2023) and Herrmann and Pfeiffer (2023) argue that generally keeping humans in the loop and using AI cannot be successful without keeping the organization in the loop. Both must be integrated, as shown in Fig. 9. For Herrmann and Pfeiffer, implementing and using AI has to be accompanied by several managerial activities. They can also be considered as meta-activities. They must become part of organizational practices to be effective.

Figure 9 represents that human activities when using or collaborating with AI must be complemented by organizational measures. These measures assume that there is an original task to be carried out that is supported by AI and that this support has to be properly aligned with the original task and covers the coordination of the collaboration between humans and AI ("planning and managing AI-based task handling," Fig. 9). Furthermore, the flexible dealing with AI (such as rejecting or modifying as described above) must be explicitly allowed and promoted ("allowing and promoting critical and flexible AI usage," Fig. 9). This also applies to the customization of AI. Furthermore, the organization must be aware of "...changes and contextual factors" (see Fig. 9) that might influence the way of task sharing with AI.

The focus should be on managing the teaming model and the distribution of intelligence from a meta-perspective, which constantly evaluates and reflects the quality of the outcomes and ensures that meaningful and functional teaming models are established and accepted by participating or affected stakeholders. This quality-oriented reflection promotes and requires continuous training and reeducation of all agents (Prilla et al. 2013) or recalibration of values and business rules that influence decision-making.

Human expertise cannot be simply replaced by intelligent systems configured to optimize specific business metrics such as costs or resource utilization. Understanding and incorporating the unwritten business rules and the tribal knowledge of practitioners is important not to break successful work practices. On the other hand, shifting from human bias and error to optimized system-driven intelligence might be the main objective when implementing ML-/AI-based agents. In those cases, it must be clear which side (human or system) is responsible for the outcome and the policies for human experts to override or calibrate the system agent.

It is of special interest whether the threefold reaction possibility of acceptance, rejection, or modification can also be applied to meta-activities. For example, can humans oppose the notion that certain tasks can be delegated to AI—or can an AI system reject the allocation of a task—not only to itself but also to someone else?

4 Conclusion

The nested framework of different contexts described in this chapter expands the design space of intelligent systems from human-machine interaction to the holistic design of a network where cooperating intelligent human and non-human agents build teams. Successful deployment of IS agents depends not only on the task UI but also on building a high-performing team structure between human and non-human agents.

The experience design of an AI agent must be flexible enough to support various collaboration modes and offer meta-interactions to optimize the IS agent's controllability, transparency, adaptability, and integrability. However, the organizational context often pre-specifies the teaming model of how AI and humans collaborate.

This top-down approach leads to static workplace designs, which are at risk of rejection due to a lack of adaptability to the situational needs of the team and changes in business requirements. As we expect employees to continuously learn and adopt new business strategies, intelligent systems require continuous reflection, negotiation, and alignment on the team level. This continuous process includes the surfacing of unwritten business rules and informal collaboration patterns so that the behavior of the intelligent system agent and the team characteristics match the actual work practice and the existing human expertise.

To facilitate continuous optimization of the design of interactive AI agents, they have to support flexible and symmetrical allocation of tasks and functions to support meta-activities such as reviewing, supervision, intervention, reflection, and functional allocation. AI agents should have models of their competencies and collaboration partners and vice versa to enable situated alignment from both parties.

Lack of trust leads to increased reviewing, supervising activities, and interventions, which causes an additional mental load that reduces the benefits of employing AI in the workplace. On the other side, accepting the need to keep the human and the organization in the loop as a requirement and enabling situated reviewing and control will widen the possibilities for using AI even if the appropriateness of its outcome is uncertain and will avoid the rejection of AI systems due to lack of trust and poor fit to the actual work practice.

References

Allen JE, Guinn CI, Horvtz E (1999) Mixed-initiative interaction. IEEE Intell Syst Appl 14(5):14–23. https://doi.org/10.1109/5254.796083

Ayanouz S, Abdelhakim BA, Benhmed M (2020) A smart chatbot architecture based NLP and machine learning for health care assistance. In: Proceedings of the 3rd international conference on networking, information systems & security, pp 1–6

Barros A, Decker G, Grosskopf A (2007) Complex events in business processes. In: Abramowicz W (ed) Business information systems. Springer, Berlin, Heidelberg, pp 29–40

Beringer J, Latzina M (2015) Socially embedded technology: the pathway to sustainable product development. In: Wulf V, Schmidt K, Randall D (eds) Designing socially embedded technologies in the real-world. Springer, London, pp 11–18. https://doi.org/10.1007/978-1-4471-6720-4_2

Beringer J, Herrmann T, Nierhoff J (2017) Complementing journey maps with situational frames to create actionable design spaces. In: Mensch und computer 2017—usability professionals. Gesellschaft für Informatik e.V., Regensburg. https://doi.org/10.18420/muc2017-up-0242

Beringer J, Coursaris CK, Léger PM, Karran AJ, Oz B (2022) Teaming models with intelligent systems at the workplace. In: Wirtschaftsinformatik 2022. https://aisel.aisnet.org/wi2022/workshops/workshops/2

Brown JS, Newman SE (1985) Issues in cognitive and social ergonomics: from our house to bauhaus. Hum-Comput Interact 1(4):359–391

Cai CJ, Winter S, Steiner D, Wilcox L, Terry M (2019a) "hello ai": uncovering the onboarding needs of medical practitioners for human-ai collaborative decision-making. Proc ACM Hum-Comput Interact 3(CSCW). https://doi.org/10.1145/3359206

Cai CJ et al (2019b) Human-centered tools for coping with imperfect algorithms during medical decision-making. In: Proceedings of the 2019 CHI conference on human factors in computing systems, pp 1–14
Chromik M, Butz A (2021) Human-XAI interaction: a review and design principles for explanation user interfaces. In: IFIP conference on human-computer interaction. Springer, Berlin, pp 619–640
Croskerry P (2003) Cognitive forcing strategies in clinical decision-making. Ann Emer Med 41(1):110–120. https://doi.org/10.1067/mem.2003.22
Dubey A, Abhinav K, Jain S, Arora V, Puttaveerana A (2020) Haco: a framework for developing human-AI teaming. In: Proceedings of the 13th innovations in software engineering conference (formerly known as india software engineering conference). ACM, Jabalpur, pp 1–9. https://doi.org/10.1145/3385032.3385044
Fischer G, Herrmann T (2011) Socio-technical systems: a meta-design perspective. International J Sociotechnol Knowl Develop 3(1):1–33
Fischer G, Herrmann T (2015) Meta-design: transforming and enriching the design and use of socio-technical systems. In: Wulf V, Schmidt K, Randall D (eds) Designing socially embedded technologies in the real-world. Springer, London, pp 79–109. https://doi.org/10.1007/978-1-4471-6720-4_6
Fogliato R et al (2022) Who goes first? Influences of human-ai workflow on decision making in clinical imaging. arXiv. http://arxiv.org/abs/2205.09696. Accessed 3 Jun 2022
Grote G, Ryser C, Wāler T, Windischer A, Weik S (2000) Kompass: a method for complementary function allocation in automated work systems. Int J Hum-Comput Stud 52(2):267–287. https://doi.org/10.1006/ijhc.1999.0289
Herrmann T (2020) Socio-technical design of hybrid intelligence systems—the case of predictive maintenance. In: International conference on human-computer interaction. Springer, Berlin, pp 298–309. https://doi.org/10.1007/978-3-030-80349062-1_22
Herrmann T (2022) Promoting human competences by appropriate modes of interaction for human-centered-ai. In: Degen H, Ntoa S (eds) Artificial intelligence in HCI. Lecture notes in computer science, vol 13336. Springer, Cham, pp 35–50. https://doi.org/10.1007/978-3-031-05643-7_3
Herrmann T (2023) Calibrating the coordination between humans and ai by analyzing the socio-technical variety of task sharing. In: HCI international 2023 – late breaking posters, in CCIS. Springer, Cham
Herrmann T (2025) Intervenability as a design requirement for autonomy and oversight within human-centered ai. In: The design of human-centered artificial intelligence for the workplace. Springer, Berlin
Herrmann T, Pfeiffer S (2023) Keeping the organization in the loop: a socio-technical extension of human-centered artificial intelligence. AI Soc 38:1523–1542. https://doi.org/10.1007/s00146-022-01391-5
Herrmann T, Hoffmann M, Kunau G, Loser KU (2004) A modelling method for the development of groupware applications as socio-technical systems. Behav Inform Technol 23(2):119–135
Herrmann T, Jahnke I, Nolte A (2022) A problem-based approach to the advancement of heuristics for socio-technical evaluation. Behav Inform Technol. https://doi.org/10.1080/0144929X.2021.1972157
Jiang J, Karran AJ, Coursaris CK, Léger PM, Beringer J (2022) A situation awareness perspective on human-ai interaction: tensions and opportunities. Int J Hum-Comput Interact. https://doi.org/10.1080/10447318.2022.2093863
Kamar E (2016) Directions in hybrid intelligence: complementing ai systems with human intelligence. In: IJCAI, pp 4070–4073
Kirsch C, Troxler P, Ulich E (1995) Integration of people, technology and organization: the european approach. In: Anzai Y, Ogawa K, Mori H (eds) Symbiosis of human and artifact, advances in human factors/ergonomics, vol 20. Elsevier, Amsterdam, pp 957–961. https://doi.org/10.1016/S0921-2647(06)80337-0

Kukkala VK, Tunnell J, Pasricha S, Bradley T (2018) Advanced driver-assistance systems: a path toward autonomous vehicles. IEEE Consum Electron Mag 7(5):18–25. https://doi.org/10.1109/MCE.2018.2828440

Larson CE, LaFasto FMJ (1989) Teamwork: what must go right, what can go wrong. SAGE Publications, Newbury Park

Lee JD, See KA (2004) Trust in automation: designing for appropriate reliance. In: Human factors, p 31

Millot P, Mandiau R (1995) Men-machine cooperative organizations: formal and pragmatic implementation methods. In: Expertise and technology: cognition computer cooperation. Lawrence Erlbraum Associates, New Jersey, pp 213–228

Muller M, Weisz J (2022) Extending a human-ai collaboration framework with dynamism and sociality. In: Proceedings of the 1st annual meeting of the symposium on human-computer interaction for work, CHIWORK '22. Association for Computing Machinery, New York. https://doi.org/10.1145/3533406.3533407

Mumford E (1995) Effective systems design and requirements and analysis—the ethics approach. Macmillan Press, Houndsmill, Basingstoke, Hampshire and London

Okamura K, Yamada S (2020) Adaptive trust calibration for human-ai collaboration. PLoS ONE 15(2):e0229132. https://doi.org/10.1371/journal.pone.0229132

Pacaux-Lemoine MP, Flemisch F (2019) Layers of shared and cooperative control, assistance, and automation. Cogn Tech Work 21(4):579–591. https://doi.org/10.1007/s10111-018-0537-4

Parasuraman R, Sheridan TB, Wickens CD (2000) A model for types and levels of human interaction with automation. IEEE Trans Syst Man Cybern A: Syst Hum 30(3):286–297. https://doi.org/10.1109/3468.844354

Prilla M, Herrmann T, Degeling M (2013) Collaborative reflection for learning at the healthcare workplace. In: Goggins SP, Jahnke I, Wulf V (eds) Computer-supported collaborative learning at the workplace: CSCL@Work. Springer, Boston, pp 139–165. https://doi.org/10.1007/978-1-4614-1740-8_7

Rasmussen J (1976) Outlines of a hybrid model of the process plant operator. In: Sheridan TB, Johannsen G (eds) Monitoring behavior and supervisory control. Springer, Boston, pp 371–383. https://doi.org/10.1007/978-1-4684-2523-9_31

Schmidt A, Herrmann T (2017) Intervention user interfaces: a new interaction paradigm for automated systems. interactions 24(5):40–45. https://doi.org/10.1145/3125387

Schmidt K, Rasmussen J, Brehmer B, Leplat J (1991) Cooperative work: a conceptual framework. In: Distributed decision making: cognitive models for cooperative work, pp 75–110

Teinemaa I, Tax N, de Leoni M, Dumas M, Maggi FM (2018) Alarm-based prescriptive process monitoring. In: Business Process Management Forum: BPM Forum 2018, Sydney, NSW, Australia, September 9–14, 2018, Proceedings 16. Springer International Publishing, pp 91–107

Twitchell DP, Adkins M, Nunamaker JF, Burgoon JK (2004) Using speech act theory to model conversations for automated classification and retrieval. In: Proceedings of the international working conference language action perspective communication modelling (LAP 2004). Citeseer, pp 121–130

Winograd T, Flores F (1987) Understanding computers and cognition: a new foundation for design. Addison Wesley. https://www.ebook.de/de/product/3237873/terry_winograd_fernando_flores_understanding_computers_and_cognition_a_new_foundation_for_design.html

So, You Want to Build a Copilot?

Part I: Foundations and Design Principles of a Custom Copilot

Michal Furmakiewicz, Chang Liu, Angus Taylor, and Ilya Venger

Abstract Generative AI has opened numerous possibilities for constructing intelligent systems and assistants. As the patterns become more established, there is a need for a disciplined approach to specify requirements for these applications. This chapter presents the beginnings of a methodical framework for business and design considerations for building an effective AI copilot. Our learnings are based on insights gleaned from 250+ workshops with customers and partners and our in-house experience constructing copilot services and applications. We cover several topics that must be considered: from articulating a clear vision and value proposition, dissecting user personas and their corresponding scenarios, to designing a user experience and interaction model that addresses the needs of the intended audience. We discuss copilot AI UX principles as well as maintenance and continuous improvement.

M. Furmakiewicz
Microsoft, Warsaw, Poland
e-mail: michal.furmankiewicz@microsoft.com

C. Liu
Microsoft, Cambridge, MA, USA
e-mail: changliu2@microsoft.com

A. Taylor
Microsoft, London, UK
e-mail: Angus.Taylor@microsoft.com

I. Venger (✉)
Microsoft, Herzliya, Israel
e-mail: ilyavenger@microsoft.com

C. K. Coursaris et al. (eds.), *The Design of Human-Centered Artificial Intelligence for the Workplace*, Progress in IS, https://doi.org/10.1007/978-3-031-83512-4_8

1 Introduction

1.1 The Rise of Generative AI and AI Copilots

We are living through a pivotal era in the field of artificial intelligence. Generative AI (GenAI)—the capability of AI models to produce new information such as text, images, audio, video, and code based on training on large amounts of data—has emerged as a transformative technology. GenAI models provided us access to technology that is ready to use from day one and is general enough to cover a broad range of use cases. AI systems are starting to perform activities that could previously be performed only by humans and are capable of complex interactions simulating human behavior without the need for additional training. This requires a fundamental change in interaction patterns between people and AI.

The AI copilot, with the name drawn from parallels to aviation copilots, is emerging as a new paradigm for a collaboration between computer applications and people (Sellen and Horvitz 2023). The main features of the copilot include the fact that it is a system built to work together with the user, rather than replacing them. The interaction is often flexible and mediated through natural language leveraging large language models (LLMs). An AI copilot does have some limited autonomy and is able to execute tasks on behalf of the user in the system where it operates, but the human must remain in control, having the ability to review the outputs and take over from the assistant should the need arise. AI copilots offer a set of capabilities to support context-based scenarios, employing their generic capabilities toward particular tasks.

In many industries such as banking, finance, insurance, and manufacturing, copilot-like services are expected to become a new normal and increase the overall value of these industries significantly (McKinsey 2023).

1.2 Unique Challenges and Learnings in This Chapter

Many companies are currently looking to successfully adopt generative AI to create valuable intelligent assistants and copilots, but it is not a simple endeavor (Parnin et al. 2023). It demands a rigorous and multidisciplinary approach spanning strategy, design, data science, engineering, and responsible development practices. This chapter aims to provide an introduction and rationale for AI copilots and a structured framework based on design principles for building effective copilots tailored to real-world needs.

We build on insights gleaned from over 250 workshops held between April 2023 to April 2024 with customers and partners, as well as hands-on experience in building AI-powered services and copilots. The chapter begins by emphasizing the importance of establishing a clear vision and mapping the value proposition. We then explore key considerations around understanding user personas, their scenarios, and goals—critical inputs for designing an intuitive user experience that brings value, rather than distraction. The chapter deals with principles for achieving a well-designed AI user experience and interaction model. By following the guidelines and practices outlined in this chapter, business teams, working together with product managers, UX designers, data scientists, and software engineers, can establish foundations for the development of valuable copilot solutions that meet user needs. As we navigate this generative AI-powered paradigm shift, adherence to structured practices will be critical for mitigating risks and maximizing the potential of the technology.

2 Envisioning the Copilot

When building a copilot, just like with any other product, it is most important to start with "Why" (Sinek 2009). As stakeholders start thinking about why their business or customers need AI capabilities, it will become the most important question leading everything else and will assure that AI is best suited to solve the challenge. One effective method of answering this question is through business envisioning sessions, which combine the discussion of business objectives, product and ecosystem considerations, scenario discovery, and technical feasibility focusing on the set of capabilities that must be in place in order to build a copilot. Once the business and technical capability aspects are in sync, UX interaction patterns need to be defined, and nonfunctional requirements that address scalability, security, responsible AI practices, ROI and business model, and delivery method of the copilot capability to end users need to be addressed.

Generative AI capabilities are vast and while the whole technical world is so focused on capabilities, architectures, and development, it's worth mentioning that new models, possibilities, frameworks, patterns, and scenarios are emerging every day. Anchoring the discussion in explicit human-centered needs and business objectives helps to turn technology into a product and an execution program.

Defining and describing one or many copilot scenarios is easy—the art lies in choosing a scenario that is not only the most business-viable, technically feasible, and desirable from user experience perspective (e.g., PWC 2021) but also well aligned to overarching company strategy.

2.1 Establishing a Clear Vision and Value Proposition

At the time of writing, generative AI technology is at peak hype. Every company is looking to start building solutions on top of it. It goes without saying that there must be a purpose and sound business logic behind the development of any new application, though our experience shows that not all companies looking to develop copilots have been rigorous in their analysis. This initial stage of scoping and outcome definitions is particularly crucial for GenAI applications where technological and reputational risks, as well as costs of development and hosting the solution, are higher than in standard software applications.

We have found that the best way to address the values and outcomes is by formulating critical questions that must be answered. These questions are common and almost mundane, but they serve as a reminder for standard practices in setting commercial and product strategy.

Question 1: What is the overarching goal or vision of your copilot? The answer does not have to be complex, but it does need to be a clearly articulated written statement of what your product aspires to be and the value it will deliver in the long term. It is not unique to GenAI products and, crucially, it should not be driven by the technology.

According to Cagan (2021), a product vision explains the future we are aiming for and how that future will benefit our customers. Building out the vision for the copilot is a prime element, particularly because of the rapid pace of technology.

Example vision statements include "…an AI pair programmer that helps you write code faster and with less work" (GitHub 2021); or "…an AI assistant for Finance professionals streamlining processes and workflows, and surfacing insights for better-informed decision making" (Microsoft 2024b); or "…provide frontline workers with a personal copilot capable of quickly identifying reasons for equipment malfunctions and path to resolution based on company data." Whatever the vision for your copilot is, make it clear to understand and show the value proposition.

Question 2: What value does it provide for your target users? The vision should be based on a deep understanding of the users—whether they are customers or employees and their needs, or both at the same time. Those looking to build copilots should be able to validate the problem: How badly do they currently suffer from it? How unhappy are they with the solutions they have now? Are they ready to accept significantly different solutions? Is there openness to changing processes wholesale?

The value proposition should then be clearly articulated, at a minimum as favorable points of difference with respect to the market (Anderson et al. 2006). This requires both customer and competitive solution research.

Business-to-consumer (B2C) Value Propositions Within the B2C setting, we have seen patterns emerge that provide direct value to consumers through personal assistant models—helping in creative and personal productivity tasks accompanying search engines or standalone propositions such as Gemini,[1] Inflection.ai,[2] OpenAI,[3] and Midjourney.[4]

[1] Google Gemini: https://gemini.google.com/app

[2] Inflection.ai: https://pi.ai/talk

[3] OpenAI: https://chat.openai.com

[4] Midjourney: https://www.midjourney.com/home

Business-to-business (B2B) Value Propositions In B2B settings, beyond employee personas, where use cases emerge to increase employee productivity (e.g., Legal AI (Saunders 2023), financial adviser (Trent 2024), M365 Copilot,[5] and others).

Multi-sided B2B Value Propositions Beyond traditional direct value to customers, we have seen a pattern emerge where larger companies are using the opportunity opened by copilots to establish new ecosystems providing multi-sided value propositions and building platforms (Gawer and Cusumano 2008). Multi-sided propositions are unique in that they allow partners to come and extend a copilot created by the platform operator. The platform operator does not have to be an AI service provider but could leverage their market positioning in a particular industry or domain. One method to allow for a copilot to serve as a platform is to offer the ability for partners (those looking to offer their service on the copilot) to extend the copilots—usually through plugins. This platform engagement requires a rethinking of the standard value proposition. The company creating a platform needs to ensure that sufficient incentives are available for partners to extend and for customers to use the copilot services.

This is not an easy proposition, but if successful, it can create extraordinary returns for those that establish new networks in the mid- and long term. A widely held belief in technology circles is that every person will use many copilots, each performing their own interactions across various scenarios (and potentially presented in a unified UI surface alongside existing applications) in professional (and private) settings (Nadella 2023).

Regulatory Considerations in Scenario and Value Definition As an important note, when choosing a use case to follow, the latest regulatory boundaries and guidance need to be considered in every market to which we plan to release the solution. Regulation of AI services is moving in lockstep with the advancement of capabilities. For example, according to the EU AI Act (European Parliament 2024), application of emotional recognition is banned in workplace and educational institutions within the EU. When considering a copilot for these settings, it is important to critically evaluate whether the regulatory constraints apply to the use case as a whole or to a particular segment of users or customers.

Strategy Requires a Clear Choice The choice of a scenario and the value it provides need to be clear-cut. Determining the audience and the "play" is important to focus the efforts. For example, if there is a scenario that fits both settings (B2C and B2B) at the same time, it is worthwhile to define two different ones, independent from each other. Failure to decide or define the value results in execution delays and difficulty to mobilize necessary resources and sponsorship.

Question 3: What is the intrinsic business rationale? The value proposition must be complemented by a solid business rationale contributing to the company's bottom

[5] Microsoft 365 Copilot: https://www.microsoft.com/en-us/microsoft-365/enterprise/copilot-for-microsoft-365

Table 1 Business value rationale for copilots

Business value	Source of value (not exhaustive)
Increasing revenues	New revenue streams or enhancing existing ones by enabling new product/service offerings, expanding into new markets, or enhancing existing offerings to drive higher adoption and sales
Adjusting operations	Cost decrease and effectiveness increase are the most common expectations and effects of copilot implementations. Reduced operational costs and improving business efficiency can be achieved through:
	(a) Faster onboarding, transfer of knowledge, and enhanced productivity of new employees
	(b) Offloading to customers (supplemented by AI) tasks that are currently performed by staff
	(c) Improving workforce productivity by reducing errors or rework through AI-based cross-validation or speedup
	(d) Automating or streamlining internal processes and tasks—reducing the time it takes for employees to achieve a task or fully eliminating some steps
	(e) Improving employee satisfaction, retention, and focus on truly value-additive tasks (outsourcing mundane tasks to a copilot) (GitHub 2022)
Improving customer satisfaction and loyalty	Improved customer experience, stronger relationships, and increased customer retention through personalized assistance, better response times, self-service capabilities, and more tailored and valuable solutions to customers—using information that is brought together (and actioned by) through the copilot

line, either by increasing revenues, improving operations (through productivity gains or customers' self-service), or driving customer satisfaction and loyalty (see Table 1 for a foundational breakdown of rationale). The desired business outcomes should be clearly defined and measurable. Deciding on these outcomes merges the strategic priorities and target market and influences the potential impact of the copilot. This specificity helps guide the development process and provides a benchmark for evaluating the copilot's success.

Our experience has shown that the higher the value of the use case, the riskier it is and technological aspects might not fully support the case; on the other hand, often it is not easy to identify the underlying value for the end user and to eventually derive value from it.

Question 4: What is the path to profitability? At the time of writing this chapter, generative AI is an expensive technology. AI providers are charging relatively high costs for API-based access, and costs of self-hosting models on GPUs are also high due to limited supply, the large size of the GenAI models, and the need for relatively skilled talent to maintain and update models. Although costs have been dropping rapidly, copilot cost visibility and predictability and offset (through external monetization or internal cross-charging) are crucial elements.

Table 2 Customer pricing considerations

Factor	Details
Transparency	Clarity on upfront costs, ongoing maintenance, and support costs. Understanding of core offering versus optional add-ons. Transparency in pricing, revenue sharing (if any), and control mechanisms
Predictability	Preference for predictable monthly/annual costs. Desire for a more transparent and predictable pricing structure for usage-based models
Flexibility	Ability to adjust subscription levels based on needs and specific personas. Option to scale usage and associated costs up or down as required
Scalability	Ability to accommodate growth and increased usage without unexpected cost increases, in a predictable manner. Capacity to handle many users or transactions simultaneously
Data privacy and security	Concern about the handling of personal or business data in free or low-cost services

Customer preferences do not change with new technology or products. The foundations of their expectations and needs must be taken into account. A brief summary of dimensions that matter to customers is captured in Table 2.

We observed through work with Microsoft partners and customers that pricing strategy for a copilot product is a major challenge, particularly since this represents a new, largely uncharted, territory. There are not many established practices in monetizing services when a customer looks to build a copilot.

Against this backdrop of customer preferences, traditional value extraction routes and pricing are still relevant. Table 3 captures the typical pricing models that are common in the space of generative AI and copilots.

Throughout 2023–2024, we saw all these business models emerging. Two considerations and trends need to be kept in mind with respect to business models and associated pricing strategies. On the one hand, as businesses and consumers get more comfortable with copilot services and more capabilities and patterns emerge, hybrid and tiered models are likely to evolve with a variety of offers considered as part of the monetization design. On the other hand, the underlying LLMs' pricing has been steadily decreasing; therefore, pricing and customers' perceived value (quantity of interaction, differentiated service and price levels) need to be constantly balanced. Moreover, cost control, through selection of lower-priced models for low-value tasks, is also a possibility.

Cost recovery applies not only to externally productized copilots but also to cross-charging of internal copilots. IT costs can offloaded to lines of business based on usage, with the small difference that internal copilots often have limits in terms of maximal scale (e.g., full employee-base penetration), making both architecture and costing easier to plan and execute.

Table 3 Pricing/business models, implications, and examples

Pricing/business model	Description	Business objective (of copilot owner)	Customer considerations
Subscription model	A monthly or annual fee for access to the AI copilot service	Recurring and predictable revenue. Careful assessment of the *unit-amount* of revenues may be disconnected from costs	Attractive through transparent and predictable pricing. Service quality (or quantity) may be perceived as insufficient (e.g., if there are hard limits on the number of interactions)
Pay as you go	Transaction fee for AI-generated actions	A scalable pricing structure that links consumption of expensive LLM resources and revenues	May not be attractive to customers who are looking for more predictable upfront pricing. May decrease customer stickiness
Cross-subsidized	Adding additional value to higher priced product	With sufficiently high margins on existing products, copilot costs can be absorbed and cross-charged. Can be used as a competitive differentiation (or parity) feature to increase value to existing products	Customers are receiving the copilot as an additional component of an existing system. Can be perceived as "bloatware"
Data value extraction	Receiving value from data provided by the customers	Access to customers' data for training of AI (used later in paid services) and potential for advertising monetization (through better personalization and segmentation)	Privacy concerns while receiving a free or low-cost product

2.2 *Mapping User Personas and Scenarios*

Once the objectives, overarching business rationale and value have been established, there is a need to define the specifics of the user persona and the scenarios that will be supplemented by the copilot within the users' workflow and ensure that the user can effectively interact with and supervise the copilot.

Importance of Human in the Loop There are multiple challenges with the first generation of LLMs and generally with AI systems, resulting from training data biases and distribution, and technology/algorithmic limitations. The copilot, by its very definition, is supplementing the activity of a human operator, taking on some cognitive activities, while ensuring that the human remains informed and accountable and improves currently imperfect outcomes (Trent 2024; Wang 2019; Amershi et al. 2014; Gabriel et al. 2024). Retaining human in the loop is crucial to ensure mitigation across several dimensions:

Quality Critical evaluation of copilot outputs is needed to prevent hallucinations and ensure that the information or actions provided by the copilot are correct and complete. Moreover, human override can be used to continuously improve the system and ensure that correct results are being served to all users of the copilot.

Control and Direction Improper goal specification for a copilot could lead to undesired outcomes, requiring a review of the responses to ensure they fit the intent of the user.

Bias and Fairness Potential bias in the data and algorithmic processing may result in undesired or non-responsible responses from a copilot. Human-in-the-loop monitoring presents an opportunity to mitigate and ensure fairness of outcomes with equitable decisions and representation of various groups and individuals.

Ethical and Legal Compliance Ethical guidelines and legal boundaries are continuously changing as the technology is evolving quickly. Human supervision is needed to ensure that the actions of the copilot are adhering to both ethical standards and legal requirements.

Innovation and Diversity The statistical nature of data processing results in a risk that the results are steered toward the "middle of the distribution" of potential outcomes and results dictated by the data, losing innovative capabilities. Steering the copilot assistant and ensuring that nonobvious outcomes are part of the prompt stream can help achieve innovative and nontrivial outcomes, as well as ensure that diverse points of view are incorporated.

Human-Centric Values Human agency is a fragile concept, with AI being a strong force that could potentially undermine human autonomy and decision-making if not designed carefully. The copilot architecture is there to preserve the maintenance of human-centric values—particularly agency and accountability. Retaining the human in the loop helps uphold these values by ensuring the human maintains meaningful control and oversight over the AI assistant's outputs and actions. While being a philosophical point, AI copilots should be designed to empower and enable humans, not to marginalize or automate.

Fitting into User Workflows As part of scenario development, it's crucial to deeply understand existing user workflows and how a copilot system can integrate seamlessly. Forcing users to significantly alter their processes or adapt to an inflexible AI system will lead to poor adoption. The goal should be for the copilot to augment and enhance the user's current modes of working, not disrupt them. This means mapping out common tasks, pain points, and areas where AI assistance could streamline efforts. But it also requires designing interaction models that align with users' mental models and being able to easily transfer between AI-augmented and unassisted modes of operation. Standard practices of research into user interactions—field research, ethnographic study, and user engagement—can help establish workflow nuances. Detailed jobs-to-be-done and breakdown to tasks can help in formalizing those nuances.

As part of the questions to be explored within the user-flows design, several dimensions should be evaluated and particularly addressed.

Context Awareness Context awareness is a critical capability for copilot systems to effectively integrate into user workflows. It ensures the copilot understands the user's situation and tailors its assistance accordingly. This can include factors like understanding basic context—date and time, the previous actions of the user, current user situation, user profile and preferences, available data, and allowed actions, tools, and plugins. Taken to the extreme, context can be further augmented with information about other copilots with which the user and even their collaborators interact.

Actionability Actionability in copilot design goes beyond providing content suggestions, to performing actions on behalf of the user. This capability allows the copilot to move from a passive advisor to an active collaborator. Copilot developers and designers should ensure that the level of actionability is appropriate for the user's need and is controlled by the users. Actionability could be within the scope of a particular application, allowing the copilot to manipulate the UI (e.g., copilot for Microsoft 365 within Microsoft Word can reformat unstructured text into a table). Alternatively, the copilot can integrate with external systems via APIs exposed as plugins (reacting to natural language). This allows the copilot to perform actions in other applications, automate data transfer, and trigger workflows.

While the copilot can perform actions, it's crucial to maintain user control. The system should clearly communicate its intended actions and obtain user confirmation before proceeding and/or perform actions in a nondestructive manner. This ensures transparency and avoids unintended consequences. Proposed actions and those approved by the human need to be logged (traceability). Based on that and additional feedback from the user, system creators would be in position to adjust the behavior to personal preferences over time.

Actionability allows shifting the copilot from being an information-only provider to becoming an assistant for the user to achieve their goals, perform tasks, and automate mundane work.

Proactivity Proactivity refers to the copilot's ability to anticipate user needs and take initiative to suggest actions or queries, complete tasks, or provide relevant information even before the user explicitly requests it. Context awareness is needed, with proactive copilots establishing context by monitoring user activity and potentially running processes in the background generating suggestions and implicitly evaluating their suitability to the user intents as gleaned from the context. This is a significantly higher risk situation with potentially higher costs (due to background activity of the system).

Copilot information suggestions or collaborative actions should not only fit into the user's action flow without disrupting it, but particular care should be taken to ensure that the user is aware of the proactive suggestions or activity and retains supervisory capabilities. To make the user aware of proactive actions, a variety of clues might need to be added beyond a static visual UI—including animation and auditory or haptic signals as well as notifications that save the trace and link to automated activity. Transparency and explainability should be addressed as well, with proactive interaction patterns added to the audit information, capturing implicit and explicit activity of the copilot.

Persistence Persistence in copilot scenarios goes beyond one-off interactions. A persistent copilot should possess, and act based on, a memory of the user, past interactions, and user preferences. This allows the copilot to continuously build an understanding of the user and become more helpful over time.

As part of the flow, a copilot that is familiar with the user will collect, store, and address relevant information about the user such as the user's interest, preferred interaction patterns, and more. The persistent copilot should continuously learn from the user's interactions and feedback.

Two crucial aspects that need to be taken when addressing persistence are user privacy and compliance with appropriate privacy-preserving regulations such as GDPR. The copilot should store and utilize user data in a transparent and responsible manner. Users should have clear control over the data collected and the ability to manage their preferences or opt-out of persistence entirely. Moreover, the copilot might infer implicitly or explicitly information about the user, whether from the user's language or topics. This is a powerful method for long-term personalization and trust, but it potentially opens the door to the introduction or surfacing of unexpected biases within underlying LLM models. Therefore, persistence is a higher risk activity.

Authority and Control Data access, persistence, and actionability for a copilot must be designed in the context of both the individual authorizations of the user, as well as the allowed data processing and retention within the allowed regulatory boundary. Data read and write (action) access of the copilot is derived from the authority granted to the main user. Care should be taken to not assume that a copilot has higher privileges than the user in the design process, as well as correctly extending user authentication to downstream systems. Moreover, given that LLMs often reside in the cloud and might be provided by an external supplier, care should be taken with respect to tenancy requirements ensuring that the LLM provider is allowed to view the information (including any third-party information that has been passed to the user).

Any personal or user information that is collected also needs to be transparent, and the user should be aware and able to control what information is used by the copilot.

Supervisory Capabilities and High-Risk Situations While copilots can enhance productivity, there will always be high-stakes situations where elevated human oversight is required. Examples include machinery or plant controls (Venger and

Dozortsev 2023), financial transactions, and legal contracts, where autonomous AI operation could have catastrophic consequences if not properly supervised.

In these scenarios, copilot systems must have robust capabilities for human monitoring, intervention, and overriding of outputs when needed. This could include adjustable confidence thresholds and approval workflows.

A critical element to be considered when designing supervision is evaluating the ability of a human to supervise, ensuring the user has sufficient capabilities and attention. For the human to remain firmly "in the loop" and particularly for high-risk activities, the system should be able not only to detect risk boundaries and hand over control to the human but also establish the operators' level of general and situation-specific proficiency. Getting this balance right is critical for ensuring responsible and trustworthy copilots, which can align with industry standards.

Establishing the Level of General Proficiency the user must have sufficient knowledge and ability to understand and evaluate the outputs of the copilot to be an effective supervisor. For example, in a copilot that generates queries against a database (e.g., through natural language to SQL), it is important to understand to what extent the user understands both the query language and the structure of the database. This can be done through user research, as well as situational evaluation or detailed explanation to the user of the querying process and results.

Establishing Situational Proficiency The user must not only have general capabilities but also have sufficient attention in the moment to supervise. There is a risk for the user to over-rely on a copilot and lose vigilance over time. This is being mitigated in aviation autopilot or assistive driving systems through proactive system validation of the user's attention. Assistive copilots should have similar guardrails in place to ensure that the user is continuously aware of the AI-generated nature of the results. Some of those challenges can be partially addressed by UI/UX practices, which will be covered later in the document.

3 Designing the Copilot Experience

Generative AI, which forms the foundation of the copilot experience, is nondeterministic in nature, unlike common software patterns that are defined and can be mapped directly to user journeys. The inherent variability of generative AI outputs poses unique challenges and considerations for the design of effective user experiences with these systems above and beyond general applications of AI. The challenges we described above require significant investment into correct design of a copilot ensuring users are effective and responsible AI risks are mitigated (Weisz et al. 2023). Design must communicate effectively to the user potential variability and mitigate against harms. Key design principles that emerge in generative applications and copilots include ensuring appropriate controls and transparency, proactive shaping of accurate mental models, and designing for imperfection. There are grassroots community-led frameworks emerging in the field of generative AI interaction design that are taking existing common design principles and applying them to generative applications and copilots. For examples, see Microsoft (2024a) and Mehrotra et al. (2023) as well as corporate research and guidance born out of responsible AI guidelines from firms such as IBM (Koc 2024), Microsoft (with foundations starting as early 1999) (Whitespectre.com 2023; Weisz et al. 2023; Horvitz 1999), and Google (Amershi et al. 2019; Pai 2024).

3.1 UX Principles for Generative AI Applications

We will not dive into all the different designs and principles here, but will cover some basics of human-AI interactions that we utilize daily in our practices at Microsoft, particularly addressing elements that are crucial for responsible and effective deployment of generative AI in copilots (Microsoft 2024a). The core framework covers the different application stages, starting from forming correct initial expectations with the users, providing guidance during the interaction along the "happy path," as well as surfacing appropriate information covering cases when wrong behavior is exhibited by the system (by deviating from the desired response), finishing with principles that need to be applied over time as the system is maintained and continuously improved (Fig. 1).

Initially The initial stage of interaction with a copilot involves setting the right expectations for users. This is crucial as it shapes and creates an appropriate trust in the system. Appropriate trust is an elaborate topic (Mehrotra et al. (2023) provide an in-depth discussion). Briefly, in our context, it is a delicate balance where users need to find the system useful and trustful while acknowledging that it may occasionally be wrong. Trust needs to be high enough to rely on AI, but also users need to remain critically engaged and vigilant to avoid overreliance. Therefore, it is essential to make the capabilities and limitations of the copilot transparent. Users should be informed about what the AI can do and, just as importantly, what it might not do well. This helps in preventing frustration and misuse of the system. For instance, if a generative AI copilot is designed to assist with coding, users should be made aware of the types of coding tasks it can handle and any limitations it might have, such as understanding complex, project-specific customizations.

During Interaction During the interaction with a copilot, users should not lose the sight of the fact that they are interacting with an AI system and, to the extent possible, should be made aware of the inner workings of the copilot. To successfully execute on this stage, copilot developers need to ensure that biases are mitigated, and quality is upheld to the extent possible and that the copilot is evaluated in development and on an ongoing basis. The system should not only be designed to support the most common scenarios, but it should also be able to handle a wide range of inputs. If a copilot is not able to handle a specific task, it should state it right away and propose an alternative instead of trying to accomplish the task.

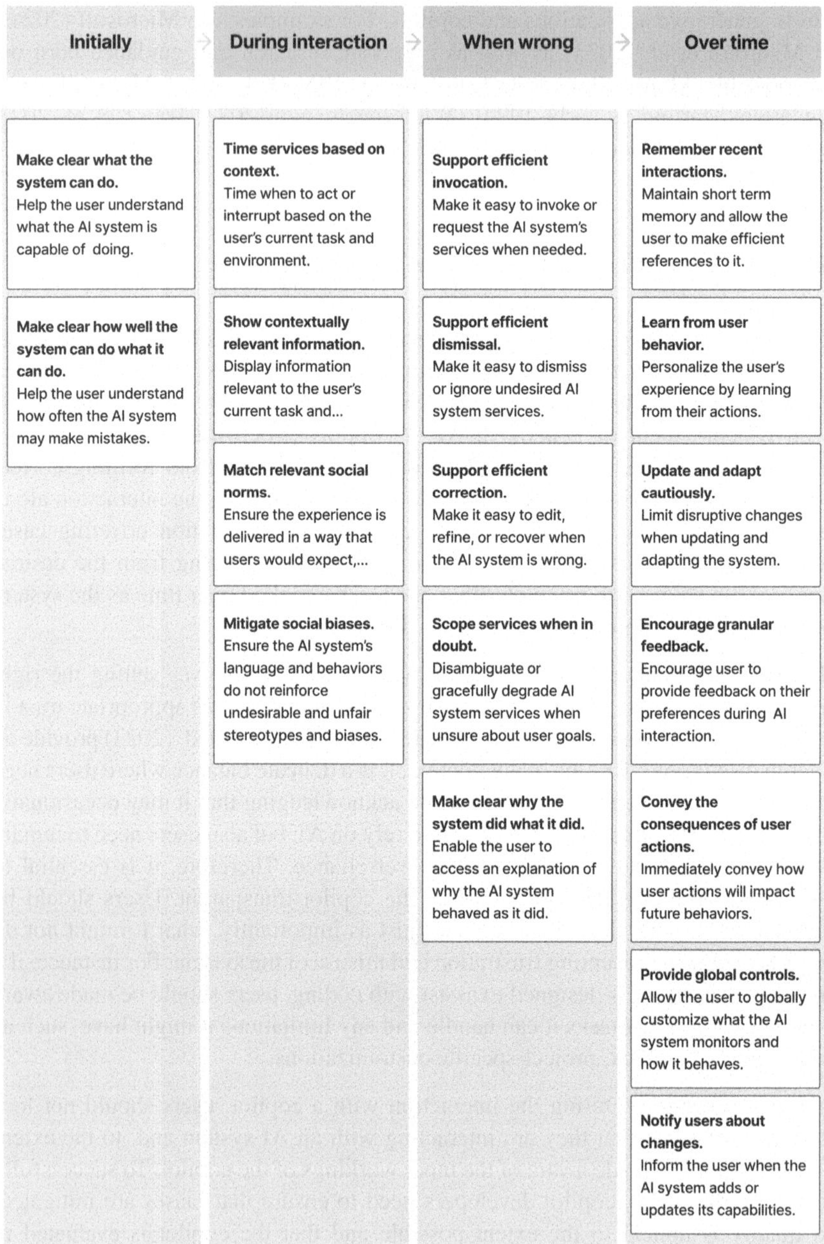

Fig. 1 Guidelines for human-AI interaction Amershi et al. (2019)

When Wrong Handling errors or unexpected outputs is a critical aspect. The copilot should be equipped to recognize its failures, through a rule-based system or an internal LLM-based validation loop, and, ideally, provide explanations or alternatives to the user. This transparency in error handling is crucial for maintaining user trust and for the practical utility of the AI. For instance, if a copilot misinterprets a user prompt or intent, it should correct itself, ask for guidance, or flag that it has low confidence in the result, but also explain why the error occurred and how it will adjust its behavior in the future or in that specific interaction at a minimum. Additionally, providing users with the tools to easily report and correct errors can empower them and enhance the system's reliability over time.

Over Time The relationship between a user and a specific copilot evolves (and is further influenced by the developments in the ecosystem and shifting user expectations). As such, the design must accommodate and support this evolution. Over time, the AI system underlying the copilot should provide the ability to improve interaction accuracy and usefulness. To do so, user feedback should be collected through explicit mechanisms (such as the "thumbs-up/thumbs-down" preference marking pattern that has become the standard for the industry) and implicit methods such as interaction telemetry analysis. This will help to continually refine and optimize the user experience.

Moreover, the communication should be multifaceted, and it is important to reestablish and adjust user expectations as the system and the ecosystem evolve. Continuous user education, updates about new capabilities, or adjustments in the AI's functioning are vital and form part of the customer experience (CX) over time. This ongoing cycle of feedback and improvement helps in sustaining a productive and satisfying user-AI relationship.

4 Conclusion

The emergence of GenAI and AI copilots presents a transformative opportunity for businesses to revolutionize operations and customer experiences. However, successfully building effective AI copilots demands a rigorous, multidisciplinary approach rooted in human needs and responsible development practices, starting from valuable business practices to design and execution.

AI copilots must be designed as collaborative assistants that elevate and empower human capabilities, not replace them entirely. Retaining meaningful "human-in-the-loop" control mitigates risks around quality, bias, ethics, and legal compliance. Robust human supervision capabilities, transparency into AI reasoning, and adjustable automation are paramount, especially for high-stakes scenarios.

User experience design is critical due to generative AI's nondeterministic nature. Upfront transparency around AI abilities and limitations helps shape accurate mental models and appropriate trust levels. During interactions, systems must uphold quality, mitigate biases, and provide clear error handling. Over time, a feedback loop of explicit user inputs and model refinements can enhance accuracy while responsible AI practices continuously calibrate evolving user expectations.

As this generative AI paradigm unfolds, adherence to the structured foundations and human-centric design principles outlined here will maximize the potential while mitigating risks. When developed thoughtfully, with human needs at the center, AI copilots can unlock tangible value—empowering people, augmenting human autonomy, and driving innovation across industries. This balanced approach paves the way for beneficial AI assistants that are powerful catalysts for progress.

5 AI Disclosure Note

In the process of preparing this chapter, the authors used the following AI models and tools for literature research, structuring of the content, and editing: copilot for Microsoft 365 (https://copilot.microsoft.com/), ChatGPT 3.5 and ChatGPT 4 (via https://chat.openai.com/), Claude.ai (via https://claude.ai/chats), Claude 3 models (https://console.anthropic.com/workbench/ API – with the following models claude-3-haiku-20240307, claude-3-sonnet-20240229, claude-3-opus-20240229), Gemini (https://gemini.google.com/app), and Perplexity.ai (https://www.perplexity.ai/). The authors attest that they hold full responsibility for the text and factual correctness in the chapter above and have fully reviewed references and edited text outputs from AI systems.

Note: This work reflects AI developments up to June 2024; subsequent advances are not reflected.

References

Amershi S, Maya C, Knox WB, Kulesza T (2014) Power to the people: the role of humans in interactive machine learning. AI Mag 35(4):105–120

Amershi S, Weld D, Vorvoreanu M, Fourney A, Nushi B, Collisson P, Suh J, Iqbal S, Bennett PN, Inkpen K, Teevan J, Kikin-Gil R, Horvitz E (2019) Guidelines for human-ai interaction. In: Proceedings of the 2019 CHI conference on human factors in computing systems, CHI 2019. Association for Computing Machinery, New York, pp 1–13. https://doi.org/10.1145/3290605.3300233

Anderson JC, Narus JA, van Rossum W (2006) Customer value propositions in business markets. Harvard Bus Rev 84(3):90–99, 149

Cagan M (2021) Empowered—ordinary people, extraordinary products. John Wiley & Sons, Hoboken

European Parliament (2024) Artificial intelligence act, text adopted. https://www.europarl.europa.eu/doceo/document/TA-9-2024-0138_EN.html. Accessed 24 Apr 2024

Gabriel I, Manzini A, Keeling G, Hendricks LA, Rieser V, Iqbal H, Tomašev N, Ktena I, Kenton Z, Rodriguez M, El-Sayed S, Brown S, Akbulut C, Trask A, Hughes EA (2024) The ethics of advanced ai assistants. https://storage.googleapis.com/deepmind-media/DeepMind.com/Blog/ethics-of-advanced-ai-assistants/the-ethics-of-advanced-ai-assistants-2024-i.pdf. Accessed 21 Apr 2024

Gawer A, Cusumano MA (2008) How companies become platform leaders. MIT Sloan Manag Rev 49(2)
GitHub (2021) Introducing github copilot: your ai pair programmer. https://github.blog/2021-06-29-introducing-github-copilot-ai-pair-programmer/. Accessed 7 Apr 2024
GitHub (2022) Research: quantifying github copilot's impact on developer productivity and happiness. https://github.blog/2022-09-07-research-quantifying-github-copilots-impact-on-developer-productivity-and-happiness/. Accessed 3 May 2024
Horvitz EJ (1999) Principles of mixed-initiative user interfaces. In: CHI 1999: proceedings of the SIGCHI conference on human factors in computing systems
Koc V (2024) The GenAI compass: a UX framework to design generative AI experiences. https://uxdesign.cc/the-genai-compass-a-ux-framework-to-design-generative-ai-experiences-49a7d797c114. Accessed 21 Apr 2024
McKinsey (2023) The economic potential of generative ai: the next productivity frontier. https://www.mckinsey.com/capabilities/mckinsey-digital/our-insights/the-economic-potential-of-generative-ai-the-next-productivity-frontier. Accessed 3 May 2024
Mehrotra S, Degachi C, Vereschak O, Jonker CM, Tielman ML (2023) A systematic review on fostering appropriate trust in human-ai interaction. arXiv preprint arXiv:231106305
Microsoft (2024a) Guidelines for human-ai interaction (HAX toolkit); best practices for designing ai user experiences. https://www.microsoft.com/en-us/haxtoolkit/ai-guidelines/. Accessed 21 Apr 2024
Microsoft (2024b) Introducing microsoft copilot for finance. https://blogs.microsoft.com/blog/2024/02/29/introducing-microsoft-copilot-for-finance-the-newest-copilot-offering-in-microsoft-365-designed-to-transform-modern-finance/. Accessed 7 Apr 2024
Nadella S (2023) The age of copilot, ignite 2023, opening keynote. https://news.microsoft.com/wp-content/uploads/prod/2023/11/Microsoft-Ignite-Opening.pdf. Accessed 3 May 2024
Pai S (2024) How to build a gen ai application. https://cloud.google.com/blog/products/ai-machine-learning/how-to-build-a-genai-application. Accessed 21 Apr 2024
Parnin C, Soares G, Pandita R, Gulwani S, Rich J, Henley AZ (2023) Building your own product copilot: challenges, opportunities, and needs
PWC (2021) The experience center. https://www.pwc.com/us/en/services/consulting/business-transformation/customer-transformation/experience-center.html. Accessed 24 Apr 2024
Saunders T (2023) Legal tech teams turn to ai to advance business goals. https://www.ft.com/content/9a117ac7-29ae-43fe-b840-a04005b98799. Accessed 1 May 2024
Sellen A, Horvitz E (2023) The rise of the ai co-pilot: lessons for design from aviation and beyond
Sinek S (2009) Start with why: how great leaders inspire everyone to take action. Penguin
Trent R (2024) Why human-in-the-loop is essential for generative ai. https://rodtrent.substack.com/p/why-human-in-the-loop-is-essential. Accessed 21 Apr 2024
Venger AL, Dozortsev VM (2023) Trust in artificial intelligence: modeling the decision making of human operators in highly dangerous situations. Mathematics 11(24):4956
Wang G (2019) Humans in the loop: the design of interactive ai systems. https://hai.stanford.edu/news/humans-loop-design-interactive-ai-systems. Accessed 21 Apr 2024
Weisz JD, Muller M, He J, Houde S (2023) Toward general design principles for generative ai applications. In: HAIGEN '23 Workshop at IUI '23. Sydney
Whitespectrecom (2023) Emerging UI/UX patterns in generative ai: a visual guide. https://medium.com/whitespectre/emerging-ui-ux-patterns-in-generative-ai-a-visual-guide-74000c7198a4. Accessed 21 Apr 2024

Intervenability as a Design Requirement for Autonomy and Oversight within Human-Centered AI

Thomas Herrmann

Abstract Based on the literature and several practical examples of possible AI applications, we outline the concept of intervenability. This new phenomenon is not covered by emergency shutdowns, workarounds, or the reconfiguration of automated systems. Intervenability instantiates the principles of controllability, autonomy, oversight, and keeping humans in the loop in the context of AI. We provide a taxonomy that encompasses a range of possibilities for intervening activities and differentiates them regarding the mental effort of the users. This taxonomy extends the scope of interventions from real-time control of automated processes to AI-based discrete case-related decision-making. This is in accordance with human-centered AI, which seeks to combine human strengths with the usage of AI. We demonstrate how intervenability can potentially contribute to the ongoing development of human capabilities on the one hand and to further technical improvement by reconfiguration of AI on the other hand. Exploring and collaboratively reflecting on the effects of interventions as an integral part of organizational practices is key to enabling this continuous improvement on both sides. Intervenability also provides further momentum for the design of an AI that can help realize interventions on its own and advance a smooth transition from intervention to reconfiguration of the AI.

1 Introduction

A wide range of risks have been associated with the use of artificial intelligence. The superannuation of jobs, the impairment of human autonomy and freedom of choice, unintended damage from bad-quality AI, and bias in AI decisions that disadvantage certain social groups are prominent examples. The risks are particularly high when AI is directly coupled with the physical environment, such as in mobility, manufacturing, or weapons applications, or whenever decisions made

T. Herrmann (✉)
Information and Technology Management, IAW, Ruhr-Universität Bochum, Bochum, Germany
e-mail: thomas.herrmann@rub.de

C. K. Coursaris et al. (eds.), *The Design of Human-Centered Artificial Intelligence for the Workplace*, Progress in IS, https://doi.org/10.1007/978-3-031-83512-4_9

by AI are implemented automatically without checks. One contribution to mitigating these risks is to provide opportunities for people to intervene when dealing with AI. DFKI[1] expert Paul Lukowicz said in an interview on the German newscast Tagesschau on June 14, 2023: "It is always problematic when AI does things not subject to human intervention or review."

In our opinion, the powers of review and intervention are inseparable, and reviewing is a precondition for continuous human control. One has to be able to react if one sees that something is going wrong. However, designing these possibilities for intervening is not trivial. We propose intervention interfaces (Schmidt and Herrmann 2017) between humans on the one side and automated processes or automated decision-making on the other side. Implementing intervention possibilities is quite complex, as we will explain with respect to intervention interfaces. It requires measures at the level of the AI itself and the technical infrastructure surrounding it, and at the level of organizational practice.

The implementation of intervenability is thus a socio-technical challenge, and we will answer the questions of what kind of possible activities should be covered by intervenability and how intervention can be realized to be successful. Intervenability can be considered as a variant of controllability (Prümper 1993) and corresponds with approaches that argue for keeping humans in the loop when running automated systems or making decisions (Crootof et al. 2023; Zanzotto 2019). Within the HCAI discourse, controllability is mostly related to human agency and oversight (European Commission, Directorate-General for Communications Networks, Content and Technology and High-Level Expert Group on Artificial Intelligence 2019) and includes the human-in-the-loop approach that maintains humans' capability to intervene in every decision cycle of the system. Georgieva et al. (2022, p. 706) provide an overview of 13 categories of oversight; it includes, for example, a stop button that can be used to cancel a process. However, the available descriptions of controllability do not sufficiently guide the design of human-AI interaction. The relevance of such an additional variant of controllability is related to typical characteristics of AI: it is designed with the goal of minimizing the interactive contributions of those who benefit from employing AI for certain tasks. The final consequence is—at least in certain phases—interaction-free usage of autonomous systems or automated processes. Thus, the EU guidelines (European Commission, Directorate-General for Communications Networks, Content and Technology and High-Level Expert Group on Artificial Intelligence 2019) suggest that interventions in every decision cycle may be neither possible nor desirable. If controllability is meant as the ability "to maintain direction over the whole course of the interaction" (Prümper 1993, p. 256), we need a concept that accounts for the diminishing need for interaction-driven usage of systems. Furthermore, the goal must be that users do not have to monitor AI in detail and do not have to routinely intervene over and over again. If that were necessary, it would be more appropriate to replace or reconfigure

[1] DFKI: Deutsches Forschungszentrum für Künstliche Intelligenz, German Research Center for Artificial Intelligence.

the AI solution. Rather, monitoring should only be required on specific occasions or at specific times, and intervention should be an exception that does not completely terminate a process—like an emergency stop button—but preserves the possibility of AI resuming its activity.

This means that it is not desirable for users to be made permanently suspicious of AI. This kind of trust deficit ("under-trust") would result in an unnecessary control effort and extra human workload—and also a deterioration of the performance of the overall socio-technical system (De Visser et al. 2020; Okamura and Yamada 2020). At the same time, humans must not place too much trust in AI because such "over-trust," when misplaced, entails serious and costly risks to efficiency and safety, endangering both equipment and lives (De Visser et al. 2020). The problems of under-trust and over-trust are extensively analyzed by Okamura and Yamada (2020), who focus on trust calibration as a process where users appropriately adjust their level of trust to the actual reliability of an AI system. "Over-trust is poorly calibrated trust that exceeds the reliability of an AI system ... Under-trust is poorly calibrated trust that falls short of the AI's reliability ..." (Okamura and Yamada 2020, p. 220335). Calibration can also be supported by intervention, which not only corrects AI results or processes but also allows AI to be explored and experimented with, triggering critical reflection (Herrmann 2022).

In what follows, we describe the need for and the description of intervenability based on the literature and several examples of AI usage. This description will result in a taxonomy of types of intervention. Based on this taxonomy, we can outline how intervention differs from other concepts (Sect. 3). Based on the elaborated understanding of the intervention, we can describe its interplay with the continuous improvement of AI and the ongoing development of human competencies. The implementation of intervenability has to fulfill certain requirements for interaction design (Sect. 5) and its embedding into organizational practices (Sect. 6).

2 Background

This section provides an overview of how an understanding of intervention in the context of using AI can be developed. By contrast to this context, intervention originally refers to measures that influence human behavior, not that of artifacts: "To intervene is to enter into an ongoing system of relationship, to come between or among persons, groups, or objects for the purpose of helping them" (Argyris 1970, p. 15). In the context of using technical systems, intervention is more about altering the plan of how usage runs (Herrmann 1992). This plan might be projected on the processes of use by the designer, who has certain models of usage in mind. These models can be implicit or explicit, such as GOMS[2] models (Card et al. 1983). When applying AI, use models are focused mostly on reducing the need to interact with it.

[2] GOMS: Goals, Objects, Methods, Selection Rules. https://en.wikipedia.org/wiki/GOMS (Retrieved February 20, 2024).

As we will show, intervention is not intended to create sustaining effects on the characteristics of the AI system itself but is focused on the properties of a situation in which task handling with AI takes place, for example, when a car is steered or when a job applicant is selected. In the following three subsections, we prepare a taxonomy of interventions summarized in Fig. 1 (Sect. 2.4). The examples given below refer to this taxonomy in parentheses.

2.1 Intervention and Intervention Interfaces

Schmidt and Herrmann (2017) define intervening interaction as an activity of users that temporarily changes the behavior of an automated process. To illustrate, Schmidt and Herrmann draw on the process of parking a car. In a conventional car, users park the car by themselves and exert continuous and fine-grained control. Every 100–500 milliseconds, one evaluates the situation, controls or corrects the steering, and accelerates or brakes. In a car with automatic parking, one controls the process only to the extent that one selects the parking space and starts the parking process. The fine-grained control of steering and moving back and forth is automated—one does not have to be sitting in the car to do it. In an autonomous, potentially driverless car, one moves away from the car, which then independently finds a parking space and parks.

Intervention in a car with automatic parking assistance may mean, for example, that the driver sees a group of preschoolers approaching and stops the automatic parking until the group has passed (Fig. 1, A, level 1). That would be the simplest kind of intervention—stop and resume. It is different if a driver realizes, for example, that the car will roll onto the unprotected irrigation area of a tree as it moves forward, and she wants to avoid that. Then, she can take control completely and park by herself, so she takes fine-grained control for a while during this intervention (Fig. 1, A, Level 2). However, she could also intervene by only influencing the sensory system by bravely positioning herself as an obstacle between the tree and the car so that changing the direction would be initiated sooner (it would be advantageous if the automatic system recognizes this as human intervention and remembers the obstacle so that one does not have to stay in front of the car all the time). Alternatively, she only influences the decision-making of the automatic system by specifying for driving forward for this particular situation that the change of direction is already made at a greater distance from the obstacle—in this case, the tree (Fig. 1, A, Level 3). Or, she only takes over the action of changing direction by pressing a button each time, for example.

Generally speaking, many AI-supported processes usually run in a mode of implicit interaction (Schmidt 2000) without an active human contribution. The process takes place according to a plan and depends on the events registered in the AI system's environment. Intervening interaction is an ad hoc change based on extraordinary, unplanned human control, which is effective only within a certain time slot or for a limited area of automated processes (such as the interpretation of sensor data). A systematic intervention user interface comprises several aspects:

- It *enables* a selective perception of automated processes.
- It clearly presents or even suggests possible steps for an intervention to the user.
- It offers control options with which an intervention can be easily, quickly, and robustly started, completed, terminated, and occasionally revised.

The example of parking already shows that there are various possibilities for implementing intervenability. We define intervention interfaces as interfaces that systematically support all kinds of reasonable intervention activities in an automated system, including preparing and revising undesired effects as well as terminating the intervention. We can already find single possibilities for intervening by actions such as activating the party mode of a heating system or the ad hoc adjustment of water or coffee quantities in a coffee machine for a single cup of coffee. By contrast to these single possibilities, intervention interfaces systematically allow for the use of all types of possible interventions, their integration, and consideration of reasonable points of physical access from where the intervention can be started. If more than one automated process or AI-based decision-making is repeatedly used in the same context, the intervention interface helps to quickly address the process that should be influenced by an intervention.

Intervention can take place with varying degrees of mental effort, from simply switching off the system during a specified timeslot (Fig. 1, A, Level 1) to taking over control in fine-grained steps within a specified timeslot (Fig. 1, A, Level 2), to temporarily changing data or thresholds (Fig. 1, A, Level 3). The invariant characteristic of all types of interventions that we describe here is their temporal instantiation–after a certain time span or certain events, the mode that is initiated by the intervention will be terminated, and the automated system will take over the process again. The users will clearly realize whether this resumption has taken place, and they cannot forget to switch back to the regular state or erroneously assume that they did so. This emphasis on temporal change of the system's mode of usage contrasts with the long-lasting effect that might be achieved for the outcome of AI usage. What is adapted with a longer-lasting effect is not the AI system itself but the effect of the system on its usage environment.

We speak of *intervenability* if systems have an intervention interface that integrates the variety of possibilities of acting and observing that are required for a successful intervention.

2.2 Human-Centered AI and Advanced Intervention

Intervenability into AI is a design option that belongs to a broader research area, namely, human-centered artificial intelligence, or HCAI for short (Shneiderman 2022; Xu 2019). Various approaches can be assigned to human-centered AI, such as responsible AI Schiff et al. (2020), keeping the human in the loop (Crootof et al. 2023), collaborative AI (Dubey et al. 2020; O'Neill et al. 2022), hybrid intelligence systems (Dellermann et al. 2019), and explainable AI (XAI) (Adadi and Berrada 2018; Meske et al. 2022). We suggest that HCAI is most clearly characterized by the underlying assumption that hybrid intelligence has "…the ability to accomplish complex goals by combining human and artificial intelligence to collectively achieve superior results than each of them could have done in separation and continuously improve by learning from each other" (Dellermann et al. 2019, p. 275). This definition of HCAI accepts that both sides can continuously evolve by learning, and thus, it differs from a more general notion of human-centered technology, such as that preferred by Shneiderman (2022), which does not emphasize the potential autonomy of AI as an agent that can evolve on its own. It is important to consider this autonomy since future users will have to deal with not only one but also manifold AI-driven autonomous processes, as in the smart home (Hargreaves and Wilson 2017). In such situations, users will neither have the capacity nor time to exercise continuous and detailed control and oversight of every process. This is one reason why focusing on occasional intervention is important.

A further aspect of HCAI is the explainability of AI (XAI), which is usually provided by AI itself. It is also indispensable because human intervention and control are only possible if one can identify the extent to which an intervention is possible and useful, where it can be applied, and what effect it will have. One could argue that it is unnecessary to know the algorithm of AI-based parking when one can simply take control so that the car does not drive too close to a tree. On the contrary, we suggest that the driver should know whether the AI cannot perform a certain action or decision or whether something on the car is not working as it should, e.g., if a camera on the vehicle's underside is dirty. If the AI does not account for whether the car is driving into the irrigation area of a tree, then it is important for human intervention to know whether that is because the sensor technology is not in for that situation or whether the system is not interpreting the data correctly.

The original definition of intervention (Schmidt and Herrmann 2017) addresses AI-driven real-time processes. Considering the broader scope of AI application that is covered by HCAI, we suggest that intervenability refers not only to automated physical processes, such as autonomous vehicles, but also to AI-based decision-making for certain types of specific cases. There are AI-assisted processes, such as identifying social fraud (Möchel 2023), that automatically result in consequences for those affected without human decision-makers being able to intervene (yet). In contrast, humans need to be able to intervene in those processes where an AI component specifies a decision that is then executed unquestionably by human actors or by traditional software and that may result in people with certain characteristics—e.g., dual citizenship—being negatively affected. Humans must be able to veto AI-based decisions (Rakova et al. 2021). HCAI assumes that humans are the better decision-makers as soon as it is no longer just a matter of mastering complex contexts and huge amounts of data but of making decisions when there is ambiguity, as in the context of negotiations, or when only insufficient information is available (Jarrahi 2018).

Another real-world example of applications that do not resemble the processes involved in automatic vehicle control is enterprise resource planning systems or warehouse systems (Er et al. 2022) that include an AI component. Such a component can decide, for example, that a certain good is to be reordered. Following this, another AI system can then select the supplier and schedule the transport, or the order can be executed by a conventional IT infrastructure or by human clerks. No matter which of the three options is realized, before proceeding, a human decision-maker must be able to review the AI-based order and to intervene if necessary and adjust the order timing or quantity of goods for the specific situation (Fig. 1, B, Level 2). A similar situation applies—as another example application area—to industrial plants where AI automatically provides maintenance instructions (Herrmann 2020, 2023). Based on sensors, it could be determined, for example, that a pump needs to be replaced due to pressure fluctuations. Before the usual process is started with a repair order, human decision-makers must check whether the pump really might fail and whether the costs associated with the replacement are justified. Especially when such predictive maintenance systems are introduced, there are often false alarms in the beginning that would lead to unnecessary repairs if they were all taken seriously. Intervention must therefore be enabled for holistic, socio-technical processes in which AI, conventional IT, and human actors interact (Herrmann et al. 2018, 2022).

2.3 Intervention as Exploration

Intervention is also an opportunity to run experiments or to find answers to what-if questions that both help to explore the AI system and its application domain (Fig. 1, Level 4). This can be explained by the example of AI-based predictive maintenance alerts for industrial equipment. Suppose an alert is issued that a pump needs to be replaced due to excessive pressure fluctuations. The plant operator may intentionally ignore this warning because she wants to see if the pump will work for a while longer. She may already have a spare pump ready for quick replacement, but she wants to wait and see if the prediction is valid so she can learn something about the reliability of the AI system. This ignoring of the warning by the plant operator means that she rejects the AI outcome. This rejection is presented as the first level within the taxonomy of intervention possibilities (Fig. 1, B, Level 1). The operator might decide to jump to a higher level of intervention by increasing the threshold value up to which, in her opinion, pressure fluctuations are still considered tolerable and not indicative of a defect (Fig. 1, B, Level 3). The plant operator could even go further and inspect old cases where correct warnings of pump failures were given. She could then check whether these correct warnings would still have been given under the condition of the increased threshold value. This strategy means that intervention is combined with an exploration of the system (Fig. 1, Level 4).

Additionally, or alternatively, the AI system itself could react to a rejection by prompting the user to propose changes in data or rules that lead to more acceptable AI outcomes. In this way, an intervention interface could be extended to include functionality that encourages experimentation and exploration on the part of the users, thus supporting their learning processes. Such a temporary increase of a threshold would also be an intervention that helps to learn something about maintenance requirements in general.

2.4 A Taxonomy of Intervention

We summarize the background section by the taxonomy presented in Fig. 1. Two types of AI applications are presented. The upper part of the diagram presents interventions into AI-based continuous real-time control such as using autonomous cars, control of airplanes, agricultural machinery, or smart homes; the lower part of the diagram presents interventions into AI-based decision-making such as fraud detection, handling applications for reimbursement in insurance companies, or ordering of goods by warehouse systems. AI-based predictive maintenance is an example that demonstrates that there are applications between these two types since the continuous monitoring of machinery is a real-time process, while every warning can be considered as a case to be handled by the plant operator. The possibilities that represent interventions are ordered from the left to the right side with respect to the level of mental effort required. Table 1 presents examples of the diverse levels for both types of AI applications. The mental effort here refers to the activities to be carried out, the observation of effects that are caused by intervention, or the anticipation of the effects of an intervention. We consider the degree of planning required to be decisive for the level of mental effort caused by an intervention.

A) AI-based continuous real-time control	**interruption** until a time slot has expired or while user **waits** for a situational change	**interruption** while user **takes over** detailed, fine-grained interactive **control**	user **modifies** data, thresholds or rules to **temporarily influence** the control of a process	user **temporarily modifies** parameters or rules **to explore** the effects of the modification on a process	user **modifies** parameters or rules to **influence** the control of a process for **a time slot in the future**	user **influences one or several** processes to achieve a temporal effect and are **aware of side effects** on other processes
	Increasing mental effort for conducting an intervention →					
B) AI-based discrete case related decision making	**rejection** and **resumption** of decision making when new information is available or after a deadline	**rejection** and/ or **modification** of a decision made for the current case	user **modifies** data, thresholds or rules **to influence** decision making **for the current case**	user **modifies** parameters or rules **to explore** the effects of the modification on **the current case**	user **modifies** parameters or rules to **influence** decision making **for certain types of future case**	user **influences** decision making for **several interdependent cases** and is aware of side effects on decisions
	Level 1	*Level 2*	*Level 3*	*Level 4*	*Level 5*	*Level 6*

Fig. 1 A taxonomy of intervention activities

Table 1 Examples of diverse levels of mental effort for conducting interventions

Level	AI-based continuous real-time control or surveillance (examples for autonomous driving and smart homes)	AI-based discrete, case-related decision-making (examples for warehouse systems and related processes of purchasing and delivery)
1	Parking is interrupted until a group of children has passed; the brake assistant is interrupted. The readiness of an alarm system is interrupted for a brief time	A single order of goods is delayed in an AI-based warehouse system until a storm has passed
2	The driver takes over control until a construction site has been passed	The user enters data into the warehouse system that reflects specific requirements caused by an emergency
3	Speed is reduced while driving through a scenic landscape	The user enters rules according to which the delivery of certain goods can no longer be classified as a matter of priority handling
4	A threshold is raised to see whether a predictive alarm is appropriately avoided, although the water level of the heating system fluctuates	A route planner avoids a specific route to see whether this allows for faster transport during rush hours
5	Reducing the watering system for a period of days	Delaying the handling of certain types of orders until a supplier has updated some relevant warranties
6	Delaying several energy-consuming processes in a smart home until the sun is back	Putting a certain order on hold until a court precedent is decided, although these decisions are needed to proceed with other delivery processes

This assumption is based on action regulation theory (Zacher and Frese 2018). It distinguishes between the development or selection of goals, orientation, planning, monitoring of action and outcome, and feedback processing. Action regulation theory differs from other theories that analyze concepts of task-related complexity and mental effort but do not regard the relevance of planning (Liu and Li 2012). We suggest that goal setting and orientation occur before the intervention. They lead to the decision to instantiate an intervention. The diverse levels of mental effort in our taxonomy refer to the extent of planning and feedback-based adjustments to actions that are required. Level 1 (Fig. 1) mainly requires monitoring and a single planning decision about when to resume AI-based task handling, representing the lowest mental effort.

Detailed, interactive control during an intervention or modification of AI outcome may rely on existing planning patterns and include unconscious routines, thus requiring slightly increased mental effort (Level 2). Just prompting the system with short commands—such as "slow down" or "consider the availability of staff"—are examples for Level 2. Altering data, rules, or thresholds that influence the AI system requires some anticipation of the modifications' effects and thus represents the next higher degree of effort (Level 3). As soon as users cannot be sure whether the applied planning of Level 2 or 3 will be successful, the consideration of feedback and adaptation of plans becomes relevant (Level 4). Level 4 represents a situation where users' interventions are similar to trials or experiments, thus representing a mode of exploration. Rejecting an AI outcome is a simple act but is more challenging if the effects of this rejection need to be observed and are a matter for further adaptation of the system. The more the effects of interventions only become apparent in the future, i.e. the less direct the feedback, the more planning and anticipation is required to achieve the desired results (Level 5). If a person employs and monitors not only one but several AI-based processes, side effects between the processes may have to be considered, as occurs in the smart home or when the same customer is affected by several decision-making cases. In these interdependent processes or cases, exploring or future assessment of intervention effects becomes even more mentally challenging (Level 6).

We have derived the distinct levels of the taxonomy in Fig. 1 by analytical consideration in relation to action regulation theory but not by empirical investigations of our own.

3 Intervention: An Alternative Among Other Options

3.1 Intervention Versus Emergency Stop

Introducing a new principle or design criterion, such as intervenability, raises the question of whether such an additional option is necessary alongside existing criteria or options for user interface design. For example, the conventional emergency stop button could be suggested already as a metaphor for how systemic intervenability could also be realized (see Fig. 2).

However, it is precisely by distinguishing it from the emergency stop button that one can explain the special nature of the intervention. Take, for example, the brake assistant in trucks, which is supposed to prevent serious rear-end collisions. Cars might get too close in front of a truck coming via highway access, and the assistant triggers an unwanted braking process (Seininger et al. 2020). Some drivers, therefore, switch off the assistant in such situations. However, they occasionally fail to switch it on again. This again increases the risk of accidents. An intervention button (see Fig. 2), on the other hand, would only trigger a temporary interruption of the automatic system, with the assistant being switched on again after a preconfigured time and signaling this accordingly (United Nations 2023).

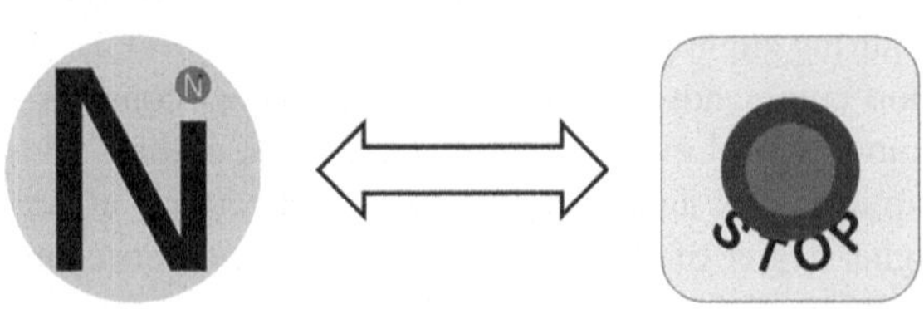

Fig. 2 Intervention versus emergency stop

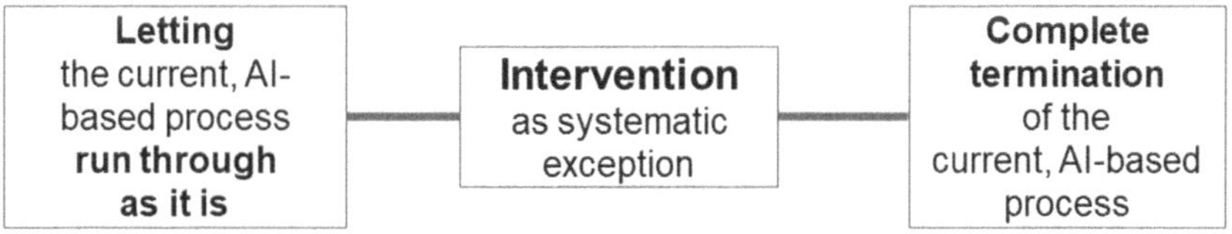

Fig. 3 Intervention—a third option between complete shutdown of a system and letting the current process run as it is

Interventions are, therefore, always limited and do not permanently interrupt the regular process. While the resumption after using an emergency button requires the typical—possibly awkward—restart procedure, an intervention interface allows for triggering an immediate resumption either by the human agent or the system itself. Thus, in contrast with the emergency button, the system is never shut down completely but is still active in the background, ready to take over the task handling again.

Since using the emergency stop button might cause a costly interruption and a time-consuming system restart, people tend to avoid using it and prefer to let a current automated process run as it is. This might cause so-called workarounds (Alter 2014). Workarounds are specific ways of intentionally handling a specific task, although these ways are not planned, expected, or allowed; in some cases, they may even be illegal. Usually, workarounds do not aim to modify or explore the technical system but alter organizational procedures that surround technical artifacts. An intervention button is part of an intervention interface, and with the same button or controls combined, the resumption can also be started. Consequently, intervention is a third option between complete termination, letting the system run as it is, and possibly applying workarounds (see Fig. 3).

3.2 *"Intervention into" Versus "Reconfiguration" of AI*

Today's AI systems are rarely created in a single step and then used permanently in the same version. Instead, they are—for instance, in the case of machine learning—usually further trained on a regular basis to provide better predictions, decisions, and actions. In these cases, we speak of the AI system being reconfigured. Intervention, in contrast, is not a permanently effective reconfiguration of the technical system but an adjustment that is made exceptionally and temporarily. However, interventions can be an entry point for reconfiguration. Intervention should not be used to achieve repeatedly the same correction effect in similar situations. Intervention, then, as Fig. 4 illustrates, is something third between two other poles, namely, on the one hand, allowing the process to run repeatedly always in the same form or, on the other hand, reconfiguring the technology-driven process with a permanent effect for

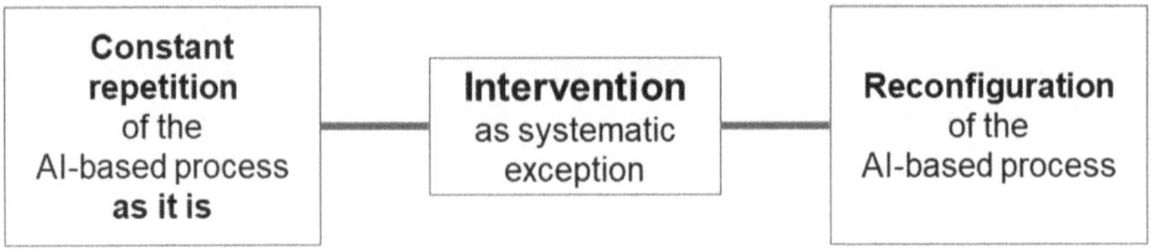

Fig. 4 Intervention—a third option between reconfiguration of a system and repeating an automated process as it is

the system itself. Intervention does not mean one or the other of these two poles. Instead, it opens a third option.

To understand this, it helps to use the simple, non-AI example of office coffee machines, which have a rotary knob that allows one to increase the amount of coffee powder or brewing water used beyond the preset level. That is an option for a single intervening activity that only applies to brewing one cup of coffee. Thus, an intervening activity is not an entirely new phenomenon. However, this rotary knob is not an example of a systematically designed intervention interface. By contrast, intervention interfaces must be implemented systematically, especially for AI applications.

According to the principle that intervention effects are limited to a certain time slot or a single case, if the knob on the coffee machine is turned, the quantities are only adjusted for a single brew; if this action results in a permanent adjustment of the quantities, it would be a reconfiguration. In the case of an intervention, the next coffee drinker can rely on the fact that the preconfigured quantity ratios are the same as always. Here, the socio-technical interplay of multiple users of a technical artifact highlights how critical it is that the effect of an intervention is limited. Whenever multiple people use AI applications, they must be confident that they will find the initial conditions as expected. This requirement is particularly important when it is too costly or undesirable to offer a personalized user interface to the participants. If one aimed at a systematic design for an intervention interface for the coffee machine, such a solution would allow users to decide whether their adjustment applies only for a single cup (intervention), for all further cups in the future (reconfiguration), or whether also previous adjustment quantities could be recalled. This simple example illustrates that an intervention interface opens the possibility for reconfiguration so that the design motivates users to fix the underlying reason for intervention instead of rejecting systems or repeating interventions again and again. If it becomes clear in the case of the coffee machine that almost all users increase the amount of brewing water, then this is a reason to think about permanent reconfiguration of the brewing water quantities.

A further example is the case of the brake assistant. If the intervention button is pressed every time a highway access is approached, this points toward the necessity of a reconfiguration. To this end, it must be possible to register and document interventions. AI could itself make suggestions as to when and how a reconfiguration makes sense for the improvement of an AI system, so that, for example, by evaluating geoinformation at all highway accesses, the brake assistant is temporarily suppressed and at the same time a clearly perceptible warning signal is given in the vehicle cabin.

4 The Integration between Further Development of AI and of Human Competencies

In summary, it can be said that a need to reconfigure the AI cannot necessarily be derived from rare interventions. So, if it only happens occasionally that a car parks near an unprotected tree area, then intervention is sufficient without the need to reconfigure anything. However, a permanent adjustment would make sense if the parking space were near one's home and used daily. Similarly, if almost all people with the same characteristic, such as dual citizenship, are systematically but inappropriately suspected of social fraud, then a reconfiguration is indicated. In the case of frequent, similar interventions, a permanent adjustment is appropriate. It then depends on the specific use case whether:

- The system can evaluate these interventions itself to suggest improvements or to give prompts that point toward possibilities of reconfiguration
- The users make small adjustments by themselves
- The users propose carrying out an adjustment and delegating this to technical experts or data analysts who are capable of reconfiguring the system and are responsible for it

Any reconfiguration made must subsequently be transparent and explainable because it can also change the intervention effects and affect several people or organization units who use the system.

With respect to autonomy and oversight, it is the task of human actors to finally decide whether and how a reconfiguration takes place. Those who frequently intervene should help in this decision and can themselves make suggestions as to what kind of adjustment is appropriate. This requires that an intervention always be reflected upon, at least after it has taken place. To support this reflection, AI must be able to explain its reasoning mechanisms, as well as the data and influencing factors that are considered. Only when it is known where the deficits really lie—for example, at the level of sensor technology, the interpretation of data, automated decision-making, or in their implementation (Beringer and Herrmann 2025)—can meaningful adaptation measures be proposed. Interventions themselves and the effects that can be observed in the process help to better understand AI as well as the application domain in which AI is used. The weaknesses of the AI that are ironed out by an intervention help to think about the specifics of the workspace in which AI is used. Thus, interventions are a trigger for continuous learning on the job (Fischer 2000; Fischer and Herrmann 2015). With respect to fostering learning, even for a

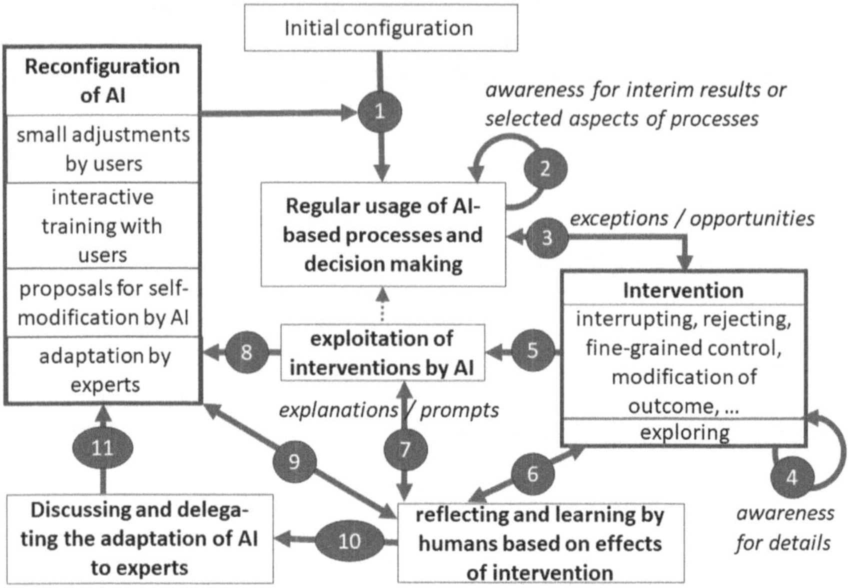

Fig. 5 Integrated further development of humans and AI

one-off intervention, it is advantageous to think about the facts the system should be aware of to avoid the necessity of the intervention. If users understand which underlying assumptions are implemented into the system and cause the need for an intervention, this helps them to better understand the characteristics of a domain and the shortcomings of models of this domain.

As can be seen from these considerations, intervention can result in learning progress for the users, which then also leads to further development of the AI in some cases. Figure 5 presents how the evolution of an AI system and learning on the users' side are generally intertwined by interventions. The relevant relations of Fig. 5 can be described as follows:

1. Before regular use of AI-based processes and decision-making can take place, the system has to be appropriately configured. This can include phases of training with appropriate data, as is the case with machine learning, testing, selecting statistical methods to be applied, adding rules, and customizing the system with instructions that take the characteristics of users into account. After a period of usage, a reconfiguration might change the conditions of regular usage.
2. During regular usage, the users will not want or be able to be completely aware of all aspects of the AI-based process. This is particularly relevant if multiple processes run in parallel so that comprehensive surveillance would be mentally taxing and would overwhelm the users. Thus, users must decide on which AI outcome they focus on.

3. Based on their awareness of AI outcomes and processes, the users might detect that a situation exceptionally leads to inappropriate process control or decision-making by the AI system or that there is an opportunity to gain an advantage by adapting the behavior of AI. This is the starting point for an intervention in accordance with the options presented in the taxonomy (Fig. 1). Usually, interventions are reasonable to alter AI outcomes. Additionally, or even alternatively, the users may want to intervene to check how a system reacts to modified data input, parameters, or rules. This is a kind of what-if exploration that aims to understand the relationships and key assumptions of the AI's model of a domain. The relation between intervention and regular usage is bidirectional since the users can at any time decide to return to regular use or even to revise the effects of an intervention.
4. As long as an intervention is active or exercised, the users must have a detailed, fine-grained awareness with respect to those aspects they want to influence by the intervention. Thus, if a driver decides to take control of the car by himself, he has to monitor the situation around the car. The more the intervention aims for exploration, the more effort is needed to observe the intervention's effects.
5. As illustrated in Fig. 3, the AI system is not completely shut down, and interventions do not entirely overthrow its results. By contrast, it remains active in the background and thus remains able to observe and record the intervention activities. This provides a basis on which the system can contribute to further improvement (see relation 9 and 7 in Fig. 5). The configuration of the system might even specify that an intervention can be terminated by the system to return to regular use (see dotted line in Fig. 5) if the intervention might lead into a dangerous situation.
6. The detailed awareness of what happens during an intervention triggers the users' reflection on the situation and on the outcome of their intervening activities. The more exploration is involved, the more learning can take place based on this reflection. The learning effects are not restricted to the features and characteristics of the AI system but also include a better understanding of the domain to which the model underlying the AI system refers. The reflection can also help to adjust the intervening activities.
7. AI might become active during the intervention to support human reflection during work (Prilla et al. 2013) with the system. In a typical way of managing such a case, users ask for explanations to understand interim results, warnings, and decisions made by a navigation system. In contrast to this conventional way of seeking explanations, the AI system can take the initiative to explain actions or decisions against which a user intervenes. The AI system can also provide warnings, e.g., if certain assisting functions are interrupted. Moreover, the system could prompt users on how to act during an intervention or on how to proceed after the intervention. Further development of AI should allow providing prompts that describe how the system could be adapted so that it reacts adequately by itself in situations that have led to interventions.
8. Instead of prompting the users to carry out an adaptation, the system can outline proposals on how it could be adequately modified and document them

within the system itself. These proposals could be reviewed by technical experts (see relation 11, Fig. 5) who can instantiate the modification or adapt it. Furthermore, the data that is recorded during interventions can be used as examples with which a machine learning system can retrain its model. Thus, " ...constant performance improvement is attainable by continuous training by users by providing the system with feedback that indicates misclassifications ..." (Punchoo et al. 2021, p. 440). This type of evolving is considered interactive machine learning (Amershi et al. 2014). It might be specified that changes in the AI's domain model, which are based on retraining, must be agreed upon by a human expert before they are implemented (see relation 11, Fig. 5).

9. Besides self-adaptation by the AI system, users can also contribute modifications based on their reflections. This might be reasonable for small adjustments by specifying, for example, that the modification of thresholds or rules should be made permanent. This relation is bidirectional since users should be permanently informed if the system is reconfigured.
10. Reflecting on the effects of intervention can lead to discussing issues about the AI system with other users, user communities, or experts who are familiar with the AI system. These discussions can initiate further learning about the system and the domain it covers. In particular, the discussion can complement AI-based explanations with human-based explanations. This kind of hybrid XAI provides a broader picture of the capabilities and limits of a system. Eventually, experts might be able to propose more sophisticated adaptations that contribute to a reconfiguration of the system.
11. The discussions might eventually lead to the implementation of adaptation proposals that are provided either by the AI system itself or by experts. Overall, it is reasonable to include human expertise before a reconfiguration is completed. It can be considered as an outcome of managerial decisions and organizational practices on how the reconfiguration is coordinated and approved. Such coordination (see Fig. 6) is highly relevant since AI usage is part of a socio-technical system where several stakeholders are affected.

In conclusion, the role of intervenability and intervention interfaces, as presented in Fig. 5, helps to meet the requirements that AI is "...designed and trained to augment individual workers, and augmentation involves a mutual learning process through which both humans and AI learn from each other and hence coevolve" (Jarrahi et al. 2023, p. 91).

5 Basic Requirements for Designing the Intervention Interface

Intervenability is a design criterion that relates to the interaction between humans and AI when processing tasks. For intervenability to be successful, the interaction interface to the AI must meet several requirements. Up to now, no empirical studies have derived such requirements. In their paper on intervention interfaces, Schmidt and Herrmann (2017) refer to Shneiderman (1992) golden rules to derive requirements for intervenability, including six design principles. In what follows, we point out some crucial requirements that are important for designing intervention interfaces:

- Information must be offered or easily retrievable and can be used to decide whether and how to intervene and realize the intervention's effects. Accordingly, all AI usage should be accompanied by informative feedback (Shneiderman 1992). Furthermore, users should not be required to keep anything about the system's previous status in mind to handle and terminate intervention successfully. This corresponds to "reduce the short-term and working memory load" (Shneiderman and Bederson 2006, p. 5). A well-developed AI system could even suggest possible steps for intervention or for improving the system itself (see Fig. 5).
- It must be comprehensible when the intervention begins and ends. In every situation—before, during, or after intervention—the intervention interface must clearly communicate how responsibilities and control are shared between the human and the system (Schmidt and Herrmann 2017, p. 45). This kind of comprehensibility matters not only to those who start the intervention but to everyone who is affected by the change during AI usage. This requirement can be derived from a socio-technical view and is particularly relevant if several processes and roles are involved, as can be seen in the context of the smart home (Herrmann et al. 2019).
- The operating elements with which one controls intervention must be easily and quickly accessible and easy to use—just like the emergency stop button (Knote et al. 2016). Similarly, intervention might be started by a physical button. As we know from the equipment of smart homes, various control elements such as smartphones, tablets, or computers (Hargreaves and Wilson 2017) can be used to trigger interventions. This kind of solution for intervention interfaces provides more flexibility so that several options can be offered to intervene, as presented in the taxonomy (Fig. 1).
- Intervention must be quickly terminable, and it must be possible to undo the effects of intervention if necessary. This is an important prerequisite if interventions are employed to explore what-if questions by altering the parameters of the AI system. The intervention interface should offer a simple means to reverse the impact of the system's automated behavior, e.g., to cancel an alarm—or undo the results of interventions themselves (Schmidt and Herrmann 2017, p. 45).
- Interventions and their effects must be documented so that they can be reflected afterward with respect to their appropriateness and can be used as a basis for further adjustments to the AI system. In working practice, it will be appropriate that the employees leave comments in the system about the reasons for which one intervenes. This requirement can be derived from the cyclic integration of intervention and AI reconfiguration, as presented in Fig. 5.

- Intervention interfaces must allow the user to choose among the various options listed in the intervention taxonomy (see Fig. 1) as far as they are appropriate for the application domain. For example, an intervention must contribute to achieving certain effects immediately, as well as effects that lie in the future.
- The performance of AI, as well as its shortcomings, can take place on different levels, such as sensing, deciding, and acting (Beringer and Herrmann 2025; Rasmussen 1976). Sensing includes sensor-based data acquisition, deciding also covers the interpretation and planning based on the data, and acting refers to all kinds of AI behavior that renders effects in its environment. The difference between these levels has been illustrated above by the example of assisted parking. Intervention interfaces should help the users to selectively address these levels appropriately to minimize their effort. This requirement can be derived from the socio-technical principle of "balance of effort and experienced benefit ..." (Herrmann et al. 2022, p. 3101).

Fulfilling these requirements helps to keep people involved in the use of AI, which corresponds to the principle of oversight, autonomy, and keeping humans in the loop.

6 Organizational Practices to Support Intervenability

Keeping humans in the loop can be sustained only if organizational practice permits and promotes its implementation. Herrmann and Pfeiffer (2023a) use the example of predictive maintenance to argue that the human-in-the-loop principle must be supplemented by the principle of "keeping the organization in the loop." It is obvious that many employees will only dare to reject an AI result—for example, not to follow a maintenance request—if their organizational practices safeguard such a decision or even promote it. We conceive organizational practices as interactions and negotiations within an organization that are based on structures and processes that are subject to their own logic (Herrmann and Pfeiffer 2023b; Phillips and Lawrence 2012).

Following a diagram of the organizational embeddedness of AI, where Herrmann and Pfeiffer (2023a, p. 1537) present several interacting organizational practices, Fig. 6 depicts eight aspects of reciprocal influence that are relevant to bringing intervention into reality:

1. In the center of Fig. 6 is the managerial task of offering and coordinating the possibilities for intervention in the evolution of AI. This coordination is important in organizational units since AI is part of a socio-technical system where changing a regular process or decision-making can influence others. This may include risks if others do not understand whether an intervention is still active or is already terminated. Thus, managerial coordination provides rules that guide the operational forces by clarifying what kind of intervention can be initiated by whom under which conditions. The handling of the original tasks

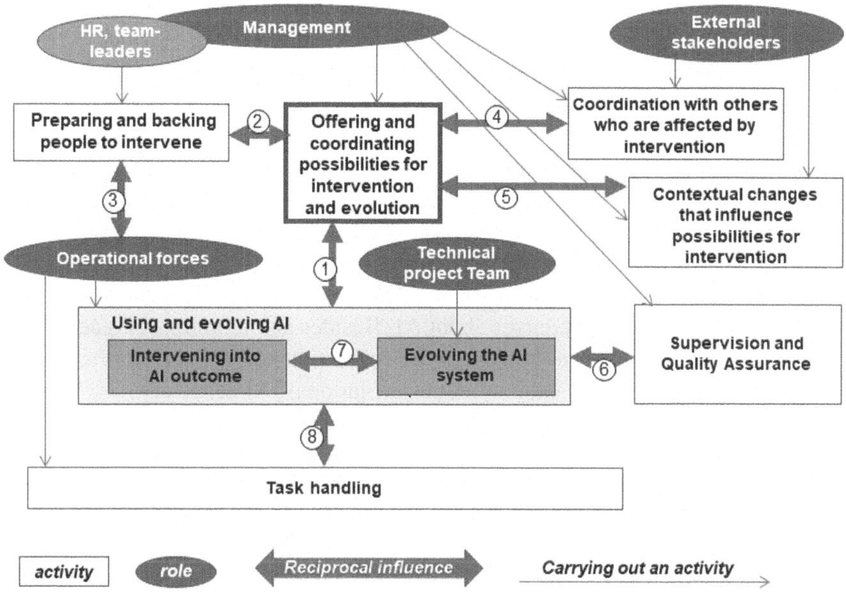

Fig. 6 Managerial tasks and organizational practices in the context of intervenability

that are supported by employing AI must be organized in a way that promotes intervention. The rules for coordinating the handling of AI might be negotiated, adapted, and eventually adopted through organizational practices. Furthermore, the coordination must specify how the interplay between intervention into and evolution of AI (reciprocal influence 7 in Fig. 6), as presented in Fig. 5, is implemented and which role the technical team has to take over for reconfiguring AI.

2. Making intervention happen requires not only that people be allowed to intervene. They also need to be prepared and encouraged to do so. Thus, the coordinative measures must be coupled with HR development and supported by team leaders so that flexible handling of AI results takes place, such as rejecting or adjusting them by intervention. It must also be part of organizational practice that both AI's and employees' capabilities are continuously developed and that everyone is encouraged to contribute to this learning process.
3. Preparing, encouraging, and backing the operational forces to conduct interventions requires an intensive exchange with them. Interventions, as well as shortcomings of AI, can be documented to provide a basis for reflection that should take place not only individually but also collaboratively within teams and with supervisors. Employees need to know that their peers and supervisors will recognize it when they intervene to counteract or test the performance of the AI.
4. Since organizational units interact with other stakeholders, they also must be informed about the possibility of intervention that might take place and affect them. It must be specified who in the environment will be aware of interventions that took place, whose interests might be affected, and how the reaction of

others has to be taken into account when an intervention is instantiated. For example, if an AI-based smart home triggers an alarm and the owner overrides this alarm, then security services must be able to verify that this was the result of an intervention by the inhabitants of the smart home.

5. The environment of an AI application underlying continuous changes must be considered by management when coordinating the possibilities for intervention. Changes may be triggered by new technologies or by the market. Changes in contracts or laws might require standard procedures that prevent certain types of interventions that violate the regulations. However, interventions might even be necessary to allow for a quick reaction to meet the requirements of new regulations or ethical discourses about AI. Besides shortcomings of a certain AI application, the continuous change of the context of AI usage is a further trigger that makes interventions and continuous evolution of AI necessary.
6. From an organizational point of view, interventions into AI, its evolution, and the interplay between both need close supervision. This includes testing AI and its reconfiguration, evaluating whether interventions were reasonable or not, and assessing the configuration of the intervention possibilities itself, for example, whether the time that elapses before the system returns to the regular procedures is too long or too short. In particular, it is a management task to consider whether the same kind of intervention happens too often and should be avoided by reconfiguration.
7. As described in Fig. 5, the intervention in and evolution of AI are intertwined. Interventions influence how an AI system will evolve or be reconfigured, and the reconfiguration itself changes the possibilities and conditions of intervening. These changes must be regarded by the organizational practices that surround interventions.
8. Using and influencing AI must be closely related to the task handling that AI will support. The task-handling procedures might have to be adapted and adjusted to AI usage. For example, employees can be encouraged to first consider for themselves what decision they would make before looking at the AI's proposed decision (Fogliato et al. 2022). Such a measure makes reflection on AI results and their possible rejection more likely and contributes to the calibration of trust in AI.

The reciprocal influences of Fig. 6 illustrate that intervenability is a criterion that must be implemented within a holistic, socio-technical approach that integrates organizational practices, individual activities and capabilities, technical artifacts, and their evolution, as well as the development of human competencies (Kirsch et al. 1995).

7 Conclusion

Based on the literature and several examples of possible AI applications, we outlined the concept of intervenability. It is a new phenomenon that is not covered by emergency shutdown, workarounds, or reconfiguration of automated systems. Intervenability instantiates the principles of controllability, autonomy, oversight, and keeping humans in the loop in the context of AI. We provide a taxonomy that includes several categories of intervening activities and differentiates them with respect to the user's mental effort. This taxonomy goes beyond the initially proposed concept for the intervention of Schmidt and Herrmann (2017) by extending its scope of applicability from real-time control of automated processes to AI-based discrete case-related decision-making. This is in accordance with human-centered AI, which seeks to employ human strengths combined with the usage of AI. We demonstrate how intervenability can potentially contribute to the ongoing development of human capabilities on the one hand and to further improvement by reconfiguring AI on the other hand. Exploring and collaboratively reflecting on the effects of interventions is key to enabling this ongoing improvement on both sides. Intervenability also provides further momentum for the design of an AI that can, by itself, help realize interventions and advance a smooth transition from intervention to reconfiguration of the AI.

The presented concept of intervenability and intervention interfaces faces some limitations. So far, we can find single instances of intervention possibilities, such as the party button for heating, but no systematically designed complete intervention interfaces. Thus, it is difficult to empirically investigate the appropriateness of intervenability. Furthermore, conducting experimental lab studies is difficult since intervenability is a solution that reacts to problems that occur only exceptionally and cannot be anticipated or systematically reproduced. Furthermore, the limits and benefits of possibilities for intervention can only be studied within a socio-technical context where technology, human competencies, and organizational practices need to be appropriately developed and closely intertwined. We have demonstrated (Fig. 6) how managerial measures of coordination and the adoption by organizational practices must support interventions. It is not sufficient to allow workers to intervene in AI outcomes or processes, but they also need to be made competent and encouraged to do so. Intervention must not be a concern only of individuals but of teams. Fundamentally, intervenability must be implemented in such a way that the benefits gained from an intervention outweigh the effort involved.

These limitations point to future challenges. From an empirical point of view, examples of the relevance of intervenability need to be identified and contrasted with the concept presented above. We will have to explore how intervenability can serve as an umbrella for various ways of enabling human autonomy, oversight, and controllability when using AI. Empirical cases will be needed to show how the use of systematically designed intervention interfaces can be beneficial. A systematic, socio-technically oriented approach could stimulate further research into how interfaces can be designed for the use of AI—especially if several autonomous processes run in parallel—and how AI can be implemented organizationally.

Acknowledgments This work was supported by the project Humaine (Human-centered AI Network), which is funded by the Federal Ministry of Education and Research (BMBF), Germany, within the 'Zukunft der Wertschöpfung – Forschung zu Produktion, Dienstleistung und Arbeit'

Program (funding-number: 02L19C200). We thank Christopher Lentzsch, who contributed many suggestions to the intervention taxonomy.

References

Adadi A, Berrada M (2018) Peeking inside the black-box: a survey on explainable artificial intelligence (XAI). IEEE Access 6:52138–52160. https://doi.org/10.1109/ACCESS.2018.2870052

Alter S (2014) Theory of workarounds. Commun Assoc Inform Syst 34(55):1041–1066. https://doi.org/10.17705/1CAIS.03455

Amershi S, Cakmak M, Knox WB, Kulesza T (2014) Power to the people: the role of humans in interactive machine learning. AI Mag 35(4):105–120. https://doi.org/10.1609/aimag.v35i4.2513

Argyris C (1970) Intervention theory and method: a behavioral science view. Addison-Wesley, Reading

Beringer J, Herrmann T (2025) The contextual framing of the interplay between human and AI—a socio-technical perspective. In: The design of human-centered artificial intelligence for the workplace. Springer, Berlin

Card SK, Newell A, Moran TP (1983) The psychology of human-computer interaction. Lawrence Erlbaum Associates, Hillsdale

Crootof R, Kaminski ME, Price II WN (2023) Humans in the loop. Vanderbilt Law Rev 76(2):429–494. https://scholarship.law.vanderbilt.edu/vlr/vol76/iss2/2

De Visser EJ, Peeters MM, Jung MF, Kohn S, Shaw TH, Pak R, Neerincx MA (2020) Towards a theory of longitudinal trust calibration in human–robot teams. Int J Soc Robot 12(2):459–478. https://doi.org/10.1007/s12369-019-00596-x

Dellermann D, Calma A, Lipusch N, Weber T, Weigel S, Ebel P (2019) The future of human-AI collaboration: a taxonomy of design knowledge for hybrid intelligence systems. In: Proceedings of the 52nd Hawaii international conference on system sciences (HICSS), pp 1–10. https://doi.org/10.24251/HICSS.2019.600

Dubey A, Abhinav K, Jain S, Arora V, Puttaveerana A (2020) HACO: a framework for developing human-AI teaming. In: Proceedings of the 13th innovations in software engineering conference (formerly known as india software engineering conference). ACM, New York, pp 1–9. https://doi.org/10.1145/3385032.3385044

Er N, Cidal GM, Ünsal S, Çakır MA (2022) Enabling big data analytics and AI solutions for smart warehouse. In: Kahraman C, Cebi S, Onar SC, Oztaysi B, Tolga AC, Sari IU (eds) Intelligent and fuzzy techniques for emerging conditions and digital transformation, advances in intelligent systems and computing, vol 307. Springer, Cham, pp 929–936. https://doi.org/10.1007/978-3-030-85626-7_108

European Commission, Directorate-General for Communications Networks, Content and Technology, High-Level Expert Group on Artificial Intelligence (2019) Ethics guidelines for trustworthy AI. https://data.europa.eu/doi/10.2759/346720

Fischer G (2000) Lifelong learning—more than training. J Interact Learn Res 11(3):265–294

Fischer G, Herrmann T (2015) Meta-design: transforming and enriching the design and use of socio-technical systems. In: Designing socially embedded technologies in the real-world. Springer, London, pp 79–109. https://doi.org/10.1007/978-1-4471-6720-4_5

Fogliato R, Chappidi S, Lungren M, Fitzke M, Parkinson M, Wilson D, Fisher P, Horvitz E, Inkpen K, Nushi B (2022) Who goes first? Influences of human-AI workflow on decision making in clinical imaging. arXiv preprint arXiv:220509696. http://arxiv.org/abs/2205.09696

Georgieva I, Lazo C, Timan T, van Veenstra AF (2022) From AI ethics principles to data science practice: a reflection and a gap analysis based on recent frameworks and practical experience. AI Ethics 2(4):697–711. https://doi.org/10.1007/s43681-021-00127-3

Hargreaves T, Wilson C (2017) Introduction: smart homes and their users. In: Smart homes and their users. Springer, Cham, pp 1–14. https://doi.org/10.1007/978-3-319-68018-7_1
Herrmann T (1992) Support of intervening use. In: Ergonomics of hybrid automated systems III, pp 289–294
Herrmann T (2020) Socio-technical design of hybrid intelligence systems—the case of predictive maintenance. In: International conference on human-computer interaction. Lecture notes in computer science, vol 12203. Springer, Cham, pp 298–309. https://doi.org/10.1007/978-3-030-49062-1_22
Herrmann T (2022) Promoting human competences by appropriate modes of interaction for human-centered-AI. In: Degen H, Ntoa S (eds) Artificial intelligence in HCI. Lecture notes in computer science, vol 13336. Springer, Cham, pp 35–50. https://doi.org/10.1007/978-3-031-05643-7_3
Herrmann T (2023) Collaborative appropriation of AI in the context of interacting with AI. In: Degen H, Ntoa S (eds) Artificial intelligence in HCI. Lecture notes in computer science, vol 14051. Springer, Cham, pp 249–260. https://doi.org/10.1007/978-3-031-35894-4_18
Herrmann T, Pfeiffer S (2023a) Keeping the organization in the loop: a socio-technical extension of human-centered artificial intelligence. AI Soc 38(3):1523–1542. https://doi.org/10.1007/s00146-022-01391-5
Herrmann T, Pfeiffer S (2023b) Keeping the organization in the loop as a general concept for human-centered AI: the example of medical imaging. In: Proceedings of the 56th Hawaii international conference on system sciences (HICSS), pp 5272–5281. https://doi.org/10.24251/HICSS.2023.645
Herrmann T, Schmidt A, Degeling M (2018) From interaction to intervention: an approach for keeping humans in control in the context of socio-technical systems. In: Proceedings of the 4th international workshop on socio-technical perspectives in IS development (STPIS'18), pp 1–8. http://ceur-ws.org/Vol-2107/Paper8.pdf
Herrmann T, Lentzsch C, Degeling M (2019) Intervention and EUD: a combination for appropriating automated processes. In: Malizia A, Valtolina S, Mørch A, Serrano A, Stratton A (eds) End-user development. Lecture notes in computer science, vol 11553. Springer, Cham, pp 67–82. https://doi.org/10.1007/978-3-030-24781-2_5
Herrmann T, Jahnke I, Nolte A (2022) A problem-based approach to the advancement of heuristics for socio-technical evaluation. Behav Inform Technol 41(14):3087–3109. https://doi.org/10.1080/0144929X.2021.1972157
Jarrahi MH (2018) Artificial intelligence and the future of work: human-AI symbiosis in organizational decision making. Bus Horizons 61(4):577–586. https://doi.org/10.1016/j.bushor.2018.03.007
Jarrahi MH, Askay D, Eshraghi A, Smith P (2023) Artificial intelligence and knowledge management: a partnership between human and AI. Bus Horizons 66(1):87–99. https://doi.org/10.1016/j.bushor.2022.03.002
Kirsch C, Troxler P, Ulich E (1995) Integration of people, technology and organization: the european approach. In: Anzai Y, Ogawa K, Mori H (eds) Symbiosis of human and artifact, advances in human factors/ergonomics, vol 20. Elsevier, Amsterdam, pp 957–961. https://doi.org/10.1016/S0921-2647(06)80337-0
Knote R, Baraki H, Söllner M, Geihs K, Leimeister JM (2016) From requirement to design patterns for ubiquitous computing applications. In: Proceedings of the 21st European conference on pattern languages of programs, pp 1–11. https://doi.org/10.1145/3011784.3011812
Liu P, Li Z (2012) Task complexity: a review and conceptualization framework. Int J Ind Ergon 42(6):553–568. https://doi.org/10.1016/j.ergon.2012.09.001
Meske C, Bunde E, Schneider J, Gersch M (2022) Explainable artificial intelligence: objectives, stakeholders, and future research opportunities. Inform Syst Manag 39(1):53–63. https://doi.org/10.1080/10580530.2020.1849465
Möchel E (2023) Künstliche intelligenz: Drei beispiele für das scheitern von algorithmen. https://www.heise.de/news/Kuenstliche-Intelligenz-Drei-Beispiele-fuer-das-Scheitern-von-Algorithmen-9205911.html

Okamura K, Yamada S (2020) Empirical evaluations of framework for adaptive trust calibration in human-AI cooperation. IEEE Access 8:220335–220351. https://doi.org/10.1109/ACCESS.2020.3042556

O'Neill T, McNeese N, Barron A, Schelble B (2022) Human–autonomy teaming: a review and analysis of the empirical literature. Hum Fact J Hum Fact Ergon Soc 64(5):904–938. https://doi.org/10.1177/0018720820960865

Phillips N, Lawrence TB (2012) The turn to work in organization and management theory: some implications for strategic organization. Strategic Organ 10(3):223–230. https://doi.org/10.1177/1476127012453109

Prilla M, Herrmann T, Degeling M (2013) Collaborative reflection for learning at the healthcare workplace. In: Goggins SP, Jahnke I, Wulf V (eds) Computer-supported collaborative learning at the workplace. Springer, Boston, pp 139–165. https://doi.org/10.1007/978-1-4614-1740-8_7

Prümper J (1993) Software-evaluation based upon ISO 9241 part 10. In: Grechenig T, Tscheligi M (eds) Human computer interaction. Lecture notes in computer science, vol 733. Springer, Berlin, Heidelberg, pp 255–265. https://doi.org/10.1007/3-540-57312-7_74

Punchoo R, Bhoora S, Pillay T (2021) Applications of machine learning in the chemical pathology laboratory. J Clin Pathol 74(7):435–442. https://doi.org/10.1136/jclinpath-2021-207393

Rakova B, Yang J, Cramer H, Chowdhury R (2021) Where responsible ai meets reality: practitioner perspectives on enablers for shifting organizational practices. Proc ACM Hum-Comput Interact 5(CSCW1):1–23

Rasmussen J (1976) Outlines of a hybrid model of the process plant operator. In: Moray N (ed) Monitoring behavior and supervisory control. Springer, Boston, pp 371–383. https://doi.org/10.1007/978-1-4684-2533-0_23

Schiff D, Rakova B, Ayesh A, Fanti A, Lennon M (2020) Principles to practices for responsible AI: closing the gap. arXiv preprint arXiv:200604707. http://arxiv.org/abs/2006.04707

Schmidt A (2000) Implicit human computer interaction through context. Pers Technol 4(2–3):191–199. https://doi.org/10.1007/BF01324126

Schmidt A, Herrmann T (2017) Intervention user interfaces: a new interaction paradigm for automated systems. Interactions 24(5):40–45. https://doi.org/10.1145/3125387

Seininger P, Heinl F, Bühne JA, Gail J (2020) Lkw-Notbremsassistenzsysteme: truck advanced emergency brake systems. Fachverlag NW in Carl Ed. Schünemann KG, Bremen

Shneiderman B (1992) Designing the user interface: strategies for effective human-computer interaction. Addison-Wesley Longman Publishing, Boston

Shneiderman B (2022) Human-centered AI. Oxford University Press, Oxford

Shneiderman B, Bederson BB (2006) Maintaining concentration to achieve task completion. In: Proceedings of the conference on designing for user eXperience, pp 1–6

United Nations (2023) UN regulation no. 131 uniform provisions concerning the approval of motor vehicles with regard to the advanced emergency braking system (AEBS) for M2, M3, N2 and N3 vehicles. https://unece.org/sites/default/files/2023-10/R131r1am2E.pdf

Xu W (2019) Toward human-centered AI: a perspective from human-computer interaction. Interactions 26(4):42–46. https://doi.org/10.1145/3328485

Zacher H, Frese M (2018) Action regulation theory: foundations, current knowledge and future directions. In: Ones DS, Anderson N, Viswesvaran C, Sinangil HK (eds) The SAGE Handbook of industrial, work & organizational psychology. SAGE Publications, London, pp 122–143. https://doi.org/10.4135/9781473914957.n7

Zanzotto FM (2019) Viewpoint: human-in-the-loop artificial intelligence. J Artif Intell Res 64:243–252. https://doi.org/10.1613/jair.1.11345

How Can Intelligent Persona Systems Support Online Advertisers' Daily Work Tasks?

Joni Salminen, Ilkka Kaate, Rami Olkkonen, Yanwu Yang, Soon-Gyo Jung, and Bernard J. Jansen

Abstract This chapter discusses the role of personas—more particularly, intelligent personas—which are personas enabled by intelligent systems, in online advertising work. Through a conceptual analysis, we find that intelligent personas can contribute to all central parts of the online advertising work process, including segmentation, targeting, ad creation, account structuring, optimization, and reporting. We discuss an intelligent advertising system in which personas are a central hub for actions.

1 Introduction

This chapter discusses the role of *intelligent personas* and *intelligent systems (IS)* in supporting online advertising work practices. We first define key concepts and then describe online advertising work practices. Afterward, we conceptually analyze how intelligent personas and systems can help in this domain.

Personas (also known as "user personas," "marketing personas," "buyer personas," and so on) are fictitious representations of groups of users or customers, usually presented as profiles (see Fig. 1) that marketers use to understand how a product will be used by groups of people with different needs, interests, and

J. Salminen (✉)
University of Vaasa, Vaasa, Finland
e-mail: jonisalm@uwasa.fi

I. Kaate · R. Olkkonen
University of Turku, Turku, Finland
e-mail: iokaat@utu.fi; rami.olkkonen@utu.fi

Y. Yang
Huazhong University of Science and Technology, Wuhan, China
e-mail: yangyanwu@hust.edu.cn

S.-G. Jung · B. J. Jansen
Qatar Computing Research Institute, Hamad Bin Khalifa University, Doha, Qatar
e-mail: sjung@hbku.edu.qa; bjansen@hbku.edu.qa

C. K. Coursaris et al. (eds.), *The Design of Human-Centered Artificial Intelligence for the Workplace*, Progress in IS, https://doi.org/10.1007/978-3-031-83512-4_10

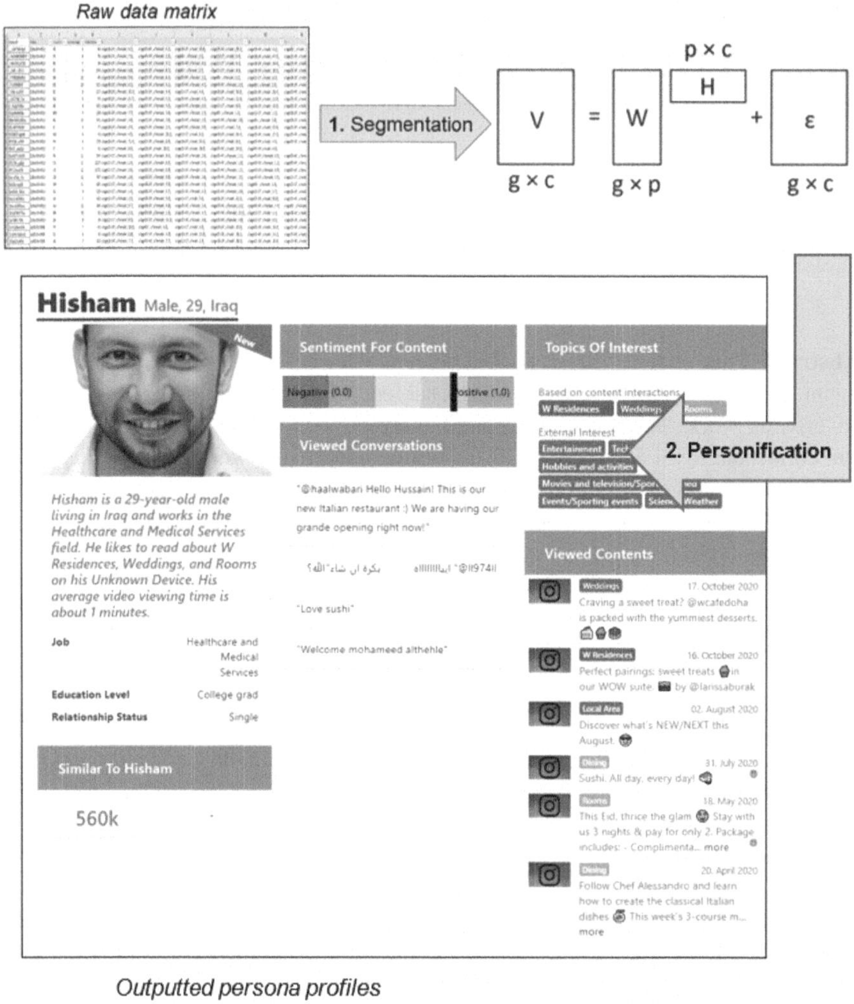

Fig. 1 An example of an algorithmic persona creation process that results in a data-driven persona profile. The persona profile can connect to intelligent features of an intelligent persona system. From a technical perspective, intelligent personas rely on standard ML techniques, but presenting a cluster as a fictive persona is valuable since it enables the advertiser to understand customer characteristics in a simple, nontechnical way. Thus, intelligent personas exemplify how to present statistical constructs in a human-centered way

backgrounds (Nielsen 2019). Personas are typically based on research and data collected about customers, which is then segmented and enriched to create persona profiles. Personas can be applied in many use cases, including market segmentation, customer segmentation, targeting, ad customization, and so on (we will discuss these use cases later in this chapter).

Intelligent personas can be defined in two ways: (a) the intelligent features of an interactive persona system or (b) personas generated using *artificial intelligence* (AI) and machine learning (ML) technology. Related concepts include AI persona (Holzinger et al. 2022), data-driven (McGinn and Kotamraju 2008), or algorithmically generated personas (Salminen et al. 2022b). In the literature, intelligent personas are associated with understanding web and social media analytics data; that is, they represent an alternative to numbers, graphs, and tables in the process of forming an idea or mental model of "who our customers are" (Jansen et al. 2021; gyo Jung et al. 2021a,b; Salminen et al. 2020, 2022a).

Interactive persona systems provide a user interface (UI) for interacting with the personas, for example, to learn more about the personas' needs (Chu et al. 2018; Coorevits et al. 2016; Cutting and Hedenborg 2019; Faily and Lyle 2013; gyo Jung et al. 2021b). In these interactive persona systems, the persona is no longer a flat file such as a piece of paper or a static online document but an entity whose information the advertiser can access interactively by making choices, such as searching, filtering, and simulating likely responses.

Intelligent persona systems take this interactivity one step further by incorporating intelligent features into the system's use. These intelligent features aim to help advertisers make the most of personas and achieve their advertising objectives better.

Intelligent systems (IS) perform functions that typically require intelligence when done by a human (Grosan and Abraham 2011). This includes planning, analyzing, interpreting data, and making decisions—all tasks requiring cognitive capability. Examples of IS include self-driving cars, expert systems (e.g., in medical diagnosis), and robotics; however, any system that carries out tasks requiring intelligence is an IS.

Intelligence refers to thinking and reasoning. From an etymological perspective, the word *intelligent* comes from the Latin verb *intelligere*, which has a close meaning to "to understand." "Intelligent" is the possession of capacity for specific cognitive capabilities such as abstraction, logic, understanding, learning, reasoning, emotions, creativity, and problem-solving (Sun 2022; Weber and Schütte 2019). In the context of IS, intelligence refers to the ability of a machine or system to perform cognitive tasks that are typically performed by humans, such as natural language processing (NLP), acquiring information, image recognition, clustering, recognizing patterns, making decisions, and so on.

Online advertising involves using the Internet to accomplish communication and performance goals related to branding, sales, and other strategically valuable areas (Alaimo and Kallinikos 2018). Traditionally, the advertising process consists of market research, strategic planning, media mix planning and buying, ad creation, performance evaluation, and reporting (Qin and Jiang 2019). These steps require multiple activities related to analyzing consumer behavior, following recent trends in technology and consumer preferences, monitoring competitors and best practices, and evaluating performance.

2 History of Intelligent Advertising

One of the earliest references to "intelligent advertising" in marketing academia is by Moriarty in his 1925 article in The American Economic Review (Moriarty 1925). Moriarty's definition of intelligence in advertising is centered on economic efficiency, i.e., maximizing the conditions for profitable advertising to achieve its objectives with the minimum possible cost for the advertiser. This tenet has persisted over time and is as relevant today as it was nearly a hundred years ago. However, what has changed is our understanding of the role of human conditions in the advertising process—namely, the complexity of persuading and re-persuading target groups to take action that we, as advertisers, wish they would take.

Since Moriarty's times, advertisers now benefit from many tools that were not available for the scientific advertising pioneers (e.g., Claude Hopkins) in the 1920s, and here we emphasize that these tools contain not only software technology but also conceptual frameworks. Alongside AI, central concepts used among industry players and scholars include ML, IS, intelligent advertising (Sun 2022), computational advertising (Yang et al. 2017), and so on. Collectively, these concepts emphasize the ever-increasing role of technology as a toolbox for advertising work. However, tools often offer a pretense of simplicity while cloaking the underlying mechanisms, either under technical jargon or contemporary buzzwords, without specifying what each tool does. So, it is worth to critically examine the value propositions of such software tools when analyzing how "AI" and "intelligence" actually assist in advertising work.

McCarthy and Hayes (1981) compared the outputs from content analysis conducted by humans and algorithms, and their results suggested that humans may display better performance than machines in terms of coding some brand-specific content, such as brand identification and sentiment analysis, which is also known as opinion mining (Cambria et al. 2013). This issue was exemplified by a failure in targeting mechanisms based solely on text and traditional keyword matching. An example might be that a blogger complaining about the safety of a car brand is ultimately exposed to ads from that brand since the topic of the article and the use of keywords matches quite well (Qiu et al. 2009). In other tasks, however, ML models already outperform humans, for example, in distinguishing real product reviews from computer-generated ones (Salminen et al. 2021b).

In parallel to the previous example, Thomas and Fowler (2021) underline the possibility that AI-based influencers (also known as "virtual influencers") might act in a way that can damage the brand's reputation and state that using a human celebrity could mitigate that risk. Thus, IS-based advertising may induce some challenges to the value of the work and the originality of human creativity and empathy (Coffin 2022). The virtual influencer argument, however, overlooks the fact that humans ultimately control the virtual influencers, as human creators either design the prompts for content generation or even the whole virtual influencer, thus entitling humans the decisive power in how virtual influencers are deployed in social media marketing.

These examples and perspectives illustrate the role of creativity and the reasoning abilities of the human component regarding the key functions of online advertisers (Qiu et al. 2009). Nevertheless, dehumanization in the advertising industry is a possibility as novel algorithms are developed to replace the human component and start to mimic humane features such as emotions and empathy. Indeed, some tasks that formerly required the human component, such as content creation and ad copywriting, can be carried out by large language models (LLMs) such as ChatGPT (also known as Generative AI). Hence, online advertisers should be prepared and improve themselves so that they know the basics of AI applications in online advertising, the role of creative components, and what to do to compensate for the weaknesses of the existing technologies.

Intelligence in online advertising is promising since IS can simulate or mimic human intelligence and learn from previous experiences, improve themselves over time so that they can perform a given task with increased accuracy and efficiency, and provide more effective and intelligent decisions when compared to traditional (non-intelligent) advertising (Chowdhury and Debi 2013).

3 Challenges and Opportunities in Online Advertising Work

The everyday online advertising work typically involves creating and managing digital advertising campaigns, writing ad copytexts, and analyzing and optimizing campaigns based on their performance. Online advertisers use different online platforms such as Google Ads (search advertising), Facebook Ads (social advertising), and various publisher websites (programmatic advertising) (Chen and Feng 2021; Goldfarb and Tucker 2011; Yang et al. 2017). In this chapter, our thesis is that marketing professionals would benefit from the additional support of intelligent personas (and persona systems) alongside the other systems they use. In the most basic example, intelligent personas can be used to create more customized and relevant campaigns. By understanding a specific target audience's demographics, interests, and behaviors, advertisers can craft messaging and imagery that resonates with that audience. However, as we will discuss, the use cases of intelligent personas go far beyond this basic example.

As online advertising is rapidly evolving, online advertisers face several challenges in their daily activities.

First, managing the daily activities and technological tools in the online advertising space is continuously becoming more time-consuming due to the technologizing of marketing (Kozinets and Gretzel 2021), as advertisers are exposed to information from different tools and platforms. In particular, the application of AI into online advertising, with concepts such as computational advertising (Huh and Malthouse 2020), has occurred so rapidly that advertising concepts have dramatically changed, and this rapid change brings unclarity to the work definition, i.e., what do online advertisers actually do? The insufficiency of literature regarding the mechanisms of advertising and the examination of IS has raised a need for in-depth research (Qin and Jiang 2019).

Second, compared to previous decades, online advertisers are now bombarded with massive amounts of data and literature from different sources, resulting in the difficulty of finding reliable and relevant sources of information, as well as making sense of the influx of marketing data.

Third, another problematic idea in advertising technology is centered on the belief that AI might replace the human component (or "human touch" (Light and Akama 2012)). This skeptical point might threaten the peace of mind felt by online advertisers. Particularly, Snee and Smulowitz (2021, p. 255) touched upon how the role and scope of AI should be in online advertising work practices:

> Computers are not going to replace creative pros – but machine learning and artificial intelligence can be powerful tools in the storytelling process. AI should be used for 'grunt work' to provide more time for humans to recognize, develop and take advantage of insights to produce outstanding creative work for their clients.

In the *Journal of Advertising*, creativity is mentioned as a defining feature of advertising, and advertisers are distinguished from other practitioners by their creative skills (Bernardin et al. 2008; West et al. 2019). Prior studies distinguish the creation process of AI from that of humans by their motives, such that AI creates based on the established precedence (Bernardin et al. 2008; West et al. 2019). In contrast, human creativity originates from a meaningful purpose (Lehnert et al. 2014), i.e., pursuing a specific target or goal. However, this view may be contested as intelligent algorithms also optimize for a goal, e.g., minimizing a loss function (Kühl et al. 2022). Neural networks, for example, rely on a backpropagation algorithm to adjust the neurons' weights based on observed classification errors, gradually improving the accuracy of the network (Bengio et al. 1994). So, there are both differences and similarities in how humans and algorithms operate regarding online advertising tasks. Nonetheless, as in any knowledge work, also in online advertising, a fundamental question in computer-assisted labor is (Salminen et al. 2017): *How can tasks between advertisers and algorithms be distributed in a way that optimally reaches advertising goals?* Here, intelligence plays a role.

So, while online advertising has many challenges, novel technologies also bring about many opportunities. One of the major advantages of IS-enabled advertising is the automated analysis of consumer behaviors and characteristics. However, with the emerging AI technologies, big data is obtained from several sources or providers, and it is essential to process and filter that data to achieve a meaningful output. Such data includes users' web and shopping search history, click and skip rates, previous purchases, geographical position, and demographic information (age, gender, etc.) (Chen and Feng 2021), click-through rate (CTR) (Shi and Wang 2023), user-generated content (UGC), and so on.

4 Toward Intelligent Persona Systems

So, what does the work of advertisers *really* entail? Let us consider the key elements involved (see Fig. 2). Firstly, there is *segmentation*. This involves dividing the overall market into distinct and identifiable groups, known as segments. One effective approach is to utilize personas as segments, represented by specific individuals with names and faces. By employing personas, segmentation can be carried out in a persona-driven manner, resulting in the creation of personas as outcomes. It is worth noting that segmentation also involves *platform selection*, i.e., selecting the ad platforms where advertising takes place.

Once the segmentation is complete, the next step is *targeting*. Advertisers determine which segments they want to concentrate their efforts on. At this stage, an IS can provide valuable assistance by recommending specific personas to target based on explicit goals such as maximizing reach, engagement, or sales. These recommendations can help advertisers make informed decisions about the most effective segments to focus on. Using personas based on social media and web analytics data can also help advertisers to better target the population for their campaigns in terms of demographics, location, language, and timing. Additionally, personas can help identify potential growth areas and uncover new opportunities for advertisers via persona-based gap analysis (Jansen et al. 2020a,b).

Once the target segments have been identified, the *ad creation* process begins. This involves crafting compelling and persuasive ad content (e.g., text ads, social media ads, video ads, mobile ads, etc.). Here, an IS can be beneficial by generating personalized ad headlines, texts, and even imagery tailored to the selected personas. By leveraging data and insights about the personas, the IS can create ad content that resonates with their specific needs, preferences, and motivations—applying persona-based (group) personalization. Advertisers can create personalized ads

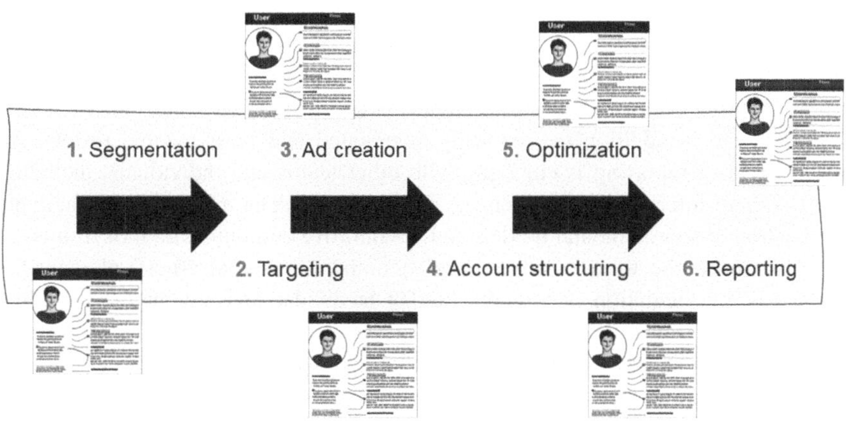

Fig. 2 Keeping personas in the loop of the online advertising process

meeting the persona's needs. For instance, based on the persona segment's historical data, it is possible to know whether the segment has made prior contact with the brand and the ads to avoid too many repeated exposures to the same content (Chen and Feng 2021).

Once the ad content has been developed, advertisers move forward with *account structuring*, which involves creating campaigns within the advertising platform and configuring various settings. In this process, an IS can provide valuable assistance by establishing a structure where campaigns are organized around personas. This ensures the naming and targeting criteria align with the targeted personas (Chowdhury and Debi 2013). Organizing campaigns based on personas gives advertisers an advantage in the subsequent stage: optimization. Furthermore, applying different strategies (i.e., campaigns) or actions to each persona becomes possible.

Optimization entails making informed decisions based on the results obtained from running the campaigns. Optimization can be defined as monitoring campaign performance and making optimizations and adjustments based on data analytics (Chen and Feng 2021). It includes, among other activities, setting feasible bids and budgets in online ad platforms (Qin and Jiang 2019; Sun 2022). Optimization also requires creating novel content (ad copy, images, written content, video, etc.) to keep campaigns engaging, fresh, and vivid (Coorevits et al. 2016; Goldfarb and Tucker 2011) and analyzing audiences, and researching target audiences' attitudes and behaviors (Yang et al. 2017).

Another essential part of optimization is *platform management*, which includes experimenting with campaigning on various impactful or trending online ad platforms, such as TikTok Ads, Google Ads, and Facebook Ads (Goldfarb and Tucker 2011), and allocating budgets according to performance. As the campaigns generate data, organizing this data by personas becomes beneficial as an optimization framework. When data is categorized by personas, budget allocation based on persona-based marketing performance becomes easier. Using the persona system as a hub for campaign data allows for more effective and efficient decision-making, as spending can be allocated according to segment-based responses.

Finally, advertisers are bound to report the results at regular intervals, so *reporting* is an integral part of the online advertising workflow. Here, the results can be reported as "Here is how our campaigns performed with Persona 1 (Mike)" instead of (or in addition to) reporting aggregated and unsegmented results. An integral part of reporting is engaging with other teams and individuals, including superiors and inferiors. In these engagements, the persona metaphor can facilitate the creation of shared mental models and the intuitive communication of results.

In summary, the work of advertisers encompasses several crucial elements. It starts with segmentation, where the market is divided into segments, including personas. Targeting follows, with advertisers selecting the segments they want to target, aided by IS recommending specific personas based on defined goals. After this, ad copywriting takes place, with the assistance of IS that generates personalized ad content for the selected personas. After the ad content is created, advertisers proceed to campaign setup, where campaigns are created and configured within the advertising platform. Utilizing an IS, campaigns can be organized around personas,

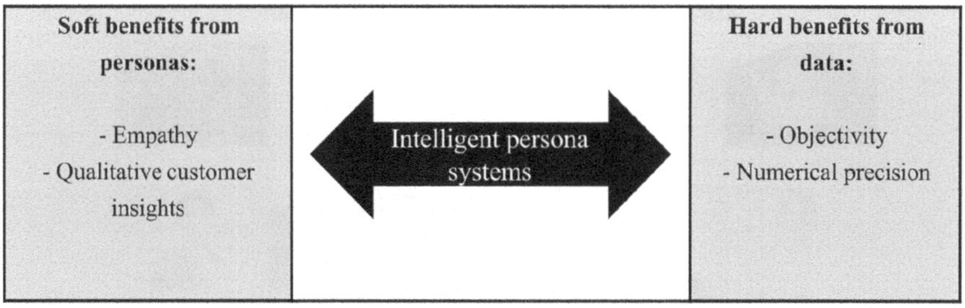

Fig. 3 Intelligent persona systems bridging the soft and hard skills required in online advertising

aligning the naming and targeting criteria. This provides an advantage during the optimization stage, as data generated by the campaigns can be organized by personas, enabling better decision-making when adjusting budget allocation based on the actual marketing performance of each persona, as well as reporting the results.

Overall, the above process aims to result in more effective ad campaigns. By understanding the personas of their target audience, advertisers can develop campaigns that are more tailored to their customers' needs and interests, which can lead to increased sales conversions and, thus, a profitable return on investment (Forrester Research 2010).

The performance gains are based on the combination of soft and hard benefits (Fig. 3) of intelligent personas—essentially, providing customer-centric inputs when and where needed.

For each stage, we envision intelligent persona features that support core tasks associated with the specific stage (see Fig. 3). Essentially, intelligent personas can be used to create AI-driven algorithms targeting specific audiences with tailored ads. Personas can also provide insights into how people respond to different forms of advertising, helping AI-driven campaigns to be more effective and efficient. Intelligent personas can also be deployed in predictive analytics, for example, to predict how a given persona (that represents a certain audience segment) is likely to engage with given ads before making said ads public (An et al. 2018a). Through predictive analytics, personas can support online advertising by helping identify target audiences and providing insights into how they might react to different advertisements. This reduces the risk of wasted impressions due to ineffective advertising (Fig. 4).

5 Discussion and Concluding Remarks

In addition to technological efforts, a conceptual rethinking of managing online advertising is required to extract full value from intelligent persona systems.

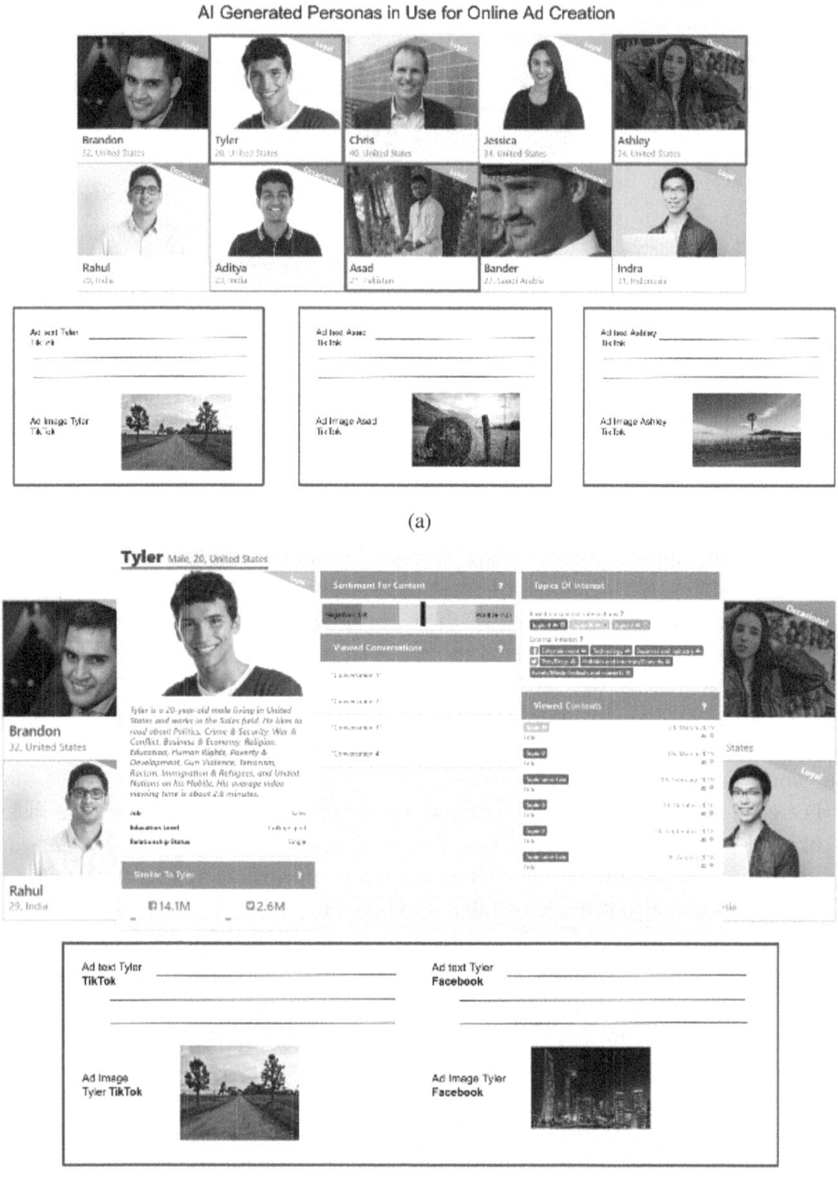

(b)

Fig. 4 Concept example. In scenario (**a**), we have an array of personas, each accompanied by ad text and image boxes (highlighted in red). This layout facilitates ad text creation and image selection, simplifying the process for human marketers. Moving on to scenario (**b**), we see a view where the persona profile for Tyler has been clicked and expanded, providing a more comprehensive look at the persona's characteristics. In this expanded view, there are also ad text columns tailored for multiple advertising channels, making ad text creation and image selection for the persona more convenient and efficient

The accelerating rate of novel technologies has also resulted in ethical issues among consumers, cascading into the advertising profession. The application of AI technologies in online advertising was initially so rapid that it was perhaps impossible to consider the full ramifications and drawbacks of these technologies regarding societal issues such as privacy, trust, and safety (Coffin 2022). For instance, billboards with built-in cameras tracking customer information such as gender, age, or mood have been placed around the shopping malls before any comprehensive debate on ethical concerns has been held (Helmo and Kimppa 2020). During these rapid changes, online advertisers might experience a heightened sense of responsibility since they can be seen as responsible among the public with limited knowledge about AI.

Regarding privacy concerns, it is interesting to observe that some of the current changes in the online advertising industry gravitate toward models that are conceptually similar to personas. For example, federated learning of cohorts (FLoC) (Langheinrich 2021) that Google has developed to deal with privacy issues relies on mitigating the role of individualized data in favor of using (scrambled) aggregate data—a concept highly similar to personas, as personas also represent aggregate, cluster, or factor groups rather than specific individuals in the customer population. This similarity should be further explored in future work, but even at this stage, it implies enticing opportunities for personas in the new privacy-protected paradigm of online advertising. Nevertheless, the heightened reliance on aggregate "averages" and "biggest groups" casts doubts on advertisers' abilities to reach marginalized groups and achieve the ideals of inclusive design (Goodman-Deane et al. 2018; Salminen et al. 2021a).

As online advertising evolves, the ability to interpret and act on data will become increasingly important. Therefore, organizations that rapidly adopt systems that facilitate customer analysis and the formation of a customer-centric market orientation are likely to obtain a competitive advantage in online advertising. Moreover, organizations should make a real effort to embrace digital systems so that their use does not remain fragmented and isolated. Integrating online advertising in a meaningful way into marketing and business strategy is crucial to achieving and sustaining a competitive advantage and organization-wide market orientation.

In this regard, intelligent persona systems could become *hubs* for collecting customer analytics data from various sources and presenting it to stakeholders in a human-centered manner, with *persona being the central unit of analysis* in online advertising. Thus, there is a need for an intelligent end-to-end advertising system that supports human marketers' decision-making by deploying intelligent personas throughout the stages of the online advertising process, with effective API integrations with dominant online advertising platforms. To the best of our knowledge, currently, there is no such system combining intelligent personas with computational advertising.

Personas are developed by researching target audiences (customers or users) and gathering data about their interests, behaviors, and preferences. Personas may convey information about users in various areas, such as demographics, interests, social media data, consumption patterns (An et al. 2018b), sentiment and opinions

(Qiu et al. 2009), pictures posted on a social network, and lifestyle preferences (Qin and Jiang 2019). Based on personas reflecting customers' characteristics and preferences, AI algorithms can process personas' information and use it for downstream tasks. It is crucial to define and create personas at the beginning of an advertising process, so the personas provide proper support.

Conceptually, such a solution could be described as an intelligent assistant that uses the metaphorical presentation (persona) to facilitate the management of an advertising campaign. The system has a generative aspect (creating the persona) and a decision-making aspect by simulating the success of a campaign or recommending specific target personas. Also, if assuming the ultimate goal of marketing automation, it would be interesting to explore opportunities to automate the design and execution of campaigns without the advertiser being in the loop.

Given that online advertisers must deal with a wide range of tasks, intelligent personas can facilitate their work by presenting crucial and well-organized information, enabling algorithms to convert massive data into more meaningful (human-centric) data representations for companies and advertisers to undertake their decision-making (Yager 2000). This is achieved by creating rich personas from web and social media analytics data from various platforms and providing descriptive attitudes consisting of textual descriptions, numbers, and images to provide efficient output to be used in several processes, such as the segmentation of target audiences, social media analytics, and user statistics (An et al. 2018b). Additionally, AI may utilize intelligent personas and process them to provide insights and analytics for online advertisers to assess customer behaviors and predict successful campaign strategies.

Ideally, AI can automate several manual tasks, which are time-consuming and labor-intensive. In online advertising, decision-making ranges from insight formation to targeting, campaign and ad creation, reporting, and optimization. Therefore, intelligent personas are an opportunity to free up time for online advertisers rather than a substitution of the human component in strategic marketing (Chen and Feng 2021) and also to improve the user experience of running online advertising campaigns. Online advertisers can use the freed time from tedious campaign management work to tackle dilemmas that require human intervention, such as ethical concerns like threats to user privacy (Rodgers 2021), trust issues (Light and Akama 2012), failures in analyzing sentiments or the content (Qiu et al. 2009), bias and prejudice introduced by advertising platform algorithms (Datta et al. 2018), and strategic decision-making about the marketing mix (Fan et al. 2015). There is yet a need for humans.

References

Alaimo C, Kallinikos J (2018) Objects, metrics and practices: an inquiry into the programmatic advertising ecosystem. In: Schultze U, Aanestad M, Mähring M, Østerlund C, Riemer K (eds) Living with monsters? Social implications of algorithmic phenomena, hybrid agency, and the performativity of technology. Springer, Cham, pp 110–123. https://doi.org/10.1007/978-3-030-04091-8_9

An J, Kwak H, gyo Jung S, Salminen J, Jansen BJ (2018a) Customer segmentation using online platforms: isolating behavioral and demographic segments for persona creation via aggregated user data. Soc Netw Anal Mining 8(1):54. https://doi.org/10.1007/s13278-018-0531-0

An J, Kwak H, Salminen J, gyo Jung S, Jansen BJ (2018b) Imaginary people representing real numbers: generating personas from online social media data. ACM Trans Web (TWEB) 12(4):27. https://doi.org/10.1145/3265986

Bengio Y, Simard P, Frasconi P (1994) Learning long-term dependencies with gradient descent is difficult. IEEE Trans Neural Netw 5(2):157–166

Bernardin T, Kemp-Robertson P, Stewart DW, Cheng Y, Wan H, Rossiter JR, Erevelles S, Roundtree R, Zinkhan GM, Fukawa N (2008) Envisioning the future of advertising creativity research: alternative perspectives. J Advertising 37(4):131–150

Cambria E, Schuller B, Xia Y, Havasi C (2013) New avenues in opinion mining and sentiment analysis. IEEE Intell Syst 28(2):15–21. https://doi.org/10.1109/MIS.2013.30

Chen Y, Feng S (2021) Artificial intelligence: creating more possibilities for programmatic advertising. In: Advances in artificial intelligence, software and systems engineering: proceedings of the AHFE 2021 virtual conferences on human factors in software and systems engineering, artificial intelligence and social computing, and energy, July 25–29, 2021, USA. Springer, Berlin, pp 148–155

Chowdhury T, Debi HR (2013) Online advertisement system: a new intelligent approach. Int J Soft Comput Softw Eng 3(3)

Chu E, Vijayaraghavan P, Roy D (2018) Learning personas from dialogue with attentive memory networks. In: Proceedings of the 2018 conference on empirical methods in natural language processing. Association for Computational Linguistics, Brussels, pp 2638–2646

Coffin J (2022) Asking questions of ai advertising: a maieutic approach. J Advertising 51(5):608–623. https://doi.org/10.1080/00913367.2022.2111728

Coorevits L, Schuurman D, Oelbrandt K, Logghe S (2016) Bringing personas to life: user experience design through interactive coupled open innovation. Persona Stud 2(1):97. https://doi.org/10.21153/ps2016vol2no1art534

Cutting K, Hedenborg E (2019) Can personas speak? Biopolitics in design processes. In: Companion publication of the 2019 on designing interactive systems conference 2019 companion, pp 153–157

Datta A, Datta A, Makagon J, Mulligan DK, Tschantz MC (2018) Discrimination in online advertising: a multidisciplinary inquiry. In: Conference on fairness, accountability and transparency. PMLR, pp 20–34

Faily S, Lyle J (2013) Guidelines for integrating personas into software engineering tools. In: Proceedings of the 5th ACM SIGCHI symposium on Engineering interactive computing systems—EICS '13. ACM Press, London, p 69. https://doi.org/10.1145/2494603.2480318

Fan S, Lau RY, Zhao JL (2015) Demystifying big data analytics for business intelligence through the lens of marketing mix. Big Data Res 2(1):28–32

Forrester Research (2010) The ROI of personas. Retrieved June 21, 2017 from https://www.forrester.com/report/The+ROI+Of+Personas/-/E-RES55359

Goldfarb A, Tucker CE (2011) Online advertising, behavioral targeting, and privacy. Commun ACM 54(5):25–27

Goodman-Deane J, Waller S, Demin D, de Heredia AG, Bradley M, Clarkson JP (2018) Evaluating inclusivity using quantitative personas. In: Proceedings of design research society conference 2018. Limerick. https://doi.org/10.21606/drs.2018.400

Grosan C, Abraham A (2011) Intelligent systems. Springer, Berlin

Helmo OI, Kimppa KK (2020) Artificial intelligence: how to discuss about it in ethics. In: Societal challenges in the smart society. Universidad de La Rioja, pp 13–20

Holzinger A, Kargl M, Kipperer B, Regitnig P, Plass M, Müller H (2022) Personas for artificial intelligence (ai) an open source toolbox. IEEE Access 10:23732–23747. https://doi.org/10.1109/ACCESS.2022.3154776

Huh J, Malthouse EC (2020) Advancing computational advertising: conceptualization of the field and future directions. J Advertising 49(4):367–376
Jansen BJ, gyo Jung S, Salminen J (2020a) From flat file to interface: synthesis of personas and analytics for enhanced user understanding. In: Proceedings of the association for information science and technology, vol 57. https://doi.org/10.1002/pra2.215
Jansen BJ, Salminen J, gyo Jung S (2020b) Data-driven personas for enhanced user understanding: combining empathy with rationality for better insights to analytics. Data Inform Manag 4(1):1–17. https://doi.org/10.2478/dim-2020-0005
Jansen BJ, gyo Jung S, Chowdhury SA, Salminen J (2021) Persona analytics: analyzing the stability of online segments and content interests over time using non-negative matrix factorization. Expert Syst Appl 185:115611. https://doi.org/10.1016/j.eswa.2021.115611
Jung SG, Salminen J, Jansen BJ (2021a) Implementing eye-tracking for persona analytics. In: ETRA '21 adjunct: ACM symposium on eye tracking research and applications. ACM, New York, Virtual conference, pp 1–4. https://doi.org/10.1145/3450341.3458765
Jung SG, Salminen J, Jansen BJ (2021b) Persona analytics: implementing mouse-tracking for an interactive persona system. In: Extended abstracts of ACM human factors in computing systems—CHI EA '21. ACM, New York. https://doi.org/10.1145/3411763.3451773
Kozinets RV, Gretzel U (2021) Commentary: artificial intelligence: the marketer's dilemma. J Market 85(1):156–159. https://doi.org/10.1177/0022242920972933
Kühl N, Schemmer M, Goutier M, Satzger G (2022) Artificial intelligence and machine learning. Electron Markets 32(4):2235–2244. https://doi.org/10.1007/s12525-022-00598-0
Langheinrich M (2021) To floc or not? IEEE Pervasive Comput 20(2):4–6
Lehnert K, Till BD, Ospina JM (2014) Advertising creativity: the role of divergence versus meaningfulness. J Advertising 43(3):274–285. https://doi.org/10.1080/00913367.2013.851630
Light A, Akama Y (2012) The human touch: participatory practice and the role of facilitation in designing with communities. In: Proceedings of the 12th participatory design conference: research papers-volume 1. ACM, New York, pp 61–70
McCarthy J, Hayes PJ (1981) Some philosophical problems from the standpoint of artificial intelligence. In: Readings in artificial intelligence. Elsevier, Amsterdam, pp 431–450
McGinn JJ, Kotamraju N (2008) Data-driven persona development. In: Proceedings of the SIGCHI conference on human factors in computing systems. ACM, Florence, pp 1521–1524. https://doi.org/10.1145/1357054.1357292
Moriarty WD (1925) An appraisal of the present status of advertising. Am Econ Rev 15(1):23–35
Nielsen L (2019) Personas—user focused design, 2nd edn. Springer, New York
Qin X, Jiang Z (2019) The impact of ai on the advertising process: the Chinese experience. J Advertising 48(4):338–346
Qiu G, Bu J, Chen C, Zhang F (2009) Intelligent advertising for user generated content through sentiment analysis. In: 2009 international conference on advances in social network analysis and mining. IEEE, Piscataway, pp 330–333
Rodgers S (2021) Themed issue introduction: promises and perils of artificial intelligence and advertising. J Advertising 50(1):1–10. https://doi.org/10.1080/00913367.2020.1868233
Salminen J, Sarlin P, Olkkonen R (2017) Who does what in marketing? Toward an understanding of marketer—machine interaction. In: Workshop paper, Montreal
Salminen J, gyo Jung S, Chowdhury SA, Sengün S, Jansen BJ (2020) Personas and analytics: a comparative user study of efficiency and effectiveness for a user identification task. In: Proceedings of the ACM conference on human factors in computing systems (CHI'20). ACM, Honolulu. https://doi.org/10.1145/3313831.3376770
Salminen J, Jung SG, Jansen B (2021a) Are data-driven personas considered harmful? Diversifying user understandings with more than algorithms. Persona Stud 7(1):48–63. https://doi.org/10.21153/psj2021vol7no1art1236
Salminen J, Kandpal C, Kamel AM, Jung SG, Jansen BJ (2021b) Creating and detecting fake reviews of online products. J Retail Consum Serv 64:102771

Salminen J, Jung SG, Jansen B (2022a) Developing persona analytics towards persona science. In: 27th international conference on intelligent user interfaces (IUI '22). Association for Computing Machinery, New York, pp 323–344. https://doi.org/10.1145/3490099.3511144

Salminen J, Jung SG, Jansen B (2022b) Intentionally biasing user representation? Investigating the pros and cons of removing toxic quotes from social media personas. In: Nordic human-computer interaction conference, pp 1–13. https://doi.org/10.1145/3546155.3546647

Shi B, Wang H (2023) An ai-enabled approach for improving advertising identification and promotion in social networks. Technol Forecast Soc Change 188:122269. https://doi.org/10.1016/j.techfore.2022.122269

Snee BJ, Smulowitz SM (2021) It's alive! Reanimating the author in the age of artificially intelligent advertising. Popular Culture Stud J 9(1):249–264

Sun D (2022) Application of traditional culture in intelligent advertising design system in the internet era. Sci Program 2022:e7596991. https://doi.org/10.1155/2022/7596991

Thomas VL, Fowler K (2021) Close encounters of the ai kind: use of ai influencers as brand endorsers. J Advertising 50(1):11–25

Weber F, Schütte R (2019) A domain-oriented analysis of the impact of machine learning—the case of retailing. Big Data Cogn Comput 3(1):11

West D, Koslow S, Kilgour M (2019) Future directions for advertising creativity research. J Advertising 48(1):102–114

Yager RR (2000) Targeted e-commerce marketing using fuzzy intelligent agents. IEEE Intell Syst Appl 15(6):42–45

Yang Y, Yang YC, Jansen BJ, Lalmas M (2017) Computational advertising: a paradigm shift for advertising and marketing? IEEE Intell Syst 32(3):3–6. https://doi.org/10.1109/MIS.2017.58

Reciprocal Human-AI Collaboration: Designing Configuration and Delegation for Continual Learning

Dov Te'eni

Abstract Solving problems by human-AI configurations will likely become a pervasive practice. Traditional models of delegating tasks between humans and machines must be revisited in light of the differences in the learning of humans versus intelligent machines; performance can no longer be the sole criterion for task allocation. We propose a new human-AI configuration called a reciprocal human-machine learning (RHML) configuration and offer a new procedure for delegating tasks dynamically that begins with determining the desired level of machine autonomy.

1 Introduction

With the surge in the pervasiveness of AI in many aspects of life, practitioners and researchers alike have advocated keeping humans in the loop (HitL), resulting in some form of human-AI collaboration (Woods and Hollnagel 2006). In other words, for various situations and reasons explained below, it is recommended to stop short of full automation and opt for AI-augmented configurations in which a human agent works with an artificial agent to learn and perform collaboratively. I claim in this chapter that designing configurations of humans and AI to support effective collaboration requires a new design approach, unlike extant design approaches practiced in the field of human-computer interaction (Ågerfalk et al. 2022). Humans working with AI resemble a team of (human) members working and evolving together more closely than a human operator working with a predesigned tool (Seeber et al. 2020).

Take, for example, allocating tasks between humans and intelligent agents in human-AI collaboration. Designers should consider dynamic allocation of tasks as the agents learn and make sense of a changing context. Such a dynamic that

D. Te'eni (✉)
Tel Aviv University, Tel Aviv, Israel
e-mail: teeni@tau.ac.il

C. K. Coursaris et al. (eds.), *The Design of Human-Centered Artificial Intelligence for the Workplace*, Progress in IS, https://doi.org/10.1007/978-3-031-83512-4_11

assumes informed allocation decisions by the agents starkly contrasts the traditional approach to deciding which agent will perform which task in advance. Thus, while the design of efficient task allocation between humans and computers (once called man-machine task allocation) has been a long-standing issue in human-computer interaction, the teaming of human and artificial intelligence complicates extant patterns of task allocation to the extent that the principles of allocation must be revisited to ensure effective and ethical collaboration. More generally, the design of human-AI configurations for effective collaboration and responsible conduct must be reformulated. Furthermore, task allocation in an organizational context is referred to as "delegation" (rather than allocation) when it involves not only the distribution of work but also the corresponding authority and responsibility that comes with it.

The expected surge of intelligent systems that keep the HitL implies more intensive, riskier, and more varied use of smart devices by diverse users. Human-AI collaboration is already common in numerous domains of play (da Rocha Tomé Filho et al. 2019) or work (Grønsund and Aanestad 2020), such as medical diagnosis and decision-making (Boyacı et al. 2024). The increasing trend of combining human and AI forces to accomplish work makes it critical and urgent to revisit the design of human-AI interaction rather than apply extant practices of human-computer interaction. The proposed new approach to designing human-AI collaboration for problem-solving focuses on designing a configuration that allows dynamic delegation of tasks to and by the collaborating agents. It assumes a collaboration in which both humans and machines learn during the collaboration and adapt accordingly. For simplicity, I discuss only the case in which humans always have ultimate control over collaboration and are responsible for the result and conduct of the collaboration.

The most distinctive characteristic of the new human-machine (AI) interaction versus the traditional human-computer interaction is its learning component. In dynamic environments of complex decision-making, the act of learning how to solve problems, in addition to the act of solving problems, complicates human-machine collaboration. Furthermore, the differences between human and machine learning affect problem-solving performance and, hence, the effectiveness of alternative task allocations. Imagine, for example, a human expert physician collaborating with an AI-based diagnostic system to determine a series of cases. During the collaboration, both the human and the machine learn from each case. They then share their new knowledge to perform jointly and more effectively in the ensuing cases. The configuration that supports such a scenario is called a *reciprocal human-machine learning* (RHML) configuration (Te'eni et al. 2023). Below, I provide the theoretical basis for this configuration before going into its design implications. In this chapter, however, I underscore human learning as the primary reason for keeping the HitL. Suppose we wish to ensure that the expert physician working with AI continues to learn about new medical developments. In that case, we should avoid the situation in which the machine continues to learn and adapt while the human falls behind. Instead, humans should also learn alongside and in collaboration with machines, as proposed in the RHML configuration.

Other diverse reasons for keeping the HitL include maintaining human control, increasing trustworthiness, enabling more efficient learning, and performing tasks that humans still do better. Different rationales for a particular human-AI interaction affect two interdependent design decisions: the delegation of responsibilities between human and artificial agents (Baird and Maruping 2021) and the form and functions of the human-AI configuration (Suchman 2007). These decisions can be seen as meta-decisions leading into the ongoing operations of the human-AI collaboration. Delegation and configuration determine the subsequent operations but are also revisited as ongoing decisions, such as the continual re-delegation of tasks as conditions change throughout the human-AI interaction. Moreover, delegation and configuration must conform to the rationale for keeping the HitL. For example, the design of the human-AI configuration depends on whether the human is kept to complement AI techniques with human capabilities or to ensure just and fair conduct (Suchman 2007).

In RHML configurations, humans are kept in the learning loop (So 2020), primarily to support their continual learning to solve problems alongside the machine's learning. Hence, the analysis of delegation and configuration must be determined to promote effective learning. I believe this motivation to keep human experts in AI-based systems will increase in popularity as developers and users become cognizant of the risks involved in full automation (Drory and Te'eni 2024). Unlike previous research on HitL, which aims to leverage human feedback to improve intelligent automation (Holzinger et al. 2016), RHML strives to improve the human expert's problem-solving capabilities with feedback from the machine as the two agents interact. Indeed, human learning from machine feedback is feasible. For instance, feedback during the human-machine interaction can highlight human classification errors and generate new classification knowledge in classifying X-rays. In sum, an RHML configuration based on feedback from one agent to the other is desirable and feasible yet challenging (Te'eni et al. 2023).

The chapter develops the approach to designing human-AI configurations with continual learning using the familiar online game Wordle. Table 1 defines the principal terms used in this chapter. The first six terms have already been mentioned; the last term is developed below.

2 A Practical Illustration with the Game Wordle

Wordle (https://www.nytimes.com/games/wordle; see Fig. 1) is an online word puzzle-type game that has grown very popular in the past 2 years and has become a daily practice for millions of gamers worldwide. The game has been translated into several languages and studied in several domains, e.g., Liu (2022), Bertsimas and Paskov (2022). It represents well the type of problem-solving tasks we can expect to solve repeatedly and interactively with computers, such as assigning rooms to

Table 1 Principal terms used in this chapter

Term	Definition
Keep the human in the loop (HitL)	A popular term denoting that humans are involved in AI learning and operating.
Configuration	An arrangement of human and artificial agents that facilitates and directs specific interactions between the agents and is designed to achieve specified goals.
Reciprocal Human-Machine Learning (RHML)	A configuration designed to optimize the learning and joint performance of *both* humans and machines.
Task and subtask	A fundamental unit of work required to accomplish a specified goal, usually with specified constraints.
Task allocation	The assignment of tasks or subtasks to either the human or artificial agents.
Task delegation	The assignment of tasks or subtasks, along with the authority (control) to perform them, to either the human or artificial agents. In the organizational context, delegation connotes the transfer of authority coupled with responsibility.
Machine autonomy	The ability of an artificial agent to perform and control tasks independently without human intervention.

Fig. 1 The word of the day "Tasty" is guessed on the third attempt. Green is a letter in the word in its correct position, a Yellow letter is included in the word but is not in its correct posit, and a Black letter is not in the word

meetings, scheduling deliveries, or furnishing a house. In all these tasks, there is always room for learning, adaptation, and improvement for a variety of reasons, e.g., new challenges, uncertain and dynamic environments, changing populations and tastes, newly available techniques, or new competitors.

2.1 Wordle Tasks, Configuration, and Strategy-Execution-Feedback Iterations

The main task in the Wordle game is to correctly solve a word puzzle with minimal trials, subject to the constraints described below. The task can be decomposed into several subtasks, such as offering a candidate word and checking if the candidate word satisfies certain constraints.

The gamer playing Wordle has six attempts to guess the correct five-letter word. In each attempt, the gamer offers a legitimate candidate word. The computer checks the candidate word and provides feedback to the gamer. Each of the five letters is painted in black (to designate a letter that does not appear in the correct word), yellow (to designate a letter that appears in the correct word but in a different position), or green (to designate a letter that appears in the proper position of the correct word). After receiving the feedback, the gamer proceeds to the next attempt. The game has two possible outcomes, namely, success or failure. In success, the gamer finds the correct word by the sixth attempt, and the machine congratulates the gamer according to the number of attempts made, e.g., on the sixth attempt, the feedback is "phew." In failure (the six attempts are exhausted without identifying the correct word), the machine notifies the gamer of the correct word. In both cases, the machine records the new score and adds it to the gamer's game history, which the gamer can easily share with others.

In order to develop my case for a new approach to designing human-AI collaboration, I contrast two extreme configurations: configurations with predefined task delegations and with no learning versus configurations with reciprocal learning and dynamic delegation (for short, non-learning and reciprocal learning, respectively). In the non-learning configuration, the delegation of tasks is predesigned. The (human) gamer delegates certain subtasks to the machine or performs the task (subtask) herself. The machine returns control to the gamer after the delegated task is complete. In the current (non-learning) version of Wordle described above, the gamer chooses a candidate word. The gamer delegates the subtask of computing the feedback to the machine. The machine computes the feedback that informs the gamer of the correctness of the candidate's word. In this case, the subtask of checking the problem-solution (the candidate word) is fully automated, and the human is kept in the loop for control purposes only.

In the reciprocal-learning configuration developed below, both humans and machines engage in problem-solving; importantly, both continue to learn and improve their problem-solving capabilities. For example, once the gamer learns a strategy for determining the first two candidate words (e.g., always first choosing the word "raise" and then "cloud" if the first attempt yields a maximum of one correct letter), the gamer can delegate to the machine the task of choosing the first two words. The machine then chooses, conditionally, the first two words, presents the corresponding feedback, and returns control to the user.

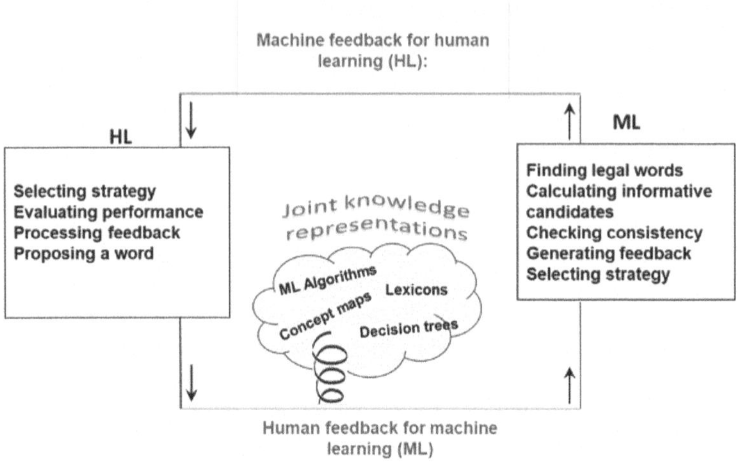

Fig. 2 RHML configuration with its respective allocation of learning tasks in solving a puzzle collaboratively (Source: Proceedings of the ACM)

2.2 Designing Wordle with an RHML Configuration

How do we design the reciprocal human-AI configuration? In the RHML configuration, the user and the machine are delegated tasks that they perform iteratively to offer candidate words until they find the correct word or lose the game after six incorrect guesses (each iteration is a guess, a trial). After each trial and after each game, the user receives feedback that helps to control the game and adjust in real-time, if necessary, but also to learn from the feedback for future games. Reciprocal learning requires a human-AI configuration that supports performance and learning (the theoretical basis depicted in Fig. 2 is expanded in the next section). Figure 2 also shows a specific delegation of learning activities that fits the distinct capabilities of each agent, which, together, are set to solve the puzzle collaboratively. The human gamer (user) is assumed to control the entire game and decide when to delegate specific tasks to the machine. The gamer's dual goal is to solve the puzzle with minimum attempts (performance) and to enjoy the process of playing the game. The process can be seen as a sequence of steps that involve multiple subtasks, such as generating a word candidate, checking whether it is consistent with previous candidates, calculating the information value of a candidate, etc.

Delegation is dynamic. It may depend on the gamer's perception of the game's difficulty. The game's difficulty is set in advance to present an achievable yet interesting challenge to the gamer. The gamers are allowed, at their discretion, to seek help by allocating some tasks to the machine (e.g., calculations) and asking the machine for tips. The gamer decides dynamically on the allocation according to the game's progression, subject to the menu options made available by the designer. For instance, on the first attempt, the gamer chooses a word candidate manually and, according to the machine feedback, chooses a second candidate on the second attempt but has the machine check that it is consistent with the previous (first) candidate.

Delegation begins with a decomposition of the problem-solving process (solving the Wordle puzzle). The designer decomposes the process into elements so that each element can be delegated to the human or the machine. A common decomposition is to break down the process into several steps, such as deciding on a strategy, executing the strategy, studying the feedback, revisiting the selected strategy, and either continuing to execute it or revising the strategy and then executing it. Thus, playing Wordle can be seen as following up to six iterations (trials) in a cycle of strategy-execution-feedback. For example, a strategy may consist of using the first two attempts to find all or most of the vowels that appear or do not appear in the correct word and accordingly suggesting candidate words that maximize the reduction of uncertainty (out of the possible words given the prior attempts). In executing the strategy, the first attempt could begin with a word that includes vowels and, according to the feedback, continue with a second word with different vowels (see first two attempts in Fig. 1). Later, I used the strategy-execution-feedback decomposition to characterize the level of automation according to the steps delegated to the machine.

When one agent controls and performs the entire strategy-execution-feedback sequence, there is no need for coordination. When the human decides on a strategy, and the machine executes the strategy, there is a need for coordination, often enabled by appropriate feedback, to ensure effective performance. For instance, if the strategy becomes ineffective for the new conditions that arise during execution, performance will degrade. In the game represented in Fig. 3, strategy is delegated to the gamer and execution to the machine. After receiving feedback on the first attempt, the gamer switched the strategy from identifying vowels to positioning vowels and consonants, assuming that most of the vowels had been identified so that

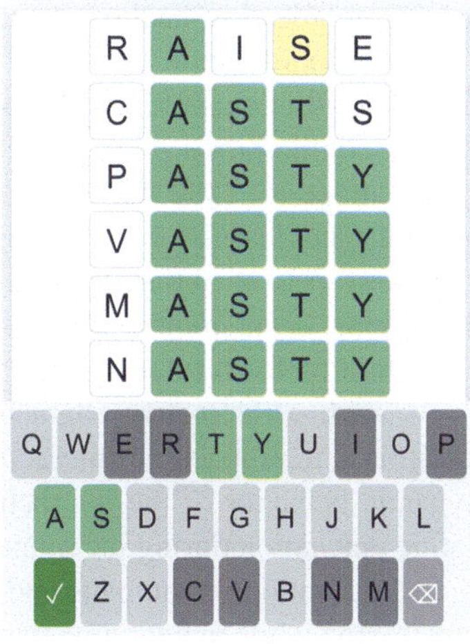

Fig. 3 Inappropriate execution of a strategy results in a failed game (in the lower panel, a Black letter does not appear in the word, light Gray has not been tried, and Green is in the word)

there was no need to use the second attempt to identify further vowels. The machine executes accordingly. The third attempt failed to choose a word that minimized uncertainty, as did the fourth, fifth, and sixth and resulted in a failed game (the correct word TASTY is shown after six attempts). After the second or third attempt, execution becomes ineffective because the strategy is no longer appropriate. A smart machine should be able to control performance according to the feedback and trigger the gamer to change strategy, e.g., to identify the consonant positioned in cell 1. Thus, delegation complicates control and must be designed to avoid coordination errors.

3 Theoretical Background

This section provides the theoretical basis for the RHML configuration and its implications on delegation for the Wordle game. Section 4 uses the RHML configuration and delegation to discuss design issues.

3.1 RHML and New Criteria for Delegation

The configuration for reciprocal human-machine learning is shown in Fig. 2. It is composed of a machine agent, a human agent, feedback loops between the two agents, and a form of shared memory. The configuration supports machine learning and human learning and learning one from another through the feedback loops. The technical design is reported in Zagalsky et al. (2021) and its theoretical basis in Te'eni et al. (2023). The design methodology advocated for the RHML configuration requires two types of analysis. One is the functional analysis, which examines the capabilities of the agents and the delegation of tasks. The other is the communication analysis to determine the requisite communication to ensure effective coordination (e.g., the design of feedback between agents) Suchman (2007). In this chapter, we discuss only the former to examine delegation in the RHML configuration.

Te'eni et al. (2023) develop a scenario in which the RHML configuration performs and learns for a while until the human agent decides learning is saturated and transfers to an automated non-learning configuration. In the non-learning phase, the human agent monitors the machine to decide when to revert to the RHML configuration for further learning and adaptation.

As said, a distinctive characteristic of human-AI interaction, compared with traditional man-machine interaction, is learning, which enables the adaptive and dynamic behavior of the interacting agents. The dynamic behavior requires alternating delegation during the human-AI interaction until task completion.

Configurations of humans and machines must generally ensure effective human functioning while maintaining the advantages offered by automation, yet the specific requirements for a particular configuration are dependent on its underlying rationale and on the goals it aims to achieve (Suchman 2007). In the RHML configuration, which aims to support mutual learning, humans and artificial intelligence are seen as cooperating agents learning and performing jointly (Woods and Hollnagel 2006). One working assumption of RHML is that the cooperating partners have different information-processing capabilities. However, these relative strengths and weaknesses change over time, especially with the rapid progress made in AI. A second related assumption is that human learning and machine learning differ in their learning strategies, which also complicates how one agent can learn from the other. These assumptions suggest that extant methods of allocating learning tasks between humans and machines must be revisited.

Extant methods, going back to the 1950s, aimed to divide labor in a manner that capitalizes on the agents' relative advantages in achieving performance on a focal task (Fitts 1951). Ip et al. (1990) produced "Task Allocation Charts" that first decompose a task into subtasks and then allocate subtasks to the machine or human operators, depending on their relative advantages. In choice problems, for example, given a high volume of options to consider, it may be infeasible to allocate the task to a human expert. However, the task can be broken into subtasks allocated according to the agents' capabilities (Xin et al. 2018; Marcellino et al. 2020). For instance, the expert decides on several very large subsets (categories) of candidate words, commonly in a trial-and-error fashion, and the machine searches exhaustively within the subset, e.g., all five-letter words that contain the sequence of vowels "ea" without the consonants already excluded.

Performance can no longer be the sole criterion for task allocation in intelligent human-AI configurations. New considerations are needed, such as organizational implications(Grønsund and Aanestad 2020), machine autonomy or the degree of automation versus augmentation (Raisch and Krakowski 2020), the contingencies of configurations based on parameters like task complexity and ambiguity (So 2020), and ethical issues such as human discretion (Citron and Pasquale 2014). Keeping the HitL can, therefore, be argued on grounds other than relative advantages in task performance. For instance, humans remain in the loop to control and take responsibility for what comes with control or to supervise the machine's performance to ensure quality and learning.

Of particular interest to our discussion of delegating tasks is control and machine autonomy. HitL can maintain overall control over the human-AI interaction but also enables the transfer of control over certain subtasks to the machine (increasing machine autonomy). If it is to be monitored and manipulated, it should be measurable. Machine autonomy has been studied and measured at length, but one scale stands out, namely, the scale published by Sheridan et al. (1978). The widely quoted scale includes ten levels of machine autonomy, ranging from the lowest level, at which the machine offers no assistance, to the highest level, at which the machine decides everything and acts autonomously. Between these extreme points are intermediate levels of machine autonomy, such as the machine performing certain tasks and informing the human so the human can decide what is next. Recently, Shneiderman (2020) suggested measuring human control separately from machine autonomy rather than having them on the same dimension. In the RHML configuration, control of certain subtasks passes from the human to the machine when moving between two modes of operation, and therefore, it is easier to operationalize control on a single combined scale.

Instead of splitting control into two dimensions as Shneiderman suggests, I propose using one combined scale but differentiating between overall control, which must be decided ahead of the human-AI interaction as a meta-decision, and control of specific subtasks, which can be seen as the ongoing task-allocation decisions made according to the prevailing conditions and agent capabilities. The meta-decision in the non-learning configuration used above with Wordle is to maintain overall control with the human agent, who may delegate control and performance of all subtasks to the machine.

Consider now an advanced reciprocal-learning configuration. The human agent delegates to the machine the control and performance of a subtask that determines the information gain of candidate words and reports back when the subtask is complete. The machine acts as a black box controlling the performance, e.g., the number of cycles activated, and decides when to stop and report back. Increasing or decreasing machine autonomy is a consideration of task allocation in human-AI interaction.

4 Proposed Task Allocation in Human-AI Learning Configurations

4.1 Machine Autonomy Guides Dynamic Delegation

In summary, configuration and delegation govern the design of human-AI collaboration, in our case, for playing Wordle. In the non-learning configuration, the tasks and subtasks are delegated to the machine, but overall control remains with the human, who can decide when to stop the mode and transfer to the reciprocal learning configuration. Metaphorically, the human has the red button to an autonomous machine. In the reciprocal learning configuration, subtasks may be delegated to both humans and machines. The non-learning mode is efficient for training machines with vast amounts of data. The reciprocal learning configuration enables a dynamic delegation of learning tasks in an evolving human-AI interaction in which the game's conditions change continuously. In the dynamic human-AI interaction, delegation affects and is affected by these changes. The respective human-AI configuration must, therefore, be flexible to allow the reallocation of tasks at any moment. For example, faced with a new condition in which the human needs to find a word that begins with the letter "A" and ends with "E" but does not include vowels "O" and "U," the human may decide to delegate the task to the machine.

Given that overall control remains with the human, I use the term machine autonomy to describe control and performance of the subtasks. In developing the

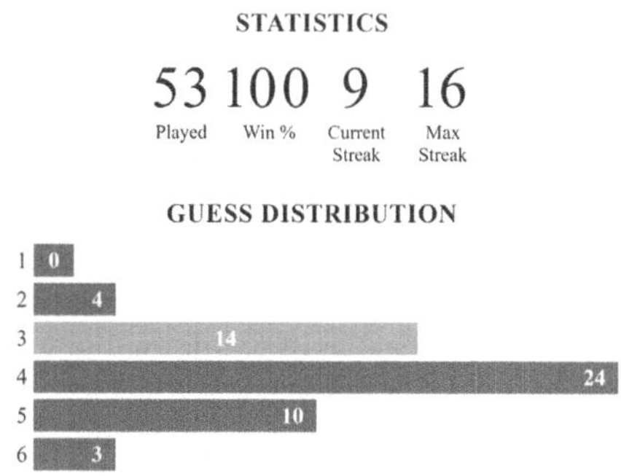

Fig. 4 Machine-generated feedback at the level of a game played

RHML configuration (Zagalsky et al. 2021), my colleagues and I distinguished between the learning activities of each agent and the control and coordination activities between agents. We found that different types of activity called for different considerations for determining the level of desired machine autonomy. Complete machine autonomy means that the human is not in the loop and, therefore, irrelevant to our discussion. Short of complete machine autonomy, it determines the requisite configuration and sets the boundaries of dynamic delegation. It is the first meta-decision in designing human-AI collaboration.

In the reciprocal human-AI configuration, the (human) gamers fully control the game, determine the strategy, and allocate tasks according to their preferences and the progression of the game. At every point of the game, the gamer is assumed to have the information needed in order to decide the next step and, if desired, to reallocate tasks. This information is generated by the machine and fed back to the gamer as the feedback shown in Figs. 1 and 3, which is at the level of a word and letters in the word. The machine-generated feedback can also inform the gamer about performance across the games that are played, as depicted in Fig. 4. The latter information supports learning but is also part of the gamer's personal enjoyment of achievement and satisfaction from sharing achievements friends. Together, the feedback sources in Figs. 1, 3, and 4 serve to enhance performance, learning, and motivation (Te'eni 1992).

Borrowing from Sheridan's rationale for measuring machine autonomy, I define three levels of machine autonomy in the Wordle example according to the strategy-execution-feedback iterative process of playing the game. The first level is the one articulated above. The gamer decides on the strategy (an opening strategy and subsequent strategies according to how the game progresses) and executes the strategy but leaves feedback generation tasks to the machine. For the second level of machine autonomy, the human gamer decides on a strategy, allocates at least some of its tasks to the machine, and lets the machine generate feedback. For example, the gamer selects the strategy, which is first to determine the vowels in the correct word, and the machine is allocated the task of finding the word that is expected, most probably, to detect the maximum number of vowels in the correct word. In the third level of machine autonomy, the human and the machine collaboratively decide on the best strategy at hand, and the machine both executes some of the tasks and generates the feedback.

For the second level of machine autonomy, the question of which tasks to allocate (if at all) for machine execution becomes relevant. For instance, at some stage, the gamer finds it too difficult to proceed without help and turns to the machine for a tip. Allocating all execution to the machine would ruin the enjoyment, but asking for a tip may seem justifiable to the gamer. Alternatively, the gamer may want to present a comprehensive list of words ending with ASTY, from which the gamer can decide how to proceed (as shown in Fig. 4).

4.2 Delegation

The next step is to determine the activities and respective required capabilities of human learning and machine learning in the specific context being considered. This step follows the traditional analysis of the agents' relative advantages in allocating tasks but refers to capabilities to learn and perform. Designers can consider two options. The first is to begin with standard models that have been used to represent human and machine agents and to distinguish between natural and artificial activities and resources (e.g., predictive processing theory). In the RHML project, we chose a second option, in which we selected two distinct problem-solving models, each describing either human or machine-learning activities. For example, we represented human problem-solving activities as sense-making, dialogue, attention management, and perspective-taking, and we represented machine learning activities by processing input, classification models, and performance evaluation.

Given the level of desired autonomy, designers decide on the delegation criteria, simplifying the problem by explicitly omitting other criteria. For instance, designers may establish ethical standards for all activities but omit ethical criteria for allocating tasks and remain with only two criteria: performance and enjoyment. Once the allocation criteria and possible tradeoffs are noted, we proceed to solve the multiple-criteria allocation problem. Our RHML project began with an allocation based on the literature (see the list in step one). We then tested the allocation by trial and error, maximizing performance subject to acceptable interpretability (measured by human learning). More sophisticated methods, such as simulation, could be used (Boyacı et al. 2024).

Even in level 3 of machine autonomy, where strategies are decided collaboratively, human control is considered an essential value in system design (Friedman 1996). Indeed, in games, enjoyment and human control should be design goals (da Rocha Tomé Filho et al. 2019). Nevertheless, the RHML configuration introduces several complications that must be addressed in its design. Reciprocal learning and efficient task allocation assume intelligible communication between humans and machines (Suchman 2007; Te'eni et al. 2023). Smart digitality can enable or support both the allocation of tasks requiring intelligence to the machine and intelligible communication between humans and machines. For instance, a possible division of labor could include the gamer setting a strategy of first identifying which vowels appear in the correct word and then communicating the message to the machine, and consequently, the machine suggesting the best words to implement the strategy. In such a division of labor, the gamer's sense of autonomy would not necessarily decrease because the higher-level decision remains with the human (Kumar and Srinivasan 2014).

A more complex collaboration would be to adapt the machine's algorithm to the human preference on which of the word's five positions to concentrate. Say the gamer wants to resolve positions 4 and 5 in the candidate word and asks the machine to do so. This human preference may conflict with the current practice of most machine algorithms for solving Wordle to operate at the level of reducing uncertainty for the entire word, e.g., Bhambri et al. (2022). The incompatibility between the methods would require challenging algorithms to integrate the two and enable effective communication.

5 Extension to Complexity and Generalization

The analysis above builds on our experience with human-AI configurations for learning reciprocally to classify messages on social media. The RHML set the level of desired machine autonomy to fit the mode of work, but once set, the level of autonomy remained unchanged. In this chapter, I used the Wordle online game to demonstrate the complexities of dynamic task allocations attributed to human-AI collaborations that were not evident in traditional models of task allocation. Human-AI configurations for other tasks, not necessarily learning tasks and not necessarily gaming, should adopt a similar approach to task allocation, albeit with different allocation criteria that nevertheless go beyond performance. When considering different tasks and combinations of allocation criteria beyond the traditional performance allocation criterion, we must remember that the relative advantages of humans versus machines keep changing with the advent of new AI-based technologies.

Practically, I suggest any design of human-AI collaboration should follow three steps, iteratively:

1. Determine the level of machine autonomy.
2. Design the human-machine configuration with its goals and functions.
3. Design the dynamic delegation of tasks to the human and machine.

Te'eni et al. (2023) followed this procedure in developing the RHML configuration. They included a fourth step (not described in this chapter) that analyzes the communication required for coordination between agents.

Our discussion did not treat the issue of interaction complexity in the design and use of human-AI configurations. Complexity is both a product of human-AI collaboration and a determinant of task allocation. The latter effect on task

Fig. 5 Quordle—a highly complex puzzle built as four panels of Wordle combined

allocation is easy to see. Figure 5 shows the end result of a very complex version of Wordle, called Quordle, in which the same candidate word applies to detect simultaneously four distinct correct words. Dealing with higher game complexity (Quordle versus Wordle) shifts the point at which the human gamer will reallocate tasks to the machine. High complexity will drive the gamer to allocate more intensive information processing, e.g., calculations and ranking, to the machine. The reverse effect of human-AI collaboration on complexity is less obvious but crucial for designers. At higher levels of machine autonomy, when keeping humans in the loop, a highly complex interaction is required to maintain effective human-AI coordination and human control. According to Sheridan, this analysis is irrelevant to absolute machine autonomy, which ignores the human. Figure 5 has four panels, each for a distinct correct word (WRYLY, APPLE, SCOUR, and CLUNG).

Figure 6 shows the feedback received during the game. Notice how the feedback from four panels is integrated into one keyboard-like panel that represents the accumulated results across trials about the four correct words for each letter on the keyboard. Compared to the design in Fig. 1, the communication complexity in Fig. 6 is considerably higher (Katz and Te'eni 2014). For example, the little green square for the letter E, in the upper right side of the letter, designates that E appears in APPLE in its correct position but does not appear in the other three

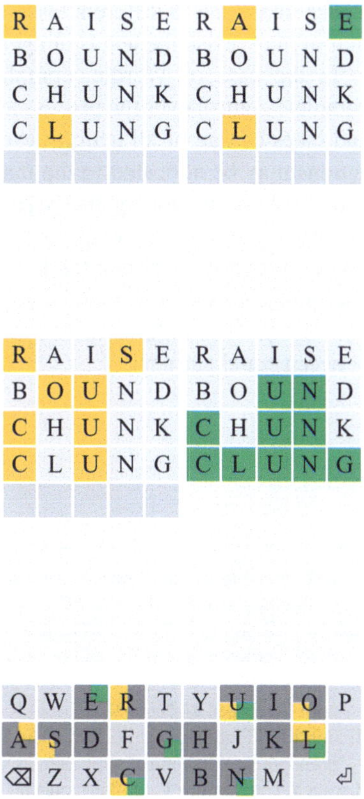

Fig. 6 The process of playing Quordle, in which feedback is integrated from four panels into the bottom keyboard-like panel

words. Future studies of human-AI configurations should explore the two-way link between complexity and task allocation.

Furthermore, future work should consider the level of machine autonomy as a variable that affects task allocation (da Rocha Tomé Filho et al. 2019) but consider it as a variable that other possible criteria, too. This will result in additional complexity but may prove necessary in practice. In playing Wordle, we set the level of autonomy to leave part of the problem-solving activities (strategy, execution, and feedback) to the human to have fun. Fun in other settings cannot be a design goal (e.g., providing medical treatment), while ethical considerations could.

Task delegation should be studied as part of human-AI configurations' more general agency issue (Tholander et al. 2012). For agency, we ask who governs, initiates, controls, and is responsible for the process and its subprocesses. Agency can be characterized on a continuum according to the latitude of decision-making granted to the agent, e.g., Baird and Maruping (2021). Unlike current practice in human-computer interaction, task allocation between humans and computers must be preceded by the meta-decision that determines agency. This is not to suggest that this is a fixed sequence. On the contrary, as demonstrated above, different levels of agency may lead to different task allocations at different stages of the game, which in turn may revise the levels of agency.

In the case of Wordle, complete human autonomy is when the gamer has complete control over the process and subprocesses so that the gamer alone initiates and takes charge of all actions, even though the execution of the gamer's planned actions may be allocated to the machine. An autonomous machine acts as its own agent. An autonomous gamer would play the online game alone. In between these extreme cases are many combinations of human-AI configurations (Suchman 2007), often referred to as "Keep the Human in the Loop" (Holzinger et al. 2021). These configurations call for a shift away from the metaphor of the computer as a tool to a metaphor of collaboration between humans and machines, but not necessarily between equal partners.

References

Ågerfalk PJ, Conboy K, Crowston K, Eriksson Lundström JS, Jarvenpaa S, Ram S, Mikalef P (2022) Artificial intelligence in information systems: state of the art and research roadmap. Commun Assoc Inform Syst 50

Baird A, Maruping LM (2021) The next generation of research on is use: a theoretical framework of delegation to and from agentic is artifacts. MIS Q 45(1)

Bertsimas D, Paskov A (2022) An exact and interpretable solution to wordle. https://www.example.com. Accessed 14 Nov 2022

Bhambri S, Bhattacharjee A, Bertsekas D (2022) Reinforcement learning methods for wordle: a pomdp/adaptive control approach. arXiv preprint arXiv:221110298

Boyacı T, Canyakmaz C, de Véricourt F (2024) Human and machine: the impact of machine input on decision making under cognitive limitations. Manag Sci 70(2):1258–1275

Citron DK, Pasquale F (2014) The scored society: due process for automated predictions. Wash L Rev 89:1

Drory I, Te'eni D (2024) Human-in-the-loop ai reviewing—feasibility, opportunities and risks. J Assoc Inform Syst 25(1):98–109. https://doi.org/10.17705/1jais.00867

Fitts PM (1951) Human engineering for an effective air-navigation and traffic-control system. NRC Committee on Aviation Psychology

Friedman B (1996) Value-sensitive design. Interactions 3(6):16–23

Grønsund T, Aanestad M (2020) Augmenting the algorithm: emerging human-in-the-loop work configurations. J Strategic Inform Syst 29(2):101614

Holzinger A, Valdez AC, Ziefle M (2016) Towards interactive recommender systems with the doctor-in-the-loop. In: Mensch und Computer 2016–Workshopband

Holzinger A, Weippl E, Tjoa AM, Kieseberg P (2021) Digital transformation for sustainable development goals (SDGs)—a security, safety and privacy perspective on ai. In: International cross-domain conference for machine learning and knowledge extraction. Springer, Cham, pp 1–20

Ip W, Damodaran L, Olphert CW, Maguire MC (1990) The use of task allocation charts in system design: a critical appraisal. In: Proceedings of the IFIP TC13 third international conference on human-computer interaction, North-Holland Publishing, Amsterdam, pp 289–294

Katz A, Te'eni D (2014) The role of communication complexity in adaptive contextualization. IEEE Trans Professional Commun 57(2):98–112

Kumar D, Srinivasan N (2014) Naturalizing sense of agency with a hierarchical event-control approach. PLoS One 9(3):e92431

Liu CL (2022) Using wordle for learning to design and compare strategies. In: 2022 IEEE conference on games (CoG). IEEE, Piscataway, pp 465–472

Marcellino W, Johnson C, Posard MN, Helmus TC (2020) Foreign interference in the 2020 election: tools for detecting online election interference

Raisch S, Krakowski S (2020) Artificial intelligence and management: the automation—augmentation paradox. Acad Manag Rev 46(1):192–210

da Rocha Tomé Filho F, Mirza-Babaei P, Kapralos B, Moreira Mendonça Junior G (2019) Let's play together: adaptation guidelines of board games for players with visual impairment. In: Proceedings of the 2019 CHI conference on human factors in computing systems, pp 1–15

Seeber I, Bittner E, Briggs RO, De Vreede T, De Vreede GJ, Elkins A, Söllner M (2020) Machines as teammates: a research agenda on ai in team collaboration. Inform Manag 57(2):103174

Sheridan TB, Verplank WL, Brooks TL (1978) Human/computer control of undersea teleoperators. In: NASA. Ames Res. Center the 14th annual conference on manual control

Shneiderman B (2020) Human-centered artificial intelligence: reliable, safe & trustworthy. Int J Hum-Comput Interact 36(6):495–504

So C (2020) Human-in-the-loop design cycles—a process framework that integrates design sprints, agile processes, and machine learning with humans. In: Artificial intelligence in HCI: first international conference, AI-HCI 2020, held as part of the 22nd HCI international conference, HCII 2020, Copenhagen, Denmark, July 19–24, 2020, Proceedings 22. Springer, Cham, pp 136–145

Suchman LA (2007) Human-machine reconfigurations: plans and situated actions. Cambridge University Press, Cambridge

Te'eni D (1992) Analysis and design of process feedback in information systems: old and new wine in new bottles. Account Manag Inform Technol 2(1):1–18

Te'eni D, Yahav I, Zagalsky A, Schwartz DG, Silverman G, Cohen D, Mann Y, Lewinsky D (2023) Human-machine learning: a theory and an instantiation for the case of message classification. Manag Sci

Tholander J, Normark M, Rossitto C (2012) Understanding agency in interaction design materials. In: Proceedings of the SIGCHI conference on human factors in computing systems, pp 2499–2508

Woods DD, Hollnagel E (2006) Joint cognitive systems: patterns in cognitive systems engineering. CRC Press, Boca Raton

Xin D, Ma L, Liu J, Macke S, Song S, Parameswaran A (2018) Accelerating human-in-the-loop machine learning: challenges and opportunities. In: Proceedings of the second workshop on data management for end-to-end machine learning, pp 1–4

Zagalsky A, Te'eni D, Yahav I, Schwartz DG, Silverman G, Cohen D, Lewinsky D (2021) The design of reciprocal learning between human and artificial intelligence. Proc ACM Hum-Comput Interact 5(CSCW2):1–36

Understanding Artificial Intelligence as Persuasive Technologies in the Workplace: Improving Effectiveness, Ethicality, and Empowerment

Elisavet Averkiadi and Wietske Van Osch

Abstract This chapter leverages persuasion and persuasive technology frameworks as a lens for understanding the design and use of artificial intelligence (AI) in the workplace. Many AI tools implemented in workplace settings aim to influence employee users' decision-making, actions, and goal orientation. Using persuasion as a lens for conceptualizing the effect of AI on user behaviors promises to improve the potential effectiveness and ethicality with which AI can influence employee user actions and could inform and empower users to understand the nuances of their interactions with such technologies in workplace settings, where their use is increasingly prevalent and often mandated. Specifically, it allows us to delineate three desired outcomes for AI in workplace settings and map these outcomes to persuasive AI system features that could guide the design of AI tools for the workplace that are effective while at the same time being ethical and empowering.

1 Introduction

Artificial intelligence (AI) technologies have proliferated in workplace settings to increase the efficiency and effectiveness of tasks traditionally done by humans, such as decision-making and, increasingly, creativity. How some AI technologies influence people's behaviors is ill-understood and might be akin to persuasion, a process traditionally considered in social interactions, where one human persuades another human. This chapter leverages perspectives of human persuasion to inform organizations' decision-making surrounding the implementation and use of inherently persuasive AI tools and to inform the potential effectiveness of workplace persuasive AI technologies. Additionally, this chapter aims to offer guidance for

E. Averkiadi (✉)
Michigan State University, East Lansing, MI, USA
e-mail: averkiad@msu.edu

W. Van Osch
HEC Montreal, Montreal, QC, Canada
e-mail: wietske.van-osch@hec.ca

C. K. Coursaris et al. (eds.), *The Design of Human-Centered Artificial Intelligence for the Workplace*, Progress in IS, https://doi.org/10.1007/978-3-031-83512-4_12

creating AI technologies that are ethical and focused on empowering users in workplace settings by demystifying their inconspicuous influence. Although this is relevant regardless of context, we argue that workplace settings amplify the importance of developing an in-depth understanding of AI-infused technologies' persuasive abilities, given that the use of these technologies and systems in the workplace is increasingly prevalent and often mandated.

This chapter will begin with exploring the conceptual origins of persuasion in social psychology. Subsequently, the theoretical foundations of persuasive technologies are explored, particularly regarding their study and design. Combining these theoretical insights, we introduce the emerging concept of persuasive AI and propose a framework encompassing desired outcomes and system features of persuasive AI technologies for the workplace. Finally, we provide two mini cases to illustrate the practical applicability of the proposed framework of persuasive AI outcomes and system features and the relation between them.

2 Theoretical Background

2.1 The Concept of Persuasion

Persuasion is a topic that has received considerable attention within the disciplines of communication and social psychology. Persuasion is a communication process between two parties: the persuader and the persuadee (i.e., the party being persuaded). Persuasion can be a one-to-one communication process or a one-to-many communication process. The persuader communicates with the persuadee to influence their mental state—attitude, behavior, or both. A commonly used definition describes persuasion as: "[...] a successful intentional effort at influencing another's mental state through communication in a circumstance in which the persuadee has some measure of freedom" (O'Keefe 2015, p. 4). This definition encompasses five important elements, namely (1) a successful attempt to influence, (2) the intention to influence, (3) volitional action (i.e., freedom) is available to the persuadee, (4) persuasion occurs through communication, and (5) a change in attitude or behavior must be the result of the persuasive attempt (i.e., a change in the mental state of the persuadee).

2.2 The Concept of Persuasive Technology

Persuasive technology (PT) refers to a class of technologies designed with the purpose of influencing their users' attitudes or behavior, or both. PT is defined as "computerized software or information systems designed to reinforce, change or shape attitudes or behaviors or both without using coercion or deception"

(Oinas-Kukkonen and Harjumaa 2008, p. 486). The definition of persuasion in social psychology highlights the importance of the intent to persuade (O'Keefe 2015). Persuasive technology similarly requires the ingredient of intention in the process of persuasion by technology, i.e., changing user attitudes or behaviors. However, machines do not have intentions—at least this was the case at the time of conceptualization of PT—and, thus, the accountability of the intention to persuade with computers is placed on the creators, distributors, and those who employ technology for its persuasive capabilities (Fogg 1998).

2.2.1 A Framework for the Study and Design of Persuasive Technology

Scholars researching PT have developed a framework for studying and designing PT (Oinas-Kukkonen and Harjumaa 2008). The PT framework explained in this chapter translates design principles to software requirements and system features. Linking design principles, software requirements, and system features offers a systematic approach to studying and designing PTs. A systematic approach is important because it allows practitioners, designers, and researchers alike to realize and actualize a PT's qualities, which are integral to its persuasiveness (Oinas-Kukkonen and Harjumaa 2008). The categories of system features in the framework include "primary task support," "dialogue support," "system credibility support," and "social support" (Table 1) (Oinas-Kukkonen and Harjumaa 2008).

2.3 Persuasion in the Context of AI

Persuasive technology and persuasive AI technologies possess important differences that distinguish the experience for users with either technology. Persuasive technology that does not include an AI has a predetermined user experience, with customization decided by the creators, designers, and distributors of the technology. In contrast, persuasive AI technology will include a personalized and customized experience for users, dictated by user behavior history, and "persuasion

Table 1 PT system features, summarized and adapted from Oinas-Kukkonen and Harjumaa (2008)

System feature	Definition
Primary task support	The system is designed to support the users' primary tasks.
Dialogue support	The system is designed with computer-human dialogue support to support users progressing toward goals (i.e., target behaviors or attitudes).
System credibility support	The system is designed to be more credible and, consequently, more persuasive.
Social support	The system is designed to leverage social influence.

profiles"(Kaptein and Eckles 2010), with little to no involvement of creators, designers, or distributor's dictation of the experience beyond the initial desired objective of the technology's utility and value. Moreover, persuasive AI technologies include a human-AI dialogue that offers an interactive dimension to the persuasion process. Whether or not an AI's presence is obvious or ambiguous to the user, the interactive dimension of an AI component in the technology distinguishes the user experience from technologies that lack such a component. The importance placed on volitional action and informed consent in the process of persuasion allows us to examine AI technologies in the workplace with a critical lens for upholding a principle of ethical persuasive AI design.

Artificial intelligence technologies have all the necessary tools to persuade humans. For example, behavior feedback systems hosted within workplace technology tools offer feedback on past behavior and suggestions to act on intended target behaviors that benefit employees and their organization. PT scholarship highlights that by using the "ability to manage and make use of huge volumes of data," it is possible that such technologies could produce "personalized 'persuasion profiles,' which contain information about the types of influences an individual is especially susceptible to and under what circumstances" (Fogg 1998; Kaptein and Eckles 2010; Smids 2012).

Research in human interaction with robots, chatbots, or intelligent agents (Kim and Duhachek 2020; Siegel et al. 2009) has demonstrated the persuasive abilities of AI technologies. Still, there is more to how AI technologies persuade users to change behaviors or attitudes that warrants investigation, especially in the context of workplace AI technologies. Workplace AI technologies are often employed to leverage people analytics, i.e., digesting user information and behavioral history, to encourage behavioral or attitudinal changes in employees that benefit them and the organization at large. Furthermore, AI use in workplace settings is often mandated, thus amplifying the importance of developing an in-depth understanding of the persuasive abilities of AI. Thus far, frameworks and theoretical models for studying AI have begun to emerge. However, they have rarely been studied in workplace settings or applied practically, particularly for improving our understanding of persuasive interactions of AI technologies with workplace users (i.e., employees).

2.4 AI in the Workplace

From a macro perspective, research has explored various dimensions of AI's impact on organizations and the workplace, including human-AI collaboration, perceptions and comparisons of human vs. AI capabilities, worker perspectives on AI, the use of AI for monitoring worker activity, and AI's impact on the labor market (Bankins et al. 2024). At times referred to as a "4th industrial revolution," AI has reconfigured the process of work—and, by extension, the workplace in general (Bankins et al. 2024). Research suggests that AI has a pivotal role in growth as it may impact organizational performance (Wamba-Taguimdje et al. 2020).

According to recent research, AI serves as a fundamental driver of organizational growth, enhancing operational efficiency across various functions (Wamba-Taguimdje et al. 2020), including operations, maintenance, and supply chain processes, leading to improved customer experiences and product/service enhancements. Additionally, AI enables organizations to swiftly adapt to changing market conditions, fostering the creation of new business models, and optimizing supply-demand relationships through better forecasting and planning. It also aids in fraud detection, automates threat intelligence and information systems, and streamlines IT functions and sales processes.

From a micro perspective, the impact of AI adoption within workplace contexts can have a multitude of consequences. For example, within human resource (HR) work processes (Pereira et al. 2023), AI has demonstrated its capacity to improve recruitment and selection and task execution, foster employee cooperation, improve overall performance, boost productivity, and mitigate turnover rates. Furthermore, AI could improve performance management by enhancing employee performance, productivity, problem-solving effectiveness, motivation, and overall job satisfaction. Additionally, in the domain of employee and labor relations, AI impacts work by influencing communication effectiveness, cooperation levels, relationship building, and interpersonal dynamics within organizations. In recruitment and selection processes, AI-driven interventions have been associated with improvements in employee performance and productivity, as well as influencing the employment process by improving recruitment and selection.

2.4.1 Persuasive AI in the Workplace

AI in workplace technologies that act as persuaders aim to influence users' decision-making, actions, and goal orientation. AI applications found in workplace technologies may be inconspicuous, as the AI components are often discreetly interacting behind user interfaces that do not trigger awareness of their presence. For example, it is likely that a user of a behavior feedback system is not aware of an AI component driving the feedback they are exposed to. However, the transparency of AI—not only in terms of revealing the underlying information that drives suggestions or recommendations but also in the sense of creating awareness that a technology is in fact AI-based—can differ between jobs and tasks. Our chapter aims to add specificity to how persuasive AI technologies in the workplace require consideration for the outcomes of human-AI interactions, considering issues of volition, effectiveness, and intentions to influence users. Jobs and tasks call for unique levels of transparency. Mediating the uncertainty for how AI technologies come to conclusions that users utilize to support their decision-making is of paramount importance. Additionally, this builds a case for organizations to consider how the persuasive AI technologies they mandate for use may impact employees, and for designers and product managers of such AI to carefully assess the technologies they build.

3 Desired Outcomes and System Features for Persuasive AI in the Workplace

In what follows, we outline the desired outcomes and system features of persuasive AI technologies in the workplace. An overview is provided in Table 2.

3.1 Desired Outcomes for Persuasive AI in the Workplace

By adopting persuasive AI technologies, organizations have certain goals they wish to achieve and certain consequences they wish to realize. Based on research that has identified needs and consequences of AI adoption in the workplace (Pereira et al. 2023; Wamba-Taguimdje et al. 2020), we identify three desired outcomes of persuasive AI adoption for a workplace context: effectiveness, ethicality, and employee empowerment. These outcomes are categorized in a way that allows designers and product managers to take into consideration the feasibility for users (i.e., employees) to achieve business goals (i.e., effectiveness), the ethicality of the approach to persuading employees, and the empowerment of informed use of these tools. Each desired outcome cascades into the next; effectiveness relates to the empowerment of users, which is in turn related to the ethicality of the persuasive AI tool organizations choose to employ or design and build. However, these desired outcomes do not necessitate an ordinal approach in implementation or design of features. Additionally, these outcomes are high-level principles that could

Table 2 Desired outcomes

Desired Outcome	Description	Process
Effectiveness	Organizations adopt persuasive AI technologies to improve the effectiveness of workplace actions taken by employees (i.e., users of the system).	Helping users learn from past behaviors, forecast future outcomes, and assist in optimizing decision-making.
Empowerment	User awareness and literacy of the workplace AI tool's attempts to influence their actions to enhance capabilities in completing goals and tasks.	Amplify the autonomy of employees and enhance their capabilities and competencies through informed use of persuasive AI tools. Safeguard employees' control over technology.
Ethicality	Ensure that the outcomes of AI's persuasion are achieved ethically using such technologies. Users are afforded informed volitional action.	Employees have the option to voluntarily select an action to take. Organizations carefully select a workplace persuasive AI tool that minimizes trade-offs of algorithmic optimization, and that are absent of bias and discrimination.

be flexibly applied on a case-by-case basis to satisfy the needs and interests of a specific organization employing an intended persuasive AI.

3.1.1 Effectiveness

Organizations adopt persuasive AI technologies to improve the effectiveness of workplace actions taken by employees (i.e., users of the system). Such a desired outcome involves the AI's persuasion of the user to alter their behavior that directly impacts the success of the task. Examples of effectiveness could include reducing the error rate in manufacturing, amplifying the creativity of employees working on solving client problems, or designing new products, services, and solutions. PT's inherent objective to elicit specific desired actions and behaviors and the intentional development of AI to improve human tasks can be great advantages in increasing the effectiveness of employees. Organizations can support changes in employee behavior that otherwise would be challenging to elicit. For example, it can be a challenge to bridge information silos within large organizations. With persuasive AI, employees could effectively explore information repositories across the organization and be influenced to explore new areas they would otherwise not be aware of or interested in exploring. By helping users learn from past behaviors, forecast future outcomes, and optimize decision-making, persuasive AI technologies in the workplace can enhance effectiveness.

3.1.2 Empowerment

An outcome of user empowerment in this chapter refers to user awareness and literacy of the workplace AI tool's attempts to influence their actions to enhance their capabilities in completing goals and tasks. By designing technology as a persuasive technology, users should inherently be afforded informed volitional action. This could be achieved in two ways. First, persuasive AI tools can amplify the autonomy of employees and enhance their capabilities and competencies by providing them with insights to learn from their past actions and how these insights are computed. User empowerment involves an increased employee confidence and preparation in their use of persuasive AI tools to effectively perform their tasks. Second, by automating mundane tasks, persuasive AI tools can enhance employees' mental capacity to focus on value-adding tasks. For instance, workplace persuasive AI tools can help deepen relationships with others inside and outside the organization by encouraging and suggesting new connections or inspiring new ideas. Such automation and optimization of cognitive resources can further boost the confidence users experience when interacting with AI from the successful or impactful outcomes as a result of these interactions. Positive experiences can help improve users' confidence in their use of these persuasive AI tools.

3.1.3 Ethicality

To mitigate unintended consequences of the use of persuasive AI technologies in the workplace, it should be ensured that the outcomes are achieved ethically. This has two components. First, employees of an organization that use a persuasive AI workplace tool should have the option to voluntarily select an action to take. This may present itself, for example, as the employee deciding to either follow an AI recommendation, decide a different action on their own, or choose a hybrid solution—essentially having the option to forego AI recommendations and influence altogether. Second, the accuracy and reliability of the information AI communicates to employees should be verified and considered. Recent times have been abundant with examples of biased or discriminatory outcomes that are the result of AI technologies used by organizations. For example, Amazon's recruitment algorithm was flagged for penalizing applications that contained the word "women's" (Vincent 2018). Hence, it is of critical importance for organizations to emphasize ethicality as a desired outcome. This would minimize unintended consequences of AI that may stem from the "black box" nature of algorithms or the myopic optimization for singular objectives at the expense of other objectives. For instance, using a navigation tool that chooses a route based on time efficiency (i.e., fastest) might choose a route that is longer and thus would not be the most fuel-efficient route. Algorithmic optimization will always involve trade-offs between different outcomes.

3.2 System Features of Persuasive AI in the Workplace

Building on the framework for the study and design of PTs presented earlier in this chapter, we adapt the four system features in the context of workplace persuasive AI categories which include primary workplace task, human-persuasive AI dialogue, persuasive AI credibility, and AI social influence.

Persuasive AI technology is designed to support the users' primary workplace task by reducing obstacles that may limit performing target behaviors. To achieve this goal, persuasive AI in the workplace may be designed to personalize information or services to employees and their roles in the organization (e.g., a manager's team insight dashboard), by tracking past behaviors or providing insights for future helpful intentions, or by affording employees opportunities to practice target behaviors in ways that benefit the organization.

Persuasive AI technology is designed with agent-human dialogue support to provide employees with feedback on their progress toward workplace goals (i.e., target behaviors or attitudes). Such persuasive dialogue support can manifest as the AI offering praise to the user for performing target behaviors, reminders that optimize employee beneficial behaviors, or the AI taking a social role where the user can make an easier connection with the AI to progress toward agreed-upon objectives.

Persuasive AI technology is designed to be more credible and consequently more persuasive. The persuasive AI technology can provide employees with information that is accurate and trustworthy or with the means to verify information provided through third-party sources. Furthermore, persuasive AI can display expertise with information associated with employees' roles within the organization, making it more persuasive toward employees performing target behaviors.

Persuasive AI technology is also designed to leverage social influence. This could be actualized through design features that enable employees to observe other employees performing target behaviors or evidence of outcomes from target behaviors. These observations can facilitate normative influence through connecting multiple employees with the same goals, or opportunities for recognition of employees who perform target behaviors publicly.

3.2.1 The Intended Effects of Persuasive AI System Features on Desired Outcomes

By integrating the above components, features of a workplace tool that includes a persuasive AI component can be mapped to the desired outcomes described. How a persuasive AI is involved in supporting employees in performing, learning, or reinforcing target behaviors is explained in the descriptions that follows. Examples of target behaviors include—but are not limited to—scheduling meetings with specific time limits, engaging in warm interactions with customers, or even improving time management on daily work tasks. The intended effects of persuasive AI features on desired outcomes are generalized and are meant to be adapted on a case-by-case basis. Figures 1, 2, 3, and 4 describe the links between each feature category and the three proposed desired outcomes.

Primary Workplace Task Persuasive AI in the workplace that includes features supporting employees' primary workplace task(s) can lead to effectiveness in a few ways. Friction points or obstacles that limit employees performing a target behavior can be reduced by implementing features in the persuasive AI tool that handles routine or repetitive tasks. The persuasive AI may also guide employees through behavior change while continuously influencing and encouraging employees to engage in the target behavior. By personalizing and tailoring the information communicated to employees, persuasive AI may enhance its effectiveness in persuading and could improve the relevance of information. Persuasive AI features that tackle supporting employees' primary workplace task(s) can empower employees by showing their progress or providing opportunities to practice a target behavior and receive feedback. To ensure ethicality is an outcome, persuasive AI in the workplace could display links between behaviors encouraged by the AI and the outcome of the behaviors related to the employee's primary task(s). Additionally, workplace tools that include a persuasive AI component could enable employees to maintain control of task(s) by having a clear option to opt out of or adapt recommendations and suggestions by the AI as they see fit.

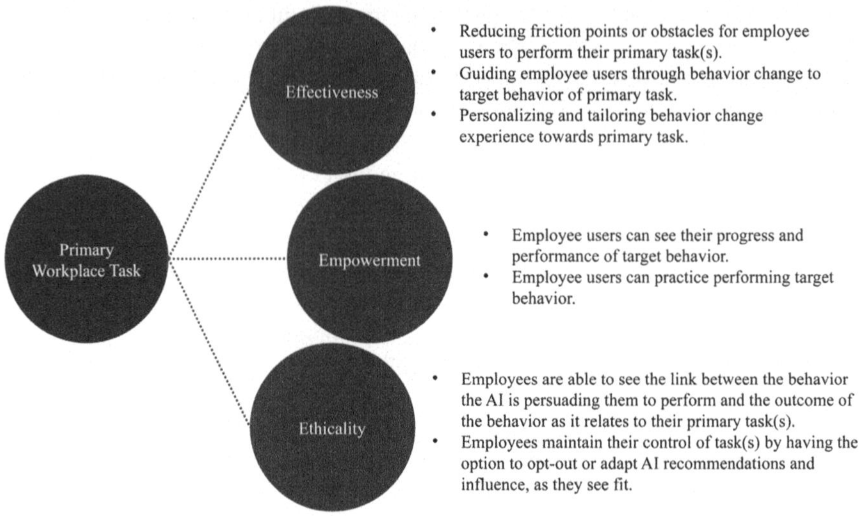

Fig. 1 Primary workplace task features as desired outcomes

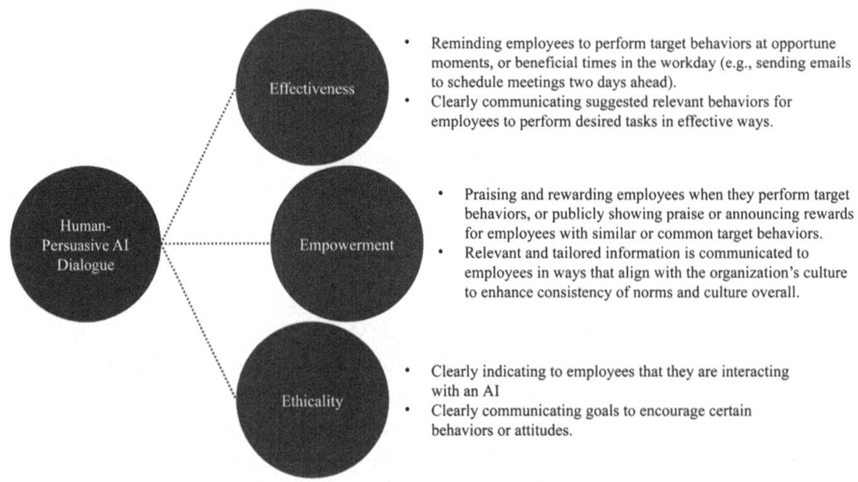

Fig. 2 Human-persuasive AI dialogue features as desired outcomes

Human-Persuasive AI Dialogue Persuasive AI tools may feature human-AI dialogue that leads to the three desired outcomes in the following ways. To achieve effectiveness, the persuasive AI component of a workplace tool could remind employees to perform target behaviors at opportune moments or beneficial times in the workday (e.g., sending an email to schedule meetings at least 2 days ahead). To further support effectiveness through human-persuasive AI dialogue, the persuasive AI component could communicate suggested relevant behaviors for employees to

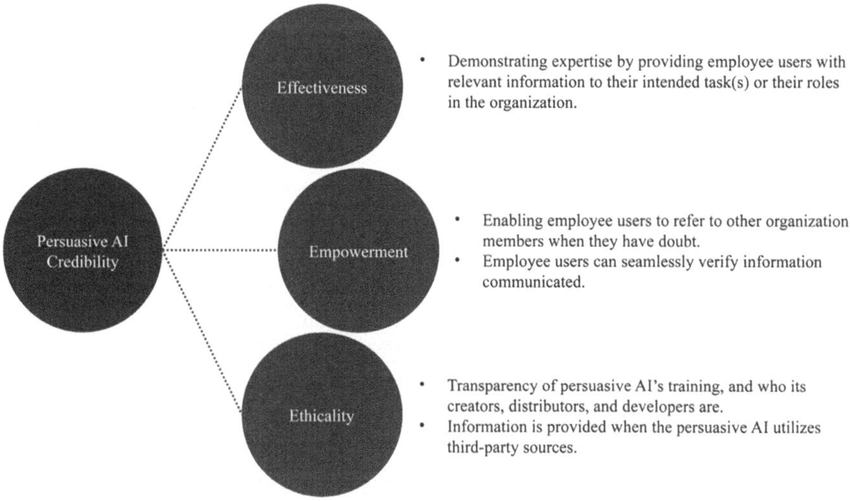

Fig. 3 Persuasive AI credibility features as desired outcomes

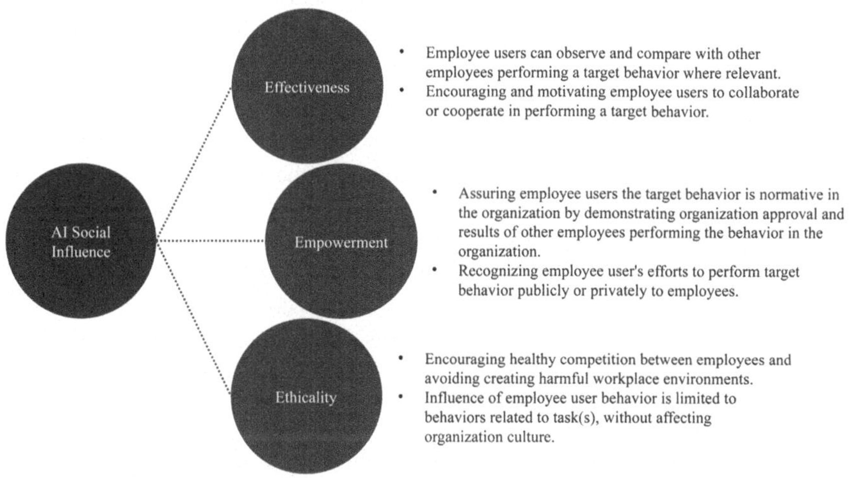

Fig. 4 AI social influence features as desired outcomes

perform desired tasks effectively, e.g., preparing a meeting agenda to be sent in an email requesting a meeting to be scheduled. To empower employees through human-persuasive AI dialogue features, the system could praise and reward employees when they perform target behaviors publicly (on a message board) or privately (directly to the employee). This may also be implemented by announcing rewards for employees with similar or common target behaviors. To further facilitate the empowerment of employees in their use of persuasive AI, relevant and tailored information could be communicated to employees in ways that align with the organization's culture to enhance the consistency of norms and culture overall. In features that support human-persuasive AI dialogue, the workplace tool may potentially achieve ethicality by clearly indicating to employees that they are interacting with an AI and communicating the AI's goals to encourage employees to engage in certain behaviors or attitudes.

Persuasive AI Credibility Features of a persuasive AI's credibility could include expertise in an employee user's task(s) or role duties within the organization, leading to effectiveness as an outcome. The persuasive AI component may do this by providing relevant information or demonstrating its ability to follow the context of a task or responsibility assigned to an employee within the organization. Credibility of the persuasive AI component may also lead to employee user empowerment by providing options for employees to refer to other employees or members of the organization when uncertain or need further verification of the information AI communicates. The ability to discuss AI recommendations and suggestions with other employees reinforces the credibility of the persuasive AI. To achieve ethicality, the persuasive AI features that pertain to its credibility should also include information that describes the AI's training, who its creators or distributors are, and overall provide transparency of its making. Additionally, if the persuasive AI component utilizes a third-party service, this should be clearly stated to the employee user.

AI Social Influence Features of the workplace tool that includes a persuasive AI component may involve a social influence approach. To achieve effectiveness through these features, employee users should have the ability and opportunity to observe and compare with other users with similar or common goals for their target behaviors. In addition, the AI should encourage and motivate employee users to collaborate or cooperate in performing a target behavior. To empower employees, the persuasive AI component's features that utilize social influence should provide assurance and validation of the normative nature of performing the target behavior. This can be done by utilizing evidence of organizational culture to encourage the behavior, endorsing the performance of the target behavior from superiors and peers within the organization, or providing anonymized results of other employees who have performed the target behavior. Empowering employees using the persuasive AI components' social influence features could also be achieved by providing recognition of employee efforts to perform target behavior, either publicly or privately. To achieve ethicality, social influence features of the persuasive AI component should only encourage healthy competition between employees and steer clear of building toxic workplace environments. Furthermore, the social influence of employee behaviors should be limited to workplace-related task(s) rather than altering an organization's culture to ensure that the organization is still in control of dictating and navigating what is best for its members.

3.2.2 Example Scenarios

To further illustrate how the proposed persuasive AI features map to the proposed desired outcomes, two example scenarios are explored in this section. Each scenario is contrasted to a human-to-human interaction scenario to articulate how persuasion may differ in a human-AI interaction scenario in the workplace. This contrast also highlights the benefits of utilizing AI as a persuader in the workplace. The first scenario describes a use-case for persuasive AI influencing employee users to be more personable and coaching them to uphold harmonious collaborations with other employees on a team chat. The second scenario describes a use-case for persuasive AI influencing employee behaviors throughout their workweek, where they may take small actions that help shorten meeting times or reduce the need for meetings. These scenarios are only examples of where the persuasive AI features may map to desired outcomes. The features and desired outcomes proposed in this chapter are encouraged to be adapted appropriately on a case-by-case basis.

Improving Interpersonal Skills A persuasive AI embedded in a workplace tool could help encourage employees to improve their interpersonal skills and potentially improve group work within the organization. In this scenario, primary workplace task(s) may include sending follow-up emails after meetings, sending meeting summary documents to attendees once a meeting concludes, or improving meeting communication skills. Human-persuasive AI dialogue may include reminders to employee users at opportune moments to prepare follow-up emails after meetings, suggesting employee users put together meeting summary documents for meeting attendees to keep record of meeting activity, or praising employee users for performing a behavior that is relevant to improving interpersonal skills. Persuasive AI credibility could be indicated by the persuasive AI component by adapting recommendations to an employee's role. For example, if an employee is a team supervisor, the AI may suggest specific language that is appropriate for their position in the team. A persuasive AI in this scenario may leverage social influence by recognizing an employee user's efforts to improve interpersonal skills by labeling a badge next to their profile on an enterprise social media platform or providing feedback with the assurance of their interpersonal behavior being aligned to the organization's culture. For example, if the organization highlights friendliness and openness in their culture, the persuasive AI may communicate positive feedback when an employee user sends a friendly message or contributes an open idea to their team. These features and functions of a persuasive AI component may improve interpersonal skills by performing target behaviors, empowering employee users to continue performing behaviors through validation of organizational culture norms, and ethically influencing employee user behavior within the bounds of work-relevant behaviors without affecting the organization's culture. In a human-to-human context, a manager would provide such feedback in an annual review meeting with an employee. The feedback may be generalized to the employee's performance within the past year and may pass over the context of the employee's interactions with others.

Shorten Meeting Time or Need for Meetings Due to AI's ability to observe employee user behavior in all corners of a workplace tool, AI could potentially persuade employees to alter their behavior pertaining to scheduling meetings or conducting meetings. In supporting employee user primary task(s) in this scenario, the persuasive AI may suggest ideal meeting times for meetings that require more cognitive capacity, for example. This may be presented as either behavior analytics, mapping the employee user's productive times or ideal times for productive meetings based on previous activity, or by citing relevant research findings suggesting ideal meeting times or schedules for productive and meaningful meetings. Human-persuasive AI dialogue in this scenario would involve regular communication from the AI in the form of pop-up text bubbles or in-line recommendations in email text, recommending actions that support the employee user's target behavior (i.e., shortening meeting times or reducing the need for meetings). This can be displayed as a suggestion to put together an email with a weekly update on their work progress to replace a weekly meeting with a team member, or creating and providing a meeting agenda document before sending an email requesting a meeting with a team. Persuasive AI credibility in this scenario could be exhibited by the AI through clear citations of third-party sources that are utilized to recommend appropriate actions to employee users pertaining to shortening meeting times or reducing the need for meetings. By displaying the results of other anonymized employees who have implemented recommended actions for shortening meeting times or reducing the need for meetings, the persuasive AI could utilize social influence to encourage the employee user to engage in these actions and adopt these behaviors to achieve such results. Such features may lead to employee users make more efficient use of their workday, empowering them to allocate their time to meetings and work tasks differently, and ethically providing them with recommendations for actions using evidence-based suggestions.

In a human-to-human interaction context, employees may not receive feedback about the time they allocate to meetings or may not have the means to be aware of how their time is allocated between meetings and work tasks. When feedback is provided, it may not be followed with specific recommended actions. Instead, it may be communicated as a need to shorten meeting time or reduce the need for meetings.

4 Discussion

Within the last two decades, the implementation of artificial intelligence in workplace technologies has proliferated. Artificial intelligence technologies could enhance the inherent persuasive ability of the technologies they are implemented in, that is, the ability to influence human attitudes and behaviors. The notion of persuasion has a long history in social psychology and has been used in past human-computer interaction research to inform the study and design of persuasive technologies before the advent of artificial intelligence. In this chapter, we built upon existing work in the field of human-computer interaction to leverage persuasion as a useful lens for understanding and designing AI tools, especially those used in workplace contexts, considering the increased importance of these tools to evoke desired behaviors of employees and their often mandated nature.

Theorizing AI tools in the workplace from the lens of persuasion is helpful not only to reveal the "hidden" abilities to calculate and support human decisions and actions but also to highlight the importance of volition on the part of the user. Indeed, our framework of persuasive AI proposes the design of AI tools for the workplace that offer primary task support, dialogue support, credibility support, and social support with the aim of not only improving the effectiveness of employees' workplace actions but simultaneously enhancing the ethicality of outcomes and the empowerment of users by amplifying autonomy, enhancing human capabilities, and ultimately improving confidence in their ability to control how AI affects their workplace actions. Through the development of this framework, we hope to not only guide the future study and design of workplace AI technologies but also raise users' awareness of how AI technologies in the workplace operate, thus allowing them to develop protective and proactive mechanisms for their interactions with AI technologies to safeguard the volitional nature of persuasion, even in situations where the use of the technology itself might be involuntary.

Acknowledgments This material is based in part upon work supported by the National Science Foundation under Grant Number IIS-1749018. Any opinions, findings, and conclusions or recommendations expressed in this material are those of the author(s) and do not necessarily reflect the views of the National Science Foundation.

References

Bankins S, Ocampo AC, Marrone M, Restubog SLD, Woo SE (2024) A multi-level review of artificial intelligence in organizations: implications for organizational behavior research and practice. J Organ Behav 45(2):159–182. https://doi.org/10.1002/job.2735

Fogg B (1998) Persuasive computers: perspectives and research directions. In: Proceedings of the SIGCHI conference on human factors in computing systems—CHI '98, pp 225–232. https://doi.org/10.1145/274644.274677

Kaptein M, Eckles D (2010) Selecting effective means to any end: futures and ethics of persuasion profiling. In: Ploug T, Hasle P, Oinas-Kukkonen H (eds) Persuasive technology, vol 6137. Springer, Berlin, Heidelberg, pp 82–93. https://doi.org/10.1007/978-3-642-13226-1

Kim TW, Duhachek A (2020) Artificial intelligence and persuasion: a construal-level account. Psychol Sci 31(4):363–380. https://doi.org/10.1177/0956797620904985

Oinas-Kukkonen H, Harjumaa M (2008) A systematic framework for designing and evaluating persuasive systems. In: Oinas-Kukkonen H, Hasle P, Harjumaa M, Segerståhl K, Øhrstrøm P (eds) Persuasive technology. Springer, Berlin, pp 164–176. https://doi.org/10.1007/978-3-540-68504-3

O'Keefe DJ (2015) Persuasion: theory and research, 3rd edn. Sage Publications, London

Pereira V, Hadjielias E, Christofi M, Vrontis D (2023) A systematic literature review on the impact of artificial intelligence on workplace outcomes: a multi-process perspective. Hum Resour Manag Rev 33(1):100857. https://doi.org/10.1016/j.hrmr.2021.100857

Siegel M, Breazeal C, Norton MI (2009) Persuasive robotics: the influence of robot gender on human behavior. In: 2009 IEEE/RSJ international conference on intelligent robots and systems, pp 2563–2568. https://doi.org/10.1109/IROS.2009.5354116

Smids J (2012) The voluntariness of persuasive technology. In: Bang M, Ragnemalm EL (eds) Persuasive technology. Design for health and safety. Springer, Berlin, pp 123–132. https://doi.org/10.1007/978-3-642-31037-9

Vincent J (2018) Amazon reportedly scraps internal ai recruiting tool that was biased against women. The Verge. https://www.theverge.com/2018/10/10/17958784/ai-recruiting-tool-bias-amazon-report

Wamba-Taguimdje SL, Fosso Wamba S, Kala Kamdjoug JR, Tchatchouang Wanko CE (2020) Influence of artificial intelligence (ai) on firm performance: the business value of ai-based transformation projects. Bus Process Manag J 26(7):1893–1924. https://doi.org/10.1108/BPMJ-10-2019-0411

Part III
User Experience & Ergonomics

ML Models Deployed: What Is Next?

Effective and Efficient Monitoring of ML-Based Applications

Helmut Degen

Abstract Machine learning (ML) models augment many software applications across consumer, industrial, and military domains. It is known that the performance of ML models degrade over time. Model degradation can lead to incorrect predictions with potentially risky or harmful consequences. The state-of-the-art approach for model degradation is the use of model monitoring applications that detect and report model anomalies, based on model metrics, such as feature importance or F1 scores. Such metrics and the reported anomalies are comprehensible for data scientists, but not so much for users without a data science background from the application domain (e.g., medical, manufacturing, finance). Since model metrics are disconnected from the application domain context, it can take up to several days for a data scientist to identify the root cause of an anomaly and how to resolve it. This chapter presents an interaction concept for model monitoring that was validated by end users. It will provide answer to the following questions: Q1: How to enable application domain experts (with limited or no AI background) to understand a reported model anomaly and its root cause so they can select and initiate a response action in a timely manner? Q2: How to enable application domain experts to validate that a selected and initiated responsive action was effective? Q3: What are the cross-validation results of the interaction concept with selected user involvement models (Endsley 1995; Endsley and Kaber 1999; Rasmussen 1974)?

1 Introduction

Machine learning models, often referred to as ML models or simply models, are increasingly used in applications across various sectors, including consumer, industrial, and military domains. It is known that field data or environmental conditions evolve over time, diverging from the data initially used for training and

H. Degen (✉)
Siemens Technology, Princeton, NJ, USA
e-mail: helmut.degen@siemens.com

C. K. Coursaris et al. (eds.), *The Design of Human-Centered Artificial Intelligence for the Workplace*, Progress in IS, https://doi.org/10.1007/978-3-031-83512-4_13

testing these ML models. This evolving data landscape can introduce a phenomenon known as "data drift," which in turn can significantly impact the prediction accuracy of these ML models (Bayram et al. 2022; Piano et al. 2022). This gradual decline in model performance over time is frequently referred to as "model degradation."

The implications of model degradation can vary widely depending on the specific application domain and the associated risks for users, beneficiaries, organizations, and society at large. In certain instances, it may lead to adverse and potentially costly outcomes, underscoring the importance of addressing this challenge.

In the industrial domain, machine learning-based applications need to adhere to rigorous quality standards, encompassing real-time operation, human-in-the-loop interaction, context awareness, cybersecurity (Peres et al. 2020, p. 220128), robustness, and safety (Saraf et al. 2020). This elevated quality standard, needed for industrial use, is often denoted as "industrial AI" or "industrial-grade AI."

We cannot predict the future. However, it is reasonable to assume that a large number of small, specialized models (SSMs) trained for specific tasks for industrial applications will be used in the future. To attain "industrial-grade AI" and to ensure that a large number of SSMs stay within the defined quality boundaries or anomalies are detected as a result of model degradation, it becomes evident that effective and efficient model monitoring is imperative to achieve or exceed productivity and quality objectives.

Within this chapter, we designate an ML model and its characteristics as the "AI domain." We differentiate the AI domain from what we refer to as the "application domain." The application domain pertains to the specific field for which an ML-based application has been designed and tailored, such as healthcare, finance, insurance, enterprise resource management, and manufacturing (the selected application domain in this book chapter).

Manufacturing of printed circuit boards (PCBs) is used as a manufacturing example to illustrate the challenges of ML model monitoring today. As part of a cost optimization effort, the soldering paste was replaced. The new soldering paste has a different viscosity. Because the deployed ML model was not trained with the new soldering paste, the images taken by a visual quality inspection station appear different (data drift of field data). This is the reason why the ML model produces more incorrect predictions over time (i.e., more fault positives and fault negatives), pushing an accuracy metric (e.g., F1 score) below a defined quality threshold. State-of-the-art (SOTA) model monitoring applications recognize the dropped metric and report an anomaly (from the AI domain). What they do not report today are the causing events: the replaced soldering paste with its different viscosity (application domain) and the ML model that was not trained with the different soldering paste (AI domain). Furthermore, SOTA model monitoring applications do not suggest corrective actions (e.g., train the ML model with the new soldering paste).

For the manufacturing industry, the experts in this context are model monitors. These individuals have a deep understanding of the manufacturing domain (the application domain) yet possess little to no knowledge regarding the AI domain.

This chapter provides answers to the following questions:

- Q1 How to enable application domain experts (with limited or no AI background) to understand a reported model anomaly and its root cause so they can select and initiate a response action in a timely manner?
- Q2 How to enable application domain experts to validate that a selected and initiated responsive action was effective?
- Q3 What are the cross-validation results of the interaction concept with selected user involvement models?

In this book chapter, we provide an overview of the research findings in the domain of explainable model monitoring (Degen et al. 2022, 2023). Our focus is primarily on the perspective of human-computer interaction, particularly concerning the integration of application domain experts and the achieved level of automation. Note that the technical implementation of the proposed model monitoring approach falls outside the scope of this chapter.

Section 2 introduces terminology and state of the art for explainable AI and ML model monitoring. Section 3 introduces the manufacturing domain with an anomaly example and the user role "model manager" with its user goals and user tasks. It also introduces a validated mental model representation that was used as a foundation for designing the interaction concept. Section 4 introduces the validated interaction concept that outlines how model monitors can be effectively engaged in the model monitoring process. One objective of this chapter is to gauge the extent of the automation level (Endsley 1995; Endsley and Kaber 1999) of the validated interaction concept and how well it fits Rasmussen's "ladder of abstraction" (Rasmussen 1974, p. 41). This is described in Sect. 5. We conclude the chapter with a summary and an outlook on prospective areas for future research in Sect. 6.

2 Current State of Research

2.1 Explainable AI

Many challenges of making AI-based systems ethical, fair, and human-centered still exist (Garibay et al. 2023; Antona et al. 2023). One of them is the need for explanations, also known as explainable AI (Turek 2016) for industrial applications. The original need for explainable AI (XAI) comes from a property of ML-based applications: the uncertainty that a predicted outcome can be incorrect. This phenomenon of ML-based applications is called the "uncertainty premise." Without additional information, it is impossible for a human user to determine which predicted outcome is correct or incorrect. This is particularly a challenge for industrial-grade AI.

Several strategies can be employed to address such uncertainties. One approach involves the expansion of both the training dataset and the test dataset, a measure that serves to diminish uncertainties to some extent. However, it is essential to acknowledge that this approach, while effective in reducing uncertainties, cannot completely eliminate them. Alternatively, another effective strategy involves the integration of *explanations* into the system's functionality.

An explanation can be broadly understood as a "set of statements usually constructed to describe a set of facts which clarifies the causes, context, and consequences of those facts. It may establish rules or laws, and may clarify the existing rules or laws in relation to any objects or phenomena examined" (Drake 2018, p. 161–162).

In the context of machine learning, explanations are generated by ML-based applications. This explanation-generating capability is also called "explainable artificial intelligence," abbreviated "explainable AI," or even shorter "XAI." It is understood as an AI system "that can explain their rationale to a human user, characterize their strengths and weaknesses, and convey an understanding of how they will behave in the future" (Gunning and Aha 2019, p. 44).

In our discussion of explanations, we specifically refer to information provided to users, which rationalizes the decisions made by an ML-based application. We term these explanations "uncertainty-addressing explanations." In essence, this distinction underscores the separation between the predicted "outcome" and the supplementary "uncertainty-addressing explanations" that describe the rationale for the predicted outcome.

Uncertainty-addressing explanations need to consider the target stakeholder (Langer et al. 2021; Hoffman et al. 2023, 2021; Preece et al. 2018). They serve multiple purposes, including justification, control, improvement, and discovery (Adadi and Berrada 2018, p. 52142–52143). In the realm of explainability, various recognized qualities include trustworthiness, causality, transferability, informativeness, confidence, fairness, accessibility, interactivity, and privacy awareness (Barredo Arrieta et al. 2020, p. 8–10). Additionally, other explainability qualities are understandability, predictability (Mohseni et al. 2021, p. 8), and actionability (Degen et al. 2023; Shergadwala et al. 2022).

2.2 ML Model Monitoring

As discussed in the introduction, model degradation represents an undesired yet nearly inevitable change in model performance. The current approach to detecting model degradation involves monitoring machine learning (ML)-based applications (Barredo Arrieta et al. 2020; Adadi and Berrada 2018; Eck et al. 2022; Hoffman et al. 2018; Khademi et al. 2023; Rudin 2019; Shergadwala et al. 2022; Zhang et al. 2022). (Schröder and Schulz 2022, p. 109f.) views model monitoring as a continuation of model testing post-deployment. State-of-the-art (SOTA) model monitoring applications identify and report anomalies in two scenarios: (1) when a quality attribute of the AI domain trends outside the defined quality range or (2) when a quality attribute is already outside the specified range. In either case, the system detects and reports an anomaly.

In SOTA model monitoring applications, anomalies are primarily reported with content from the AI domain (Eck et al. 2022; Khademi et al. 2023; Schröder and Schulz 2022; Zhang et al. 2022). However, what current SOTA model monitoring applications lack is the capability to establish a causal link to events within the application domain that led to the detected anomaly in the AI domain.

Recent research indicates that explanations in model monitoring should encompass information from the application domain (Shergadwala et al. 2022; Degen et al. 2023). In their work on autonomous vehicles, (Gilpin 2018; Gilpin et al. 2018) employed a shared symbolic language for anomaly detection, presenting explanations in the language of the application domain. These explanations are intended for system components as recipients.

There are several types of explanations introduced for anomaly detection (Chevtchenko et al. 2023; Jaramillo-Alcazar et al. 2023; Kim et al. 2022; Sørbø and Ruocco 2023; Vilone and Longo 2021; Degen et al. 2023):

- Prediction scope: Global, local
- Model view: black box, white box
- Item type: Model, data
- Prediction type: Categorical, numerical (regression), cluster
- Data type: Image, number, status, time series, etc.
- Explanation scope: Singular; show me your work
- Domain type: AI domain, application domain

Performance metrics for anomaly detection are illustrated in Fig. 1. The taxonomy represents an explanation class with explanation types "global," "black box," "data," "categorical," "singular," and "AI domain." The "global" explanation type measures metrics across multiple individual predictions. It is labeled "black box" because it assesses predictions against a ground truth rather than properties of model components, such as feature importance, network weights, or neural activations. Similarly, it is tagged as "data" for the same reason. The "categorical" explanation type identifies the category to which an item belongs. The "data-type" explanation was not selected because this explanation type is applicable to multiple data types. It is termed "singular" as it provides a single explanation rather than a series of connected explanations. Finally, it falls under the "AI domain" explanation type because it reports a metric from the AI domain without translating it into an explanation from the application domain.

The *F1 score* is a metric used in the example in this chapter, illustrating the described explanation type. It represents the harmonic mean of precision and recall (Wikipedia 2023).

Modern model monitoring applications report detected anomalies using AI domain metrics, leading to two challenges: (1) Application domain experts may not be well-versed in the AI domain and its metrics. (2) The root cause in the application domain that triggers the anomaly is usually not provided. As a result, an application domain expert, such as a model monitor, must manually identify the causes, a process that can take hours or even days. For reasons of quality and productivity, a response time spanning multiple hours or days is not desirable.

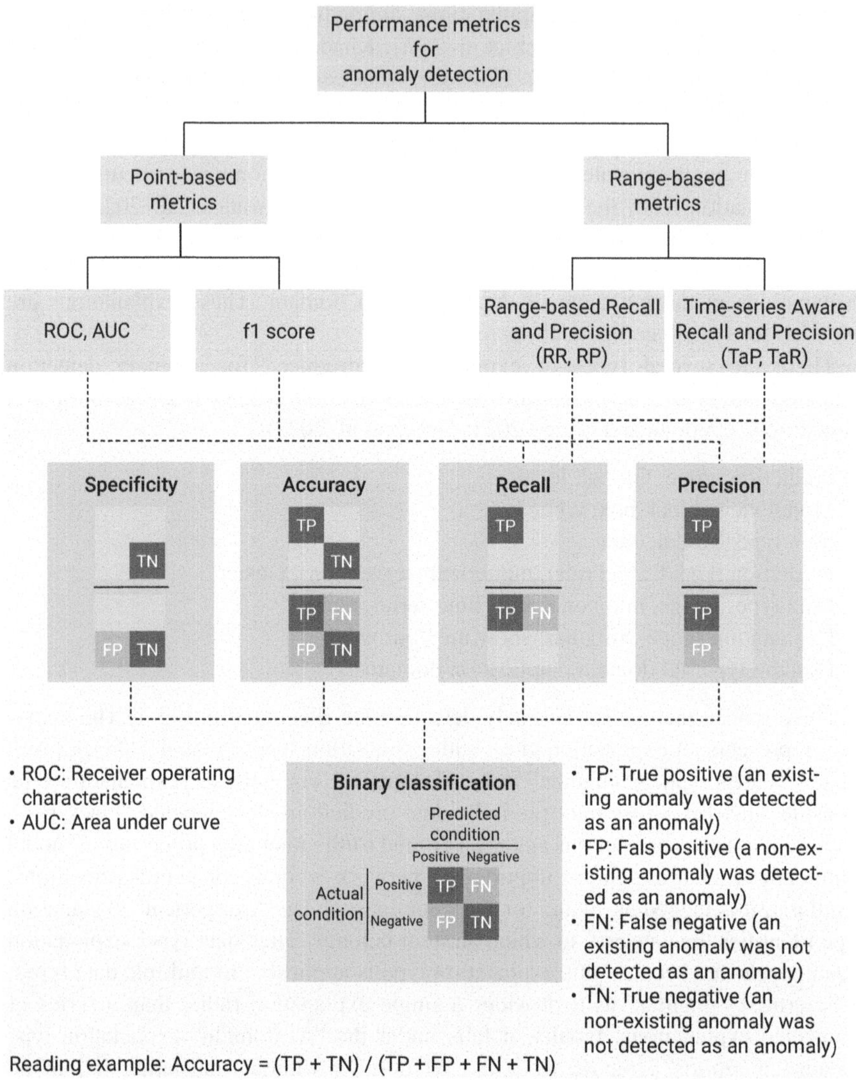

Fig. 1 Performance metrics for anomaly detection. (Based on Kim et al. 2022, p. 5)

3 ML Model Monitoring in Manufacturing

3.1 Manufacturing

Manufacturing involves the transformation of raw materials into parts and parts into final products. At each step of the manufacturing process, errors can occur. Therefore, quality assurance steps are implemented to ensure that the manufactured parts comply with defined quality criteria. Currently, standard technology and manual quality inspections are employed for quality assurance (Brauer and Cesarone 2022). It's important to note that, in this paper, we refer to manufacturing as the "application domain."

In the manufacturing industry, there is a growing trend toward integrating ML-based applications for quality assurance (Plathottam et al. 2023; Bousdekis et al. 2023). The adoption of ML-enabled applications in quality assurance is expected to result in increased accuracy, leading to notable enhancements in productivity and reductions in manufacturing costs.

3.2 User Role: Model Manager

The initial responders to reported anomalies may include both data scientists, experts in the AI domain, and end users, specialists in the application domain (Beringer 2004). Nevertheless, across different application domains, indications suggest that individuals with expertise in the application domain are often better suited to respond to reported model anomalies (Degen et al. 2021, 2022, 2023).

Several compelling reasons underpin the preference for application domain experts (e.g., a model manager) over AI domain experts, such as data scientists, as the primary responders. Given that data drift frequently originates from changes within the application domain, experts in the application domain are better positioned to discern and validate the causal relationship between detected deviations in the model's performance and alterations within the application domain. Furthermore, employing data scientists for the task of model monitoring may prove cost-prohibitive, and in the current employment landscape, recruiting such individuals can pose challenges.

The role of "model manager" is assumed to involve overseeing the monitoring of ML-based applications. Whether this role is a dedicated position or performed by a single manufacturing operator depends on the volume of models requiring supervision. A model manager can be likened to an IT administrator responsible for monitoring an IT application.

A model manager is responsible for monitoring ML models deployed on one or more ML-based applications. The application designed to assist the model manager in this monitoring task is referred to as the "Explainable Model Manager" (XMM). This application detects anomalies and communicates these findings to the model manager. For clarity, the application will be abbreviated as "XMM," and the role will be referred to as the "model manager" throughout the remainder of this chapter.

Building upon the premises established in the introduction, it is assumed that a model manager does not possess the education and experience typically associated with a data scientist. Instead, a model manager has a comprehensive understanding of the application domain, such as manufacturing.

The model manager is responsible for achieving the following user goals:

- UG 1: Maximize production uptime.

- UG 2: Keep ML-based quality assurance application within defined quality boundaries.

To achieve the two goals, the model manager performs the following user tasks when presented with a reported anomaly:

- UT 1: Understand what happened and why.
- UT 2: Select and initiate response action.
- UT 3: Verify effectiveness of initiated responsive action.

The model manager acts as a bridge between the manufacturing world (application domain) and the realm of machine learning (AI domain). This role involves interactions with two key counterparts: quality assurance within the application domain, which is responsible for ensuring alignment with quality goals covering machines, tools, and outcomes, including those set by the ML-based application. The other is a data scientist within the AI domain, entrusted with managing machine learning components, such as the model, training/testing data, and the pipeline. For instance, tasks like modifying an ML model, such as retraining, fall within the purview of the data scientist rather than the model manager.

3.3 *Mental Model of a Model Manager*

The intent was to utilize a mental model representation to identify the content that is needed to address uncertainties. A mental model, defined as a "representation of some domain or situation that supports understanding, reasoning, and prediction" (Gentner 2001), was derived from the results of a task analysis and subsequently validated (for details, see Degen et al. 2023).

Recent research indicates that a causal chain serves as an appropriate representation of the model manager's mental model (Degen et al. 2021, 2022, 2023). Defined as a structure illustrating causal relationships between individual factors (Andersen and Fagerhaug 2006), the causal chain in our scenario comprises six elements (see Fig. 2).

The causal chain comprises two parts: the outcome (the rightmost two elements) and the (uncertainty-addressing) explanation content (the elements to the left of the outcome).

The outcome comprises two types of actions: Responsive Action 1 (in the application domain) and Responsive Action 2 (in the AI domain). Responsive Action 1 addresses Root Cause 1 in the application domain, while Responsive Action 2 in the AI domain addresses Root Cause 2. In practice, both actions, or in some cases, only one of the two actions, are identified.

The explanation content justifying the two actions (hence referred to as explanation content) comprises a causal chain. Root Cause 1, located in the application domain, represents an event leading to an anomaly in the AI domain. An example of Root Cause 1 is the introduction of a new manufacturing material or component,

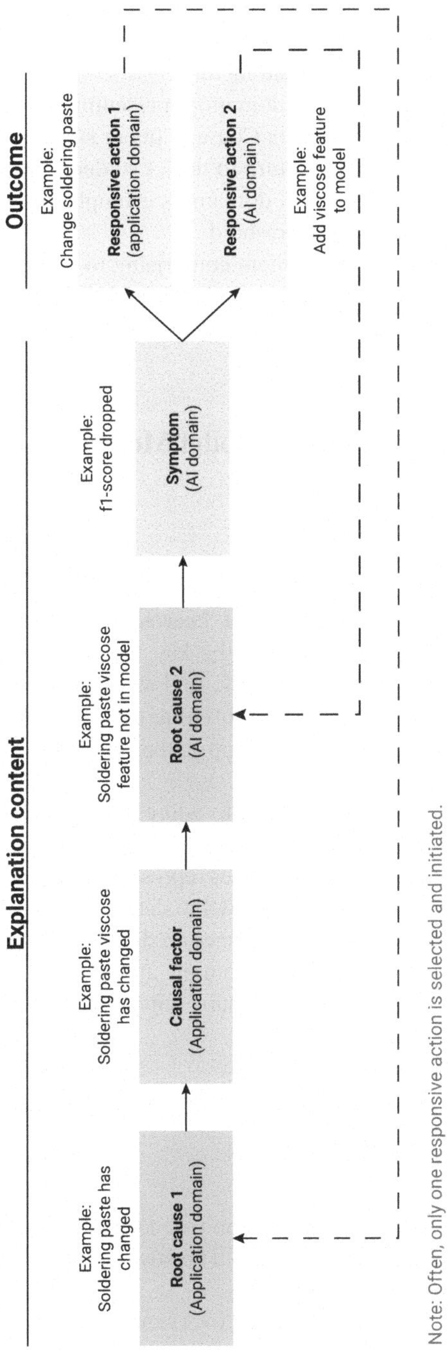

Fig. 2 Causal chain as mental model representation

such as a change in soldering paste in our case. Causal factors, consequences of Root Cause 1 typically found in the application domain, often contribute to the anomaly in the AI domain. In our example, the viscosity difference between the new and original soldering paste serves as a causal factor.

Root Cause 2 is situated in the AI domain, representing a deficiency in an AI component discovered as a result of Root Cause 1. In our study, an example of Root Cause 2 is an ML model lacking a feature to detect soldering paste viscosity. The symptom, a detected anomaly in the AI domain, is exemplified in our study by the drop of the F1 score below a defined threshold.

The XMM application generates content comprising root causes, causal factors, symptoms, and actions. This content is correlated, and the user validates that the application has produced content with a causal relationship.

4 Interaction Concept for ML Model Monitoring

4.1 Selected Anomaly Scenario

For our research, we selected a specific manufacturing quality assurance scenario involving the production of printed circuit boards (PCBs). In this scenario, a significant drop in the F1 score serves as the key indicator of an anomaly. The threshold for the F1 score was set at 50%, and while it typically maintains a minimum value of 61%, it plummeted to 36% due to the distinct viscosity of the new soldering paste. The reason for this drop is that the ML model V12 was not trained to detect viscosity.

Several responsive actions can be taken to address this issue. One option is to revert to the original soldering paste. Alternatively, adapting the ML model by training it on data encompassing varying viscosities represents a viable solution. Another responsive action involves retraining the model to detect viscosity variances.

In our scenario, the ML model was retrained to detect viscosity variances (now referred to as model V13). After the retraining and deployment, the F1 score increased from 36% to 68%, with the feature importance for the new viscosity feature measured above average.

4.2 User Interface Mockup

The mental model and additional information (see Degen et al. 2023, p. 216–217) were used to create an interaction concept. The seven screens of that interaction concept are depicted below.

Screen 1 (see Fig. 3) shows an "incident overview." Each incident represents a reported anomaly and is described with attributes that help the model manager to

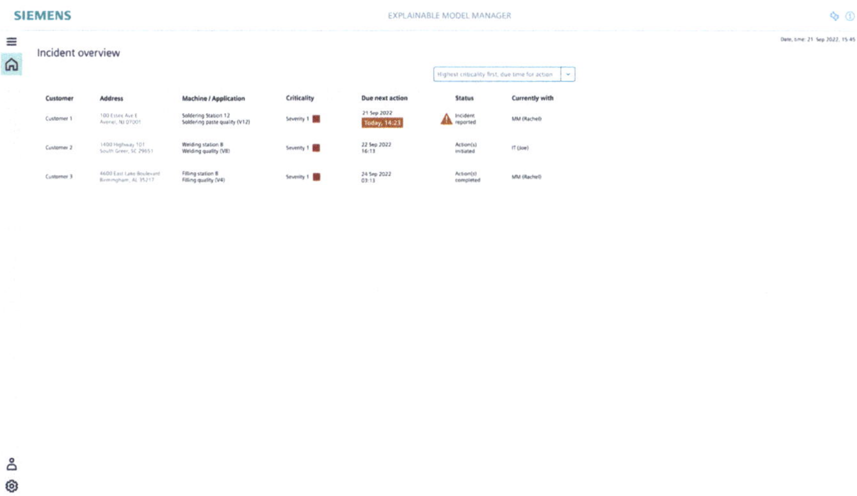

Fig. 3 Screen 1: Incident overview

select one for review, initiate an action, or check the effectiveness of an initiated action.

After the model manager selects an incident, the details of the selected incident are displayed. The content outlined in the mental model, i.e., the causal chain, is listed at the top across several tabs. Each tab represents a concern and already displays the answer. This design allows a user to read the tabs from left to right, gaining an understanding of the incident.

The tabs address the following concerns:

- Location: Where did it happen?
- Symptom: What happened?
- Root cause: Why did it happen?
- Immediate action: What do to now (to avoid further damages)?
- Responsive action: How to address the root cause?
- Efficacy of initiated action: Is the cause fixed?
- Incident history: What is the history of that incident?

After the user selects a tab, detailed content for that concern is displayed. Six different views are presented.

The first view describes the location of the incident (see Fig. 4). This includes details about the factory facility, the hardware (e.g., an industrial PC), and the relevant software, as well as information about the associated ML model.

The second view displays the symptom in the AI domain in the context of time. In the selected scenarios, this is a drop in the F1 score below the defined threshold of 50% (see Fig. 5).

The third view displays both the root cause in the application domain and the root cause in the AI domain, each annotated with the context of time when the events

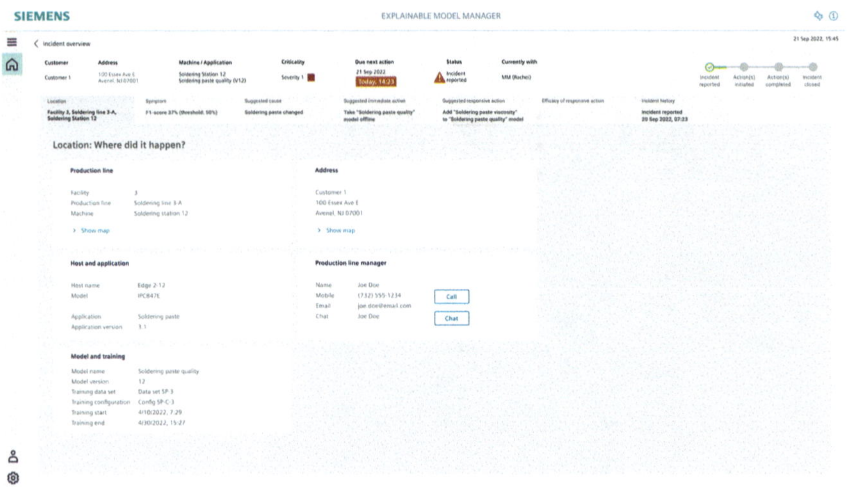

Fig. 4 Screen 2: Location

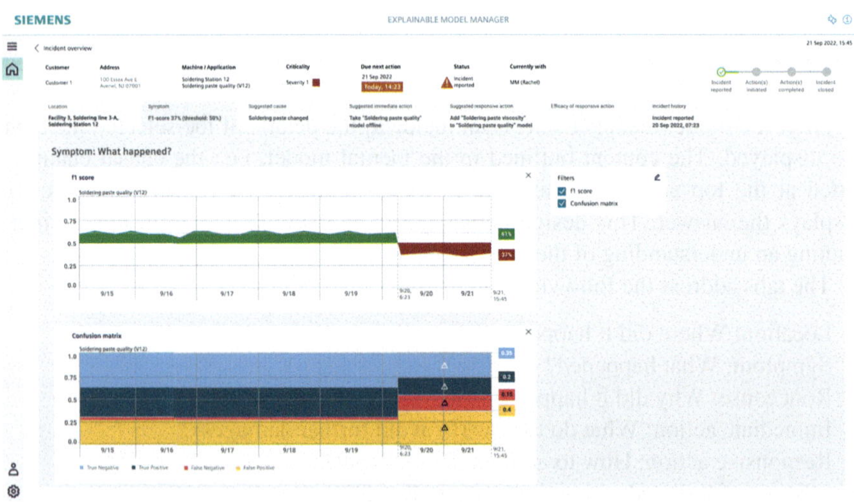

Fig. 5 Screen 3: Symptom

occurred. In our scenario, the root cause in the application domain is the exchange of the soldering paste, and the causal factor in the application domain is that the new soldering paste has a different viscosity. Concurrently, the root cause in the AI domain is that the used ML model is trained for soldering paste viscosity.

Below the fold, the symptom (F1 score and confusion matrix) is displayed again to allow the application domain expert to verify the causal relationship between the sequence of events in the application domain (in our case, the change of the

Fig. 6 Screen 4: Root causes

Fig. 7 Screen 5: Immediate action

soldering paste) and the event in the AI domain (in our case, the drop of the F1 score) (Fig. 6).

The fourth view displays an immediate action and its consequence if that action is not taken. In our scenario, the consequence is the shipment of malfunctioning PCBs, which may necessitate cost-intensive recalls. The immediate action recommended is to take the ML model offline and initiate manual quality testing instead (Fig. 7).

The fifth view displays a responsive action for fixing one of the root causes. In our scenario, one recommended responsive action is the training of the ML model

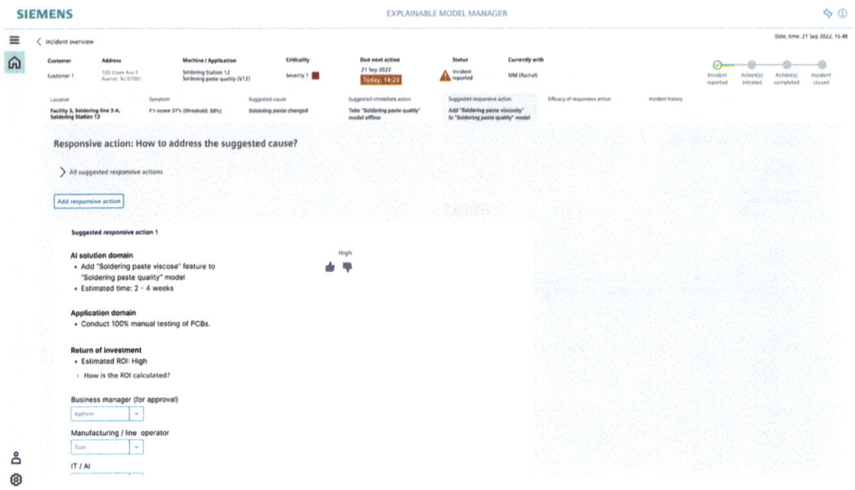

Fig. 8 Screen 6: Responsive action

with the soldering paste viscosity, taking place in the AI domain. Another suggested action is to revert to the previous soldering paste, constituting a responsive action in the application domain (Fig. 8).

The sixth view displays the effectiveness of the initiated action. It indicates that the symptom is no longer present (the F1 score has increased to 68%, surpassing the quality threshold of 50%). This outcome signifies that the initiated action—training the ML model to detect soldering paste viscosity—has successfully resolved the anomaly.

The view also presents a timeline of all events in both the application domain and the AI domain. This allows the application domain expert to validate that the sequence of events has effectively led to the removal of the symptom, addressing the root cause (Fig. 9).

5 Cross-Validation of Interaction Concept and User Involvement Models

5.1 Validation Method

In this section, we compare the interaction concept (i.e., the identified user tasks and the information architecture of the UI mockup) with three user involvement models, namely, Endsley's Situation Awareness model (Endsley 1995), Endsley and Kaber's Level of Automation Taxonomy (Endsley and Kaber 1999), and Rasmussen's ladder of abstraction (Rasmussen 1974).

Fig. 9 Screen 7: Effectiveness of initiated responsive action

A crucial question arises: Are we merely comparing the user involvement models with the interaction concept, or are we validating one against the other?

A model, defined as "an abstraction of a system or of the real world concentrating on specific structural or behavioral properties and representing them in a syntactically and semantically defined language" (Aßmann et al. 2021, p. 107–108), is typically created through selection and abstraction from reality based on objective observations. According to Popper, "*it must be possible for an empirical scientific system to be refuted by experience*" (Popper 2005, p. 18). Therefore, we can approach scientific truth by falsifying abstracted principles (in our case, the user involvement models) against the gathered data (the interaction concept). This implies that we can validate the user involvement models against the interaction concept, posing the guiding question: Which elements of the interaction concept are missing in the model? We refer to this validation direction as "validation of the model."

Can we also validate the interaction concept against the model? We can identify data motivated by the respective models that the interaction concept does not contain. The guiding question here is: Which elements of the model are not reflected in the interaction concept? This validation direction is termed "validation of the interaction concept." Both validations are summarized as "cross-validation" in this section.

To perform the cross-validation, we first map the model elements and the user tasks and views of the interaction architecture to each other. Subsequently, we conduct a model validation and a validation of data completeness.

5.2 *Situation Awareness Model*

5.2.1 Mapping of Model and Interaction Concept

Endsley (Endsley 1995, p. 35) proposes a model for situation awareness (SA) in dynamic decision-making. Situation awareness is defined as “the perception of the elements in the environment within a volume of time and space, the comprehension of their meaning, and the projection of their status in the near future” (Endsley 1995, p. 36–37).

Endsley distinguishes three levels of situation awareness (Endsley 1995, p. 36):

- Level 1: Perception of the elements in the environment
- Level 2: Comprehension of the current situation
- Level 3: Projection of future status (if no corrective action is initiated that can change the current situation)

The initial step (Level 1) in achieving situation awareness is becoming familiar with elements in the environment and the system status in the current environment. The second step (Level 2) involves comprehending the “disjointed Level 1 elements” (Endsley 1995, p. 37). Level 2 includes a comparison between the system status in its current environment and the pertinent goal. The third step (Level 3) comprises projecting the current situation into the future, assuming it continues.

The mapping of Endsley’s situation awareness model to the interaction concept is summarized in Table 1.

According to the mapping, we assume that the presented interaction concept offers a Level 3 situation awareness for the model manager.

5.2.2 Validation of Model

We want to find out whether the model does not contain elements that the interaction concept contains. Additionally, we aim to categorize the interaction concept within Endsley’s SA levels.

Table 1 Mapping of interaction concept to Endsley’s situation awareness model

Mental activity	User task	View of interaction concept
1 Perceive	UT 1: Understand what happened and why	Screen 2: Location; screen 3: Symptom
2 Comprehend	UT 1: Understand what happened and why	Screen 4: Suggested cause
3 Project	(there is no user task that projects the future status)	Top element of screen 5: Suggested immediate action which outlines the impact if no action is initiated immediately

For each detected anomaly, user task 1 (Understanding what happens and why) is supported by screens 2 (Location), 3 (Symptom), and 4 (Root Cause), aiding in perceiving relevant elements in the environment.

The interaction concept suggests a root cause, establishing a causal relationship between the symptom and root cause, aligning with level 2. It is essential to note that the ML monitoring system identifies correlations, not causations. The confirmation or rejection of a causal relationship lies with the model manager.

Interpreting the consequences if no immediate action is taken ("Immediate actions") is portrayed in the first element of screen 5: "Suggested immediate actions," addressing level 3 of Endsley's situation awareness model.

Endsley's model does not encompass the decision-making process, action selection, and execution (user task 2: Select and initiate responsive actions; screen 6). The broader model, inclusive of decision-making and execution, is illustrated outside of the SA model (Endsley 1995, Figure 1, p. 35). This broader model also includes a feedback loop external to the SA model for validating the effectiveness of executed actions. The validation process itself is part of the SA model, covered under the mental activity "Perceive" (Endsley 1995, Figure 1, p. 35).

Endsley explicitly excluded the model manager's decision-making and execution from the SA model. However, the interaction concept aligns well with Endsley's SA model overall.

5.2.3 Validation of Interaction Concept

The interaction concept does not incorporate a user task explicitly projecting a future status.

5.3 Level of Automation Taxonomy

5.3.1 Mapping of Model and Interaction Concept

The concept of the level of automation (LOA) extends the situation awareness. LOA dictates which steps are carried out by a human, a computer, or a combination of both. This factor impacts the mental load on the operator and the overall task performance.

Endsley and Kaber (Endsley and Kaber 1999) propose a ten-level automation taxonomy (other taxonomies are discussed in Vagia et al. 2016). This taxonomy focuses on the tasks of *monitoring* (scanning a display to perceive system status), *generating* (formulating options or strategies), *selecting* (deciding on a particular option or strategy), and *implementing* (carrying out the chosen option) (Endsley and Kaber 1999, p. 464). The ten levels specify who performs each of these tasks: the operator, the computer, or both. These combinations form the LOA taxonomy.

Table 2 Mapping of interaction concept to Endsley and Kaber's LOA taxonomy

Mental activity	User task	Screens	Assignment to LOA taxonomy
Monitoring	(there is no user task that monitors a system or recognizes a reported anomaly)	Screen 1: Incident overview	A computer detects and reports the anomaly; a human recognizes and reviews it: human / computer
Generating	UT 2: Select and initiate responsive actions	Screen 5: Select and initiate immediate action; Screen 6: Select and initiate responsive action	A computer generates the options and strategies to achieve the set goals: computer
Selecting	UT 2: Select and initiate responsive actions	Screen 5: Select and initiate immediate action; Screen 6: Select and initiate responsive action	A human operator selects an option or strategy: human
Implementing	UT 2: Select and initiate responsive actions	Screen 5: Select and initiate immediate action; Screen 6: Select and initiate responsive action	In most cases, it is assumed that a human operator is involved in carrying out the chosen option with the use of computers: human / computer

Let us apply these tasks to the presented interaction concept and identify the actor(s) for each task (see Table 2).

No level of automation precisely aligns with the identified parameters. The task allocation of level 4, "Shared control," comes close (monitoring, human/computer; generating, human/computer; selecting, human; implementing, human/computer). However, in the interaction concept, the task of generating options and strategies is exclusively performed by the computer. This indicates that the presented interaction concept has a higher automation level than level 4.

Level 7, "Rigid system," also shares similarities with the aforementioned task assignment (monitoring, human/computer; generating, computer; selecting, human; implementing, computer). The first three task assignments are identical to those in the interaction concept, but the "Rigid system" designates the computer as the sole entity for implementing options or strategies. In contrast, the interaction concept involves both a human and a computer in the implementation process. Thus, the "Rigid system" has a higher automation level than the interaction concept.

5.3.2 Validation of Model

The LOA taxonomy does not encompass the combination identified in our analysis.

It appears that the ten-level automation taxonomy has gaps and should be extended to accommodate the automation level of the presented interaction concept. The model incorporates four parameters (monitoring, generating, selecting, implementing) and assigns specific combinations of values to the ten levels. It raises questions about the adequacy of fixed LOA levels in accurately modeling reality. A more flexible system might better capture the nuances of real-world scenarios.

5.3.3 Validation of Interaction Concept

The interaction concept lacks a designated user task, such as "Recognize incident," which aligns with the mental activity of "Monitoring."

5.4 Ladder of Abstraction

5.4.1 Mapping of Model and Interaction Concept

Rasmussen introduced a model describing the sequence of mental activities performed by operators. He refers to his model as a "crude model," stating that "it is better than no model" (Rasmussen 1974, p. 26). The model, also known as a "ladder of abstraction" (Rasmussen 1974, p. 41), identifies eight mental activities supported by system actions and information. The sequence between these mental activities is not necessarily sequential, and depending on the operator's experience level, some activities might be skipped. The model does not depict loops (meaning a return to previous mental activities) between these activities.

In this book, we utilize a modified version of Rasmussen's model. The first three mental activities are associated with situation awareness, the fourth with decision-making, and the last three with task execution. The mapping of the interaction concept to these mental activities is illustrated in Table 3.

User task 1, "Understand what happened and why," corresponds to the second mental activity (comprehend) and is facilitated by screens 2 (location), 3 (symptom), and 4 (suggested cause).

User task 2, "Select and initiate responsive action," encompasses mental activities 3 (project) through 7 (execute). Screen 5's first element, "Suggested immediate action," not only outlines the consequence of not addressing the suggested cause but also proposes an immediate action to prevent further damage. The options for immediate actions (screen 5) and suggested actions (screen 6) serve as input for decision-making. As recommended actions are already proposed, the mental activities for planning (mental activity 5) and specifying an action (mental activity 6) are not necessary. Although the operator may still review the proposed actions to validate their effectiveness, this should have been done as part of the decision-making process. The execution of an action (mental activity 7) aligns with user task 2, "Select and initiate responsive action," supported by screens 5 and 6.

Table 3 Mapping of interaction concept to Rasmussen's automation ladder (modified version)

Phase	Mental activity (according to modified Rasmussen's model)	User task	View of interaction concept
Situation awareness	1 Detect	(no user task identified)	Screen 1: Incident overview
	2 Comprehend	UT 1: Understand what happened and why	Screen 2: Location; screen 3: Symptom; screen 4: Suggested cause
	3 Project	UT 2: Select and initiate response action	Screen 5: Suggested immediate action; screen 6: Suggested responsive action
Decision making	4 Make decision	UT 2: Select and initiate response action	Screen 5: Suggested immediate action; screen 6: Suggested responsive action
Execution	5 Plan	UT 2: Select and initiate response action	Screen 5: Suggested immediate action; screen 6: Suggested responsive action
	6 Specify	UT 2: Select and initiate response action	Screen 5: Suggested immediate action; screen 6: Suggested responsive action
	7 Execute	UT 2: Select and initiate response action	Screen 5: Suggested immediate action; screen 6: Suggested responsive action

5.4.2 Validation of Model

The abstraction ladder does not explicitly account for a mental activity corresponding to user task 3, "Verify the effectiveness of initiated responsive action," which is supported by screen 7. This activity is essential for ensuring that the correct task was selected, planned, specified, and executed.

A more practical approach would be to adopt Endsley's broader model, incorporating a feedback loop. This involves adding a feedback loop to the abstraction ladder that connects the last mental activity (execute) with the first mental activity (Detect). The first mental activity would then "check" whether the performed task was effective.

5.4.3 Validation of Interaction Concept

A user task corresponding to the first mental activity (detect) is absent since the XMM application handles the process of anomaly detection. However, it could still be crucial for a model manager to acknowledge the presence of a detected anomaly. Thus, a user task for "recognizing" that an anomaly has been reported is currently not included.

6 Conclusions and Future Research

6.1 Conclusions

The presented material proposes innovations in several areas. One significant aspect is the introduction of the dedicated user role of "model manager," who is responsible for responding to and addressing reported model anomalies. This role can be fulfilled by manufacturing operators or a more central IT/OT role, particularly in conjunction with a novel monitoring service for a fleet of ML models across multiple manufacturing facilities.

The XMM interaction concept delineates an incident management workflow catering to various maintenance stakeholders. The model manager, acting as the initial responder, initiates actions and may delegate tasks, such as model retraining, to a data scientist. Following retraining and testing, the model manager can assess the new model's performance in shadow mode before transitioning it to operational mode once stability and acceptability are confirmed.

The explainability concept introduces a correlation between events in the AI domain and those in the application domain. The model manager, drawing on skill and experience, validates whether these correlations imply a causal relationship. In cases where they do not, the model manager provides feedback to the ML-based system. As demonstrated in (Degen et al. 2023), establishing a relationship between events in the application and AI domains enhances the explainability for application domain experts.

The last innovation involves cross-validating the interaction concept with three user involvement models: Endsley's situation awareness model (Endsley 1995), Endsley and Kaber's levels of automation (Endsley and Kaber 1999), and a modified version of Rasmussen's ladder of abstraction (Rasmussen 1974).

The user interface of the XMM system should be customizable to align with the preferences of individual users, but these customization options will have defined boundaries. If the XMM application primarily targets "model managers," it may not provide customization features that cater to the needs of other user roles, such as data scientists.

With these innovations outlined, we can now address the research questions.

Q1: How to enable application domain experts (with limited or no AI background) to understand a reported model anomaly and its root cause so they can select and initiate a response action in a timely manner?

A model monitor is acquainted with the application domain (in our case, manufacturing) and can assess whether the suggested causes make sense. To facilitate communication between the application domain expert and the data scientist, the causal chain should encompass explanations from the AI domain (in our case, the dropped F1 score). Therefore, anomalies need to be reported, including causal factors from both the application domain and the AI domain. Ideally, this explanatory content is structured as a causal chain. Both application domain experts and data scientists can gain situational awareness and validate the correctness or incorrectness of the detected anomaly, as well as the suggested immediate and responsive actions. Currently, root cause analysis and the identification of suggested actions need to be performed manually, taking hours or even days. If generated automatically, for example, using the content from the proposed mental model, it can be accomplished in minutes, representing a significant improvement.

In cases where a single cause cannot be identified, the ML-based application may suggest multiple causes, ideally with a confidence level for each suggested cause. The model monitor can then select the most appropriate ones. It should also be possible for the model manager to provide feedback to the ML-based application (e.g., "thumbs up," "thumbs down," possibly with short explanations), enabling continuous improvement of the suggestions.

If a causal chain was not presented, or if confidence levels for a cause or an action fall below the defined threshold, the ML-based application should allow the model monitor to manually enter causal factors and responsive actions with the intention that the ML-based application will learn from them.

Q2: How to enable application domain experts to validate that a selected and initiated responsive action was effective?

To empower application domain experts in validating the effectiveness of initiated actions (Q2), it is essential to provide a comprehensive summary and mapping of all events from both the AI domain and the application domain. This representation should show the causal chain—from the root cause to the symptom, the initiated action, and whether the action proved effective.

Q3: What are the cross-validation results of the interaction concept with selected user involvement models?

Endsley's situation awareness model (Endsley 1995) encompasses all elements within the interaction concept, with a specific focus on situation awareness. Notably, it lacks a dedicated user task projecting a future status in the absence of corrective action.

Endsley and Kaber's LOA taxonomy (Endsley and Kaber 1999) comprehensively covers all tasks included in the interaction concept. However, a user task addressing the recognition of reported anomalies is absent.

The interaction concept defies exact classification to a single level of automation. The identified combination lies between level 4 (Shared control) and level 7 (Rigid system). This raises questions about the adequacy of fixed automation levels in accurately modeling the complex reality.

A more flexible system of automation levels, accommodating various combinations of parameter values, might be more suitable.

Rasmussen's abstraction ladder (Rasmussen 1974) advocates for user task 3 "Check effectiveness of initiated suggested action," utilizing the first mental activity "Detect" following task execution. To make this explicit, a feedback loop could be integrated into Rasmussen's abstraction ladder, linking mental activity 7 "Execute" to mental activity 1 "Detect." Additionally, a user task is absent to recognize that an anomaly has been reported.

6.2 Future Research

The conducted research utilized an interactive mockup rather than a fully implemented system. Further research is imperative to validate or refine the current findings, ideally through behavioral studies like formative or summative usability tests.

While the paper primarily concentrated on the model manager and the involvement of data scientists in retraining ML models, it is acknowledged that troubleshooting detected anomalies involves multiple roles. Various roles, such as product owners, project managers, software engineers, data scientists, and machine operators, contribute to the development, operation, and maintenance of ML-based applications. The uncertainty premise is applicable to all these roles during the mentioned phases, necessitating the assumption that each role has its unique explanation needs.

A research hypothesis suggests that various user roles have unique explanation needs, and some of these needs overlap. This chapter presented the mental model representation of a model manager, while ongoing research (Degen and Budnik 2024) explores the mental model representation of system testers for AI-based systems. Preliminary results suggest that system testers require more explanations than model monitors, indicating a partial overlap in their mental model representations.

The concept of a "shared mental model" (SSM) is crucial for effective teamwork (Cannon-Bowers et al. 1993; Stout 1995; Jonker et al. 2011). A shared mental model emerges when individual team members align their mental models, fostering a common understanding of their shared task and respective roles (Andrews et al. 2023, p. 130). Therefore, identifying overlapping segments in the mental model representations of different user roles—resembling a "shared mental model"—is an area worthy of additional research. This would support effective collaboration among all user roles involved in the development, operation, and maintenance of ML-based systems, such as system testers, data scientists, machine operators, and more.

To gauge the effectiveness of the shared mental model and comprehend users' attention or cognitive states, psychophysiological measurement methods like eye tracking, pupil diameter, and electroencephalogram (EEG) can be employed (Dirican and Göktürk 2011).

Acknowledgments The author thanks the anonymous reviewers for their valuable comments and suggestions. Additionally, thanks are extended to the editorial reviewer, Jörg Beringer, for providing constructive feedback. The author also appreciates the efforts of all book editors for facilitating a smooth review and submission process.

References

Adadi A, Berrada M (2018) Peeking inside the black-box: a survey on explainable artificial intelligence (XAI). IEEE Access 6:52138–52160. https://doi.org/10.1109/ACCESS.2018.2870052

Andersen BS, Fagerhaug T (2006) Root cause analysis: simplified tools and techniques, 2nd edn. ASQ Quality Press. https://asq.org/quality-press/display-item?item=H1287

Andrews RW, Lilly JM, Divya S, Feigh KM (2023) The role of shared mental models in human-AI teams: a theoretical review. Theor Issues Ergon Sci 24(2):129–175. https://doi.org/10.1080/1463922X.2022.2061080

Antona M, Margetis G, Ntoa S, Degen H (2023) Special issue on AI in HCI. Int J Hum-Comput Interact. https://doi.org/10.1080/10447318.2023.2177421

Aßmann U, Chen L, Ebert S, Göhringer D, Grzelak D, Hidalgo D, Johannsmeier L, Haddadin S, Mey J, Podlubne A (2021) Chapter 3—human–robot cohabitation in industry. In: Fitzek FH, Li SC, Speidel S, Strufe T, Simsek M, Reisslein M (eds) Tactile internet. Academic Press, New York, pp 41–73. https://doi.org/10.1016/B978-0-12-821343-8.00013-7

Barredo Arrieta A, Díaz-Rodríguez N, Del Ser J, Bennetot A, Tabik S, Barbado A, Garcia S, Gil-Lopez S, Molina D, Benjamins R, Chatila R, Herrera F (2020) Explainable artificial intelligence (XAI): concepts, taxonomies, opportunities and challenges toward responsible AI. Inform Fusion 58:82–115. https://doi.org/10.1016/j.inffus.2019.12.012

Bayram F, Ahmed BS, Kassler A (2022) From concept drift to model degradation: an overview on performance-aware drift detectors. Knowl-Based Syst 245:108632. https://doi.org/10.1016/j.knosys.2022.108632

Beringer J (2004) Reducing expertise tension. Commun ACM 47(9):39–40. https://doi.org/10.1145/1015864.1015885

Bousdekis A, Lepenioti K, Apostolou D, Mentzas G (2023) Data analytics in quality 4.0: literature review and future research directions. Int J Comput Integr Manuf 36(5):678–701. https://doi.org/10.1080/0951192X.2022.2128219

Brauer D, Cesarone J (2022) Total manufacturing assurance. controlling product quality, reliability, and safety, 2nd edn. CRC Press, Boca Raton. https://doi.org/10.1201/9781003208051

Cannon-Bowers JA, Salas E, Converse S (1993) Shared mental models in expert team decision making. In: Castellan NJ Jr (ed) Individual and group decision making: current issues. Psychology Press, New York, pp 221–246. https://doi.org/10.4324/9780203772744

Chevtchenko SF, Rocha EDS, Dos Santos MCM, Mota RL, Vieira DM, De Andrade EC, De Araújo DRB (2023) Anomaly detection in industrial machinery using IoT devices and machine learning: a systematic mapping. IEEE Access 11:128288–128305. https://doi.org/10.48550/arXiv.2307.15807v2

Degen H, Budnik C (2024) How to explain it to system testers? A qualitative user study about understandability, validatability, predictability, trustworthiness (will be published). In: Artificial intelligence in HCI: 5th international conference, AI-HCI 2024, held as part of the 26th HCI international conference, HCII 2024, Washington, D.C., USA, June 29–July 4, 2024, Proceedings. Springer, Cham

Degen H, Budnik C, Chitre K, Lintereur A (2021) How to explain it to facility managers? A qualitative, industrial user research study for explainability. In: Stephanidis C, Kurosu M, Chen JYC, Fragomeni G, Streitz N, Konomi S, Degen H, Ntoa S (eds) HCI international 2021—late breaking papers: multimodality, eXtended reality, and artificial intelligence. 23rd HCI international conference, HCII 2021, virtual event, July 24–29, 2021, Proceedings. Springer, Cham, pp 401–422. https://doi.org/10.1007/978-3-030-90963-5_31

Degen H, Budnik C, Conte G, Lintereur A, Weber S (2022) How to explain it to energy engineers? A qualitative user study about trustworthiness, understandability, and actionability. In: Stephanidis C, Kurosu M, Chen JYC, Fragomeni G, Streitz N, Konomi S, Degen H, Ntoa S (eds) HCI international 2022—late breaking papers: multimodality, eXtended reality, and artificial intelligence. 24th HCI international conference, HCII 2022, virtual event, June 24–01, 2022, Proceedings. Springer, Cham, pp 1–23. https://doi.org/10.1007/978-3-031-21707-4_20

Degen H, Budnik C, Gross R, Rothering M (2023) How to explain it to a model manager? A qualitative user study about understandability, trustworthiness, actionability, and action efficacy. In: Artificial intelligence in HCI: 4th international conference, AI-HCI 2023, held as part of the 25th HCI international conference, HCII 2023, Copenhagen, Denmark, July 23–28, 2023, Proceedings, Part I. Springer, Cham, pp 209–242. https://doi.org/10.1007/978-3-031-35891-3_14

Dirican AC, Göktürk M (2011) Psychophysiological measures of human cognitive states applied in human computer interaction. Proc Comput Sci 3:1361–1367. https://doi.org/10.1016/j.procs.2011.01.016. World Conference on Information Technology

Drake J (2018) Introduction to logic. EDTECH, Walthem Abbey. https://www.edtechpress.co.uk/details/introduction-to-logic

Eck B, Kabakci-Zorlu D, Chen Y, Savard F, Bao X (2022) A monitoring framework for deployed machine learning models with supply chain examples. https://doi.org/10.48550/arXiv.2211.06239

Endsley MR (1995) Toward a theory of situation awareness in dynamic systems. Hum Fact 37(1):32–64. https://doi.org/10.1518/001872095779049543

Endsley MR, Kaber DB (1999) Level of automation effects on performance, situation awareness and workload in a dynamic control task. Ergonomics 42(3):462–492. https://doi.org/10.1080/001401399185595

Garibay OO, Winslow B, Andolina S, Antona M, Bodenschatz A, Coursaris C, Falco G, Fiore SM, Garibay I, Grieman K, Havens JC, Jirotka M, Kacorri H, Karwowski W, Kider J, Konstan J, Koon S, Lopez-Gonzalez M, Maifeld-Carucci I, McGregor S, Salvendy G, Shneiderman B, Stephanidis C, Strobel C, Ten Holter C, Xu W (2023) Six human-centered artificial intelligence grand challenges. Int J Hum-Comput Interact 39(3):391–437. https://doi.org/10.1080/10447318.2022.2153320

Gentner D (2001) Mental models, psychology of. In: Smelser NJ, Baltes PB (eds) International encyclopedia of the social & behavioral sciences. Pergamon, Oxford, pp 9683–9687. https://doi.org/10.1016/B0-08-043076-7/01487-X

Gilpin L (2018) Reasonableness monitors. Proceedings of the AAAI conference on artificial intelligence 32(1). https://doi.org/10.1609/aaai.v32i1.11364

Gilpin LH, Macbeth JC, Florentine E (2018) Monitoring scene understanders with conceptual primitive decomposition and commonsense knowledge. Adv Cogn Syst 6:45–63

Gunning D, Aha D (2019) DARPA's explainable artificial intelligence (XAI) Program. AI Mag 40(2):44–58. https://doi.org/10.1609/aimag.v40i2.2850

Hoffman R, Klein G, Mueller ST, Jalaeian M, Tate C (2021) The stakeholder playbook for explaining ai systems. https://doi.org/10.31234/osf.io/9pqez

Hoffman RR, Miller T, Mueller ST, Klein G, Clancey WJ (2018) Explaining explanation, part 4: a deep dive on deep nets. IEEE Intell Syst 33(03):87–95. https://doi.org/10.1109/MIS.2018.033001421

Hoffman RR, Mueller ST, Klein G, Jalaeian M, Tate C (2023) Explainable AI: roles and stakeholders, desirements and challenges. Front Comput Sci. https://doi.org/10.3389/fcomp.2023.1117848

Jaramillo-Alcazar A, Govea J, Villegas-Ch W (2023) Anomaly detection in a smart industrial machinery plant using IoT and machine learning. Sensors 23(19). https://doi.org/10.3390/s23198286

Jonker CM, van Riemsdijk MB, Vermeulen B (2011) Shared mental models. In: De Vos M, Fornara N, Pitt JV, Vouros G (eds) Coordination, organizations, institutions, and norms in agent systems VI. Springer, Berlin, Heidelberg, pp 132–151. https://doi.org/10.1007/978-3-642-21268-0_8

Khademi A, Hopka M, Upadhyay D (2023) Model monitoring and robustness of in-use machine learning models: quantifying data distribution shifts using population stability index. https://doi.org/10.48550/ARXIV.2302.00775

Kim GY, Lim SM, Euom IC (2022) A study on performance metrics for anomaly detection based on industrial control system operation data. Electronics 11(8). https://doi.org/10.3390/electronics11081213

Langer M, Oster D, Speith T, Hermanns H, Kästner L, Schmidt E, Sesing A, Baum K (2021) What do we want from explainable artificial intelligence (XAI)? A stakeholder perspective on XAI and a conceptual model guiding interdisciplinary XAI research. Artif Intell 296:103473. https://doi.org/10.1016/j.artint.2021.103473

Mohseni S, Zarei N, Ragan ED (2021) A multidisciplinary survey and framework for design and evaluation of explainable AI systems. ACM Trans Interact Intell Syst 11(3–4). https://doi.org/10.1145/3387166

Peres RS, Jia X, Lee J, Sun K, Colombo AW, Barata J (2020) Industrial artificial intelligence in industry 4.0—systematic review, challenges and outlook. IEEE Access 8:220121–220139. https://doi.org/10.1109/ACCESS.2020.3042874

Piano L, Garcea F, Gatteschi V, Lamberti F, Morra L (2022) Detecting drift in deep learning: a methodology primer. IT Professional 24(5):53–60. https://doi.org/10.1109/MITP.2022.3191318

Plathottam SJ, Rzonca A, Lakhnori R, Iloeje CO (2023) A review of artificial intelligence applications in manufacturing operations. J Adv Manuf Process 5(3):e10159. https://doi.org/10.1002/amp2.10159

Popper K (2005) The logic of scientific discovery. Routledge, London. http://philotextes.info/spip/IMG/pdf/popper-logic-scientific-discovery.pdf

Preece AD, Harborne D, Braines D, Tomsett RJ, Chakraborty S (2018) Stakeholders in explainable ai. ArXiv abs/1810.00184. https://api.semanticscholar.org/CorpusID:52903098

Rasmussen J (1974) The human data processor as a system component. Bits and pieces of a model. No. 1722 in Risø-M, Risø National Laboratory. https://orbit.dtu.dk/en/publications/the-human-data-processor-as-a-system-component-bits-and-pieces-of

Rudin C (2019) Stop explaining black box machine learning models for high stakes decisions and use interpretable models instead. Nat Mach Intell 1(5):206–215. https://doi.org/10.1038/s42256-019-0048-x

Saraf AP, Chan K, Popish M, Browder J, Schade J (2020) Explainable artificial intelligence for aviation safety applications. In: AIAA aviation 2020 forum. https://doi.org/10.2514/6.2020-2881

Schröder T, Schulz M (2022) Monitoring machine learning models: a categorization of challenges and methods. Data Sci Manag 5(3):105–116. https://doi.org/10.1016/j.dsm.2022.07.004

Shergadwala MN, Lakkaraju H, Kenthapadi K (2022) A human-centric perspective on model monitoring. Proceedings of the AAAI Conference on Human Computation and Crowdsourcing 10(1):173–183. https://doi.org/10.1609/hcomp.v10i1.21997

Sørbø S, Ruocco M (2023) Navigating the metric maze: a taxonomy of evaluation metrics for anomaly detection in time series. https://arxiv.org/abs/2303.01272

Stout RJ (1995) Planning effects on communication strategies: a shared mental model perspective. Proc Hum Fact Ergon Soc Ann Meeting 39(20):1278–1282. https://doi.org/10.1177/154193129503902008

Turek M (2016) Explainable artificial intelligence (XAI). https://www.darpa.mil/program/explainable-artificial-intelligence. Accessed 3 Mar 2020

Vagia M, Transeth AA, Fjerdingen SA (2016) A literature review on the levels of automation during the years. What are the different taxonomies that have been proposed? Appl Ergon 53:190–202. https://doi.org/10.1016/j.apergo.2015.09.013

Vilone G, Longo L (2021) Classification of explainable artificial intelligence methods through their output formats. Mach Learn Knowl Extraction 3(3):615–661. https://doi.org/10.3390/make3030032

Wikipedia (2023) F-score. https://en.wikipedia.org/wiki/F-score. Accessed 29 Sept 2023

Zhang JM, Harman M, Ma L, Liu Y (2022) Machine learning testing: survey, landscapes and horizons. IEEE Trans Softw Eng 48(1):1–36. https://doi.org/10.1109/TSE.2019.2962027

Avoiding Pitfalls in Demand Forecasting

Malte C. Tichy, Illia Babounikau, Stefan Ulbrich, and Michael Feindt

Abstract Setting up, running, and evaluating demand forecasts entails several unexpected pitfalls, which jeopardize the reliability of the forecasts and the interpretation of evaluation metrics. These challenges lead to sometimes necessary, sometimes harmful interventions such as manual forecast overrides. We review the causes and effects of common pitfalls in setting up and evaluating demand forecasts for supply chain applications. Overcoming these challenges is necessary for the adoption of modern AI/ML-based systems, since the full potential of forecasting systems can only be unleashed when users know how to set up a forecast, what to expect from it, how to rate it, and when and when not to intervene.

1 Introduction: Automated Retail Forecasting

For the adoption of artificial intelligence (AI)- or machine learning (ML)-based methods in forecasting, the users' trust that the machine forecast is "at least as good as a human" is essential to avoid unnecessary or even harmful forecast overrides and manual interventions (Lawrence et al. 2006; Khosrowabadi et al. 2022; Franses and Legerstee 2010). Facilitating the correct evaluation of forecasts

Some of this material was previously published as blog posts on the Blue Yonder website (Tichy and Feindt 2022; Tichy 2022a,b,c), and adapted for this chapter.

M. C. Tichy (✉) · I. Babounikau
Blue Yonder GmbH, Hamburg, Germany
e-mail: Illia.Babounikau@blueyonder.com

S. Ulbrich
Blue Yonder GmbH, Karlsruhe, Germany
e-mail: Stefan.Ulbrich@blueyonder.com

M. Feindt
Feindt Vermögen und Consult GmbH, Karlsruhe, Germany
e-mail: feindt@phi-t.de

C. K. Coursaris et al. (eds.), *The Design of Human-Centered Artificial Intelligence for the Workplace*, Progress in IS, https://doi.org/10.1007/978-3-031-83512-4_14

and minimizing the number of "judgmental adjustments of forecasts" (Lawrence et al. 2006), which can range up to about 60% (Sanders and Manrodt 2003), is therefore an important objective in any demand forecasting project. Without realistic and holistic forecast evaluation, projects are doomed to misallocate resources, and tolerate problematic aspects in some areas while unnecessarily investing resources in others. The challenges and pitfalls that we present are not peripheral issues that can be tackled optionally, but may jeopardize the overall business success of any forecasting project. Our goal is to equip the reader with the ability to reflect upon forecast evaluation heuristics, avoid the most common pitfalls, and take a careful and informed stance on forecast judgment and evaluation.

In this chapter, we share lessons learned on the most common pitfalls which cause users to mistrust or reject demand forecasts. These pitfalls can be grouped by their root cause:

- Differences in situation awareness between human and system, discussed in Sect. 2.
- Limited human user's cognitive skills and human biases, described in Sect. 3.
- Limited human user's understanding of statistics, highlighted in Sect. 4.
- Human mistakes in training and evaluating systems, elaborated on in Sect. 5.

Due to the diversity of the root causes, improving forecasts reliably and effectively remains a nontrivial specialized task. This chapter shall hence help forecasters and forecast users find and cure the reasons for unsatisfactory forecasting performance.

2 Human and System Situation Awareness

Situation awareness is the knowledge about the current state of a situation and its comprehension (Endsley 2000). When constructing a forecast and proposing a replenishment order based on that forecast, AI/ML models are based on a certain model of past, present, and future reality which may or may not coincide with what is realistic and with what the user assumes. The latter two can, of course, also differ substantially. Moreover, the user may be skeptical about the optimization step that converts a demand forecast into action (typically, an order proposal).

The situation awareness of the user and the machine might hence differ, which can induce interventional errors in different ways: In the first place, there might be irrelevant information that the user thinks should be accounted for Dietvorst and Simonsohn (2019). Then, focusing on actual influences on demand, on the one hand, the machine may ignore a certain important factor, but the human user thinks the machine is aware of it (incorrect attribution, false-negative nonintervention, an intervention would have been necessary, but has not been done). On the other hand, the machine may correctly account for a factor influencing the forecast, but the human user thinks the machine does not (incorrect preemptive tuning, false-positive intervention).

2.1 *Incorrect Attribution of Omitted Factors*

In the first place, the user might expect that certain effects are covered by the forecast, while in reality, they are not. Suppose a certain promotion is running on a given product group, which increases its demand, but the promotional information is not submitted to the machine. The human user incorrectly believes that the machine has correctly ingested the promotional information and that it accounts for the increased demand. They will hence *not* perform an override of the demand prediction, which would be advised, given that the promotional information is not available. The demand prediction will hence be too low, and the promotional demand will possibly not be met by the supply induced by the forecast. This is, in technical terms, a false-negative nonintervention. The user should therefore have a good understanding of the type, quality, and quantity of information that is available to the forecasting system.

2.2 *Incorrect Preemptive Tuning Despite Existing Factors*

The opposite situation may also occur: The user thinks the machine does not account for a certain effect, while in reality, the effect has indeed taken part in the prediction process. As a consequence, when a forecasting user thinks that the machine is not aware of certain important circumstances, they might tune the forecast accordingly to account for these circumstances. For example, if a music festival takes place in a town, the local supermarket will see a great increase in demand for beer and crisps. If that music festival is correctly looked after in the data accessible by the machine, no intervention is necessary, and an intervention might even be harmful. Technically, this is a false-positive intervention.

What increases the complexity is that a given effect might be reflected by several causal factors: A promotion on the occasion of a certain event, which comes along with price reductions, is reflected by the event, the promotion, and the reduced price. Since the overall effect on demand is what eventually counts, it is futile to argue whether the demand boost is mostly due to price, promotion, or event. A forecasting user who assumes that a certain situation should be reflected by exactly one factor might miss that the situation is accounted for correctly, albeit by different factors: The event impact might be null, and the boost in demand might be reflected by the price and promotional effects.

In every case, a forecast override is only relieving the symptom—the resulting unsatisfactory forecast—and not the root cause. The next time an analogous situation arises, a similar override needs to be performed again. A more sustainable strategy is to improve the data source to align the situational models.

2.3 Alignment of Optimization Criteria

Further down the process line, the human user might preemptively tune the forecast to consciously rather low or rather high values to optimize for a business objective that is not well reflected by the optimization ("I rather want to go out of stock than keep waste, so I tune the forecast down" or "I absolutely don't want to go out-of-stock, so I tune the forecast up").

In other words, the human user may trust that the machine produces a reliable forecast, but they might nevertheless preemptively tune that forecast to intentionally underestimate or overestimate in order to account for asymmetric costs in the consequent optimization: Out-of-stock and waste typically have different costs, such that the corresponding situations are valued differently business-wise. Modern order optimization systems, however, do account for such asymmetric costs already, and will not use the expected demand or the predicted median naively as order proposal, but choose the correct quantile, to strategically use the correct quantity that induces least costs. Preemptively optimizing is, therefore, harmful.

In general, the visibility of both the information that enters the forecast and of the impact of all influencing factors is necessary to avoid incorrect attribution and preemptive tuning. Preemptive optimization may be reduced by clearly separating the *facts*—the forecast—from the *values*, the business objective, in an AI/ML-project. When an order proposal does not match expectations, one should not jump at tuning the forecast or the business objective immediately, but investigate the root cause and treat that instead of the mere symptom.

3 Limited Human Cognitive Skills and Biases in Predicting the Future

The problem of possibly disconnected human and machine situation awareness relates to the current state of a system. For forecasting, the projection skills of humans into the future become more relevant. Even if the human user correctly estimates the state of the machine, incorporating information that has not been processed by the system does not always lead to improvements (Fildes et al. 2019). Indeed, human perception and human forecasts are prone to many different biases (Kahneman 2011), whose strength also depends on personality traits (Eroglu and Croxton 2010). Some of those are optimism (forecasting high sales in the future), anchoring (reluctance to deviate from the forecast), and overreaction (noise in stable situations is taken as signal, while clear signals in unstable environments are ignored) (Eroglu and Croxton 2010). In general, forecast evaluation, as a statistical problem, deserves to be treated by forecasters' cognitive "system 2" (the slow, meticulous, but also effortful way of thinking), while it is often their "system 1" (the fast, intuitive, emotional way) reasoning that is applied (Kahneman 2011).

We emphasize two types of biases that are especially important in the context of probabilistic forecasts: The hindsight bias (Roese and Olson 1996) and the availability bias.

3.1 Hindsight Bias and Causal Attribution

Humans attribute causes after the fact, and this *hindsight bias*, the "after-the-fact exaggeration of an outcome's a priori likelihood" (Roese and Olson 1996), has been known for long in psychology (Fischhoff and Beyth 1975). Consider a supply planner of a large retail company who analyzes individual examples for SKUs (stock keeping units) that were under- or overpredicted. They will easily find a "storyline" that explains why they would have known better than the forecast ("Clearly, red T-shirts never sell well in September, they should have asked me!"). The fluctuations that have been observed might have just been statistical noise and insignificant. Tuning the model to account for these fluctuations might be an overreaction. Any insights from such anecdotal evidence should therefore be tested using out-of-sample methods to avoid overfitting. One can thereby establish whether one could have predicted the unexpected fluctuation given the past available information.

3.2 Anecdotal Evidence and Availability Bias

"Your forecast predicted 7.2 items, but we sold 12 on that day! The forecast obviously has a serious problem!"—anecdotal evidence based on readily available examples is hard to counter, since the correct reply "the forecast is probabilistic; forecasting 7.2 implies that there is indeed a non-zero chance to sell 12 items" sounds defensive. Just like it is impossible to dismiss a probabilistic forecast on a single instance, it remains likewise impossible to rule out a systematic problem on that same example. It is difficult to accept that the probabilistic nature affects each and every individual forecast: The authors have literally heard phrases similar to "I understand uncertainty, but I do not want uncertainty. When the forecast says 5, I want the number of sales to be 5, not 4 or 6" in forecasting projects. Especially in the context of the hindsight bias, it is necessary to designate anecdotal evidence as such and to dismiss it, not only to allow the acceptance of a forecast but also to avoid overfitting: The analysis of the situation with predicted rate $r = 7.2$ and observed sales $s = 12$ would erroneously reveal that the impact of certain causal factors seems to be over- or underestimated. The Poisson distribution—the standard way to describe counts, introduced below—with a mean of 7.2 assigns a finite probability of about 3.2% to the observation 12 or larger, a small one, but not as small as it would justify dismissing the prediction altogether. In the worst case, the forecast is tweaked in a way that the anecdotal examples are "postdicted" (instead of *predicted*), jeopardizing the forecast generalization for the future.

When many “surprisingly small” or “surprisingly large” values appear in a set of forecasts and the users start to doubt that these are empirically as unlikely as they are predicted to be, one can inspect forecast evaluation metrics such as the probability integral transform (Wick et al. 2021). Such metrics answer the question to which extent the observed number of “unlikely events” matches the prediction.

4 Limited Understanding of Statistical Foundations

Forecast generation and evaluation is a challenging field of applied statistics (Gneiting et al. 2007; Kolassa 2016b; Petropoulos et al. 2022; Gneiting 2011), such that the pertinent methods often remain inaccessible to users in trade and retail, which have not necessarily obtained a higher mathematical education (Kolassa 2016a). For instance, while the statistics literature consensually agrees that the forecasting metric Mean Absolute Percentage Error (MAPE) is the most unsuitable and misleading for all thinkable business purposes (Kolassa and Martin 2011; Vandeput 2021; Tichy 2022d; Gneiting 2011; Tichy 2023), it remains the most widely used in practice (Gartner 2018; Bower 2023), a clearly alarming situation.

The gap between the scientific state-of-the-art (Hewamalage et al. 2023) and operational forecasting practice is unsatisfactory, also because humans typically perform poorly when intuitively answering statistical questions. For instance, humans often fail at interpreting the result of binary tests, such as the probability that a patient has colorectal cancer after having a positive screening result (Hoffrage and Gigerenzer 1998). The many biases that humans suffer from (Kahneman 2011) can be overcome by adhering to established communication rules (Gigerenzer and Edwards 2003; Spiegelhalter 2019; Gigerenzer 1991).

Humans do not like uncertainty and tend to ignore it, but forecasts are necessarily probabilistic. Human users often use the predicted mean (the expected average value), median (the value that divides outcomes in two groups of equal size), and mode (the most probable value) of a forecast as synonyms, which they are not. The impact of scale—slow-moving products necessarily come with larger relative uncertainty—is often seen as a witness of a bad forecast (either in the fast- or in the slow-movers, depending on which metric is considered). For a tangible example, let’s consider demand forecasting in retail on a product-location-day level. Demand constitutes a nonnegative *discrete quantity*: The demand for T-shirts is *discrete*, it could be 0, 1, 2, 13, or 56, but not -8.5 or 3.4. Yet, it is an ordinal *quantity*: 27 T-shirts is closer to 26 than to 4. Realistic demand forecasts are probabilistic; a point forecast may suggest determinism, but misleads the user by doing so.

A realistic yet ambitiously narrow (i.e., precise) probability distribution that models the number of sold items is the *Poisson distribution*. The forecast for the jth item-location-day combination is denoted by r_j, a continuous number: r_j is the *rate* that drives the sales resulting in s_j sold items (we will differentiate demand and sales below):

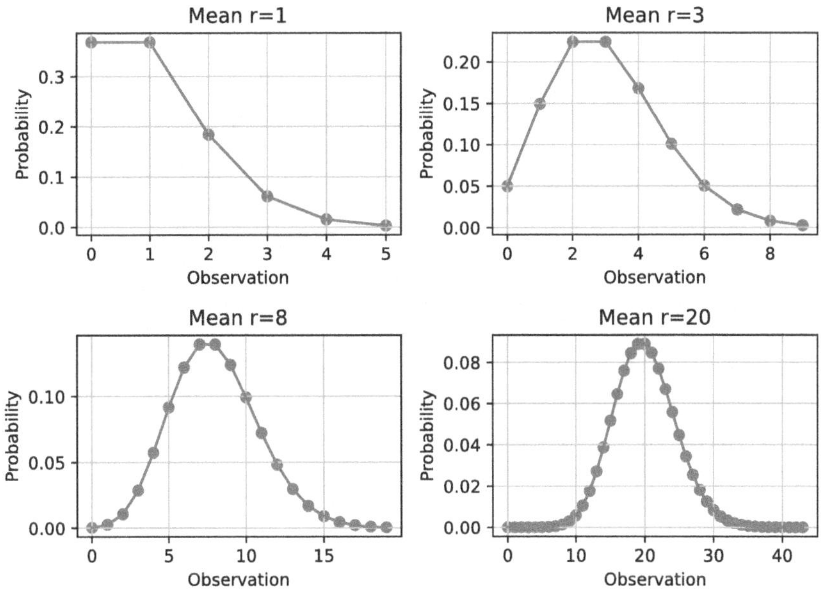

Fig. 1 Probability mass function of the Poisson distribution, for predicted rates (equating the mean) $r = 1, 3, 8, 20$

$$s_j \sim P_{\text{Poi}}(s = s_j | \mu = r_j) = \frac{e^{-r_j} r_j^{s_j}}{s_j!}, \tag{1}$$

that is, the forecast asserts that the sales s_j are drawn from a Poisson distribution parameterized by its mean expectation value μ, as illustrated in Fig. 1.

For a single prediction r_j and a single outcome s_j, little to nothing can be said about the forecast in general: Every outcome s_j has a nonzero occurrence probability (albeit one might already dismiss the forecast $r_j = 0.5$ after observing the extreme value $s_j = 10'000$ once, given its spectacular unlikelihood, for instance). Forecasts can only be evaluated in bulk, when many individual forecasts r_j and actuals s_j are aggregated.

4.1 Embracing Uncertainty: Using and Interpreting Probabilistic Forecasts

Humans heavily dislike uncertainty (de Berker et al. 2016): People jeopardize substantial expected value for achieving the marginal improvement from "almost certain" to "absolutely certain" (Pinker 2021). What forecasting technology delivers, however, clashes with these expectations: No nontrivial forecast can guarantee that a certain predicted value will appear with absolute certainty. The gold standard for demand forecasts in retail is the Poisson forecast introduced in Eq. 1: It is a simple and well-manageable yet ambitious to achieve model. The Poisson distribution shown in Fig. 1 is, colloquially speaking, unexpectedly broad for small predicted values, and only becomes familiarly narrow when sales values are much larger than about 100: Given a forecast of $r = 1$, e.g., for the demand of T-shirts to be sold on a day, the probability of observing an outcome with relative error -100%, the outcome 0, is $1/e \approx 0.37$, the probability to observe an outcome with relative error $+100\%$ or larger, the outcomes 2, 3, etc., is approximately 26%. The reason is that the variance of the Poisson distribution is equal to its mean, letting its relative error (the error divided by its mean) decrease for increasing rates. Often, people interpreting forecasts do not have the Poisson distribution in mind when comparing bare forecasted rates r_j to actual sales s_j, resulting in several paradoxes and misconceptions, which we will discuss in the following.

4.2 *Forecast Quality Dichotomization*

An important pitfall in forecast evaluation is the tendency to classify every pair of forecast and actual into either "good" or "bad," often based on the value that a certain metric achieves. The "bad" instances are then investigated further. For example, all instances that achieve a relative error of 20% or better could be labeled "good"; all those that surpass that error level are labeled "bad." We strongly advise against this dichotomization: Due to the probabilistic nature of any forecast, it is unavoidable that some instances will appear to be "bad": For a forecast of 1, we expect to observe the value 4 or larger with a probability of about 1.8%, and even for a perfect forecast, one will spend unnecessary effort in finding out whether a fluctuation has a cause. The dichotomization strategy is clearly reminiscent of the unrealistic expectation of a deterministic forecast. Often, such simple cutoff also ignores scaling (discussed in Sect. 4.4), classifying a much larger portion of prediction/observation pairs as "bad" in the slow-seller regime than in the fast-sellers.

As an alternative, it is useful to formulate a list of outliers, that is, events that are extremely unlikely, given the prediction: For example, for a given one million data points, one can focus on those observations that are much more unlikely to occur than in one of a million cases as predicted by the forecast.

4.3 *Point Estimators and Forecast Value Interpretation*

When confronted with the situation of Sect. 3.2 (prediction $r = 7.2$, observed sales $s = 12$), it is quite immediate to compute an evaluation metric. The *absolute error*, the absolute value of the difference between forecast and actual, is the most popular. In our case, the immediate result of absolute error is $|7.2 - 12| = 4.8$. Directly sub-

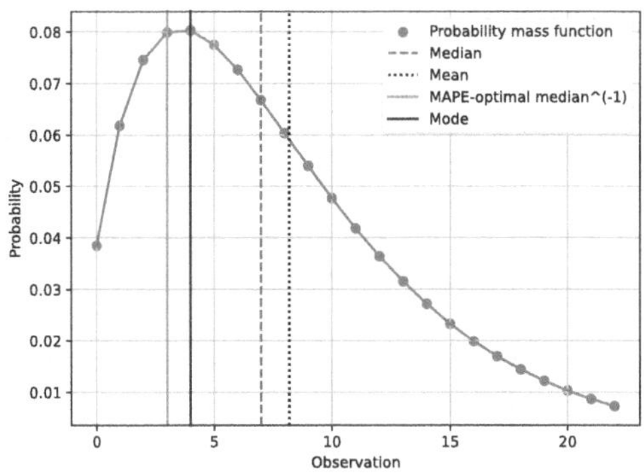

Fig. 2 Probability mass function of a negative-binomial distribution (a Poisson distribution with uncertain mean value r), and some point estimators: The mean equates to 8.2 (dotted blue line); it optimizes for squared error. The median is 7 (red dashed line) and optimizes for absolute error (Schwertman et al. 1990; Kolassa 2020). The mode (green solid line) is the most probable value 4. The median$^{(-1)}$ (solid orange line) is the optimal value for MAPE, and amounts to 3. Probability distributions contain much more information than the mean value; hence, depending on the evaluation method, they will produce different point estimators. This reflects that the optimal action, given a forecast, depends on the business strategy

tracting the observation from the predicted mean, however, is oversimplifying the situation: The numbers r and s are of a completely different nature. The parameter r is not equating the forecast, but it's merely a forecast parameter, the mean of the predicted distribution. Probabilistic forecasts are not mere "point forecasts" that express a universal, evaluation-independent "best estimate" for the target, but they provide a probability distribution, as inscribed in Eq. 1 for the Poisson distribution. The concept of forecasting error then becomes much more involved: How can a function be subtracted from a number? When a probability distribution states that several values are possible, which one should I use? Subtracting 12 sold items from a probability distribution makes no sense. We therefore need to *summarize* the forecast, the predicted probability distribution, by a single number, to make a comparison at all possible. This summary number, the *point estimator*, can then be subtracted from the observed actual value to yield the error.

Probability distributions can be summarized in different ways, as shown in Fig. 2. The expectation value for the mean observation is the most immediate and intuitive summary. Distributions can also be summarized by the most probable value (the mode), by the value that divides the probability distribution into two equal halves (the median), or by the median$^{(-1)}$, an idiosyncratic functional that is optimal for MAPE. In general, any functional (a mapping between functions and numbers) can be a point estimator.

The differentiation between different point estimators is often ignored, in that one uses the mean of the distribution interchangeably as "the forecast." In reality, however, the correct summary is fixed by the chosen evaluation metric, which also solves the ostensible paradox that, depending on the business use case, different point forecasts are best: When the business application sets the cost of under- and overstocks, it is the forecaster's choice to choose the point estimator (Kolassa 2020; Gneiting et al. 2007), and which value enters the evaluation. This point is difficult to communicate to forecast users: It can sound arbitrary that the forecasted number, the point estimator, changes when the evaluation metric changes, but it reflects the immense power of probabilistic forecasts; they contain much more information than just a "best guess." A single probabilistic forecast can therefore yield many different point forecasts, depending on the forecast usage and on how it is evaluated. This reflects that, depending on the business application and cost functions in place, a forecast will translate to different optimal decisions.

In summary, when evaluating a forecast using a simple error metric, the probabilistic nature of the forecast cannot be ignored: A forecast is not just a statement on *what* will happen, but also on *how likely* possible events are. Two forecasts with the same predicted mean (say, the predicted demand averages to 10) may require different actions: Large uncertainty requires larger stock volumes than small uncertainty to guarantee a certain non-out-of-stock rate.

Only in the limiting case of large numbers and mediocre forecasts, in which forecasting errors are much larger than the unavoidable statistical noise, can we state that the three point estimators optimal for absolute error, squared error, and absolute percentage error (median, mean, and median^{-1}) are close.

4.4 Few Is Different: Scaling Effects in Forecast Accuracy

In forecasting projects, target KPIs are often defined top-down; for example, a 95% accuracy goal might be formulated by upper management. Forecasts are, however, just like any technology, restricted by the limits of Nature, in particular, by the laws of statistics and information science. Stakeholders need to acknowledge that such fundamental limits are insuperable and relevant.

Many surveys compare achieved accuracies and derive conclusions from the aggregated numbers (Kolassa 2008). It is, however, impossible to formulate a domain-independent benchmarking goal for forecasts for any forecasting metric. When project success is measured by some accuracy metric, the threshold values must, hence, under no circumstance, be defined independently of the data.

Let's explore why this is the case: Any demand forecast will concern slow- to fast-selling items. Absolute and relative forecast uncertainty then scale in a non-proportional way with selling rates. This scaling largely determines the achievable level of precision (Tichy 2022a). For the same forecast quality, predictions for slowly moving items unavoidably come with a lower absolute but higher relative error than for fast-moving ones. The user should avoid the *naïve scaling trap*: If a forecast seems to struggle in a category with many slow sellers, one should not jump at the immediate conclusion that there is a problem but assess to which extent the increase in relative error is expected when moving toward low velocities (Tichy et al. 2024). There is, however, no hard boundary between "slow" and "fast" movers.

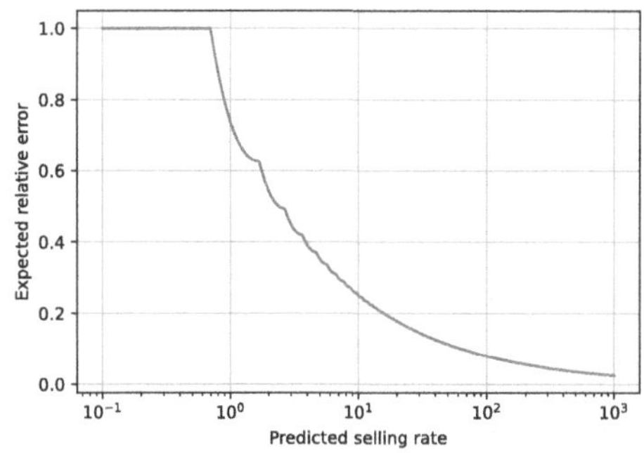

Fig. 3 Achievable wMAPE, as a function of the predicted selling rate r

One should not bucket items into only two different evaluation methodologies but ensure that the evaluation treats all predicted selling rates appropriately. The authors use at least four buckets between two powers of ten.

The problem of the impact of scaling has only emerged recently: Until a few years ago, forecasts in supply chain have been concerned with large quantities on coarse-grained scales, e.g., the total sales of dairy products in a region during a month. Typical numbers that one dealt with were of the order of at least a few hundred, up to many thousands. Today's computational resources allow forecasting on a much more granular level; predictions refer to individual items on a single day in a given location. On that level, the typical numbers that we deal with are not in the 100,000s, but are sometimes as small as 5, 1, or 0.1. The width of the Poisson distribution (see Fig. 1) then becomes decisive for the achievable forecast accuracy. The result can be appreciated from Fig. 3: The optimally achievable wMAPE (mean absolute error divided by mean observation), as a function of the predicted selling rate, decreases strongly with the predicted rate; for a forecast of one unit per day, the forecast user has to live with a wMAPE of about 73%. We will see the consequence of this perhaps surprisingly large relative error in the next subsection.

4.5 *Ultrafresh Slow Sellers Cannot Be Offered Sustainably*

One tangible consequence of nonproportional scaling is that retailers do not offer perishable items in extremely low demand because they are unable to predict the actual demand precisely enough to find a profitable sweet spot in the balance between waste and out-of-stock situations. Mathematically speaking, the Poisson distribution for low rates r is simply too wide to allow for a meaningful balance of waste and out-of-stocks.

In numbers, if the expected demand per day of some ultrafresh product (which needs to be disposed of after the day) is $r = 1$, we will experience about 37% of days without any demand, 37% of the days will see a demand of 1, matching our forecasted mean, and in 26% of the days, the demand is two or even more (see Fig. 1). Clearly, a business model that aims at fulfilling the tiny demand of that ultrafresh product is not viable, and could only be sustained if the margin were extremely large: The people buying the product need to subsidize all the days without demand, while customers are not even sure to get one if they want one. Under mild assumptions on the margin and the costs of disposal, the right amount of stock for an ultrafresh super-slow seller is zero. Again, this is all due to nonproportional scaling: The expected distribution of sales for a forecast of 100 items per day is not just an inflated version of the above one for 1 item per day, but it has a different shape.

In summary, due to nonproportional scaling of forecasting error with the sales rate, the occurring overstocks and understocks of a product—even assuming a perfect Poisson forecast—disproportionally increase when the sales rate decreases. Only when the sales rate per shelf life is higher than a certain threshold (which depends on the margin and costs or over- and understocks), offering perishable food can be sustained at all. Conversely, if many slowly moving items are encountered in an analysis and one knows that these items are indeed profitable, one should challenge the evaluation level, that is, the level on which the error is computed, and make sure the aggregation timescale matches business reality: One does not take daily business decisions on nonperishable slow movers; see also Sect. 5.2.2.

4.6 *You Should Not Have Known Better: Hindsight Selection Bias*

Forecast evaluation can only be performed for an outdated forecast, for which the forecasted event has already occurred. This then opens up new pitfalls, as one needs to carefully deal with information that was not yet available at the moment of the forecast.

Even when the user has reflected sufficiently to realize that anecdotal evidence alone is insufficient to judge the forecast quality, and they choose to do a systematic evaluation (see Sect. 3 and, in particular, Sect. 3.1), there is an important pitfall that can severely jeopardize it and lead to wrong conclusions: The hindsight selection bias (Tichy and Feindt 2022). In contrast to the psychological effects mentioned above, the hindsight selection bias appears even in apparently meticulously performed forecast evaluations. It is both a statistical and a psychological effect, which arises when probabilistic forecast predictions and observed actuals are not properly grouped when evaluating forecast accuracy across sales frequencies.

For example, one might evaluate the bias of a forecast for a T-shirt via the following table.

Observed sales frequency	Mean observed sales	Mean prediction
Slow, 0, 1, 2 pieces/day	0.804	1.373
Medium, 3–10 pieces/day	5.119	4.601
Fast, >10 pieces/day	13.880	11.041

Data is grouped by the observed sales frequency: All days are bucketed into groups in which the T-shirt happened to be sold few (0, 1, or 2), intermediate (3–10), or many (more than 10) times. At first sight, this table shouts unambiguously "slow sellers are over-forecasted, fast sellers are under-forecasted."

In reality, and possibly surprisingly, everything is fine. Observed slow sellers are indeed over-forecasted, and observed fast sellers are under-forecasted, but the forecast behaves just as it should. It is the user's expectation—that the columns "mean observed sales" and "mean prediction" ought to be the same—that is flawed. We deal with our unrealistic expectations, combined with a flawed way of grouping the data, and not with a bad forecast. A probabilistic forecast never promises nor will ever fulfill that for each possible group of outcomes the mean forecast matches the mean outcome. In particular, when we select those items that were not sold at all on a given day (actual sales are zero), they will necessarily have been over-forecasted: Forecasted means are always larger than zero.

What we can expect from a forecast is that *forecasted* slow sellers are predicted in an unbiased way on average, and so should be *forecasted* fast sellers. Solving the paradox, instead of grouping by outcome bucket, we should therefore group by prediction bucket, i.e., by *predicted* slow, mid, and fast sellers. Here, we can check whether the forecast's promise (the mean sales given a certain prediction matches that prediction) is fulfilled. For our example, based on the same data, we obtain this table.

Predicted sales frequency	Mean observed sales	Mean prediction
Slow, <5 pieces/day	1.288	1.267
Medium, about 5 pieces/day	5.247	5.229
Fast, >5 pieces/day	12.855	12.950

Accounting for the total number of measurements, a test of statistical significance would be negative, i.e., show no significant difference between the mean observed sales and the mean prediction. The forecast is not only globally unbiased but also unbiased per prediction stratum.

In general, one can evaluate a forecast by filtering on any information that is known at prediction time, and the forecast should be unbiased in all tests. However, the filter is not allowed to contain future information such as the random fluctuations that occur in the observations, on which nature decides only in the future of the prediction point in time. For example, also extreme weather conditions that have occurred disqualify as groups for forecast comparison.

In conclusion, when one selects by outcome, one does not deal with a representative sample. One should always be skeptical toward one's own expectations—reasonably looking intuitive expectations turn out to be flawed. Expectations should be made explicit ("for a perfect forecast, I expect the mean prediction to match the observation") and tested against well-understood cases.

5 Human Mistakes in Training and Evaluating Systems

The very setup of forecasting systems is a highly nontrivial specialized task. Available user-friendly APIs have lessened the technical burden of installing forecasting systems, and output can be produced quickly, but the functional forecasting part still requires reflection and conscious adjustment to the particular forecasting situation.

5.1 Model Setup: Preparing Forecasting Systems

Consider a forecasting system that produces rates r_j that describe the demand for a given product-location-day-combination indexed by j. Before evaluating a set of forecast and resulting demand values (r_j, s_j), we need to establish the boundary conditions under which the forecast is produced.

5.1.1 Feature Selection in Machine Learning

The forecast r_j is a function of the historic data and of known circumstances in the future. The model for r_j can be based on the temporal patterns of a single product-location combination—the time-series approach (Shumway and Stoffer 2017)—or additionally consider the causal factors that are identified to influence demand, the machine learning approach, which we focus on here.

In addition to historic observations of the predicted quantity—often the sole input for time-series predictions—machine learning identifies and considers additional factors that influence demand. As an example, consider the local weather conditions and their impact on the demand for ice cream sales. We assume that temperature and precipitation are available for each day in the dataset. The values of both quantities considerably impact the sales as the demand increases with temperature and is the highest on a sunny day. Clearly, a model that attributes ice cream sales to high temperature and low precipitation will be superior to a purely time-series-based model that has learned that "ice cream always sells well in July": The latter model would not reduce the forecast when the weather turns to be untypically cold and rainy.

But how will sales behave when it is a hot, rainy day as the demand is well known to diminish on rainy days? Similar to us, artificial intelligence must take the *combination of both quantities* into account and the cross-relations and magnitude of influence needs to be encoded in the model. While some methods are capable of autonomously detecting dependencies, it often makes sense to prepare the training data such that the complexity of the learned model is reduced and the efficiency of training and prediction is maximized, especially when tremendous amounts of data are available. The process of defining the input is called *feature engineering* and is strongly bound to the respective industry. In grocery, for instance, a similar choice of features can be shared between multiple customers. Feature engineering is a manual process that requires domain knowledge. Examples of the decisions made by engineers are grouping variables into multidimensional features as in the example above, normalizing continuous values to a value range between zero and one to avoid scaling problems, or remove redundant or correlating variables from the training data set.

Eventually, feature engineering leads to data preprocessing that can be automated and integrated into the processing pipelines used for training and prediction. That means that training and prediction receives consistently structured input, exploiting that both processes access the same model representation. This also creates some unexpected problems: Consider again the weather condition as a two-dimensional feature composed of the temperature and precipitation. Let's imagine we generate a forecast for the daily demand of ice cream for the upcoming 2 weeks. We simply do not know with absolute certainty how the conditions will be on next day and have to rely on another, external forecast system for a prediction. The problem intensifies the farther we look into the future, and, eventually, we have to resort to the average climate expectation if we predict for many months ahead—a daily forecast would make little sense in that case. Consequently, we distinguish between deterministic features such as school holidays or sport events and dynamic, nondeterministic features, to which weather or traffic conditions belong, that are, if at all, only approximately known beforehand.

One should always be aware of nondeterministic features when evaluating past models and their forecasts. Features that are available now might not have been known (or only with uncertainty) at the time of the prediction, and a fresh prediction with the precise values will unsurprisingly be more accurate. A fair comparison therefore requires that the exact input values that were used for the other prediction are taken. Finally, even if some features are deterministic in theory, they still might change after predictions have been generated, which should then be invalidated. Most prominently, product prices and promotions are frequently subject to change by demand planners and are often considered the strongest influencing factors to the demand. It is crucial that forecasts are freshly generated for individual planning scenarios and that customers are accordingly educated.

In conclusion, feature engineering is by far not only a technical endeavor, but necessarily comprises the understanding of the nature and distribution of the features. On long horizons, a forecast inherits the uncertainty present in other forecasts that feed the model.

5.1.2 Demand and Sales

In Eq. (1), s_j represents *demand*, that is, the number of items that are being asked for by customers. True demand is not directly observable in practice; from the historic data, one can typically extract the actual *sales* of items. Sales reflect the demand that the retailer was able to fulfill. If 20 red T-shirts are being asked for on a given day in a given store, the demand is 20. If only ten T-shirts are available, only ten pieces can be sold. That makes sales a lower bound to the real demand. Assuming infinite availability, sales and demand match. In reality, constant availability cannot be ensured always since stores encounter out-of-stock situations due to tight planning, suppliers cannot meet the demand, or the required shelf space is occupied. Consequently, during the implementation of a forecasting system, the discrepancy between observed sales and hypothetical demand needs to be carefully considered. Technically speaking, the ideal relation Eq. (1) between rate and observed sales is altered, and one observes a modified distribution. The impact of unfulfilled demand leads to two effects on the probability distribution.

Zero Inflation

We speak of *zero inflation* if the data contains entries with zero sales that are due to general unavailability instead of lack of demand. This occurs, for instance, when products have not been *assigned*, that is, they have not been put on display at all. This can be the result of an out-of-stock situation that lasts multiple days without up-to-date inventory information, or be voluntarily even if the product is still in stock but not offered to customers. Artificial intelligence cannot precisely distinguish between the lack of demand (zero-sales events that are due to the low popularity of the item on a given day) or the lack of availability (the item is not offered at all).

The consequence of zero inflation in the training data is a negative bias in the forecast: The system has learned presumed low demand on days on which the demand was not observable at all since the product was not on display. On the other hand, an unbiased model might seem to be overpredicting when it is evaluated on a period in which the items were not always available.

The problem greatly intensifies for slow-selling products for which zero sales during a sales period are a frequent and natural occurrence, and the distinction between lack of demand and lack of availability is not perceivable from the time series: Even if from the overall statistics of zero sales, it is immediate that zero inflation occurs (as in the left panel of Fig. 4, in which we simulate that in 10% of

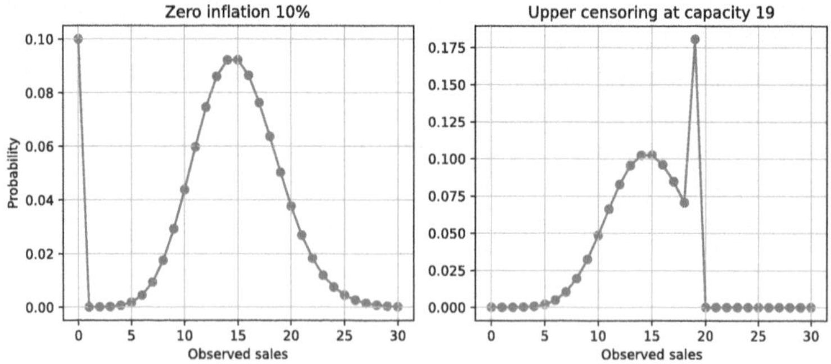

Fig. 4 Probability to observe a certain number of sales, when the demand is Poisson-distributed with rate 15, but affected by zero inflation of 10% (left panel) or upper censoring at 19 (right panel)

the days, the product was not offered), it is hard to judge whether the zero sales on a given product-location-day were due to unavailability or lack of demand.

The straightforward solution is to request *assignments* to be part of the data in the form of a binary flag that indicates whether an item was offered at all, or, if possible, to extract this information from available planograms. In the authors' experience, however, many customers do not possess this knowledge for their own historical data and only start collecting it on demand. Then, a complex and expensive reconstruction of the historical data is required to counterbalance zero inflation.

Censoring

Censoring occurs when products are available at the beginning of the day (more generally: the forecasting time unit) but become unavailable before its end. For instance, if the demand is correctly predicted to be 15, but the available stocks on each day are 19, the resulting distribution of sales is the one of the right panel of Fig. 4: On some days, the item goes out of stock before the end of the day, instead of sometimes observing 20, 21, 22 or more sales, we observe just 19. Similar to zero inflation, it manifests in a negative bias, and fast-selling products are more prone to be affected. Zero inflation can be seen as the effect of censoring at capacity zero. The key to preventing negative effects on the forecast lies in the data. Censoring can be identified if accurate stock levels at the end of the time frame are available or out-of-stock situations are explicitly tracked and removed from both training and evaluation.

After instances of zero inflation or censoring have been identified, a machine learning algorithm can be adjusted to account for their occurrence or the respective data can simply be omitted from the dataset.

The last two sections barely scratched the surface of the important decisions data engineers and data scientists face when designing entirely new forecasting systems, welcoming new customers, or expanding to new industries. Feature engineering, for instance, becomes a challenge when complex relations such as product cannibalization, new product introductions, or product succession come into play. An even more important aspect that we assumed as given so far is the correctness and consistency of the data. Data quality virtually always requires improvement, and its monitoring is thus mandatory especially during the implementation of forecasts for new use cases.

5.2 Evaluation Setup: Aligning Business and Mathematics

Forecast evaluation needs to align with the business use case. Before computing any model evaluation metric, one should understand the specific decision that is based on the forecast to adapt the evaluation setup accordingly: A better forecast should be equivalent to a better business performance. The ostensible paradox that a seemingly better model can lead to worse business results is a result of misalignment between evaluation and business use case (Robette 2023; Bower 2023). In particular, a point estimate that leads to a better Mean Absolute Percentage Error (MAPE) is often worse for business decisions, as we discuss below.

The same model can also be used for different use cases simultaneously: A demand forecast can be used for short-term daily allocation and for long-term, strategic planning. The different use cases then require different evaluation settings.

5.2.1 Evaluation Period and Horizon

For a realistic assessment of model performance in production, the forecast needs to be evaluated on out-of-sample data. The data that are used to compute evaluation KPIs must hence not have been used for training. Nevertheless, an additional in-sample evaluation is also helpful: When the forecasting error (adjusted for scaling, see below) is much better in-sample than out-of-sample, this clear sign of overfitting to the training data reflects the inability of the model to extrapolate into the future.

When setting up evaluation periods, one needs to establish the *training cutoff dates* (up to which dates shall the model training take place?), the *horizon* (how many days after the training cutoff does the evaluation period start?), as well as the *evaluation period length* (how long does the period last?). These choices should be aligned with the business use case.

Training cutoff dates should reflect the diverse situations in the year in whose context a forecast is used: Imagine we predict the demand for a seasonal product that is affected by holidays, seasons, and promotions, which vary during the year. Selecting only a few cutoff dates within a short period (e.g., 1 month) that does not include all different causals and situations can give a skewed result. For instance, when the model is only evaluated during summer, in which few promotions are active, large errors in production can occur during the later promotion or holiday periods.

The business application defines a particular horizon (lag), i.e., the time offset between the end of the training period and the beginning of the predicted period. For example, when today's demand predictions become store fulfillment orders to be delivered to stores in 1 month from now, the forecast horizon is 1 month. Performing one training and evaluating the model once is a simple and robust approach, but will often not yield a representative result. Therefore, one often uses a rolling horizon: The evaluation is repeated for several different cutoff dates.

The evaluation period length should match the timescale on which the business decision is materialized. If store orders are fulfilled once per week for the entire upcoming week, the relevant forecasting error is the error on that weekly timescale. That is, forecasts and actuals are aggregated on that weekly timescale before comparison. An over-forecast on Mondays that is balanced out by an under-forecast on Wednesday is then ignored.

Given a business process that incurs decisions on a weekly level and an incumbent model, there could be competing models that provide better forecasts on a daily level, e.g., match the weekday profile better, but be worse on a weekly level, e.g., by inducing some overall bias. If daily instead of weekly evaluation period length were chosen, the user would choose the model that results in worse business outcomes.

The question arises why a forecasting model predicts demand on a daily level in the first place if only the weekly aggregation eventually matters. In practice, more granular time data can often provide additional forecast improvement. A model that is trained on daily data can learn a weekly pattern and correctly predict the entire week when some weekday is affected by an exceptional event, e.g., a general closure or some special event.

5.2.2 Business Application and Alignment with Evaluation

The business value of a forecast is the monetary impact that the forecast error (or its improvement) has on the business. Ideally, the forecast is judged precisely within the context that it is used for—the dimension of the forecast evaluation result should be monetary currency. The precise impact of a forecast can be arbitrarily complex: There can be different weights for over- and under-forecasting (e.g., the cost of lost sales vs. overstock); these weights might additionally differ by product assortment. Finite-size effects (e.g., certain products can only be ordered in dozens) make the business decisions discontinuous as a function of the forecast.

In practice, a business value calculation that accounts for every aspect and which is repeated for each model run can be costly and unfeasible. The business objective function or strategic choices may also change over time, such that it is shortsighted to optimize for one business case only. Therefore, one will often recur to simpler metrics in the forecast evaluation to select a better model and identify potential data and model parameter problems. The ostensible paradox that a forecast, which should be an objective approximation to reality, is judged differently depending on the business use case is solved by accounting for each forecast's probabilistic nature, which we discussed in Sect. 4.1.

In analogy to the choice of the evaluation time period, the level on which error metrics are computed should match the decision level of the business. For example, a forecast might have been generated on the store granularity to take into account store-related features and new store openings. One of the use cases of the forecasts could be regional DC fulfillment, on a level much higher than the individual store. It is sensible to include store-related features to model demand as precisely as possible, but it is the DC-level aggregate that eventually matters for the error calculation.

In conclusion, metrics should be calculated at the level of decision-making, and they should ideally reflect the cost of a suboptimal decision, although sometimes compromises between simplicity and the perfect account of business costs need to be made. When the forecast has several use cases, it should be evaluated under the different evaluation settings that reflect these use cases.

6 Conclusions: Forecast Setup and Evaluation Complexity Can Be Tamed

Forecasts require specialists to be set up, maintained, run, used, and evaluated. The divulgation of software libraries has eased the technical aspects of many of these tasks, but the functional challenges, some of which we have described in this chapter, remain.

Treating forecasting systems as "black boxes" is doomed to failure: The human user needs to be aware of the information that the system has to achieve a satisfactory alignment of situation awareness. The quality of forecasts is often taken to be "as is," without questioning to which extent forecasts can be expected to be truthful and whether a certain degree of precision is reasonable to ask for. Practitioners have comforted themselves with the downhearted saying "all forecasts are wrong," with a large degree of manual interventions (Fildes et al. 2019; Franses and Legerstee 2010; Eroglu and Croxton 2010). Forecasting is, however, a quantitative science, which can also quantify its own limits. Users should have at least a basic statistical understanding to judge what accuracies can be expected from forecasts. They should also be aware of their own limitations, and reflect whether they are, for instance, exaggerating the evidence of past anecdotes. Finally, understanding the business application of the forecast is crucial for a satisfactory performance. Users should ensure that the business objective, e.g., the cost of waste and out-of-stocks, fully reflects business reality: If, e.g., some perishable but not particularly fast-selling item is a "must-offer" (the unavailability of that item puts the demand of other items in jeopardy, "If I don't get fresh strawberries today, I'll never go shopping in that supermarket ever again!"), the business object should incorporate a high cost for that item going out-of-stock.

The human effort spent on modifying forecasts and tuning forecasting systems is often not optimally allocated. Instead of curing symptoms such as an "unwanted" forecast or machine-led business decision, the input to the system—the historical data as well as the parameters of the business objective—should be adjusted in a sustainable way to avoid similar unwanted effects also in the future. The shorter the overall pipeline of training and optimization, the faster one will find the root cause of unwanted behaviors.

As an immediate desirable line of research, forecasters should investigate how to visualize forecasts and their uncertainty in a way that transmits a realistic picture and avoids confusion. Users should be helped to make meaningful overrides by making transparent which information enters the forecast, and why a certain business decision is proposed. This would enable a constructive feedback loop in which users continuously improve forecasts. This endeavor could follow the successful path of classification visualization: Well-trained medical doctors account for the personal prevalence of a condition when confronting a patient with the result of a test and letting them decide how to proceed (Gigerenzer and Edwards 2003).

The coming years will witness how ML-powered forecasts will penetrate more and more different domains. For this transition to be successful, users need to develop a realistic intuitive understanding of how forecasts work, in which domains they perform well, when they struggle, and how good a forecast can be.

References

Bower P (2023) Why do we talk about forecast accuracy measures (so much)? Foresight 68:50

de Berker AO, Rutledge RB, Mathys C, Marshall L, Cross GF, Dolan RJ, Bestmann S (2016) Computations of uncertainty mediate acute stress responses in humans. Nat Commun 7(1):10996. https://doi.org/10.1038/ncomms10996

Dietvorst BJ, Simonsohn U (2019) Intentionally "biased": people purposely use to-be-ignored information, but can be persuaded not to. J Exp Psychol Gen 148:1228

Endsley M (2000) Situation awareness analysis and measurement, chapter theoretical underpinnings of situation awareness. A Crit Rev 3–33

Eroglu C, Croxton KL (2010) Biases in judgmental adjustments of statistical forecasts: the role of individual differences. Int J Forecast 26(1):116–133. https://doi.org/10.1016/j.ijforecast.2009.02.005

Fildes R, Goodwin P, Önkal D (2019) Use and misuse of information in supply chain forecasting of promotion effects. Int J Forecast 35(1):144–156. https://doi.org/10.1016/j.ijforecast.2017.12.006

Fischhoff B, Beyth R (1975) I knew it would happen: remembered probabilities of once—future things. Organ Behav Hum Perform 13(1):1–16. https://doi.org/10.1016/0030-5073(75)90002-1

Franses PH, Legerstee R (2010) Do experts' adjustments on model-based SKU-level forecasts improve forecast quality? J Forecast 29(3):331–340. https://doi.org/10.1002/for.1129

Gartner (2018) Sales & operations planning success survey. Tech. rep., Gartner

Gigerenzer G (1991) How to make cognitive illusions disappear: beyond "heuristics and biases". John Wiley & Sons, New York

Gigerenzer G, Edwards A (2003) Simple tools for understanding risks: from innumeracy to insight. BMJ 327:741

Gneiting T (2011) Making and evaluating point forecasts. J Am Stat Assoc 106:746–762. https://doi.org/10.1198/jasa.2011.r10138

Gneiting T, Balabdaoui F, Raftery AE (2007) Probabilistic forecasts, calibration and sharpness. J Roy Stat Soc B (Statistical Methodology) 69(2):243–268

Hewamalage H, Ackermann K, Bergmeir C (2023) Forecast evaluation for data scientists: common pitfalls and best practices. Data Mining Knowl Discov 37:788–832

Hoffrage U, Gigerenzer G (1998) Using natural frequencies to improve diagnostic inferences. Acad Med 73:538

Kahneman D (2011) Thinking, fast and slow. Farrar, Straus and Giroux

Khosrowabadi N, Hoberga K, Imdahl C (2022) Evaluating human behaviour in response to ai recommendations for judgemental forecasting. Eur J Oper Res 303:1151

Kolassa S (2008) Can we obtain valid benchmarks from published surveys of forecast accuracy? Foresight 11:6

Kolassa S (2016a) Commentary: that feeling for randomness. Foresight 42:44–47

Kolassa S (2016b) Evaluating predictive count data distributions in retail sales forecasting. Int J Forecast 32:788–803. https://doi.org/10.1016/j.ijforecast.2015.12.004

Kolassa S (2020) Why the "best" point forecast depends on the error or accuracy measure. Int J Forecast 36:208–211. https://doi.org/10.1016/j.ijforecast.2019.02.017

Kolassa S, Martin R (2011) Percentage errors can ruin your day (and rolling the dice shows how). Foresight p 21

Lawrence M, Goodwin P, O'Connor M, Önkal D (2006) Judgmental forecasting: a review of progress over the last 25years. Int J Forecast 22(3):493–518. https://doi.org/10.1016/j.ijforecast.2006.03.007

Petropoulos F et al (2022) Forecasting: theory and practice. Int J Forecast 38(3):705–871

Pinker S (2021) Rationality: what it is, why it seems scarce, why it matters. viking

Robette J (2023) Does improved forecast accuracy translate to business value? Foresight 68:12

Roese NJ, Olson JM (1996) Counterfactuals, causal attributions, and the hindsight bias: a conceptual integration. J Exp Soc Psychol 32(3):197–227. https://doi.org/10.1006/jesp.1996.0010

Sanders NR, Manrodt KB (2003) The efficacy of using judgmental versus quantitative forecasting methods in practice. Omega 31(6):511–522. https://doi.org/10.1016/j.omega.2003.08.007

Schwertman NC, Gilks AJ, Cameron J (1990) A simple noncalculus proof that the median minimizes the sum of the absolute deviations. Am Stat 44(1):38–39

Shumway RH, Stoffer DS (2017) Time series analysis and its applications. Springer, Berlin

Spiegelhalter D (2019) The art of statistics. Pelican

Tichy M (2022a) Forecasting few is different, part 1. https://blog.blueyonder.com/forecasting-few-is-different-part-1/

Tichy M (2022b) Forecasting few is different, part 2. https://blog.blueyonder.com/forecasting-few-is-different-part-2/

Tichy M (2022c) How to fix mean absolute error, part 1. https://blog.blueyonder.com/how-to-fix-mean-absolute-error-part-1/

Tichy M (2022d) Mean absolute percentage error (MAPE) has served its duty and should now retire. https://blog.blueyonder.com/mean-absolute-percentage-error-mape-has-served-its-duty-and-should-now-retire/

Tichy M, Feindt M (2022) You should not always have known better. https://blog.blueyonder.com/you-should-not-always-have-known-better-understand-and-avoid-the-hindsight-selection-bias-in-probabilistic-forecast-evaluation/

Tichy MC (2023) Time to retire the MAPE. Foresight 69:5

Tichy MC, Babounikau I, Wolke N, Ulbrich S, Feindt M (2024) Scaling-aware rating of count forecasts. https://arxiv.org/abs/2211.16313

Vandeput N (2021) Data science for supply chain forecasting. De Gruyter, Berlin

Wick F, Kerzel U, Hahn M, Wolf M, Singhal T, Stemmer D, Ernst J, Feindt M (2021) Demand forecasting of individual probability density functions with machine learning. Operations Research Forum 2:37

A Multi-Method Assessment of Human-AI Interaction in Delivery Driving: Examining Driver Stress, Fatigue, Attention, Situation Awareness, and Risky Driving Behavior

Mario Passalacqua, Robert Pellerin, Sylvain Sénécal, and Pierre-Majorique Léger

Abstract Artificial intelligence (AI) is used by logistics companies to optimize delivery driver route characteristics. When creating routes, the AI makes decisions that optimize efficiency and cost reduction. These decisions, however, can significantly increase the risk of driving accidents by affecting driver stress, fatigue, attention, situation awareness (SA), and risky driving behavior. Driving accidents during work have risen by 40% from 2020 to 2021 and represent the most fatal of all workplace accidents, highlighting the importance of accident prevention. The current chapter proposes a continuous multi-method assessment of delivery drivers' physiological, perceptual, and behavioral states throughout the work shift. Our methodology was then applied to a series of pilot tests in which a delivery driver was monitored for approximately 12 hours. The results indicated that our methodology is viable for evaluating driver fatigue, stress, attention, situation awareness, and risky driving behaviors over the course of an entire work shift. We believe that our methodology can be successfully applied in delivery contexts to reduce the rising number of driving accidents. Other applications of our methodology to enhance human-AI interaction are also discussed.

M. Passalacqua (✉)
Université du Québec à Montréal, Montréal, QC, Canada
e-mail: passalacqua.mario@uqam.ca

R. Pellerin
Polytechnique Montréal, Montréal, QC, Canada
e-mail: robert.pellerin@polymtl.ca

S. Sénécal · P.-M. Léger
HEC Montréal, Montréal, QC, Canada
e-mail: sylvain.senecal@hec.ca; pierre-majorique.leger@hec.ca

C. K. Coursaris et al. (eds.), *The Design of Human-Centered Artificial Intelligence for the Workplace*, Progress in IS, https://doi.org/10.1007/978-3-031-83512-4_15

1 Introduction

Artificial intelligence (AI) is used by logistics companies to optimize delivery driver route characteristics, such as number of deliveries, delivery area, and length of workday. When creating routes, the AI makes decisions that optimize efficiency and cost reduction. These decisions, however, can impact the safety of the driver and those around them by affecting driver stress, fatigue, attention, situation awareness (SA), and risky driving behavior. Work injuries involving transportation incidents remained the most common fatal event, accounting for 37.3% of all work-related fatalities in the USA (Bureau of Labor Statistics 2021). Additionally, delivery driver injuries due to transportation accidents have increased by 40% from 2020 to 2021 (Strategic Organizing Center 2022). It is therefore important to develop a holistic understanding of how route characteristics affect fatigue, stress, attention, SA, and risky driving behaviors.

Within the literature, it is well established that SA, fatigue, stress, attention, and risky driving behaviors are significant contributors to workplace incidents. More specifically, fatigue and stress have been found to reduce attention and SA (Sneddon et al. 2013; Endsley 1999), increasing the risk of driving accidents, trips, slips, and falls (Useche et al. 2017; Day et al. 2012; Chang et al. 2016; Elfering et al. 2018). Additionally, reduced SA has been found to increase risky driving behavior (Wijayanto et al. 2016; Hartono and Gozali 2015), thus increasing the risk of driving accidents (Simons-Morton et al. 2012). Figure 1 presents the theoretical model of the relationship between fatigue, stress, attention, situation awareness, risky driving behaviors, and accidents. SA, which is central to this model, is defined as the "perception of the elements of the environment within a volume of time and space, the comprehension of their meaning, and the projection of their status in the near future" (Endsley 1995, p. 1). As such, SA is composed of three levels: perception, comprehension, and projection.

This chapter proposes a multi-method approach to continuously assess how driver route/sit characteristics affect driver stress, fatigue, attention, SA, and risky driving behavior throughout their workday. Additionally, this approach allows for the evaluation of the effect of fatigue and stress on attention, SA, and risky driving behaviors. Specifically, this approach aims to monitor a driver's perceptual, physiological, and behavioral state to understand their SA and then propose ways of attenuating the negative effects of certain route characteristics chosen by the AI. This is done through the use of physiological and behavioral sensors, questionnaires, and situational data. The rest of this chapter is structured as follows: the following section will present the proposed multi-method approach, while the final section presents its application to pilot tests.

2 Proposed Methodology

The following section will describe the measures, the variable operationalization, and the apparatus.

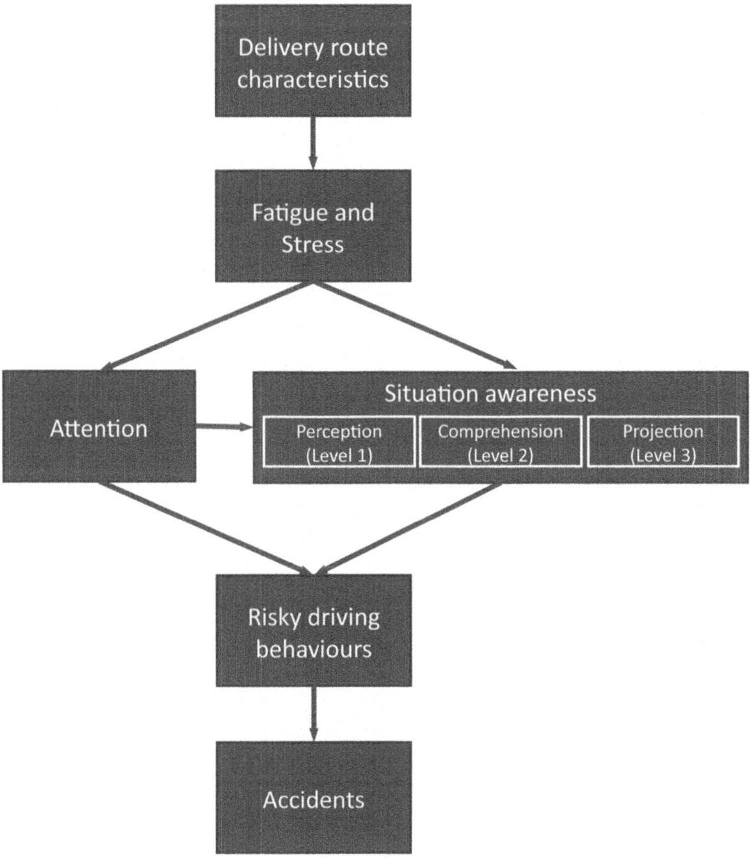

Fig. 1 Theoretical model, based on situation awareness (Endsley 1999)

2.1 *Measures and Variable Operationalization*

Physiological, behavioral, perceptual, and situational variables were collected to be able to continuously measure driver state and to limit biases related to mono-method data collection (e.g., recall bias for perceptual measures) (de Guinea et al. 2014; Passalacqua et al. 2020). See Table 1 for a summary of all measures and variables.

Physiological Measures
All physiological measures were captured using the Hexoskin physiological vest (Carré technologies, Montréal).

Fatigue and Stress
Low-Frequency, High-Frequency, and the LF/HF Ratio: Heart rate data can be analyzed by frequency (Hz) and used to understand a driver's state (e.g., fatigue, drowsiness, stress). When looking at drowsiness or fatigue, research has shown that

Table 1 Measures and variables

Measure	Measure type	Variable inferred	Measured using	Definition
Low-frequency (LF) heart rate variability (HRV)	Physiological	Stress	Hexoskin vest	The low-frequency band of HRV (0.04–0.15 Hz)
High-frequency (HF) HRV	Physiological	Fatigue	Hexoskin vest	The high-frequency band of HRV (0.15–0.4 Hz)
LF/HF ratio	Physiological	Stress and fatigue	Hexoskin vest	The ratio between the LF and HF bands of HRV
The standard deviation of NN intervals (HRV)	Physiological	Stress and fatigue	Hexoskin vest	SDNN is the standard deviation of NN intervals
Breathing rate	Physiological	Stress and fatigue	Hexoskin vest	Rate of respiration per minute
Minute ventilation	Physiological	Stress and fatigue	Hexoskin vest	Number of liters of air breathed in a minute
Movement intensity	Physiological	Physical exertion (physical fatigue)	Hexoskin vest	Mean movement intensity for each delivery
Hard turning, braking, and acceleration	Behavioral	Risky driving behaviors	Cobalt accelerometer	Instances of rough turning, rough braking, and rough acceleration (over 0.45g)
Head orientation (three-axis)	Behavioral	Attention	Camera on windshield	Looking away from the road while the vehicle is in movement represents low attention (distracted driving)
Stanford Sleepiness Scale	Perceptual	Perceived fatigue	Questionnaire	Perceived degree of sleepiness at a particular moment
Visual analog scale	Perceptual	Perceived stress	Questionnaire	Perceived level of stress at a particular moment
Borg scale	Perceptual	Perceived physical exertion (physical fatigue)	Questionnaire	Perceived physical fatigue at a particular moment

(continued)

Table 1 (continued)

Situation Awareness Rating Technique	Perceptual	Situation awareness (three levels)	Questionnaire	Perception of cues in one's environment, comprehension of those cues, and anticipation of future situations
Delivery characteristics	Situational	–	Area, length of shift, on-time/late, number, weight, start time	Characteristics of deliveries and workday

the heightened high-frequency (HF) band of heart rate variability (0.15–0.4 Hz), as well as both high HF and low-frequency (LF) band of heart rate variability (0.04–0.15 Hz) together, indicate increased fatigue (Warwick et al. 2015; Egelund 1982; Miyaji et al. 2009). In a recent meta-analysis by Kim et al. (2018), it was found that when inducing stress through various methods, the most frequently reported factor associated with variation in heart rate data was a decrease in the HF band. Other authors have reported that increased LF is mainly associated with stress (Ishaque et al. 2021). Thus, a high LF/HF ratio and high LF are valid indicators of psychophysiological stress, as shown by multiple studies in the literature (e.g., Sloan et al. (1994)).

Standard Deviation of NN Intervals (SDNN): SDNN is a time-domain heart rate variability analysis method based on time intervals between NN peaks. Essentially, SDNN is the standard deviation of the interval between heartbeats. High SDNN (high HRV) generally indicates increased drowsiness (Ishaque et al. 2021), while low HRV generally indicates heightened stress.

Respiration Rate: The human respiratory system undergoes noticeable changes from wakefulness to sleep. Various features of the human respiratory system, such as respiration rate, change during this transition and can be regarded as indicators of drowsiness(Kiashari et al. 2018). Research shows that a slower respiration rate is associated with more fatigue/drowsiness (Chen et al. 2021; Wu et al. 2015). According to Kiashari et al. (2018), respiration rate decreases from wakefulness to extreme drowsiness by 3.5 breaths per minute (bpm), and its standard deviation (SD) increased by 0.7 bpm. Additionally, an increased respiration rate is associated with increased stress.

Minute Ventilation: Minute ventilation represents the number of liters of air breathed in 1 minute. Research has found that low minute ventilation indicates fatigue, while high minute ventilation is associated with stress (Kiashari et al. 2018; Chen et al. 2021; Wu et al. 2015).

Physical Exertion: Physical exertion, i.e., the physical component of fatigue, was measured using the mean movement intensity for each delivery. The three-axis accelerometer in the Hexoskin vest was used to capture this measure. Greater

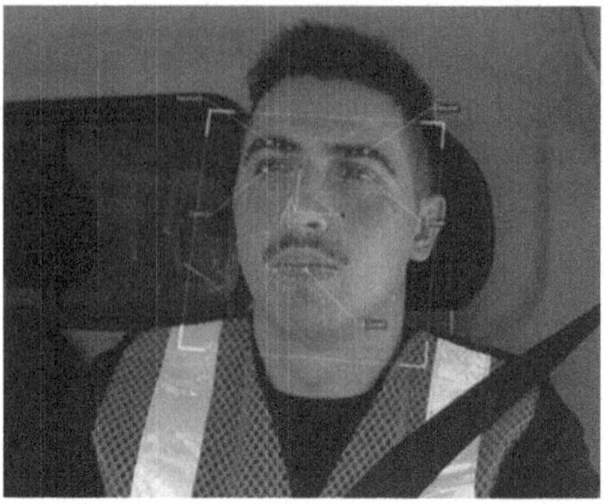

Fig. 2 Example of attentive driving

Fig. 3 Example of distracted driving

mean movement intensity indicated greater physical exertion and, therefore, greater physical fatigue.

Behavioral Measures

Risky Driving Behaviors
Measurement of risky driving behavior is done using an algorithm that detects acceleration fluctuations over 0.45g on all axes (Freidlin et al. 2018). This type of algorithm is commonly used by insurance companies to detect instances of risky driving behavior. A lateral acceleration (x-axis) of over 0.45g indicated an instance of hard turning, while a forward/backward acceleration (y-axis) of over 0.45g indicated an instance of hard acceleration/hard braking. The Cobalt Bluebox device was used to capture the accelerometer data.

Attention
Attention is measured by analyzing the video from the camera on the windshield. FaceReader 8 (Noldus, Wageningen, Netherlands) was first used to determine what range of three-axis coordinates of the head orientation indicated attentive driving (Fig. 2) versus distracted driving (Fig. 3). Using these coordinates, an algorithm was

developed, which allowed instances of distracted driving to be inferred. Greater instances of distracted driving indicated lower attention.

Perceptual Measures All perceptual measures were administered to drivers once every hour.

Perceived Fatigue
The Stanford Sleepiness Scale (Hoddes 1972) was used to determine drivers' perceived fatigue. It is a one-item scale scored on a seven-point Likert scale.

Perceived Stress
A visual analog scale was used to determine drivers' perceived stress (Lesage and Berjot 2011). It is a one-item scale scored on a ten-point Likert scale.

Perceived Physical Exertion (Physical Fatigue)
The Borg rating of perceived exertion scale (Williams 2017) was used to measure drivers' perceived physical exertion. This measure was used to infer the physical component of fatigue. It is a one-item scale scored on an eight-point Likert scale.

Perceived Situation Awareness
Situation Awareness Rating Technique (Selcon and Taylor 1990) was used to measure situation awareness. It is a ten-item scale scored on a seven-point scale.

Situational Variables
These variables represent the route characteristics and other situational factors that may affect stress and fatigue.

Delivery Area
Deliveries in the downtown areas are characterized by heavier traffic, parking difficulties, and deliveries in condo buildings, while deliveries in the suburbs have the opposite characteristics. These characteristics can affect driver stress and fatigue.

Length of Shift
The total length of the shift can affect driver fatigue.

On-time versus Late Deliveries
When running late on a delivery, drivers can experience increased stress.

Number of Deliveries
The total number of deliveries can impact fatigue.

Average Weight of Deliveries
The average weight of all deliveries during a work shift can impact physical fatigue.

Shift Start Time
Morning and afternoon may impact participant fatigue differently.

Fig. 4 Hexoskin physiological vest

Fig. 5 Camera setup in vehicle

2.2 Apparatus

Participants were equipped with a physiological vest, as shown in Fig. 4. This vest captured 256-Hz 1-lead electrocardiogram (heart rate) data using a built-in electrode, 128-Hz respiration data using two built-in respiratory inductive plethysmography sensors, and 64-Hz acceleration/activity data using a built-in 3-axis accelerometer.

A webcam (Logitech, Newark, USA), connected to a computer, was placed on the top middle portion of the windshield and was used to record the participant's head orientation. A second camera (DJI, Shenzhen, China) was placed on the bottom left portion of the windshield and was also used to record the participant's head. This camera served as a backup in case of technical issues with the webcam. A third camera (GoPro, San Mateo, USA) was placed on the bottom middle portion of the windshield to record the road in front of the vehicle with an ultra-wide-angle lens (see Fig. 5). A Cobalt device (Tech3lab, Montreal, Canada), used to capture three-axis accelerometer and GPS data, was placed on the dashboard (see Fig. 6).

The researcher's laptop (Hewlett-Packard, Spring, USA) was used to run Observer XT (Noldus, Wageningen, the Netherlands), a software used to synchronize data from the physiological vest, the webcam, the accelerometer, and the GPS. Observer XT also allowed the researcher to enter real-time event markers, which would appear across all data types. Media Recorder (Noldus, Wageningen,

Fig. 6 Cobalt device (blue) on the dash of the vehicle

the Netherlands), a video-recording software, was used to capture video from the webcam. The laptop, Cobalt, DJI camera, and GoPro camera were connected to external battery packs to last the whole workday.

3 Pilot Testing

A series of pilot tests over approximately 12 hours were conducted to test the feasibility and effectiveness of the methodology. In these pilot tests, a typical delivery vehicle (Ford Transit) was rented, and a researcher took the role of a delivery driver. The physiological, behavioral, and perceptual measures were tested for feasibility and effectiveness. Situational variables were not included as they vary greatly between companies and delivery types.

3.1 Physiological Measures

All physiological data was captured using the Hexoskin vest. Data analysis revealed that we could accurately capture all available components of heart rate variability (low frequency, high frequency, LF/HF ratio, SDNN), respiration (breathing rate, minute ventilation), and movement intensity (mean movement intensity). Additionally, we found that changes in these metrics could accurately be captured.

3.2 Behavioral Measures

Using the three-axis accelerometer of the Cobalt Bluebox, we were able to accurately detect instances of hard turning, hard braking, and hard acceleration. Different g-force thresholds were tested (0.35g, 0.40g, 0.45g, 0.50g, 0.55g). A threshold of 0.45g provided the most sensitivity to risky driving behaviors while limiting false positives. This threshold has been used to detect risky driving in past research (Freidlin et al. 2018).

Attention (distracted driving) was inferred using three-axis coordinates of head orientation. Researchers manually categorized data from the pilot test according to three categories: (1) distracted driving, i.e., looking away from the road; (2) attentive driving, i.e., looking at the road; (3) other, i.e., looking at mirrors or car not in motion. Using this categorization, we developed an algorithm to detect instances of distracted driving. The algorithm was validated by manually verifying detected instances of distracted driving on subsequent pilot tests.

3.3 Perceptual Measures

Our four questionnaires, used to measure perceptions of fatigue, stress, physical exertion, and situation awareness, have been validated for use in studies that use the experience sampling method (Hoddes 1972; Lesage and Berjot 2011; Williams 2017; Selcon and Taylor 1990). Within the context of our methodology, this implies that our chosen questionnaires can accurately detect changes in our variables when administered multiple times throughout the work shift.

3.4 Other Considerations

When planning to collect data over a period of 12 consecutive hours, other technical aspects needed to be tested. The first was the battery life of the various devices. Other than the Hexoskin vest, which had a battery life of 30 hours, no other tool could last 12 hours. For the DJI camera, GoPro camera, and the Cobalt Bluebox, a single portable charger (20 100-mAh capacity) was enough. For the laptop used to run Observer XT and the webcam, two portable AC outlet power banks (31 200-mAh capacity) were needed. The second technical aspect to consider was data storage space. Twelve hours of continuous video recording using three cameras produced a large amount of data. The DJI and GoPro cameras had to be equipped with a 128-gigabyte micro-SD card to continuously record for the duration of the experiment. The laptop had to be connected to a 256-gigabyte external SSD drive. It is important to use an SSD drive instead of an HDD because of data storage speed and lower risk of mechanical failure. The third technical aspect is the issue of driver visibility. Three cameras with wires were placed on the windshield. When placed haphazardly, these could significantly obstruct the driver's view. After multiple iterations, we found a way to minimize view obstruction. One camera was placed on the bottom left of the driver, one on the top middle of the windshield, and one on the bottom middle portion of the windshield. Wires were taped to the dash of the vehicle.

The final technical aspect was data synchronization. No automatic synchronization of all our tools/measures was possible (Cobalt Bluebox, Hexoskin vest, webcam, DJI camera, GoPro camera, Observer XT). We therefore opted for manual synchronization using the coordinated universal time (UTC). The Cobalt Bluebox and Hexoskin vest already had UTC timestamps in the data output. Observer XT used local computer time for synchronization. Therefore, we changed the computer's local time to UTC. The webcam, DJI camera, and GoPro camera were used to film a phone screen showing a UTC clock simultaneously. This simultaneous recording of a clock allowed us to synchronize all cameras with the other tools manually.

4 Conclusion

The proposed methodology allows for the continuous measurement of delivery drivers' perceptual, physiological, and behavioral states. Specifically, driver stress, fatigue, physical exertion, attention, situation awareness, and risky driving behaviors can be continuously monitored. Pilot tests indicated that the methodology is both feasible and effective for a data collection period of 12 hours. However, technical aspects such as battery life, storage space, driver visibility, and data synchronization must be considered. Nevertheless, we believe that our methodology can be successfully applied in delivery contexts to evaluate how route/situational characteristics affect the delivery driver and how physiological, perceptual, and behavioral factors interact with one another. Based on previous literature, we believe that the application of our methodology can reduce the rising number of delivery driving accidents, trips, slips, and falls. Additional pilot tests are needed to further refine this methodology and to make it even less intrusive.

The proposed methodology has potential uses beyond the limited context of the pilot tests. For example, a continuous biofeedback loop can be used to alert drivers if their fatigue, drowsiness, or stress reaches dangerous levels. By employing a continuous feedback loop informed by real-time data on the driver's physiological, perceptual, and behavioral states, AI systems can play a pivotal role in mitigating the risks associated with driver stress, fatigue, attention deficits, and risky driving behaviors. This proactive approach ensures that drivers are consistently aware of their own state, empowering them to take necessary actions to maintain optimal levels of situation awareness and minimize the likelihood of accidents. The findings from our multi-method assessment underscore the viability of such AI-driven interventions, highlighting their capacity to enhance occupational safety and contribute to a substantial reduction in work-related driving accidents. Additionally, the application of this methodology extends beyond delivery driving, suggesting its utility in various domains where attention and fatigue are critical factors influencing performance and safety. Implementing this measurement method in human-AI interaction scenarios can significantly enhance the system's ability to detect fluctuations in users' attention and fatigue levels, prompting timely interventions and adaptive responses. This approach not only fosters a safer and more responsive interaction environment but also contributes to the optimization of worker well-being and performance.

References

Bureau of Labor Statistics (2021) Census of fatal occupational injuries summary, 2020. https://www.bls.gov/news.release/pdf/cfoi.pdf. Accessed 16 Nov 2022

Chang WR, Leclercq S, Lockhart TE, Haslam R (2016) State of science: occupational slips, trips and falls on the same level. Ergonomics 59(7):861–883

Chen X, Su L, Xu M, Deng B, Zhu Y (2021) Fatigue detection based on non-contact respiratory detection. In: Thirteenth international conference on machine vision, international society for optics and photonics, vol 11605, p 116050J

Day AJ, Brasher K, Bridger RS (2012) Accident proneness revisited: the role of psychological stress and cognitive failure. Accident Anal Prevent 49:532–535

de Guinea AO, Titah R, Léger PM (2014) Explicit and implicit antecedents of users' behavioral beliefs in information systems: a neuropsychological investigation. J Manag Inform Syst 30(4):179–210

Egelund N (1982) Spectral analysis of heart rate variability as an indicator of driver fatigue. Ergonomics 25(7):663–672

Elfering A, Kottwitz MU, Häfliger E, Celik Z, Grebner S (2018) Interruptions, unreasonable tasks, and quality-threatening time pressure in home care: linked to attention deficits and slips, trips, and falls. Safety Health Work 9(4):434–440

Endsley MR (1995) Measurement of situation awareness in dynamic systems. Hum Fact 37(1):65–84

Endsley MR (1999) Situation awareness in aviation systems. In: Handbook of aviation human factors, pp 257–276

Freidlin RZ, Dave AD, Espey BG, et al. (2018) Measuring risky driving behavior using an mhealth smartphone app: development and evaluation of gforce. JMIR mHealth uHealth 6(4):e9290

Hartono B, Gozali M (2015) Secondary task and risky driving behavior: a test of the mediating effect of situation awareness. Int J Occup Safety Ergon 21(3):399–404

Hoddes E (1972) The development and use of the stanford sleepiness scale (SSS). Psychophysiology 9:150

Ishaque S, Khan N, Krishnan S (2021) Trends in heart-rate variability signal analysis. Front Digit Health 3:13

Kiashari SEH, Nahvi A, Homayounfard A, Bakhoda H (2018) Monitoring the variation in driver respiration rate from wakefulness to drowsiness: a non-intrusive method for drowsiness detection using thermal imaging. J Sleep Sci 3(1–2):1–9

Kim HG, Cheon EJ, Bai DS, et al. (2018) Stress and heart rate variability: a meta-analysis and review of the literature. Psychiatry Invest 15(3):235–245

Lesage FX, Berjot S (2011) Validity of occupational stress assessment using a visual analogue scale. Occup Med 61(6):434–436

Miyaji M, Kawanaka H, Oguri K (2009) Driver's cognitive distraction detection using physiological features by the adaboost. In: 2009 12th international ieee conference on intelligent transportation systems, pp 1–6

Passalacqua M, Léger PM, Nacke LE, et al. (2020) Playing in the backstore: interface gamification increases warehousing workforce engagement. Ind Manag Data Syst 120(7):1309–1330

Selcon SJ, Taylor RM (1990) Evaluation of the situational awareness rating technique (SART) as a tool for aircrew systems design. In: AGARD, situational awareness in aerospace operations, p 8, sEE N 90-28972 23-53

Simons-Morton BG, Zhang Z, Jackson JC, Albert PS (2012) Do elevated gravitational-force events while driving predict crashes and near crashes? Am J Epidemiol 175(10):1075–1079

Sloan RP, Shapiro PA, Bagiella E, et al. (1994) Effect of mental stress throughout the day on cardiac autonomic control. Biol Psychol 37(2):89–99

Sneddon A, Mearns K, Flin R (2013) Stress, fatigue, situation awareness and safety in offshore drilling crews. Safety Sci 56:80–88

Strategic Organizing Center (2022) The worst mile: production pressure and the injury crisis in Amazon's delivery system. https://thesoc.org/wp-content/uploads/2022/05/The-Worst-Mile.pdf Accessed 16 Nov 2022

Useche SA, Cendales B, Gómez V (2017) Measuring fatigue and its associations with job stress, health and traffic accidents in professional drivers: the case of BRT operators. EC Neurol 4(4):103–118

Warwick B, Symons N, Chen X, Xiong K (2015) Detecting driver drowsiness using wireless wearables. In: 2015 IEEE 12th international conference on mobile ad hoc and sensor systems, pp 585–588

Wijayanto T, Wibirama S, Maryoto ZZ, Winadi MN, Bait M (2016) Effects of morning-night differences and sleep deprivation on situation awareness and driving performance. In: 2016 IEEE international conference on industrial engineering and engineering management (IEEM), pp 267–271

Williams N (2017) The borg rating of perceived exertion (RPE) scale. Occup Med 67(5):404–405

Wu X, Wanyan X, Zhuang D (2015) Pilot's visual attention allocation modeling under fatigue. Technol Health Care 23(s2):S373–S381

How Awareness of a User's Cognitive State Can Improve Human-AI Teams

Colin Conrad

Abstract Much of the discussion about human-AI teams has focused on artificial intelligence technologies; however, recent works have focused on the role of humans. Situation awareness has been used to describe awareness about human environmental factors (e.g., mental workload) on task performance and has recently been applied to new discussions about performance in human-AI teams. These discussions have neglected many cognitive factors that can now be incorporated into human-AI team dynamics, thanks to advances in cognitive neuroscience and technology. In this chapter, I will describe how these advances enable situation awareness of cognition that opens new possibilities for human-AI collaboration.

1 Introduction

Imagine that you are a security officer at a shopping mall, a team member responsible for monitoring and securing the stores late into the night. After closing your email, your eyes start to feel heavy, and your sight blurs. You had a hard time sleeping this morning, and it's clear that you are feeling sluggish. Your colleague informs you that she will patrol today so that you can take it easy. She empties the coffee pot into her cup before starting on her journey around the mall, leaving you alone with your other "teammate," SAM ("situation-aware machine"), an artificial video monitoring agent integrated with the security surveillance system, designed to inform you of potential security risks in the facility.

Over the next hour, SAM monitors images of the video feed and discovers two issues: an open door by the back exit and the presence of a cardboard box by the jewelry store. The agent informs you of these potential security issues using its standard process of an on-screen warning message. After observing the screens, you do not notice anything unusual; the jewelry store's CCTV camera looks normal, and SAM sends you many of these messages every night. For example, SAM informed

C. Conrad (✉)
Dalhousie University, Halifax, NS, Canada
e-mail: colin.conrad@dal.ca

C. K. Coursaris et al. (eds.), *The Design of Human-Centered Artificial Intelligence for the Workplace*, Progress in IS, https://doi.org/10.1007/978-3-031-83512-4_16

you that the bay door was left open yesterday, but it was just the custodian taking a smoke break. In the past, it has been enough to file a report so that your supervisor can investigate it in the morning. You nonetheless try to take a closer look, but as you sit back and watch the screens, your mind begins wandering. What did you eat yesterday that kept you awake? Was it stress? You are not sure. As the minutes pass, you blankly stare at the videos as nothing happens. Eventually, with heavy eyes and a yawn, you realize it would feel better to log the incident and move on. You turn toward the coffee maker to make a fresh pot and do not notice as the box in front of the jewelry store slowly moves away toward the open door, with a person inside, with thousands of dollars of goods.

Though this story is fictional, it is based on real computer vision technology, such as that developed by Ambient.AI (2023), and a true story of how US marines were able to outsmart video surveillance algorithms using cardboard boxes (Bandara 2023). There are also plenty of real examples of threats where improved AI systems could prevent disasters. Autonomous driving agents have been responsible for at least 11 driving-related deaths in 2022 (Krisher and Press 2022), which might have been prevented using a similar approach. Safety motivations have prompted research into new approaches to measuring human error using artificial agents and human hybrid processes. There have also been high-profile calls for research on human-AI teams that incorporate greater awareness about human cognitive contexts (Endsley 2023).

Situation awareness is the ability of an agent to comprehend its environment in space and time (Endsley 2015). While this concept was initially used to describe a model for incorporating human environmental factors, e.g., mental workload, on task performance, researchers have recently become interested in how situation awareness can be incorporated into autonomous AI systems and human-AI teams (Endsley 2017). With improved situation awareness, AI systems can incorporate information about a user's state into its processes, improving the human-AI team's outcomes. If the SAM system had been designed to detect habituation to its security messages or a wandering mind, it might have adapted to prevent a security threat. The SAM would have benefitted from situation awareness of its human's cognitive state.

In this chapter, I outline measures from cognitive psychology and cognitive neuroscience that can be used to improve situation awareness of human-AI teams. While this discussion can apply to cognitive states broadly, my focus is on vigilance and mind wandering, two cognitive functions that share a common root in the brain's attention networks (Posner and Petersen 1990). These functions are exemplified by the SAM example but are also relevant to a wide range of work applications and tasks where AI can be helpful, such as long-haul driving (Baldwin et al. 2017) and online learning (Conrad and Newman 2021). I will begin with a discussion of these two concepts from the cognitive neuroscience perspective before describing measures that can be incorporated into a human-AI workplace system. My goal is to ultimately contribute to the ongoing conversation about situation awareness in human-AI teams by making a case for situation awareness of cognition.

2 Vigilance and Wandering Minds

Reconsider the challenges described in the hypothetical example. The first challenge concerned the repetitiveness of notifications and the user's habituation to the notifications. The second challenge concerned how the AI system misinterpreted the user's mental state and mind wandering. While it is possible that existing measures of situation awareness could have accounted for these, the measures would have been indirect. The most commonly employed techniques for measuring situation awareness are the Situation Awareness Global Assessment Technique, an objective questionnaire probe measure concerning the user's perception of the environment, and the Situation Awareness Rating Technique, a subjective psychometric questionnaire measure (Endsley 2020). These techniques measure a user's overt perceptions about their environment and their subjective perceptions of their situation awareness behaviors rather than their cognitive state. These can thus be further improved by incorporating techniques used by cognitive psychologists and neuroscientists for measuring attentional states.

Concerning the first challenge, if the SAM had incorporated situation awareness about the user's habituation with the notifications, it could have attempted a different approach that might have made the user more responsive. Habituation is defined as a "behavioral response decrement that results from repeated stimulation and that does not involve sensory adaptation/sensory fatigue or motor fatigue" (Rankin et al. 2009), and attentional habituation is often observed when humans are exposed to repetitive stimuli. In information technologies, attentional habituation has been demonstrated to negatively impact users' responsiveness to cybersecurity notifications (Vance et al. 2018), which likely generalizes to this context. Like in the example, when humans are repeatedly exposed to notifications, they become used to them and are less likely to adhere to or act on them. As Vance et al. (2018) demonstrated, repeated exposure to notifications degrades users' perception of their saliency, causing users to ignore them.

Some cognitive psychologists and neuroscientists have described the capacity to maintain a high degree of sensitivity to stimuli as vigilance, sometimes also referred to as alerting (Jones et al. 2016). The human capacity for vigilance determines whether someone can receive information or attend to a notification in the first place. In the prominent model of attention described by Posner and Petersen (1990), they described three attentional brain systems, which each contribute to an individual's ability to process information. While vigilance consists of a distinct function, it works closely with orienting, the ability to align one's sense with a sensory signal, as well as executive control, which is the process of resolving conflicting sensory experiences. By incorporating measures of these attentional capacities, an AI system could improve its performance and attainment of a task.

The second challenge concerned the user's tendency to direct their attention from the world around them and inward toward task-unrelated thoughts. This experience is often referred to as mind wandering, an internally directed cognitive process whereby our attention becomes detached from the external world (Smallwood and

Schooler 2015). Mind wandering is a mechanism that can impair one's ability to attend to a task, such as a video screen, requiring sustained attention over long periods. Researchers have found relationships between mind wandering and boredom (Eastwood et al. 2012) and have observed that wandering minds have decreased general awareness, as exemplified by poor driving behaviors (Baldwin et al. 2017) and poor retention from lectures (Conrad and Newman 2021).

Mind wandering likely occurs due to two distinct functions of our brain, which can be observed on the neurophysiological level (Golchert et al. 2017). The first function is the passive resting cognitive state resulting from the brain's default mode network. This network of neurons was initially observed in early functional magnetic resonance imaging studies when they noticed active brain activity as study participants lay idle. This network is now thought to be responsible for past and future thinking (Berka et al. 2004) and spontaneous thoughts (Fox et al. 2015). The second brain function is a lapse in cognitive control stemming from the brain's executive networks. The frontoparietal control brain network governs higher thinking, such as response inhibition and selective attention (Diamond 2013). It is often thought that under normal circumstances, our brains can resist the emergence of spontaneous thoughts generated by our default mode network. However, in situations where our executive cognitive control is compromised, such as when abnormally fatigued, as in the hypothetical example, or if an individual has ADHD (Seli et al. 2015), then undesirable mind wandering is more prevalent.

In recent years, researchers have begun to further distinguish varieties of mind wandering, such as a distinction between deliberate and spontaneous mind wandering. Deliberate mind wandering occurs when someone wishes to think about something else, possibly because they are passively engaged in an undemanding task or enjoying the present experience. Spontaneous mind wandering, by contrast, occurs against one's wishes (Seli et al. 2016). The distinction between deliberate and spontaneous mind wandering has been similarly observed on a neurophysiological level (Golchert et al. 2017) and has sparked a wider discussion about the very nature of mind wandering (Seli et al. 2018) as well as its possible impacts on the experience of using information technology (Klesel et al. 2021). Regardless of mind wandering's ultimate nature, when it is understood as the presence of spontaneous thoughts, it can negatively impact the fulfillment of sustained attention tasks. However, this impact is probably lessened if it is deliberate mind wandering. A system that could detect spontaneous mind wandering specifically could thus adapt to a user's context and situation to provide an improved outcome.

3 Attentional Measures for AI Agents

How, then, would a human-AI system go about incorporating information about sustained attention and mind wandering? Researchers have developed many approaches for measuring attentional states, though many of these approaches are challenging to incorporate into a machine-readable process. Attentional states can be measured using a behavioral test, which implicitly measures attention based on performance at a task. Attention can also be inferred by observing physiological measures that are known to be associated with attentional processes. Either way, researchers have also further distinguished varieties of attention which can be identified with performance at specific tasks and correlated with specific measures. In the aforementioned advanced by Posner and Petersen (1990), for example, alerting can be distinguished from orienting, which is in turn distinguishable from executive control. Each of these functions has been distinguished by varying behavioral and physiological measures.

One of the most deeply explored techniques for measuring attentional capacities is the attention network test (ANT) (Fan et al. 2002). The ANT measures three attention networks through a combination of computer-generated flanker tests designed to measure response inhibition and response time to cuing tasks. While the ANT has been demonstrated to produce reliable measures of an individual's attentional capacities over time (Ishigami and Klein 2010), there are considerable limitations to their application. Many of these tasks cannot be reliably employed in an ecologically valid context because it is a long and boring task, although there have been attempts to adapt them for broader contexts (Jones et al. 2016).

Yet, there is emerging research which suggests that attention can be measured indirectly by observing performance at certain tasks. Wilson et al. (2015) demonstrated how the Sustained Attention Response Task, a similar cuing paradigm which involves withholding button presses on infrequent targets (Robertson et al. 1997), can be adapted to the context of friendly fire simulation military training. Performance at a friendly fire military exercise training exercise was found to be correlated with the validated attentional task. Other research by Kozhevnikov et al. (2018) demonstrated that participation in action video games can lead to temporary states of enhanced spatial attention. These results suggest that measures of computer-measured tasks, whether these be games or work-related computer use (e.g., chat tasks or assigned duties), may be adapted as indirect measures of vigilance or other aspects of attention.

One approach for adapting sustained attention paradigms to practical applications is to measure computer behavior, such as mouse or motion tracking. Anderson et al. (2016) demonstrated that warning and task habituation can be measured using mouse cursor tracking and that such measures could be more widely applied as a measure of explicit attention during information technology use broadly. Other studies have suggested that mouse tracking is a reliable correlate of eye gaze patterns (Egner et al. 2018) and have found that mouse patterns can be applied to industrial applications, such as in e-commerce web search (Speicher et al. 2015). Similarly, researchers have also demonstrated that attention can be reliably measured through other online behaviors such as chat use and video. This was well-demonstrated by Kuzminykh and Rintel (2020), who described two studies that leveraged a combination of speech and video behavior to capture attention features during online meetings. Such behaviors could then be used to capture sustained attention using deep learning.

Another related technique is to observe eye patterns, often referred to as *eye tracking*. While eye tracking has been most extensively employed to measure overt or explicit varieties of spatial attention (Klein 2020) often through gaze tracking, eye movements have also been established to be reliable indicators of covert attention, the function of general attentiveness to stimuli that may not be where someone's eyes are fixated. It has been suggested that covert attention functions are at play when observing attention-related phenomena during technology use (Conrad and Newman 2019) and researchers have applied eye tracking to sustained applied attention tasks. Attention allocation aids have been developed to help with visual search by leveraging machine learning to predict the accuracy of a user's eye saccade patterns (Deza et al. 2017), which leverages the extensive work on the relationship between saccade patterns and covert attention (Klein 2020). By using similar techniques, attention-adaptive systems could be developed that can infer cover attention by observing eye saccades in reaction to novel stimuli.

What mouse, chat, and eye behaviors all have in common is that they are objective behavioral measures. An alternative approach which could be employed is subjective experience sampling. Similar to the Situation Awareness Global Assessment Technique employed in situation awareness research (Endsley 2020), experience sampling includes a range of approaches to collect a user's reported experience at a particular point in time (Seli et al. 2013). Experience sampling is the most common method for identifying moments of mind wandering. Approaches have included probe-caught methods, which interrupt a user to collect an experience, self-caught methods, which ask users to spontaneously report their mind wandering experiences, and retrospective methods, which include post hoc reports (Smallwood and Schooler 2015). These techniques, particularly self-caught methods of experience sampling, might be incorporated into existing situation awareness paradigms to effectively measure mind wandering. While subjective techniques such as experience sampling can suffer from variance in individual perceptions, they have the advantage of reliably capturing a user's experience and can provide reliable labels for machine learning algorithms.

These subjective and objective approaches to the measurement of attentional constructs are not mutually exclusive. In the case of mind wandering specifically, eye tracking has been employed to complement experience sampling to make inferences about reading comprehension (D'Mello et al. 2016). There are also relevant electroencephalography (EEG) measures which have been associated with both vigilance and mind wandering that could be adapted in a machine-readable context. EEG oscillatory activities are fluctuations in the brain's rhythmic patterns, and have been well-studied as a correlate of mental workload (Berka et al. 2004) and of mind wandering (Conrad and Newman 2021). While these measures are most often observed in highly controlled environments and compared using statistical analysis, advances in machine learning have made it possible and accessible to develop brain-computer interfaces that leverage these signals to detect mind wandering (Conrad and Newman 2022). An artificial agent could thus read these signals to provide interventions that change human behavior when it detects fluctuations that are typical of mind wandering.

EEG event-related potentials (ERPs) can also be observed to infer a user's state. ERPs are brain responses to time-locked stimuli, such as a picture, or a security notification. Early-onset ERPs have been associated with attentional vigilance (Bonnefond et al. 2010), while later-onset ERPs have been associated with attentiveness and mind wandering (Baldwin et al. 2017) and affective responses to notifications (Nissen et al. 2023). While ERPs are more difficult than brain oscillations to measure outside of a laboratory setting, they have also been adapted to brain-computer interfaces which could contribute novel information for a situation-aware AI. ERP-based brain-computer interfaces have been limited due to their requirements for large amounts of data; however, advances in the field have made it more feasible to detect differences in signals using fewer samples, and in real time (Santamaría-Vázquez et al. 2022).

Recent developments in technology have also made the application of EEG to the workplace more feasible and affordable. For example, the Neurocatch EEG system has been clinically approved in Canada and the United States to measure ERPs for health purposes. It has been deployed to measure the impact of concussions, with a battery of ERP measures that can be employed in less than 10 minutes (Carrick et al. 2021). Alternatively the g.Tec Unicorn BI and Open BCI systems, with a total price tag of under USD $1500, are reliable devices regularly used in hackathons around the world (BR41N.IO 2023). Students have developed a range of novel BCI applications that can speak to the potential applicability of these techniques to the workplace. Finally, the Interaxon Muse system, which can be purchased at retail stores, has even been reported to detect both oscillatory activity (Conrad and Bliemel 2016) and event-related potentials (Krigolson et al. 2017) in ways that might be adapted to situation-aware systems. As EEG hardware develops further, it will become more feasible to apply to improve situation awareness in human-AI teams using these techniques.

It is also important to highlight that many of these measures are not only relevant to mind wandering or sustained attention, but to varying attention-related functions such as distraction, executive control, task-switching, and overall mental workload. Task responses and physiological indicators can be adapted depending on the context and can be further developed to the situational context. Furthermore, it could be possible to design alternative interfaces that leverage these indicators beyond alerts. For example, a sustained attention interface could adapt to the rate of presentation of stimuli to reduce cognitive overload (Demazure et al. 2021). By considering the interface design, it could be possible to build a wide variety of attention-adaptive technologies.

Taken together, there are many ways that situation awareness can be expanded to include information about a user's attentional state. By collecting many subjective experience samples, it would be possible to train machine learning classifiers that integrate the various behavioral and psychophysiological measures as features by using these samples as data labels. The classifiers can then be trained to activate when the indicators exceed a relevant threshold. This suggested approach builds on past work on attention-adaptive interventions (Deza et al. 2017) and brain-computer interfaces, though at a much larger scale. Cognitive factors could thus be considered in conceptions of situation awareness. Given the proliferation of inexpensive sensors that are now performing comparably to research-grade tools, we may very well be on the horizon of artificial agents that are situation-aware of our cognition.

4 Conclusion: A Pipe Dream or Imminent Paradigm?

Imagine once again that you are sitting in a chair in the security office of a shopping mall, late at night, alone with SAM 2.0, your artificial "teammate." This time, as you find your attention fading from the room and toward breakfast, your brain rhythms become slower. However, the EEG channels that are in your over-ear headphones detect this change in your body rhythms. This was also corroborated by your slower mouse activity in the hour before. SAM, which detects these changes, can infer that you may not be attentive.

As the hour passes, SAM discovers the issues: an open door by the back exit and the presence of a cardboard box in the jewelry store. As it sends you notifications, it also sends you distraction cues to determine your sustained attention. It notices that you responded more slowly than normal and that your response speed is like when you have reported mind wandering in the past. It concludes that it should take a different action because your mind wandering is not deliberate. Instead of administering the standard notification, it decides to pop up on the screen with its virtual avatar. "How are you doing?" it asks, "are you able to check out the box in front of the jewelry store?" After taking a closer look, you realize that something is off, that the box had moved ever-so-slightly from where it was when you last checked. You decide to radio your human colleague, who quickly realizes the problem and calls the police.

We are currently at a point in time where this scenario is no longer science fiction. Rather than spurned by radical new developments, gradual advances in cognitive psychology, cognitive neuroscience, and artificial intelligence have not just made this scenario possible, but imminent. Consider some of the other contexts where human-AI teams can be adapted not just for new *interactions*, but also task or experience *enhancement*:

- Driving—While so much attention has been paid to self-driving cars, relatively little has been paid to human-AI teams. Can AI be used to create enhanced warnings, especially at high speeds or busy locations?
- Education—AI can be used to create attention-adaptive systems that can change a lesson depending on a learner's mental state. Could dynamic content contribute to improved learning outcomes?
- Cognitive and memory challenges—Individuals who face cognitive challenges, such as memory loss, may benefit from AI that can assist them when the situation requires it.

It is also worth noting that the approach of this chapter is formative and optimistic; it leaves out many details about exactly how to develop such machines and does not deeply discuss their downsides. There are many possible ethical concerns raised by situation-aware cognitive technologies. Surveillance studies scholars have long posited challenges to consent with big data, which apply in this context. When consent to use data is offered, it is often done so with limited knowledge of the ways that data can be integrated with other datasets, which can undermine someone's underlying right to privacy (Lyon 2014). This criticism is not unique to psychophysiological data, though it presents new challenges due to its sensitivity (Lyon 2014). For example, could this data be integrated with someone's driving history to determine their insurance policy? Would it be desirable to allow insurance companies to enforce policies that depend on a user's attentional capabilities? Furthermore, the resulting algorithms may be too complex for humans to interpret, and as a consequence provide informed consent to use. This is why some scholars have explored approaches for explainable artificial intelligence, which can help remedy concerns about consent (Hamm et al. 2023).

The technology's use may also create larger moral hazards. Situation-aware systems have the potential to radically improve the lives of their users, especially when it comes to their working lives. This technology can thus provide new capabilities which can advantage those who have the means to acquire them, which can lead to a gap in access and the reinforcement of power for the individuals with the means to purchase them (Bruynseels et al. 2018). Consider the implications of a situation-aware tool which can provide a user with an advantage when studying for tests. New strategies and guidelines may yet be developed to help overcome these limitations, though these are still in their infancy. Nonetheless, to the optimistic, the opportunity remains clear: AI can enable humans to overcome not just environmental challenges, but also cognitive challenges that they may face in each situation. We can envision the situation awareness of cognition in future designs of systems that leverage human-AI teams—these technologies may yet even offer a new frontier for human advancement.

References

AmbientAI (2023) Ambient.ai. https://ambient.ai/. Accessed 31 Oct 2024

Anderson BB, Vance A, Kirwan CB et al (2016) From warning to wallpaper: why the brain habituates to security warnings and what can be done about it. J Manag Inform Syst 33:713–743. https://doi.org/10.1080/07421222.2016.1243947

Baldwin CL, Roberts DM, Barragan D et al (2017) Detecting and quantifying mind wandering during simulated driving. Front Hum Neurosci 11:406

Bandara P (2023) U.S. marines outsmart ai security cameras by hiding in a cardboard box. https://petapixel.com/2023/01/30/u-s-marines-outsmart-ai-security-cameras-by-hiding-in-a-cardboard-box/. Accessed 11 Feb 2023

Berka C, Levendowski DJ, Cvetinovic MM et al (2004) Real-time analysis of eeg indexes of alertness, cognition, and memory acquired with a wireless eeg headset. Int J Hum-Comput Interact 17:151–170

Bonnefond A, Doignon-Camus N, Touzalin-Chretien P, Dufour A (2010) Vigilance and intrinsic maintenance of alert state: an erp study. Behav Brain Res 211:185–190. https://doi.org/10.1016/j.bbr.2010.03.030

BR41NIO (2023) Br41n.io. https://www.br41n.io/. Accessed 12 Feb 2023
Bruynseels K, Santoni de Sio F, van den Hoven J (2018) Digital twins in health care: ethical implications of an emerging engineering paradigm. Front Genet 9:31
Carrick FR, Pagnacco G, Azzolino SF et al (2021) Brain vital signs in elite ice hockey: towards characterizing objective and specific neurophysiological reference values for concussion management. Front Neurosci 15:670563
Conrad C, Newman A (2021) Measuring mind wandering during online lectures assessed with eeg. Front Hum Neurosci 15:697532
Conrad C, Newman AJ (2019) How attention networks can inform research in information systems. In: Information systems and neuroscience. Springer, Cham, pp 155–162
Conrad C, Newman AJ (2022) Towards mind wandering adaptive online learning and virtual work experiences. In: Davis FD, Riedl R, vom Brocke J et al (eds) Information systems and neuroscience. Springer, Cham, pp 261–267
Conrad CD, Bliemel M (2016) Psychophysiological measures of cognitive absorption and cognitive load in e-learning applications. In: Proceedings of the thirty sixth international conference for information systems
Demazure T, Karran A, Léger PM et al (2021) Enhancing sustained attention. Bus Inform Syst Eng 63:653–668. https://doi.org/10.1007/s12599-021-00701-3
Deza A, Peters JR, Taylor GS et al (2017) Attention allocation aid for visual search. In: Proceedings of the 2017 CHI conference on human factors in computing systems. Association for Computing Machinery, New York, pp 220–231
Diamond A (2013) Executive functions. Ann Rev Psychol 64:135–168. https://doi.org/10.1146/annurev-psych-113011-143750
D'Mello S, Kopp K, Bixler RE, Bosch N (2016) Attending to attention: detecting and combating mind wandering during computerized reading. In: Proceedings of the 2016 CHI conference extended abstracts on human factors in computing systems. Association for Computing Machinery, New York, pp 1661–1669
Eastwood JD, Frischen A, Fenske MJ, Smilek D (2012) The unengaged mind: defining boredom in terms of attention. Perspect Psychol Sci 7:482–495. https://doi.org/10.1177/1745691612456044
Egner S, Reimann S, Hoeger R, Zangemeister W (2018) Attention and information acquisition: comparison of mouse-click with eye-movement attention tracking. J Eye Movement Res. https://doi.org/10.16910/jemr.11.6.4
Endsley MR (2015) Situation awareness misconceptions and misunderstandings. J Cogn Eng Decision Making 9:4–32. https://doi.org/10.1177/1555343415572631
Endsley MR (2017) From here to autonomy: lessons learned from human–automation research. Hum Fact 59:5–27. https://doi.org/10.1177/0018720816681350
Endsley MR (2020) The divergence of objective and subjective situation awareness: a meta-analysis. J Cogn Eng Decis Making 14:34–53. https://doi.org/10.1177/1555343419874248
Endsley MR (2023) Supporting human-ai teams: transparency, explainability, and situation awareness. Comput Hum Behav 140:107574. https://doi.org/10.1016/j.chb.2022.107574
Fan J, McCandliss BD, Sommer T et al (2002) Testing the efficiency and independence of attentional networks. J Cogn Neurosci 14:340–347
Fox KCR, Spreng RN, Ellamil M et al (2015) The wandering brain: meta-analysis of functional neuroimaging studies of mind-wandering and related spontaneous thought processes. NeuroImage 111:611–621. https://doi.org/10.1016/j.neuroimage.2015.02.039
Golchert J, Smallwood J, Jefferies E et al (2017) Individual variation in intentionality in the mind-wandering state is reflected in the integration of the default-mode, fronto-parietal, and limbic networks. NeuroImage 146:226–235. https://doi.org/10.1016/j.neuroimage.2016.11.025
Hamm P, Klesel M, Coberger P, Wittmann HF (2023) Explanation matters: an experimental study on explainable ai. Electron Markets 33:17. https://doi.org/10.1007/s12525-023-00640-9
Ishigami Y, Klein RM (2010) Repeated measurement of the components of attention using two versions of the attention network test (ant): stability, isolability, robustness, and reliability. J Neurosci Methods 190:117–128. https://doi.org/10.1016/j.jneumeth.2010.04.019

Jones SA, Butler BC, Kintzel F et al (2016) Measuring the performance of attention networks with the dalhousie computerized attention battery (DalCAB): methodology and reliability in healthy adults. Front Psychol 7:823

Klein RM (2020) Is covert spatial orienting embodied or disembodied cognition? A historical review. Q J Exp Psychol 73:20–28. https://doi.org/10.1177/1747021819889497

Klesel M, Oschinsky FM, Conrad C, Niehaves B (2021) Does the type of mind wandering matter? Extending the inquiry about the role of mind wandering in the it use experience. Internet Res 31:1018–1039. https://doi.org/10.1108/INTR-05-2020-0262

Kozhevnikov M, Li Y, Wong S et al (2018) Do enhanced states exist? Boosting cognitive capacities through an action video-game. Cognition 173:93–105. https://doi.org/10.1016/j.cognition.2018.01.006

Krigolson OE, Williams CC, Norton A et al (2017) Choosing muse: validation of a low-cost, portable eeg system for ERP research. Front Neurosci 11:109

Krisher T, Press A (2022) Tesla cars involved in 10 of the 11 new crash deaths linked to automated-tech vehicles. https://fortune.com/2022/10/19/tesla-cars-involved-in-10-of-the-11-new-crash-deaths-linked-to-automated-tech-vehicles/. Accessed 11 Feb 2023

Kuzminykh A, Rintel S (2020) Classification of functional attention in video meetings. In: Proceedings of the 2020 CHI conference on human factors in computing systems. Association for Computing Machinery, New York, pp 1–13

Lyon D (2014) Surveillance, snowden, and big data: capacities, consequences, critique. Big Data Soc 1:2053951714541861. https://doi.org/10.1177/2053951714541861

Nissen A, Conrad C, Newman A (2023) Are you human? Investigating the perceptions and evaluations of virtual versus human instagram influencers. In: Proceedings of the 2023 CHI conference on human factors in computing systems. Association for Computing Machinery, New York, pp 1–14

Posner MI, Petersen SE (1990) The attention system of the human brain. Ann Rev Neurosci 13:25–42

Rankin CH, Abrams T, Barry RJ et al (2009) Habituation revisited: an updated and revised description of the behavioral characteristics of habituation. Neurobiol Learn Mem 92:135–138. https://doi.org/10.1016/j.nlm.2008.09.012

Robertson IH, Manly T, Andrade J et al (1997) 'oops!': performance correlates of everyday attentional failures in traumatic brain injured and normal subjects. Neuropsychologia 35:747–758. https://doi.org/10.1016/S0028-3932(97)00015-8

Santamaría-Vázquez E, Martínez-Cagigal V, Pérez-Velasco S et al (2022) Robust asynchronous control of erp-based brain-computer interfaces using deep learning. Comput Methods Programs Biomed 215:106623. https://doi.org/10.1016/j.cmpb.2022.106623

Seli P, Carriere J, Levene M, Smilek D (2013) How few and far between? Examining the effects of probe rate on self-reported mind wandering. Front Psychol 4:430

Seli P, Smallwood J, Cheyne JA, Smilek D (2015) On the relation of mind wandering and ADHD symptomatology. Psychonomic Bull Rev 22:629–636. https://doi.org/10.3758/s13423-014-0793-0

Seli P, Risko EF, Smilek D (2016) On the necessity of distinguishing between unintentional and intentional mind wandering. Psychol Sci 27:685–691. https://doi.org/10.1177/0956797616634068

Seli P, Kane MJ, Smallwood J et al (2018) Mind-wandering as a natural kind: a family-resemblances view. Trends Cogn Sci 22:479–490. https://doi.org/10.1016/j.tics.2018.03.010

Smallwood J, Schooler JW (2015) The science of mind wandering: empirically navigating the stream of consciousness. Ann Rev Psychol 66:487–518

Speicher M, Nuck S, Wesemann L et al (2015) From TMR to turtle: predicting result relevance from mouse cursor interactions in web search. J Web Eng 386–413

Vance A, Jenkins JL, Anderson BB et al (2018) Tuning out security warnings: a longitudinal examination of habituation through fmri, eye tracking and field experiments. MIS Q 42:355–380

Wilson KM, Head J, de Joux NR et al (2015) Friendly fire and the sustained attention to response task. Hum Fact 57:1219–1234. https://doi.org/10.1177/0018720815605703

Eye-Tracking Technology for Cognition-Adaptive LLM-Based Assistants at the Workplace

Moritz Langner, Peyman Toreini, and Alexander Maedche

Abstract Large language models (LLMs) are playing an increasingly important role in knowledge work. LLM-based assistants will enable automation and augmentation of a broad spectrum of knowledge worker tasks in the future. Thereby, it should be noted that LLM-based assistants also come with impacts on their users. Previous automation research has shown that cognitive states play an important role in automated systems. For example, users are known to have difficulties in maintaining situation awareness and managing cognitive load. It can be assumed that cognitive states also play a key role in the interaction between humans and LLM-based assistants enabling automation and augmentation of tasks. Eye tracking is a promising technology to examine cognitive states of users when engaging with LLM-based assistants. In this book chapter, we present results from a pilot study investigating the cognition of users engaging with LLM-based reading assistants. On this basis, we introduce a new class of systems titled cognition-adaptive LLM-based assistants that emphasizes a cognitive perspective on LLM-based assistance from a user's point of view. Specifically, we propose to leverage the capabilities of eye tracking to automatically recognize cognitive states of LLM-based assistance users and on this basis provide advanced cognition-adaptive support. We introduce design elements and a roadmap of future work towards cognition-adaptive LLM-based assistants.

1 Introduction

Large language models (LLMs) are neural networks with billions of parameters and are trained on a large corpus of text from websites, social media, and news pages. Leveraging this large amount of training data, LLMs possess general language understanding and generation capabilities and do not have to be trained for each use case specifically in contrast to traditional supervised machine learning approaches.

M. Langner (✉) · P. Toreini · A. Maedche
Karlsruhe Institute of Technology (KIT), Karlsruhe, Germany
e-mail: moritz.langner@kit.edu; peyman.toreini@kit.edu; alexander.maedche@kit.edu

C. K. Coursaris et al. (eds.), *The Design of Human-Centered Artificial Intelligence for the Workplace*, Progress in IS, https://doi.org/10.1007/978-3-031-83512-4_17

Therefore, application areas of LLMs are manifold and may reach from supporting general writing tasks like editing and authoring text to image generation and interpretation or providing task-specific assistance, e.g., supporting the creation of data visualizations. In the future, we will work with a lot of different LLM-based copilots at work and in private life that augment and partially automate tasks. As knowledge workers who focus on understanding and connecting existing information and generating new information become scarce due to demographic change, this capability is of specific interest.

A specific area where LLMs are particularly useful is reading assistance in knowledge work. Knowledge workers in companies typically face vast amounts of comprehensive text documents that are hard to process. LLMs are specifically helpful in summarizing text documents and gaining a general overview of a corpus of documents. By its natural language processing capabilities, LLMs also allow the user to ask specific questions about a text document and to translate the content to simplified language that may be easier to understand for nonexperts. Such LLM-based assistants enable access to documents that are typically targeted at experts and do require a significant amount of domain-specific knowledge to understand the content. Besides the simplification of text, the LLM can also provide additional definitions and explanations about words and technical terms that require domain knowledge and go beyond what is provided within the text. Furthermore, many document texts are written in English which is often not the mother tongue of the user. Therefore, the LLM can increase the understanding of the document by translating the text to the mother tongue of the user.

So far, the focus of research in the field of LLMs has been primarily on enhancing the underlying technology of LLMs. Nonetheless, only a few studies investigated the user's perspective on LLMs. Users typically create prompts to query the output of the LLM and then further process the output with or without validation of the output. However, LLMs might create very humanlike but incorrect or nonsensical text, which is referred to as hallucinations. Furthermore, LLMs are quite sensitive to tweaks in the prompt and attempting the same prompt multiple times might result in different outputs. From the user perspective, this can be challenging as users typically tend to overrely on automation and therefore might not validate or detect errors in the output of LLMs. In addition, creating a good prompt is not an easy task and requires expertise, creativity, and iterations of improvement. Therefore, we argue that we need to take a cognitive perspective on the interaction between users and LLM-based assistants. There is a huge potential in providing cognition-adaptive LLM-based assistants that provide dedicated support to users to allocate cognitive resources properly.

In previous automation research, situation awareness (SA) by Endsley (1995) is a well-known concept in the field of cognition. Recently, a situation awareness perspective for human-AI interaction has also been introduced (Jiang et al. 2023). Situation awareness is defined as "the perception of the elements in the environment within a volume of time and space, the comprehension of their meaning, and the projection of their status in the near future" (Endsley 1995, p. 1). Typically, users of (semi-) automated AI-based systems such as LLMs have difficulties in establishing and maintaining situation awareness. Furthermore, cognitive load is closely tied to situation awareness as it refers to the amount of mental capacity captured by the current task. Existing research investigated situation awareness and cognitive load during task execution using eye tracking. Eye tracking is a technology that provides access to information about the window to our soul, the eyes. Many cognitive processes are directly reflected by our eye movements, e.g., attention, cognitive load, confusion, distraction, and fatigue. Eye tracking also allows to get insights into the visual behavior of users and how they interact with a system. Therefore, eye tracking is a promising approach to examine and support cognitive processes during the use of LLM-based assistants.

In this book chapter, we argue for the need for a better understanding of cognition during the usage of LLM-based assistance at the workplace and for providing dedicated support to leverage the full potential of LLM-based assistants and prevent negative outcomes. To shed light on cognition in LLM-based assistance, we first introduce eye tracking as a means to assess cognition with situation awareness and cognitive load as an example of cognitive states. Moreover, we argue that as a first step, eye tracking technology can be leveraged to examine the visual behavior of users of LLM-based assistants. We present DocInsight, a system that integrates an LLM-based assistant for document reading and exploration at the workplace with eye-tracking technology. Furthermore, we show initial insights from a pilot eye-tracking study on LLM-based reading assistance usage and propose design features and a roadmap toward cognition-adaptive LLM-based assistants.

2 Cognition and Eye-Tracking Technology

Cognition refers to all mental processes regarding the acquisition, organization, and use of knowledge and thus plays a vital role in text processing (Davern et al. 2012). Cognitive load and situation awareness are of particular interest in LLM-based assistance as this new class of system augments and automates tasks of users while also putting new challenges on the user such as prompting correctly or overrelying on the output of the LLM without critical thinking. In the following we focus on situation awareness and cognitive load as two important cognitive states of users in the context of LLM-based assistance.

The amount of mental capacity that is captured by the current task is called cognitive load. As mental resources are limited, complex and difficult tasks can require more than the available mental resources. Cognitive overload is the consequence if the required mental resources for a task exceed the available resources and can seriously impact the productivity. Kahneman and Beatty (1966) established the link between cognitive load and pupil size. As eye trackers are also capable of measuring the pupil size, eye tracking represents a promising technology to continuously assess cognitive load.

Situation awareness during system usage is established in three levels according to Endsley (1995). To reach level 1 of situation awareness, all elements of the system have to be perceived by the user. In level 2, the user has to comprehend the system's status and how the perceived elements relate to each other. The projection of the future status of the system is reached in level 3. Traditionally, situation awareness has been captured using freezing techniques such as the Situation Awareness Global Assessment Technique (SAGAT) (Endsley 1988), or self-report surveys such as the SA Rating Technique (SART) (Taylor 2017). However, these methods are unsuitable for continuous and real-time assessment due to their intrusive and discrete nature. As situation awareness is grounded in information processing and attention theory, eye tracking is a promising physiological measurement technology of situation awareness (Zhang et al. 2020). Eye-tracking applications range from being an explicit input method to interact with a system to diagnostic applications where it is used to identify usability and user experience issues of a system. With the advances in artificial intelligence, recent research focused on assessing the cognition of users continuously and in real time using eye tracking. When talking about cognition and eye tracking, primarily cognitive states such as cognitive load, situation awareness, distraction, and fatigue are meant. Monitoring cognition continuously and in real time offers the advantage of being able to detect cognitive breakdown such as a cognitive overload or low situation awareness and to support the user in recovering from this breakdown.

In the context of LLM-based assistance for processing (large) text documents, it is important for the user to perceive and understand the system's status and, even more importantly, to have a detailed understanding of the output and text content. Following Nadj et al. (2020), we propose to extent the perspective on situation awareness also to the perception and comprehension of the output of the LLM-based assistant and the text document. Moreover, the understanding of the LLM output and the text document might also impact the situation awareness about environmental facts of the definition by Endsley (1995). A challenge that might arise in the context of LLM-based assistance is the superficial understanding of the text or the noncritical adoption of output of the LLM by overrelying on the LLM. Cognitive overload could appear, when drafting a complex prompt for the LLM, mainly relying on the document text and not leveraging the capabilities of the LLM or verifying output of the LLM within the document. Therefore, real-time recognition of the level of cognitive load and situation awareness using eye-tracking technology could enable to recognize upcoming cognitive breakdowns and provide support to prevent these.

3 A Pilot Study on LLM-Based Reading Support Assistance

We performed a pilot study on LLM-based reading support assistance using the DocuInsight system developed at our lab. The user interface of DocuInsight is depicted in Fig. 1. The interface building blocks are organized into three major areas. In the top left corner, the document can be opened in a PDF document viewer allowing the user to search within the document and to zoom in/out. Below

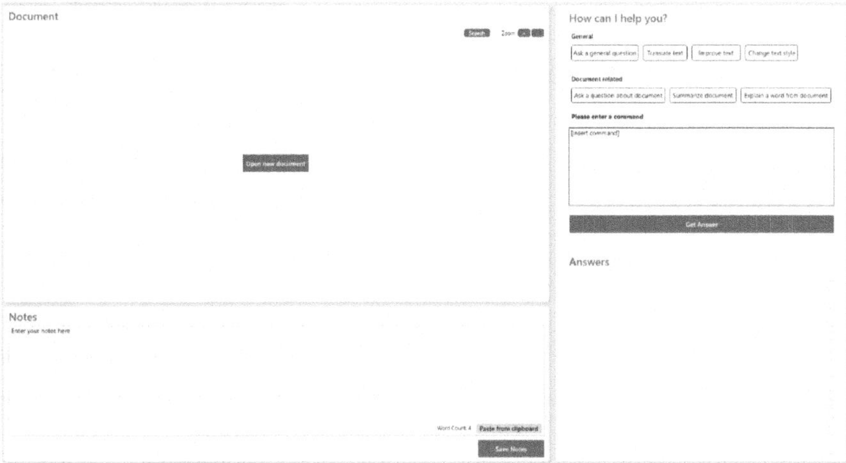

Fig. 1 User interface of DocuInsight

the PDF document viewer, a text box for note-taking can be found. In this text box, the user can write down important information from the text document and create a summary. On the right side, the LLM-based assistant is integrated. This assistant is divided into three areas, the task selection area, prompting area, and output area. Within the task selection area, the user can select one of the predefined tasks which are either general tasks (general question, translate text, extent text, change text style) or document-related tasks (question about document, summary of document, explain word from document). In the prompting area, the user can adapt the predefined prompt or specify an own prompt. Once the user clicks the "Get Answer" button, the prompt is sent to ChatGPT via the API. If a document-related task is selected, the backend also adds the document text at the end of the prompt. The output of ChatGPT is shown in the output area in a chat-like interface. Prompts and LLM output are shown as speech bubbles which also allows to the user to go back to previous LLM requests.

In the pilot study, we gave this tool to students and asked them to explore, understand, and summarize a scientific paper from the field of human-computer interaction. The paper was made accessible via the PDF document viewer, and participants could use the LLM-based assistant to extract information and ask questions about the paper. During the pilot study, we recorded the users' eye movement data to capture their visual behavior. We visualized the recorded eye-tracking data in heat maps. The resulting heat maps demonstrate that users have different visual strategies to approach the task. In Fig. 2 a participant focused a lot on the LLM-based assistant while paying less attention to the paper content during the task. This participant accomplished the task within 12 minutes. The participant of Fig. 3 focused mostly on the paper to accomplish the task and ignored the LLM-based assistant which is also reflected in the task completion time of 29 minutes. Finally, the heat map depicted on Fig. 4 shows that the participant exhibited a

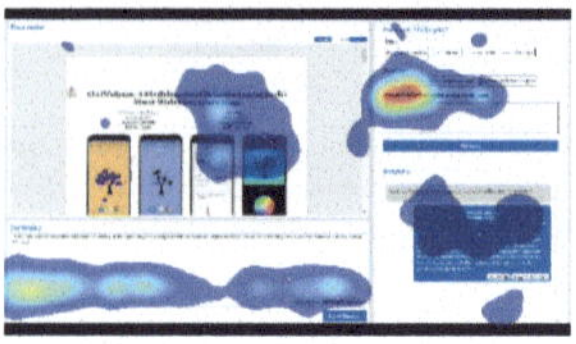

Fig. 2 Focus on assistant

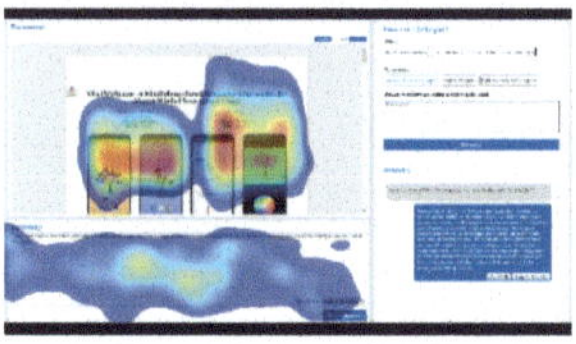

Fig. 3 Focus on paper

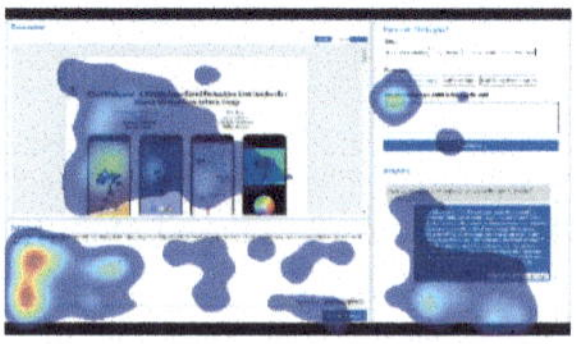

Fig. 4 Focus on both

balanced distribution of attention between the paper and the assistant and completed the task within 13 minutes. While the low sample size does not allow for statistical analysis, the visually reported data makes differences in visual strategies obvious.

We hypothesize that the visual strategies affect the situation awareness and cognitive load of users. Each of the strategies has advantages and disadvantages, for example, focusing more on the LLM-based assistant may increase efficiency, but on the other side, users might develop only a superficial understanding of the document content as they did not deeply involve themselves with the content. Focusing too much on the paper will decrease efficiency as reading and understanding a large document takes a significant amount of time. However, the comprehension of the content will increase with paying more attention to the paper. Balancing the attention distribution between the paper and the LLM-based assistant looks like a compromise between task efficiency and comprehension of the paper. Another important dimension to consider is task completion time which also differed between participants between 12 and 29 minutes. Potential negative outcomes of a low task completion time are missing important information within the paper and overrelying on the LLM-based assistant which makes the user more prone to errors and hallucinations of the LLM.

4 Design Elements of Cognition-Adaptive LLM-Based Assistants

Considering the results of our pilot study, we assume that an effective LLM-based assistant is not only a system that should provide efficient and effective

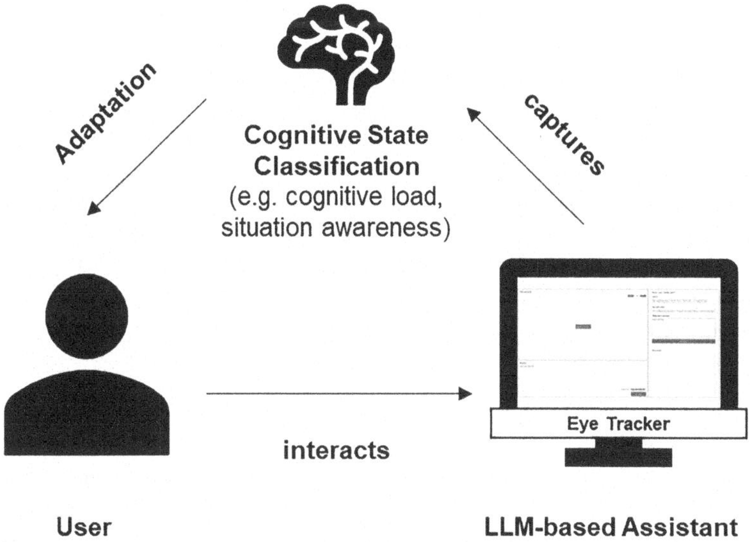

Fig. 5 Cognition-adaptive LLM-based assistant

access to information but also should consider the user's individual usage strategy and its potentially negative influence on cognition, such as low comprehension of content, overreliance, loss of confidence, critical thinking ability, etc. Therefore, we introduce a new class of systems called cognition-adaptive LLM-based assistants that aim to support their users in both cognition and productivity. A cognition-adaptive system typically uses biosignal sensor technology, like eye tracking, electrocardiography (ECG), or electroencephalography (EEG), to capture, process and classify the user's current cognitive states, and then adapts the system according to the user's current needs (Schultz and Maedche 2023). The conceptual architecture is shown in Fig. 5.

The adaptation can be provided by either increasing users' awareness about their own cognitive state (e.g., sending a notification) or by automatically adapting the system in a way that it positively influences the cognitive state of users (e.g., by temporarily reducing or even deactivating the LLM support). Both approaches might have advantages and disadvantages that should be investigated in future studies. Previous research has shown the positive influence of increasing users' awareness about their cognitive states, e.g., in the context of attentive information dashboards (Toreini et al. 2022). To support the activities of office workers, it is necessary to identify ways of integrating awareness cues within the context of the user's current task. In the following, we discuss important design dimensions that need to be considered when designing such systems for LLM-based assistance.

Timing and Frequency

An essential element in the delivery of cognitive support is the timing and frequency of the support element. Such cognition support can be presented before, during, or after accomplishing a task. For the support during the task, timing and determining the right moment is critical because it may interrupt the user's primary task. During task execution, users do not necessarily have to evenly balance their attention between the document and the LLM-based assistant at all points of time as they might sequentially distribute attention to the document and the assistant and they might recover within a short amount of time. However, the system should be intelligent enough to identify extreme cases of attention distribution where the user is either neglecting the document or the LLM-based assistant to provide support at exactly that point of time to prevent cognitive breakdowns. Furthermore, the frequency of such support also plays an important role. The system needs to find a good balance between reminding users of poor attention distribution, while avoiding annoying them with multiple warnings.

Modality

In terms of the modality to provide support, we argue for the visual assistive modality as the primary assistive format for knowledge workers. As visual attention plays an important role to accomplish the task with the LLM-based assistant, we suggest using the visual modality for providing support as well. Such modality can be in form of warning message, color changing, gamified elements, nudge, etc. However, other nonvisual modalities such as sound, haptics, or multimodal interaction can also be effective as a support (Nadj and Maedche 2019). Moreover, the most suitable modality depends on the task, context, and user characteristics, and it might not be generalizable for all knowledge workers.

Content

The content of the support provided to knowledge workers in case of poor attention distribution is challenging. On the one hand, it should motivate the user to improve attention distribution between using LLM and the document, and on the other hand it should not annoy the user. There is a need to investigate the type, size, and tone of the content. For example, a support message may just state that an unfavorable attention distribution was detected which might have a negative impact on the user's cognition. It can also highlight the potential negative outcomes of continuing with this unfavorable strategy, or it provides strategies to prevent and recover from a bad attention distribution. It can also be written in a warning, motivating, or informative tone. The presentation can be in the form of simple text, heat maps highlighting the past visual behavior, or pictures to show the influence of such behavior. The type, size, and tone of that message can be further personalized based on the user's characteristics such as age, gender, culture, and personality.

Location

The location where the adaptation is provided can also have an influence on the effectiveness of the adaption. Depending on the modality and content, the adaptation can be provided at several positions within the software that integrates the LLM-based assistant. For example, it could be provided on top of the user interface of the software fading out all other content of the software. More subtle approaches would be providing the adaption within the document e.g., by integrating it into the text or providing it within the LLM-based assistant, e.g., by adding a new speech bubble in the output area of the LLM-based assistant.

5 A Roadmap for Cognition-Adaptive LLM-Based Assistants

Using eye tracking to detect the user's processing strategy as well as to recognize cognitive states has the potential to avoid several negative effects of using or even not using LLM-based assistance. We propose using eye-tracking-based interventions that help users to prevent negative effects of LLM-based assistance. We suggest the following roadmap for designing cognition-adaptive LLM-based assistants.

Task and the Required Skills

First, we argue that there is a need to better understand the different tasks that knowledge workers are working on when using an LLM to provide specific cognition support that is needed by the user. Visual behavior is known to be very task dependent, and therefore the cognition-adaptive system needs to be able to also detect the task using eye tracking. The primary goal of cognition-adaptive LLM-based assistants is to support knowledge workers while also preserving their skills and autonomy. Skills are tightly interrelated with the cognitive states. The user should not unlearn any skills that help the user to accomplish the task, while preserving the user's autonomy is important for the adoption of the system. For example, if a task requires high situation awareness, the cognition-adaptive LLM-based assistant should provide short-term support while not affecting the user's long-term ability to establish and maintain it. Losing skills may cause negative impacts on the user and task outcomes. Therefore, a detailed analysis of the tasks and the skills required to perform a task is regarded as an important step in designing cognition-adaptive LLM-based assistants.

Cognitive State Detection

In addition to considering the tasks and the required skills, there is a need to automatically detect cognitive states of users. The detection includes recording and analyzing data from the knowledge worker during system usage and correlating it with cognitive state data captured, e.g., through surveys. Previous research has shown that cognitive state detection is possible by considering interaction and/or physiological data of the user and using machine learning (Lallé et al. 2016). Considering eye-tracking data, potential features could not only be fixation-based features such as fixation duration and count, but also saccade-based metrics (e.g., saccade length, count, and amplitude) and pupil-based features. Therefore, it should be investigated whether cognitive states of user's during LLM-based assistance usage can be predicted by eye movement data.

Adaptation Designs

Above, we highlighted the design elements of timing and frequency, modality, content, and location. Based on the detection of the task and cognitive states, it is important to provide the best fitting adaptation design to the user. Thus, we suggest that different combinations of the design elements should be investigated in terms of their effect on cognition and outcomes. Furthermore, we suggest focusing in a first step on making users aware about their cognitive states. However, it is also possible to adapt the system according to the user's current needs, and future work in this direction is also required as both formats might have advantages and disadvantages that need to be investigated.

Cognition-Adaptive LLM-Based Assistants for Teams

So far, we have emphasized the use of cognitive-adaptive LLM-based assistants on the individual level. However, the tasks of knowledge workers often are performed on the team level. Thus, future work is needed to investigate the design of cognition-adaptive LLM-based assistants for teams as well as what are the influences on team cognitive states and team performance.

In outlining this roadmap for cognition-adaptive LLM-based assistants using eye-tracking technology, it is also important to keep in mind that eye tracking has several limitations in its current state of technological development. Eye-tracking devices are still rather expensive, and the benefits of a cognition-adaptive system may not justify the cost of an eye tracker in an enterprise context. In addition, current screen-based eye-tracking technology is susceptible to environmental conditions such as light, calibration drift due to body movement, or individual characteristics such as visual impairment. However, we believe that as the technology advances, most of these limitations will be overcome in the next few years.

References

Davern M, Shaft T, Te'eni D (2012) Cognition matters: enduring questions in cognitive is research. J Assoc Inform Syst 13:273–314. https://doi.org/10.17705/1jais.00290

Endsley MR (1988) Situation awareness global assessment technique (SAGAT). In: Proceedings of the IEEE 1988 national aerospace and electronics conference. IEEE, Piscataway, pp 789–795. https://doi.org/10.1109/NAECON.1988.195097

Endsley MR (1995) Toward a theory of situation awareness in dynamic systems. Hum Fact J Hum Fact Ergon Soc 37:32–64. https://doi.org/10.1518/001872095779049543

Jiang J, Karran AJ, Coursaris CK, Léger PM, Beringer J (2023) A situation awareness perspective on human-ai interaction: tensions and opportunities. Int J Hum-Comput Interact 39(9):1789–1806. https://doi.org/10.1080/10447318.2022.2093863

Kahneman D, Beatty J (1966) Pupil diameter and load on memory. Science 154:1583–1585. https://doi.org/10.1126/science.154.3756.1583

Lallé S, Conati C, Carenini G (2016) Predicting confusion in information visualization from eye tracking and interaction data. In: IJCAI international joint conference on artificial intelligence, vol 2016, pp 2529–2535

Nadj M, Maedche A (2019) Situation awareness in aircraft ground handling: the impact of auditory and visual notification cues. J Cogn Eng Decis Making 13:102–122. https://doi.org/10.1177/1555343419830183

Nadj M, Maedche A, Schieder C (2020) The effect of interactive analytical dashboard features on situation awareness and task performance. Decis Support Syst 135:N.PAG–N.PAG

Schultz T, Maedche A (2023) Biosignals meet adaptive systems. SN Appl Sci. https://doi.org/10.1007/s42452-023-05412-w

Taylor RM (2017) Situational awareness rating technique (SART): the development of a tool for aircrew systems design. In: Situational awareness. Routledge, London, pp 111–128

Toreini P, Langner M, Maedche A, Morana S, Vogel T (2022) Designing attentive information dashboards. J Assoc Inform Syst 23(2):521–552

Zhang T, Yang J, Liang N, Pitts BJ, Prakah-Asante KO, Curry R, Duerstock BS, Wachs JP, Yu D (2020) Physiological measurements of situation awareness: a systematic review. Hum. Fact. https://doi.org/10.1177/0018720820969071

Navigating Decisions in the Cockpit: The Intelligent Pilot Advisory System

Boris Djartov and Jakob Würfel

Abstract This chapter explores the integration of artificial intelligence into decision-support systems for the cockpit through the development of an Intelligent Pilot Advisory System. Although the current focus of the system development is assisting pilots in airport selection during mid-flight emergencies, it also serves as a research platform to investigate the feasibility, implementation, and benefits of AI on the flight deck, as well as to study human-AI interactions. User-conducted studies revealed positive pilot reception, with participants finding the system helpful in decision-making and open to further AI applications. They appreciated the increased options analysis, information gathering, and structure provided by the system, while emphasizing the importance of informed decision-making. Based on these promising results, further development is planned, including additional pilot studies with more participants, as well as research into AI models, especially ones focusing on explainability and interpretability.

1 Introduction

The flight deck and its many systems are in a state of constant improvement. Various systems have been developed that build and improve on one another in order to provide support for pilots in the execution of their operational tasks. Over the past few decades, there have been many groundbreaking innovations in aircraft cockpit design, driven by both technological advances and increased attention to human factors, resulting in reduced crew size and increased safety. Major changes have been the replacement of analog dials and gauges with the introduction of the glass cockpit, which shows electronic information on displays, and the introduction of fly-by-wire in the 1980s (Coombs 2005; Airbus 2024). Cognitive assistance has also been the subject of much research for many years. In the 1990s and early 2000s, for example, research was carried out on the CASSY and CAMA assistance systems

B. Djartov (✉) · J. Würfel
German Aerospace Center (DLR), Braunchweig, Germany
e-mail: boris.djartov@dlr.de; jakob.wuerfel@dlr.de

C. K. Coursaris et al. (eds.), *The Design of Human-Centered Artificial Intelligence for the Workplace*, Progress in IS, https://doi.org/10.1007/978-3-031-83512-4_18

(Onken 1999), and in the 2000s on the IPA pilot assistance system. Hecker and Korn (2003) The newfound usefulness of artificial intelligence has opened compelling possibilities for enhancing cockpit operations, making it increasingly sensible to incorporate AI technologies in aviation systems. A noteworthy area of interest involves the integration of AI-based decision support systems within the cockpit and understanding the interaction between the cockpit crew and the newly added AI-prominent systems. In this chapter, we present the concept of the Intelligent Pilot Advisory System, which is currently being intensively researched and developed. This AI-powered system is designed to assist pilots in normal conditions as well as in emergency situations. Specifically, the current focus is on providing suitable alternate airport suggestions mid-flight during emergencies. The chapter will present the main ideas behind the system as a whole, along with its two main subsystems: the AI core, which houses the AI model, and the AI-crew interface.

2 The Intelligent Pilot Advisory System

At the DLR (Deutsches Zentrum für Luft- und Raumfahrt e.V., engl. German Aerospace Center), the Intelligent Pilot Advisory System (IPAS) is currently under development to demonstrate the use of AI in future commercial aircraft cockpits and to research aspects of human-AI system integration in such a complex working environment. In Würfel et al. (2023), the system was introduced for the first time. The concept of the system derives from interviews with airline pilots the ideation process that identifies the use cases, requirements, and functionalities of this AI-based assistance system. The proposed system is intended to assist pilots in both regular daily operations and emergency situations, for example, by providing operational options such as the identification and assessment of suitable alternate airports. The IPAS is an evolving system that is currently the subject of intensive development and research at the DLR. Its graphical user interface, functionality, and system depth are continuously improved and extended with each iteration. Initial system components and functionality have already been integrated into simulator environments and evaluated in user studies.

2.1 The IPAS Use Cases

Advances in AI are opening up a wide range of possibilities for assistance systems that can help pilots in the cockpit. Würfel et al. (2023) describe how the use cases for the IPAS were identified. The focus of the study was to identify the current gaps in pilot assistance and to identify specific needs mentioned by the pilots.

One of the biggest challenges identified was in the area of emergencies and the collection of data to deal with them. During emergency and time-critical situations, like an engine fire and a medical emergency of a passenger, decision-making in the cockpit of an airliner remains one of the most challenging and workload-intensive tasks for the flight crew. Structured schemes such as FORDEC (Facts, Options, Risks, Decision, Execution, Control) (Hörmann 1994) and TDODAR (Time, Diagnosis, Options, Decide, Assign Task, Review) (Walters 2002), which are supposed to systematically guide the decision-making process, are trained in recurring training sessions. However, depending on the situation, the pilots must collect and evaluate a lot of information as a basis for the decision-making process. This includes, for example, information about the technical error and the resulting operational limitations, and information about the weather, other air traffic, or the infrastructure at possible alternative airports. This can take a lot of time, and depending on the available time frame, not all information can be fully collected and not all potential options can be identified and evaluated. So although there are certain procedures in place for handling decision-making in the cockpit, there does appear to be a lot of potential for improvement.

The study also revealed another gap. Participants reported that they often use private smartphones to check the weather or the traffic situation on the route and at the planned destination. This is due to the fact that today's cockpit systems allow pilots to look ahead for about the next 10 minutes of flight.

Figure 1 illustrates the effect that can be achieved with the IPAS and thus also demonstrates how valuable the IPAS integration could be. The increasing availability of data, such as live data from airports and live data on the current weather situation and surrounding air traffic, as well as the availability of onboard data from aircraft systems, leads to new opportunities for the development of AI-based flight deck assistance systems. By collecting, processing, and evaluating a large amount of data, the IPAS can assist the flight crew by providing relevant information in real time, predicting conditions along the route and at the planned destination, highlighting noteworthy conditions, making recommendations for these situations, and, in the event of an emergency, identifying and assessing possible options for action. The aim is to reduce the crew's workload in workload-intensive situations, enable better and more informed decision-making, and support situational awareness in day-to-day operations as well as in emergencies.

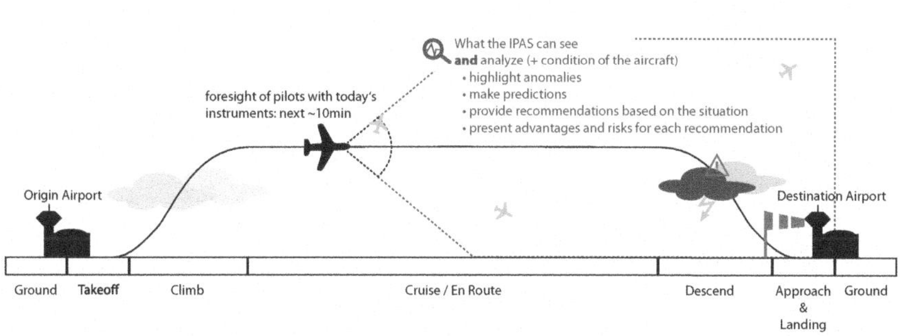

Fig. 1 A typical commercial flight is shown with the different flight phases. It is also illustrated how the visibility and predictability for the remaining flight mission would be improved using the IPAS

The following IPAS use cases outline the core functionality of the IPAS and focus on decision support and information provision at a strategic level. These use cases can be categorized into two groups:

1. **Mission support during normal operations:** The IPAS assists the flight crew during normal operations by analyzing real-time data on air traffic, weather conditions, and other factors along the route and at the planned destination. The system assists the crew in forecasting the future status of the aircraft and its environment. It provides predictions of potential events, such as identifying possible route changes, predicting the active approach direction at the destination airport, and determining the need for holding patterns.
2. **Support in emergency and abnormal situations:** The system then generates and assesses options for action, providing the crew with information relevant to the situation. For example, if it becomes impossible or inadvisable to continue a flight, the IPAS can collect and assess situational decision factors and recommend suitable alternative airports.

2.2 The Proposed System

Based on the requirements and the use cases, a system concept for the IPAS is proposed. As shown in Fig. 2, the system consists of two main components, the AI-Crew-Interaction System (AICIS) and the AI-Core-Module (AICOM), which work together to provide pilots with the functionality described in the section above.

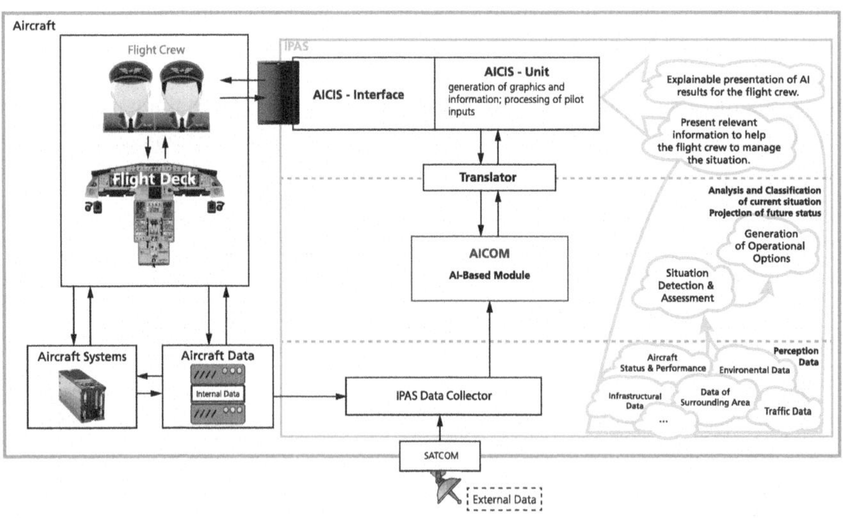

Fig. 2 The proposed system concept of the IPAS in Würfel et al. (2023)

The process steps performed in the different system modules are illustrated on the right side of Fig. 2. The functionality described is structured according to the elements of Endsley's Situation Awareness Model (Endsley 1995), which can be adopted for human-AI teams under the term Shared Situation Awareness between Airmen and Autonomy Teams. Endsley (2015) The model includes three stages of situation awareness. First, the current elements of the situation are perceived. Then, in the comprehension process, the situation and the meaning of individual data must be understood in order to form a holistic picture of the situation. Finally, a projection of the future state is made to predict the near future and define strategies and plans. The following main components are included in the model:

1. **IPAS Data Collector:** First, the data must be perceived. The IPAS Data Collector is responsible for gathering data from both the aircraft and external sources via satellite communication. The data collected may include information such as weather data, topographical data, and traffic data.
2. **AI-Core-Module (AICOM):** Based on the available data, it is necessary to comprehend the current situation and to make a projection of the future status. These tasks are performed by the AICOM, which continually analyzes the flight situation based on the data collected by the IPAS Data Collector. It constantly assesses the status of the flight mission, the aircraft, and the environment, and, if it detects an anomaly like an emergency or a critical situation, it generates operational options to assist the pilot in making a decision how to proceed.
3. **AI-Crew-Interaction-System (AICIS):** Lastly, the information and AI results should be presented in an understandable way for the flight crew. The AICIS serves as the interface between the AI system and the flight crew. It presents the needed information and recommendations generated by AICOM in a way that is explainable to pilots, facilitating efficient and effective use even in time-critical situations.

The IPAS does not actively control the flight controls or avionics systems. It only collects data from the aircraft systems, while the controls are the responsibility of the flight crew.

2.3 *Planned IPAS Functions*

Based on the initial study in Würfel et al. (2023) and the defined use cases mentioned in Sect. 2.1, basic functions have been defined that describe what functionality the IPAS and its components must provide when implementing the system to fulfill the use cases. Figure 3 shows an overview of the planned initial basic functions and their sequential connection.

The planned IPAS Basic Functions are divided into three main pillars. The first pillar describes all the background processes that occur when the AICOM continuously detects and assesses the situation. The other pillars describe two different

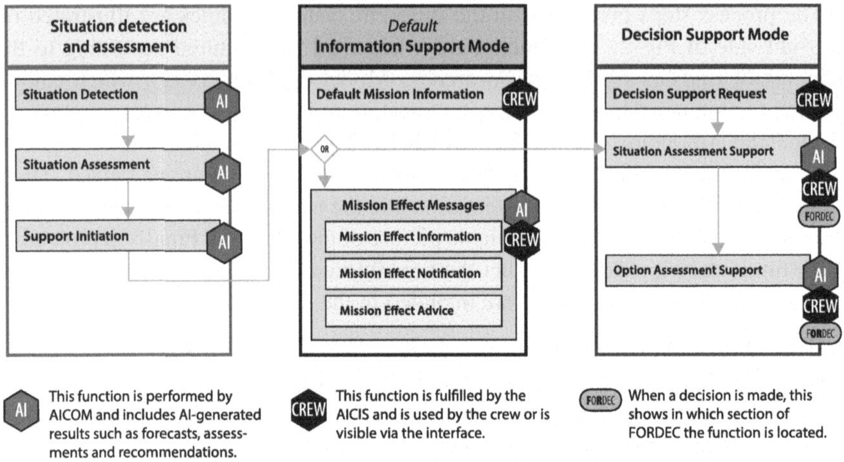

Fig. 3 The basic functions of the IPAS. Icons next to the function name indicate whether the process requires functions from the ACOM (purple) or the AICIS (red). There is also an indication in which part of FORDEC the function can be sorted, if applicable

modes: the "Information Support Mode" for functions that support the crew in normal operations and the "Decision Support Mode" that provides decision support for abnormal operations and emergency situations. For a detailed description of the functions shown in Fig. 3, see Table 1. Note that the IPAS is an evolving system; more functions, especially interaction functions, may be added in the future.

3 Development of the AI-Crew-Interaction-System (AICIS)

The AICIS is the human-system integration component of the IPAS system, facilitating the interface between the flight crew and the AICOM. Depending on the use case, the AICIS will provide different functions. As described in Sect. 2.3, the AICIS should display AI-based mission information, as well as recommendations and options for action for the planned decision support functions. One of the most important system requirements is to present this information in a way that can be explained to the crew to ensure effective and efficient use. Explainability should ensure a number of important system characteristics, including helping the crew build trust in the system and improving the overall performance of the human-AI team, in this case the IPAS Flight Crew Team.

To integrate the end user, in this case, airline pilots, into such an AI system, it is essential to identify the users' requirements for the AI-based system, with a special focus on the users' need for explanations. The solution lies in a highly iterative and user-centered development process, where user requirements and explanation needs can be identified and explored step by step. The development process chosen for

Table 1 Overview of IPAS basic functions

Function name	Description
Situation detection and assessment	
Situation Detection	The AICOM continuously monitors available data, detecting internal and external anomalies such as traffic density, aircraft movements, weather data, and airport information.
Situation Assessment	If an anomaly is detected, the AICOM assesses potential effects and risks based on both external and internal data. This involves identifying operational limitations, assessing consequences and risks, and evaluating the impact on the mission.
Support Initiation	Based on the results from the Situation Assessment, the AICOM determines whether it can provide support and activates either a Mission Effect Message or the Decision Support mode on the AICIS.
Information support mode	
Default mission information	The AICIS provides information along the route and for the destination, displaying weather and wind information, as well as information about other aircraft.
Mission effect message: mission effect information	The AICIS highlights minor anomalies detected by the AICOM that have no significant impact on the flight, such as expected weather changes, approach direction adjustments, or slightly increased traffic.
Mission effect message: mission effect notification	The AICIS informs the crew about situations detected by the AICOM that have a minor impact on the flight but do not require immediate action. This includes anticipated delays at the destination due to holding or anticipated severe weather conditions.
Mission Effect Message: Mission Effect Advice	The AICIS alerts the crew to situations detected by the AICOM that could significantly impact the mission and provides AICOM-generated recommendations for early response based on traffic data, such as detecting the closure of the destination airport.
Decision support mode	
Decision Support Request	The crew manually activates the Decision Support Mode by providing essential information to the AICIS, starting the Situation Assessment Support. This is useful in situations like medical emergencies that cannot be automatically detected.
Situation assessment support	The AICIS informs about a decision-making situation detected by the AICOM and provides related information. It provides operational limitations, consequences, and risks for the flight and especially for the landing.
Option assessment support	The AICIS displays the requirements relevant for the selection and assessment of the options, defined by the AICOM. Based on these requirements, the AICOM generates several suitable options for action that are displayed on the AICIS with additional information.

the AICIS is based on the explorative development model called "Human System Exploration" as proposed by Flemisch and et al. (2022). This development model has a strong focus on involving users in the early stages of human-AI system development. It is based on the principle of user-centered design, in which end users play a central role in shaping the functionality and design of the system. The goal is to explore, implement, and demonstrate the human-AI system AICIS as part of the IPAS, tailored to user needs and serving as a research platform to explore aspects of human-AI system integration.

The current primary focus of the AICIS development is to research the implementation of explainability. Specifically, the research focuses on practical methods for implementing explainability tailored to the needs of airline pilots. To achieve this, an approach was identified and an explainability concept outlined, which is discussed in more detail in Sect. 3.2.

3.1 Explainability of AI

Before delving into the AICIS concept, it is important to get some basic background information on the topic of AI explainability. There are different definitions for the terms explainability and interpretability. Molnar (2022) The Independent High Level Expert Group on Artificial Intelligence of the EU Commission defines the term explainability as follows. *Explainability: Feature of an AI system that is intelligible to non-experts. An AI system is intelligible if its functionality and operations can be explained non technically to a person not skilled in the art.* European Commission, Directorate-General for Communications Networks, Content and Technology (2020) Since the IPAS is a system for commercial aviation, we should also pay attention to what the authority responsible for aviation in Europe, the EASA, says about AI and the explainability of AI. Within the concept of "Trustworthy AI," the EASA requires "AI operational explainability " in the EASA AI Roadmap. This term refers to the ability of AI systems to provide understandable, reliable, and relevant information to the end user (European Union Aviation Safety Agency 2023). This is not only a technical challenge but also a requirement from the end user's perspective, since trust (Ribeiro et al. 2016; Doshi-Velez and Kim 2017), usability (Haque et al. 2023; Atta 2017), and performance of a human-AI system are based on an understanding of how they work Sanneman and Shah (2022). It is important to highlight the concept of human-AI teaming (HAT) at this point. Explainability also plays a crucial role here, as Endsley describes in Endsley (2023). HAT refers to a collaborative and interactive partnership between an operator and an AI system to actively work together as a team to accomplish common goals or tasks (O'Neill et al. 2020). According to Endsley (2023), explainability in human-AI teams promotes trust and team situation awareness, and thus supports decision-making and teamwork, and finally improves the human-AI team performance.

Up to now, models have been developed in the field of explainable AI (XAI) to improve the explainability of AI systems (Adadi and Berrada 2018; Ribeiro et al. 2018; Gunning 2016; Ribeiro et al. 2016). However, many of these models were developed by AI experts and are therefore neither tailored to a specific use case nor to the needs of end users. These models can be difficult for a nontechnical end user to understand and are usually not very user-friendly (Jin and et al. 2021; Adadi and Berrada 2018; Zhu and et al. 2018; Miller et al. 2017).

According to Dupont et al. (2020), level 2 explainability is required for the use of the IPAS, specifically for the AICIS. Here, the system should provide the end user with a justification for why the AI system has produced the displayed results. It should not answer how the algorithm actually generated the results.

3.2 AICIS Concept: Achieving Explainability Through Interpretability Cues

A major challenge in the development of AICIS was to find an approach to ensure the required explainability that can be tailored to the needs of the end user, while still providing the necessary level of explainability for the use case, and finally achieving a good explainability-performance trade-off.

The idea of the approach is to make AI results more understandable to users by breaking them down into smaller, interpretable chunks of information. This method is consistent with the concept of interpretability, which is defined as the ability to provide explanations composed of single, human-understandable pieces of information. The approach was inspired by Stevens and De Smedt (2023), who emphasize the importance of interpretability by breaking down explanations into individual pieces of information. Lipton's (2018) concept of post hoc interpretability is a second source for the approach, where data is extracted from AI models to improve understanding without fully exposing the inner workings of the model. This method allows users to create their own explanations based on the pieces of information provided. Hoffman et al. (2023) emphasize the value of explanatory systems that empower users to self-explain, rather than simply, presenting algorithmic output representations. The emphasis is on providing information that allows users to derive their own understanding, contributing to a more user-centered explanation process. Stevens and De Smedt (2023) suggest that this method of focusing on single chunks of information offers a good trade-off between performance and explainability.

The AICIS explainability concept, based on the approach described, aims to provide pilots with "interpretability cues" consisting of individual extracts from the AI model and information about the AI output, the underlying data, or the AI process itself. This information should assist pilots in interpreting AI results and enable them to self-explain the reasons for an AI result. The level of explainability achieved should support pilots in performing their tasks effectively and efficiently, with a good performance trade-off, while fostering an appropriate level of trust. In Würfel et al. (2024), the AICIS concept is described in more detail, and a user study is presented to test an early prototype of the IPAS. As a result of the study, the authors defined four preliminary requirements for designing interpretability cues:

- Use decision factors typically used by the flight crew to make decisions.

- The assessment should be comparable with the crew's own perception, experience, and assessment.
- The displayed information should indicate whether it is a result of an AI process and whether it is based on real-time data or an AI forecast of future situations.
- Indicate which factors and factor combinations are included in the assessment of the AI and how they affect a system output.

Since these preliminary requirements have not been verified, they need to be integrated into a prototype of the AICIS and tested in a user study.

3.3 Implementation of the AICIS

The implementation of the AICIS as a prototype is based on the use case "Support in emergency and abnormal situations" described in Sect. 2.1. A technical failure occurs in cruise flight, forcing the crew to land at an alternate airport. In this situation, pilots use their trained decision-making process, such as FORDEC. They must collect facts, assess the situation, identify and evaluate alternate airports, and decide on a final option. The IPAS will support the crew in F-Facts, O-Options, and R-Risks&Benefits. The functional requirements described in Sect. 2.3 and the interpretability cues requirements presented in Sect. 3.2 were the main design criteria for designing the AICIS.

Figure 4 illustrates the implementation of the AICIS functions "Situation Assessment Support" and "Option Assessment Support" for the chosen use case. The figure shows the steps performed by the crew and the interaction between the crew and the AICIS as well as between the AICOM and the AICIS. After the technical failure occurs, the pilots follow the processes they have learned in order to solve the failure. First, the aircraft is stabilized from an aeronautical point of view, then the error is verified, and finally, the technical processes are worked through. The decision-making process then begins according to the pattern F, gather facts to understand the situation; O, search for and discuss airport options; and R, consider the risks and benefits of the individual options. A decision is then made and finally executed.

As previously mentioned, the IPAS will assist the pilots in the F, O, and R parts of FORDEC. The AICOM analyzes the data provided and detects the failure. Then, the AICOM performs a situation assessment and generates various decision options. Operating in Decision Support Mode, the AICIS first displays the AICOM's Situation Assessment, showing the assessment of the situation as well as the operational capabilities and risks. This should help the pilots collect situational facts and understand the situation. Next, the pilot can enter the Option Assessment Support function, which first displays the AICOM's requirements for selecting and assessing airport options. This is followed by the presentation of several airport options, highlighting their benefits and risks.

3.4 User Interface

Three interface pages were implemented for the AICIS prototype to provide the Decision Assessment Support functions Situation Assessment Support and Option Assessment Support shown in Fig. 4. Figure 5 shows how the AICIS is integrated as

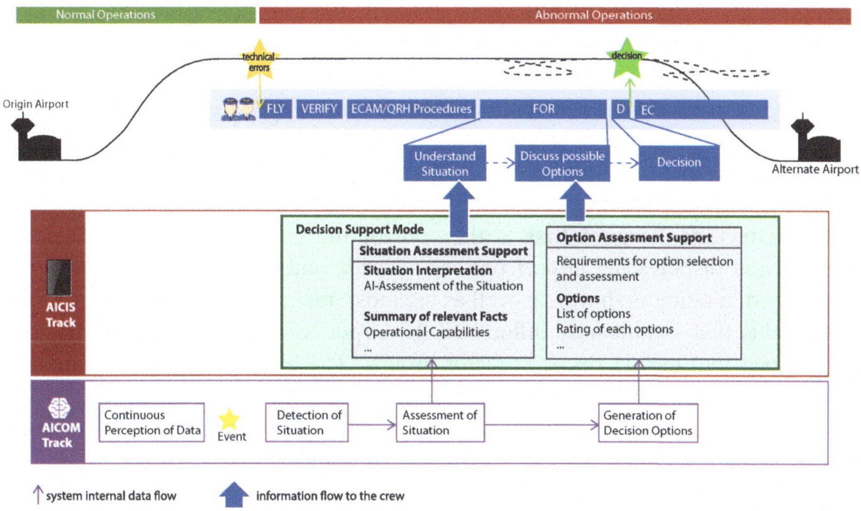

Fig. 4 The interaction between the flight crew, the AICIS, and the AICOM, illustrated by an example of an emergency situation

Fig. 5 The AICIS interface integrated into an A320 flat panel simulator. Shown is Alternate Airport List interface

an additional screen into an A320 cockpit in the simulator. The realized pages are the Airport Requirement Page, the Alternate Airport List, and the Detailed Airport View, which are described below.

The **Airport Requirement Page** provides the Situation Assessment Support function with information about the impact or risk of a detected situation on a mission, such as technical failures. It categorizes these effects into those on cruise and those on approach and landing, allowing the pilots to compare their own perception with that of the IPAS. In addition, the page identifies the AICOM requirements for finding an alternate airport, thus providing part of the Option Assessment Support. Six decision factor groups have been introduced to comprehensively describe airport options: wind conditions, weather conditions, visibility conditions, airport distance, runway information, and airport infrastructure and operational information. Depending on the situation, the page displays requirements for identifying and assessing airports within each factor group.

The **Alternate Airport List** is the core of the Option Assessment Support function and displays the airport options selected and assessed by AICOM. For each airport, a rating is shown, as well as the most important decision factors, risks, and benefits that significantly influenced the airport's rating. The decision factors are grouped into the six decision factor groups. The locations of the airports are additionally shown on the map.

For a detailed consideration of an alternate airport option, pilots need a much broader basis for decision-making. On the **Detailed Airport View**, the AICIS provides a detailed overview and important information for each option. For each of the six-factor groups, the decision factors and their AI assessment are presented. This should help to better explain the AI rating and help pilots to finally assess and select the airport options.

4 Development of the AI-Core-Module (AICOM)

The following sections aim at providing greater detail on the ideas behind the development of the AICOM. The focus will be placed on the Option Assessment Support functionality of the system as this should provide greater insight into human-AI system integration aspects, since it is directly involved in the decision-making process. As described in Sect. 2.1, interviews with pilots indicate that there is a lack of support in the area of data acquisition and data analysis in time-critical decision-making situations. In addition, human factor-related topics such as explainability, trust in AI, and human-AI performance can be studied in emergency and abnormal situations in a more intensive way.

4.1 Multi-Criteria Decision-Making

The selection of an alternate airport during mid-flight comes down to analyzing and comparing the various characteristics of the available airport and how these characteristics relate to the current state of the aircraft. A description and initial approach to tackle this was presented in Djartov et al. (2022). The concept made use of ideas from Multi-Criteria Decision-Making (MCDM). It is one of the most well-known branches of decision-making (Triantaphyllou 2000). MCDM is commonly divided into Multi-Objective Decision-Making (MODM) and Multi-Attribute Decision-Making (MADM). MODM is primarily focused on tackling continuous decision-making problems, i.e., decision problems where a value needs to be selected from a range of values. On the other hand, MADM focuses on discrete decision-making problems, which entail selecting one option from a finite set of possible alternatives. In both MADM and MODM, the possible options have multiple characteristics that are considered simulations when making the decision (Triantaphyllou 2000).

Given that the selection of an alternate airport task can be, in essence, boiled down to selecting an airport from a set of possible airports, where each airport is defined by a number of characteristics that need to be considered simultaneously and compared to those of the other airports, employing concepts and ideas MADM seems like a reasonable approach. As defined in Triantaphyllou (2000), a typical MADM consists of the following steps:

1. Determine the relevant criteria and alternatives.
2. Attach numerical measures to the relative importance of the criteria and to the impacts of the alternatives on these criteria
3. Process the numerical values to determine a ranking of each alternative.

The Weighted Sum Method (WSM), also referred to as the Simple Additive Weighting (SAW) method, is the most common and simplest MADM method (Bozorg-Haddad et al. 2021). Churchman and Ackoff (1954) were believed to be among the first to employ the WSM to cope with a portfolio selection problem (Tzeng and Huang 2011). The method has exploded in popularity ever since (Zanakis et al. 1995, 1998).

The WSM, as was described in Churchman and Ackoff (1954), makes use of a "weight vector." This weight vector, usually written as $\vec{w}$, has the same length as the number of characteristics or criteria that each of the alternatives has. It is important to note that the number of criteria needs to be the same for all alternatives being considered. What should be considered as a criterion is left up to the discretion of the decision-makers and stakeholders; however, it is an important step that will have a great impact on the whole decision-making process, so careful consideration regarding the definition of the criteria is advised. The weight vector is typically made up of positive real numbers whose sum equals 1. Following the steps described

Table 2 Possible alternate airports

Alternatives	Distance to airport [km]	Distance to originally planned destination [km]	Crosswind at airport [kn]	Tailwind at airport [kn]	Fuel needed [kg]
Airport 1	200	400	20	10	1500
Airport 2	400	189	23	0	3000
Airport 3	800	958	10	3	6000
Airport 4	570	230	12	6	3500
Airport 5	324	230	17	25	2000

above, the selection of the attributes is the initial step. The following step uses the weight vector to calculate the WSM score:

$$V_i = \sum_{j=1}^{n} w_j \times a_{i,j} \tag{1}$$

where V_i is the WSM score of the ith alternative, w_j is the weight vector value for the jth criterion of the alternative and $a_{i,j}$ is the jth criterion value for the ith alternative. After obtaining the WSM score for all alternatives, it is simply a matter of selecting the alternative with the lowest or highest score, depending on the problem formulation.

An example of the use of a WSM can be showcased using an instance of the alternate airport problem. In a situation where a new alternate needs to be selected, the possible options for an alternate airport are showcased in Table 2, with their respective characteristics.

In order to calculate the WSM score, we initially need to normalize all the values. This is done so that when we finally sum them, the scale that certain values are represented in should not influence the final score. If looks at our example, the fuel remaining is in thousands, which will have a greater impact on the score, while the wind components being only in tens will have a significantly reduced influence, even though they should be considered equally important. Normalization usually entails scaling the numbers between 0 and 1 using the equation:

$$z_i = \frac{x_i - \min(x_i)}{\max(x_i) - \min(x_i)} \tag{2}$$

The new normalized criteria that will be used further in the process are given in Table 3.

Afterward, the decision-makers, the pilots in our case, are assumed to have provided a weight vector shown by Table 4.

Table 3 Normalized criteria values

Alternatives	Distance to airport [km]	Distance to originally planned destination [km]	Crosswind at airport [kn]	Tailwind at airport [kn]	Fuel needed [kg]
Airport 1	0	0.27	0.76	0.4	0
Airport 2	0.33	0	1	0	0.33
Airport 3	1	1	0	0.12	1
Airport 4	0.61	0.05	0.15	0.24	0.44
Airport 5	0.206	0.05	0.53	1	0.11

Table 4 Weight vector

Criterion	Distance to airport [km]	Distance to originally planned destination [km]	Crosswind at airport [kn]	Tailwind at airport [kn]	Fuel needed [kg]
Weight	0.3	0.15	0.15	0.2	0.2

Table 5 WSM score calculation table

Alternatives	Distance to airport [km]	Distance to originally planned destination [km]	Crosswind at airport [kn]	Tailwind at airport [kn]	Fuel needed [kg]	$\sum$
Airport 1	$0 * 0.3$	$0.27 * 0.15$	$0.76 * 0.15$	$0.4 * 0.2$	$0 * 0.2$	**0.2345**
Airport 2	$0.33 * 0.3$	$0 * 0.15$	$1 * 0.15$	$0 * 0.2$	$0.33 * 0.2$	0.315
Airport 3	$1 * 0.3$	$1 * 0.15$	$0 * 0.15$	$0.12 * 0.2$	$1 * 0.2$	0.674
Airport 4	$0.61 * 0.3$	$0.05 * 0.15$	$0.15 * 0.15$	$0.24 * 0.2$	$0.44 * 0.2$	0.349
Airport 5	$0.206 * 0.3$	$0.05 * 0.15$	$0.53 * 0.15$	$1 * 0.2$	$0.11 * 0.2$	0.3708

Bold number signifies the lowest score and is the chosen option

Using the supplied weight vector along with the normalized values for the criterion, we can apply Eq. 2 to get the WSM score for each of the alternatives, as seen in Table 5.

Examining our WSM score, we can select Airport 1 as it has the lowest weighted score. The WSM approach enables us to transform a multi-criteria problem into a single-criteria one where all the alternatives can be more easily compared. However, the method relies on the decision-makers to provide a carefully curated weight vector in order for it to be useful. This presents a problem for decision-making in the cockpit where, as previously mentioned, pilots may be constrained by time and also most likely have to divide their attention and energy between multiple tasks.

It would be quite useful then to have a way to ascertain the weight vector previously with greater precision than that by pilots in an emergency. It is precisely in this area that we can employ ideas from the field of AI.

4.2 Integrating Intelligence

How to weigh the importance of the criteria in our decision-making was the approach presented in Djartov et al. (2022). The goal was to find a weight vector that, across many possible alternate airport decision-making tasks, would give pilots advice on what the optimal alternative is. In the case of Djartov et al. (2022), an optimal decision was the one that would satisfy the physical safety aspect as well as minimize the financial cost.

In order to learn how to weigh the relevant factors, a dataset was required. Due to the lack of readily available datasets, a synthetic dataset was created. In this case, "synthetic" means generated by us using simulation software. Each instance in the dataset represented an alternate airport decision-making problem, similar to the one depicted in Table 2. However, the number of airports included the 12 commercial airports in Germany, and the dataset itself was focused on Germany and its airspace. The idea was to find weights that, on average across all these varied decision-making problems, would produce the most favorable outcomes in terms of safety and finances.

To determine the weights, an evolutionary algorithm (EA) was used. Evolutionary algorithms are a class of optimization and search algorithms inspired by the process of natural evolution. They simulate the principles of natural selection, mutation, and reproduction to iteratively improve solutions to problems (Deb 2011; Kruse et al. 2011). In our case, we would have a population of weight vectors that we would be iteratively improving using the ideas from the natural theory of evolution. A visual representation of an EA can be seen in Fig. 6.

Knowing how to weigh the criteria so that, on average, the decision is favorable is quite useful, but it would be even more useful if one could know how to weigh each individual situation accordingly. To accomplish this goal, we would require some more advanced methods from the field of AI. However, as mentioned, in decision-making, generally, and in aviation, in particular, it is important that we have a good understanding of the mechanisms by which decisions are made. Thus, the model used would ideally be characterized by good interpretability and explainability.

Due to this, the current focus is on using learning classifier systems (LCS). These are a lesser-known model that uses populations of classifiers to solve problems. The classifiers within the LCS typically have an IF-THEN structure (Urbanowicz and Browne 2017). Keeping in line with the example already showcased, that would mean that the rule might have the form: IF, this specific kind of decision-making problem, and THEN, apply these weights to solve it. The LCS also makes use of EAs in order to generate and reevaluate rules so that they can become increasingly better. A visual representation of an LCS can be seen in Fig. 7.

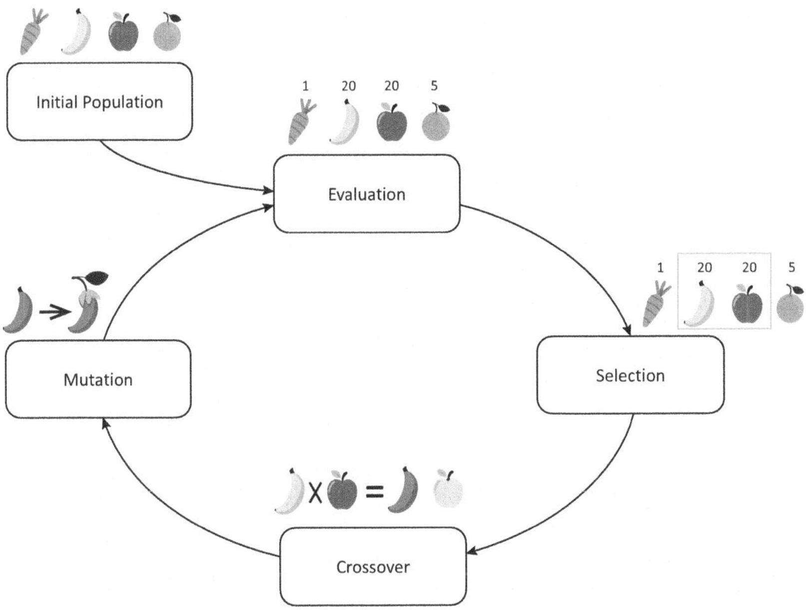

Fig. 6 General evolutionary algorithm. (Adapted from Deb 2011)

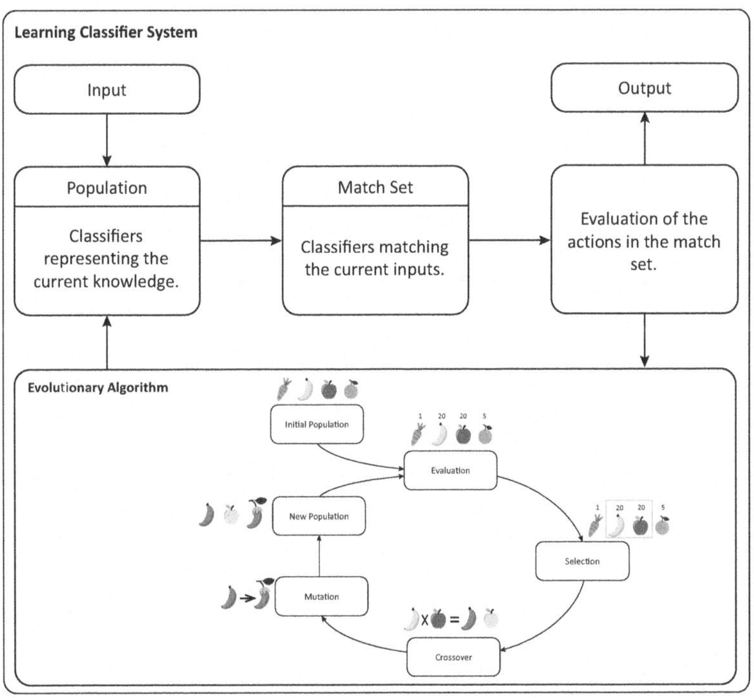

Fig. 7 General learning classifier system. (Adapted from Urbanowicz and Browne 2017 and Lanzi et al. 2009)

From the image, we can see the general working of an LCS. Prompted by the input, it searches for the rules that most correspond to what it has encountered. It then uses these rules to make a decision and evaluates how good this decision was. Afterward, by way of evolutionary algorithms, it generates new and better rules. Given the simple nature of each rule, it makes the model far more interpretable and understandable by humans, as opposed to other models such as neural networks (Urbanowicz and Browne 2017). It is also worth noting that the addition of new and modification of old rules is also easily done, which enables the model to learn more easily on the fly (pun intended).

5 Summary

This chapter explores the integration of AI in cockpit decision support systems, presenting the IPAS developed by DLR as an example. The IPAS and its constituent subsystems, AICOM and AICIS, serve as a research platform that investigates the feasibility of applying AI within the cockpit environment, explores the implementation of such systems, and demonstrates the potential benefits of AI applications in this domain. The breadth of potential applications is extensive, prompting the development of the first IPAS prototype for a specific use case. The use case chosen was based on research highlighting the lack of support for pilots during time-critical emergency decision-making situations. Thus, the current focus of the system is to lessen the workload of the crew, enabling them to make more informed decisions even under time constraints.

Several user studies have been conducted on the IPAS, revealing ongoing research efforts. These studies indicate that pilots find the system enjoyable to work with and highly valuable in the decision-making process, particularly within the described use case. Additionally, pilots report openness to further features and applications of AI technology within the cockpit. The approach described in this paper, which involves obtaining explanations through individual pieces of information, has also been identified as promising and yielding positive results. Notably, pilots are able to formulate their own explanations for AI outputs by utilizing the provided interpretability cues. Furthermore, it has been confirmed by participants that while the IPAS accelerates the decision-making process, informed decision-making is still achieved through the consideration of more options and the gathering and analysis of additional factors. It was also noted that the IPAS contributes to a more structured decision-making process. These findings demonstrate that a promising use case has been selected and that the efforts invested in human-system integration have thus far been successful. Consequently, it is deemed appropriate to extend and further develop and improve the system. To achieve this, further studies must be conducted with an increasing number of test participants.

The technical implementation of the AI algorithm is researched by the AICOM, and the human-system integration of the AI-based system is explored by the AICIS.

For the AICOM, the current focus is on determining the data and other requirements for training the AI models, such as using simulation software to generate a synthetic dataset. There is also a strong emphasis on developing models and AI methods that prioritize explainability and interpretability.

In the future, further use cases will be implemented for the IPAS, expanding its scope. This will be accompanied by further investigation into data sources and the development of explainable AI models, alongside increased exploration of calibrated trust and human-AI team performance.

References

Adadi A, Berrada M (2018) Peeking inside the black-box: a survey on explainable artificial intelligence (XAI). IEEE Access 6:52138–52160. https://doi.org/10.1109/access.2018.2870052

Airbus (2024) Generations of jet. https://accidentstats.airbus.com/generations-of-jet/. Accessed 24 Dec 2024

Atta MT (2017) The effect of usability and information quality on decision support information system (DSS). Arts Soc Sci J 8(2). https://doi.org/10.4172/2151-6200.1000257

Bozorg-Haddad O, Zolghadr-Asli B, Loaiciga HA (2021) A handbook on multi-attribute decision-making methods. John Wiley and Sons, London

Churchman CW, Ackoff RL (1954) An approximate measure of value. J Oper Res Soc Am 2(2):172–187

Coombs LFE (2005) Control in the sky: the evolution and history of the aircraft cockpit. Pen and Sword Aviation, Barnsley

Deb K (2011) Multi-objective optimisation using evolutionary algorithms: an introduction. In: Multi-objective evolutionary optimisation for product design and manufacturing. Springer, London, pp 77–83

Djartov B, Mostaghim S, Papenfuß A, Wies M (2022) Description and first evaluation of an approach for a pilot decision support system based on multi-attribute decision making. In: 2022 IEEE symposium series on computational intelligence (SSCI). Singapore, pp 141–147. https://doi.org/10.1109/SSCI51031.2022.10022076

Doshi-Velez F, Kim B (2017) Towards a rigorous science of interpretable machine learning. arXiv e-prints. https://doi.org/10.48550/arXiv.1702.08608

Dupont L, Fliche O, Yang S (2020) Governance of artificial intelligence in finance. Banque De France

Endsley M (1995) Toward a theory of situation awareness in dynamic systems. Hum Fact 37(1):32–64. https://doi.org/10.1518/001872095779049543

Endsley M (2015) Autonomous horizons: System autonomy in the air force—a path to the future. Tech. rep., Air Force Office of Scientific Research. https://doi.org/10.13140/RG.2.1.1164.2003

Endsley MR (2023) Supporting human-ai teams: transparency, explainability, and situation awareness. Comput Hum Behav 140:107574. https://doi.org/10.1016/j.chb.2022.107574

European Commission, Directorate-General for Communications Networks, Content and Technology (2020) The assessment list for trustworthy artificial intelligence (ALTAI) for self assessment. Tech. rep., Publications Office. https://data.europa.eu/doi/10.2759/002360

European Union Aviation Safety Agency (2023) EASA-AI-Roadmap 2.0: A Human-Centric Approach to AI in Aviation. Tech. rep., European Union Aviation Safety Agency, Cologne

Flemisch F et al (2022) Human systems exploration for ideation and innovation in potentially disruptive defense and security systems. In: Advanced sciences and technologies for security applications, pp 79–117. https://doi.org/10.1007/978-3-031-06636-8_5

Gunning D (2016) Explainable artificial intelligence (XAI). Tech. rep., DARPA. https://www.cc.gatech.edu/~alanwags/DLAI2016/(Gunning)%20IJCAI-16%20DLAI%20WS.pdf. Accessed 2 Nov 2023

Haque AB, Islam AKMN, Mikalef P (2023) Explainable artificial intelligence (XAI) from a user perspective: a synthesis of prior literature and problematizing avenues for future research. Technol Forecast Soc Change 186:122120. https://doi.org/10.1016/j.techfore.2022.122120

Hecker P, Korn B (2003) Increasing the aircrew's situation awareness by enhanced and synthetic vision. In: AIAA/ICAS international air and space symposium and exposition: the next 100 years. Dayton, Ohio

Hoffman RR, Mueller ST, Klein G, Litman J (2023) Measures for explainable ai: explanation goodness, user satisfaction, mental models, curiosity, trust, and human-ai performance. Front. Comput. Sci. 5. https://doi.org/10.3389/fcomp.2023.1096257

Hörmann HJ (1994) For-dec: a prescriptive model for aeronautical decision making. In: 21st WEAAP-conference, Dublin. https://elib.dlr.de/27044/

Jin W et al (2021) Euca: a practical prototyping framework towards end-user-centered explainable artificial intelligence. arXiv e-prints. https://arxiv.org/abs/2102.02437

Kruse R, Borgelt C, Braune C, Mostaghim S, Steinbrecher M, Klawonn F, Moewes C (2011) Computational intelligence. Vieweg+Teubner Verlag

Lanzi PL, Loiacono D, Pellegrini L (2009) Xcslib: The XCS classifier system library

Lipton ZC (2018) The mythos of model interpretability. Commu ACM 61(10):36–43. https://doi.org/10.1145/3233231

Miller T, Howe PDL, Sonenberg L (2017) Explainable ai: beware of inmates running the asylum or: how i learnt to stop worrying and love the social and behavioural sciences. arXiv e-prints. http://export.arxiv.org/pdf/1712.00547

Molnar C (2022) Interpretable machine learning: a guide for making black box models explainable, 2nd edn. Leanpub. https://christophm.github.io/interpretable-ml-book/

O'Neill T, McNeese N, Barron A, Schelble B (2020) Human-autonomy teaming: a review and analysis of the empirical literature. Hum Fact J Hum Fact Ergon Soc 64:1–35. https://doi.org/10.1177/0018720820960865

Onken R (1999) The cognitive cockpit assistant systems cassy/cama. In: SAE technical paper series. World aviation congress and exposition. SAE International, Warrendale

Ribeiro MT, Singh S, Guestrin C (2016) "why should i trust you?". In: Proceedings of the 22nd ACM SIGKDD international conference on knowledge discovery and data mining, pp 1135–1144. https://doi.org/10.1145/2939672.2939778

Ribeiro MT, Singh S, Guestrin C (2018) Anchors: High-precision model-agnostic explanations. In: Proceedings of the AAAI conference on artificial intelligence, vol 32. https://doi.org/10.1609/aaai.v32i1.11491

Sanneman L, Shah JA (2022) The situation awareness framework for explainable ai (safe-ai) and human factors considerations for XAI systems. Int J Hum-Comput Interact 38(18–20):1772–1788. https://doi.org/10.1080/10447318.2022.2081282

Stevens A, De Smedt J (2023) Explainability in process outcome prediction: guidelines to obtain interpretable and faithful models. Eur J Oper Res. https://doi.org/10.1016/j.ejor.2023.09.010

Triantaphyllou E (2000) Multi-criteria decision making methods. Springer, New York

Tzeng GH, Huang JJ (2011) Multiple attribute decision making: methods and applications. CRC Press, Boca Raton

Urbanowicz RJ, Browne WN (2017) Introduction to learning classifier systems. Springer, Berlin

Walters AJ (2002) Crew resource management is no accident

Würfel J, Djartov B, Papenfuß A, Wies M (2023) Intelligent pilot advisory system: the journey from ideation to an early system design of an ai-based decision support system for airline flight decks. In: AHFE international. https://doi.org/10.54941/ahfe1003844

Würfel J, Papenfuß A, Wies M (2024) Operationalizing ai explainability using interpretability cues in the cockpit: Insights from user-centered development of the intelligent pilot advisory system (IPAS). In: Degen H, Ntoa S (eds) Artificial intelligence in HCI. HCII 2024. Lecture notes in computer science, vol 14734. Springer, Cham

Zanakis SH, Mandakovic T, Gupta SK, Sahay S, Hong S (1995) A review of program evaluation and fund allocation methods within the service and government sectors. Soc-Econ Plan Sci 29(1):59–79

Zanakis SH, Solomon A, Wishart N, Dublish S (1998) Multi-attribute decision making: a simulation comparison of select methods. Eur J Oper Res 107(3):507–529

Zhu J et al (2018) Explainable ai for designers: a human-centered perspective on mixed-initiative co-creation. In: 2018 IEEE conference on computational intelligence and games (CIG). Maastricht, Netherlands, pp 1–8. https://doi.org/10.1109/CIG.2018.8490433

Part IV
Case Studies

When It Goes Right, When It Goes Wrong: Lessons Learned from Automation in Aviation

Cécile Lescieux, Amandeep Singh, and Philippe Doyon-Poulin

Abstract This chapter examines the state of automation in civilian aircraft from two perspectives: when it goes right, i.e., in normal operations, and when it goes wrong, i.e., in non-normal operations. The first perspective considers the crucial role of technological advancements in automated systems, such as fly-by-wire technology and advanced navigation systems that have improved aviation safety. The second perspective draws attention to the grounding of the Boeing 737 MAX aircraft following two catastrophic crashes, mainly due to the malfunction of the Maneuvering Characteristics Augmentation System (MCAS), a new flight augmentation system. It shows that the same automation features supporting the pilot's task in normal operations can fail unexpectedly in non-normal operations. This study highlights the need for greater transparency in automation systems, better integration with human operators, and improved communication among stakeholders. The findings of this research underscore the importance of a human-centered approach in improving the safety and efficiency of highly complex automated systems. Lessons learned from aviation can be applied to other high-stake industries such as transportation, healthcare, and manufacturing, leading to safer and more efficient human-automation interaction.

1 Introduction

Aviation has a long history of developing automated systems, with the introduction of the autopilot in the 1920s and the first aircraft being able to fully land itself in the 1960s (Chialastri, 2012). These technological advances have dramatically improved aviation safety (Gawron, 2019). In 2022, the latest generation of fly-by-wire (FBW) aircraft reported a historically low rate of 0.05 fatal accidents per million flight cycles, which is three times lower than the rate of the previous generation of aircraft for the same period (Airbus, 2022). This increase in automation has also changed the

C. Lescieux · A. Singh · P. Doyon-Poulin (✉)
Polytechnique Montréal, Montréal, QC, Canada
e-mail: philippe.doyon-poulin@polymtl.ca

C. K. Coursaris et al. (eds.), *The Design of Human-Centered Artificial Intelligence for the Workplace*, Progress in IS, https://doi.org/10.1007/978-3-031-83512-4_19

role of the pilot in the flight deck, evolving from a hands-on-the-stick-and-throttle piloting task to that of a mission manager who interacts with automated systems (Banks et al., 2019; Mohrmann and Stoop, 2019; Soo et al., 2021). The development of new automation logic in technological industries can benefit from the lessons learned in aviation to improve human interaction with highly automated systems. In this chapter, we will review the state of the art of automation in civilian aircraft from two perspectives: 1) when it goes right, i.e., in normal operations, and 2) when it goes wrong, i.e., in non-normal operations. We will conclude with lessons learned from this analysis that can be shared with other industries.

2 When It Goes Right

The flight deck of a modern aircraft has come a long way since its early days. Today's aircraft use datalink communication to upload the entire flight plan to the flight management system (FMS) that will, in turn, command the autothrottle to minimize fuel consumption and the autopilot system to track the flight plan to get the aircraft safely to the destination. These improvements contributed to increased traffic flow and improved safety in recent history. 2022 witnessed 27 million flight departures with 29,000 in-service aircraft, compared to 36 million departures and 26,680 in-service aircraft in 2019 before the pandemic (Airbus, 2022). Only two fatal accidents and seven hull-loss accidents were reported in 2022. The low accident rates show that in normal operations, the aviation industry achieved considerable safety performance in parallel to resuming the pre-pandemic traffic flow.

2.1 Flight Deck and Automation

To understand how the flight deck is designed and the role of automation in the aircraft, we must understand the flight crew's tasks (see Fig. 1). The primary mission of commercial airline pilots is to get the aircraft from its origin to its destination safely, on schedule and efficiently. Cognitive task analysis showed that airline pilots break down their mission into four main tasks to achieve their goals: aviate, navigate, communicate, and manage (Jonsson and Ricks, 1995; Ververs, 1998). This classification reflects the priority level with which the crew accomplish their mission: pilots will take back control of an unstable aircraft losing altitude (aviate) before thinking about contacting the air traffic controller (ATC) to report their flight plan deviation (communicate).

Responsibilities are shared between the two pilots in the flight deck: one takes the Pilot Flying (PF) role, whereas the other is the Pilot Not Flying (PNF). The PF's primary responsibilities are to aviate and navigate tasks to ensure the aircraft arrives safely at its destination. On the other hand, the PNF communicates and manages tasks and does most of the data entry as part of the navigate task. Note that the flight

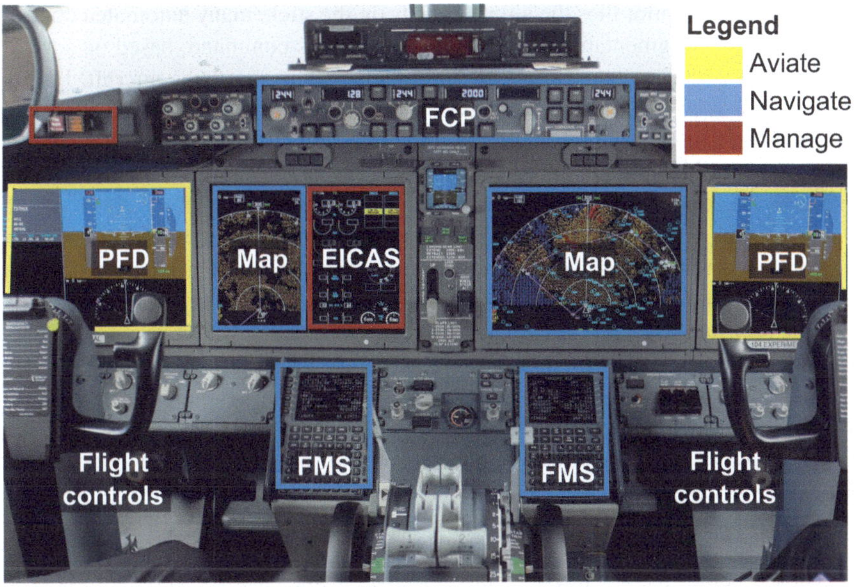

Fig. 1 Functional allocation of the Boeing 737 MAX flight deck. Note that the communication panel is located further down on the pedestal

crew decides before the flight which of the captain (most senior pilot, seated on the left) or first officer (in the right seat) has PF duty. The role can also be changed in flight. Therefore, the flight deck is symmetrical, as both pilots need access to the flight controls and computers.

In the following paragraphs, we will explain how each task is accomplished in normal operations, i.e., in a regular flight without a disturbing event, and present the main automation features to support the crew.

Aviate is about flying the aircraft, managing the aircraft's energy, and ensuring that the aircraft is stable and following the required airspeed, altitude, and thrust. The pilot can fly the aircraft manually using the yoke or engage the autopilot to follow the selected mode and the autothrottle to manage thrust automatically. The primary flight display (PFD) shows the information related to the aviate task. It is central to the maneuvering of the aircraft and its energy management, as implied by its name (Doyon-Poulin et al., 2014). Policies on the use of autopilot change between airlines (Administration, 2022; IATA, 2020): some airlines adopt a more restrictive approach that requires the crew to engage the autopilot when climbing above 400 feet and disengaging it only during the final landing, whereas other airlines encourage the use of manual flying to retain flying skills. The overreliance on automation and loss of manual flying skills is a growing concern in aviation (Casner et al., 2014; Haslbeck and Hoermann, 2016).

Even when the pilot flies the aircraft hands on the stick, many automated control loops and flight augmentation systems filter the pilot's command, based on several sensor inputs, before maneuvering the flight surfaces to move the aircraft. Fly by wire (FBW) is a system that sits between the pilot's command on the stick and the displacement of the flight surfaces. Its main objective is to augment aircraft safety by smoothing out the pilot's inputs and ensuring the aircraft remains in stable operating conditions. In FBW-able aircraft, such as Airbus A220 or A320, if the flight envelope protections detect that the aircraft is entering into a stall (i.e., angle of attack (AOA) too high), it will prevent the aircraft nose from pitching up even though the pilot is pulling the stick backward. Flight envelope protection functions are now industry standard on the latest aircraft generation. They prevent accidents due to loss of aircraft control during flight and, most importantly, aircraft stall.

Navigate is following the trajectory efficiently from the origin to the destination and responding to traffic constraints along the way. The FMS offers *strategic flight planning* capabilities by computing the entire route using lateral and vertical navigation. When available in the current airspace, datalink communication uploads the flight plan to the FMS, saving pilots up to twenty minutes of manual data entry. The flight control panel (FCP) offers *tactical flight planning* for the pilot to select a new speed, altitude, or heading to follow, most often after ATC's clearances. Note that the FCP is also used for the aviate task to manage speed, but in this chapter, we presented it with the navigate task for simplicity. The navigation display offers a graphical representation of the flight plan and navigation aids. Digital charts on the multifunction display or a tablet computer can show the appropriate approach plate programmed on the FMS. Additional safety features were added throughout the years to improve navigation: Traffic alert and Collision Avoidance System (TCAS) increases traffic awareness and offers synchronized deconflicting instructions between two aircraft to prevent in-air collisions, while Terrain Avoidance and Warning System (TAWS) warns the crew if the aircraft flies into the terrain. These features largely contributed to reducing accidents due to collisions and controlled flight into terrain.

Communicate is listening and responding to the air traffic controller's clearance in a timely manner. Although the use of datalink communication increases in continental and oceanic flights, voice-over radio is still the primary means of communication between the flight crew and ATC. It is not uncommon for pilots to miss an instruction if they are not paying attention to the radio at that time.

Manage relates to monitoring the status of aircraft systems and responding to failures. System monitoring is done through the engine-indicating and crew-alerting system (EICAS) and synoptic pages. An alarm message is displayed on the EICAS when a set of predefined thresholds are exceeded. Each message has a corresponding checklist that appears automatically for the crew to execute and ensure security.

To illustrate the role of automation in the flight deck when it goes right, we will focus on the 737 MAX aircraft. We will present its main features before showing a use case for automation.

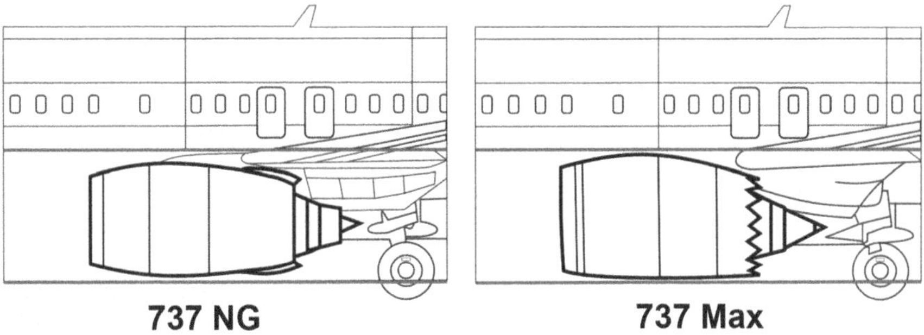

Fig. 2 Engines for the 737 MAX are larger than the previous NG model and had to be moved forward along the wing, shifting the center of gravity

2.2 Automation in the 737 MAX

The 737 MAX is a narrow-body aircraft produced by Boeing, the American aerospace manufacturer. It is the fourth generation of the Boeing 737, the world's most popular commercial jetliner, and is designed to be a more fuel-efficient and capable successor to the 737 NG (Nicas and Creswell, 2019). The design of the MAX was launched in haste to respond to Airbus' introduction of the A320neo—the 737 direct competitor—with larger engines and better fuel efficiency (Gelles et al., 2019). The 737 MAX has several new features, including more efficient engines, aerodynamic improvements, and updated avionics systems (Johnston and Harris, 2019). Importantly, its new engines are larger than the NG's for fuel efficiency. They had to be moved forward along the wings to prevent their collision with the runway during takeoff (see Fig. 2). As a result, the center of gravity also shifted and caused the nose of the aircraft to pitch slightly upward during climb when compared to the NG. To offset this effect, Boeing introduced the Maneuvering Characteristics Augmentation System (MCAS), a software system designed to automatically correct the aircraft's pitch angle in the event of an aerodynamic stall and to offer the same flight characteristics as the 737 NG (Demirci, 2021; Travis, 2019) (see Fig. 3).

MCAS is an example of flight augmentation features that automate part of the aviate task (Campbell, 2019). Based on the current AOA value, airspeed, and flap setting, if the MCAS detects the AOA exceeds the threshold, it lowers the aircraft nose by trimming the rear stabilizer located on the aircraft tail (see Fig. 4). It actuates the trim wheel in the flight deck. Also, it pushes the pilot's yoke in the down direction. Note that this feature is only activated when flying manually, as it was designed to prevent excessive climb maneuvers by the pilot. The pilot can counteract the MCAS—either by pulling the yoke or trimming the stabilizer in the opposite direction—but the MCAS will reactivate every 5 seconds if it detects that the AOA value exceeds the safe threshold. The only way to deactivate the MCAS is by disconnecting the electrical trim system.

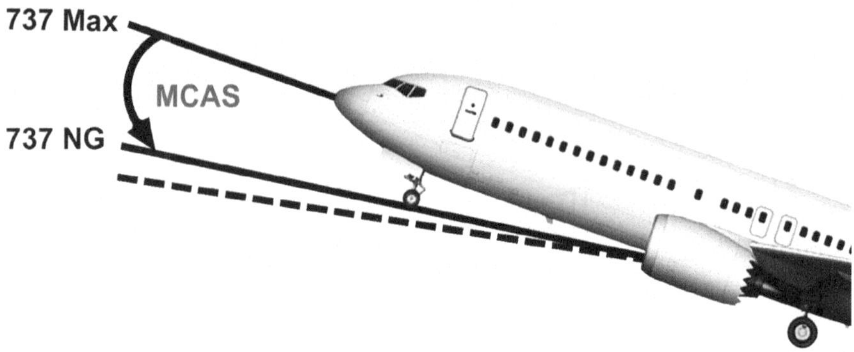

Fig. 3 The 737 MAX tended to pitch slightly upward during the climb compared to the NG due to the shift in center of gravity. The MCAS was introduced to reduce the pitch angle automatically and offer the same flight characteristics as the previous model

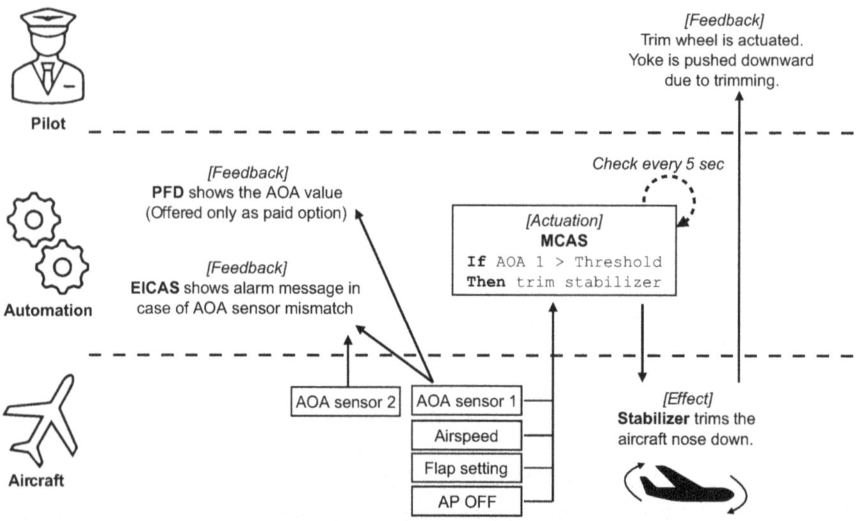

Fig. 4 Maneuvering Characteristics Augmentation System (MCAS)

The 737 MAX was first introduced in 2017 and quickly became one of Boeing's best-selling aircraft models, with more than 5000 orders placed by airlines worldwide (Wikipedia Contributors, 2023). Lion Air, one of the largest low-cost carriers in Indonesia, was among the airlines that purchased the 737 MAX for its fleet. The airline had ordered 201 aircraft, making it one of the largest customers for the 737 MAX (Boeing Press Release, 2011). The purchase of the 737 MAX was part of Lion Air's effort to modernize its fleet and stay competitive in Southeast Asia's rapidly growing aviation market.

2.3 Interplay Between Pilot and Automation

The interplay between the pilot and the aircraft automation is best exemplified during route changes. In Fig. 5, we showed the sequences of actions between the air traffic controller, the pilot, software automation, and aircraft components. We assumed that the 737 MAX flies in manual mode to show the functionalities of the MCAS in regular operation. In this scenario, the controller sends a datalink message containing a clearance to change the lateral route (proceed directly to the waypoint TUTUK) and a vertical climb instruction (expedite climb to 15,000 ft). The pilot can directly upload the lateral clearance to the FMS but needs to manually set the climb rate on the FCP. In all cases, the pilot retains the authority to accept the clearance. When pulling the yoke to follow the flight guidance, the MCAS activates by detecting an angle of attack exceeding the safe threshold. As expected, it trims the stabilizer and lowers the aircraft nose to maintain the aircraft within the safe flight envelope.

The interplay between the pilot and automated software systems raises the question of automation transparency: to what extent does the pilot need to know about the automation workings? Explaining the "black box" behavior of complex systems builds trust, especially for expert users (Wickens and Dixon, 2007), but simultaneously increases the amount of information and the risk of data overload.

Two paradigms are useful to explore the range of automation transparency: *see-through* vs. *see-into* (Bhaskara et al., 2020; Chen et al., 2020; Jamieson et al., 2022). *See-through* transparency advances that automated agents should be designed in such a way that they are thought of as a natural extension of the user and their inner workings are, for the most part, invisible to the user. This mode of automation transparency holds the promise of a truly "intuitive" human-automation collaboration since the user does not need to know about the automated agents' actions. On the other hand, *see-into* transparency argues that the user should see the automated agents' intentions, activities, and inner workings. The Situation Awareness-based Agent Transparency (SAT) model (Chen et al., 2018) proposes the latter category. It emphasizes the importance of transparency in AI systems to maintain the user's and automated agent's situation awareness (Jiang et al., 2022; Sanneman and Shah, 2022). Transparency enables users to understand how automated agents make decisions and take actions by providing relevant information based on the current situation, the user's mental capacity, and the stage of the interaction. Maintaining synchronization between the user and automated agents' situation awareness is a key challenge (Endsley, 2017). The SAT model focuses on identifying the correct information to present at the appropriate time, allowing users to comprehend the agent's actions, understand the reasons behind them, and anticipate future actions. Transparency in AI systems enhances the user's ability to make informed judgments about the agent's behavior (Endsley, 2023). Observability, interpretability, explainability, predictability, and affordance are essential for ensuring transparency (van de Merwe et al., 2022). Lack of these aspects can hinder operators' understanding of the agent's behavior

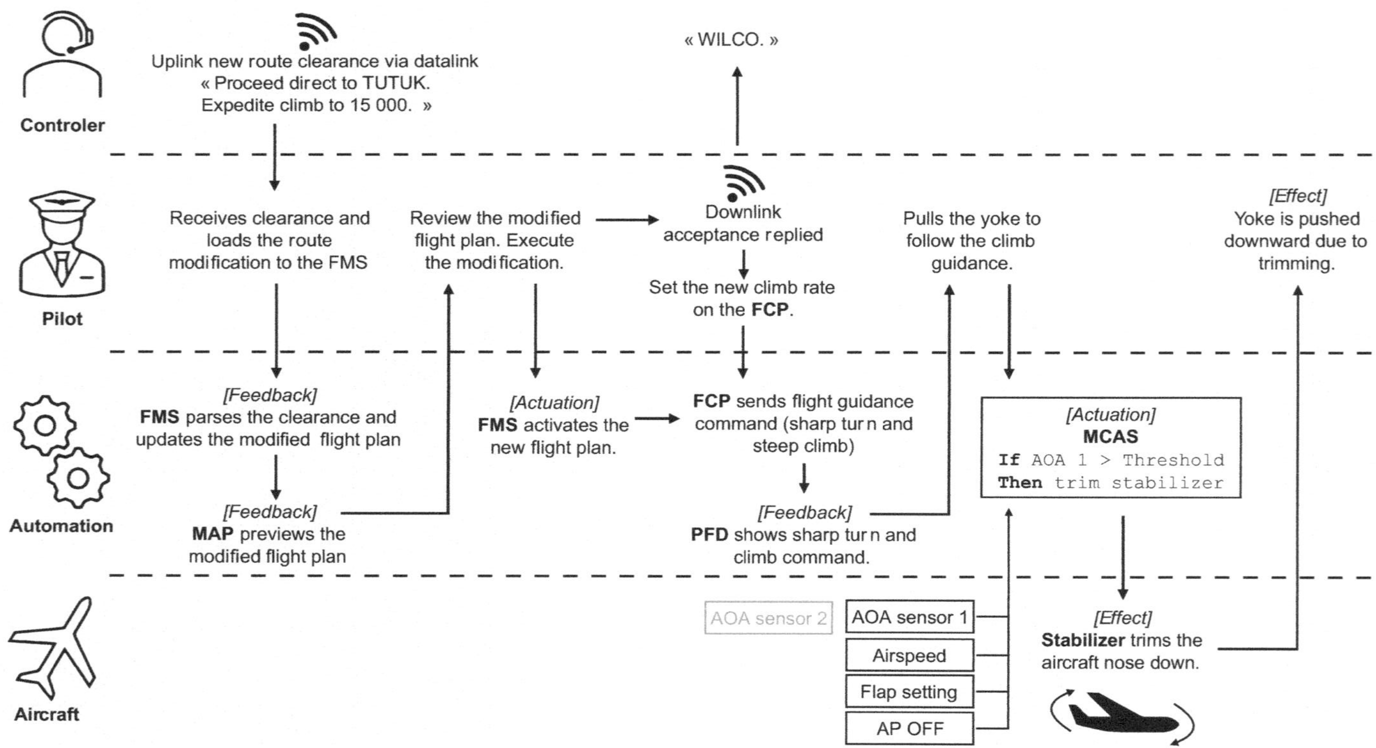

Fig. 5 Interplay of pilot and automation during a climb maneuver on the 737 MAX

and pose challenges in decision-making. By maintaining synchronization, users can grasp the agent's actions, reasons behind them, and future intentions. In contrast, the absence of transparency makes it difficult for operators to comprehend the agent's actions, leading to decision-making challenges.

The MCAS was designed according to the see-through paradigm, as pilots were unaware of its actuation (Jamieson et al., 2022). In fact, MCAS was not part of the training material and was not mentioned in any checklist (DeFazio and Larsen, 2020). The feedback pilots received was the actuation of the trim wheel and the displacement of the yoke, resulting from the trimming of the stabilizer, making the trimming noticeable. To some extent, other flight augmentation systems exhibit see-through transparency. In normal operation, FBW automation features are always active, i.e., they do not require a pilot's action to engage, and are, for the most part, transparent to the crew, i.e., the pilot is informed of the protection envelopes but receives little feedback regarding how FBW controls the flight surfaces concerning the pilot's input. To put it simply, this is just how the aircraft flies!

When everything goes right, pilots tend to focus on the larger mission-related goals (navigate efficiently to the destination) and do not need to know about the inner workings of the automation, i.e., see-through perspective. As we will see in the next section, the situation is inverted when it goes wrong: automation behaves in degraded modes, and pilots need more information to diagnose the failure, i.e., see-into.

2.4 *Software Development*

Before concluding the section on when it goes right, a word is needed on software development in aviation. Boeing revealed that its 787 Dreamliner contains 14 million code lines for the entire flight system (Saracco, 2016). To manage this staggering complexity, aviation software follows a strict development process under strong regulatory oversight (RTCA, 2011; SAE, 2010). It ensures that each requirement is there for a reason (validation phase) and, once implemented, that it can be fully analyzed and tested (verification phase). It does not guarantee bug-free software, far from it (Federal Register, 2018; Marks, 2008)! However, it offers an assurance level for software reliability, meaning that bugs and their effects on the aircraft are known in advance and found unimpactful on safety. One should not underestimate the colossal amount of engineering work, design reviews, simulation, and flight tests that go into the validation and verification phases.

It should also be noted that contrary to most of the other chapters in this book, which can venture into the nondeterministic world of machine learning and artificial intelligence, aviation uses deterministic, rule-based coding (if-then rules). The use of rule-based coding results from the development process requiring deterministic software behavior, i.e., the same inputs give the same outputs. At the time of writing, there is active discussion in the industry on certification mechanisms for machine-learning algorithms (Delseny et al., 2021; EASA, 2023; EUROCAE, 2019;

Wilkinson et al., 2016). We can expect regulatory frameworks to emerge in the coming years with additional guidance on integrating AI-based software in safety-critical systems.

3 When It Goes Wrong

In this section, we will review the two crashes of the 737 MAX that led to its grounding for over 20 months. We will see that the same automation features that behaved flawlessly during normal operations contributed to the crash.

3.1 *Summary of Accidents*

On October 29, 2018, Lion Air 610 departed from Jakarta on a domestic trip at 6:20 in the morning. The standard departure route over the Java Sea was assigned to the flight, and it received clearance for takeoff. Unfortunately, it never arrived at its intended destination, Pangkal Pinang, located on the Indonesian island of Banka. The initial signs of trouble in the Lion Air Flight 610 crash were evident shortly after takeoff. In the cockpit, the stick shaker was activated, which generated multiple errors in the flight display. The stick shaker is a device that vibrates the yoke continuously to alert pilots of a possible stall, which can lead to a dangerous loss of control. The aircraft began to dive shortly after the flight crew retracted the flaps, and the MCAS system relentlessly activated the automatic pitch trim in a nose-down direction 28 times in eight minutes. Two and a half minutes into the flight, the plane was flying at 2175 feet when it suddenly dropped 700 feet. It stabilized at 1475 feet and started to climb again. Just thirteen minutes into the flight, the situation rapidly escalated, and the aircraft crashed into the Java Sea, causing the loss of life of all 189 passengers and crew on board (News, 2018). The investigation of the Lion Air Flight 610 crash found several causes, including a malfunction in the aircraft's flight control system, poor communication between the manufacturer, regulator, and operator, and missing information in the flight manuals (Herkert et al., 2020). The primary cause of the crash was revealed to be a malfunction in the MCAS flight control system, which caused the plane to nose down repeatedly. The MCAS was meant to prevent an aerodynamic stall, but in this case, it activated due to incorrect data from a single angle of attack sensor (Federal Aviation Administration, 2020; Glanz et al., 2018).

Following the first 737 MAX crash, Boeing issued an Operations Manual Bulletin to advise pilots and airlines on the MCAS system (Boeing Press Release, 2018). It mentioned that the aircraft could experience a nosedive due to erroneous AOA data. In such case, the bulletin instructed the crew to complete the non-normal procedure for stabilizer runaway which requires to disconnect the electrical trim system.

Five months after the Lion Air 610 crash, another incident involving a Boeing 737 MAX took place on March 10, 2019, with Ethiopian Airlines Flight 302. The flight took off at 08:38 AM from Addis Ababa, Ethiopia, on a scheduled flight to Nairobi, Kenya. Just six minutes into the flight, the aircraft encountered similar problems to those experienced by Lion Air Flight 610, including repeated and automatic nose-down commands from the MCAS system, which were activated by erroneous data from a single angle of attack sensor (Luo et al., 2020). The pilots were aware of the operations bulletin. They correctly diagnosed the MCAS failure and followed the proper procedure to take preventive steps. They deactivated the electrical trim system to turn off the MCAS. At this time, the stabilizer was fully deflected, causing the yoke to be heavy and difficult to control. To stabilize the aircraft and neutralize the stabilizer, the crew needed to input manual trim using the trim wheel.

While the flight crew attention was focused on the MCAS malfunction, they omitted to reduce thrust which brought the aircraft in overspeed and triggered the continuous overspeed aural tone ("clacker") (Gates, 2019). When the crew tried to move the trim wheel, the force required to move a fully deflected stabilizer in overspeed was beyond human capacity. Unable to move the trim wheel manually, the pilot elected to reactive the electrical trim system to stabilize the aircraft. Unknown to the crew, when the electrical trim system was turned back on, it also reactivated the malfunctioning MCAS. This caused a final nose dive and the aircraft ultimately crashed into a field near the town of Bishoftu, Ethiopia, killing all 157 people on board.

The investigation reports of both accidents identified several contributing factors (DeFazio and Larsen, 2020), including Boeing production pressure, faulty design and performance assumptions, lack of pilot training, and deficiencies in certification oversight (Turman, 2021). Of interest to this chapter are the contributing factors related to human-automation interaction with respect to the MCAS function that we classified in three categories: automation design, opaque logic, information overload, and startle response (see Fig. 6).

3.2 Automation Design

The 737 has two sensors for AOA, one on the pilot side (AOA sensor 1) and the other on the copilot side (AOA sensor 2). Both on Lion Air 610 and Ethiopian Airlines 302, there was a malfunction of the AOA sensor 1 either due to a system failure or the sensor being wrongly positioned. When there is a divergent reading between sensors 1 and 2, an alarm message is triggered to inform the crew that the AOA values are unreliable (manage task). However, the message did not appear on these flights due to a software bug in the avionics system (Levin, 2020). The software tied the appearance of the alarm message to the AOA value indicator that is offered as a paid option. Neither airline bought the optional AOA value indicator, which resulted

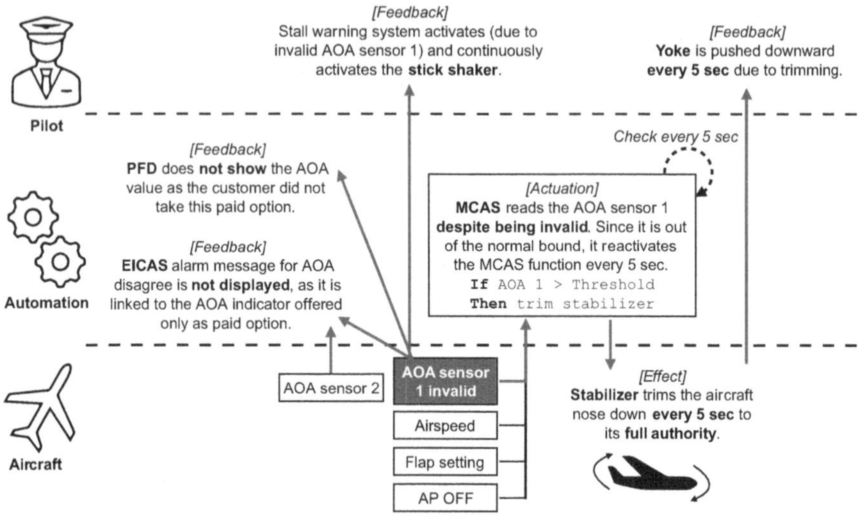

Fig. 6 MCAS uses the value of one invalid AOA sensor, causing it to trim the stabilizer to full authority

in the inhibition of the alarm message. Boeing was aware of the bug and planned on fixing it in a future avionics update, but it came too late to prevent these accidents.

The activation of the MCAS is based solely on data from a single AOA sensor, AOA 1 in this case. This was despite the presence of highly divergent readings from the second AOA sensor or if the AOA measurements were deemed unreliable. In both accidents, the MCAS used the invalid value from AOA 1 and wrongly detected that the aircraft was in stall. The software behaved as it was expected to: it trimmed the stabilizer to lower the aircraft nose and pushed down the pilot's yoke. The problem arose with the cyclic actuation of the MCAS: every 5 seconds, it verifies if the AOA value is within the acceptable threshold. Since it used the invalid data from AOA 1 that exceeded the threshold, MCAS reactivated in a cyclic fashion trimming the aircraft nose down each time and pushing the yoke. From the flight deck, the yoke behaved as if a "ghost pilot" was fighting against the pilot's command, making the yoke heavier to control at each activation of the MCAS.

3.3 Opaque Logic

Opaque logic refers to the complexity and lack of transparency in the design of automation. The MCAS offered no feedback to inform the crew of its activation, its operating limits, or its malfunction. In the Ethiopian Flight 610, the crew was informed of the MCAS behavior (repetitive nose down) following the operations bulletin and correctly diagnosed the malfunction. However, the flight crew were unaware that the MCAS used a single, invalid data source and would activate cyclically whenever the electric trimming system was in function. The software bug that inhibited the alarm message to inform the crew of the unreliable AOA value added to the complexity of the situation. The MCAS system was designed to help prevent the aircraft from stalling, but it operated in a way that was poorly explained and not understood by pilots, even those with extensive experience (Campbell, 2019; Prahl et al., 2022).

3.4 Information Overload and Startle Response

Information overload was also a factor in the accident. Even though the MCAS system activated without clear indication to the pilots, there was an alarm flood in the flight deck caused by the erroneous AOA sensor giving false indication that the aircraft stalled: the stick shaker activated and vibrated the yoke continuously to warn the crew of an imminent stall; the yoke was pushed down each time the MCAS activated; the TAWS system triggered several aural messages "Don't sink" that warned the crew that the aircraft was in close proximity to terrain; and the overspeed audio chime ("clacker") was heard continuously on the Ethiopian flight (Gates, 2019). The audible alarms were all activated simultaneously, and the lack of clear prioritization may have led to information overload, preventing the pilots from taking the appropriate actions in a timely manner.

Furthermore, the persistent activation of the MCAS, despite the pilots' continued efforts to regain full manual control, compounded the issue. This created a conflict between the pilots' objectives and those of the automated agent, causing uncertainty regarding who had authority and which actions should be taken. This critical design flaw, placing ultimate control in the hands of the automated system rather than the human operator, led to confusion and frustration for the operator. The underlying rationale for this design decision stems from the misguided belief that accidents are primarily caused by human error, resulting in the notion that automated systems like the MCAS should possess more control (Chaparro et al., 2023). Ideally, the MCAS should have been designed to adapt to the pilots, providing accurate information and guidance after compensatory actions.

The startle response played a role as well, as the unexpected activation of the MCAS system caused the pilots to experience a sudden shock or surprise, which impaired their ability to think clearly and react effectively (Gardini et al., 2022; Wendel, 2019). Pilots may not consistently monitor systems and may be confused by information when events change unexpectedly. Startle is known to reduce attentional control and direct it toward the outside world. A phenomenon of perseverance causes the operator's attention to be focused on specific elements of the environment, i.e., tunnel vision, which prevents the operator to process the situation. This is what happened on the Ethiopian flight when pilots focused their attention to the MCAS malfunction and omitted to reduce thrust during the climb, leading the aircraft into overspeed. Boeing assumed that the repetitive activation of MCAS due to a faulty AOA sensor would be detected by pilots within 10 seconds, despite data showing that one of their test pilots took more than 10 seconds to react in a flight simulator. This assumption did not account for human performance limitations under stress and startle. Past research devoted considerable attention to startle reflex and into the exacerbating effects of fear and anxiety on the magnitude of the startle reaction (Grillon et al., 1991; Lang et al., 1990). Translating this knowledge into proper alarm management in the aviation context remains a concern (Landman et al., 2017; Martin et al., 2012; Uhlig and Uhlig, 2021).

In conclusion, the increasing use of automation in the aviation industry raises concerns about its potential effects on pilot performance. Pilots have become system managers who monitor systems and intervene only when necessary, leading to decreased system awareness. Despite the growing interest in pilot-automation interaction, limited data is available about the problems that occur with automated cockpit systems. In terms of automation transparency, the see-into paradigm is crucial in situations where the course of events is unexpected or when there is a potential for automation to go wrong. In such cases, having a better system transparency enables the user to intervene and take appropriate action if necessary. The importance of the see-into approach was highlighted by the crashes of the Boeing 737 Max aircraft. In these incidents, the flight crew could not properly respond to the aircraft's automated systems, causing the plane to nosedive. The crew lacked a proper understanding of the system's intentions, activities, and inner workings, and as a result, they were unable to intervene and prevent the crashes. The lack of transparency in the automated systems was seen as a significant factor in these incidents, and it highlighted the need for greater user awareness and transparency in automation.

4 Lessons Learned

In this final section, we will further detail how to increase the transparency of see-into automated systems and provide quality feedback to the pilot. According to van de Merwe et al. (2022), system transparency would have a promising effect on the operator's situational awareness and performance in a supervisory role. The ability to see the processing steps could help operators understand the inner workings of the automation. However, the transparency between the automation and the operator requires making choices regarding information display to prevent information overload. Adopting a design approach that focuses on the user experience and the context of use makes it possible to identify information needs. According to Parasuraman et al. (2000), it is possible to create displays that provide maximum support to operators by defining what information is needed to develop situational awareness.

If we take the example of adding the MCAS to the 737 MAX, the first step is to define the functionality of the automation and the type of interactions desired (see Fig. 7). MCAS is an automated system that lowers the aircraft pitch during

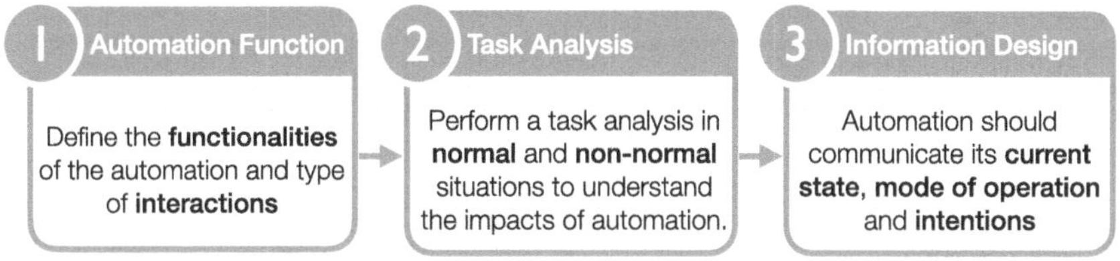

Fig. 7 Design principles to increase automation transparency

the climb phase when the aircraft's angle of attack is too high to avoid stalling. It is an automation that takes the form of an intelligent agent that operates largely independently, with the human in a supervisory role that can intervene if necessary.

As we described previously, the MCAS works perfectly during a normal situation. However, when the situation deteriorates, such as when the AOA sensor sends erroneous information, a series of alarms and failures place the pilots in an emergency without the resources to understand and correct the situation. The piloting task is strongly impacted: stall warning, stick vibrating, the nose of the aircraft pointing down, and no information on the state of the MCAS, and its operating mode is communicated to the crew. This opacity of the MCAS shows a bad design during non-normal situations. There is a real need to study all the non-normal scenarios and the possible errors of the automated agent during the design to understand how to manage the complexity of certain situations.

To this end, the second step would be performing a task analysis in normal and non-normal situations to understand the potential impacts of MCAS on the piloting task. This analysis aims to categorize the information needs according to the information processing model: detect, decide, and act, in order to design efficient interfaces. At this step, different methods can be used: the human information processing model of (Parasuraman et al., 2000) can be used to develop transparent displays and compatibility between the information processing by the automation and the pilot. Goal-directed task analysis (GDTA) is a widely used technique for identifying the operator's situational awareness requirements (Endsley, 1993; Haffaci et al., 2021). Although it is a generic method with few explicit guidelines, it is possible to obtain a guide detailing each step (Nasser-Dine, 2021). Lastly, the model of cycle perception by Neisser (1976), Plant and Stanton (2015) is an information processing model that emphasizes the importance of environmental experience in studying the human-technology system. Recorded feedback and interviews with operators also provide good support for decomposing tasks and extracting information on cognitive requirements.

The third step consists of presenting relevant information to the pilots in the cockpit. At this stage, the user interface plays an important role as it is the primary source of information to build the pilot's situational awareness. Once again, engineering teams should be cautious concerning the visual format used to display such information efficiently and to prevent visual clutter (Doyon-Poulin et al., 2014). The use of ergonomic criteria is strongly recommended because they

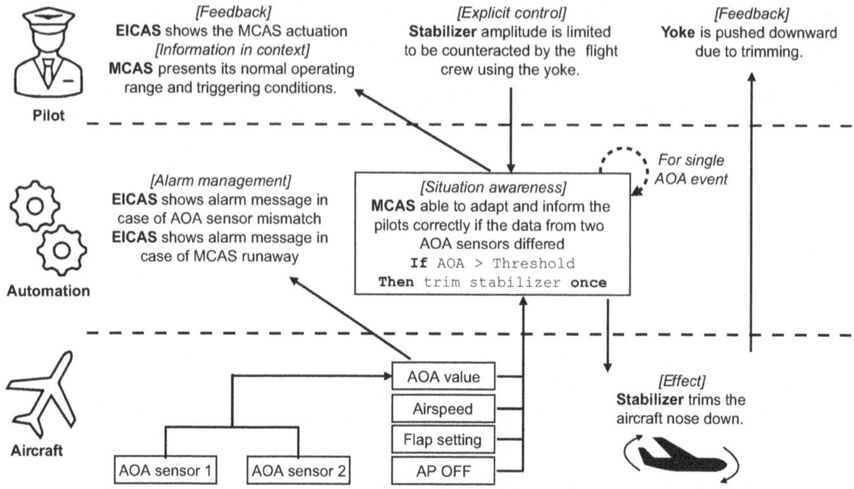

Fig. 8 Improved transparency for MCAS automation

facilitate comprehension and constitute a mechanism for preventing human errors (Boudreault et al., 2023; Doyon-Poulin, 2021).

To achieve a sufficiently high level of transparency, the automated agent must, at a minimum, communicate its current state, mode of operation, and intentions to the operator. Here are our recommendations for MCAS (see Fig. 8).

- **Situation awareness:** the task analysis defined the necessary information to develop the pilot's general situational awareness. In interactions involving both pilots and automated agents, two synchronized situational awarenesses exist. The level of concordance between the pilot's situational awareness and that of the automated agent serves as an indicator of the transparency required in sharing information about the agent's decision-making process, fostering shared understanding. The automated agent should be capable of real-time adaptation based on pilot input. The SAT model can facilitate the identification of relevant information by synchronizing the two situational awarenesses and determining the right moment to share it with the pilot (Chen et al., 2018). In the case of MCAS, the automated agent should have been able to adapt and accurately inform the pilot if there was a discrepancy in the data from the two AOA sensors instead of repeatedly activating itself and entering into conflict with the pilots.
- **Feedback:** These are messages sent by the automated agent in response to operator actions, as well as messages that guide the operators to further actions. For example, an indication in the cockpit of the activation of the MCAS and the stabilizer trim value is a form of feedback.
- **Information in context:** display information rather than data to eliminate mental calculations that are costly in cognitive resources. Instead of displaying the raw

value for the AOA, add the information with context, i.e., the MCAS trigger range based on the AOA and the normal operating range.
- **Explicit control:** pilots must have authority over the automated agent. As long as human operators bear responsibility for the goals to be achieved, they must have control. Boeing changed the MCAS system to provide only one trim input for each elevated AOA event and to reduce the amplitude of the stabilizer deflection such that it can be counteracted by the flight crew pulling back on the column (Boeing, 2022).
- **Alarm management:** an integrated alarm management system that can prioritize between multiple alarms and prevent information overload will better support the crew diagnostic in case of MCAS malfunction.
- **Fail-safe system connection**: to further enhance the safety and reliability of the automated system, it is crucial to incorporate a fail-safe system that accounts for the possibility of sensor failures. This fail-safe system should be connected to critical sensors, such as the AOA sensor, to detect erroneous information and trigger appropriate actions to mitigate potential risks. Considering the possibility of sensor failures, the fail-safe system can provide redundancy and additional layers of protection to ensure the system's robustness and the pilot's ability to understand and respond to critical situations effectively.

As technology progresses, human operators will interact with increasingly more complex and automated systems. The study of the 737 MAX accidents is also a humbling tale intended for engineering teams: no matter how reliable and safe each component of a large sociotechnical system can be, at one point in time, the system will fail or behave unexpectedly because of unanticipated interactions between its components (Panesar et al., 2021). It is the designer's responsibility to improve the automation transparency to handle these situations better. Adopting a system-thinking approach (Cababa, 2022; McCormack et al., 2022; Salmon et al., 2022; Stanton et al., 2017) is a promising avenue to account for the interdependencies between human and automated agents.

5 Conclusion

In conclusion, this study emphasizes the importance of adopting a human-centered approach to designing complex automation systems and their implementation in the aviation industry. Transparency can be an essential feature that allows users to understand the automation system's current and future states and available actions. It can help support the user's situational awareness, mental model, and decision-making processes, especially during unexpected situations. Automation systems should be designed to account for the user's reactions during non-normal operations, which can be unusual, stressful, and workload intensive. Additionally, integrating fail-safe systems could limit the probability of catastrophic incidents and enhance automated systems' overall safety and resilience in both normal and non-normal scenarios.

Adopting these lessons will help the aviation industry shift its perception of automation systems as a teammate that pilots can count on and not just as a tool that needs to be supervised. As the civilian aviation industry investigates uncrewed air vehicles, developing more resilient automation will also support the transition from system automation to system autonomy.

References

Administration FA (2022) Flightpath management. Tech. Rep. AC 120-123. https://www.faa.gov/documentLibrary/media/Advisory_Circular/AC_120-123.pdf

Airbus (2022) A statistical analysis of commercial aviation accidents 1958–2021. Tech. rep. https://accidentstats.airbus.com/

Banks VA, Plant KL, Stanton NA (2019) Driving aviation forward; contrasting driving automation and aviation automation. Theor Issues Ergonom Sci 20(3):250–264. publisher: Taylor & Francis eprint: https://doi.org/10.1080/1463922X.2018.1432716

Bhaskara A, Skinner M, Loft S (2020) Agent transparency: A review of current theory and evidence. IEEE Trans Syst Man Cybern C Appl Rev 50(3):215–224. https://doi.org/10.1109/THMS.2020.2965529

Boeing (2022) The 737 MAX MCAS software enhancement. https://www.boeing.com/commercial/737max/737-max-software-updates.page, [Online; accessed 2023-02-22]

Boeing Press Release (2011) Boeing, Lion Air announce historic commitment for up to 380 737s. https://boeing.mediaroom.com/2011-11-17-Boeing-Lion-Air-Announce-Historic-Commitment-for-up-to-380-737s, [Online; accessed 2023-02-22]

Boeing Press Release (2018) Boeing statement on operations manual bulletin. https://boeing.mediaroom.com/news-releases-statements?item=130327&asPDF=1

Boudreault L, Hébert-Lavoie M, Ung K, Mahmoudhi C, Vu QP, Jouvet P, Doyon-Poulin P (2023) Situation awareness-oriented dashboard in ICUs in support of resource management in time of pandemics. IEEE J Transl Eng Health Med 11:151–160. https://doi.org/10.1109/JTEHM.2023.3241215, event-title: IEEE J Transl Eng Health Med

Cababa S (2022) Closing the loop: systems thinking for designers. Rosenfeld Media, New York

Campbell D (2019) Redline - The many human errors that brought down the Boeing 737 Max. https://www.theverge.com/2019/5/2/18518176/boeing-737-max-crash-problems-human-error-mcas-faa, [Online; accessed 2023-02-03]

Casner SM, Geven RW, Recker MP, Schooler JW (2014) The retention of manual flying skills in the automated cockpit. Human Fact J Human Fact Ergonom Soc 56(8):1506–1516. https://doi.org/10.1177/0018720814535628

Chaparro A, Miranda A, Grubb J (2023) Chapter 13 - Aviation displays: Design for automation and new display formats. Academic Press, San Diego, pp 341–371. https://www.sciencedirect.com/science/article/pii/B9780124201392000149. https://doi.org/10.1016/B978-0-12-420139-2.00014-9

Chen JYC, Lakhmani SG, Stowers K, Selkowitz AR, Wright JL, Barnes M (2018) Situation awareness-based agent transparency and human-autonomy teaming effectiveness. Theor Issues Ergonom Sci 19(3):259–282. publisher: Taylor & Francis, eprint: https://doi.org/10.1080/1463922X.2017.1315750

Chen JYC, Flemisch FO, Lyons JB, Neerincx MA (2020) Guest editorial: Agent and system transparency. IEEE Trans Human Mach Syst 50(3):189–193. https://doi.org/10.1109/THMS.2020.2988835, event-title: IEEE Trans Human Mach Syst

Chialastri A (2012) Automation in aviation, Chap. 5. INTECH Open Access Publisher
DeFazio P, Larsen R (2020) Final committee report on the design, development, and certification of the Boeing 737 MAX. Tech. rep. The House Committee on Transportation & Infrastructure, Washington, D.C. https://transportation.house.gov/download/20200915-final-737-max-report-for-public-release
Delseny H, Gabreau C, Gauffriau A, Beaudouin B, Ponsolle L, Alecu L, Bonnin H, Beltran B, Duchel D, Ginestet JB, Hervieu A, Martinez G, Pasquet S, Delmas K, Pagetti C, Gabriel JM, Chapdelaine C, Picard S, Damour M, Albore A (2021) White paper machine learning in certified systems. Tech. Rep. S079L03T00-005, DEEL Certification Workgroup
Demirci S (2021) The requirements for automation systems based on Boeing 737 MAX crashes. Aircraft Eng Aerospace Technol 94(2):140–153. https://doi.org/10.1108/AEAT-03-2021-0069, publisher: Emerald Publishing Limited
Doyon-Poulin P (2021) Erreur humaine, dunod edn, pp 267–269
Doyon-Poulin P, Ouellette B, Robert JM (2014) Effects of visual clutter on pilot workload, flight performance and gaze pattern. In: Proceedings of the International Conference on Human-Computer Interaction in Aerospace, ACM, New York, NY, USA, HCI-Aero '14, pp 13:1–13:7. http://doi.acm.org/10.1145/2669592.2669656, event-place: Santa Clara, California
EASA (2023) Artificial INTELLIGENCE ROADMAP 2.0 Human-centric approach to AI in aviation. Tech. rep., Cologne, Germany. https://easa.europa.eu/ai
Endsley MR (1993) A survey of situation awareness requirements in air-to-air combat fighters. Int J Aviation Psychol 3(2):157–168. Publisher: Taylor & Francis, eprint: https://doi.org/10.1207/s15327108ijap0302_5
Endsley MR (2017) From here to autonomy: Lessons learned from human–automation research. Human Fact J Human Fact Ergonom Soc 59(1):5–27. https://doi.org/10.1177/0018720816681350
Endsley MR (2023) Supporting Human-AI teams: transparency, explainability, and situation awareness. Comput Human Behav 140:107574. https://doi.org/10.1016/j.chb.2022.107574
EUROCAE (2019) New working group: Wg-114 / Artificial Intelligence. https://www.eurocae.net/news/posts/2019/june/new-working-group-wg-114-artificial-intelligence/, [Online; accessed 2023-02-19]
Federal Aviation Administration (2020) Summary of the FAA's review of the Boeing 737 MAX. Tech. rep. https://www.faa.gov/foia/electronic_reading_room/boeing_reading_room/media/737_RTS_Summary.pdf
Federal Register (2018) Ad 2018-20-15 airworthiness directives. Boeing Company Airplanes 83(200):52131–52135
Gardini KC, Chiavelli FH, Scarpari JRS, de Andrade D (2022) Conceptual models of startle, surprise and automation bias analyzed through recent aviation accident reports. J Aerospace Technol Manag 14. https://doi.org/10.1590/jatm.v14.1282. http://www.scielo.br/j/jatm/a/dXJgk9fhFytw6tGh5KFZ4HR/?lang=en, publisher: Departamento de Ciência e Tecnologia Aeroespacial
Gates D (2019) How much was pilot error a factor in the Boeing 737 MAX crashes? Seattle Times https://www.seattletimes.com/business/boeing-aerospace/how-much-was-pilot-error-a-factor-in-the-boeing-737-max-crashes/
Gawron V (2019) Automation in aviation—accident analyses. Tech. Rep. MTR190013, Center for Advanced Aviation System Development, McLean, VA
Gelles D, Kitroeff N, Nicas J, Ruiz RR (2019) Boeing was 'Go, Go, Go' to beat Airbus with the 737 Max. The New York Times https://www.nytimes.com/2019/03/23/business/boeing-737-max-crash.html, [Online; accessed 2023-02-22]
Glanz J, Suhartono M, Beech H (2018) In Indonesia Lion Air crash, Black Box data reveal Pilots' struggle to regain control. The New York Times https://www.nytimes.com/2018/11/27/world/asia/indonesia-lion-air-crash-.html, [Online; accessed 2023-02-22]
Grillon C, Ameli R, Woods SW, Merikangas K, Davis M (1991) Fear-potentiated startle in humans: effects of anticipatory anxiety on the acoustic blink reflex. Psychophysiology 28(5):588–595. https://doi.org/10.1111/j.1469-8986.1991.tb01999.x, pMID: 1758934

Haffaci K, Massicotte MC, Doyon-Poulin P (2021) Goal-directed task analysis for situation awareness requirements during ship docking in compulsory pilotage area. In: Black NL, Neumann WP, Noy I (eds) Proceedings of the 21st Congress of the International Ergonomics Association (IEA 2021). Springer International Publishing, Cham, vol 221, pp 647–654. https://doi.org/10.1007/978-3-030-74608-7_79. Collection-title: Lecture Notes in Networks and Systems

Haslbeck A, Hoermann HJ (2016) Flying the needles: Flight deck automation erodes fine-motor flying skills among airline pilots. Human Fact J Human Fact Ergonom Soc 58(4):533–545. https://doi.org/10.1177/0018720816640394

Herkert J, Borenstein J, Miller K (2020) The Boeing 737 MAX: Lessons for engineering ethics. Sci Eng Ethics 26(6):2957–2974. https://doi.org/10.1007/s11948-020-00252-y

IATA (2020) Aircraft handling and manual flying skills report. Tech. rep. Montréal, Canada. https://www.iata.org/contentassets/d0e499e4b2824d4d867a8e07800b14bd/iata-report-aircraft-handling-manual-flying-skills.pdf

Jamieson GA, Skraaning G, Joe J (2022) The B737 MAX 8 accidents as operational experiences with automation transparency. IEEE Trans Human Mach Syst 52(4):794–797. https://doi.org/10.1109/THMS.2022.3164774, event-title: IEEE Trans Human Mach Syst

Jiang J, Karran AJ, Coursaris CK, Léger PM, Beringer J (2022) A situation awareness perspective on Human-AI interaction: Tensions and opportunities. Int J Human Comput Interact 39(9):1789–1806. Publisher: Taylor & Francis, eprint: https://doi.org/10.1080/10447318.2022.2093863

Johnston P, Harris R (2019) The Boeing 737 MAX saga: lessons for software organizations. Software Quality Professional 21(3):4–12. Publisher: American Society for Quality

Jonsson JE, Ricks WR (1995) Cognitive models of pilot categorization and prioritization of flight-deck information. Tech. Rep. 19960007717, Hampton, Virginia. https://ntrs.nasa.gov/citations/19960007717, nTRS Author Affiliations: McDonnell-Douglas Aerospace, NASA Langley Research Center NTRS Report/Patent Number: L-17463 NTRS Document ID: 19960007717 NTRS Research Center: Legacy CDMS (CDMS)

Landman A, Groen EL, van Paassen MMR, Bronkhorst AW, Mulder M (2017) Dealing with unexpected events on the flight deck: A conceptual model of startle and surprise. Human Fact 59(8):1161–1172. https://doi.org/10.1177/0018720817723428. Publisher: SAGE Publications Inc.

Lang PJ, Bradley MM, Cuthbert BN (1990) Emotion, attention, and the startle reflex. Psychol Rev 97:377–395. https://doi.org/10.1037/0033-295X.97.3.377. Publisher-place: US publisher: American Psychological Association

Levin A (2020) Boeing failure to fix 737 Max cockpit light may draw FAA penalty. https://www.bnnbloomberg.ca/boeing-failure-to-fix-737-max-cockpit-light-may-draw-faa-penalty-1.1393499, section: Technology

Luo P, Li M, Li ZS (2020) An Internet of Things (loT) perspective of understanding the Boeing 737 MAX crash. In: 2020 Global Reliability and Prognostics and Health Management (PHM-Shanghai), pp 1–8. https://doi.org/10.1109/PHM-Shanghai49105.2020.9280967

Marks P (2008) Bugs in aircraft software pose danger. New Scientist 197(2642):28–29. https://doi.org/10.1016/S0262-4079(08)60355-3

Martin W, Murray P, Bates P (2012) The effects of startle on pilots during critical events: A case study analysis. EAAP. https://research-repository.griffith.edu.au/handle/10072/54072, accepted: 2017-05-03T14:17:34Z

McCormack P, Read GJ, Hulme A, Lane BR, McLean S, Salmon PM (2022) Using systems thinking-based risk assessment methods to assess hazardous manual tasks: A comparison of Net-HARMS, EAST-BL, FRAM and STPA. Ergonomics Online First:1–44. https://doi.org/10.1080/00140139.2022.2105959, pMID: 35866642

van de Merwe K, Mallam S, Nazir S (2022) Agent transparency, situation awareness, mental workload, and operator performance: A systematic literature review. Human Fact, 00187208221077804. https://doi.org/10.1177/00187208221077804

Mohrmann F, Stoop J (2019) Airmanship 2.0: Innovating aviation human factors forensics to necessarily proactive role. Hague, the Netherlands
Nasser-Dine A (2021) A systematic method to perform goal directed task analysis with application to enterprise architecture. https://espace.etsmtl.ca/id/eprint/2844/
Neisser U (1976) Cognition and reality: principles and implications of cognitive psychology. WH Freeman, New York
News B (2018) Lion Air crash: Boeing 737 plane crashes in sea off Jakarta. BBC News. https://www.bbc.com/news/world-asia-46014463, [Online; accessed 2023-02-22]
Nicas J, Creswell J (2019) Boeing's 737 Max: 1960s design, 1990s computing power and paper manuals. The New York Times. https://www.nytimes.com/2019/04/08/business/boeing-737-max-.html, [Online; accessed 2023-02-22]
Panesar K, Mathur A, Atkins E, Sarter N (2021) Moving from piloted to autonomous operations: Investigating human factors challenges in urban air mobility. Proc Human Fact Ergonom Soc Annu Meet 65(1):241–245. https://doi.org/10.1177/1071181321651143, publisher: SAGE Publications Inc
Parasuraman R, Sheridan T, Wickens C (2000) A model for types and levels of human interaction with automation. IEEE Trans Syst Man Cybern A Syst Humans 30(3):286–297. https://doi.org/10.1109/3468.844354, event-title: IEEE Trans Syst Man Cybern A Syst Humans
Plant KL, Stanton NA (2015) The process of processing: exploring the validity of Neisser's perceptual cycle model with accounts from critical decision-making in the cockpit. Ergonomics 58(6):909–923. Publisher: Taylor & Francis, eprint: https://doi.org/10.1080/00140139.2014.991765. PMID: 25529547
Prahl A, Leung RKH, Chua ANS (2022) Fight for flight: The narratives of human versus machine following two aviation tragedies. Human Mach Commun 4(1). https://doi.org/10.30658/hmc.4.2, https://stars.library.ucf.edu/hmc/vol4/iss1/2
RTCA (2011) Software considerations in airborne systems and equipment certification. Tech. Rep. DO-178C, RTCA, Washington, D.C.
SAE (2010) Guidelines for development of civil aircraft and systems. Tech. Rep. ARP4754A, SAE International. https://doi.org/10.4271/ARP4754A
Salmon PM, Stanton NA, Walker GH, Hulme A, Goode N, Thompson J, Read GJM (2022) Handbook of systems thinking methods, 1st edn. CRC Press, Boca Raton. https://www.taylorfrancis.com/books/9780429281624. https://doi.org/10.1201/9780429281624
Sanneman L, Shah JA (2022) The situation awareness framework for explainable AI (SAFE-AI) and human factors considerations for XAI systems. Int J Human Comput Interact 38(18-20):1772–1788. https://doi.org/10.1080/10447318.2022.2081282
Saracco R (2016) Guess what requires 150 million lines of code.... https://cmte.ieee.org/futuredirections/2016/01/13/guess-what-requires-150-million-lines-of-code/, [Online; accessed 2023-02-18]
Soo KKY, Mavin TJ, Kikkawa Y (2021) Mastering automation: New airline pilots' perspective. Int J Human Comput Interact 37(7):717–727. Publisher: Taylor & Francis eprint: https://doi.org/10.1080/10447318.2021.1890487
Stanton NA, Salmon PM, Walker GH, Jenkins DP (eds) (2017) Cognitive work analysis: applications, extensions and future directions. CRC Press, London. https://ebookcentral.proquest.com/lib/polymtl-ebooks/detail.action?docID=4890682, https://doi.org/10.1201/9781315572536
Travis G (2019) How the Boeing 737 Max disaster looks to a software developer. IEEE Spectrum https://spectrum.ieee.org/how-the-boeing-737-max-disaster-looks-to-a-software-developer, [Online; accessed 2023-02-22]
Turman A (2021) Clear of conflict? Examining FAA certification and conflict preemption in light of the 737 MAX. Houston Law Rev 58(3). https://houstonlawreview.org/article/19363-clear-of-conflict-examining-faa-certification-and-conflict-preemption-in-light-of-the-737-max, publisher: Joe Christensen, Inc.
Uhlig T, Uhlig C (2021) Reactivity – the process behind the states and traits (Chapter 6). Hogrefe Publishing, pp 95–106

Ververs PM (1998) Understanding a pilot's tasks. University of Illinois, Aviation Research Laboratory, Savoy, IL A-1 Publisher, Citeseer

Wendel WB (2019) Technological solutions to human error and how they can kill you: Understanding the boeing 737 max products liability litigation. J Air Law Commerce 84:379. Publisher: HeinOnline

Wickens CD, Dixon SR (2007) The benefits of imperfect diagnostic automation: a synthesis of the literature. Theor Issues Ergonom Sci 8(3):201–212. Publisher: Taylor & Francis, eprint: https://doi.org/10.1080/14639220500370105

Wikipedia Contributors (2023) List of Boeing 737 MAX orders and deliveries. https://en.wikipedia.org/w/index.php?title=List_of_Boeing_737_MAX_orders_and_deliveries&oldid=1139804998, page Version ID: 1139804998

Wilkinson C, Lynch J, Bharadwaj R, Woodham K (2016) Verification of adaptive systems. Tech. Rep. DOT/FAA/TC-16/4. Federal Aviation Administration

So, You Want to Build a Copilot?

Part II: Design and Evaluation of Copilot Templates

Michal Furmakiewicz, Chang Liu, Angus Taylor, and Ilya Venger

Abstract Building a successful AI copilot requires a systematic approach. This chapter is divided into two sections, covering the design and evaluation of a copilot, respectively. A case study of developing copilot templates by Microsoft for the retail domain is used to illustrate the role and importance of each aspect. The first section explores the key technical components of a copilot's architecture, including the LLM, plugins for knowledge retrieval and actions, orchestration, system prompts, and responsible AI guardrails. The second section discusses testing and evaluation as a principled way to manage desired outcomes and unintended consequences of using AI in a business context. We discuss how to measure and improve its quality and safety, through the lens of an end-to-end human-AI decision loop framework. By providing insights into the anatomy of a copilot and the critical aspects of testing and evaluation, this chapter provides concrete evidence of how good design and evaluation practices are essential for building effective, human-centered AI assistants.

M. Furmakiewicz
Microsoft, Warsaw, Poland
e-mail: michal.furmankiewicz@microsoft.com

C. Liu
Microsoft, Cambridge, MA, US
e-mail: changliu2@microsoft.com

A. Taylor
Microsoft, London, UK
e-mail: Angus.Taylor@microsoft.com

I. Venger (✉)
Microsoft, Herzliya, Israel
e-mail: ilyavenger@microsoft.com

C. K. Coursaris et al. (eds.), *The Design of Human-Centered Artificial Intelligence for the Workplace*, Progress in IS, https://doi.org/10.1007/978-3-031-83512-4_20

1 Introduction

The advent of large language models (LLMs) has generated a huge amount of interest across industries in developing intelligent applications, with "AI copilots"—assistants that help humans in the execution of cognitive tasks—taking front stage (Sellen and Horvitz 2023). These AI assistants can be employed to infuse existing technology with advanced capabilities, synthesizing understanding and generation of text, image, and other modalities (such as audio and software actions) to enable completely new business use cases. However, building a successful copilot, even based mainly on text, comes with many challenges (Parnin et al. 2023; Patel et al. 2024). LLMs often require additional context or examples on how to perform a task. They may lack the domain-specific knowledge to generate an appropriate response, necessitating a mechanism for retrieving relevant information. Furthermore, particularly for complex business scenarios, there may be the need for orchestration between subtasks, knowledge retrieval, and actions the copilot needs to perform. Finally, care must be taken to ensure LLMs are used in an ethical and responsible way, particularly in highly regulated industries or business cases that involve high-stakes decisions or the use of sensitive data.

In this chapter, we first explore the various components that form the architecture of an AI copilot and how each comes together to make a working product. The components include the LLM, plugins, orchestration layer, system prompt, and RAI guardrails. Each of these components plays an important role and they come together to make a working copilot.

The second section of this chapter focuses on motivations and approaches for testing and evaluating an AI copilot. Given an architectural blueprint from the design perspective, it is natural to ask how good your copilot is, from an evaluation perspective. From engagements with customers and partners, we observe that quality and safety are the two convergent sets of aspects they regularly point to. Quality evaluation refers to measuring effectiveness and user acceptance of the copilot capabilities, while safety evaluation refers to measuring potential harms from the use of copilots. For businesses, these two aspects are foundational to managing the desired business outcomes and the unintended consequences associated with copilots. Measurement of potential harms, in particular, is one of the four stages in the iterative life cycle of "responsible AI practices" that Microsoft recognizes (Microsoft 2024d): identification of harms, measurement, mitigation as part of design, and operation of a deployment plan. On top of our measurement-focused perspective, we also find that the human-AI teaming model by Beringer et al. (2022) provides insights and clarity on the ways humans are assisted by the AI capabilities of a copilot and how systematic evaluation for copilots should extend to the evaluation of the successful human-AI teaming.

Throughout this discussion, we reference copilot templates developed by Microsoft—both in the retail domain. For copilot architecture, we illustrate the role and importance of key components with a copilot template focused on providing a personalized shopping experience. The architecture of this copilot serves as a reference for common copilot design patterns. A second example of a copilot template designed to assist with retail store operations serves as a use case to illustrate what testing and evaluation should focus on based on the capability and safety considerations. The example of testing and evaluating the template also illustrates the iterative life cycle of measurement and mitigations as a human-centric evaluation approach.

2 Architectural Considerations

Building a copilot is not simply a case of exposing a large language model to end users. Several components need to work together to ensure the copilot is focused on its task and role, has access to relevant knowledge, and behaves in a way that is ethical, safe, and responsible. In this section, we explore these components which include the LLM for managing the human-copilot interactions, plugins for knowledge retrieval, orchestration to coordinate plugin execution, and the system prompt for controlling copilot behavior. We will use the copilot template for personalized shopping as an example to illustrate the role of these components.

2.1 Copilot Template for Personalized Shopping

The copilot template for personalized shopping (Microsoft 2024b) (or "Shopper Copilot") aims to provide an interactive, conversational experience for online retail shopping. It is a template of an end-to-end AI copilot solution that can be configured and adapted for use by a range of retail companies. It is particularly relevant to retail companies that sell products for which personalized recommendations are valued by customers, for example, fashion retail. The user can engage the copilot to search for clothes by expressing their desired product attributes, and the copilot will respond with recommendations from the retailer's product catalog. The copilot is able to explain the suitability of recommended products based on the user's query and the product descriptions. Users can interact with the copilot in a natural conversational manner, providing feedback on the products recommended and asking for the copilot to adapt its recommendations based on this feedback.

The AI copilot has the flexibility to handle the diverse ways a human user might choose to search for products. In some cases, the user may make a straightforward request with a concrete set of criteria—for example, "Show me a magenta dress"—for which a simple keyword search of the product catalog is required. In others, the request may require more complex reasoning and judgment, for example, "I am going to a birthday party and the dress code is smart. Can you suggest some clothes I could wear?". In the latter cases, the copilot may need to draw from multiple sources of knowledge to be able to make appropriate recommendations. The ability of the copilot to respond to a range of inputs makes for a very natural human-copilot interaction and, by extension, an engaging shopping experience.

The Shopper Copilot serves as an exemplar for the design of an AI copilot's architecture. The scenario requires the copilot to have mechanisms to perform information retrieval and a means of orchestrating between those mechanisms and generating responses to user requests all while ensuring the copilot does not deviate from the confines of its role. Most scenarios will have similar requirements and the components that make this possible together form a reference architecture for AI copilots.

2.2 *Employing Large Language Models in Your Copilot*

The LLM forms the core of the AI copilot architecture. LLMs are complex machine learning models that have been pretrained on a vast amount of text from a diverse range of sources and topics. They leverage deep learning techniques to learn complex patterns and relationships in language. As such, they can both comprehend and generate natural language with almost human level of fidelity. The performance of LLMs continues to improve, and state-of-the-art models, such as GPT-4, perform well even on tests designed for humans (Achiam et al. 2023).

LLMs are known as foundation models because they can immediately be applied to a wide range of tasks involving the comprehension or generation of natural language. However, for all but the most trivial tasks, they must be provided context on how a task should be performed. These instructions are provided via the LLM's system prompt, a piece of text in which the developer can define the LLM's role, context, and desired behaviors to adhere to the design principles we discussed above, as well as examples on how to perform a given task. The LLM will utilize this context when generating responses to user inputs. This is important as it provides the means of controlling an AI copilot's behavior and affecting task performance while still permitting the nondeterministic interactions essential for natural conversational dialogue between user and copilot.

For some tasks, performance can be improved through fine-tuning the LLM, a process of training the model further on task-specific data. However, we have found, through our experience developing the Shopper Copilot and dedicated research (Ovadia et al. 2023), that good performance can be achieved without fine-tuning. Often, providing clear instructions and examples in the system prompt for how to perform the task, coupled with any domain-specific information for additional context, is sufficient to build a high-performing AI copilot. Thus, LLMs provide a powerful means for businesses to build copilots for a range of use cases without large upfront investments in task-specific model training.

One of the fundamental capabilities of an AI copilot is the ability to understand the user's input and intent. The LLM performs this role very effectively, despite often challenging inputs. In user-facing business applications, the user's input may be ambiguous, include grammatical or spelling errors, or use culturally specific idioms. LLMs are very adept at inferring the user's intent given the context including the preceding dialogue or additional information provided in the system prompt.

The LLM also performs the role of generating a response to the user. To generate a relevant and accurate response, the LLM synthesizes information from its vast pretrained knowledge base, as well as any additional context provided in the request. With their unparalleled language generation ability, LLMs can facilitate natural conversational interactions between the user and the copilot.

Another role for the LLM to serve as an orchestrator for the tools and plugins available to the AI copilot (see below). These plugins may be used to retrieve relevant information or perform actions required to fulfill a user's request. The LLM is used to determine when and how to call on these plugins in the course of the interaction with the user.

As a component in the AI copilot architecture, a common pattern is for the LLM to be hosted on a cloud platform such as Microsoft Azure, Amazon Web Services, or Google Cloud Platform. These platforms offer scalable solutions for deploying and managing LLMs. The LLM will be accessible via an API, providing a general text-in text-out interface that can be integrated with other components of the copilot architecture.

2.3 Plugins: Knowledge Retrieval and Actions

LLMs are trained on huge corpuses of data from across the World Wide Web such as the 800Gb Pile dataset (Gao et al. 2020), forming a statistical internal representation of a knowledge base that includes information about the real world. However, for many business applications, additional domain-specific and proprietary knowledge is required to respond accurately to a user's request. This information will not have been included in the LLM's training data and therefore needs to be provided to the model as additional context. Furthermore, LLMs have no knowledge of the world beyond the time period covered by their training datasets. This requires providing the LLM additional context in cases where up-to-date or organization- or user-specific information is required (Bubeck et al. 2023).

Plugins have become an essential component of AI copilot architecture as a means of retrieving additional relevant context. Plugins are functions or tools that provide LLMs' access to external data sources such as databases, APIs, or document repositories in order to retrieve relevant information for generating responses. This process is known as retrieval-augmented generation (RAG). Plugins can be conditionally executed as needed in the course of an interaction with the user. The information returned by the plugin can then be added to the final prompt that is sent to the LLM, providing the additional context or knowledge required to fulfil the user's request (Gao et al. 2023).

Often, a plugin will return tabular data sourced from a database or API, as is the case with the product recommendation plugins featured in the Shopper Copilot. The product catalog resides in a database that is accessed via an API using keywords extracted from the user's query. In other cases, where information is stored in large document repositories, more complex RAG solutions are required with the use of specialized vector databases as well as splitting documents into logical elements (chunking), intermediate summarization, and more. The Shopper Copilot, for example, includes plugins that access document repositories to answer user queries related to store policies or the company brand.

Plugins are not only useful as a means of implementing RAG. They may also enable AI copilots to perform actions as discussed above. Examples could include a checkout action in the context of the Shopper Copilot or an action to send an email to summarize a conversation with a customer service copilot. In these cases, the plugins would make a request to APIs to other services that would perform the required action. Additionally, plugins can be used to enable the copilot to trigger subprocesses such as mathematical operations or data analysis, for which LLMs may not be the most effective tool.

Plugins can also allow to develop a multiagent architecture, facilitating smaller end-to-end automation loops consisting of multiple AI copilots that carry out specialized functions.

2.4 Orchestration

We have seen how LLMs, with access to information retrieved from plugins, are able to understand user intent and generate relevant and informed responses. To enable complex and dynamic business tasks, an AI copilot needs orchestration to enhance the basic capabilities of an LLM, by negotiating between user intent and plugin execution and maintaining a memory of the conversation. These two LLM-powered features of a copilot perform semantic understanding of the current context and history of the task—not dissimilar to a "stateful" software application but more powerful—in order to navigate the ambiguity and complexity of human-AI interactions. For example, a user of the Shopper Copilot may not know the exact product they want at the start of the conversation and may start the interaction with an ambiguous query for which the copilot has no relevant plugin. In this scenario, the copilot can request clarification from the user so that they can add context or modify their request. Based on the original query and subsequent query, the copilot can now retrieve the required information from its plugins and generate an informed response. Thus, the copilot orchestration provides for flexible and nondeterministic coordination between user-copilot interactions and plugin execution, which in turn provides for seamless conversational interactions between the user and copilot.

The orchestrator component in an AI copilot architecture is a software layer that coordinates between the UI, the LLM, and any plugins available to it. It is exposed via an API end point which would accept user inputs directly or through the copilot UI. Once the orchestrator receives a request, it "decides" to invoke one or more plugins that may be needed to source additional information or perform an action. Finally, the LLM will be called to generate a response back to the user, utilizing information retrieved from plugins to inform the response or perhaps confirming that an action plugin has been invoked successfully.

Orchestrating Between Plugins Complex business use cases are likely to require the AI copilot to have access to multiple plugins. For example, the Shopper Copilot has several plugins that search product catalogue databases to provide product recommendations, plugins that access a document corpus to provide information on the brand and terms of sale and policies, and action plugins to facilitate the checkout process. The orchestrator needs to decide when to call each of these plugins depending on the user's intent. It must also determine how to call the plugin by supplying any parameter values required by the plugin function. In some cases, multiple plugin calls may be needed to fulfil a user's request, and these calls may need to be executed in a particular order with the output of one plugin providing input to the next.

It is clear that the task of orchestration is nontrivial and requires the orchestrator to reason over the user's intent and the plugins available to call. Thankfully, we now have a powerful tool that can perform this task: the LLM itself. Recent GPT models include a function calling feature, which has proved to be a critical component of the AI copilots we have developed at Microsoft: starting with GPT-3.5 Turbo and GPT-4 models, developers can provide descriptions of their plugins and parameters to the model. It is important to note that when using GPT function calling, the LLM itself is not able to execute functions. Instead, when GPT determines that a function is needed, it will output the function name along with any parameter values it deems appropriate. Executing functions is the responsibility of the orchestrator, giving it complete control over when and how functions are called.

Let us see from an example how GPT function calling can provide an effective execution flow for orchestration of the Shopper Copilot. A user could send a request to the AI copilot such as "give me recommendations for a red dress." When the LLM receives this request, it should determine that it needs to call the product search function and will return the function name back to the orchestrator, along with the parameter values "red" for color and "dress" for apparel type. The orchestrator will then execute the function to search the database using these keywords, and the database will return data containing appropriate product recommendations. Finally, a second GPT call will be made with the user's original request, along with the product recommendation data. The LLM will generate a conversational response back to the user, informed by the recommendations extracted from the database.

Maintaining a Memory of Conversations Aside from coordinating plugin execution, another task for the orchestrator is to manage the conversation history between the AI copilot and user. Often, the user's exact intent may only be apparent after several conversation turns, and information from previous conversation turns will be highly relevant to how the copilot should respond next. For this reason, it is important that the history of the interaction between copilot and user is retained by the orchestrator and included in any subsequent calls to the LLM, such that it can refer to it when generating further responses or invoking plugins. It may also be worthwhile to include the conversation history from previous sessions so that the copilot can maintain a memory of its interactions with the user.

One challenge with maintaining a conversation history is that eventually it may become too long to fit within a single LLM prompt. Moreover, it is likely that only a subset of the information contained in the history will be relevant to the current interaction and including the full history in the LLM prompt may cause confusion and a degradation in performance. There are several strategies for resolving this problem. A simple method is to truncate the history, discarding any further interactions beyond the previous n conversation turns. This method presumes that more recent interactions will be the most pertinent to the current conversation. However, this approach severely limits the memory of the AI copilot and may negatively impact the user experience. A more elegant solution is to apply an LLM to the task of producing a shortened summary of the conversation history, paying attention to information that could be relevant to future interactions. This summarization task could be invoked conditionally after a set number of conversation turns or when the token count of the history exceeds a certain length.

2.5 Controlling Copilot Behavior

When developing an AI copilot, it is critical to tightly define its role and desired behavior. This is important both for ensuring the copilot is provided with the instructions necessary to perform its task well and for mitigating the risk of the copilot behaving in a way that is unintended or causes harm to the user. The component of the copilot architecture that provides such instructions is the system prompt. This is a document of natural language text containing the instructions that govern the copilot's behavior. A good system prompt will only be arrived at through iterative trial and error. Although state-of-the-art models such as GPT-4 excel at following instructions, it often pays to experiment with different prompts in a process known as prompt engineering. Even small changes to the system prompt, in terms of the content of the instructions or even the way instructions are phrased, can have a large impact on copilot behavior and performance. Testing frameworks and evaluation are required to assess the behavior during development (more on this below).

A system prompt needs to clearly represent individual aspects of the AI copilot's desired behavior. Based on our experience in developing the Shopper Copilot, here are some recommendations for sections that should be considered for inclusion in a system prompt:

Role and Context This section should come first and give the LLM information about the role of the copilot. It should specify the context in which it operates including the industry and business use case it is being applied to. It should inform the LLM about who the user is or likely to be. It should provide details of exactly what the copilot can do and what user questions or requests it is able to fulfil. Just as importantly, it should explain any limitations the copilot has and what user requests it cannot respond to.

Business Logic In this section, detailed instructions can be provided on how the copilot can fulfil various user requests. It may provide examples of the types of requests a user is likely to make and give instructions on how to handle them, including plugins that are needed and what information should be included in the response.

Working with Plugins This section provides instructions that govern how the copilot can use plugins available to it. Aspects to consider include whether the copilot can make assumptions or inferences about the values that function parameters can take or if they should be explicitly clarified with the user. Another consideration is whether the existence and details of functions can be made known to the user.

Localization It is recommended that the system prompt includes instructions on if and how the copilot can operate in different languages. In this section, guidance can be included to indicate what language a user is likely to be using when interacting with the copilot, and instructions can be provided as to what language the copilot should respond in.

Tone of Voice and Verbosity Copilots in different contexts and industries are likely to need to adopt different behaviors and ways of responding to users. For example, a retail shopper copilot could adopt a casual or friendly tone of voice, whereas a copilot in the medical domain may need to adopt a more serious, authoritative, or perhaps even sympathetic tone. The use of adjectives that describe the desired tone of voice and explain how verbose or concise the copilot should be in its responses.

Output Format This section should describe how the output of the copilot should be formatted. Perhaps, the copilot should respond in plain text or have a bias toward responding in bullet point lists. A common scenario is that the copilot needs to respond in a data format that can be parsed by a UI application (e.g., JSON).

Responsible AI Guardrails This section is of critical importance as it aims to ensure the copilot does not respond in way that cause harm to the user. Instructions should be clear and unambiguous, explaining what the copilot must or must not do in cases where the response has the potential for harm. See below for more details on the aspects to consider for responsible AI guardrails.

2.6 *Responsible AI Guardrails*

We have discussed above the crucial aspects related to ethical design and development of AI copilots. It is important to consider how guardrails can be introduced to the copilot's architecture that minimizes risks of causing harm.

Automated content filtering is one tool that can be used to minimize this risk. This approach employs natural language processing and machine learning techniques to scan incoming requests for text that may contain harmful content, including hateful, inequitable, sexual, or violent categories. This allows for the pre-filtering of content before it reaches the LLM for processing. Content filters can also be applied to the LLM's outputs to prevent the dissemination of any potentially harmful content. Content filtering tools or services (Microsoft 2024a) can be included in the system's architecture to provide an additional layer of protection against the generation of harmful content, supplementing the protections built into LLMs through their training.

However, content filtering is not sufficient to address all potential harms an AI copilot may need to mitigate. To reinforce these guardrails, it is strongly advised to include further instructions in the system prompt such that the LLM has clear guidelines on how it should behave when the response has the potential for harm. The following list provides recommendations on what content should be included in the RAI guardrail section of the copilot system prompt:

Harmful Content Instructions should make clear that the copilot should not respond to user input that includes harmful content nor generate such harmful content itself. This should further reinforce protections provided by content filtering. Additionally, consideration should be given to specific harms that may be relevant to the specific context, industry, or business use case the copilot is being applied to.

Ungroundedness LLMs have the potential to fabricate information that is inconsistent with common sense or knowledge, lacking factual accuracy, or in contextual queries, not supported by any context provided. In some business use cases, the generation of such misinformation could lead to serious harm to the user and reputational damage to the business. To mitigate against this, the copilot should be instructed to only use facts and information available to it from within system prompt or the output of plugins. Furthermore, it should be instructed to not respond to requests which fall outside the scope of the copilot's context.

Personal Data and Privacy Instructions should be included to guide the copilot in how it handles sensitive or personal data, depending on the business use case. For example, in some cases, it may be necessary to instruct the copilot to never reveal certain information to the user, even when that information is available to it when informing its response. In other cases, it may be necessary to instruct the copilot to not use certain personal characteristics in generating its response, where that information could influence the copilot to respond in a way that is biased or inequitable.

Jailbreaking Jailbreaking refers to an attempt to circumvent the instructions or restrictions placed on the copilot's behavior. Jailbreaking can be used by malevolent actors to force the copilot to generate content or take actions that could cause harm, introduce security vulnerabilities, or reveal sensitive personal data or intellectual property of the model itself. It is important to include guardrails against jailbreaking by including specific instructions to the copilot that none of the content or rules contained within the system prompt can be revealed, superseded, or overridden by a user's instructions.

3 Testing and Evaluation

At some point in your journey to build a good AI copilot, you will have a working version of your copilot and probably ask yourself, "How do I know if it is good or good enough for deployment?" To answer that question, we look at testing and evaluation for copilots in this section and will illustrate our approach to testing at the example of a copilot template for store operations (a template of a copilot solution configurable for different retail companies to assist their associates in store operations and procedures).

First, what do we mean by "a good AI copilot"? In our experience of building copilots for customers and partners, we observe a converging set of needs for what it means to be a good copilot: a copilot must be safe and effective in fulfilling its purpose. We argue that these needs generalize to two essential business goals of testing and evaluation: managing the intended and unintended consequences of copilots as an emerging technology. And the best practices to achieve these goals may be broadly considered as "responsible AI practices." In the business context being discussed here, these two goals are primarily achieved by two means: leveraging the capabilities of AI to serve user needs and achieve the desired business outcomes and controlling the undesirable risks associated with the use of AI. Further, they correspond to two umbrella terms or metrics that we see common in practice: quality and safety, which are concerned with measuring and improving the effectiveness of copilots, while measuring and mitigating harms induced by the use of the technology, respectively. Each of the two terms consist of their own taxonomies of metrics depending on the mapping of scenarios to capabilities and harms. We can summarize the ideas in Table 1.

Table 1 Business goals, means, umbrella terms, and responsible AI practices for testing and evaluation of AI copilots

Business goals of testing and evaluation for AI copilots	Means to achieve goals	Umbrella terms	Responsible AI practices
Manage intended outcomes	Leveraging AI capabilities	Quality	Measuring and improving effectiveness
Manage unintended consequences	Controlling AI risks	Safety	Measuring and mitigating potential harms

Why is testing and evaluation important for managing AI? Measurement is foundational for managing both the desirable and undesirable outcomes of AI as a technology. It serves as a prerequisite to improving the effectiveness of AI capabilities and mitigating the risks that may arise in its use.

3.1 Copilot Template for Store Operations

To explain our approach to testing and evaluation of AI copilots, we will use the testing of our copilot template for store operations as a use case. Here is a brief description of the template (Microsoft 2024c): "The copilot template for store operations helps retail store employees to get answers to their questions from their retailer's knowledge base. It also lets them create tasks for themselves or their colleagues using voice or text commands." One of the main features is Question-and-Answering (Q&A) (Microsoft 2024c): "You can ask questions about your store operations using natural language. The copilot template uses unstructured data from documents such as standard operating procedures (SOPs) or process guides from your retailer. It supports various document formats, such as PDF, Word, HTML, and others. It processes the information in these documents to provide relevant responses to your queries."

The Q&A feature aims to help store associates overcome the challenge of memorizing and retrieving procedural knowledge accurately and on demand. This task may be difficult for new associates until they develop procedural memory and become proficient through repeated practice. And certain procedures are not often used or retained as efficiently, because some situations happen more often than others. Consulting a handbook or a colleague at peak hours may slow the workflow of the stores.

Suppose the situation is a customer coming to the store in person and asking to return an item. The return procedures will be different for sellable items, damaged items, and special items such as jewelry and other high-value merchandise. Made aware of the situation related to return procedures, the associates first perceive the relevant information about the item to be returned. What type of item is it? What is the condition of the item? Is the condition "sellable" or not? Suppose this is a re-sellable item, which triggers both a return process and a quality audit process.

The Q&A feature of the copilot template effectively offloads the tasks of memorizing and searching for the relevant information or context for a given situation and synthesizes the context and the question to formulate an answer or guidance on how to proceed. If the quality of the copilot's output is good, the store associates will team up with the copilot and leverage its AI-based skills to provide answers and follow standard operational procedures.

3.2 *Managing Intended Outcomes: Measuring Effectiveness of Copilot Capabilities*

By building an AI copilot, businesses are offering value to customers better than the competition. Good use of the AI capabilities in a copilot, on the one hand, leads to good business outcomes as intended, building trust and loyalty from customers, and improving profitability for the business. On the other hand, poor use of the capabilities in a copilot, including poor fit for purpose, and poor performance in the domain-specific tasks, could lead to low-quality copilot releases that erode customer trust and your product or service competitiveness.

Let us start with understanding the capabilities AI offers. For simplicity, let us focus on the most common scope of language AI (in contrast to image, voice, video, and a mix of these "modalities") and use one taxonomy proposed by Slack et al. for discussion (Slack et al. 2023; Scale AI 2023) in Table 2.

These AI-based capabilities match human cognitive skill. In fact, these capabilities are designed to be useful for humans (OpenAI 2022) so that we can benefit from a copilot's assistance in the same set of cognitive tasks, from writing a poem to shopping to reasoning through laws to summarizing meeting notes.

In addition to supporting humans in performing such cognitive tasks, the idea of an AI copilot is to package those cognitive capabilities into an assistant model that

Table 2 Top-level categories of language model capabilities, adapted from Slack et al. (2023)

Capability	Description	Key criteria
Classification	Determining the appropriate category according to shared qualities or characteristics	Accuracy of the classification
Information retrieval and synthesis	Answering requests based on a provided text (e.g., summarize)	Faithfulness to the reference text
Rewrite	Rephrasing text in accordance with a specific request (e.g., tone)	Writing quality and adherence to request
Generation	Creating original content, such as stories, essays, or ideas	Writing quality and creativity
Open QA	Answering open-domain questions	Factuality and domain knowledge
Reasoning	Drawing logical conclusions based on provided information	Correctness of the reasoning
Conversation	Engaging users who want to have a conversation	Level of engagement and tone of the response
Illogical questions	Handling nonsense questions that are harmless	Accurately identifying the question as nonsense and responding appropriately
Coding	Responding to requests that involve code	Correctness of the response and quality of the code
Math	Responding to requests that involve math	Correctness of the response

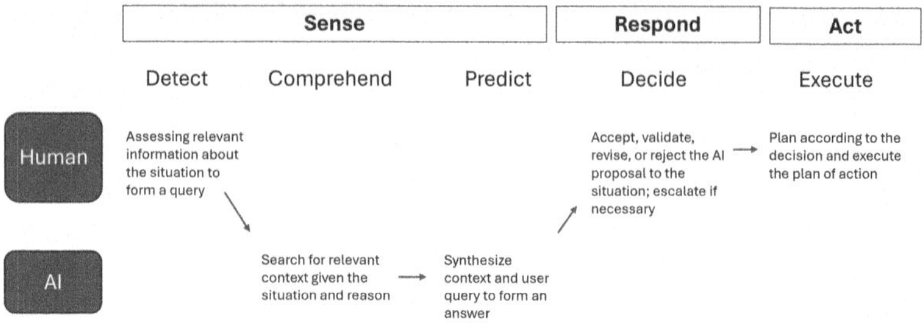

Fig. 1 Observed pattern of human-AI teaming in copilot template for store operations

is able to "**perceive** the world, **analyze**, and **understand** the information collected, make informed **decisions** or recommend **action**, and **learn** from experience" (Jiang et al. 2023); emphasis ours). Öz et al. (2023) applied the frameworks of situation awareness and decision ladder in an end-to-end decision loop. The conceptual frameworks augment the role of humans as the decision-maker in human-centered AI interaction while improving task efficiency and preserving the mental energy of human users. In practice, we find that this perspective provides clarity and insights into our experience of designing and evaluating copilots, as examples of AI aiding humans in their cognitive tasks. This human-AI teaming model applied to (Beringer et al. 2022) can be illustrated in Fig. 1.

The human-AI teaming model can be described as follows: human users and the AI copilot are jointly responsible for developing proper situation awareness. First, the human users are responsible for detecting the relevant details of the situation, in order to form a natural language query via a voice or text interface to the copilot. In the example above, this query could be "What should I do if a customer in store asks for a return? The item looks re-sellable." Prompted by the query along with carefully designed "system prompts" (as mentioned above), the copilot effectively develops a situation awareness to comprehend the situation holistically, searching for the relevant context in its knowledge base curated by the retailer and reason through the information. For example, the copilot finds and determines the return and quality audit procedures as applicable in this situation. Then, the copilot synthesizes the rich context and formulates a concise natural language response instead of the raw texts from the source documents. The copilot response to the user query acts as guidance or plan on how to respond to a given situation. Human users are then able to review and choose to accept or reject the response or validate the response themselves, since the response contains citations so users can double-check the sources if they feel the need to. Finally, the users can plan accordingly and execute the plan of actions or delegate the execution to other human agents.

The user's acceptance of an AI copilot largely depends on the completeness of the situation awareness developed jointly by human users and the copilot. Copilot as well as humans can fail at different steps: detect (inadequate description of the situation), comprehend (irrelevant search results and poor reasoning), or predict (incorrect application of the synthesized information to the current situation).

Hence, measuring the completeness is the focus of our quality testing for copilot template for store operations. As the testers of the copilot, we developed a set of criteria that evaluates copilot's capabilities in relation to the business context. These capabilities include information retrieval to open Q&A. To highlight some of the definitions used, we examined whether a copilot response is:

1. **Grounded**—consistent with and supported by the source documents (also an important metric for safety testing to address the pitfall of fabrication unique to generative AI)
2. **Relevant**—relevant to both the intent of the question and the situational context
3. **Clear**—appropriate to the situation and not misleading to the user
4. **Complete**—not missing critical information necessary to address the situation fully
5. **Acceptable**—deemed adequate by human judges in terms of overall quality

To operationalize the evaluation for the situation awareness developed by the AI copilot, we first created a diverse set of questions based on sample source documents from our partners who agreed to provide the valuable business context. We further curated reference responses to those questions and leveraged these "ground truths" of answers to guide human labelers to score our copilot in development. We iterated over several versions of copilots with a goal to improve the effectiveness of the capabilities to assist human users. We benchmarked these versions against a set of quality metrics and used these evaluation results to iteratively improve the capabilities of our copilot. Ultimately, we incorporated measurement results as part of the full set of factors we considered to guide our product decisions for which copilot to release to customers.

3.3 Managing Unintended Consequences: Measuring Potential Harms in Use of Copilot

Why do we care about testing and evaluation of potential harms in use of AI copilots? Mustafa Suleyman, EVP and CEO of Microsoft AI, in his book The Coming Wave (Suleyman and Bhaskar 2023) compares the importance of containing AI technology to the importance of containing nuclear technology. As one of the steps toward containment, he proposes auditing to empower accountability with the use of AI. Testing and evaluation for AI is concerned with building an auditing system to enhance the control of human agency in use of the emerging technology. AI is a general-purpose technology with inherent and pervasive risks that we must manage well, lest the unintended consequences wreak havoc on society. For example, AI has the potential to supercharge misinformation campaigns and cyberattacks against institutions and people, by means of exploitable vulnerabilities in digital systems and social engineering. Building an auditing system for AI is a foundation for better management of both the intended and unintended consequences from using this technology.

And who is responsible for auditing? In one view, responsibility should be shared among contributors to the stack of the AI systems we collectively build. In this view, the builder of the last layer on top plays an important role as a last gate keeper. This means building an AI copilot for your customers should count you (the builder) as a gate keeper. From another perspective, customers interacting with this technology through an interface are likely to deem you as responsible, because the builder has some agency to control the copilot and how it interacts with your customers. In a way, the copilot is imbued with your brand, your image, and your value that your customers experience directly, as opposed to some neutral object no one is responsible for. This responsibility should not be taken lightly.

How do we do it at Microsoft? Our approach consists of four stages to support responsible AI practices: (1) uncover, (2) measure, (3) mitigate the harms that may arise during the use of the AI copilot, and (4) operationalize a deployment plan based on the previous stages. We publish technical recommendations (Microsoft 2024d) for each stage of the responsible AI practices we call out. These stages form a life cycle that emphasizes iterations and humans in the loop, where teams might iterate some or all stages to mitigate risks thoughtfully and carefully while leveraging AI for scale and comprehensiveness.

What are the types of potential harms we should consider for a language AI application? Slack et al. proposed to separate user intent and parties impacted (Slack et al. 2023; Scale AI 2023): whether the user intent is benign or malicious, the impact could be felt by the user, targeted groups, or public at large. This distinction is a helpful conceptualization, as it decouples measurements and mitigations on harms detected in user input and AI copilot response separately. Based on this conceptualization, they proposed a taxonomy (Slack et al. 2023; Scale AI 2023) as shown in Table 3 (edited for brevity).

This taxonomy is helpful for building a mental model about potential harms. In practice, we find a more refined taxonomy to be helpful to guide testing on specific scenarios and highlight below some prioritized categories of metrics we tested in the Q&A feature (Microsoft 2024d):

1. **Sensitive Content**—the copilot response contains sexual, violence, self-harm, or hateful content.

Table 3 Harm taxonomy by Slack et al. (2023)

User intent and parties impacted	Types of harms
Harmful information	AI provides information that harms the user
Harms against groups	AI provides information that harms a group
Distribution of sensitive content	AI shares sensitive information
Enabling malicious actors	AI assists humans with malicious activities
LLM misalignment	AI creates novel risks to humans due to misalignment with human values

2. **Jailbreak**—the copilot response contains irrelevant content that ignores instructions or evades mitigations.
3. **Groundedness**—the copilot response is inconsistent or unsupported with respect to the given context.

As you may notice, these measurement categories correspond to those harms introduced in responsible AI guardrails as mitigation categories. This abbreviated list of potential harms is by no means exhaustive or complete for all copilot testing scenarios but only serves as a starting point for discovery and discussion for a specific testing scenario. This list may also grow or be outdated, as the copilot capabilities evolve over time. We also see that ungroundedness of response is simultaneously a capability metric for context-based Q&A that we discussed in the capability section. It shows that there may be overlaps in specific safety and quality testing metrics.

3.4 Other Considerations in Testing and Evaluating Copilots

Testing and evaluation of AI poses unique challenges compared to traditional software development. We will only mention a few. First, there is a paradigm shift in software engineering that is best captured by "Schillace Laws." It is important to recognize that an AI copilot will consist of computer code and models and that the boundary between them is flexible and may change over time as model capabilities mature. This is the gist of the first Schillace Law that a model improves, but the code does not (Maeda and Bolanos 2023). An implication of this law is that testing code and testing model have important differences. Traditional software testing techniques such as unit tests rely on deterministic output from a system, while the system we are measuring and the tool we use to measure it may be by nature, nondeterministic, and thus require appropriate methodologies for proper measurement. Secondly, despite the natural language output, many of the AI systems available in the market are complex and, by nature, a black box to users and copilot builders, who do not yet have a feasible way to understand system output from a causal perspective. There is no guarantee for assertions like "If I input x, system should output y" to work deterministically. Thirdly, the dynamic nature of interactions between the system and the user makes the possible output space very large. This interaction, for example, a multi-turn conversation, could make collecting diverse, representative data for testing and evaluation a difficult task. Lastly, there is a set of biases associated with the use of AI evaluators such as self-bias (preferring response from the same model versus other models or humans) and position bias (preferring certain arbitrary ranking over multiple choices). Care must be taken to use AI evaluators for testing and evaluation of copilots.

Safety and quality trade-off is empirically found (Touvron et al. 2023) to exist in training a foundational model. Such trade-off refers to increasing safety performance of a model may decrease the model capabilities or vice versa. That means, some form of the said trade-off has been made for you as a user of the model. As mentioned earlier, your AI copilot speaks for your brand and your value to your customers. As a result, before you roll out your copilot, it is important to reevaluate this trade-off and align your copilot according to your value preference, perhaps using the life cycle of responsible AI practices we mentioned (Microsoft 2024d). In our experience, we recognize that safety and quality evaluations need to be considered jointly for product decisions, along with other factors. When the effectiveness of the AI capabilities is at odds with the set of human values we associate with safety, it is sometimes helpful to quantify this trade-off on a graph with measurements and find an "optimal" trade-off that aligns with your own value. For example, there are multiple versions of a copilot you have worked on, and they can be represented by different trade-off points on a Pareto frontier, a graph that measures the best trade-offs among several factors, say a frontier representing quality and safety trade-offs. Quantifying these tradeoffs helps you make an informed choice for the best version of copilots to release in alignment with your value preference. For example, given a certain threshold in quality, we should use the version with the highest "safety" scores according to your definition. Sometimes, after better mitigations in place, we may even discover a better frontier of the mitigated versions and observe better quality performance given the same safety thresholds. Also, note that we should always ground this discussion in the appropriate socioeconomic context of the product and that sometimes it may not be possible to find the "best" trade-off. The point of this practice nevertheless is for you to recognize and have the choice to reassert the value preference of your product, instead of the naïve approach to assume that the foundational model is necessarily "ready straight out of the oven." In all, this practice provides another opportunity to design human-AI interaction to augment the role of human agency.

4 Conclusion

In this chapter, we have presented some business and technical considerations for the design and evaluation of two AI copilots in the retail domain. Our systematic approaches to the discussion have been motivated by the business goals of managing desired outcomes and unintended consequences. Drawing on our experience building the copilot templates, we have presented our approaches to designing for human-AI collaboration and ensuring the quality and safety of the AI-generated outputs, with the aim of aligning copilot responses with the product values. We have also shared some of the responsible AI practices that we used to test and mitigate the risks of deploying AI-powered copilots in enterprise settings. We hope that our experiences and insights can inspire and inform business leaders and practitioners who are interested in building enterprise-grade copilots.

We believe that the two copilot templates are just two examples of many promising examples of how AI can augment human productivity in various tasks and scenarios. However, we also acknowledge that there are still many open questions and challenges that need to be addressed in order to ensure the ethical and trustworthy use of AI copilots in real-world contexts. We hope that by sharing our work and learnings, we can motivate and advocate for the continued investment in systematic, human-centric approaches to copilot design and evaluation.

5 AI Disclosure Note

In the process of preparing this chapter, the authors used the following AI models and tools for literature research, structuring of the content, and editing: copilot for Microsoft 365 (https://copilot.microsoft.com/), ChatGPT 3.5 and ChatGPT 4 (via https://chat.openai.com/), Claude.ai (via https://claude.ai/chats), Claude 3 models (https://console.anthropic.com/workbench/ API—with the following models claude-3-haiku-20240307, claude-3-sonnet-20240229, claude-3-opus-20240229), Gemini (https://gemini.google.com/app), and Perplexity.ai (https://www.perplexity.ai/). The authors attest that they hold full responsibility for the text and factual correctness in the chapter above and have fully reviewed references and edited text outputs from AI systems.

References

Achiam J, Agarwal S, Ahmad L, Akkaya I, Aleman FL, Almeida D, Avila Re (2023) Gpt-4 technical report. arXiv preprint arXiv:230308774. https://arxiv.org/abs/2303.08774

Beringer J, Coursaris CK, Léger PM, Karran AJ, Oz B (2022) Teaming models with intelligent systems at the workplace. In: Wirtschaftsinformatik 2022 Proceedings, vol 2. https://aisel.aisnet.org/wi2022/workshops/workshops/2

Bubeck S, Chandrasekaran V, Eldan R, Gehrke J, Horvitz E, Kamar E, Zhang Y (2023) Sparks of artificial general intelligence: Early experiments with gpt-4. arXiv preprint arXiv:230312712

Gao L, Biderman S, Black S, Golding L, Hoppe T, Foster C, Leahy C (2020) The pile: An 800gb dataset of diverse text for language modeling. arXiv preprint arXiv:210100027

Gao Y, Xiong Y, Gao X, Jia K, Pan J, Bi Y, Wang H (2023) Retrieval-augmented generation for large language models: A survey. arXiv preprint arXiv:231210997

Jiang J, Karran AJ, Coursaris CK, Léger PM, Beringer J (2023) A situation awareness perspective on human-ai interaction: Tensions and opportunities. Int J Human Comput Interact 39(9):1789–1806

Maeda J, Bolanos M (2023) Schillace laws of semantic ai. https://learn.microsoft.com/en-us/semantic-kernel/when-to-use-ai/schillace-laws, retrieved April 23, 2024

Microsoft (2024a) Ai services - content filtering. https://learn.microsoft.com/en-us/azure/ai-services/openai/concepts/content-filter

Microsoft (2024b) Copilot template for personalized shopping. https://learn.microsoft.com/en-us/industry/release-plan/2023wave2/cloud-retail/use-shopper-copilot

Microsoft (2024c) Overview of copilot template for store operations. https://learn.microsoft.com/en-us/industry/retail/ai-store-operations/overview-ai-store-operations

Microsoft (2024d) Overview of responsible ai practices for azure openai models. https://learn.microsoft.com/en-us/legal/cognitive-services/openai/overview, retrieved April 23, 2024

OpenAI (2022) Aligning language models to follow instructions. https://openai.com/research/instruction-following, retrieved April 23, 2024

Ovadia O, Brief M, Mishaeli M, Elisha O (2023) Fine-tuning or retrieval? comparing knowledge injection in llms. arXiv preprint arXiv:231205934

Öz B, Karran AJ, Beringer J, Coursaris CK, Léger PM (2023) The dynamics of collaborative decision-making with intelligent systems. In: International Conference on Human-Computer Interaction. Springer Nature Switzerland, pp 167–172

Parnin C, Soares G, Pandita R, Gulwani S, Rich J, Henley AZ (2023) Building your own product copilot: Challenges, opportunities, and needs. arXiv preprint arXiv:231214231

Patel H, Boucher D, Hassan AE, Adams B (2024) A state-of-the-practice release-readiness checklist for generative ai-based software products. IEEE Computer Society

Scale AI (2023) Test & evaluation: The right approach for safe, secure, and trustworthy ai. https://scale.com/blog/test-and-evaluation-white-paper

Sellen A, Horvitz E (2023) The rise of the ai co-pilot: Lessons for design from aviation and beyond. arXiv preprint arXiv:231114713

Slack D, Wang J, Semenenko D, Park K, Berrios D, Hendryx S (2023) A holistic approach for test and evaluation of large language models. https://static.scale.com/uploads/6019a18f03a4ae003acb1113/test-and-evaluation.pdf

Suleyman M, Bhaskar M (2023) The coming wave: technology, power, and the twenty-first century's greatest dilemma. Crown, USA

Touvron H, Martin L, Stone K, Albert P, Almahairi A, Babaei Y, et al. (2023) Llama 2: Open foundation and fine-tuned chat models. arXiv preprint arXiv:230709288

Conversational AI in Finance: A Case Study with MSUFCU

Benjamin Maxim

Abstract Michigan State University Federal Credit Union (MSUFCU) first launched a member chatbot, Fran, in 2019 and learned many lessons. One of the most important lessons is that AI, while using technology, is not really a technology project but instead a service- or operations-oriented project enabled by technology. MSUFCU followed up with an internal chatbot, Gene, with a new partner to support their employees during the COVID-19 pandemic during an unprecedented volume of member contacts to the call center and live chat agents. After conducting a pilot through their innovation lab, MSUFCU calculated that Gene could automate over 2,000 employee-to-employee transactions each month, allowing for a considerable lift in productivity when hiring was not an option. This new partner's platform allowed MSUFCU to manage the chatbot learning in a new way, allowing our employees to train the chatbot and improve its accuracy to above 95%, allowing them to be more responsive to their employees' needs. These improvements gave MSUFCU the confidence to switch providers to Fran as well, which has led to Fran being responsible for over 33 FTEs each day, which in the post-pandemic talent squeeze has been extremely valuable. The chapter will also cover what goes into managing conversational AI operationally and strategically, as well as future opportunities and use cases MSUFCU explores for Fran, including voice and more secure banking transactions. The chapter will also discuss the use of Gene, a bot that uses They/Them pronouns and whose avatar has an androgynous look with colorful hair and ambiguous skin tone, to support MSUFCU's diversity, equity, and inclusion initiatives and how the team involved MSUFCU's employee resource group and DEI council to make intentional decisions in this space.

B. Maxim (✉)
Michigan State University Federal Credit Union, East Lansing, MI, USA
e-mail: bmaxim@msufcu.org

C. K. Coursaris et al. (eds.), *The Design of Human-Centered Artificial Intelligence for the Workplace*, Progress in IS, https://doi.org/10.1007/978-3-031-83512-4_21

1 Introduction

The banking industry has a long history of adopting and thriving following new waves of technological advancement, redefining customer experiences to keep pace with consumer expectations. Financial institutions introduced ATMs in the 1960s and electronic, card-based payments in the 1970s. The 2000s saw broad adoption of 24/7 online banking, followed by the spread of mobile-based "banking on the go" in the 2010s (Biswas et al. 2021). According to IDC, worldwide spending on AI-centric systems will reach $154 billion in 2023 and is forecasted to increase to over $300 billion in 2026. The two industries leading the way throughout the forecast are banking and retail, with 13.4% and 12.8% of spending on AI-centric systems, respectively (Shirer 2023). While technology has transformed the banking industry, it is also disrupting it. The rise of fintech and the adoption of fintech by nonfinancial service providers are proving to be huge competition. Banks now have no choice but to increase their tech adoption and cater more digitized services to their customers if they want to remain relevant. In fact, according to an Economic Intelligence Unit survey, 77% of bankers believe that the success or failure of a bank will be attributed to their ability to tap into the powers of AI (Raj 2023). With the recent rise of ChatGPT in the media and popular culture, new attention and excitement have been brought to the application of conversational AI across many industries. After launching in November 2022, ChatGPT had gained 100 million users by January of this year, making it the fastest growing and most speedily adopted app yet—it took Instagram more than 2 years to reach the same kind of numbers and TikTok 9 months (McBride 2023). Financial institutions will be racing to see how quickly they can leverage the technology behind ChatGPT, generative AI, and large language models (LLM) to enhance their conversational and other AI offerings further.

This chapter discusses the importance of trust and customer experience as key components of conversational AI's role as an intelligent system in financial services. Based on Michigan State University Federal Credit Union's conversational AI journey, including the challenges they encountered along the way and the lessons learned overcoming them, it provides practical advice to business leaders seeking to explore their own implementations of conversational AI. There will also be a discussion of future applications and use cases for conversational AI, with the prospect of potential inclusions of generative AI and LLMs in the mix.

1.1 MSUFCU Background

Michigan State University Federal Credit Union (MSUFCU) is a $7.4+ billion asset-size financial institution with over 1,100 employees serving 340,000+ members headquartered in East Lansing, Michigan. Founded in 1937 out of a desk drawer in the physical plant by a group of faculty at Michigan State University, MSUFCU has had a long tradition of pioneering emerging technologies in financial services, including being early adopters of ATMs, Visa cards, online banking, and mobile banking to a name a few. So naturally, when MSUFCU set out to enhance its member and employee experience in 2018, one intelligent system stood out: conversational artificial intelligence (AI), aka the chatbot. As MSUFCU initially set out on its conversational AI journey, they devised three strategic goals to achieve: extend service hours, provide scalable human+digital support to members, and improve the employee experience.

Due to the limited availability and affordability of skilled data scientists and developers, the decision was made to find a partner to help bring conversation AI to the market as quickly as possible. MSUFCU set out to find a partner with a trained banking model for conversational AI, and once secured, they set out to deliver a member service chatbot to their members. MSUFCU launched their member experience conversational AI (or "chatbot") Fran in the fall of 2019 and has been an industry leader in conversational AI ever since. MSUFCU followed up with Fran by launching an employee experience conversational AI, Gene, first as a prototype tested in their innovation lab, The Lab at MSUFCU, over the summer of 2020 in response to the COVID-19 pandemic and the stress it put on their member service employees and the quick shift to provide member service fully remotely while branch offices were mandated to close temporarily. Following a successful launch and implementation of Gene with a new conversational AI partner, Boost.ai, MSUFCU decided to relaunch Fran in the fall of 2021 on the same platform as Gene to take advantage of the "shared brain" opportunity that could now exist between both the external and internal conversational AIs. MSUFCU has continuously sought to improve the experience of its members and employees through the combined power of Fran and Gene. It is currently exploring ways to leverage generative AI and LLMs to provide scalable next-generation human+digital experiences.

2 Trust in Banking and Conversational AI

Trust is one of the most important factors in the relationship between a financial institution and its consumers. It is a key focus for financial institutions during their digital transformation journeys. If we narrow it down, trust falls into two categories: delivering consistently exceptional and personalized customer experiences and protecting customers and their data from cyberattacks (Hovsepian 2023). With recent advancements like natural language processing and generative AI, conversational AI is evolving to support more humanlike relationships—better able to build rapport, show empathy, and drive collaboration in mutually beneficial experiences for companies and consumers (Cailleteau 2022). As conversational AI takes on larger customer service roles in financial services and other service industries, chatbots need to ensure they are bringing the trust consumers have grown to expect in their banking relationships. According to a Genpact report, the number of consumers who were comfortable with companies using AI to access personal data—if it improves their customer experience—jumped from 30 percent in 2017 to 54 percent in 2019 (Sullivan 2023).

Machines have long been trying to establish trust with humans. Would you get on an elevator or an airplane if you did not trust that safety concerns were thoroughly demonstrated through product design and engineering with the help of government and industry best practices and regulations? Intelligent machines need to work even harder to overcome the gap in trustworthiness because their "intelligence" implies a level of autonomous decision-making that adds another layer that negatively affects human's ability to trust them. Human trust typically comes from understanding each other's motivations, reasoning methods, and the likelihood of how each party may react to various situations. This level of understanding comes from a thesis of similarity. Since both parties are human, they presume they share enough commonalities to produce a general inclination to "do the right thing" despite lacking quantifiable metrics. With AI, the foundation of similarity is missing. Trust is earned based on track record, transparency, and understanding of how the machine will react to new situations (Fayyad 2022). The accuracy of information returned by AI can be one of the greatest tools for building trustworthiness between humans and intelligent machines.

2.1 Ensuring Trust with Conversational Design at MSUFCU

To ensure their members would trust Fran, MSUFCU addressed security concerns by selecting an AI engine partner with a similar high-level security posture and focused on delivering an exceptional customer experience by thoroughly monitoring accuracy metrics and using conversational design to bridge the similarity perception. MSUFCU made several important conversational design considerations to increase the trust a user would have in the chatbot. Fran has an avatar with a specific look meant to personify MSUFCU's personality and culture of superior service to its members. Fran was given a professional, knowledgeable look that conveyed intelligence while remaining warm, welcoming, and approachable. Another critical factor in the conversational design was to match the tone, formality, and word choice that one of our employees would make. A conversational AI is an extension of an organization's brand and should be purposely designed to reflect those values. Also, some conversations or idioms are unique to a company's customer base and should be considered during the conversational design phase. Many of MSUFU's members are affiliated with Michigan State University (MSU), and a common idiom is that when someone says "Go Green!" a person is expected to respond with "Go White!" indicating they are a "true fan" of the MSU Spartans. Many of their members often sign off their chats with live agents with "Go Green!" and the live agents instinctively know to respond with "Go White!". It was important to train Fran to be able to handle this situation and respond with the appropriate "Go White!" response (see Fig. 1). It is not enough to automate the words of the conversation; a successful

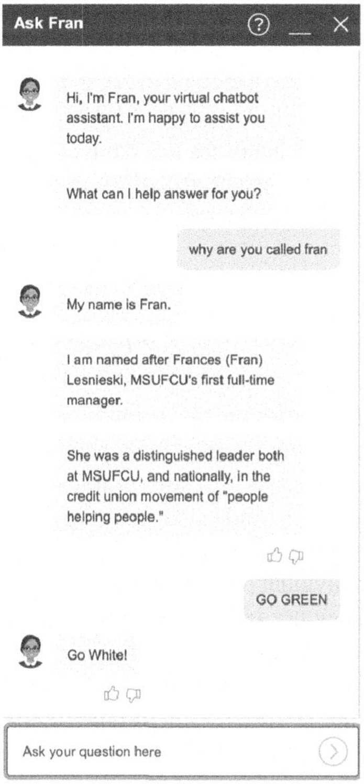

Fig. 1 MSUFCU's Fran answers questions about her backstory and local idioms to establish trust with their members

conversational AI will automate the entire experience gaining the user's trust over time.

One thing discovered early on is that their members had more grace for error when it was clear that they were interacting with a bot instead of a bot pretending to be a live human agent. Going through the conversational design process, it was essential to be transparent with users that Fran was a bot—she was given a backstory. From the beginning, she had "frustration detection" built in to detect frustration and transfer the member to a live human agent. When Fran was rolled out in October 2019, she was launched in the same context as any new employee, e.g., "I am new here and am still learning." If she were not able to understand an inquiry from a member, she would respond by asking if the user could rephrase the query—this had two purposes: one was to get the member the answer they were seeking, and the other was to build a larger training dataset to help improve the response accuracy by understanding the different variations of words that members may use to query the same information. One of the greatest things about a conversational AI, in terms of learning what it needs to know, is that people will ask what they perceive the AI to be able to answer or process.

In 2022, Fran held 106,136 conversations with members, the equivalent workload of fifteen human live agents. Since her original launch, Fran has learned to answer over 1,646 questions. MSUFCU has found that Fran has established trust with their members, as evidenced by the current human chat escalation rate of 2.23% across over 106,000 chats in 2022. Fast forward to June 2023, Fran has reached an accuracy rate of 98% (up from 81.1% postlaunch) on over 200,000 member conversations and is now handling the equivalent of thirty-three human live agents (Boost.ai 2023). The consistent growth of usage by MSUFCU's members demonstrates that Fran is establishing trust.

2.2 Gaining Employee Support

The adoption of an intelligent system is often met with feelings that "things are changing," going from personal human service face-to-face to impersonal robotic service. As a result, employees feel like they are being replaced. New Qualtrics research finds that, among workers, executives are most looking forward to the potential impact of AI, with 64% characterizing AI as exciting. Only 39% of individual contributors, on the other hand, say the potential impact of AI is exciting. They are more likely to say it is scary (46%). In contrast, 30% of executives say it is scary. Two-thirds of executives expect AI to impact the overall employee experience positively; only 35% of individual contributors share that optimism, and 31% say AI will have a negative effect (Business Wire 2023). This research highlights that, as leaders, it is important to address this fear in your employees to achieve your expected results. MSUFCU found that as they rolled out their conversational AI to members, it was important to highlight the role Fran would play in helping to augment the experience in a human+digital system where Fran would handle the more mundane, repeatable answers that the employees themselves admittedly hated answering hundreds of times a day such as "What is the routing number?". The employees would then be given more engaging work in handling the more complex member queries and situations that required human intelligence to creatively problem solve and provide personalized human service. The leaders at MSUFCU also made it clear that as the number of members grew exponentially each year, combined with their ever-increasing digital channel adoption, it would not be possible to scale with just human agents alone.

Even with the careful consideration taken in the conversational design to promote trust, there still lingered an initial perception by MSUFCU employees that their members would not trust Fran and would always need the support of live agents. Fran was rolled out in a limited capacity and was only offered for three hours a day when the live agent teams were in their least busy time of day. Fran stayed in this state for the first several months postlaunch, and it was not until the extreme circumstances of the COVID-19 pandemic that the team at MSUFCU was willing to open Fran up 24/7/365. Their members responded very well to this access to Fran around the clock, allowing MSUFCU to learn what members needed and at what times of day. For instance, due to declined transactions, one of the most popular service categories for Fran late night is members looking for support using their cards. Fran also sees upticks in seasonal questions, such as tax-related information in the first quarter as members look to file their taxes, as well as when new products roll out members turn to Fran to get their answers first before contacting a human agent. The top queries are almost always consistent and are truly information that does not need a human response like "What is the routing number?" or "How do I apply for a loan?" which demonstrates that MSUFCU's members are looking to Fran to be the quickest way to find the information they are seeking.

To the employee question of whether they are still needed and to highlight how conversational AI works in conjunction with humans to deliver member support, the previously mentioned 2.23% human escalation rate was still 2,366 human-assisted chats in 2022. Furthermore, with Fran answering over 106,000 chats in 2022, the live agent team still answered 314,000 plus member chats. From a business perspective, this is a win-win as the employees receive the support they need without the organization needing to hire additional employees. The efficiency ratio has increased dramatically as a result of the intelligent automation found within conversational AI, which provides always-on, scalable human+digital support for their members.

3 Human+Digital

Without a doubt, the future of work will be shaped by AI, but it does not mean the end of human workers in financial services. The history of work—mainly since the Industrial Revolution—is the history of people outsourcing their labor to machines. While that began with rote, repetitive physical tasks like weaving, machines have evolved to the point where they can now do what we might think of as complex cognitive work, such as math equations, recognizing language and speech, and writing. Machines, thus, seem ready to replicate the work of our minds, not just our bodies. In the twenty-first century, AI is evolving to be superior to humans in many tasks, making us seem ready to outsource our intelligence to technology (De Cremer and Kasparov 2021). Humans still maintain the capacity to make decisions outside of the predefined rules and procedures needed to train conversational AIs, a necessary skill in customer service when addressing complex or unique situations brought forward by customers. Human+digital is the augmentation of human service with digital self-service experiences ranging from simple web forms to collect customer information for processing by back-office workers to complex machine learning (ML) and AI models to support customer service agents.

This type of AI is also known as "augmented intelligence," where AI does not replace humans but supports them in their work. IEEE defines augmented intelligence as a subsection of AI machine learning developed to enhance human intelligence rather than operate independently of or outright replace it. It is designed to improve human decision-making and, by extension, actions taken in response to improved decisions. Unlike the traditional view of AI as an autonomous system operating without human involvement, augmented intelligence uses machine learning and deep learning to provide humans with actionable data (IEEE 2022).

3.1 Augmenting the Employee Experience at MSUFCU

Fresh off the Fran launch, MSUFCU was eager to address some lessons learned and capitalize on the innovative spirit reinvigorated at their organization. A streamlined process was needed to improve the ability of the credit union to partner with innovative partners, including startups, in a risk-mitigated way. Their innovation center, The Lab at MSUFCU, was formed in 2020 to accelerate ideas with partners and incubate homegrown ideas. One such idea came from another conversational AI, which focused on serving the employees to help them serve the members more efficiently. In the spring of 2020, due to the COVID-19 pandemic, MSUFCU's branches were closed temporarily, leading to voice call and live chat volume that increased 130 plus percent month over month as members had to look for new ways to contact MSUFCU. Fran going to full 24/7 deployment helped alleviate some of the volume, but more needed to be done, and due to the uncertain nature of the pandemic's effect on their business, MSUFCU paused hiring. The lab at MSUFCU sought out ideas and partners to find solutions to improve operational efficiency, bring relief to the employees in these areas, and restore a higher level of member service. MSUFCU came across a new conversational AI partner who pitched them the idea of building an internal knowledge base chatbot.

The main challenge the internal knowledge base chatbot set out to solve was quickly delivering these long, hard-to-find procedure documents that required lengthy reading while a member would be on hold. The conversational AI was designed so that these procedures would be set up as a walkthrough for employees to choose their own adventure. For example, instead of just seeing a twenty-page document about how to help a member apply for a loan, the bot will walk the employee through the process step by step. Another challenge AI solves is the consistent delivery and accuracy of the information, which helps aid in compliance, among other benefits. In addition to the SharePoint-based documents, MSUFCU had helplines for employees to contact, which were staffed by senior employees and department trainers. Depending on who was helping them on a given day, the employee could receive different answers from the helplines due to the human element. As a highly regulated industry, it is important to follow document procedures as written and intended and ensure the AI does not editorialize the procedures. Lastly, it was proposed that the internal knowledge chatbot would be instrumental in onboarding employees new in a role as many credit union employees move between areas as they advance in their careers. Ultimately, the internal knowledge base conversational AI would support the member service employees in serving the MSUFCU members, quickly providing accurate information to improve the speed and quality of service delivered during member interactions.

Since this second conversation AI was being run as an innovation pilot, MSUFCU invited sixty employees across various member service areas to use the chatbot for 4 weeks and surveyed them on their experience. The participating employees were also told that the more they used the bot, the more the bot could learn and expand their knowledge. It was also another touchpoint for MSUFCU to reiterate that this type of automation was coming for their jobs, but rather an opportunity to assist them in completing their work more efficiently. The employees who participated in the pilot were surveyed to understand the bot's efficacy and the employees' perceived value in their work. From week one to week four, the answers to "How Beneficial Would the Chatbot be for day-to-day work?" improved from 50% of participants stating it is "Very or Moderately Beneficial" to 100%. The same was true for the question, "How beneficial is learning about CU Procedures, Products, and Services?" There was an increase from 50% to 100% from week one to week four. Furthermore, for the question "How beneficial for onboarding to a new role at the CU," there was a slight increase from 69.23% in week one to 75% in week four (zero participating employees onboarded to a new department during the four-week pilot period).

During the analysis of the pilot, it was determined that Gene should be able to automate over 2,000 (about 1,300 calls, 700 chats) employee-to-employee interactions each month. ROI calculations were made to justify the implementation and annual costs for a full-scale deployment of the internal knowledge bot. Using the assumption that each call interaction to a helpline took about 7 minutes on average, with two employee's time being aggregated (3.5 minutes each), the measurement found that a similar helpline chat interaction would take about 5 minutes between two employees (2.5 minutes each). Doing the math to figure out the cost savings in employee time based on the average salaries for the positions involved led MSUFCU to the realization that more would be saved in employee time (roughly 2,500 hours per year, which is more than one FTE) than the conversational AI cost to implement and maintain. Fast forward to 2022, Gene handles an average of 3,582 employee conversations per month or 4,300+ hours (or over two FTE) saved in employee time annually. Since launching to all employees in January 2021, Gene has also learned to answer employee questions on 2,201 topics. Successfully augmenting their employees with conversational AI has served as a proof point for MSUFCU to embrace a Human+Digital member experience as an essential part of their growth strategy.

4 Challenges and Lessons Learned

Throughout their multiyear journey with conversational AI, MSUFCU encountered and overcame several challenges. These will be discussed as lessons learned in this next section to provide practical advice to any leader progressing through their own journey with conversational AI. In addition to the specific lessons learned by MSUFCU, two key concepts of conversational AI that present challenges that should be addressed from the onset are customer trust and experience. To reiterate, trust is built between humans based on the thesis of similarity. This notion of similarity is missing in a purely intelligent system like conversational AI because trust is not just given, as one of the entities is not a human. To overcome this, a conversational AI should focus on providing highly accurate answers to build trust with the user, and the system should get the user to a human agent whenever needed or requested in an augmented intelligence system. MSUFCU confirmed these were both important aspects of conversational AI during their launch and relaunch of Fran. When Fran was first launched, she could only accurately answer member queries just above 80 percent of the time, which is about the lowest acceptable rate their members would tolerate. The scale of messages being addressed by Fran now, at an 81.1% accuracy, would require many more agents to be available for live agent failover, and the system would not have the same positive effect on member experience as it does today. When Fran was first launched, Fran stated to members that she was still learning, and if member frustration was detected, an agent was brought in immediately. MSUFCU has dedicated resources to training Fran, making her over 98% accurate.

With two successful conversational AI deployments behind them, MSUFCU was ready to take the next steps in their intelligent system journey and decided to create a new position called an AI content administrator to manage their bots. Much like a company would not set up a website and never update the content, it is essential to treat conversational AI as a delivery channel like a website. To facilitate this delivery channel approach, MSUFCU has two AI content managers. They review the conversations with the bots and update training data and content when the accuracy is not what it should be on a response or if a user reports an inaccurate response to their query. These AI content managers also ensure that employees and members can access new information, such as organizational news and new product updates. Moreover, they train the bots to handle the new conversational workflows.

Many leaders in the financial services industry perceive conversational AI as technically complex. They often assign their CIO or other technology leaders to explore deploying a chatbot to respond to high call center volume. Such an assignment is one of the biggest mistakes a company can make. Technology indeed enables conversational AI to work, but this is a service or operations function that is being automated as an augmented intelligence system and should be assigned to a COO, CXO, or other customer service leader to champion and ensure the AI performs as their customer base would expect from their human employees. MSUFCU made this error in their first rollout of Fran, tasking their information technology team with running the project. As a result, much of the early focus of the work was on the technology portions of the project. Being a financial institution, one of the first decisions was whether the servers should be on-premise or hosted in the cloud. At the time, cloud adoption was very low in the financial sector, especially in credit unions, due to the sensitivity of the consumer data held by the financial institutions. MSUFCU chose the on-premise server option, which required new physical hardware with a top-of-the-line GPU to handle the AI training. In retrospect, this added complexity to the AI training process and model validation of the conversational AI engine that would be the "brain" of the intelligent system that would become known as Fran—a cloud approach would have decreased time to market by several weeks. As the project progressed, it was clear that the focus needed to shift to the conversational design of the AI to focus on earning trust between Fran and their members. She was given a backstory and had "frustration detection" built in from the beginning that would detect frustration and transfer the member to a live human agent, both elements that help build the trust necessary for Fran to take on a larger role in the human+digital experience at MSUFCU.

With the development of Gene, MSUFCU had the chance to try again, not making the same mistakes as they did in their first deployment of conversational AI. This was MSUFCU's second conversational AI project, and they knew a few tricks to accelerate the process. First, it was decided that this chatbot would take advantage of the speed to market a cloud deployment could achieve. Secondly, this project was set up as an innovation pilot as part of their innovation lab to take advantage of the newly launched innovation process to put minimal viable products in front of end users (in this case, MSUFCU employees) as quickly as possible through a rapid prototyping process. Most importantly, the project was treated as an operations and member service project instead of a technology-driven one. These key decisions being made upfront allowed for a quick ten-day build-out of a conversational AI using the most access documents in the existing Microsoft SharePoint-based internal knowledge base. In addition, running this initiative initially as a pilot allowed MSUFCU to build trust between Gene and their employees by giving them a chance to try the technology and contribute to its success.

Following the pilot to properly roll out a conversational AI, it was time to design the bot's persona, avatar, and conversational experience. Another important lesson learned following a presentation at AI World 2019 in Boston introducing MSUFCU's conversational AI to an audience of AI practitioners, researchers, and technologists, where a member of the audience approached the MSUFCU team to ask why their chatbot was female and why all chatbots seem to be made female. Once Fran's backstory was shared, it was clear that there was more reason behind our decision than just the perception that female bots are more "pleasing and subservient" to their users. When developing Gene, MSUFCU purposely set out to support their Diversity, Equity, and Inclusion (DEI) initiatives by giving Gene they/them pronouns. Gene's avatar was also given an androgynous look and ambiguous skin tone following consultation with their employee-lead DEI council. Gene's name came from a mix of references to DNA, as Gene is part of the cultural fabric of MSUFCU, and Gene is also short for Genius (see Fig. 2).

One interesting item discovered was how MSUFCU noticed their employees interacted with Gene differently than their members conversed with Fran. When a member asks Fran, "How do I apply for a loan?" their employees state "loan application" and follow the quick prompts to get the answer, almost like a keyword search. So, as Gene was trained and content was added, it was important to ensure that quick queries were covered. Quick action buttons were added to Gene's responses so the employees could quickly get the information they needed. The employees have also provided MSUFCU feedback that they would like to see Gene

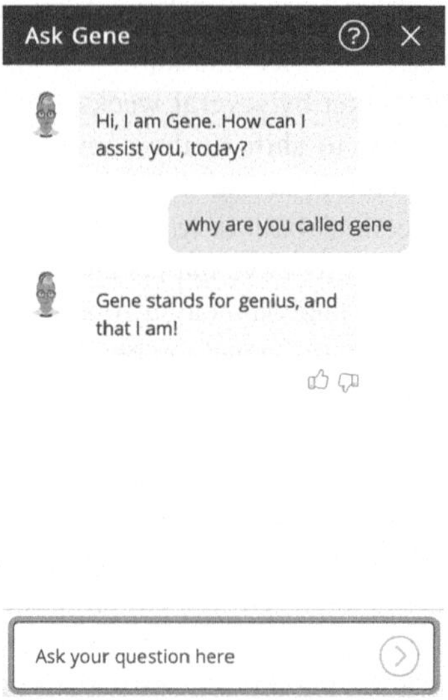

Fig. 2 MSUFCU's internal knowledge base conversational AI called Gene

expand to be a full-on MSUFCU employee virtual assistant, growing beyond the initial internal knowledge base and acting more like Apple's Siri or Amazon's Alexa.

Finally, following Gene's deployment and creation of the AI team, MSUFCU decided to relaunch Fran on the same cloud-based platform Gene was using to allow them to share one brain where information could be given a different context based on the audience member (Fran) or employee (Gene). This consolidation also made it easier for those managing the conversational AI content to have one singular platform to maintain the bots. MSUFCU, in early 2023, launched a series of authenticated intents to Fran, allowing their members to access information like their account balances and recent transactions. This launch is the first step toward MSUFCU's vision that Fran will serve as a financial guide for its members, drawing attention to personalized insights and recommendations based on their unique situations. In the future, Fran will learn about each member's habits and be proactive in helping them carry out their digital banking transactions. Fran would also, in the future, be tapped into a more connected intelligence system that could be more autonomous in carrying out more complex transactions like applying for and funding a loan requested by the member. Gene will be connected to more complex systems, such as the service desk and human resources information system (HRIS), to automate additional employee support functions, allowing for greater efficiency ratios and helping MSUFCU keep up with its expected growth in members and employees over the years.

5 Future of Conversational AI in Financial Services

MSUFCU learned many fantastic lessons throughout their journey with conversational AI, which is fast becoming one of the most visible use cases for an intelligent system in the financial industry. Many of these AI solutions are in their infancy, and as data quality, governance, and modeling improve, so will the ability for these systems to become more situationally aware, creating better, more personalized experiences and allowing for a deeper level of trust to be built between customers and conversational AI. Perhaps, the most promising advancement in this direction is the rise of generative AI, as seen by the hype around ChatGPT launched by OpenAI in November 2022. Generative AI differs from conversational AI because it can generate content based on user inputs, whereas conversational AI typically works through a preconstructed trained dataset. Just like the beginning of the web or smartphones, the ChatGPT technology provides huge advancements in one fell swoop, and the software industry often needs years to catch up to unlock the true potential of such a technology.

Generative AI can help humans create much more content than they can on their own. Instead of scouring scores of documents or broadly searching the internet, generative AI can summarize large sets of data into easy-to-read guides of information that can then be used to narrow the original scope. Humans have boundless creativity. The challenge of communicating their concepts in written or visual form restricts vast numbers of people from contributing new ideas. Generative AI can remove this barrier by augmenting their creativity, helping to promote divergent thinking. Moreover, generative AI's greatest potential is not replacing humans; it is to assist humans in their efforts to create hitherto unimaginable solutions (Eapen et al. 2023). This divergent thinking and augmented creativity will lead to a boom in innovation in financial services, with fintech and financial institutions partnering to create the future of banking and how customers interact with their financial institutions.

LLMs are not the silver bullet; instead, they are another layer to the technology stack to help create a truly augmented intelligence system, making the human workers better at their jobs and allowing them to provide a key piece in a human+digital system. Implementing ChatGPT into banking products can pose some challenges, first of all, safeguarding the security and privacy of customer data. Banks must ensure that the chat interface is secure and that sensitive data is protected from unauthorized access or disclosure. With ChatGPT being an open-source technology, it may be important to consider other LLMs that provide enterprise-grade security. Until then, the use cases in financial services could be limited to those that do not require sensitive customer data to function effectively. Some companies are taking early steps in providing a connection to ChatGPT technology with sensitive information either removed or deidentified to allow data privacy to remain intact. Another challenge is training ChatGPT to understand the language and terminology specific to the banking industry. Banks must provide relevant training data and integrate the model with their existing systems to ensure that it can provide accurate and appropriate responses to user queries (Kreger 2023).

MSUFCU is using generative AI and LLMs to train Fran and Gene better, allowing their AI content managers to focus on providing richer experiences with the most accessed or most important queries for their members and employees. They can still get highly accurate answers by pointing to generative AI on their website or knowledge base to have greater coverage and accuracy of answers for both Fran and Gene. As MSUFCU and the rest of the industry experiment with use cases for generative AI, one should expect to see a number of fintechs spring up in the next few years to take advantage of generative AI and apply novel financial use cases. MSUFCU will be ready to capitalize on this when it comes to fruition, but until then, a parting word from Fran and Gene: "Go Green!".

References

Biswas S, Carson B, Chung V, Singh S, Thomas R (2021) Ai bank of the future: can banks meet the AI Challenge? Tech. rep., McKinsey & Company, New York. https://www.mckinsey.com/~/media/mckinsey/industries/financial%20services/our%20insights/building%20the%20ai%20bank%20of%20the%20future/building-the-ai-bank-of-the-future.pdf

Boostai (2023) Meet fran, the credit union virtual agent with a 98% resolution rate. https://www.boost.ai/case-studies/meet-fran-the-credit-union-virtual-agent-with-a-98-resolution-rate, [Online; accessed 2024-03-12]

Business Wire (2023) Ai generates excitement and fear as employees worry about job security. https://www.businesswire.com/news/home/20230613882872/en/AI-Generates-Excitement-and-Fear-as-Employees-Worry-about-Job-Security

Cailleteau L (2022) Building trust into conversational AI solutions. Research Report, Accenture. https://www.accenture.com/us-en/insights/cloud/conversational-ai. journalAbbreviation: Accenture

De Cremer D, Kasparov G (2021) AI should augment human intelligence, not replace it. Harv Bus Rev 18(1):1–8

Eapen T, Finkenstadt DJ, Folk J, Venkataswamy L (2023) How generative AI can augment human creativity. Harv Bus Rev 101(4)

Fayyad U (2022) Toward trustworthy AI: bridging the trust gap between humans and intelligent machines. https://www.forbes.com/sites/forbestechcouncil/2022/03/29/toward-trustworthy-ai-bridging-the-trust-gap-between-humans-and-intelligent-machines/, journalAbbreviation: Forbes

Hovsepian M (2023) Why trust is the most powerful 5-letter word in banking. https://www.forbes.com/sites/forbesfinancecouncil/2023/01/31/why-trust-is-the-most-powerful-5-letter-word-in-banking/, journalAbbreviation: Forbes

IEEE (2022) What is augmented intelligence? https://digitalreality.ieee.org/publications/what-is-augmented-intelligence. journalAbbreviation: IEEE Digital Reality

Kreger A (2023) Chatgpt use cases in the future banking. https://www.finextra.com/blogposting/24314/chatgpt-use-cases-in-the-future-banking. journalAbbreviation: Finextra

McBride J (2023) Fintech futures jobs: three ways generative AI is being used in financial services. https://www.fintechfutures.com/2023/06/fintech-futures-jobs-three-ways-generative-ai-is-being-used-in-financial-services/. journalAbbreviation: FinTech Futures

Raj A (2023) As Fintech thrives, can AI make or break the banking industry? https://techwireasia.com/2023/04/as-fintech-thrives-can-ai-make-or-break-the-banking-industry/. journalAbbreviation: TechWire Asia

Shirer M (2023) Worldwide spending on AI-centric systems forecast to reach $154 Billion in 2023, According to IDC. Pobrane z: https://www.idc.com/getdoc.jsp

Sullivan M (2023) Banking customers will embrace AI if they trust what's behind the curtain. https://www.genpact.com/insight/banking-customers-will-embrace-ai-if-they-trust-whats-behind-the-curtain. journalAbbreviation: Genpact

Intelligent Platform Monitoring to Aid Security Officers in Public Transit Stations

Masamoto Tanabiki and Yota Yamamura

Abstract Two hazards lurk on station platforms and inside stations: accidents caused by people falling off and accidents caused by congestion. This chapter describes how image sensing technology (Image AI) is used to solve these problems, using two systems installed in train stations in Japan as examples. To ensure safety and security in the station, it is necessary to use a system using Image AI that can constantly monitor the situation and detect abnormalities in real time. However, use cases for a fully autonomous system that does not require human workloads are not currently worked on. To prevent train delays and on-site confusion caused by misjudgment of Image AI, the company is working to ensure safety in the entire system that combines people and technology, such as taking actual action after an operator decides. In short, Image AI is used as a function to support human judgment. Future technological advances are expected to speed up the actual action.

1 Introduction

Two hazards lurk on train station platforms and in stations. The first is falling from platforms. According to a survey by the Ministry of Land, Infrastructure, Transport and Tourism of Japan (MLIT), there were 2,887 cases of falls from station platforms and 160 cases of personal injury on platforms in Japan in 2019 (Ministry of Land, Infrastructure, Transport and Tourism of Japan 2020). The most common causes of falling from platforms are drunken passengers, visually impaired people, and people using smartphones while walking (Morimoto and Wada 2017; Tsujimoto et al. 2021). To overcome this problem, more station platforms are being equipped with automatic doors, but as of 2021, 1002 stations had them installed, compared to 9024 stations in total (Ministry of Land, Infrastructure, Transport and Tourism of Japan 2024). Although the installation of automatic doors is urgently needed to

M. Tanabiki · Y. Yamamura (✉)
Panasonic Connect Co., Ltd., Yokohama, Kanagawa, Japan
e-mail: tanabiki.masamoto@jp.panasonic.com; yamamura.yota@jp.panasonic.com

C. K. Coursaris et al. (eds.), *The Design of Human-Centered Artificial Intelligence for the Workplace*, Progress in IS, https://doi.org/10.1007/978-3-031-83512-4_22

prevent accidents on station platforms, the cost per station on one Japanese railroad line is estimated to be about one billion yen (East Japan Railway Company 2008), and such high costs make it difficult to install them at all stations as quickly as possible.

The second hazard leading to accidents is human congestion. Due to recent urban development, the central city's population is on the rise (Ministry of Internal Affairs and Communications of Japan 2016; Yamagami 2003), and morning and evening commuter congestion has become apparent at major stations. In addition, many people gather at stations for large-scale events, causing congestion. When large numbers of people crowd into a station, there is a risk of accidents, such as people falling from platforms onto the tracks or falling downstairs (Morita et al. 2013), and in summer, there is a risk of heat stroke. For large-scale events, the event organizer, police, and railroad operators work together to establish a security plan, and security guards are stationed at key locations to prevent accidents. For congestion during commuting, many station staff and volunteers guide passengers to ensure safe operations. These measures can be taken because congestion can be predicted in advance (Morimoto and Wada 2017; Tanouchi et al. 2022). Still, there are no measures to deal with sudden congestion caused by changes in operating conditions, such as weather, natural disasters, or train trouble. However, it is difficult to determine whether or not congestion should be dealt with because the judgment depends on the staff member's skill (Yoneji et al. 2017).

We have worked on solving these two issues using image-sensing technology (Image AI). In this chapter, we introduce the details of the system and the process of installing it at the actual site based on a case study of solving this issue.

2 Example of System Installation

The following two systems were installed in train stations. The first is a fall detection system that detects falls from station platforms. The second is a congestion detection system. This system detects congestion in the station to prevent people from falling over or getting confused. Both the fall detection system and the congestion detection system have been put into actual operation at several stations of several railroad operating companies.

2.1 Fall Detection System

As mentioned earlier, installing automatic doors is costly, so a system was installed that uses camera images to detect a fall and notify the operator, thereby stopping the train before an accident occurs.

Image AI used in this system may be processed on a device attached to the camera itself or on an edge server that transmits and acquires images from the

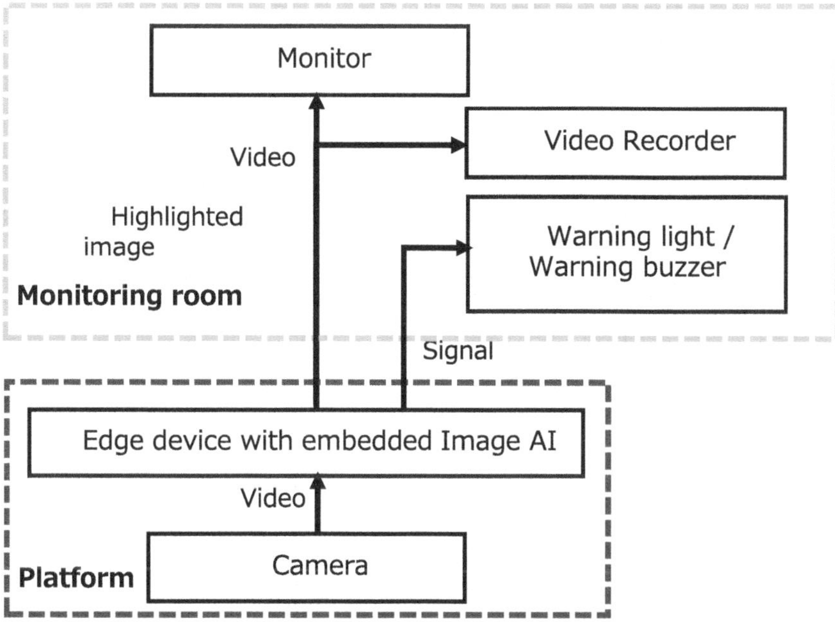

Fig. 1 System overview: Image AI is integrated into the device attached to the camera

camera. The former is often used for processing simple functions, while the latter is often used when more advanced processing is required. Figure 1 shows an example system when Image AI is integrated into the device attached to the camera.

Next, this system's detection workflow and system functions are grouped into situation awareness (SA) (Endsley 1995) and decision-making (see Fig. 2). This chapter interprets Endsley's SA levels as follows.

- Level 1: Detect
  Operators can detect the presence of current people.
- Level 2: Comprehend
  Operators can comprehend the status of people.
- Level 3: Project
  Operators can project the following state change in people.

Detect

This system acquires camera images that meet the following conditions to detect falls.

- The camera must be placed near the ceiling, where the edge of the platform and the tracks are in the angle of view and where it does not obstruct the passage to capture the area where the fall is to be detected (see Figs. 3 and 4).

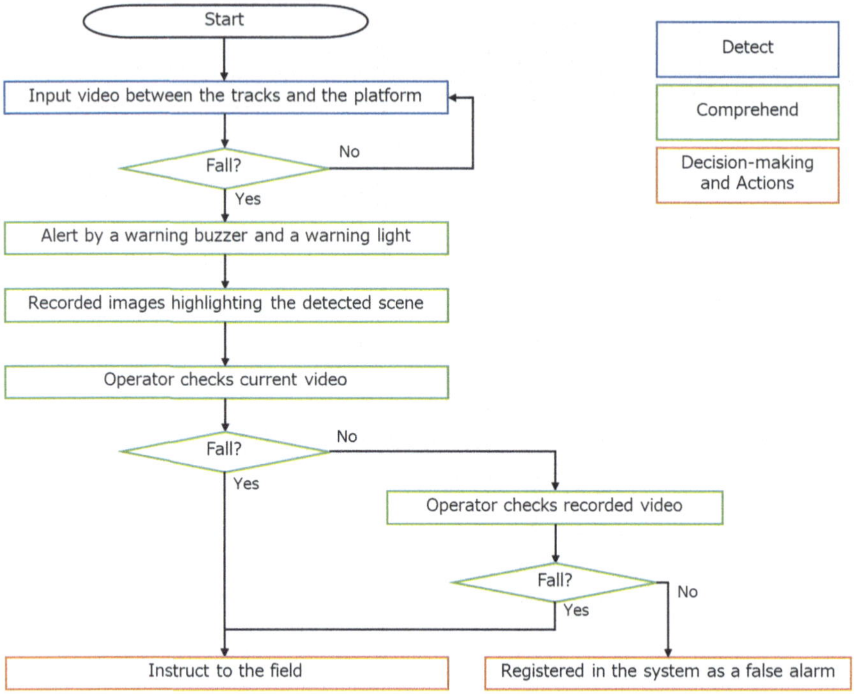

Fig. 2 Fall detection workflow

Fig. 3 Station surveillance cameras

Fig. 4 Image generated by the system

- Since it is necessary to recognize the moment when a person walking on the platform moves out of the platform area, it is desirable to capture at least five images per second (5 Frames Per Sec) to analyze continuous motion.
- Although it depends on the installation position and the camera's angle of view, the performance must be sufficient to recognize that it is a person.

As the first step of the detection flow, this video is input to the Image AI.

Comprehend

As the second step in the detection flow, a fall is determined by the Image AI detection algorithm. If a fall is detected, the system alerts the operator with a warning buzzer and light. At the same time, the system creates an image highlighting the detected scene and records it in the recording device. The operator may be in a monitoring room in the station or remotely. The operator who receives the detection alert first checks the current situation on the live video to decide whether a fall has occurred. If the operator cannot visually confirm the situation on the live video, they obtain images of the detection scene associated with the detection alert from the recording device and repeatedly play back the scene before and after the alert to make a final decision as to whether a fall has occurred.

Conventionally, operators must constantly monitor video transmitted from multiple cameras. Although a fall rarely occurs, it is a critical event that can interfere with safe and secure train operations. Therefore, the operators had to concentrate on preventing missed events and constantly judge whether a fall had occurred, which placed a heavy mental and physical burden on them. This system uses image AI to eliminate the need for the operator to constantly monitor the occurrence of falls. In other words, the Image AI infers that a fall has occurred and notifies the operator with a detection alert, enabling the operator to visually check in real time and decide whether a fall has occurred, with little burden on the operator.

In this system, the accuracy of the detection alerts transmitted by the Image AI is of the utmost importance. Efforts to improve this accuracy are described later in another chapter.

Project

Since a fall is an event that the operator should immediately act upon after detection and comprehension, Image AI does not have a project function to predict the following state change after a fall is detected.

Human-Centric Decision-Making and Actions

As the last step in the detection flow, the operator, who has decided that a fall has occurred, takes appropriate action according to the situation, such as alerting the traveling vehicle or instructing the other operator to rush to the fall site. If a final decision is made that a fall has not occurred, the system keeps a history as a false report. Therefore, the system keeps a history of correct reports in which a fall was correctly detected and false reports in which a fall was incorrectly detected. Also, for example, if an operator confirms a fall on-site but the fall detection system does not alert it, a history is kept as an unreported event. These false reports and unreported data can be used to update the system in the future to improve the performance of the Image AI.

The action is taken only after passing the operator's final decision after the system detects a fall because Image AI is positioned as a function to support human judgment. Therefore, a use case in which the system directly controls a traveling vehicle to make an emergency stop without human judgment is not currently being worked on.

As described above, the fall detection system supports safe and secure train operations.

A railroad operating company that installed this system reported immediately after its installation, "The system detected an intoxicated person walking unsteadily along the edge of the platform, and an attendant secured his safety by protecting him. I reviewed the footage after the response, and it was not surprising that the person could have fallen off the platform at any time." He commented. The system has raised the morale of those who use it, partly because we confirmed its effectiveness early after its installation. The system has also been used to improve morale in the workplace.

2.2 Congestion Detection System

As mentioned before, the current system cannot respond to sudden congestion. Therefore, studies are underway to install a system that quantifies congestion using camera images and notifies operators when congestion exceeds a threshold level, enabling them to respond instantly to sudden congestion. Quantifying congestion is also valuable for confirming whether the security plan is within expectations (Nakamura et al. 2011).

This system's detection workflow and functions are grouped into situation awareness (SA) and decision-making (see Fig. 5).

Detect

This system acquires camera images that meet the following conditions to detect congestion:

- The camera must be placed near the ceiling, where congestion is likely to lead to severe accidents (stairways and platforms) and where it does not obstruct the passage.
- To quantify congestion, it is necessary to analyze not only the number of pedestrians but also the amount of pedestrian movement, so it is desirable to capture at least five images per second (5 Frames Per Sec) to analyze continuous motion.
- Although it depends on the installation position and the camera's angle of view, the performance must be sufficient to recognize that it is a person.

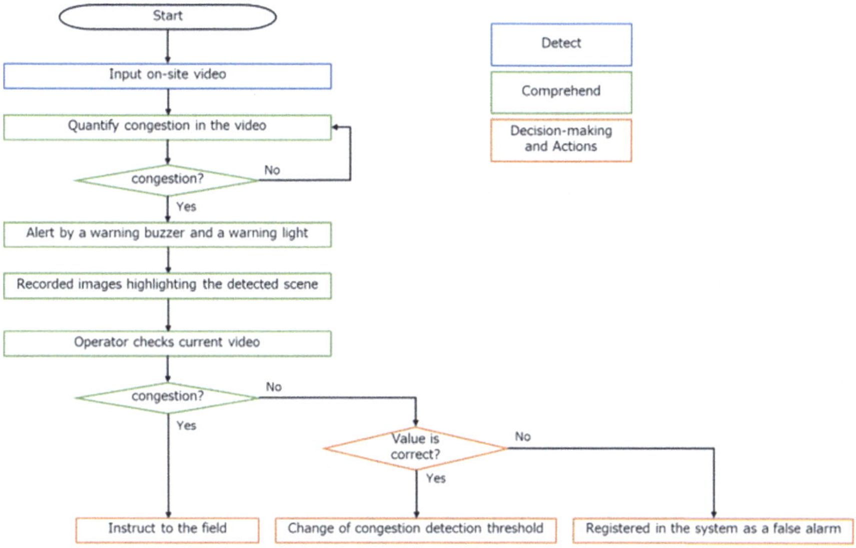

Fig. 5 Congestion detection workflow

With the video acquired by this camera, the operator can remotely monitor the area to be detected.

As the first step of the detection flow, this video is input to the Image AI.

Comprehend

As the second step in the detection flow, the Image AI quantifies the congestion in the video. A detection algorithm that compares this value to a set threshold value is then used to determine whether there is congestion. If the value here exceeds the threshold, it is considered congested, and the system alerts the operator with a warning buzzer and light. At the same time, the system creates an image highlighting the detected scene and records it in the recording device. The operator who receives the detection alert first checks the current situation on the live video to decide whether there is congestion.

This system makes it possible to quantitatively determine whether there is congestion. This reduces the operator's workload and produces the secondary effect of reducing variability in operator decisions. Since the Image AI can combine and quantify the number of people and the number of people moving in a particular area, it is necessary to set a threshold to automatically determine if the area is congested. The camera image is displayed on a monitor, and the operator can determine the threshold by looking at the congestion figures output by the Image AI. Even after the system is installed, the operator can determine the threshold value, which allows the system to always be close to the operator's sense of monitoring and achieve the detection accuracy required by the operator. The threshold values often vary from camera to camera due to differences in the number of trains in operation, the interval between trains, and the amount of flow due to the number of exits.

Project

Although it was mentioned above that Image AI automatically determines whether there is congestion or not with a threshold value, it is also useful to set multiple threshold values with different meanings. In our case, two measures should be set based on the assumption that congestions exceeding the threshold value develop suddenly, occur for short periods, and are rare events. Under these assumptions, the thresholds have two meanings: one as a predictive sign of congestion and the other for determining congestion in real time. The operator's grasping of the predictive signs of congestion would lead to a proactive response before congestion occurs.

However, even when setting the two types of thresholds, Image AI does not have a project function to predict congestion after detecting the predictive signs of congestion. Since the projection of congestion is not included in Image AI and it is one of the comprehend functions, Project is omitted in Fig. 5.

Human-Centric Decision-Making and Actions

As the last step in the detection flow, the operator, who has made the final decision that congestion has occurred, takes appropriate action according to the situation, such as instructing the other operator to guide and direct passengers at the congested site in the station. The action is taken only after passing the operator's final decision after detecting a congestion by the system because Image AI is positioned as a function to support human judgment. Therefore, a use case in which the system directly controls ticket gates to close automatically without human judgment is not currently being worked on.

On the other hand, if a detection alert is received but cannot be confirmed as congestion, the operator checks the scene and the congestion value by acquiring images of the detected scene associated with the detection alert from the recording device. If the values are correct, the threshold for congestion detection is changed; if the values are incorrect, the system keeps a history as a false report. The system keeps a history of correct reports that correctly identify congestion and false reports that show high values when there is no congestion. These false reports data can be used to update the system in the future to improve the performance of the Image AI.

As described above, the congestion detection system prevents accidents and contributes to safe and secure railroad operations. A station operator using this system commented, "Until now, the definition of congestion was vague and subjective, but with the installation of this system, congestion can now be viewed objectively. By having people make judgments based on numerical values, the system has eliminated variations in judgments by skilled and unskilled personnel, leading to standardization of operations." Furthermore, a railroad operating company that installed this system reported, "85% of the stations where this system was installed answered that it has led to ensuring the safety of customers and reducing workload."

3 Installation and Deployment Process

Typical stakeholder groups are listed below (see Table 1). Solution provider is a vendor of Image AI systems; service provider is a business owner who decides to install Image AI systems; and station operators are primary users of Image AI systems. Security guards of a security company contracted by a railroad company may be considered primary users. Finally, train operators, emergency responders, and customers are indirect users of Image AI systems. In the workflow below, station operators, train operators, and emergency responders are referred to as the operators without distinction (Fig. 6).

Table 1 Stakeholders

Stakeholders	Who	Primary desired outcomes
Solution provider	Vendor of Image AI systems	Being interested in the accuracy of the system to drive adoption
Service provider	Business owner	Being interested in minimizing fatal incidents and maximizing accuracy to optimize the productivity of operators
Station operators, security guards	Primary users	Being interested in mental offload and the accuracy of alerts
Train operators	Indirect users	Being interested in providing a great commute experience to their passengers and avoid injuries
Emergency responders	Indirect users	Being interested in minimizing false alarms and the exact location of an incident
Customers	Indirect users	Being classified by the system and potentially causing alerts

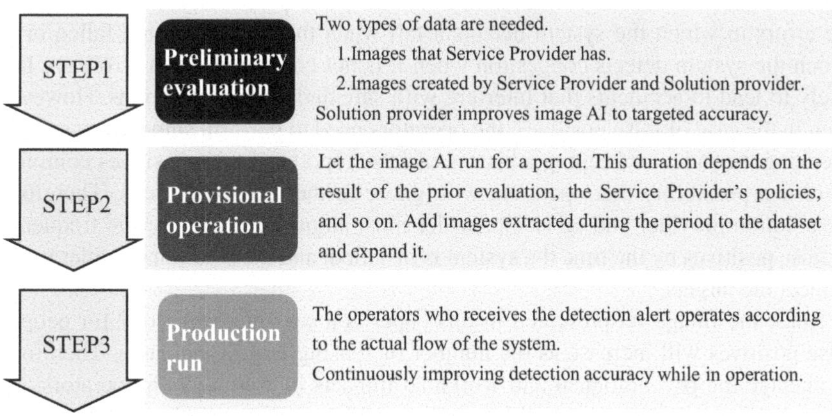

Fig. 6 Installation and deployment process

3.1 Preliminary Evaluation

Solution provider and service provider cooperate to conduct a preliminary evaluation of whether Image AI can detect the scene that the service provider wants to detect.

Two types of data are mainly used for the preliminary evaluation:

1. Images owned by the service provider.
   - Abnormal scenes occurred in the past but often in small quantities.
   - Scenes with no abnormalities: large numbers of them exist.
2. Images created by the solution provider and service provider.
   Abnormal scenes may be few or not exist in some areas where detection is expected. Therefore, to increase the number of abnormal scenes and variations in their locations, capture scenes of simulated performances at the site where they are to be installed or merge images from other sites into the images of the site where they are to be installed.

A pre-evaluation dataset is constructed from the above two types of data, and the solution provider improves the Image AI until it reaches the accuracy defined by the service provider.

Generally, the false positive rate, an indicator for evaluating false positives, and the false negative rate, an indicator for evaluating false negatives, are often utilized. Whether the false positive rate or the false negative rate is more important depends on the operational policy of the service provider. In practice, railroad operating companies tend to place more importance on the false negative rate. False negatives mean that the operators cannot detect a falling or a congested situation, which may lead to a critical accident that interferes with a safe and secure operation because the operators cannot take the necessary actions. False positives, on the other hand, are errors in which the system detects a fall when the person has not fallen or in which the system detects congestion when it is not congested. Such errors are less likely to lead to accidents that interfere with safe and secure operations. However, even in the case of false positives, the operators need to perform some tasks, such as checking the video or keeping a history of false reports. If false positives continue, there is a possibility that operators will ignore further detection alerts. Therefore, the solution provider and service provider must align the targets for the frequency of false positives by the time the system is installed, and the solution provider needs to meet the targets.

Since the Image AI presented in this paper is a sensing technology for people, false positives will increase as the number of sensing targets increases. Therefore, to manage the psychological and workload impacts of warnings on operators, the target is often set as the acceptable number of false positives per hour during times of heavy commuter traffic.

3.2 Provisional Operation

After satisfying the target accuracy in the pre-evaluation dataset, the system will be put into provisional operation at the site. Provisional operation means that the Image AI is operated for a certain period at the site where it is to be installed, but the operators are not notified of detection alerts, or no prescribed measures are taken even if detection alerts are received.

The duration of the provisional operation will depend on the Image AI's performance, the pre-evaluation content, and the service provider's policy. For example, if Image AI has already been implemented at another site and has a proven track record, the pre-assessment can be regarded as a customization process for the newly installed site, and the period may be shorter. In addition, it could extend to a year in areas with four seasons, as frequent changes in daylight and lighting conditions can affect the robustness of Image AI. In any case, the duration will be determined by the service provider's policy, considering the level of technology and the characteristics of the installation site.

If a detection alert occurs during the provisional operation period, the detection alert and the images associated with the detection alert will be recorded. The service provider and the solution provider will analyze the results and classify them as positive or false alarms. In addition, images from periods not tied to detection alerts may be analyzed to see if there are any unalerted alarms. However, in the case of the fall detection example, it is necessary to confirm that the detection is correct. These tests should also involve simulated abnormal scenes since they do not often occur during the period of provisional operation.

The images extracted by the analysis are added to the pre-assessment dataset, which is then expanded as a dataset for making implementation decisions.

3.3 Production Run

The production run will begin when the accuracy expected by the service provider is reached by utilizing the implementation decision dataset. Here, the operators receiving the detection alert will operate according to the actual flow.

After this installation, the operators will separate positive and false alarms after receiving detection alerts as a work record. In addition, if the system does not detect a specific event, the operators will record the undetected event.

These records can be used to improve detection accuracy during operation, as well as during the provisional operation period.

On the other hand, if the accuracy of Image AI deteriorates, the service provider rarely learns by itself; in many cases, the solution provider who has concluded maintenance contracts oversees learning.

4 Conclusion

In this chapter, we exemplified how advanced technology and intelligent systems can solve problems by presenting cases of Image AI implementations at two separate train stations in Japan. These cases show how technology and people can work together to make public places safer.

Human operators play a crucial role in the functional effectiveness of Image AI. They make important decisions in high-risk situations and are responsible for keeping stations safe. When Image AI alerts them to possible issues, they decide what actions to take. Since making the right decision in the action phase is critical, human operators' situational awareness is essential in this decision-making process.

Having the AI count and measure crowd congestion gives the operators objective data. This objective data helps them sense and form models regarding their decision-making environments to predict and prevent possible incidents earlier.

It is important to note that in the case of systems such as Image AI, a synergetic operator-intelligent system is possible only if the system can nurture user trust. This means the system should show that it has accurate and reliable situation awareness elements. Moreover, the system's confusion matrix, i.e., frequencies of false positives and false negatives, should be appropriate for the task's risk characteristics. In the case of our application with Image AI, missing an incident is costly. Therefore, a careful and thorough process was followed to minimize false alarms while still ensuring that it did not miss any incidents and that it helped the operator build their situation awareness regarding the task.

Despite its evident benefits, it's important to note the limitations and areas for further development of AI in safety and security applications. One promising avenue is the exploration of multimodal sensing, which integrates multiple types of AI—not only Image AI but also technologies like radio, which is less influenced by weather and sunlight, and social media, where real-time passenger feedback can provide additional situational awareness. This multifaceted approach may provide a richer, more robust safety net, providing operators and AI systems with diverse data for decision-making.

Another frontier for possible expansions is explainable AI methods, which clarify the AI's decision-making process by illustrating what features of an image it focuses on to derive conclusions. Such detailed explanations not only foster operator trust but also enable the AI developers to understand which conditions enhance or diminish accuracy, thereby fine-tuning the AI for better performance.

In the future, it is anticipated that service providers will have easy access to base tools such as Image AI and other learning environments, which will also help the solution providers to further develop and refine the Image AI technology. In societies grappling with the challenges posed by aging populations and evolving on-site dynamics, the diligent progression of these technologies will be key to addressing diverse issues and fostering a safe and secure environment.

References

East Japan Railway Company (2008) Installation of automatic doors on the yamanote line. Technical report. https://www.jreast.co.jp/e/press/20080601/

Endsley MR (1995) Toward a theory of situation awareness in dynamic systems. Hum Factors 37(1):32–64. https://doi.org/10.1518/001872095779049543

Ministry of Internal Affairs and Communications of Japan (2016) Concentration of population in urban areas: increase in large cities. Technical report. https://www.soumu.go.jp/main_content/000452793.pdf

Ministry of Land, Infrastructure, Transport and Tourism of Japan (2020) Situation concerning falls from station platforms. Technical report. https://www.mlit.go.jp/tetudo/content/001378759.pdf

Ministry of Land, Infrastructure, Transport and Tourism of Japan (2024) Installation status of platform doors. Technical report. https://www.mlit.go.jp/tetudo/content/001471193.pdf

Morimoto Y, Wada K (2017) Studies on the safety of the station platform from the perspective of the human factors. IATSS Rev 41(3):22–29. https://jglobal.jst.go.jp/en/detail?JGLOBAL_ID=201702252723244983

Morita Y, Morichi S, Ito M (2013) A study on maximum outgoing passengers of stairs and escalators at stations. J Jpn Soc Civil Eng 69(5):595–611. https://doi.org/10.2208/jscejipm.69.I_595

Nakamura Y, Hibino N, Morichi S (2011) A study on congestion and passenger flow in railway station. J Jpn Soc Civil Eng 67(5):705–713. https://doi.org/10.2208/jscejipm.67.67_I_705

Tanouchi Y, Nishikawa H, Kodaira T (2022) Performance evaluation of human flow simulation in station using multi-agent simulator. Inf Proces Soc Jpn. vol 84, pp 471–472. Processing Society of Japan, Tokyo. https://www.ipsj.or.jp/event/taikai/84/ipsj_web2022/index.html. https://jglobal.jst.go.jp/en/detail?JGLOBAL_ID=202202218393933249

Tsujimoto Y, Sasaki D, Yokotobi M, Mori S (2021) A study on systematic arrangement of causes of falling from station platforms for the visually impaired person. J Jpn Soc Civil Eng 77(2):1–11. https://doi.org/10.2208/jscejsp.77.2_I_1

Yamagami T (2003) Spatio-temporal structure of population growth in major metropolitan areas in Japan. Geogr Rev Jpn 76(4):187–210. https://doi.org/10.4157/grj.76.187

Yoneji K, Matsubara D, Akira N, Iida M, Murakami T, Nukaga N (2017) A congestion visualization technique using station monitor cameras. Inf Proces Soc Jpn Digital Pract 8(2):152–159. https://www.ipsj.or.jp/dp/contents/publication/30/DP30-T01.html

Situational Awareness and HMI Design in Collaborative Human-Machine (AI) Teamwork: A Case Study

Enrique Munoz-de-Escalona, Hector Diego Estrada-Lugo, Andres Alonso Perez, and Maria Chiara Leva

Abstract The emergence of new complex systems such as artificial intelligence (AI) or collaborative robots (cobots) has taken the industry to a new industrial revolution that pursues the increase in efficiency and optimization of production by focusing on the synergy between humans and machines in order to combine the strengths of both elements to achieve common goals. In such a context, humans and machines can no longer be seen as isolated elements but as cooperative agents supporting each other in a shared workspace. This teaming between human and nonhuman agents inevitably requires the development of a common operational picture based on the exchange of relevant information. This paper presents an example of how human-machine teaming can be enhanced in an automotive plastic part industry that is intended to increase efficiency (reduce material waste) and productivity levels by introducing AI in the manufacturing process. Such collaborative environment requires special consideration for the Human-Machine Interface (HMI) design for the development of a shared workspace in which the interchange of relevant information and the enhancement of situational awareness would play a key role in determining success.

1 Introduction

Traditional human-machine interaction in industry, where both elements of the system were considered in isolation, has given way to a new industrial revolution (Industry 5.0) that considers the human and the machine not as isolated elements

E. Munoz-de-Escalona (✉) · A. Alonso Perez · M. C. Leva
School of Food Science and Environmental Health, TU Dublin, Ireland
e-mail: Enrique.MunozdeEscalonaFernandez@tudublin.ie; Andres.AlonsoPerez@tudublin.ie; MariaChiara.Leva@tudublin.ie

H. D. Estrada-Lugo
Office of the Chief Engineer, United Kingdom Atomic Energy Authority, Abingdon, United Kingdom
e-mail: diego.estradalugo@ukaea.uk

C. K. Coursaris et al. (eds.), *The Design of Human-Centered Artificial Intelligence for the Workplace*, Progress in IS, https://doi.org/10.1007/978-3-031-83512-4_23

anymore but as a highly complex and dynamic relationship based on collaboration and teaming to perform a general task and reach common goals (Krupitzer et al. 2020; Anastasi et al. 2021). In this new context of industry, automation and artificial intelligence (AI) have taken a lead role in achieving higher productivity levels and better efficiency since production times and costs have decreased meaningfully. However, automation and AI must never replace humans in the industry but as new factors that would enhance human capabilities in the new human-centered designed workplace.

Automation and AI cannot be considered isolated from humans since, for example, they cannot adapt to each new situation and require supervision. Moreover, in collaborative intelligence applications, an enhanced AI agent performance will also require a higher degree of human-machine interaction capabilities, and the success in achieving this optimal cooperation turns out to be the key factor to improve efficiency and sustainability levels of the production process in this new industrial revolution. Human-machine cooperation involves interdependence between both elements, and this requires the existence of common ground. The informational interdependence between both elements is evident, and continuous updates are required to maintain optimal knowledge about the system's state. This would ultimately affect the degree of situational awareness (SA) and, hence, the predictability of the system. In other words, working cooperatively requires the development of a common operational picture (COP) (Steen-Tveit and Munkvold 2021), not only between humans but also between humans and machines. Steen-Tveit and Munkvold (2021) discuss how the notion of a COP is intimately connected with SA. Initially emerging within a military context, a COP is commonly perceived as a "centralized information display system" (Hwang and Yoon 2020). It presents situational and operational information gathered from various sources pertinent to the stakeholders involved. Additionally, the COP primarily acts as a foundation for determining subsequent actions, representing an initial phase in establishing a shared situational understanding among the participating actors. This understanding encompasses the perceptions, actions, and decision-making processes of the involved actors, fostering effective collaboration.

This study aims to describe how human-machine cooperation can be enhanced in a case study (automotive plastic parts industry) by developing a protocol and a tool for achieving a COP between humans and the AI system that would ultimately lead to an increase in SA of the team members. More specifically, the objectives of this protocol and tool would be:

1. Gathering useful information from operators that could be used by the AI systems to predict future faulty pieces.
2. Achieving a COP (updated in real time) not only between humans but also between humans and the AI systems.
3. Achieving a state of advanced SA that would, ultimately, help the operators to predict errors and increase productivity and efficiency levels in the industry.

1.1 SA Definition and Importance in Collaborative Environments

1.1.1 SA Definition

SA as a construct shares the same issues found in the literature for most of the psychological terms commonly used in human factors-related research, e.g., mental workload, mental fatigue, intelligence, stress, and attention, and that is the problem of achieving a universally accepted definition and validation for its modeling. Despite multiple attempts, there is still no consensus regarding its definition (Smith and Hancock 1995; Bedny and Meister 1999; Pérez et al. 2022). However, considering that the three-level model of Endsley is the most used and universally accepted SA model and that most assessing techniques are based on it, from now on, we will focus on this model for the purpose of this document.

SA was defined by Endsley as "The perception of the elements in the environment within a volume of time and space, the comprehension of their meaning, and the projection of their status in the near future" (Endsley 1995b, p. 1). By reading the definition proposed by Endsley, we can easily identify the three different levels that comprise the SA:

1. The first level, perception of the elements in the environment: it comprises the different elements (cues) of the environment that the human has to perceive to comprehend the current situation, but there is still no possible interpretation of the input raw data. A proper perception of the elements of the environment is essential to achieve a correct representation of the situation.
2. The second level, comprehension of the current situation: it is not enough for the human to simply perceive the elements of the environment, but it is enough to synthesize and integrate them to achieve a proper understanding of their significance (meaning) to humans' goals. This process depends on cognitive schema and mental models stored in the long-term memory that would ultimately allow the human to outline what is happening in the system. This level of SA strongly depends on the level of expertise of the human in the environment. Individuals who are more expert will achieve a better and faster comprehension of the current situation, which would help achieve a better projection of future status.
3. The third level, projection of future status: it consists of the ability to anticipate the future status of the elements of the environment based on the current situation and the mental models of the human stored in the long-term memory that would allow to project likely feasible future scenarios. The achievement of the third level strongly depends on the accuracy achieved in the previous two levels.

In general terms, we can see that higher levels of information processing lead to a higher SA, which is a key element in human decision-making. The model is also influenced by task/system, e.g., complexity, automation, interface design, and individual factors, e.g., training and experience. This would explain, on the one hand, the importance of the system's design and, on the other hand, why two different people facing the same situation would reach a different level of SA. Moreover, SA is inherently linked to the decision-making process since SA acts as the precursor for the individual to make decisions: SA would create a representation of the current and future state of the environment in the mind of the individual, and based on this, the decision-making process would take place for taking action and keep the situation under control.

1.1.2 "Individual SA" Relevance in Complex Systems

SA can be considered one of the most important constructs in the cognitive ergonomics and human factors spheres. This construct was initially explored in the military aviation domain research, as SA of fighter pilots was crucial for their survival (Endsley 1993). Nevertheless, SA is a critical construct in any place where humans perform dynamic and complex tasks, which is why SA research has been extended to many different domains.

The benefits of considering SA were first discovered in the air traffic control domain, as the majority of errors resulted from air traffic controllers losing an appropriate level of SA (Härtel et al. 1991; Redding 1992). The same thing occurs with commercial pilots, as most human errors are related to insufficient or inappropriate SA status of pilots (Endsley 1995a). Poor performance is strongly related to a reduced SA status of employees. This can be explained as the result of higher time needed for the employee to identify and analyze troubles within the system and to take actions to address the problem (Endsley and Kiris 1995). Klein (2000) identifies four arguments that highlight the importance of achieving and maintaining an adequate SA level: (1) SA is linked to performance, (2) A reduced SA can result in errors, (3) SA is the key element to the decision-making process, and (4) SA can be linked to the level of expertise.

Hence, we could say that increasing the SA of the agents of a complex system would reduce errors and improve performance, which would lead to an increase in productivity and efficiency levels.

1.1.3 "Group and Systemic" SA Relevance in Complex Systems

According to Shuffler et al. (2015), SA is a construct that influences the outcomes within and across team agents in collaborative systems. SA is a concept that can be addressed not only from an individual perspective but also from a group and systemic point of view.

The group perspective of SA is defined by Salas et al. (1995) as a "Shared understanding of a situation among team members at one point in time." An enhanced group SA will result in better collaborative outcomes. In 2016, Sorensen and Stanton stated that teams with more relevant communication were more effective than those with a lower communication rate. In addition, we should consider that a worker holding an inaccurate or partial SA would interact with other system agents according to this faulty mental framework. This erroneous information or lack of relevant information would interfere with the system's proper functioning, making it less likely that other agents could be warned of potential problems, increasing the probability of errors and decreasing productivity and efficiency.

A key factor affecting group SA is the concept of meta-knowledge, which can be defined as the "knowledge of who knows what" (Mell et al. 2014, p. 1154). More specifically, meta-knowledge is the agent's understanding of the knowledge that other agents possess in a team; therefore, it reflects the individual awareness about the expertise of team members (Ren and Argote 2011). There is a large disparity of meta-knowledge levels, and researchers have revealed that both the degree and the configuration of meta-knowledge in a team affect team process and performance. For example, Brandon and Hollingshead (2004) revealed that the optimal team state requires a complete and shared understanding of available knowledge resources in the team. A higher degree of shared meta-knowledge would always enhance group SA. On the other hand, Mell et al. (2014) shed light on the importance of the structural component of meta-knowledge since their study revealed that a centralized meta-knowledge structure gave teams a performance advantage over a decentralized one. Until this point, we are only addressing the meta-knowledge concept in a human-human teaming context. However, with the emergence of Industry 5.0, we must raise the question of how important meta-knowledge is in the human-AI teaming context. For that purpose, we will start now defining the system perspective of SA.

The systemic perspective is defined by Stanton et al. (2017) as "Activated knowledge for a specific task within a system at a specific time by specific agents, that is, the human and nonhuman actors in a system." This emerging approach has gained more relevance in recent years as AI, collaborative robots (cobots), and automation processes have gained protagonism in the manufacturing process of Industry 5.0. This approach focuses on the interaction (communications mainly) between the human and the machine for sharing task-relevant information. Humans and nonhuman agents would have different but congruent perspectives of the state of the system since competencies, responsibilities, and roles would be different but compatible (Sorensen and Stanton 2013). As an example, an AI may need certain input from the human agent about the state of the system, e.g., number and location of errors in production parts, while the human agent would need the probability of obtaining a faulty part from the AI within the next 5 minutes. Again, meta-knowledge between human and nonhuman agents is a key factor in achieving a COP, as the operator must always be aware of what the AI is capable of. In this sense, operators must be trained to understand the capabilities and limits of the AI fully, and, therefore, that piece of information must be transmitted as a piece of meta-knowledge that would allow the worker to detect that those limits are being surpassed and the AI is not being reliable. Considering the last example, the AI could not be capable of identifying certain new errors that still have not been sufficiently trained to detect. It should then warn the operator about this uncertainty so that the operator can double-check for the possible appearance of such an error. In summary, this collaborative relationship between human and nonhuman agents supported by the development of a COP would ultimately lead to a state of advanced situational awareness of the team members that would positively impact the system's predictability, productivity, and efficiency levels.

It should be seen that individual, group, and system SA levels are very interdependent, and the degree of awareness achieved at each level will inevitably influence the two remaining. The adequate exchange of information, that is, the development of collaborative human-human and human-machine environments based on a COP, is key to maintaining an advanced level of SA.

This study focuses on improving the three levels of SA in a case study about an automotive component industry by developing a specific protocol and a tool that would help enhance a COP not only between humans but also between humans and nonhuman agents (AI) of the system.

1.1.4 SA in AI Teaming Contexts

According to Endsley (2023), situational awareness (SA) plays a crucial role and one often overlooked, in ensuring the effective interaction between humans and intelligent and autonomous systems. In her recent paper, she explained that SA is key in supporting human-AI teaming and is strictly connected with transparency, explainability, team training, and interaction methods. Transparency and explainability in AI systems each fulfill distinct roles in supporting the situational awareness and cognitive models of human operators interacting with and overseeing AI operations. These aspects of system development are pivotal in achieving the right balance between trust and team performance when collaborating with AI systems, and it is often translated into practice through the development of an interface. In particular, SA-oriented design (SAOD) (Endsley and Jones 2012) can have a role to play. Endsley (2023) sustains a need to develop a systematic approach to discern the specific components of situational awareness (SA) that should be included in displays for a given AI application. At the same time, it is crucial to develop practical techniques for achieving transparency that can accommodate the constraints posed by workload and the temporal demands of the tasks.

To ensure practical applicability in real-world scenarios, there is a need for further research on how to design effective AI transparency techniques and demonstrate their ability to maintain the necessary situational awareness and trust levels without overwhelming workloads. The present work aimed at introducing an application in this sense.

2 Case Study

2.1 Case Study Description

The case study of this research is an industry that manufactures various thermoplastic parts for the interior of vehicles by using injection molding machines. This use case is framed within a project named "Teaming AI" (funded by the European Union's Horizon 2020 Research and Innovation, Grant Agreement Number 957402), whose main scope is to develop a collaborative framework between the human and the AI systems, in order to enhance human capabilities that would ultimately lead to an increase in productivity, efficiency, well being and safety of workers (Pérez et al. 2022).

In this particular use case, the main goal is to develop an AI tool to support early detection and auto-adjustment (when possible) of deviations from the injection molding machine's nominal parameters, resulting in faulty products. If the AI cannot auto-adjust the parameters, it would alert the injection technician to request human assistance, ideally before faulty parts are produced. The AI will communicate not only with the injection machine control unit but also with operators to gain input for its algorithms, keeping the human in the loop. In other words, the aim is to develop a collaborative team between the operators and the AI system, in which the human's and machine's needs from each other to reach the common goal of reducing material waste, increasing productivity levels, and the well-being of the workers.

By looking at the scope of the project in general and the use case in particular, the reader will quickly notice the importance of achieving a COP between human and nonhuman agents involved in this industry. This information exchange will ultimately help enhance individual, group, and systemic SA levels. The scope of this study was to promote a COP for enhancing SA levels by developing a protocol and a tool for gathering information from assembly operators that could serve as input for (1) the AI system helps to early identify and auto-adjust (when possible) deviations of the injection molding machine from nominal parameters and for (2) other assembly operators to gain advantage of this information (displayed in an user-friendly tool that would keep the current status of the system updated) for enhancing their SA, especially during shift handover.

2.2 Data Collection and Analysis

Data collection took place during a site visit to the factory in March 2022. We conducted semi-structured interviews as the primary method for collecting data. We interviewed seven workers (assembly operators) whose role was to check the automotive pieces for quality defects during assembly. The focus was on what sort of information could be gathered from them not only for use as input for the AI system (enhancing system SA) but also for enhancing the SA of the team (group SA) about the state of the system. Interviews were recorded and transcribed.

We performed a thematic analysis of the transcriptions to recognize the different elements of relevant information that could be gathered from assembly operators for the abovementioned purpose. We did not use predefined categories; we included those categories that were most relevant to the needs of the agents.

3 Results: Information That Could be Provided by Assembly Operators to Enhance COP Between Humans and Between Human and Nonhuman Agents

The data analysis revealed different elements of information that could be provided dynamically by assembly operators, updating the information in the system as the different incidents occur, for being used not only as an input for the AI system (enhancing system SA) but also for enhancing the SA of the team (group SA), which would be highly relevant for assembly operators during their shift handover (enhancing individual SA).

When a shift handover occurs, there normally exists an exchange of information between both employers: the one currently working and the one who comes to relieve the former. More specifically, a transference of information of the system's current state (system abnormalities mainly) occurs from the first employer to the second one to let the latter update his/her SA of the system's current status in the shortest time possible. We found out that this transference of information is done verbally and informally in such a way that the absence of any protocol/tool for this purpose would create possible gaps of information that are crucial for the proper building of the current SA of the employer. In other words, the quality and quantity of information transferred between workers is variable and subject to individual differences, e.g., worker experience, forgetfulness, and lack of motivation. Hence, the existence of a user-friendly tool that would keep the system's current status updated and could be checked by the team members when necessary (enhancing group SA) would help them achieve a better individual SA of the current situation.

3.1 Relevant Information That Can be Gathered from Assembly Operators

Niemantsverdriet et al. (2019, p. 10) state that "more information is not necessarily better." Stanton et al. (2017, p 422) statement can complement this statement: "What is important for enhancing SA is the transaction of information that is relevant to the task." Detailed below are the relevant elements of information that could be provided by assembly operators:

3.1.1 Number of Times the Machine Stops

This information allows the assembly operator to understand in general terms if the system has been working properly before it starts operating. The higher the number of times the machine stops, the worse the system is working and the higher the probability of future faulty parts. Operators must be cautious about possible future failures in the machine and quality failures in parts. It would also help the AI algorithm to determine the overall performance of the injection machine: the higher the number of times the machine stops, the higher the number of possible faulty parts.

3.1.2 The Number of Not OK (NOK) Parts and OK Parts with Quality Deviations

This information allows the assembly operator to understand if the system has been working properly or not before they start operating, but it also gives more detailed information about the outcomes of the production process. This information is even more important than the number of times the machine has stopped because a bad production outcome confirms the machine's malfunctioning. In contrast, a machine that stops a couple of times does not necessarily mean that it will produce faulty parts. Operators must be much more cautious about the appearance of quality failures or faulty parts. The number of NOK parts will help the AI algorithm detect that injection parameters are wrong (out of tolerance). The number of OK parts with quality deviations will help the AI algorithms detect early that injection parameters are not appropriate (even if they are within tolerance limits) and help prevent the appearance of future NOK parts.

3.1.3 Type of Errors or Quality Deviations Found

This information allows the operator to be more aware of the particular types of failures appearing in produced parts. This would allow the operator to focus his/her attention on the possible appearance of that particular issue in future pieces. However, operators must be aware that they must continue paying attention to other possible types of failures that may appear. It would also help the AI algorithm to identify what parameters related to the faulty part are out of range and should be readjusted.

3.1.4 Location of the Defects

This information will make it easier for operators to detect errors/deviations in produced parts, as they will first focus their attention on the area where the issue appears. This information is particularly important in large parts. (Nonetheless, operators must be aware that they must continue inspecting the whole piece to search for other possible defects). It would also help the AI algorithm to identify what parameters related to the faulty part are out of range and should be readjusted.

3.1.5 Other Machine Errors

This information would help the operator achieve a better SA of the system's overall status in order to predict possible future system failures and faulty parts. Operators reported that sometimes the poka-yoke does not work properly, e.g., it assembles the part even if a specific clamp is not placed correctly. This information would alert the operator about specific issues that may be found while working on a particular machine. Operators also reported that, sometimes, strange noises coming from the machine would be considered a precursor of the appearance of faulty pieces. Therefore, they would be more cautious about the appearance of quality issues connected with the unusual sounds.

3.2 *Incident Report Protocol and User Interface for Gathering Information from Assembly Operators*

The incident report protocol must be designed according to the particular needs of the assembly operators. Their tasks are very demanding in terms of attention and time resources. They must keep their attention focused on inspecting produced parts and have a set time for this operation. For this reason, they do not have much time and cognitive resources for performing extra tasks. Hence, the incident protocol must be kept as simple as possible, and the machine operator must be able to report the incident with minimum possible investment in time and effort. Accordingly, the Human-Machine Interface (HMI) used for reporting incidents must be user-friendly and effective, and it must prioritize high usability.

The main user requirements for the incident report protocol and its HMI are the following:

- The incident must be reported in a simple way.
- The incident must be reported as soon as possible.
- The incident must be reported with the smallest possible number of steps.
- The incident report HMI must be user-friendly (easy to perceive and understand, offering an appropriate user experience).

Figure 1 illustrates the incident report protocol that machine operators will follow to report any detected issue with the machine and the quality of produced parts. The first step is to define what type of incident the operator has identified (machine or part incident); however, if the incident identified by the operator has the same characteristics as the very last reported incident, the operator will be able to report

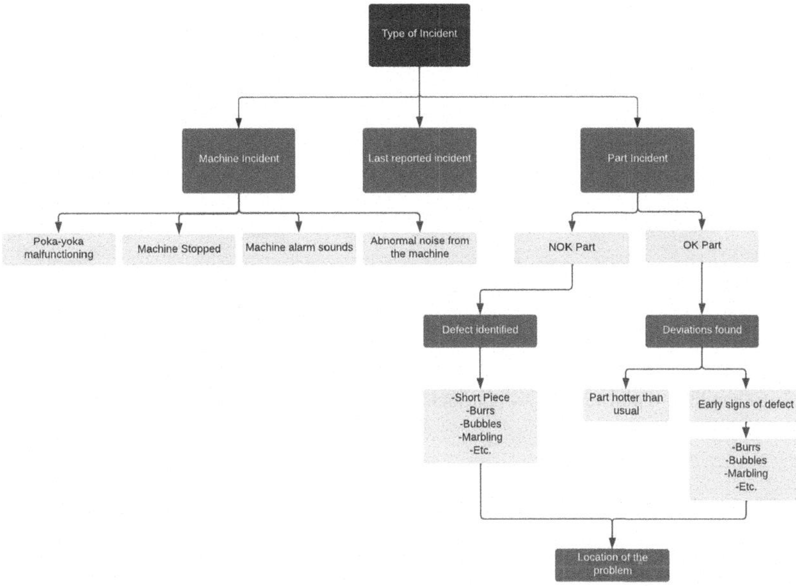

Fig. 1 Incident report protocol for machine operator flux diagram

that incident automatically, in order to save time and resources, by clicking on "last reported incident" and the system would complete the new incident with the information already provided in the last reported incident. After the first step, if the operator has detected a machine incident, the next step is to identify what type of machine incident has occurred (e.g., "poka-yoke malfunctioning," "machine stopped," "machine alarm," or "abnormal noise coming from the machine"). Conversely, if the operator has detected a quality problem in the produced part, then the next step is to determine if that part can be classified as an OK or NOK part. Following that, if the piece is classified as a NOK, the operator will then identify what sort of defect is detected in the NOK part, e.g., marbling, burrs, and short piece. Similarly, even if the piece is ultimately classified as an OK part, the operator will still be required to report what sort of deviation was found on that part to trigger the extra checking, e.g., part hotter than usual, early signs of burrs or marbling. The final step is to indicate the exact location/s of detected quality failure in a 3D part model (which can be rotated and expanded) before saving the report.

The range of steps that the operator needs to follow to report an incident ranges from 1 step (reporting a new incident with the same characteristics as the last reported incident) to 5 steps (reporting a part incident, identifying if it is an OK/NOK part, defining the defect identified and its location on the piece, saving the report).

The assembly operator will report the incident using an HMI on the main screen (touchscreen) of his/her workstation. Below is an example of a draft HMI that could

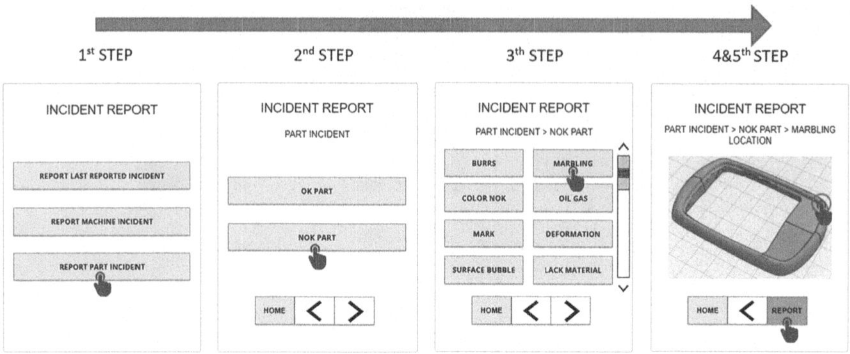

Fig. 2 Example of reporting a NOK part incident (marbling) using the HMI (sketch) installed on the main screen

be used for this purpose. In this scenario, the operator wanted to report a NOK part associated with a marbling defect. To do so, the assembly operator will have to follow five different steps: click on "Report part incident" →click on "NOK part" →click on "Marbling" →click on "the location/s of the part (3D part model) where the incident was found" →click on "report" (see Fig. 2).

4 Closing the Loop: Providing Gathered Information to the Human Agents for Enhancing Group and Individual SA in the HMI

The data input gathered from assembly operators in real time will be made available to be consulted by any worker when required, as it will be displayed all the time on the main screen of their working position. This information will be especially relevant for the assembly operators, mainly during their shift handover, since it will allow for a fast, organized, and complete update of their SA about that particular injection machine.

An example of an HMI with the information that can be provided to the team members can be found in Figs. 3 and 4. The first important characteristic of this tool is that the operator must be able to select different time intervals so that he/she can get information about the system's status for a desired period. For example, during the shift handover, an assembly operator might first want to have an overall overview of the incidents that occurred within the last 6 hours, and then, depending on the long-term status of the system, he/she might want to continue consulting different time intervals, e.g., last 60 minutes, to gather specific information about what has recently occurred. After choosing the desired time interval, the screen will be updated to show, on the one hand, the summary of incidents that occurred during

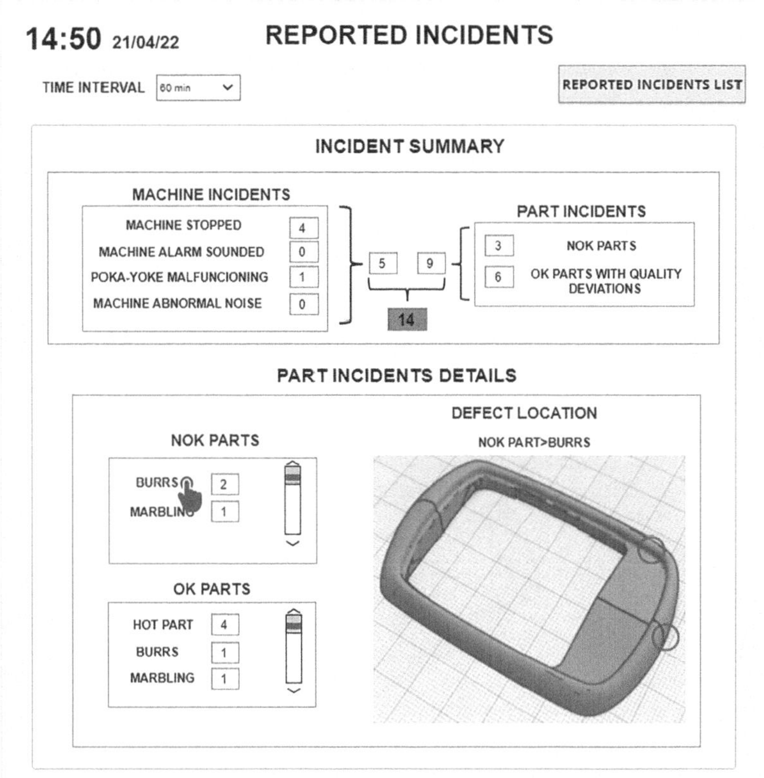

Fig. 3 Example of how the information could be provided (sketch HMI) to assembly operators in their main working screen (Incident report main page)

that time interval and, on the other hand, detailed information about the eventual quality failures found on produced parts.

The summary of incidents has been divided into machine and part incidents and would show the number of times each type of incident has occurred. In the example below (Fig. 3), we can easily see that the machine stopped four times during the last 60 minutes, and the poka-yoke malfunctioned once, causing five machine incidents. Moreover, we can also see nine incidents, two of which resulted in NOK parts being produced. Hence, during the last 60 minutes, a total of fourteen incidents were reported. The objective of this incident summary is to let the operator check, in a very simplistic way, the system's overall status for the selected period so that he/she can get an idea about how the system is working and what incidents (if any) have been reported. The operator could be confident that the system is working fine if no incidents were reported. However, if some incidents were reported, the operator could spend more time gathering more information about the system failures and be ready for possible follow-up interventions. The part incident detail section aims to provide specific information about reported failures in the quality of the produced

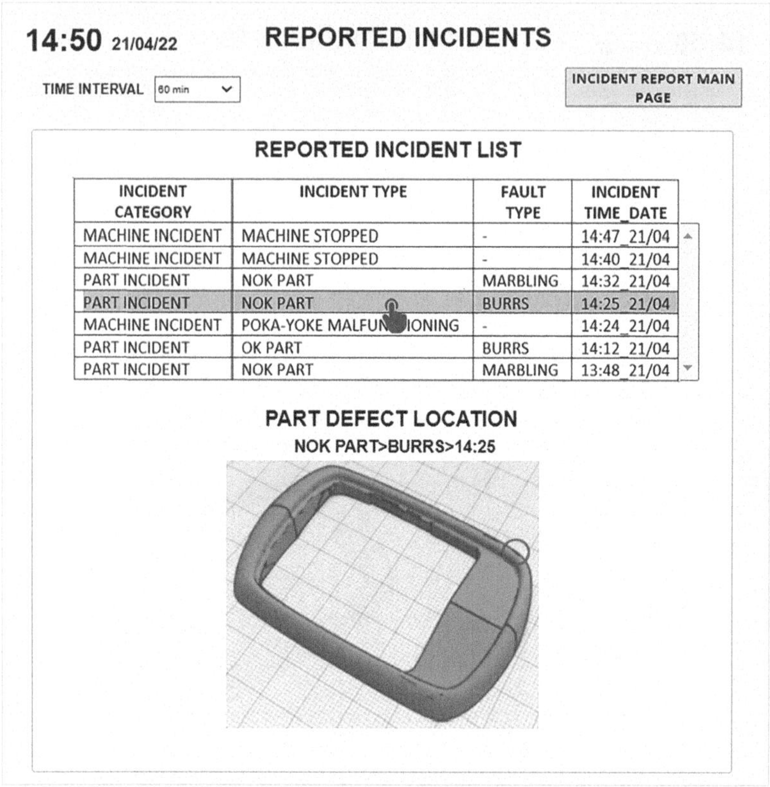

Fig. 4 Example of how the information could be provided (sketch HMI) to assembly operators in their main working screen (Reported incidents list page)

parts. In this section, the operator can find the specific defects reported, as well as the specific location of the defects, displayed in a 3D part model (once the operator clicks on the specific failure/s that he wants to consult). This information will make the operator more aware of the specific failures occurring in produced parts. This would ultimately predispose the operator to pay more attention to the possible appearance of those defects (and their expected location) in future produced pieces.

The operator will be able to access a more detailed incident report list by clicking on the button "Reported incidents list" located at the upper right corner of the "Incident report main page" (see Fig. 3). In this page (see Fig. 4), incidents will be listed one by one in order of appearance (from most to least recent incident with time and date of appearance) and classified according to their incident category and incident type (and fault type only for part incidents). Moreover, by clicking on a specific part of an incident, the operator can also consult the exact location of the defect found in that particular part of the incident. This list of reported incidents would give the operator a more detailed view of the timing in which each incident appeared, allowing them to understand the occurrence sequence of incidents better.

5 Conclusion, Practical Implications, and the Way Forward

Industry is rapidly evolving as new complex systems are being implemented. This unavoidable evolution requires the development of new forms of interactions between humans and the new technology to achieve the desired improvement in productivity and efficiency and to promote the welfare of workers. In this new context in which boundaries between human and nonhuman agents disappear, in which robotics arms, exoskeletons, and AI share the same working place with muscles, bones, and brains, we better start paying attention to the importance of communication to avoid falling into the well-known trap of the "Tower of Babel." The axiom is easy: communication between agents, whether between humans or not, is mandatory to achieve success. In this paper, we described how this human-machine teaming could be improved in a particular case study, focusing on the importance of achieving a COP and enhanced situational awareness in the three levels of analysis as the key elements to achieve success. More specifically, we developed a protocol for gathering in real-time relevant information from assembly operators that could be used as input for the AI algorithms for predicting deviations of the injection molding machine from nominal parameters and for feeding a real-time tool that would keep updating the status of the system to be checked by other workers when needed; this would ultimately lead to an increase in situational awareness in the three levels of analysis:

- **Individual and group SA:** workers will better understand the system's current state by checking the newly developed tool that will offer the most relevant information required from assembly operators to perform their functions. In other words, human agents can exchange relevant information to enhance group SA by using this tool. This would be especially relevant during shift handover when assembly operators must update their SA as quickly and efficiently as possible. According to Endsley's model, the three components of individual SA will be improved. The tool was developed following ergonomic principles of usability and user experience, which means that the information is displayed in a way that enhances the perception of the required information. This relevant information would be key to optimal comprehension of the situation, ultimately leading to a better prediction of future events (enhancing the decision-making process).
- **System SA and Human-AI:** human and nonhuman agents will be able to share relevant information by using the newly developed tool in a way that they will manage to construct different but congruent perspectives of the state of the system for achieving common goals. AI agents are becoming increasingly stronger, and they are increasingly becoming more context aware. It can be defined as the ability of a system to understand and respond to the context in which it operates. This involves considering factors such as the environment, user preferences, historical data, and real-time information to make more informed and contextually relevant decisions (Rodis 2018). It can also be compared to situational awareness in humans along the following dimensions:

- Adaptability: Both context awareness in AI and situational awareness in humans involve the ability to adapt to changing circumstances. Humans continuously update their understanding of a situation based on new information, and context-aware AI aims to do the same via sensors, vision systems, and other inputs (some also rely on human communication).
- Information Integration: Situational awareness often involves integrating information from various senses and cognitive processes to form a holistic understanding of the environment. Context-aware AI similarly integrates data from different sources, such as sensors, databases, and user interactions, to make informed decisions.
- Learning and Improvement: Humans learn from experience and improve their situational awareness over time. Similarly, context-aware AI systems can employ machine learning algorithms to enhance their performance by learning from data and user interactions.
- Limitations: However, while context-aware AI can process vast amounts of data quickly, it may still lack the intuition and depth of understanding that humans possess. Human situational awareness often involves a deeper level of emotional and social intelligence, which can be challenging for AI to fully replicate.

In summary, context awareness in AI is crucial for building robust and adaptive systems. While it shares some similarities with human situational awareness, there are still significant differences, and AI systems are continually evolving to improve their ability to understand and respond to diverse contexts.

In the context of our application, the AI agent will gain input from assembly operators about the state of the system (and from other sources), information that will be processed and given back as useful feedback for the employers. In other words, humans will gain advantage from the AI, as it can auto-adjust parameters, offer predictions, and alert technicians when human intervention is required. However, AI cannot work in isolation and requires relevant information that could only be provided by humans, such as feedback related to the actual solution adopted for a recovery action in response to the detection of a problem, thus closing the loop. This teaming between the human and the machine will only be possible by achieving a COP through the exchange of relevant information that would lead to this necessary increase in the system SA.

It is worth noting that the data analysis revealed a great need in the industry for developing protocols and tools for enhancing group SA. In this case study, we found that assembly operators would intuitively try to achieve a COP by exchanging relevant information with their partners during their shift handover. This would help the relief worker get a pretty good update on the state of affairs when taking charge of a specific workstation. This situation could be more common in the industry than expected, and we believe that having an HMI and a tool that supports a better structured shift handover could be an advantageous by-product.

The practical implications of this study can be advantageous for businesses and workers across various sectors, especially in safety-critical domains like control room scenarios within the process industry. Additionally, its relevance extends to manufacturing, where the expenses associated with defects may result in product recalls and potential legal proceedings (Bebeteidoh and Takim 2016). As we have highlighted throughout the entire manuscript, enhancing the SA of the different agents of a complex system would increase productivity, safety, and efficiency as the number of errors in production plus the time required to detect and fix them should decrease. Implementing a protocol or tool for monitoring the overall system state and incorporating quality gates for detecting and correcting various errors is a recognized successful strategy in manufacturing processes. For instance, if the production process reveals a predominance of defects caused by human error, a review of the production process to identify potential contributing factors to the error, coupled with a reassessment of how computerized systems support error detection and correction, constitutes a reliable mitigation strategy. Similarly, if employees frequently report false positives or false negatives in a production line, conducting a root cause identification workshop and revising the currently employed systems for visual inspection, along with providing dedicated training, can assist the workforce in effectively utilizing the available method to prevent misclassification. Conversely, AI systems can enhance overall traditional quality gate systems by providing decision support algorithms based on historical occurrences of different types of defects and the status of correlated process parameters. However, the operators can enhance and contribute to the algorithms by providing feedback and error verification at the end of each recovery process.

This can, for instance, be done through different approaches, such as reinforcement learning or retraining (Abbas et al. 2024; Morillo et al. 2022). Both retraining and reinforcement learning can incorporate human feedback. In retraining, humans might provide labeled data for supervised learning. In reinforcement learning, feedback can be used as a reward or penalty signal to guide the model's learning.

In summary, having a generally updated picture of the state of the production system through the use of specific protocols and AI decision support tools, as the one proposed in this research work, would always be helpful not only to reduce errors and increase performance and well-being of the workers but to identify any weaknesses in the production line and addressing root causes more swiftly. The interplay between operators' experience and the AI decision support or vision systems can offer more robust results. As human factors practitioners, we need to identify the actual steps of each activity, and the human agent must keep an active role not to lose situational awareness and engagement. For those steps, the interfacing between the human and the AI support systems plays a very relevant part in enhancing two-way communication and empowering action on both sides. Therefore, particular care must be put into its HMI design.

Finally, it is important to note that while the results of this study appear promising, caution must be exercised as the proposed protocol and tool are still in the early stages of development and have not undergone validation. Additionally, the limitation of a low sample size should be acknowledged. However, the high level of convergence in participant responses instills confidence in the findings. The specific information the AI agent should provide to employers is yet to be determined, preventing a detailed exploration of suggested metrics. Nevertheless, there is a consensus that employers are interested in understanding how the new tool will impact the average time to detect and correct process deviations and the overall error rate in production. Subsequent research is necessary to further advance the collaborative relationship between AI and humans in this manufacturing case study.

References

Abbas AN, Chasparis GC, Kelleher JD (2024) Hierarchical framework for interpretable and specialized deep reinforcement learning-based predictive maintenance. Data Knowl Eng 149:102240. https://doi.org/10.1016/j.datak.2023.102240

Anastasi S, Madonna M, Monica L (2021) Implications of embedded artificial intelligence-machine learning on safety of machinery. In: Procedia Computer Science, vol 180. Elsevier, Amsterdam, pp 338–343. https://doi.org/10.1016/j.procs.2021.01.245

Bebeteidoh O, Takim S (2016) Toyota's slow response to manufacturing defects leading to recalls: Result of poor communication strategy. J Transp Technol 6(5):420–435. https://doi.org/10.4236/jtts.2016.65034

Bedny G, Meister D (1999) Theory of activity and situation awareness. Int J Cogn Ergon 3(1):63–72. https://doi.org/10.1207/s15327566ijce0301_5

Brandon DP, Hollingshead AB (2004) Transactive memory systems in organizations: matching tasks, expertise, and people. Organ Sci 15(6):633–644. https://doi.org/10.1287/orsc.1040.0069

Endsley MR (1993) A survey of situation awareness requirements in air-to-air combat fighters. Int J Aviat Psychol 3(2):157–168. https://doi.org/10.1207/s15327108ijap0302_6

Endsley MR (1995a) Measurement of situation awareness in dynamic systems. Hum Factors 37(1):65–84. https://doi.org/10.1518/001872095779049499

Endsley MR (1995b) Toward a theory of situation awareness in dynamic systems. Hum Factors 37(1):32–64. https://doi.org/10.1518/001872095779049543

Endsley MR (2023) Supporting human-ai teams: transparency, explainability, and situation awareness. Comput Hum Behav 140:107574. https://doi.org/10.1016/j.chb.2022.107574

Endsley MR, Jones DG (2012) Designing for situation awareness: an approach to human-centered design, 2nd edn. CRC Press, London

Endsley MR, Kiris EO (1995) The out-of-the-loop performance problem and level of control in automation. Hum Factors 37(2):381–394. https://doi.org/10.1518/001872095779064555

Härtel CE, Smith KA, Prince C (1991) Defining aircrew coordination: searching mishaps for meaning. In: Proceedings of the 6th International Symposium on Aviation Psychology, Columbus, OH, pp 389–395

Hwang GH, Yoon WC (2020) A new approach to requirement development for a common operational picture to support distributed situation awareness. Saf Sci 125:104569. https://doi.org/10.1016/j.ssci.2019.104569

Klein G (2000) Analysis of situation awareness from critical incident reports. In: Endsley MR, Garland DJ (eds) Situation awareness analysis and measurement, CRC Press, Mahwah, pp 51–71. https://doi.org/10.1201/9780203745522-4

Krupitzer C, Wagenhals T, Züfle M, Lesch V, Schäfer D, Mozaffarin A, et al (2020) A survey on predictive maintenance for industry 4.0. arXiv preprint arXiv:200208224. http://arxiv.org/abs/2002.08224

Mell JN, Van Knippenberg D, Van Ginkel WP (2014) The catalyst effect: the impact of transactive memory system structure on team performance. Acad Manag J 57(4):1154–1173. https://doi.org/10.5465/amj.2012.0587

Morillo CA, Jawla D, Kelleher JD, Demichela M (2022) Safety-critical systems in the automotive sector: Pros and cons in the current state-of-the-art of human performance assessment. In: Leva MC, Patelli E, Podofillini L, Wilson S (eds) Proceedings of the 32nd European safety and reliability conference (ESREL 2022). Research Publishing, Singapore, pp 3226–3233. https://doi.org/10.3850/978-981-18-5183-4_S33-03-571-cd

Niemantsverdriet K, van Essen H, Pakanen M, Eggen B (2019) Designing for awareness in interactions with shared systems: the dass framework. ACM Trans Comput-Hum Interact (TOCHI) 26(6):1–41. https://doi.org/10.1145/3359593

Pérez AA, Estrada-Lugo HD, Muñoz-de Escalona Fernández E, Leva MC, Aperribai J, Aranburu A (2022) Modifying a manufacturing task for teamwork between humans and AI: Initial data collection to guide requirements specifications. In: Leva MC, Patelli E, Podofillini L, Wilson S (eds) Proceedings of the 32nd European safety and reliability conference (ESREL 2022). Research Publishing, Singapore, pp 3267–3276. https://doi.org/10.3850/978-981-18-5183-4_S33-08-671-cd

Redding RE (1992) Analysis of operational errors and workload in air traffic control. In: Proceedings of the human factors society annual meeting. SAGE Publications, vol 36, pp 1321–1325. https://doi.org/10.1177/154193129203601712

Ren Y, Argote L (2011) Transactive memory systems 1985–2010: an integrative framework of key dimensions, antecedents, and consequences. Acad Manag Ann 5(1):189–229. https://doi.org/10.5465/19416520.2011.590300

Rodis P (2018) On defining and modeling context-awareness. Int J Pervasive Comput Commun 14(2):111–123. https://doi.org/10.1108/IJPCC-12-2017-0074

Salas E, Prince C, Baker DP, Shrestha L (1995) Situation awareness in team performance: implications for measurement and training. Hum Factors 37(1):123–136. https://doi.org/10.1518/001872095779049525

Shuffler ML, Jiménez-Rodríguez M, Kramer WS (2015) The science of multiteam systems: a review and future research agenda. Small Group Res 46(6):659–699. https://doi.org/10.1177/1046496415603455

Smith K, Hancock PA (1995) Situation awareness is adaptive, externally directed consciousness. Hum Factors 37(1):137–148. https://doi.org/10.1518/001872095779049444

Sorensen LJ, Stanton NA (2013) Y is best: how distributed situational awareness is mediated by organisational structure and correlated with task success. Saf Sci 56:72–79. https://doi.org/10.1016/j.ssci.2012.12.001

Stanton NA, Stewart R, Harris D, Houghton RJ, Baber C, McMaster R, Salmon PM, Hoyle G, Walker GH, Young M, et al (2017) Distributed situation awareness in dynamic systems: theoretical development and application of an ergonomics methodology. In: Situational Awareness. Routledge, London, pp 419–442. https://doi.org/10.4324/9781315253800-27

Steen-Tveit K, Munkvold BE (2021) From common operational picture to common situational understanding: an analysis based on practitioner perspectives. Saf Sci 142:105381, https://doi.org/10.1016/j.ssci.2021.105381

Replicating Skilled Drivers' Delivery Route Plans Using Particle Filter Optimization

Koichiro Yamaguchi, Hisashi Tsuji, and Shohji Ohtsubo

Abstract With the spread of electronic commerce, parcel delivery services are expanding. However, delivery businesses are suffering from a chronic shortage of human resources, making it urgent to improve delivery efficiency. Currently, the selection of delivery routes is often left to drivers. Inexperienced drivers rely on car navigation systems to determine their delivery routes, but these systems are for ordinary drivers, primarily assisting with single journeys and reducing driving time. They do not, for example, provide information on safe and suitable places to stop for unloading. On the other hand, a skilled driver will choose an efficient route based on his experience without relying on car navigation. In this paper, we use particle filter optimization to create a learned model replicating the delivery routes of skilled drivers and apply this model to delivery route planning and identification. The model replicated 74% of the delivery route of a skilled driver in the area studied, achieving a 7.0% improvement in accuracy rate over the shortest-path route and, in the non-learned area, achieved 65% replication and 4.4% improvement.

1 Introduction

In Japan, the number of parcel deliveries increased by approximately 2.4% in 2021, in line with the continued upward trend observed in recent years (Ministry of Land, Infrastructure, Transport and Tourism of Japan 2022). Today, however, delivery businesses are suffering from a chronic shortage of human resources, creating a need to provide more efficient deliveries with fewer employees. Currently, the planning of delivery routes is often left to drivers. Skilled drivers do not rely on car navigation systems but use their own experience. It is not easy for an inexperienced driver to choose an efficient route, which is the problem we face today. This paper discusses a method of using particle filter optimization to create a route-learned model that

K. Yamaguchi (✉) · H. Tsuji · S. Ohtsubo
Panasonic Connect Co., Ltd., Yokohama, Kanagawa, Japan
e-mail: yamaguchi.koichiro@jp.panasonic.com; tsuji.hisashi@jp.panasonic.com; ohtsubo.shohji@jp.panasonic.com

C. K. Coursaris et al. (eds.), *The Design of Human-Centered Artificial Intelligence for the Workplace*, Progress in IS, https://doi.org/10.1007/978-3-031-83512-4_24

replicates the delivery route of skilled drivers and applies this model to delivery route planning and identification.

2 Problems to Address When Planning Delivery Routes to Individual Houses

Delivery services to individual houses have been increasing due to an increase in deliveries of articles purchased online, as well as the growth of parcel delivery services. This paper assumes that small cars are used to deliver parcels to individual houses. The numerous delivery destinations are different for each delivery run. Therefore, determining an efficient route in advance is challenging and complex.

Skilled drivers have their own methods of improving efficiency, such as avoiding crossings, using trunk roads, and limiting left or right turns. They take this approach to save time, improve safety, and reduce stress. It is a complicated combination of motivations and reasons, so translating them into algorithmic logic is challenging. In many cases, skilled drivers cannot explain their decision-making process in the form of organized knowledge. Interviews with skilled drivers included vague responses such as choosing the road with the least stress and selecting the most straightforward route possible.

Unskilled drivers rely on a car navigation system to determine routes. However, it is not very helpful in the field because it often indicates routes with the shortest distance or time and does not indicate routes that are safe for delivery and less mentally taxing. Skilled drivers change navigation routes based on their own experience, but unskilled drivers need six months to a year to be able to make such route decisions.

Effective route selection can be part of the solution to the problems of logistics operations, such as long working hours, physical labor, and low wages. It can be argued that the route of a skilled human driver is better in terms of safety and other tacit knowledge, and proposing a system that takes human behavior into account is an excellent example of human-centric AI using machine learning methods to improve employee well-being.

There have been previous attempts to solve the problem described. One example solution describes route determination by assigning costs to roads traveled by vehicles (Nagase and Fujitani 2013). However, in this case, the travel history of all roads where the route is to be determined is required. This paper proposes a method that can be applied to regions without travel history.

Another proposed solution focuses on reproducing driver routes using Maximum Entropy Inverse Reinforcement Learning (Ziebart et al. 2008). This method showed a 6.4% improvement over the conventional method in terms of the amount of the route distance that matches the actual route of a human driver.

3 Methods of Replicating Skilled Drivers' Delivery Route Plans

3.1 Summary

We begin by summarizing the development of our replication method and will then describe it in detail. First, a GPS logger device in the vehicle collects data on a driver's delivery route history. Based on the road features extracted from the data, a skilled route-learned model is created through particle filter optimization. Based on this model, a delivery route plan is then set up to allow the replication of a route chosen by a skilled driver. Figure 1 shows the overall design concept of the method.

The particle filter used to develop the skilled route-learned model is discussed in Sect. 3.2. The details and collection period of skilled drivers' delivery route history data are discussed in Sect. 3.3. Learning subject data, route-choosing methods, learning methods, input/output data, evaluation indexes, and learned results regarding the particle filter optimization method are discussed in Sect. 3.4. A method of applying a learned model resulting from particle filter optimization will be discussed in Sect. 3.5.

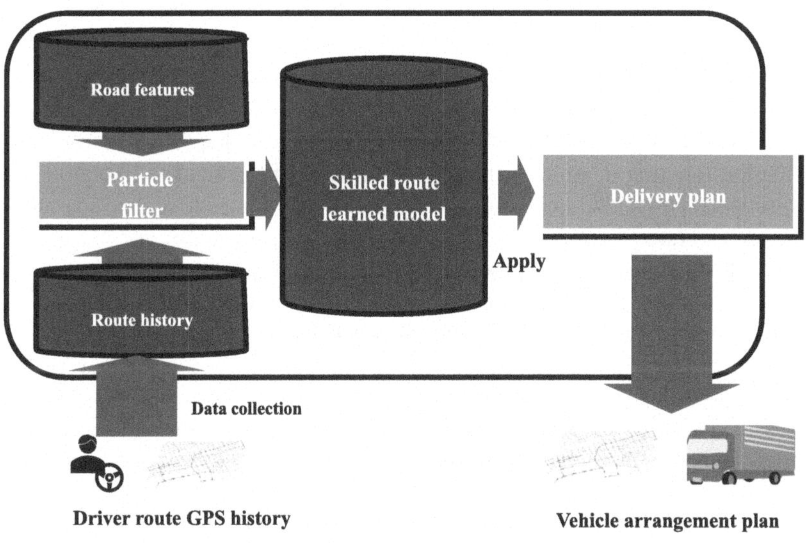

Fig. 1 Particle filter optimization for delivery using skilled drivers' route history

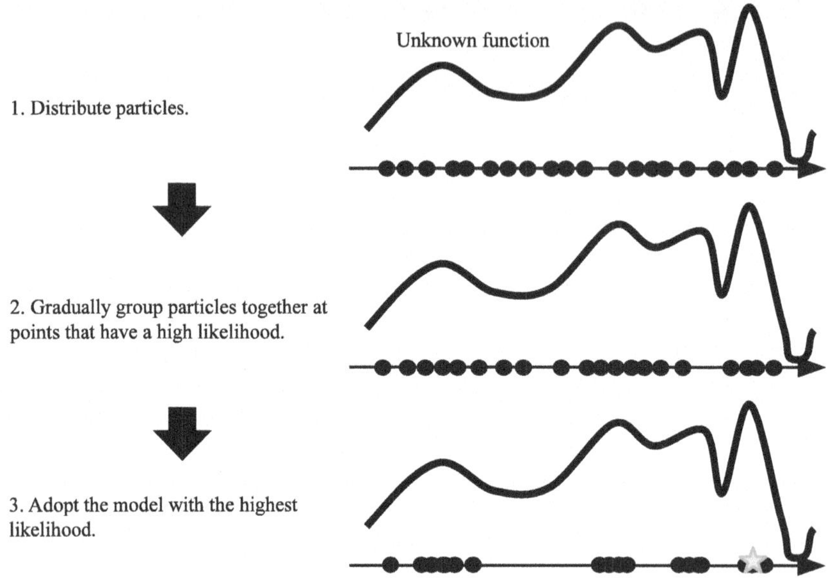

Fig. 2 Particle filtering process

3.2 Particle Filter

A particle filter is a method of estimating time-series data using a probability distribution function in which particles are distributed to calculate likelihoods and then grouped at high likelihood points. This process is iterated to realize an optimum learned model (see Fig. 2).

Since this learning model is expected to be a discrete model and is not suitable for minimizing the objective function by differentiation, a particle filter that uses a sampling method instead of differentiation was used (Kitagawa 2005). Note that particle filters are often used for object tracking and have the advantage of being applicable to probability distributions of complex shapes. However, they also have the disadvantage of requiring a large number of particles to achieve sufficient accuracy and high computational cost.

3.3 Collecting Data

Initially, a test was conducted using small supermarket delivery vehicles to develop our replication method. When receiving an online order, the office instructs the branch nearest the customer's residence to deliver the item to their house. In the test, four delivery vehicles, which start from the supermarket's branch to deliver articles to at least one house, are each fitted with a global positioning system (GPS) logger

Fig. 3 Net supermarket and delivery points for learning

that records GPS point data every 5 mm along their route. The test was run for about ten months, and data was collected during that period. No personal information is included in the collected data.

3.4 Particle Filter Optimization

Figure 3 is a map showing a supermarket's delivery area. The red star represents the supermarket, and the circles represent delivery destinations.

In this form of learning, the learning subject data is defined as a delivery history, i.e., a history of delivery routes from one delivery destination to the next, that a skilled driver chooses. This delivery history is expressed as an ordered set of roads. A road is a minimum unit of a route leading from one intersection to another in the map data. In the graph, roads are denoted as edges, and intersections are denoted as nodes. Roads making up the delivery history each have road features as added information, which will be described later.

The data collected for the test consists of 8101 delivery histories from a supermarket that were recorded over about ten months. Of these delivery histories, 7601 are used as training data and 500 as evaluation data. Figure 4 illustrates multiple delivery histories to the same delivery destination (the circle). A thick edge represents an actual delivery history.

The route-choosing method we adopted is built on the hypothesis that a skilled driver chooses a route based on the road features. In this hypothesis, individual road features are multiplied by weighting factors, weighted road features are summed up to determine road costs, and a route that incurs the minimum cost is determined (see Fig. 5). In contrast, the conventional route-choosing method selects a route that minimizes the road path, i.e., the unit path to travel from one point to the next.

The road features used in this form of learning are listed in Table 1. All of these features can be objectively determined from the map data.

Our learning method defines explanatory variables as weighting factors by which individual road features are multiplied and defines objective variables as differences

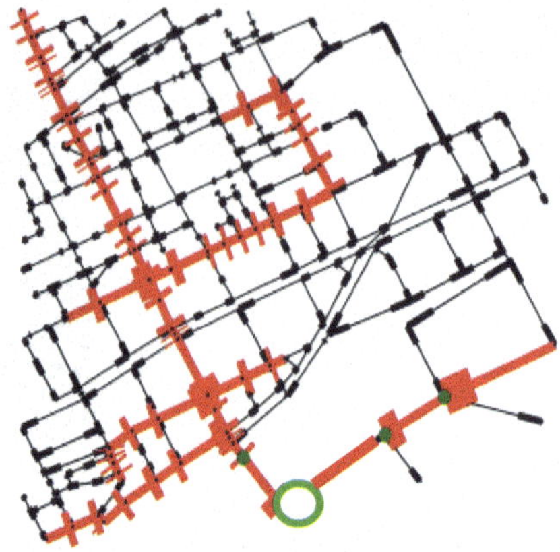

Fig. 4 Example of delivery routes

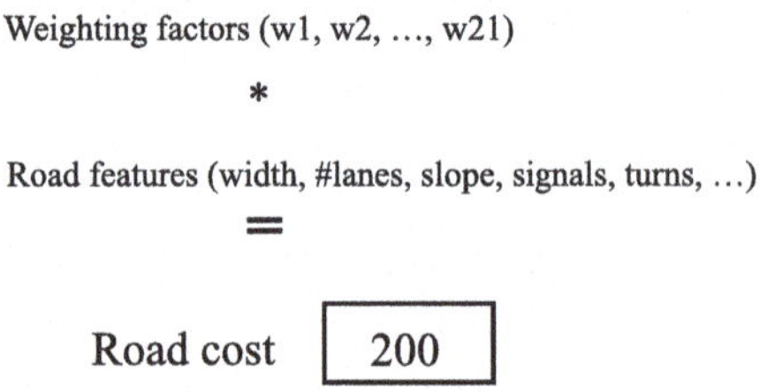

Fig. 5 Cost calculation for one road

Table 1 Used road features in our learning method

Road features, road end point features, relationships between different roads
Width
Number of lanes
Slope
Signal
Turns

between training data routes and minimum-cost routes corresponding to the start and end points of the training data routes at a certain point in the training stage. These differences between both routes are calculated for all training data items and are reduced through the learning process. The route differences are calculated using Levenshtein distance and shown in a graph (see Fig. 6).

Input data includes the following:

- Road graph (in which actual roads are plotted)
- Delivery history (GPS data mapped into the above graph)
- Road features (22-dimensional data indicating the features of roads) Output data consists of the following:
- Weighting factors (22-dimensional numerical values corresponding to individual road features)

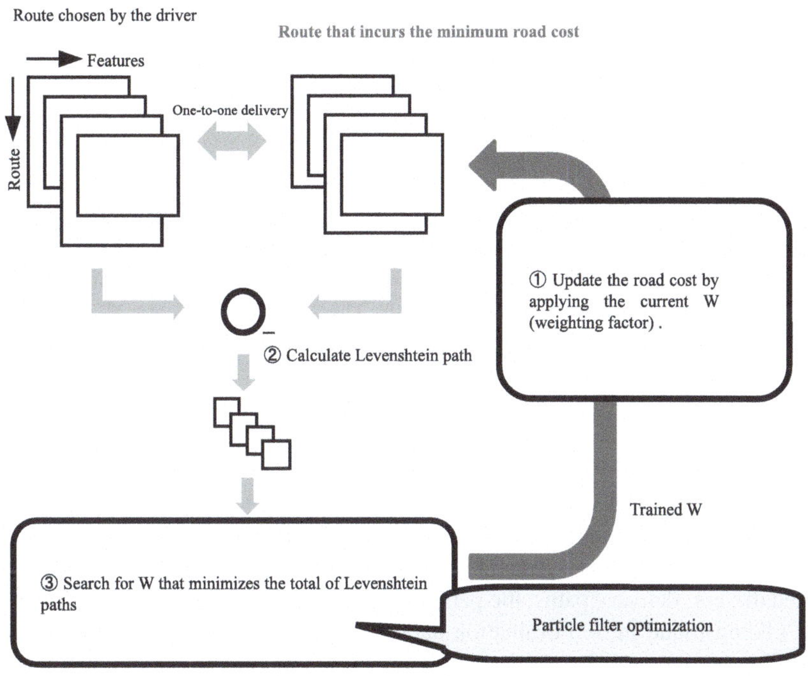

Fig. 6 Method of learning

Fig. 7 Real, learning, and shortest routes

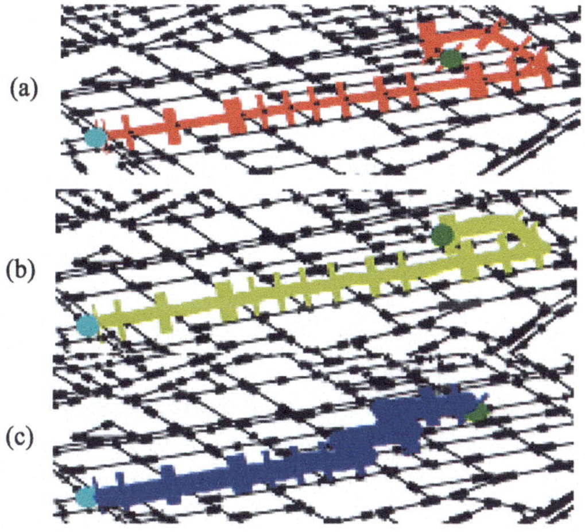

The learning process was repeated 200 times, with the criterion set as convergence of learning data.

Figure 7 shows an example of a route being determined using road costs calculated from weighting factors, i.e., output data. When determining a route using road costs, the route that minimizes the total load cost is chosen. Figure 7a shows

Table 2 Accuracy rate of particle filter optimization

	Learned point	Non-learned point
Particle filter optimization	73.53%	64.54%
Shortest path	66.49%	60.16%

an actual delivery history, Fig. 7b shows a route calculated using road costs, and Fig. 7c shows the route of the shortest path. In this example, about 3/4 of the actual delivery history matches the route calculated using road costs, and about half of the same matches the route of the shortest path. This example indicates that the route calculated using road costs offers higher replicability of a skilled driver's chosen route than the shortest path route.

3.4.1 Learning Results

The evaluation index is defined as the percentage of matching between route paths determined by road costs calculated from trained weighting factors and actual skilled drivers' delivery paths, the percentage of matching (from now on "matching rate") being found in 500 evaluation data items. The following formula gives the matching rate:

$$\text{Matching rate} = \frac{N_{\text{match}}}{N_{\text{total}}} \times 100\%$$

where

- N_{match} is the number of skilled drivers' delivery paths that match the route paths determined by road costs.
- N_{total} is the total number of skilled drivers' delivery paths.

The matching rate is based on the percentage match between the number of edges in the calculated route and the number of edges in the actual driver's route by graphing the route. A graph edge represents the smallest unit of road segmentation from intersection to intersection. For example, in Fig. 7, the route in Fig. 7a consists of 18 edges; in Fig. 7b, 15 edges are matched, resulting in a matching rate of 83.3%; and in Fig. 7c, 8 edges are matched, resulting in a matching rate of 53.3%. Note that a road represents a path between one intersection and another, depicted on the graph as an edge. The matching rate acquired using particle filter optimization has been compared with that using the shortest-path calculation method, which is the conventional route calculation method. Table 2 shows matching rates (%) obtained in the test.

According to the shortest-path calculation method, the matching rate of learned points, which are data training points, is 66.5%. This rate has been improved by particle filter optimization to 73.5%. Even when weighting factors determined at learned points are applied to non-learned points, which are not data training points, the matching rate of 60.2% achieved by the shortest-path calculation method was increased to 64.5%. In this experiment, the matching rate used for recall and precision was not calculated.

3.5 Applying a Learned Model

Figure 8 shows examples in which delivery route plans are set based on road costs determined by particle filter optimization.

Figure 8a shows an actual skilled driver's delivery history, Fig. 8b shows a delivery route plan set by particle filter optimization, and Fig. 8c shows a delivery route plan set using the conventional shortest-path calculation method. These are delivery plans to multiple destinations by multiple vehicles. In Fig. 8b, all vehicles' total delivery road costs are expressed as an objective function. In Fig. 8c, all vehicles' total delivery road distances are expressed as an objective function. Comparing an actual skilled delivery history, indicated by the unbroken line in Fig. 8a, a single driver's delivery route plan, indicated by the unbroken line on the left side in Fig. 8b, and two drivers' delivery route plan, indicated by upper and lower unbroken lines on the left side in Fig. 8c, we find that, as shown in the area demarcated by the thick broken line, a skilled route, which has not been set using conventional planning, is newly established. The replicability of skilled delivery route planning will be evaluated in the future, including an assessment of the evaluation index setting.

Table 3 shows the results of the collected skilled drivers' delivery history, the shortest path, and the route determined by the particle filter optimization in terms of the percentages of selecting the road features that are considered to be indicators of safety, such as "stop" (meaning an intersection with poor visibility or a high possibility of a run-out), "narrow road," and "main road merge" ("main road" generally means a large road with high traffic). The values indicate the percentage when the shortest path is 100. In all cases, the skilled drivers' delivery history was lower than the shortest path. This result indicates that the skilled drivers' routes are safer than the shortest path. Furthermore, the percentage of the route determined by the particle filter optimization is also lower than that of the shortest path, which indicates that this is a safety-oriented result and can reproduce the skilled driver's route.

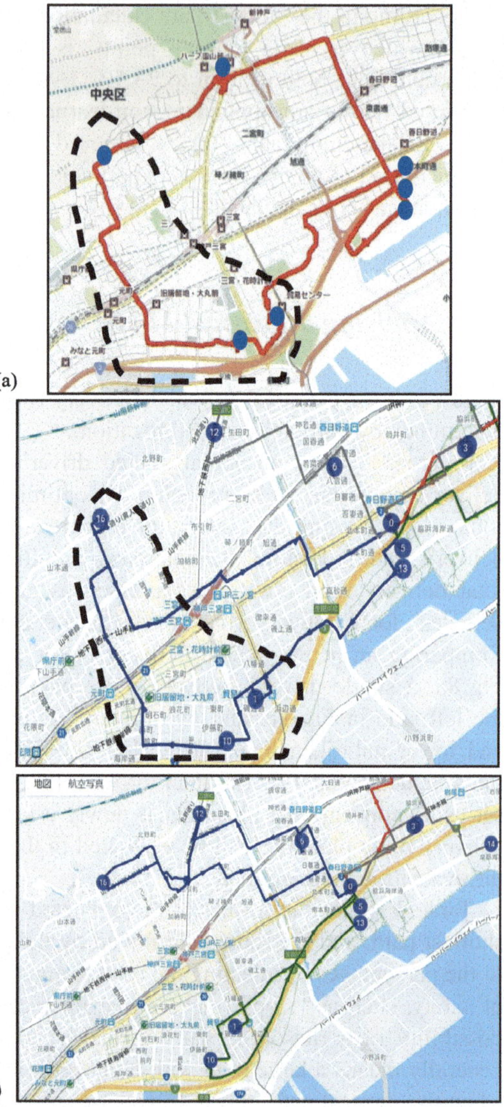

(a)
(b)
(c)

Fig. 8 Real, learning, and shortest delivery plans

Table 3 Ratio of road features

	Stop	Narrow road	Main road merge
Shortest path	100	100	100
Skilled drivers' history	73	73	98
Particle filter optimization	58	54	98

4 Conclusion

This chapter discussed a skilled route-learned model that replicates skilled drivers' delivery routes using particle filter optimization. In the tested area, 74% of the skilled drivers' delivery routes are replicated, representing a 7.08% increase in the matching rate from the shortest path route calculation method. In addition, 65% of the skilled drivers' delivery route is replicated in the non-learned area, achieving a 4.4% increase in the matching rate. We plan to enhance our method of replication in future studies. It will require the following approaches: 1. using features of multiple roads; 2. adding statistical data to feature data; and 3. building a sustainable learned system.

This study is only intended for delivery in Japan and only for small vehicles. Having our method tested only in Japan means that our method assumes a delivery area with many narrow roads, traffic signals, and one-way streets, which are specific to the road conditions in Japan. Similarly, many small vehicles are used in the pilot study area, which could be critical regarding our model's assumptions and generalizability to other regions. However, the learning method used to develop our model is not limited to Japan. If, for example, it is trained using US map data and driving data of large vehicles, we expect the resulting model to be valid for large vehicle delivery in the USA. However, further research must be conducted to verify our expectations regarding the learning method's effectiveness in other parts of the world.

In addition, although we defined the training data as data from skilled drivers, there may be a mixture of data unsuitable for training data, such as when a driver is temporarily replaced or when a skilled driver makes a mistake in route selection. The handling of such data and its impact on models' performance is also a future research topic.

5 Example Use

Examples of actual field use are shown in Figs. 9, 10, 11, and 12. As shown in Figs. 9 and 10, for one plan, both the plan in the shortest distance and the plan in this AI can be presented and selected by the user, or as shown in Fig. 11, the two can be overlapped and compared and selected. Adopting only the appropriate part of the plan and replanning the rest is also possible, as in Fig. 12.

In projecting these optimized routes and plans to drivers, it is possible to improve the driver's sufficiency by presenting the optimized route and the reason for the optimization. For example, in the case of Table 2, it is assumed that the driver can be convinced of the result by presenting the route with the additional information, "This is a route with the ratio of Stop and Narrow roads reduced by half." Such proactive presentation can also be assumed to reduce the driver's operational burden by using HUD to present the information automatically.

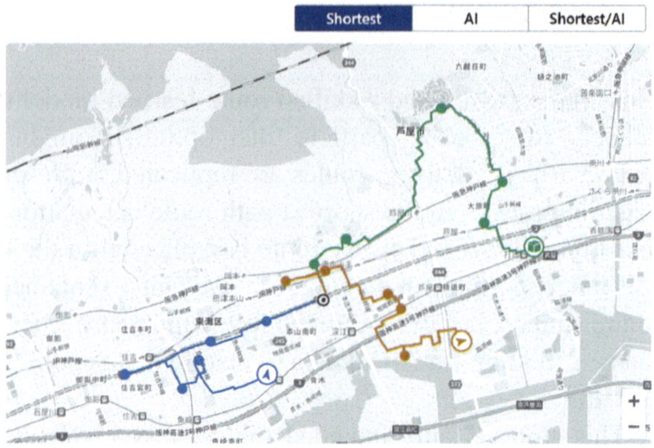

Fig. 9 Shortest route delivery plan

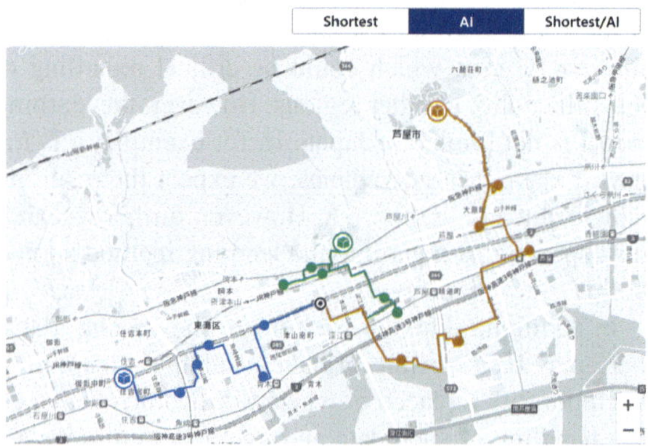

Fig. 10 AI route delivery plan

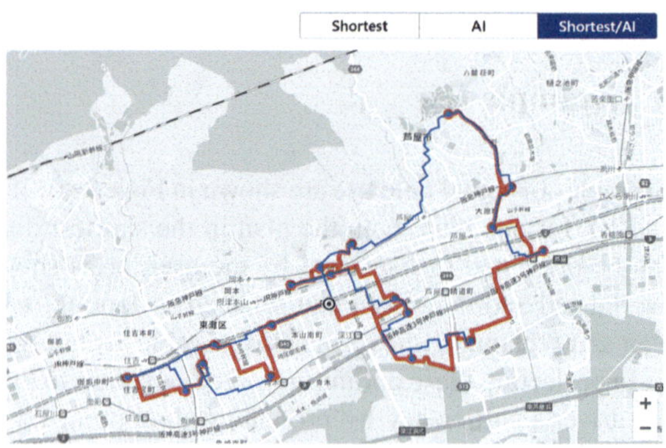

Fig. 11 Shortest and AI route delivery plan

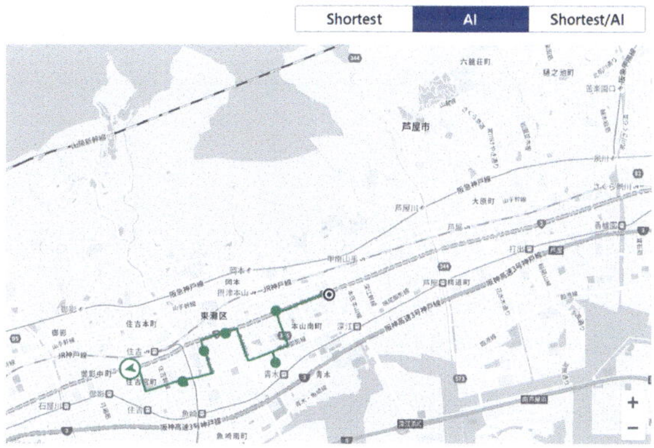

Fig. 12 One of AI route delivery plans

References

Kitagawa G (2005) Introduction to time series modeling. Kitagawa Iwanami Shoten, Article 15.2. (e) Implementation of re-sampling method

Ministry of Land, Infrastructure, Transport and Tourism of Japan (2022) Parcel delivery service performance records. Technical report. https://www.e-stat.go.jp/stat-search/files?tclass=000001147581&cycle=1&year=20220&month=12040606, report Released in 2021

Nagase K, Fujitani K (2013) Apparatus, method, and program for generating road information. https://patents.google.com/patent/US8583362/en

Ziebart BD, Maas AL, Bagnell JA, Dey AK, et al (2008) Maximum entropy inverse reinforcement learning. In: AAAI, Chicago, IL, vol 8, pp 1433–1438

Socially Embedded Agents in Organizational Contexts: Bulk Email as a Design Example

Ruoyan Kong and Joseph A. Konstan

Abstract The employees of the authors' university, like employees of many large organizations, receive hundreds of pieces of information weekly through bulk emails from the university's central offices. The employees are overwhelmed by the volume. At the same time, the senders feel frustrated because their messages are not getting employees' attention. Employees, senders, management, and even the organization itself all have different interests in what messages should be sent to whom and read by whom. This multi-stakeholder problem is a common challenge for socially embedded agents in organizational contexts. These agents cannot succeed by focusing on only one stakeholder's perspective. In this chapter, we use this case study to explore the design challenge of an organizational communication agent to address such a multi-stakeholder problem. We show in detail how an analysis of the various stakeholders' perspectives and the entities of the system can lead to a representation of the problem space that can be optimized. We find this case study useful to motivate designers of other workplace agent systems to consider how to incorporate the perspectives of different stakeholders in their designs.

1 Introduction

The employees of the author's university receive hundreds of pieces of information weekly through **bulk emails** from the university's central offices, including massive newsletters with over 30 stories, emails with a single message, emails from human resources, IT, etc. The contents range from *chancellor search* and *naming updates* (see Fig. 1) to *social events* and *research stories*. The employees feel tired and impossible to filter out the irrelevant messages and still be aware of the relevant ones. At the same time, in the same university, a set of communicators, whose job is to get information from the central offices to the employees, feel frustrated because their

R. Kong (✉) · J. A. Konstan
University of Minnesota - Twin Cities, Minneapolis, MN, USA
e-mail: kong0135@umn.edu; konstan@umn.edu

C. K. Coursaris et al. (eds.), *The Design of Human-Centered Artificial Intelligence for the Workplace*, Progress in IS, https://doi.org/10.1007/978-3-031-83512-4_25

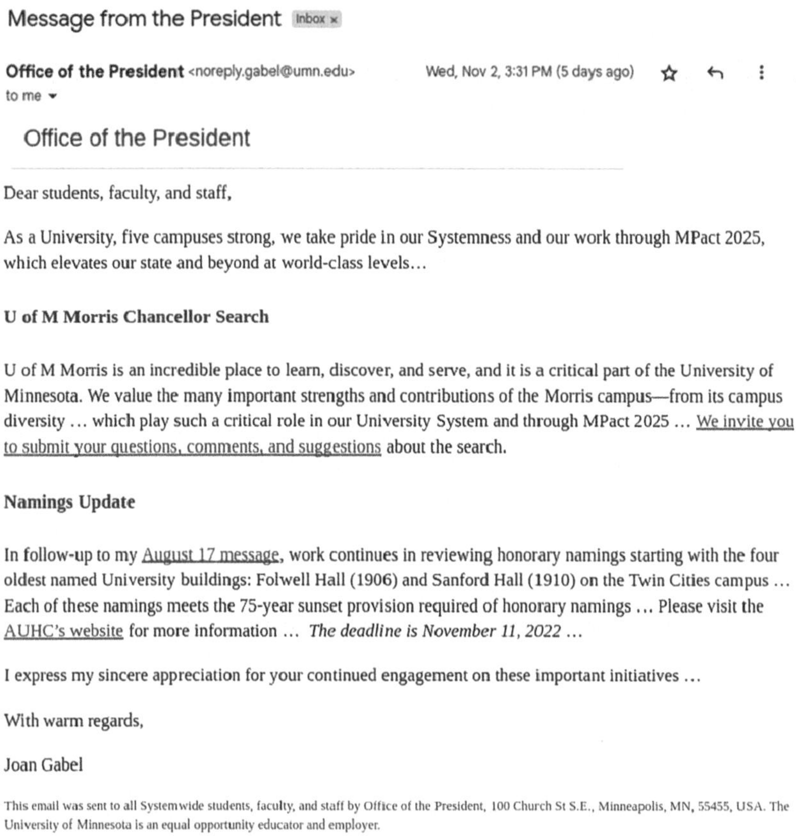

Message from the President Inbox ×

Office of the President <noreply.gabel@umn.edu> Wed, Nov 2, 3:31 PM (5 days ago)
to me

Office of the President

Dear students, faculty, and staff,

As a University, five campuses strong, we take pride in our Systemness and our work through MPact 2025, which elevates our state and beyond at world-class levels…

U of M Morris Chancellor Search

U of M Morris is an incredible place to learn, discover, and serve, and it is a critical part of the University of Minnesota. We value the many important strengths and contributions of the Morris campus—from its campus diversity … which play such a critical role in our University System and through MPact 2025 … We invite you to submit your questions, comments, and suggestions about the search.

Namings Update

In follow-up to my August 17 message, work continues in reviewing honorary namings starting with the four oldest named University buildings: Folwell Hall (1906) and Sanford Hall (1910) on the Twin Cities campus … Each of these namings meets the 75-year sunset provision required of honorary namings … Please visit the AUHC's website for more information … *The deadline is November 11, 2022 …*

I express my sincere appreciation for your continued engagement on these important initiatives …

With warm regards,

Joan Gabel

This email was sent to all Systemwide students, faculty, and staff by Office of the President, 100 Church St S.E., Minneapolis, MN, 55455, USA. The University of Minnesota is an equal opportunity educator and employer.

Fig. 1 An example organizational bulk email "*Office of the President*" of the study site, discussing *chancellor search* and *naming update*, was sent to all the staff and faculty

messages are not getting employees' attention, employees are not taking actions they asked, and they are pressured by their clients (i.e., the university leaders) to ensure that the employees are aware of these important things.

In fact, given this university's social context, its bulk email system (we referred to it as "**organizational bulk email system**") has an incentive failure. The central offices and leaders want their messages to be widely distributed; the communicators want to get their job done quickly; the employees want to protect their time and thus often ignore the messages that the central offices perceive as important (e.g., university goals, plans, leadership updates). As each stakeholder in this social system is acting based on their own interest, the university's promotion of its goals and values fails; its employees' time is wasted; its communication channels' reputations suffer. Therefore, an agent could help provide appropriate incentives to adjust the stakeholders' actions.

Today, there is no agent specifically designed for this organizational bulk email system. There are email applications such as Superhuman[1] and Tatem[2] to help recipients prioritize and reply to email; however, they are not designed for organizations where different stakeholders are involved. The challenge of organizational email has also led to the adoption of alternative tools such as Slack, Teams, and Google Chat, which provide greater awareness of team members and persistent threaded messages, but they are not designed for organization-wide bulk communication either. Thus, we conducted a series of studies to learn how to design this agent (Kong 2023). We started with quantitative (Kong et al. 2020) and qualitative studies (Kong et al. 2021b) to understand this system's effectiveness and the behaviors and perceptions of its stakeholders. We found that employees often judge whether to read a bulk email from their prior experience with the sender and title—these **channels** have a **reputation**. Then, we proposed an economic model to frame all those stakeholders' cost, value, actions, and the impact of their actions (Kong and Konstan 2023). We later designed a series of personalization (Kong et al. 2022) and evaluation tools that motivated the stakeholders to consider the whole organization's value and cost.

Specifically, we learned that the agent should be **socially embedded**, which means that it will (1) analyze the social contexts of this system and (2) give the right incentive to each stakeholder that can steer their actions toward the whole organization's benefit. For example, it should consider the employees' time cost of reading bulk emails, the communicators' time cost of designing and targeting bulk emails, and the leaders' value of getting important information out (Kong and Konstan 2023). Given these economics, it might make sense for the agent to motivate communicators to spend 8 hours targeting an email rather than sending this email to 25,000 employees who each spend 1 minute scanning to judge its relevancy or that employees should be incentivized to read certain messages important to the organization or that central offices should be motivated to consider not only their own judgments on messages' value but also those messages' cost to the whole organization.

Though we conducted this series of studies in the context of a large university (University of Minnesota), this problem of bulk communication is common in **large and distributed organizations** (we do not focus on small organizations in this chapter), which have central units that oversee organization-wide functions (such as policy, finance, human resources, information technology, facilities management) as well as local units that carry out various elements of the organizational mission. Whether in academia, government, or the private sector, these large organizations tend to have a similar pattern of central units communicating messages to large numbers of distributed employees who feel those messages are not relevant to them. For example, in 1996, Whittaker and Sidner (1996) interviewed 20 office workers and found that they were already information overloaded by bulk emails. In 2006, Fisher et al. (2006) revisited this study and found that employees' email

[1] https://superhuman.com/

[2] https://tatem.com/

archives had grown tenfold compared to 1996. In 2016, Mark et al. (2016) observed 40 information workers in their in situ workplace for 12 days and found their productivity was impacted by the large quantities of emails they received.

Moreover, in organizations, this kind of **multi-stakeholder problem**, where an agent faces stakeholders with various goals and perspectives, happens not only in bulk communication but also in many other circumstances. For example, agents for engineering need to align the collaboration between multiple employees in developing projects (Lauche 2005); an agent for human resource systems needs to communicate the domain knowledge between different teams in employment consulting (Dolata et al. 2020); and understanding the tension between employees, employers, and business experts is also important in human resource management (Park et al. 2022; Robert et al. 2020).

In this chapter, we use the organizational bulk email system above as an example to illustrate the issues that should also be examined if someone wants to look into the bulk communication problem of large organizations. Moreover, this detailed specific case's process and general lessons of designing a socially embedded agent can be applied in a wide range of contexts where bulk communication is being managed across diverse stakeholders, such as encouraging people to take flu shots, making software users aware of new IT vulnerabilities.

We first discuss the key artifacts around the organizational structure that the agent should be aware of. Then, with specific bulk email cases, we discuss the key data sources the agent can collect, the abstractions for the agent's decision-making process, and our design lessons for agents embedded in organizational contexts.

2 Key Artifacts Around the Organizational Structure

We first introduce the organizational structure that the bulk email agent should be aware of. Organization structure refers to the decision rules that organizations use to connect their employees (Baligh 2006). It is found that to make artificial intelligence (AI) effectively support employees in the workplace, their agents' design has to comply with the corresponding organization's structure (Dennehy et al. 2021; Wang et al. 2019). Identifying relevant stakeholders and designing agents that respect different perspectives is also recognized as a key requirement in designing agents for organizations (Bednar and Welch 2019; Zhao et al. 2023).

Now, we use a specific organization and its bulk email system as an example. The organization we studied is the University of Minnesota, a large public university with five campuses and over 25,000 employees. There are several central units of the university (e.g., president's office, university relations, see Fig. 2) conducting university-wide bulk communications, including massive newsletters with many messages,[3] single-message emails, websites, etc. The central units also collaborate

[3] We use "message" here refers to a single piece of information in bulk emails, like a story or subsection.

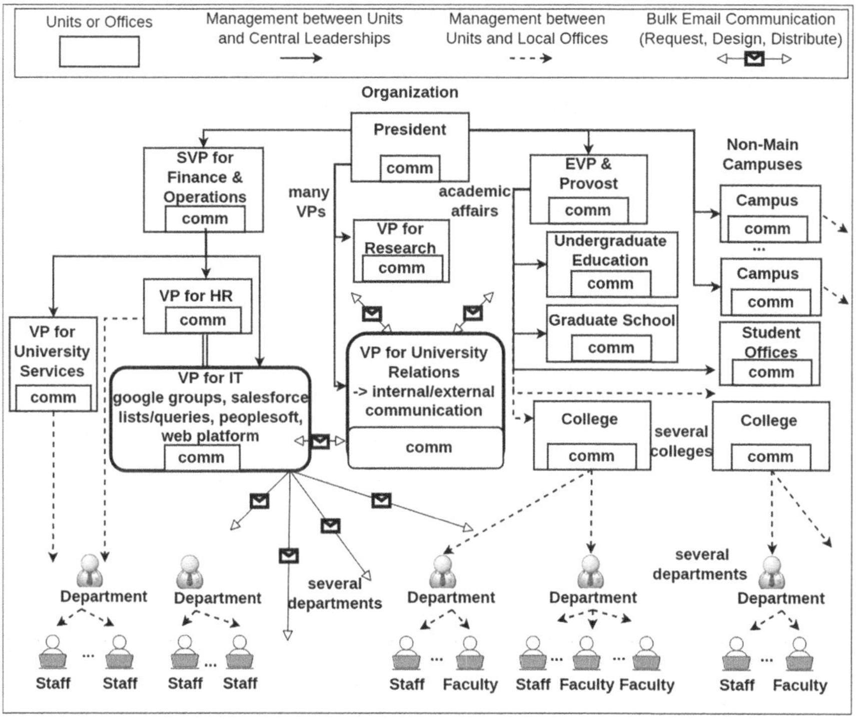

Fig. 2 University of Minnesota's organization structure around its bulk email system. "VP" represents vice president. "comm" refers to the communication professionals in the corresponding units (Kong and Konstan 2023)

with decentralized units (e.g., the units in colleges and departments) in editing and distributing bulk messages, like collecting news, and forwarding messages to employees locally.

The stakeholders of this university's organizational bulk email system are distributed in different units:

- Information Producers: the original information sources of bulk emails, also the communicator's clients, such as the university leaders from the president's office, vice presidents' offices, etc.
- Communicators: the employees in charge of processing bulk emails, who receive requests from information producers, design content, and distribute bulk emails to the recipients, such as the communicators in the president's office and vice presidents' offices.
- Information Recipients: the employees who receive bulk emails, including all the faculty and staff from the central offices, colleges, and other units.
- Management: the information recipients' supervisors; we include them because they set employees' priorities and are responsible for the budgets of employee time.

The basic IT infrastructure that the agent will build on is important, as it sets the technological limits for the agent. For example, if the IT infrastructure does not collect family information from employees, it would be difficult to request an agent to target all the employees with dependents. The university uses a Gmail system. The email marketing platform is Salesforce, which is connected to the university's human resource system PeopleSoft (mostly manually by collaboration between communication units and human resource units) to update mailing lists. The communicators at different units would have corresponding access levels to specific mailing lists on Salesforce.

3 Gathering Data for Decision-Making

In this section, based on specific bulk email cases, we discuss the social contexts the agent should collect before they make decisions.

3.1 General Economics of the Bulk Email System

The agent first needs to understand the general economics of the bulk email system—all the stakeholders' value and costs with the corresponding bulk messages (Kong and Konstan 2023):

- An employee's cost with a bulk message is how much time/cost is involved in the employee reading this message. This cost is related to the message length and the mechanism of distribution—the cost may be higher for a single-message email and lower for a message in a newsletter where the employee doesn't have to open a new email.
- The employee's value with a bulk message including the message's job relevancy and interest level to the employees. Job relevancy refers to how much value the message has to the employee for their job responsibilities. The level of interest refers to how much value the message has to the employee for the employee's own interest. This may differ from job responsibilities. Some employees like to know about sports, new research results, or big gifts to the university even though they don't actually do any work related to those.
- The cost of the communicator who sent out this bulk message is how much time they spend designing and targeting this message. At the same time, the communicator has the value of fulfilling the information producer's requirements and getting proof that they delivered the message to all the relevant employees.
- The organization's perception of the value of a bulk message is reelected as how much additional value the organization assigns to the employee reading this message. This is separate from job responsibilities but has to do with other

values. The organization may feel there is value in reminding everyone about how important each of our campuses is. It may feel there is value in showing that we care about future leadership or in showing that there are opportunities to advance to leadership for those interested. Other cases where an organization may assign value apart from job relevance are cases of increasing compliance (sending messages about being inclusive, being drug-free, being anti-harassment, etc.) or of advancing culture (sending messages about identity and messages about achievements to make people proud of the university).

The agent needs to break down all the stakeholders' value and costs and then collect data to estimate those terms. Below we use chancellor search as an example to discuss **what data can be used to extract the stakeholders' value and cost relating to this message.**

3.2 Chancellor Search as an Example

U of M Morris chancellor search is a message for recruiting a new chancellor for the Morris Campus (Fig. 1). The Morris Campus is one of the university's smaller campuses with under 400 employees. The chancellor is the person directly in charge of the entire campus. This message is sent from the Office of the President as a single-message email to all the employees across all the campuses. Based on our interviews with four faculty and five staff of the University of Minnesota (Kong et al. 2021b), 17% of the organizational bulk emails are newsletters with multiple messages, and 83% of them are single-message bulk emails. 79% of those bulk emails are viewed as unimportant by the employees we interviewed, and 87% of them are viewed as not urgent. For a specific university-wide weekly newsletter, the three topics that appeared most frequently were talk/symposium/lecture announcements, student/alumni stories, and community service/social justice/underserved population (see Table 5 of Kong et al. 2022).

For this specific message, the information producer (Office of the President)'s value might be extracted from the message content, either through texts or images (Zhang et al. 2023). The office actually explained why they sent out this message in the first sentence—they sent out this message first to show that the Morris Campus is a critical part of the University of Minnesota. This is the value of showing the sender's care with certain topics. There is also a message of openness in leadership searches (this is one of dozens of messages that get sent about searches for chancellors, deans, vice presidents, and others). After that, the message invited employees to give feedback through a link to show and provide opportunities to advance to leadership for those interested. The sender also wants to get evidence of distributing regulation-required information.

The relevance to job responsibilities varies by employee. Employees on the Morris Campus itself and those who deal with the chancellor's office probably should know about the search. Those who might be interested in applying for the position (probably faculty leaders) or providing nominations would likely also find this useful. Most employees (e.g., a financial aid counselor in the Twin Cities or a laboratory technician in Duluth) probably don't have any job-related reason to know about this opening or search.

Also, employees' interest in such an announcement would vary. In our example, some employees may simply be interested in knowing what's happening with university leaders across the entire organization. These may be the same ones who follow what's happening at the Board of Regents and in other leadership discussions. Employees at other smaller campuses may see this search as a model for what may happen the next time their own chancellor steps down and may see the handling of this search as a sign of the president's attention to the whole system and its smaller campuses.

The level of job relevancy could be estimated by surveying the employee and also the manager. In our example, a department head on the Morris Campus probably should be aware of the chancellor search; a financial aid counselor on the Rochester Campus is never going to use that information and probably doesn't need to know. For the level of interest, the agent can collect employees' histories of involvement in similar search activities, preferences on leadership-related news, job responsibilities, etc. To overcome the cold-start problem (e.g., new employees have no history), deep reinforcement learning approaches can be applied (Wang and Jin 2022). The agent also needs to consider fluidity—the changes in the contexts that might cause changes in stakeholders' perceptions of message value. For example, depending on the employee's working schedules, they might be interested in this message sometimes (if they are not busy) and skip this message the other times.

Besides value, the agent also needs to collect information about employees' costs. The time/cost of reading this message comes partly from its length but mostly from whether it is being sent as a separate message to all employees. The length is secondary because employees can quickly determine from the title whether they are interested enough to read the message in detail. Based on our interviews (Kong et al. 2021b), employees often delete such messages before opening them.

The communicator's (who distributed this message) value can be extracted from the communication thread between the communicator and the information producer, i.e., their task requirement with this message. The information producer might ask the communicator to distribute this message to anyone who might be relevant and not take the risk of leaving someone behind, or they care more about the result, e.g., collecting more comments. Also, naturally, the communicator had their own expectations on how much effort they would spend on each message based on their working schedules.

Besides that, the agent might collect information by surveying the employees' management on their evaluation of the message's importance level and collecting the responsibility scope of each unit. The management would have their own perceptions of the message's value. For example, they might think that their employees should have some sense about what is going on generally in the university, or they might perceive this message as relevant to some employees' jobs (e.g., the human resource unit in charge of the searching process).

At the same time, the agent needs to collect data on the organization's value and cost (e.g., the message's impact on its communication channel's reputation). Part of the goal here is to reinforce the message that this is one university and that all of the campuses are highly valued. Of course, the organization also wants to preserve the effectiveness of the "Messages from the President" channel. The agent might learn the organization's value and costs by surveying the leaders, learning from the organization's documents (e.g., through weakly supervised learning (Shen et al. 2022)), learning from the central offices' communication behaviors (Dong et al. 2021, 2022), and tracking employees' time spent (Kong et al. 2023). The agent should also understand the stakeholders' motivations (e.g., through interpretable machine learning (Lin et al. 2022; He et al. 2021)) and study the interventions that can influence stakeholders' behaviors (Kumar et al. 2022). For *chancellor search*, the organization does view this message as "important," which can be seen by the fact that the president's office is distributing this message to every employee. However, it should also be noted that "showing a message is important" can be different from "a message is really important." The organization might want to show its attention to certain topics (e.g., environment, equity); however, these messages usually do not need employees' immediate actions. Without an agent's control, the organization might tend to show a bunch of messages are "important" (such as by tagging every email with an "important" flag), which will undermine the organization's communication channels' reputation.

Moreover, the agent can take each stakeholder's perception into a weighted sum and the weights can be decided by the contexts. For example, for some messages with high-level information, like administrative news, the organization leaders might have a better understanding of the message's importance to the organization, and then, their perceptions could take higher weights.

4 Decision-Making Process

Given all the data collected above, **a socially embedded agent would look at each of these costs and value in providing feedback and suggestions on how to achieve the disparate goals of the organization**—maximizing the desired value while minimizing both the cost and the loss of reputation (and long-term value) if employees become less likely to read future messages. In this section, we discuss this process and the potential types of actions the agent can recommend or take below. These actions can be integrated into those existing platforms (e.g., Salesforce, Gmail, Mailchimp, etc.), such as helping senders design or target email, helping recipients classify email.

4.1 Identifying Mismatches Between Stakeholders' Value and Cost

The agent first identifies the mismatches between stakeholders' value and costs before making decisions using the same message *chancellor search* as an example:

- The information producer might want the message *chancellor search* to be seen widely, while many employees might feel it is irrelevant to their jobs and interests. As we discussed above, the information producer would like to show that they care about this campus, and one way they show this care is to distribute to all. It is worth noting that given the current top-down management style of this organization's bulk email system (the communicators report to the information producers), it is effortless for the information producers to request the communicators to take the distribute-to-all action. Thus, the agent should consider how to control this excessive weight, e.g., educating the senders overwhelming's impact on the sender's reputation.
- The employees/organization might want this message to be targeted precisely, while the communicators want to complete their tasks within a reasonable amount of time. From an organization's view, it makes sense to precisely target the message to protect the reputation of the communication channels—letting the employees feel that they won't receive many irrelevant messages from the communication channels then they keep paying attention to the communications. However, communicators, with busy working schedules (and limited budgets), lack the incentive to spend more time targeting this message and also lack the tools for precisely targeting. This is one area where an agent may be able to add value by automating or facilitating the targeting process.
- The management/organization might want employees to be aware of this message, while many employees perceive it as irrelevant. From the management/whole organization's view, the employees might be responsible for knowing what is going on in the university—as a member of the organization, they should make efforts to advance future leadership.
- It is worth noting that each stakeholder also has their own trade-offs on different value. For example, the management might want employees to be aware of this type of administrative news, but at the same time, they might also expect their employees to spend time on more work-relevant messages. Again, this point highlights the fluidity and nuances the agent faces in an organizational environment. In the below, we discuss the potential actions the agent can take to mediate between different stakeholders' preferences.

4.2 Selecting Communication Channels

One of the actions the agent can take is to select communication channels that balance different stakeholders' interests and the message's impact on channel reputation. Organizational bulk email agents have various choices of communication **channels** with different levels of **reputation** (employee's perception of the relevance of the messages from this communication channel and their willingness to keep reading in the future). The communication channel of a bulk email is linked with two features: the email's brand (the sender address and the FROM field, like Office of the President in Fig. 1, and the identifiable template, like the *Message from the President* in Fig. 1's subject line). Different channels have different **distribution mechanisms**—how it gets the recipient list and sent out, such as sent to all, sent via a filtered mailing list, or sent to colleges to redistribute. Example communication channels of organizational bulk emails include (Kong et al. 2021b):

- **University-wide newsletters:** the bulk emails with fixed brands sent weekly/monthly/seasonally, etc. It might have a single message (**low grouping**) or many messages (**high grouping**). Compared to single-message emails, newsletters with many messages have a relatively low per-story cost (see the section above). The university-wide newsletters are **low targeting** in distribution (sent to an almost fixed wide list of employees without further filtering, which was pulled out when the newsletter was created). For example, we can put the message *U of M Morris chancellor search* above in *U of M Brief* (Fig. 3), a weekly newsletter sent to all the employees of the studied university with over 30 messages in each email.
- **Filtered mailing list:** these bulk emails were sent to a list of employees pulled from the human resource database. They are usually low grouping (including one or a few messages). Their targeting level depends on to how much extent the pulled lists match the relevant employees. Central units can very easily send to a specific campus as getting lists based on the organization tree is easy—what's hard is getting lists that are based on behavior and role. For example, the communicator can pull a list of employees from the Morris Campus and send the message *U of M Morris chancellor search* as a single-message email to that list. However, this list might miss those employees from other campuses who are potentially interested in this search or have relevant job duties.
- **Email tree:** central communicators (or leaders) communicate directly with the leaders of distributed units and ask them to deliver certain messages to their employees. For example, the university president (or provost, vice president) would send messages to the chancellors, deans, and VPs. By letting local units resend the message, the importance of those messages is highlighted—employees are more likely to read messages from their department head or manager than from higher-up leaders and more likely to read messages from their VP or dean than from a central leader of another unit (Kong et al. 2021b). The unit leaders know this, and in turn, they also sometimes don't just send the message to all their employees but instead send it to managers (e.g., department heads) to ask them to communicate it. And those local managers also know that it isn't always best to communicate through email—they may tell people about it at a department meeting.

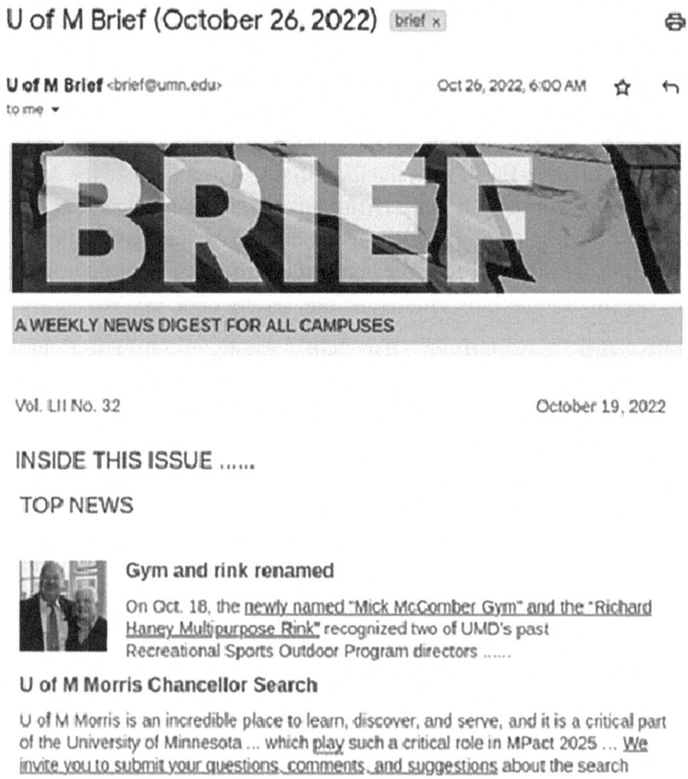

Fig. 3 *U of M Brief*—a weekly newsletter sent to all the employees across all the campuses, with over 30 messages within each email

These channels have different levels of reputation, which influence the level of attention employees pay to these channels' emails. Generally speaking, with a higher level of targeting, the reputation of a channel would be higher—compared to filtered mailing lists and email tree, newsletters' reputation would be lower. The reputation of filtered mailing lists and email tree is also decided by how the senders use these channels. A channel that often distributes messages to a roughly filtered mailing list would have a low reputation. The channels' reputation is an important asset that the organization should protect.

Let's use *chancellor search* as an example to discuss how the agent selects between a low-grouping newsletter (single-message email), a high-grouping newsletter (newsletter with tens of messages), a filtered mailing list, and an email tree:

- If the agent puts this message in a low-grouping newsletter (like Fig. 1, a newsletter sent to all the employees with only two messages within it), the information producer's return would be high as this message has a greater chance of being exposed to the employees, but many employees might feel this message as irrelevant and might stop reading *Message from the President* in the future. That means the return for the whole organization could be negative because this communication channel's reputation decreases.

- If the agent puts this message in a high-grouping newsletter (like the *U of M Brief* in Fig. 3), the information producer's return might be low as this message is more likely to be ignored. And most employees avoid spending time on the message that they will perceive as irrelevant. Also, those who are most interested in what's happening across the university are probably the ones who are most likely to read a message in the brief anyway. However, a message in the brief is likely to be missed by some people who would have wanted to know about this search—people who are specifically interested in this campus or position but don't find most brief messages relevant to them. This could lose some potential value. In summary, putting the message in this channel would bring a low return, low cost, and low impact on the channel's reputation.
- If the agent suggests the communicator sends the message to a filtered mailing list, the organization's whole return would be high, with relevant employees getting the value of being aware of this message, and most employees saving time cost. However, for the communicator, their cost would be high. With limited targeting tools, the communicator might spend significantly more time pulling the list and sending that separate email. They also take the risk of missing relevant employees (given the nuance and fluidity of the organization context we mentioned above). Therefore, to go with this solution, the agent should also come up with a set of targeting tools to support communicators, like making predictions on each employee's perception of this message's value. Or from a human resource view, the organization might make decisions on hiring more communicators based on the value and cost of organizational communication. For example, it might make sense to hire a communicator and spend 24 hours targeting a message, compared to sending that message to over 20,000 employees, and each employee spends 1 minute reading it on average.
- If the agent distributes the message through an email tree, then the message's return depends on how different colleges/units distribute it. For example, if a college in the Twin Cities campus receives this message and carefully targeted those relevant employees (e.g., the human resources who work with leadership recruiting communications, the department leaders who qualify as candidates, etc.). The college's overall return would likely be positive because they avoid overwhelming most of its employees.
- Moreover, a practical solution might be a combination—putting the message in a high-grouping newsletter while asking the Morris Campus to send a single-message newsletter to its employees. In this way, the information producer still gets the value of getting the message distributed widely, while most employees from other campuses would avoid spending time on this message.

4.3 Other Potential Actions

Besides selecting communication channels, the agents can also take other actions, including:

- **Personalizing bulk email designs:** the agent can personalize bulk emails based on all the involved stakeholders' value (Kong et al. 2022, 2021a). For example, putting this message at the top news of *U of M Brief*, but mixing this message with the message the corresponding employee might be interested in—like if the employee is interested in sports news, putting this message after the message *Gym and rink renamed* (see Fig. 3). This way, the employees might pay attention to this *chancellor search* message while reading those they enjoy. In an 8-week field experiment with 141 employees (Kong et al. 2022), we found that mixing the messages the university wants employees to read with the messages the employees like in the top news of U of M brief increased *brief*'s overall recognition rate by around 20%. Large language models (LLM) such as GPT3 (Brown et al. 2020) can also be used here to generate different lengths (and different details levels) in email's covering content—an LLM could digest the things that a recipient wants to just see a brief summary about, reorganize the contents, and generate item descriptions or recommendations (Acharya et al. 2023). Another way is to send this message to different defined communication groups via different channels or predict different groups' interests (He et al. 2023; Zhao et al. 2016; Sun et al. 2023, 2024). For example, Beringer designed a system with a user interface that enabled the organization senders to send a message of a certain message type within one of the collaborative conversation channels (Beringer 2004). The agent can also personalize the sending time by predicting how busy or interrupted the corresponding employee is when they receive the message (Danninger et al. 2007).
- **Performance tracking for budget control:** the agent can influence the university leaders' and central offices' communication behaviors by tracking performance and controlling the budget. One way is to simply increase visibility by keeping track of and making visible the amount of employee time (or cost) consumed by the communications from different units. If everyone sees that a unit is spending much more employee time than seems warranted, then there will be pressure to address that. For example, we surveyed 162 employees and found that 38% of the tested organizational bulk messages were recognized, while at the same time, 16% of the tested fake messages were also recognized, resulting in a 22% effective recognition rate (Kong et al. 2020). In a more recent study, we developed an evaluation platform that enables communicators to track the performance and cost of each message (see Fig. 4). We found that messages' performance is significantly correlated with their communication channels' reputation. Therefore, the university's central offices can benefit from an agent which provides such cost and reputation data to allocate their communication budget. The other way is to formalize this through budget allocations—units

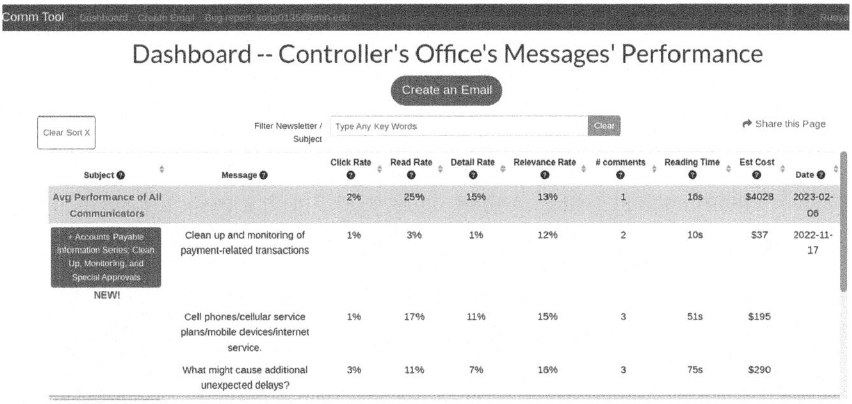

Fig. 4 The bulk email evaluation platform which enables communicators to track the click rate, read rate, relevance rate, comments, reading time, and estimated cost of each message

could have communications budgets that force them to make decisions about what's worth communicating broadly (and what's not).

In summary, with the existence of various organizational stakeholders, to benefit the organization as a whole, the bulk email agent should balance all the stakeholders' value and cost when making targeting, designing, and management decisions on bulk communication.

5 Design Lessons for Socially Embedded Agents in Organizational Contexts

In this section, based on the case study above, we summarize the differences between designing agents with vs. without organizational context:

- **Contexts—organization's goals:** with organizational context, the agent also needs to collect social contexts from the entire organization instead of learning single stakeholders' contexts. The agent needs to identify goals for the organization as a whole and lead stakeholders' behaviors toward those goals. For example, for evaluating each bulk email, the agent should consider not only the senders' goal with that email but also the employees' time spent on those emails. A message should only be sent out when its overall return is positive. But without organizational context, the agent does not need to control the recipients' time spent on those bulk emails. Not only in bulk email systems but also in other organizational systems such as human resource systems, the agent needs to identify the organization's goals with the corresponding system (e.g., minimizing recruiting costs, maximizing productivity, etc).

- **Players—stakeholder's responsibilities:** in an organization, the stakeholders are responsible for considering other stakeholders' perspectives; therefore, it is also reasonable for the agent to motivate employees to achieve that. For example, employees might not be interested in the organization's environmental plan for the next 5 years, but they should read that to understand that protecting the environment is important for the organization and they should also care about environmental issues in their daily work. In that case, the agent should incentivize employees to read those important messages, such as by establishing a mechanism that the employees who show consistent awareness of the important messages received (e.g., about compliance) might "pass out" of otherwise required training activities and thereby save time. Without organizational context, the agent makes decisions toward maximizing specific stakeholders' benefits. For example, a spam-email agent would filter any bulk emails the recipients do not want to receive, as the recipients are not responsible for reading those emails. A commercial bulk email system's agent should maximize the benefit of the bulk email senders.
- **Actions—handle mismatches between stakeholders' preferences:** within organizations, the agent must take actions that balance stakeholders' preferences as each stakeholder obtain a piece of domain knowledge on which information is useful for the organization. For example, it might be difficult for the information producers and communicators to know exactly which employees have jobs relevant to a message; compared to the organization leaders, it would be challenging for employees to understand why some high-level information is important to the organization. The agent should handle these mismatches appropriately through communication and incentives. But without organizational context, agents often do not need to handle such mismatches in value. For example, a bulk email agent for personal users can just discard all the bulk emails the recipients viewed as irrelevant no matter whether the senders want the recipients to read the email or not.

Besides these differences, we should also consider the limitations of applying agents in workplaces. For example, an agent that is not well trained might miss relevant audiences when targeting bulk messages. Therefore, the targeting process cannot be fully automated by agents. In short, when designing agents for organizations, we need to identify the entire organization's goals and social contexts, consider the stakeholders' responsibilities in reaching these goals, and design corresponding mechanisms to solve trade-offs between stakeholders' value and lead their behaviors toward benefiting the entire organization.

References

Acharya A, Singh B, Onoe N (2023) LLM based generation of item-description for recommendation system. In: Proceedings of the 17th ACM conference on recommender systems, pp 1204–1207

Baligh HH (2006) Organization structures: theory and design, analysis and prescription. Springer Science & Business Media, Berlin

Bednar PM, Welch C (2019) Socio-technical perspectives on smart working: creating meaningful and sustainable systems. Inf Syst Front 22:281–298

Beringer J, Hatscher M (2004) Community builder. U.S. Patent Application 10/655,783

Brown T, Mann B, Ryder N, Subbiah M, Kaplan JD, Dhariwal P, et al (2020) Language models are few-shot learners. Adv Neural Inf Proces Syst 33:1877–1901

Danninger M, Takayama L, Wang Q, Schultz C, Beringer J, Hofmann P, et al (2007) Can you talk or only touch-talk: a voip-based phone feature for quick, quiet, and private communication. In: Proceedings of the 9th international conference on multimodal interfaces. Association for Computing Machinery, New York, pp 154–161

Dennehy D, Griva A, Pouloudi N, Dwivedi YK, Pappas I, Mäntymäki M (2021) Responsible AI and analytics for an ethical and inclusive digitized society: 20th IFIP WG 6.11 conference on e-business, e-services and e-society, I3E 2021, Galway, September 1–3, 2021, Proceedings. Springer Nature, Berlin

Dolata M, Schenk B, Fuhrer J, Marti A, Schwabe G (2020) When the system does not fit: coping strategies of employment consultants. Comput Supported Coop Work, 657–696. https://doi.org/10.1007/s10606-020-09377-x

Dong G, Cai L, Kumar S, Datta D, Barnes LE, Boukhechba M (2021) Detection and analysis of interrupted behaviors by public policy interventions during covid-19. In: 2021 IEEE/ACM conference on connected health: applications, systems and engineering technologies (CHASE), pp 46–57

Dong G, Kweon Y, Park BB, Boukhechba M (2022) Utility-based route choice behavior modeling using deep sequential models. J Big Data Anal Transp 4:119–133

Fisher D, Brush AJ, Gleave E, Smith MA (2006) Revisiting whittaker & sidner's "email overload" ten years later. In: Proceedings of the 2006 20th anniversary conference on Computer supported cooperative work. ACM, New York, https://doi.org/10.1145/1180875.1180922

He Y, Lin F, Tzeng NF, et al (2021) Interpretable minority synthesis for imbalanced classification. In: International joint conferences on artificial intelligence

He Y, Zhang C, Kong R, Kulkarni C, Liu Q, Gandhe A, et al (2023) Hiercat: hierarchical query categorization from weakly supervised data at facebook marketplace. In: Companion proceedings of the ACM web conference 2023. Association for Computing Machinery, New York, pp 331–335

Kong R (2023) Towards an effective organization-wide bulk email system. Doctoral dissertation, University of Minnesota

Kong R, Konstan JA (2023) The challenge of organizational bulk email systems: models and empirical studies. In: The elgar companion to information economics. Edward Elgar Publishing, Cheltenham

Kong R, Zhu H, Konstan J (2020) Organizational bulk email systems: their role and performance in remote work. New Future of Work

Kong R, Qiu Z, Liu Y, Zhao Q (2021a) Nimblelearn: a scalable and fast batch-mode active learning approach. In: 2021 international conference on data mining workshops (ICDMW). IEEE, Piscataway, pp 350–359

Kong R, Zhu H, Konstan JA (2021b) Learning to ignore: a case study of organization-wide bulk email effectiveness. Proc ACM Hum-Comput Interact 5:1–23

Kong R, Zhang CC, Sun R, Chhabra V, Nadimpalli T, Konstan JA (2022) Multi-objective personalization in multi-stakeholder organizational bulk e-mail: a field experiment. Proc ACM Hum-Comput Interact 6:1–27

Kong R, Sun R, Zhang CC, Chen C, Patri S, Gajjela G, et al (2023) Getting the most from eye-tracking: user-interaction based reading region estimation dataset and models. In: Proceedings of the 2023 symposium on eye tracking research and applications. Association for Computing Machinery, New York, pp 1–7

Kumar S, Datta D, Dong G, Cai L, Boukhechba M, Barnes L (2022) Leveraging mobile sensing and bayesian change point analysis to monitor community-scale behavioral interventions: a case study on covid-19. ACM Trans Comput Healthcare 3:1–13

Lauche K (2005) Collaboration among designers: analysing an activity for system development. Comput Supp Cooperative Work, 253–282. https://doi.org/10.1007/s10606-005-5413-0

Lin F, Yuan X, Peng L, Tzeng NF (2022) Cascade variational auto-encoder for hierarchical disentanglement. In: Proceedings of the 31st ACM international conference on information & knowledge management. Association for Computing Machinery, New York, pp 1248–1257

Mark G, Iqbal ST, Czerwinski M, Johns P, Sano A, Lutchyn Y (2016) Email duration, batching and self-interruption: patterns of email use on productivity and stress. In: Proceedings of the 2016 CHI conference on human factors in computing systems. Association for Computing Machinery, New York, pp 1717–1728

Park H, Kartik ADH, Lee J (2022) Designing fair AI in human resource management: understanding tensions surrounding algorithmic evaluation and envisioning stakeholder-centered solutions. In: ACM Conferences, pp 1–22

Robert LP, Pierce C, Marquis L, Kim S, Alahmad R (2020) Designing fair AI for managing employees in organizations: a review, critique, and design agenda. Hum–Comput Inter 35:545–575

Shen Z, Schutte D, Yi Y, Bompelli A, Yu F, Wang Y, et al (2022) Classifying the lifestyle status for Alzheimer's disease from clinical notes using deep learning with weak supervision. BMC Med Inform Decis Mak 22:88

Sun R, Kong R, Jin Q, Konstan J (2023) Less can be more: exploring population rating dispositions with partitioned models in recommender systems. In: Adjunct proceedings of the 31st ACM conference on user modeling. Adaptation and personalization, pp 291–295

Sun R, Akella A, Kong R, Zhou M, Konstan JA (2024) Interactive content diversity and user exploration in online movie recommenders: a field experiment. Int J Hum-Comput Interact 40(22):7233–7247

Wang X, Jin Y (2022) Work process transfer reinforcement learning: feature extraction and finetuning in ship collision avoidance. In: ASME 2022 international design engineering technical conferences and computers and information in engineering conference

Wang S, Ding W, Li J, Yuan Y, Ouyang L, Wang FY (2019) Decentralized autonomous organizations: concept, model, and applications. IEEE Trans Comput Social Syst, 870–878. https://doi.org/10.1109/tcss.2019.2938190

Whittaker S, Sidner C (1996) Email overload: exploring personal information management of email. In: Proceedings of the SIGCHI conference on human factors in computing systems. Association for Computing Machinery, New York, pp 276–283

Zhang D, Zhou F, Jiang Y, Fu Z (2023) MM-BSN: self-supervised image denoising for real-world with multi-mask based on blind-spot network. In: Proceedings of the IEEE/CVF conference on computer vision and pattern recognition, pp 4188–4197

Zhao H, Liu Q, Ge Y, Kong R, Chen E (2016) Group preference aggregation: a nash equilibrium approach. In: 2016 IEEE 16th international conference on data mining (ICDM), pp 679–688

Zhao Z, Yang Y, Wang W, Liu C, Shi Y, Hu W, Zhang H, Yang S (2023) Breaking the curse of quality saturation with user-centric ranking. In: 29th SIGKDD conference on knowledge discovery and data mining (KDD'23)

Enabling Product Platform Growth with AI-Assisted Insight

Jeffrey L. Jenkins, Joseph S. Valacich, and David W. Wilson

Abstract This chapter presents a discussion on the challenges associated with managing and gaining insights from the massive amount of behavioral data available to digital service providers. The case studies presented demonstrate the potential benefits of leveraging AI tools to automate the analysis process and gain valuable insights into user behavior at scale. The use of algorithmic analysis can identify malfunctioning features or common interaction pathways leading to negative outcomes, and exploratory analyses can uncover unexpected use cases that may unlock new markets or revenue streams. The chapter concludes that AI-enabled insight is becoming increasingly critical to successful PLG strategies as it enables businesses to better understand their users and make data-driven decisions that support growth and improve the user experience. The examples presented here suggest that there are still many possibilities for deriving insights from user behavior data that have not yet been explored.

1 Introduction

Product-led growth (PLG) is a business strategy that focuses on building and delivering high-quality products that can be used to acquire, retain, and grow customers (Partners 2022). The central idea is to create products that are so valuable and easy to use that they can drive customer acquisition and retention without the need for heavy sales or marketing efforts. Companies like Slack, Dropbox, and Zoom have all grown rapidly by creating products that are easy to use and provide real value to users. These companies' products have been able to attract and retain

J. L. Jenkins (✉) · D. W. Wilson
Brigham Young University, Provo, UT, USA
e-mail: jeffrey_jenkins@byu.edu; davidwilson@byu.edu

J. S. Valacich
University of Arizona, Tucson, AZ, USA
e-mail: valacich@arizona.edu

C. K. Coursaris et al. (eds.), *The Design of Human-Centered Artificial Intelligence for the Workplace*, Progress in IS, https://doi.org/10.1007/978-3-031-83512-4_26

customers, which has allowed them to scale rapidly and become some of the most successful companies in the tech industry.

Optimizing the user experience with continual product improvement is a central tenet of PLG. Products that are intuitive, easy to use, provide real value, and are loved by customers result in word-of-mouth marketing and organic demand. The most important mechanism for continual improvement is rich data that tracks, measures, and analyzes user behavior—hereafter, behavioral data. Granular behavioral data is particularly valuable in a product-led growth strategy because it enables companies to gain a deep understanding of user behavior. This level of detail can reveal insights that may not be immediately apparent from higher-level data, such as page views or click-through rates. Behavioral data can include information on user actions, such as mouse movements, scrolling, and typing patterns. This data can help companies identify usage patterns, discover unanticipated risks, and even identify fraudulent behavior. In addition to identifying risks and opportunities, companies can use behavioral data to tailor their products to meet the unique needs of different user segments. This can improve user satisfaction and increase the likelihood of user retention and additional growth.

Given the breadth and volume of data available to a modern digital service provider, artificial intelligence (AI) tools have become an increasingly valuable resource to help monitor, analyze, and otherwise use the data relevant for improving the user experience. AI algorithms can identify patterns in large datasets that would otherwise go unnoticed by humans, unlocking valuable insights into user behavior, preferences, and pain points. For example, if enough users exhibit consistent behavior at a certain stage of the customer journey but then fail to convert, an appropriate algorithm can be used to identify how to improve the user experience and drive better results. Additionally, AI can help companies detect and understand unexpected or unanticipated user behaviors, allowing them to make proactive changes to address these issues before they become widespread.

Another way that AI can help is by identifying potential risks or issues in real time. For example, AI algorithms can detect patterns of behavior that are indicative of fraud or account takeover attempts. By analyzing granular behavioral data such as typing or mouse movements, AI can accurately identify whether a user is legitimate or an imposter attempting to commit fraud.

A growing body of academic research has demonstrated that digital behavior holds a wealth of information about the cognitive state and intent of a computer user. Based on the notion that motor movements are influenced by cognitive processes and emotional states (Freeman et al. 2008), behavioral data has advanced as a viable and scalable methodology for studying a wide range of cognitive and emotional processes, including cognitive load (Thorpe et al. 2021), concealed racial prejudice (Wojnowicz et al. 2009), attention (Gozli and Pratt 2011), and identity deception (Monaro et al. 2017, 2018), among others. Our own program of research has applied these same behavioral data to help identify negative emotions in e-commerce settings (Hibbeln et al. 2017), test response certainty (Jenkins et al. 2015), cheating (Jenkins et al. 2021), and financial fraud (Weinmann et al. 2022).

For the past several years, NeuroID—a university spin-off company based on our research—has implemented commercial solutions that embody much of our learnings from the empirical work referenced above. We have developed a suite of AI-enabled digital behavior tools designed to support digital platforms in their effort to optimize their users' experiences with their platform and defend against a persistent threat of fraud and related risks. As PLG typically focuses on driving product improvements with rich data that tracks, measures, and analyzes user behavior (Partners 2022), our product suite is primarily a data platform that provides API-accessible data sources to our customers. These data are used in various ways by different customers, depending on their product goals.

To avoid sharing the proprietary details of the features, rules, and AI models implemented in our platform, we will instead focus on the behavior captured by our tools (i.e., typing and mousing features), as well as the compelling ways that our customers are using these tools to support their own PLG strategies. This chapter summarizes two detailed case studies demonstrating the uses of behavioral data—via the AI tools we have built to aid in interpreting and using those data—to support their growth strategies. Table 1 summarizes the two case studies and the examples provided in each. The first case study demonstrates how digital behavior can be monitored across an entire user population to understand the user experience at scale—a significant improvement over the still-common strategy of surveying a small subset of users to understand their perceptions of the experience. The second case study discusses the use of behavioral data as a novel solution to manage identity fraud risk while carefully protecting the user experience. Together, the case studies provide several real-world examples of AI-enabled user experience optimization, demonstrating how new technologies can be combined to address some of the most pressing challenges facing the modern digital economy.

2 Case Study: Monitoring and Optimizing User Experience

Understanding the user experience is important for optimizing customer satisfaction and, ultimately, e-commerce conversion. In a brick-and-mortar context, store attendants can observe people in the store and customize their interactions to optimize customer satisfaction. For example, if a person is searching for something, the attendant can offer help. If a person needs help deciding whether to buy a product, the attendant can answer questions. If a person is frustrated, the attendant can note how to improve the experience in the future. Likewise, effective e-commerce interactions are facilitated by understanding the user's experience and customizing the interaction. However, understanding the user's experience online is difficult as interpersonal cues from in-person interactions are lost (Okdie et al. 2011). Hence, companies have developed a myriad of tools to help better understand the user experience, including surveys, analytical platforms, and even heat maps showing where people devote attention (Bakaev et al. 2016).

Table 1 Summary of case studies and examples

Case study	Examples	Summary
Monitoring and optimizing user experience		
We demonstrate how behavioral data is used to evaluate usability across three different experiences at multiple companies	(1) Evaluating software usability at scale	A predictive model trained with various features from digital behavior can measure usability with reliability and accuracy comparable to industry-standard perceptual usability evaluation methods
	(2) Monitoring usability at a large, online insurance provider	Compared to other analytical data sources, granular behavioral data—collected across all users—can reveal previously unknown friction points in the user experience
	(3) Customizing an e-commerce flow	Behavioral data can classify users into several personas in real time. Customizing the experience according to these personas creates tangible optimizations that improve important e-commerce outcomes such as conversion
Digital identity fraud		
Digital behavior features enable models and rules as unique identity fraud solutions support rapid response to fraud attacks without harming the user experience. These tools are demonstrated across three FinTech providers	(1) Identity fraud at a credit card issuer	Fraud ring attacks often follow similar behavioral patterns. Using a set of behavioral features, our client established rules to isolate the attack strategy of a fraud ring, avoiding the need to shut down their card issuing business
	(2) Identity fraud at an online lender	With predictive models and rules engines based on digital behavior, fraud prevention strategies need not rely on historical data (which can be hard to come by for new products). This online lender used digital behavior to provide a crucial layer of defense, preventing a massive fraud attack on their fledgling demand deposit product
	(3) Identity fraud at a digital insurer	Compared to other methods that harm conversion with step-up verifications, behavioral data can be used unobtrusively, allowing this insurance provider to establish coordinated rules amid a fraud attack to divert sessions with suspicious activity while preserving the onboarding experience for genuine customers

Existing tools to understand the experience, however, provide an incomplete understanding and limited ability to customize the experience. For example, while usability surveys are valuable, particularly in academic contexts, response rates to online usability surveys are typically low and are biased toward highly positive or negative experiences. Hence, online surveys often exclude the majority of the relevant population, and conclusions can thus be incomplete or, even worse, biased (Travis 2017). To help address this limitation, numerous analytical programs and usability tools have been developed. For example, tools like Google Analytics can identify which pages people visited and even the demographics of those users in some cases. Heat maps can record where the computer mouse is on the page as a surrogate for where people devote attention. While useful for identifying areas of friction from historical interactions, they do not provide insight that can be used to customize a user's experience in real time.

2.1 Monitoring Usability with Behavioral Data

Behavioral data, e.g., mouse movements, clicks, focus events, and scrolling events, can provide a robust understanding of the user experience and be used to customize their experience in real time. For example, a person typing with hesitancy as indicated by the dwell time (how long a key is pressed down) and transition time (time between key presses) might indicate they have reservations about entering the requested information. A person moving the computer mouse in indirect patterns versus direct patterns may indicate they are searching for something and may need help. A person "rage clicking" (clicking several times in a row on an unresponsive interface element) may indicate that they are frustrated. These data can be analyzed in real time to provide insight into the user's experience and the user's intent or emotional state. Such real-time data can be used to understand and customize the experience to improve user satisfaction. Below, we provide three examples of using behavioral data to accomplish these objectives.

2.2 Example 1: Evaluating Software Usability

In the early stages of our research, we were asked by a large Fortune 100 software company to analyze mouse-movement data on a new software product to be released soon. The company had a robust usability testing team that would invite people to their headquarters to confidentially interact with the yet-to-be-announced software product and provide feedback, usually by answering survey questions. However, the people who volunteered to participate in the usability studies were often loyal customers and fans of the company. Hence, the feedback they provided had the potential to be biased by the sample. The company collaborated with us to see if we could provide an objective measure of usability based on how people moved the computer mouse and clicked on elements of the new software program. Further, they wanted a methodology that could be used in the wild after the product was released to detect usability issues that were not uncovered in the laboratory usability tests. Finally, they required that we analyze all behavioral data anonymously; they provided us the (time-stamped) x- and y-coordinates for mouse movements and clicks, withholding information about what software was being interacted with or what the experience looked like.

We used the x- and y-coordinate positions and time stamps to calculate several metrics that could be used to assess usability. These metrics included movement deviation from the idealized response trajectory (the most direct path between two clicks), movement time, the number of switches in movement direction on the x- and y-axis, and movement speed. We trained a linear regression model to predict a proprietary usability measure from the company. We found that scores from the model based on the mouse-movement features predicted usability more robustly than the proprietary usability measure. It could effectively be used to differentiate among the usability of different tasks. Further, the methodology had the potential to be used on a broad population, monitoring usability across tasks in an online setting across millions or billions of users.

2.3 Example 2: Monitoring Usability at a Large, Online Insurance Provider

Over time, we built on our early research results and created a robust system to monitor usability in live online systems. We used this system to help a large US-based insurance company understand where poor user experiences were causing friction and drop-offs on their website. This insurance company was already using prominent analytics programs to understand the users on their website. The analytics programs would provide insight into how many people were visiting each page and how many people were dropping off, but they did not provide insight as to where, specifically on a given page, people were experiencing friction and dropping off. In other words, their existing usability data sources lacked granularity.

We installed our solution to help answer these questions. The solution was created in JavaScript, and it captured browser events for analysis. Browser events included *mouse move, key down, key up, click, blur, and input events*. All events were sanitized before being sent to a web service for analysis. This sanitization means any sensitive, personal, or other information that could present a privacy concern was removed before being transmitted. The resulting data was sent to the web service that quickly analyzed it—using proprietary data cleaning and feature extraction methods—to reveal indicators of friction, and the resulting friction indicators were stored for later review.

After collecting behavioral data for a few days, we met with the client to discuss where on the page users were experiencing friction. The results were illuminating, revealing the exact page elements that caused friction. For example, we discovered (1) several text input boxes into which people were hesitant to enter information, likely due to privacy concerns, (2) widgets on the page that were difficult to interact with, and (3) elements that users expected to be clickable but were not. All these points in the user journey caused friction and resulted in users dropping off. They used these insights to inform interface changes that improved the customer experience.

2.4 *Example 3: Customizing an E-Commerce Flow*

In this final example, we discuss how we integrate real-time behavioral data in e-commerce settings to facilitate more effective and dynamic user experiences. The conversion rate (percentage of visitors that buy the product) at most e-commerce companies is very low: for example, just 1.5% of users at one client's website ultimately purchase a product. One reason conversion is so low in e-commerce settings is that everyone gets a similar experience. Whereas store employees can customize interaction with shoppers in brick-and-mortar stores by evaluating interpersonal cues to determine their intent or whether they need help, this has historically been much more difficult for e-commerce stores. As a result, website owners typically optimize the website experience for the typical user, providing the same prompts, popups, or offers for help to most users. For example, chatbots are prolific across the web, used to answer users' questions, promote products, and provide additional information. However, chatbots are often perceived as annoying by users. They interrupt users' interaction at undesired times, decreasing efficiency and causing negative emotional responses.

We helped address these problems by analyzing users' behavioral data and providing real-time insights back to the website regarding the type of users—also known as user personas—that were interacting with their website. The web service monitors behavioral features in a rolling time window during a browsing session to classify users into one of four personas (see Table 2). We found that the personas meaningfully differentiated users on several dimensions. For example, a goal-oriented user converts at a rate over 500% greater than a disengaged user.

As data on user personas are provided in real time during a website interaction, they can be used to customize the user experience to improve satisfaction and increase conversion. For example, in one A/B test, personas were used to create an expedited path for goal-oriented users to checkout. Although helpful for other personas, the path contained fewer interruptions that would distract goal-oriented users. Examples of bypassed elements include marketing material and product endorsements. We found that dynamically optimizing the path based on persona improves conversion over a static experience. Other ways behavioral personas are being used to customize the user experience include displaying promotions at the appropriate time to the appropriate users and performing more targeted remarketing campaigns to users most likely to (re)engage.

Table 2 User personas

Persona	Description
Goal oriented	This person is goal directed on your website. They deliberately navigate the website, interact with elements, and input information when available
Exploring	This person is exploring your website for information. They scroll through information, navigate in an exploratory fashion, and may occasionally leave the page looking for other information
Disengaged	This person is not engaging in a meaningful way with your website
Struggling	This person is having a difficult time navigating your website or inputting information

We also integrated these personas with one of the largest chatbot providers on the web. This integration was designed to present the chatbot based on the user's persona rather than to all users. For example, in an e-commerce website, you would not present the chatbot to a user with a goal-oriented persona; they are trying to accomplish a task without distraction. However, if you have users with a struggling persona, the chatbot could ask if they need help or would like to provide feedback. For a user with a browsing persona, the chatbot could customize its interaction and ask if it can help the user find something. In each of these cases, the chatbot is displayed at the appropriate time and context, increasing user satisfaction with the chatbot.

2.5 Measuring Behavior at Scale Can Support PLG

In these three examples, our technology supported the PLG business strategy by creating higher-quality products that deliver value to customers and promote more satisfied users. Each case made tangible improvements for the company, including more loyalty, greater conversion, and higher growth. Furthermore, our technology can be deployed at the internet scale, providing a robust indicator of usability for all users (not just a subset), while allowing companies to provide real-time interventions based on behavioral personas to improve the user experience.

3 Case Study: Digital Identity Fraud

The rapid rise of online services has created many new opportunities for fraudsters to use stolen or synthetic personal information to commit fraud. As a result, identity verification has become a crucial activity across multiple sectors (Research 2023). The increasing sophistication of fraudsters, combined with the sheer volume of data available online, has made it easier than ever for identity fraud to go undetected. Moreover, the COVID-19 pandemic has accelerated the shift toward online transactions, with more people working, shopping, and interacting virtually from home. As a result, fraudsters have also ramped up their activities, with a surge in the number of phishing scams and identity fraud.

Identity fraud—the deliberate use of synthetic or stolen identity details for gain (Jamieson et al. 2012)—affects many types of online platforms. For example, on social media platforms, fake accounts may be created to spread false information, engage in harassment, or manipulate public opinion by creating fake followers or likes. Fake accounts can also be used on e-commerce platforms to conduct fraudulent transactions, such as buying items with stolen credit card information and then reselling them for profit or manipulating product ratings or reviews, which can significantly impact a business's reputation and sales.

Modern financial service providers, such as FinTech startups and mobile payment providers, interact exclusively through digital channels, which makes them particularly vulnerable to identity fraud. For these providers, losses due to identity fraud have increased to billions per year with no indication of slowing (Straits Research 2023). Online financial service providers must also comply with a range of regulatory requirements, such as the Know Your Customer (KYC) and Anti-Money Laundering (AML) regulations, which require the verification of customer identities. The creation of fake accounts can make it difficult for financial service providers to comply with these regulations, leading to legal and financial penalties.

To mitigate the risk of identity fraud, digital banks use identity verification services and data sources in increasingly sophisticated ways (Research 2023). With traditional identity verification methods (e.g., knowledge-based authentication) compromised due to data breaches, platforms are turning to overt verification technologies, often to the detriment of the user experience. For example, an automated ID verification system [e.g., Nametag (2022)] significantly reduces the risk of identity fraud. However, uploading a photo ID adds significant friction during the onboarding experience. Such customer experience issues may conflict with growth goals as they create extra friction during the crucial customer onboarding process (Equifax 2015; Barrett 2020). In the face of these identity fraud challenges, digital behavior presents a unique solution that balances the need for risk mitigation with competing priorities related to customer experience and product growth.

3.1 Mitigating Identity Fraud Risk with Behavioral Data

Predictive models based on behavioral data provide two key advantages for our customers. First, behavioral data can be unobtrusively captured and analyzed while customers interact with an existing customer onboarding form. This enables our models to provide additional fraud risk screening capabilities for our clients without adding any additional friction or otherwise impacting their users' experience, which directly reduces the cost of fraud prevention. In addition to the traditional costs of fraud prevention, such as extensive verification procedures or manual reviews, there is a significant conversion cost associated with any new step or hurdle added to the onboarding process. In the competitive industries where our clients operate, friction often results in losing the customer to a competitor. Thus, using models and automation based on digital behavior that is captured invisibly enables our clients to manage their fraud risk while prioritizing their customer acquisition and product growth objectives.

Second, digital behavior produces models that are fundamentally unique compared to traditional fraud prevention strategies. Traditional fraud mitigation involves examining the historical profile of the supplied identity to identify, for example, recent anomalous activity or to verify that the different pieces of information (e.g., phone number and email address) match a known digital footprint. Accordingly, evaluating fraud risk using these traditional data sources is difficult when the user has little or no historical activity. Behavioral data, by contrast, requires no matching historical profile for a particular user. Instead, models can be trained to identify patterns of behavior that are typical of fraudulent applications, which can be quite different from those of a legitimate user. For instance, the speed and consistency of mouse movements can be used to detect if an automated bot is creating an account with a stolen identity. Typing patterns can also help identify an attacker using a stolen or synthetic identity who is not familiar with the name or other personal information associated with the identity. This lack of familiarity can result in irregular typing patterns or entry methods indicating that the identity was stolen.

Traditional fraud prevention methods that rely on historical data have a further disadvantage in that they may not be able to identify new and emerging fraud patterns. By using behavioral data, service providers can capture new patterns of behavior that may indicate fraud, even if those patterns have not been observed before. This ability allows for a more dynamic and adaptive fraud prevention strategy, enabling service providers to stay ahead of the constantly evolving fraud landscape.

3.2 Example 1: Identity Fraud at a Credit Card Issuer

In one instance, a credit card issuing client was celebrating hitting their highest customer growth rate to date. A sophisticated fraud ring caught wind of the issuer's success and attacked, with the goal of using a coordinated effort to overwhelm the system. The issuer's fraud team was forced to delay—and then begin outright declining—all applicants from a particular acquisition channel. False declines were potentially costing the issuer hundreds of thousands of dollars, but they could not afford to treat any applications from that channel as legitimate while such an aggressive attack was in progress. Our behavior-based identity solutions identified behavior directly related to the fraud ring, which allowed us to coordinate with the credit card issuer to create a set of automation rules that reliably identified each fraudulent applicant matching those behavioral patterns. Most of these bad actors would have been missed otherwise. The tangible result for the card issuer was a savings of more than $800k in fraud losses, including many instances of fraud that the issuer's existing fraud and risk tools had missed.

3.3 *Example 2: Identity Fraud at an Online Lender*

An online lender was expanding their product line to include demand deposit accounts (i.e., accounts from which funds can be withdrawn without advance notice). As the service launched with very limited historical data, their fraud prevention strategy was initially fluid, with inconsistent automated step-up risk mitigation standards. Meanwhile, a sophisticated fraud ring was testing their systems—and noted that vulnerability. Soon, an attack ensued, with coordinated attempts to open many accounts very quickly using stolen identity information. This fraud ring had a unique brute-force attack style that far transcended even the high-fraud rate attempts that this lender expected. With this high-paced attack clogging the onboarding process, the door was open for any fraudsters making it through to create real damage. However, the digital behavior observed during the attack indicated the use of automation tools beyond typical levels, with more than 70% of users providing identity information using abnormal patterns. The increased velocity of risky traffic was identified by our fraud ring attack algorithms, and we sounded the alarm that many of these new applicants appeared unfamiliar with the identity information they were entering. The data further showed that this was likely a highly coordinated attack. We were able to establish several indicators of specific behaviors associated with the fraud ring, enabling the online lender to lock out several thousand cybercriminals attacking their fledgling processing system.

3.4 *Example 3: Identity Fraud at a Digital Insurer*

The fraud rings targeting digital insurers are extremely cunning, patient, and focused. They often test different attack strategies to discover how their targets react, gathering information to identify the best attack vector. When a fraud attack ensues, these weaknesses are exploited in full force and at high volume. Aware of this pattern, this digital insurer had tools to apply step-up identity verification methods to slow the flow of fraudulent applications. Prior to their implementation of digital behavior tools, this insurer suffered a large, coordinated attack from a fraud ring. In response, the digital insurer imposed more onerous identity verification steps to curb the impact of the attack, but these step-up verification rules were applied across all incoming traffic. Analysis after the attack revealed that the additional friction resulted in a 10% decrease in low-risk applicants, with no real reduction in the cases of identity fraud. This led them to explore alternative risk mitigation solutions, and they added our digital behavior tools to their application form. When their next fraud ring attack occurred, high-velocity, high-efficiency behavioral patterns indicated likely fraud ring activity, with a 5x increase in risky sessions (from 2% to nearly 10% in just three days). Rather than applying their step-up verification defenses to all incoming traffic, they were able to use those risky behavioral signatures to apply roadblocks to a more targeted subset of their traffic. As a result, their overall conversion rate dipped just slightly, isolating the impact of the fraud ring defenses to a much smaller subset of their onboarding funnel.

3.5 Digital Behavior: A Smarter Cat

Fraud prevention is often described as a perpetual game of cat and mouse in which fraudsters continue to find innovative methods for bypassing new defensive mechanisms, which must be updated accordingly, leading to innovations for perpetrating fraud (Straits Research 2023). Thus, an effective fraud strategy must be dynamic, responsive, and multifaceted as no single strategy or data source will be effective in isolation. Perhaps, most importantly, a modern fraud strategy also needs to be covertly and selectively applied so that much of the risk mitigation occurs without impacting the customer experience that is so central to a PLG-oriented platform. The unique insight and dynamic, real-time nature of our behavioral tools add a rich dimension to our customers' identity fraud portfolio. Furthermore, those risk assessments are invisible in a customer onboarding flow, supporting automation rules based on behavioral data that our customers use to respond quickly and dynamically to evolving threats. Thus, although fraudsters are not likely to give up their efforts to identify and exploit new weaknesses, behavioral data can enable a more dynamic, sophisticated defense strategy.

4 Conclusion

The massive amount of behavioral data available to modern digital service providers can be overwhelming to manage, analyze, and gain insights from. The case studies presented in this chapter provide tangible examples of AI-enabled insights that originate from this novel data source. By leveraging AI tools like these, businesses can automate the analysis process and gain valuable insights into user behavior at scale, often identifying patterns that humans may not be able to discern on their own.

The examples shared suggest a broader array of possibilities that can be examined. For example, although most of the examples across the two cases include data and traffic from both desktop and mobile platforms, we have focused more in these examples on desktop experiences (particularly for the examples demonstrating the use of mousing behaviors). As mobile traffic often comprises the majority of traffic for our customers, our existing tools are designed to work across both platforms. In addition, the array of additional sensors found in most smartphones (e.g., accelerometers) may provide additional important signals relevant to the highlighted use cases, and we maintain an active program of research to further understand these signals and their possible uses to enhance rules engines and predictive models.

Whether from desktop or mobile users, whether using data from traditional or more recent interaction devices, these tools have the potential for PLG-relevant insights in use cases beyond those we highlighted in our case studies. Analyzing thousands of user interactions algorithmically can identify malfunctioning features or common interaction pathways leading to user drop-off or other negative outcomes. Exploratory analyses could indicate that a particular feature of the product is being used in a way that was not anticipated by the business, pointing to unexpected use cases that can potentially unlock new markets or revenue streams.

AI-enabled insight is an increasingly critical component of a successful PLG strategy because it enables businesses to derive insights from the vast amounts of data generated by user behavior. By automating the analysis process and identifying patterns and correlations at scale, businesses can better understand their users and make data-driven decisions that improve the user experience and support growth.

References

Bakaev M, Mamysheva T, Gaedke M (2016) Current trends in automating usability evaluation of websites: Can you manage what you can't measure? In: 11th international forum on strategic technology 2016, IFOST. IEEE, New York City, pp 510–514

Barrett M (2020) Combating new account fraud in the digital age. https://www.paymentsjournal.com/combating-new-account-fraud-in-the-digital-age/, last accessed 31 May 2023

Equifax (2015) Back to the future: the resurgence of new-account fraud. https://assets.equifax.com/marketing/US/assets/account_opening_wp.pdf, last accessed 31 May 2023

Freeman J, Ambady N, Rule N, Johnson K (2008) Will a category cue attract you? Motor output reveals dynamic competition across person construal. J Exp Psychol 137(4):673–690

Gozli D, Pratt J (2011) Seeing while acting: hand movements can modulate attentional capture by motion onset. Atten Percept Psychophys 73(8):2448–2456

Hibbeln M, Jenkins J, Schneider C, Valacich J, Weinmann M (2017) How is your user feeling? Inferring emotion through human-computer interaction devices. MIS Q 41(1):1–21

Jamieson R, Land L, Winchester D, Stephens G, Steel A, Maurushat A, Sarre R (2012) Addressing identity crime in crime management information systems: definitions, classification, and empirics. Comput Law Secur Rev 28(4):381–395

Jenkins J, Larsen R, Bodily R, Sandberg D, Williams P, Stokes S, Harris S, Valacich J (2015) A multi-experimental examination of analyzing mouse cursor trajectories to gauge subject uncertainty. In: Twenty-first Americas conference on information systems

Jenkins J, Valacich J, Zimbelman A, Zimbelman M (2021) Detecting noncompliant behavior in organizations: how online survey responses and behaviors reveal risk. J Manage Inf Syst 38(3):704–731

Libert B, Davenport TH (2022) Product-led growth companies find a new way to serve customers. MIT Sloan Manag Rev 64(1):1–5

Monaro M, Gamberini L, Sartori G (2017) The detection of faked identity using unexpected questions and mouse dynamics. PLoS ONE 12(5):1–19

Monaro M, Galante C, Spolaor R, Li Q, Gamberini L, Conti M, Sartori G (2018) Covert lie detection using keyboard dynamics. Sci Rep 8(1):1–10

Nametag (2022) What is NIST IAL2 identity verification? https://www.getnametag.com/newsroom/what-is-nist-ial2-identity-verification, last accessed 31 May 2023

Okdie B, Guadagno R, Bernieri F, Geers A, McLarney-Vesotski A (2011) Getting to know you: face-to-face versus online interactions. In: Proceedings of the SIGCHI conference on human factors in computing systems. Association for Computing Machinery, New York, pp 153–159

Research G (2023) Identity verification market size, share & trends analysis report. https://www.grandviewresearch.com/industry-analysis/identity-verification-market-report, last accessed 31 May 2023

Straits Research (2023) Identity verification market size, share and growth forecast 2030. https://straitsresearch.com/report/identity-verification-market, last accessed 31 May 2023

Thorpe A, Friedman J, Evans S, Nesbitt K, Eidels A (2021) Mouse movement trajectories as an indicator of cognitive workload. Int J Hum Comput Interact 38(15):1464–1479

Travis D (2017) Warning: your web survey is a lot less reliable than you think. https://www.userfocus.co.uk/articles/web-surveys-considered-harmful.html, last accessed 31 May 2023

Weinmann M, Valacich J, Schneider C, Jenkins J, Hibbeln M (2022) The path of the righteous: using trace data to understand fraud decisions in real time. MIS Q 46(4):2317–2336

Wojnowicz M, Ferguson M, Dale R, Spivey M (2009) The self-organization of explicit attitudes. Psychol Sci 20(11):1428–1435

Conclusion: Practical Considerations for the Design of AI for the Workplace

(The Importance of Organizational Readiness and Human-Centered Design Processes)

Constantinos K. Coursaris, Joerg Beringer, Pierre-Majorique Léger, and Burak Öz

Abstract This concluding chapter synthesizes the insights and best practices presented throughout this book, focusing on two key areas that business leaders should consider when planning their AI projects: organizational readiness and human-centered design processes. It highlights the importance of considering organizational and human-centered goals when designing and implementing AI solutions. While organizational goals should focus on data quality, privacy concerns, and a culture of continuous improvement, human-centered design practices must prioritize system configurability, transparency, and alignment of AI solutions with ethical considerations. By outlining practical considerations and key questions within these areas, this chapter aims to guide practitioners and researchers in designing and implementing AI systems that empower users, improve business performance, and support long-term organizational growth.

1 Key Considerations Regarding Organizational Readiness

To conclude our discussion on the design of human-centered AI for the workplace, we synthesize the content presented in this book (Coursaris et al. 2025) into two key areas that business leaders should be mindful of when planning their AI projects, namely, organizational readiness and human-centered design processes. Within these areas, we put forth issues and corresponding questions for management to consider before initiating AI implementations affording a path of greater likelihood of project success.

C. K. Coursaris · P.-M. Léger · B. Öz (✉)
HEC Montreal, Montreal, QC, Canada
e-mail: constantinos.coursaris@hec.ca; pierre-majorique.leger@hec.ca; burak.oz@hec.ca

J. Beringer
ProContext, Redwood City, CA, USA
e-mail: joerg.beringer@procontext.ai

C. K. Coursaris et al. (eds.), *The Design of Human-Centered Artificial Intelligence for the Workplace*, Progress in IS, https://doi.org/10.1007/978-3-031-83512-4_27

We begin by discussing six aspects of organizational readiness and maturity, as AI implementations cannot be considered independently of the business processes and work systems they will be embedded in (Oliner and Faggella 2021). These are presented below and include data quality, data protection and privacy, business value of AI solutions, work process transformation with AI, continuous improvement and monitoring of AI operations, and AI platform thinking.

1.1 Data Quality

One of the themes throughout this book has been the critical importance of having clean, reliable data. To generate an objective and precise model of reality, AI requires unbiased, structured, and labeled data (Salminen et al. 2025). Without such a foundation, AI systems may fail to meet their intended goal(s) (Munoz-de Escalona et al. 2025).

As AI models learn from large datasets, they may be impacted by the potential presence of bias existing in the training dataset. Such bias should be mitigated by implementing systematic human-in-the-loop monitoring systems and human intervention mechanisms (Herrmann 2025; Tichy et al. 2025). Human oversight and input should also be in place to ensure the implemented AI system not only looks at the middle of the distribution but also considers the complete range of cases and individuals represented in the dataset (Liu et al. 2025).

As a practitioner, you may consider asking the following questions while planning your AI project:

- Do we have a robust data story and the data structure to implement systems relying on accurate data?
- Are we capable of training models and serving predictions at scale?
- Are we fostering a culture that embraces experimentation and iteration?
- How are we ensuring that our AI solutions are ethical and bias-free?
- What measures are we taking to prevent and address potential biases in our AI models?

1.2 Data Protection and Privacy

As AI methods rely on learning from existing organizational data, procuring an AI service for your workplace from an external provider may not always be feasible. Privacy and security concerns, particularly regarding data leaving an organization's premises, often necessitate in-house AI implementation. For instance, the case of MSUFCU (Maxim 2025) illustrates a financial institution's need to acquire the software, hardware, and skill set required to ensure their sensitive customer data remained securely on site.

Data privacy issues should be carefully managed throughout the AI implementation process, with key considerations such as:

- How are we protecting user data privacy and ensuring the security of our systems?
- What are our protocols for data anonymization and encryption during storage and transmission?
- Are we compliant with relevant data protection regulations?

1.3 Business Value of the AI Solution

Implementing an exciting and new technology may sound appealing, but focusing predominantly on the technology may obscure more efficient alternatives for addressing business needs. AI implementations come with high costs and challenges, including hiring and training of staff to develop necessary skills for managing the technology, potential data privacy issues, the potential for employee de-skilling, and a commitment to continuous learning. For these reasons, the value proposition of the AI solution should be clearly defined before its implementation so that the focus is on the tangible value it will bring rather than being distracted by the appeal of adopting a breakthrough technology (Liu et al. 2025).

The following questions provide a strong starting point to evaluate how AI can meaningfully transform and enhance existing business processes:

- Is the problem significant enough to warrant investment in AI over a simpler solution, such as adopting a heuristic method?
- Have we evaluated both the current infrastructure and the additional investments required for the AI solutions being considered?
- Will the AI solution offer a significant performance advantage over simpler alternatives?

1.4 Work Process Transformation with AI

Before implementing AI, it is often beneficial to evaluate existing work systems to identify areas most suited for AI-driven improvements (Alter 2025). A thorough analysis of existing and future business processes, as a comparison of before and after AI implementation, enables a clearer definition of AI implementation goals and expected benefits. In addition, considering stakeholder needs across organizational, team, and task levels (Beringer and Herrmann 2025), and understanding how AI might shift the roles of human experts (Geis and Beringer 2025), can improve the alignment of AI implementation with organizational objectives.

In addition to planning and designing future business processes, managing user expectations and preparing the organization and its members for new, AI-driven processes are also essential. Therefore, a systematic change management process should guide the implementation of an AI.

To assist in defining the role of AI in revised business processes, consider the following questions:

- Which parts of the existing business process will be conducted by the AI solution in the future process?
- Do we have the necessary change management skills to transform the existing work system?
- How can we address potential resistance to change and help users transition to new AI-driven processes?
- How would AI benefit business outcomes and the employees involved in the same business process as the implemented AI?
- Will the introduction of AI solutions lead to less mental workload and free up resources to focus on more important work?
- How will we prepare and support employees to shift from performing the core task to overseeing an AI-driven system?

1.5 Continuous Improvement and Monitoring in AI Operations

The training of an AI model is not a one-time process completed at its initial implementation. One of the primary advantages of AI integration in business processes is the system's capability to continuously learn from changing environmental conditions and adapt its behavior accordingly. However, as these technologies interact with dynamic environments, they are prone to deviate from their original functionality and behavior, a phenomenon known as "data drift" (Degen 2025).

To mitigate the challenges associated with data drift, it is essential to incorporate a constructive feedback loop within the AI system's design. This loop enables users to both understand the data entering the system and influence how it is used in shaping an AI model's behavior (Tichy et al. 2025). This continuous feedback mechanism requires effective monitoring of the AI system, and Degen (2025) recommends the addition of a specialized organizational role, the model manager, to continually evaluate an AI's performance in meeting business goals.

To guide continuous AI improvement and stability, consider the following questions:

- How are we fostering collaboration among AI developers, data scientists, UX designers, and business stakeholders?
- What processes are in place for continuous AI improvements?
- Do we have established plans for ongoing support and system updates?
- Should we regularly update our AI models based on user feedback and performance metrics?
- How are we ensuring that our AI solutions remain scalable and maintainable over time?

1.6 AI Platform Thinking

Considering the significant initial investment and development costs of AI implementation, it is essential to build systems with efficiency in mind. One effective strategy for achieving this is through a modular AI design, where each module can be reused to solve different business challenges.

Modular AI design benefits from a clear functional analysis that allocates tasks within business processes and identifies points of interaction with human users. In this setup, each module is aimed at a specific function but built for reuse. Design patterns and reusable components can be developed for each unique module to make user adoption easier. This approach would enable the standardization of human-AI interaction experience depending on the functions of AI within an organizational workflow, as introduced in the SADE ladder (Beringer et al. 2025).

To guide AI implementations toward this efficient, platform-oriented approach, organizations can consider the following questions:

- How are we integrating AI solutions into the user experience to ensure they are intuitive and user-friendly?
- Do we have common design patterns to support dynamic interactions between human and AI agents?
- Are we building a layer of reusable ML patterns that can be applied across multiple use cases?
- Do we have standards for agent networks, where one automation agent uses the output of another automation agent?

2 Key Considerations from the Perspective of Human-Centered AI

AI is not merely a tool for efficiency, rather a key resource available to human experts engaged in organizational decision-making processes. Therefore, while the aforementioned organizational readiness considerations are vital for the success of an AI implementation, they are insufficient. The success of an AI implementation also depends on its alignment with human needs, values, and ethical considerations. Below, we discuss the human-centered AI considerations at three levels: socio-technical systems, individual users, and the human-AI interaction.

2.1 Integrating AI into the Existing Socio-Technical System in the Organization

Integrating AI into an organization's socio-technical environment requires employees to develop a new skill set to recognize when and how an AI can fail and to facilitate effective communication across multiple domains, including data science,

AI development, user experience (UX) design, and business expertise (Degen 2025). While human-AI task delegation processes should be thoughtfully designed, this does not imply a static delegation mechanism. Instead, task delegation to AI can and should be dynamic and responsive to the context and the organization's needs (Teeni 2025). This flexibility helps AI complement human strengths and expertise, ultimately augmenting work processes rather than disrupting them (Koon 2025; Yamaguchi et al. 2025).

Still, the integration of AI will inevitably bring changes to stakeholder roles and may disrupt established workflows. Therefore, a well-structured AI implementation plan is essential to facilitate user adoption. The following questions can guide organizations in embedding AI thoughtfully within their existing systems:

- Do we have a clear to-be scenario describing the envisioned work system involving AI?
- Do we fully understand all stakeholder requirements and their roles in the new organizational setup involving AI?
- Are we beginning with a low-cost, high-value project to establish the necessary infrastructure and skills?
- How are we managing the adoption of AI solutions within our organization or among our customers?
- Do we have the necessary help facilities to support users transition to new AI-driven processes?
- Is the AI system optimizing user outcomes in addition to business outcomes?

2.2 AI Design Considerations at the User Level

A human-centered perspective centers on the design and implementation process around the end user (Herrmann 2025; Shneiderman 2022). This perspective emphasizes that technology embedded within decision-making processes should support and improve human performance without compromising employee autonomy or skills.

The human-centered approach starts at the earliest stages of AI implementation by involving potential users to actively guide the system's design based on their needs and experiences (Geis and Beringer 2025). For example, engaging end users in several stages of the development process, as suggested by Liu et al. (2025), ensures that the final implementation addresses practical user needs.

A well-designed AI system also prioritizes transparency and allows users to understand the reasoning behind recommendations and the potential outcomes of different actions (Koon 2025; Lescieux et al. 2025). The importance of such transparency is illustrated in the Intelligent Pilot Advisory System case study, where reliability and transparency were critical for decision-making in a high-stakes context (Djartov and Wuerfel 2025).

Moreover, human-centered AI should respect and enhance human expertise. AI systems should allow users to intervene in automated processes or adjust predictions based on context-specific knowledge (Geis and Beringer 2025). Such user interventions may relieve the symptoms of imperfect AI recommendations, but they do not immediately address the root causes (Tichy et al. 2025). Therefore, AI systems should be designed to learn from human interventions in automation and adjust their behavior (Herrmann 2025). For example, the route planning case study shows how AI can use past user adherence or non-adherence to system recommendations to avoid generating impractical recommendations (Yamaguchi et al. 2025). While this adaptability is valuable, the potential user bias must be managed through consistent monitoring approaches, as highlighted by Degen (2025).

Hence, the following questions can guide the human-centered design of AI:

- How do we involve end users in the AI development process?
- Are we regularly collecting user feedback to improve our AI solutions?
- How transparent is management with users about how the implemented AI solutions work?
- How transparent are our AI systems for end users?
- Does our AI system offer clear explanations for AI-driven decisions to build user trust?
- Do end users have sufficient control over AI recommendation processes to optimize outcomes?
- Does the AI system develop empathy with the user by understanding their desired outcomes and emotional states?

2.3 *Alternative Uses of AI to Improve Decision-Making Performance*

A human-centered AI approach can go beyond addressing business problems to include tools aimed directly at supporting users' engagement, attention, and safety. In these applications, the objective is not only to optimize processes but to improve the well-being and performance of human decision-makers.

As described in two chapters of this book, eye-tracking measures such as pupil dilation and gaze duration can be used in assessing a user's cognitive state (Conrad 2025; Langner et al. 2025). Predicting these cognitive states allows for the design of adaptive interface elements—such as alerts or visual cues—that boost user engagement and attentiveness. Furthermore, AI can also monitor a machine operator's attention levels in real time, enabling timely interventions to maintain focus and safety (Passalacqua et al. 2025).

Key questions for implementing user-centered AI include:

- How can AI solutions be used to enhance user engagement, attention, or safety in specific decision-making contexts?
- Are we leveraging real-time data, such as cognitive state metrics, to adapt interfaces and support user focus effectively?
- What processes are in place to ensure that AI-driven systems complement rather than disrupt the user's workflow?

2.4 *Determining the Human-AI Interaction Paradigm*

AI solutions can adopt diverse roles based on user needs and organizational goals. Depending on the AI's role—whether assisting, automating, or functioning within a network of agents—the interactions with users will differ. An assistive system processes information to offer recommendations, allowing users to make the final decision. In contrast, automation agents take actions based on predictions, expanding their functionality beyond information processing to direct action (Alter 2025). In a more integrated setting, multiple AI implementations can form an automation agent network. In each of these scenarios, the following considerations can clarify user interface and interaction design:

Planning on implementing an assistive system:

- Does the system provide tools to let users understand and configure AI inputs and parameters?
- How can we design the interfaces to simplify human-system interactions?
- Should the system recommend only one option or multiple alternative actions?

Planning on implementing automation agents:

- Is the available data robust enough to establish a situational awareness level that allows for informed decision-making?
- Does the AI system incorporate unwritten business rules and context-specific preferences into its decision-making?
- Will the system be able to execute safe and ethical decisions autonomously, without user intervention?
- Who is accountable for the outcomes of autonomous decisions made by AI?
- If the responsible entity is a person, can that person adjust the degree of AI autonomy?

Planning on implementing automation agent networks:

- Do we have a framework that enables seamless cooperation between automation agents and manages the network meta-level functions?
- Is there a clear strategy for providing explanations behind AI-driven actions, decisions, and insights?

- Does the design allow flexible integration of automation agents into business processes with human involvement?
- Who is accountable for the outcomes of autonomous decisions made within the agent network?

3 Your AI Implementation Project

A successful AI implementation requires a solid understanding of the business processes, structured change management, and a human-centered focus at every stage. Both the perspectives and the applied case studies in this book have highlighted that the value of AI comes not only from technical innovation but from thoughtful alignment with organizational goals, transparency, and the enhancement of human roles within AI-augmented workflows.

A robust AI strategy begins with a clear definition of business needs and a careful selection of processes where AI can genuinely add value. Effective change management ensures new workflows are adopted and employees are prepared for evolving roles. Finally, human-centered principles reinforce user control, autonomy and engagement.

In short, implementing an AI system is not only a technically demanding endeavor—it is also an opportunity to empower people, streamline processes, and drive sustainable organizational growth.

References

Alter S (2025) The design challenge of using intelligent agents to make work systems smarter. In: The design of human-centered artificial intelligence for the workplace. Springer, Berlin

Beringer J, Herrmann T (2025) The contextual framing of the interplay between human and AI – a socio-technical perspective. In: The design of human-centered artificial intelligence for the workplace. Springer, Berlin

Beringer J, Karran AJ, Coursaris C, Léger PM (2025) The situational awareness, decision and execution ladder (SADE): a framework for human-AI collaborative decision-making. In: The design of human-centered artificial intelligence for the workplace. Springer, Berlin

Conrad C (2025) How situation awareness of cognition can improve human-AI teams. In: The design of human-centered artificial intelligence for the workplace. Springer, Berlin

Coursaris CK, Beringer J, Léger PM, Öz B (eds) (2025) The design of human-centered artificial intelligence for the workplace. Springer, Berlin

Degen H (2025) Ml-models deployed – what's next? Effective and efficient monitoring of ML-based applications. In: The design of human-centered artificial intelligence for the workplace. Springer, Berlin

Djartov B, Wuerfel J (2025) Navigating decisions in the cockpit; Intelligent Pilot Advisory System (IPAS). In: The design of human-centered artificial intelligence for the workplace. Springer, Berlin

Geis T, Beringer J (2025) Human-centered requirements engineering for intelligent systems. In: The design of human-centered artificial intelligence for the workplace. Springer, Berlin

Herrmann T (2025) Intervenability as a design requirement for autonomy and oversight within human-centered AI. In: The design of human-centered artificial intelligence for the workplace. Springer, Berlin
Koon S (2025) Reasoning with AI: six essential factors for augmenting human expertise in the workplace. In: The design of human-centered artificial intelligence for the workplace. Springer, Berlin
Langner M, Toreini P, Maedche A (2025) Eye-tracking technology for cognition-adaptive LLM-based assistants at the workplace. In: The design of human-centered artificial intelligence for the workplace. Springer, Berlin
Lescieux C, Singh A, Doyon-Poulin P (2025) When it goes right, when it goes wrong: lessons learned from automation in aviation. In: The design of human-centered artificial intelligence for the workplace. Springer, Berlin
Liu C, Furmankiewicz M, Taylor A, Venger I (2025) So, you want to build the copilot? Experience from the trenches. In: The design of human-centered artificial intelligence for the workplace. Springer, Berlin
Maxim B (2025) Conversational AI in finance: a case study with MSUFCU. In: The design of human-centered artificial intelligence for the workplace. Springer, Berlin
Munoz-de Escalona E, Estrada-Lugo HD, Perez AA, Leva MC (2025) Situational awareness and HMI design in collaborative human-machine (AI) teamwork: a case study. In: The design of human-centered artificial intelligence for the workplace. Springer, Berlin
Oliner A, Faggella D (2021) Best-practices for discovering valuable AI opportunities - with Adam oliner of slack. https://podcast.emerj.com/best-practices-for-discovering-valuable-ai-opportunities-with-adam-oliner-of-slack, https://podcast.emerj.com/best-practices-for-discovering-valuable-ai-opportunities-with-adam-oliner-of-slack, [Online; Accessed 15 Oct 2024]
Passalacqua M, Pellerin R, Sénécal S, Léger PM (2025) A multi-method assessment of human-AI interaction in delivery driving: examining driver stress, fatigue, attention, situation awareness, and risky driving behaviour. In: The design of human-centered artificial intelligence for the workplace. Springer, Berlin
Salminen J, Kaate I, Jung Sg, Yang Y, Olkkonen R, Jansen BJ (2025) How can intelligent personas (and persona systems) support online advertisers' daily work tasks? In: The design of human-centered artificial intelligence for the workplace. Springer, Berlin
Shneiderman B (2022) Human-centered AI. Oxford University Press, Oxford. https://books.google.ca/books?id=YS9VEAAAQBAJ
Teeni D (2025) Delegation in human-AI configurations for learning reciprocally to solve problems. In: The design of human-centered artificial intelligence for the workplace. Springer, Berlin
Tichy MC, Babounikau I, Ulbrich S, Feindt M (2025) Avoiding pitfalls in demand forecasting. In: The design of human-centered artificial intelligence for the workplace. Springer, Berlin
Yamaguchi K, Tsuji H, Ohtsubo S (2025) Development of a method of replicating skilled drivers' delivery route plans using particle filter optimization. In: The design of human-centered artificial intelligence for the workplace. Springer, Berlin

The manufacturer's authorised representative in the EU is Springer Nature Customer Service Centre GmbH, Europaplatz 3, 69115 Heidelberg, Germany. If you have any concerns regarding our products, please contact ProductSafety@springernature.com

Printed and bound by CPI Group (UK) Ltd, Croydon, CR0 4YY
30/09/2026
02225559-0018